ALSO BY DANIEL SCHULMAN

*Sons of Wichita: How the Koch Brothers Became
America's Most Powerful and Private Dynasty*

THE MONEY KINGS

THE MONEY KINGS

THE EPIC STORY OF THE JEWISH IMMIGRANTS WHO
TRANSFORMED WALL STREET AND SHAPED MODERN AMERICA

DANIEL SCHULMAN

ALFRED A. KNOPF NEW YORK 2024

THIS IS A BORZOI BOOK
PUBLISHED BY ALFRED A. KNOPF

Copyright © 2023 by Daniel Schulman

Published in the United States by Alfred A. Knopf,
a division of Penguin Random House LLC, New York,
and distributed in Canada by
Penguin Random House Canada Limited, Toronto.

www.aaknopf.com

Knopf, Borzoi Books, and the colophon are registered
trademarks of Penguin Random House LLC.

Library of Congress Cataloging-in-Publication Data
Names: Schulman, Daniel, author.
Title: The money kings : the epic story of the Jewish immigrants who
transformed Wall Street and shaped modern America / Daniel Schulman.
Description: New York : Alfred A. Knopf, 2023. |
Includes bibliographical references and index.
Identifiers: LCCN 2023004044 (print) | LCCN 2023004045 (ebook) |
ISBN 9780451493545 (hardcover) | ISBN 9780451493552 (ebook)
Subjects: LCSH: Businesspeople—United States. | Investment bankers—
United States. | Wall Street (New York, N.Y.) | Immigrants—
Economic aspects. | Finance—United States.
Classification: LCC HB615 .S3716 2023 (print) | LCC HB615 (ebook) |
DDC 332.0973—dc23/eng/20230530
LC record available at https://lccn.loc.gov/2023004044
LC ebook record available at https://lccn.loc.gov/2023004045

Front-of-jacket image: Banker Jacob Schiff at the Liberty Loan Parade, 1917.
Bettmann / Getty Images
Back-of-jacket image: Curb brokers on Broad Street, NYC, c. 1900s.
Bettmann / Getty Images
Jacket design by Jenny Carrow

Manufactured in the United States of America
Reprinted One Time
Third Printing, February 2024

For Stacey, Wesley, and Reid

and

In memory of Bernard Schulman (1930–2022)

CONTENTS

A Debt

On my thirtieth birthday, my dad and I drove the six miles from his apartment on New York's Upper East Side to Williamsburg, where he grew up until middle school, before his family moved across the borough to Bensonhurst. His old neighborhood was just twenty minutes away, but he measured the distance in decades. "I spent half my life trying to get out of Brooklyn," he joked. "Why go back now?"

We ate lunch at Peter Luger, the iconic steakhouse, situated in the shadow of the Williamsburg Bridge. Founded in 1887, it was once a mecca for local power brokers. This was Dad's first visit. His parents kept a kosher household, and besides, money was tight. Afterward I suggested we try to locate his childhood home, a five-story brick tenement on McKibbin Street, where his family had lived in a two-bedroom apartment on the third floor. He and his two brothers had occupied one small room, their parents the other. My father, the youngest in their family of five, recalled often sleeping on the living room couch to escape the claustrophobic twin bed he shared with his middle brother, Marvin. So many of his most vivid memories were rooted on McKibbin Street: the transcendent aroma of his mother's *gribenes*, the Jewish delicacy of fried onions and chicken skins; the sound of the iceman clomping up the stairs to make his deliveries; the soothing breeze on the rooftop on sweltering summer nights; the sweet sting of a broom handle connecting with a Spaldeen during neighborhood stickball games.

The apartment also conjured bitter recollections—of a short-tempered and abusive father who imposed order with his belt strap and his fists and eventually left their family for a mistress, and of the fear, anger, and uncertainty that followed.

Dad gazed out the window as we passed the boutiques and bars of Bedford Avenue, as if he were studying a Martian landscape. These were not the gritty streets of his Depression-era youth. Finally, we turned on to his old block, a shabby and graffiti-covered one-way street off Bushwick Avenue. The building, we discovered, had been demolished. The area was at once vastly different and surprisingly recognizable. It remained a neighborhood of immigrants, but where Yiddish had once been spoken, now Spanish was.

We parked and walked around, my dad pointing out the landmarks he remembered: P.S. 147, where he attended elementary school; the squat brick library down the street. "We lived almost like we were in Europe," he remarked, explaining that when he was coming up, each of the surrounding streets might as well have been separate countries. "The Italians were on the next block," he said, pointing. The Roma "lived in the storefronts." Jews—his people—resided on McKibbin Street.

The wealthy and assimilated German Jews who lived uptown in Manhattan called his people *Ostjuden*, "eastern Jews." They were the persecuted and impoverished immigrants from what is today Hungary, Poland, Russia, and Ukraine, who during the late nineteenth and early twentieth centuries spilled off steamships in New York Harbor by the hundreds and scattered to the Lower East Side, Williamsburg, and other Jewish enclaves, packing into tenements like the one on McKibbin.

My grandmother Lena immigrated to New York in the early 1900s from Peremyshlyany, a town in what is today western Ukraine and was then part of the domain of the Austro-Hungarian Empire. She was eight years old and traveled alone, wearing a sign around her neck so an uncle she had never met would recognize her when she disembarked (or so the story goes in my family). My grandfather Elias—Al, everyone called him—also came to New York as a child, departing from the port city of Libau, in present-day Latvia, with his parents and siblings in the fall of 1905, during a spasm of anti-Jewish violence in the Pale of Settlement, the territory on the western fringe of the Russian Empire where the czar permitted Jews to live.

Lena was a candy dipper for a Manhattan confectioner; Al, a neighborhood tough guy, worked as a chauffeur, salesman, and mover. Through his contacts in the local Democratic Party machine, he eventually landed a patronage job with the Internal Revenue Service.

They lived a world apart from the protagonists of this book, who moved in rarefied circles and resided in palatial Manhattan mansions containing Baroque masterworks worth more than Al and Lena could have hoped to earn in several lifetimes.

Yet their two worlds were inextricably, and at times uncomfortably, tethered, bound by their common religion and by the proud yet sorrowful history of struggle and displacement the Jewish people shared.

My grandparents would have been familiar with Jacob Schiff, the investment banking mogul who bridged both spheres. Perhaps they first heard his name mentioned reverentially by a fellow immigrant who had coal in his furnace, or a job, or had learned English thanks to one of the many social welfare programs supported by "Unser Yankele" (our little Jacob). Or maybe they overheard a Zionist denounce the financier, incensed by Schiff's contention that establishing a Jewish homeland risked transgressing their American patriotism. But during Al and Lena's formative years, Schiff was ever present. He was the self-appointed leader of American Jewry, presiding benevolently—if paternalistically—over the immigrant masses. On Wall Street, his only equal was the fearsome John Pierpont Morgan.

Schiff used his fortune unreservedly to ensure a future for the Jews, at a time when their long-term existence seemed very much in doubt. During the prelude to World War I, as conditions in Eastern Europe and Russia worsened and cablegrams reporting massacres and mob violence piled up, Schiff worked to ensure that the United States remained a refuge for immigrants. This was no simple task. The fractious immigration debates of that era were strikingly like those of today. Politicians called for harsh restrictions and stoked fears of disease-carrying foreign criminals invading the United States, degenerating the country's character, and becoming public charges. The nation's doors constantly seemed on the verge of slamming closed to immigrants. Eventually—and with tragic consequences—they did shut.

During Schiff's lifetime, he and members of other wealthy German-Jewish banking clans successfully mobilized against efforts to curb Jewish immigration. Between 1890 and 1920, the years Schiff was most active, the Jewish population of the United States swelled from 400,000 to 3.4 million. Jewish philanthropists, with Schiff at their vanguard, founded and sustained a head-spinning network of organizations and social programs, from schools and hospitals to orphanages and job training centers, to assist the new arrivals and speed their acculturation. Banding together (not always harmoniously), Schiff and his fellow communal leaders formed what amounted to the first American-Jewish lobby, forcefully advocating for the rights of Jews abroad and pressing for liberal immigration policies at home.

Al and Lena and their sons, my father and his brothers, owed more to Schiff and his allies than they might have realized. Absent the advocacy and philanthropy undertaken by Schiff and his friends, their American story—and mine—might not have been possible. Millions of American Jews, descendants of the Russian and Eastern European immigrants who sought and found opportunity in the United States at the turn of the century, owe a similar debt.

This is a book about the evolution of modern finance, about Wall Street pioneers who formed towering institutions such as Goldman Sachs, Kuhn Loeb, and Lehman Brothers, and who shaped, to an astonishing degree, the world we live in today. It is also a tale of how immigrants such as Al and Lena arrived in this country and why they thrived.

These seemingly disparate threads overlap, forming part of the same remarkable story.

INTRODUCTION

Salem Fields

September 28, 1920, was supposed to be a joyful day. A Tuesday, it fell during Sukkot, the weeklong Jewish harvest festival that follows Yom Kippur, the somber Day of Atonement. Sukkot was usually a time of revelry and jubilation, singing and feasting. Instead, grief and gloom shrouded New York City.

The weather itself was "unsettled," according to the forecast, the air sticky with humidity and rain on the way. Judges adjourned their courts that morning, and flags flew at half staff in the financial district. The streets of the Lower East Side, where crowds typically jostled among a labyrinth of pushcarts, were unnervingly serene. Peddlers covered their wares. Merchants locked their shops. Tucked into the windows of closed storefronts, and hanging in the entryways of tenements, settlement houses, and orphanages, were placards, in English and Hebrew, reading, "The East Side mourns the loss of Jacob H. Schiff."[1]

The banker and philanthropist, head of the formidable Wall Street house of Kuhn Loeb, had died several days earlier. He was a diminutive man—he claimed five feet six on his passport, though he might have been rounding up generously—but a colossus in finance and Jewish life, whom one New York paper described as "the foremost world-representative of his race."[2] During his lifetime, he had dueled with J. P. Morgan for railroad industry dominance, gone toe-to-toe with U.S. presidents over immigration and foreign policy, and warred with an entire empire on behalf of his oppressed religious brethren. He left the world a vastly different place than it had been when he entered it seventy-three years earlier in Frankfurt am Main.

Perhaps the mourners felt it. They were saying farewell not just to a man but to an age.

Built to accommodate two thousand worshippers, Temple Emanu-El, the hulking Moorish-revival-style synagogue on 43rd Street and Fifth Avenue, was filled to capacity, its polished walnut pews thick with VIPs. The presidents of the Union Pacific and Pennsylvania railroads, a mining tycoon and a precious gems magnate, a former ambassador and a future one, the Civil War general who captured Jefferson Davis, the founder of Sears, the publisher of *The New York Times*—these eminences were just part of the twenty-three-man contingent of honorary pallbearers, which also included one of the most famous New Yorkers of that era, Schiff's Kuhn Loeb partner Otto Kahn, the debonair and mustachioed financier-statesman who was said to have formed part of the inspiration for the Monopoly man.

But the most amazing sight was not to be found inside Emanu-El's cavernous sanctuary; rather, it came into view as Schiff's funeral procession traveled down Fifth Avenue from the banker's mansion near the corner of 78th Street. For block upon block stood thousands of people, many of them poor Jewish immigrants from the East Side, who had come to pay their respects, their heads bowed low as Schiff's flower-laden casket passed.

After the service, crowd members fell in with the funeral cortege, some of New York's lowliest citizens mixing with some of its loftiest. They marched to the Queensborough Bridge, from which Schiff's casket continued to Salem Fields, the sprawling cemetery that the Emanu-El congregation had established on a vast and gently rolling tract that straddled Brooklyn and Queens. Stately mausoleums, some containing stained-glass windows by Louis Comfort Tiffany depicting biblical tableaus, speckled the hillsides. Interred within were some of America's greatest financial minds, men Schiff had known well: Jesse and Joseph Seligman, whose prolific sale of U.S. bonds during the Civil War and afterward helped to sustain and strengthen the fragile nation; Marcus Goldman, a trailblazer in the commercial debt market; Emanuel and Mayer Lehman, the commodities-trading wunderkinds who helped found the New York Cotton Exchange.

Schiff's majestic tomb, assembled from twenty-ton granite slabs and evoking a Roman temple, overlooked the rest. He was among the last in a line of German-Jewish dynasts—and in many ways the most consequential—who played a pivotal part in America's progression into a financial, and thus global, superpower. Their firms—J. & W. Seligman & Co., Goldman Sachs, Kuhn Loeb, Lehman Brothers— capitalized railroads and transit systems, utilities and industrial giants, cities and nations. They helped give rise to some of the nation's most iconic companies: B.F. Goodrich, General Motors, Kodak, Macy's, Paramount, Polaroid, Sears, Studebaker, U.S. Rubber, Western Union, Westinghouse, Woolworth, and many others. And that was merely one facet of their seismic influence on the twentieth century.

"He was one of the small but powerful group who have made the higher commercial life of New York City what it is today," one of Schiff's intimates remarked on the day of his funeral. "The future historian of American business and industrial affairs must set forth their careers as dominating an epoch which, with all its faults, had been no less than majestic in its power, its distinction and its forward movement among the ages."[3]

Wandering the narrow, tidy lanes of Salem Fields, where the found- ing partners of Goldman Sachs reside a short stroll from the Lehman brothers, and where the Schiff and Seligman clans are entombed sev- eral hundred feet from each other, is a humbling, sometimes over- powering experience. Here the through lines of the past converge, the manicured grave sites forming the guideposts to the modern era. The proximity of these titans and their families in death hints at their intimacy in life. They were allies (and occasional rivals) in business, partners in philanthropy, friends, and in some cases in-laws. They worshipped together and celebrated one another's milestones. Each dynasty established a legacy that was exceptional on its own but is disorienting in scale when the aperture widens to take in their col- lective impact.

Families such as the Goldmans, Lehmans, Sachses, Schiffs, Selig- mans, and Warburgs are said to belong to "our crowd," members of a close-knit German-Jewish aristocracy in New York dominant dur- ing the Gilded Age. That became the ubiquitous descriptor for their social milieu, following the publication of Stephen Birmingham's dishy best-selling 1967 book of the same name, which colorfully chronicled the interwoven, near-incestuous, and outrageously opu- lent world of Manhattan's German-Jewish upper crust. In Birming- ham's telling, their high society paralleled that of the Christian elite, who held them at arm's length: namely, the "Four Hundred," Caroline Astor's roster of New York's haute monde. "They have referred to themselves as 'The One Hundred,'" Birmingham wrote. "They have been called the 'Jewish Grand Dukes.' But most often they have simply called themselves 'our crowd.'"[4]

Yet it's not clear that they did refer to themselves this way, which is why I largely avoid this appellation. Birmingham's own correspondence and other letters concerning his book's publication raise questions about the origins of this phrase. "I have never heard of these families referring to themselves as 'the One Hundred,' or calling themselves 'our crowd,'" Geoffrey Hellman, a *New Yorker* writer and great-grandson of Joseph Seligman, complained to Birmingham's publisher.[5] Hellman had been one of Birmingham's key sources, as was Frances Lehman, granddaughter of Mayer Lehman, who phoned the author after *Our Crowd*'s publication to express similar bewilderment.[6] In a letter to Hellman, Birmingham defended the title as "satiric" (because there was considerable rivalry within this supposedly cohesive group—essentially, crowds within "our crowd") and said that he had plucked the name from *Red Damask*, a 1927 novel about a wealthy German-Jewish family in New York, authored by Emanie Sachs, the first wife of Goldman Sachs scion Walter Sachs. The phrase "our crowd," he noted, was sprinkled throughout the text.[7] It was a useful literary device, but there is little historical basis to suggest that "our crowd" was anything more than that.

I set out to tell a different tale than Birmingham—less a social history than a financial, political, and philanthropic one—that focuses on a handful of dynasties whose members were particularly close, whose legacies were startlingly profound, and whose lives form an elemental part of the story of how modern America, the modern world, really, came to be. The annals of their firms reveal the nation's financial evolution, from the rough-and-tumble rise of Wall Street to the ascent of some of the twentieth century's quintessential companies and industries. Their philanthropy and institution-building are the bedrock on which American-Jewish life is built. Their support for the fine arts, literature, film, and music, and for libraries, museums, and universities, is embedded in the nation's cultural DNA.

The title of this book comes from the term that newspapers often used to describe Jacob Schiff and his fellow financial heavyweights—as in "Money King on Witness Stand," when Schiff testified before the New York legislature as it probed the life insurance industry, or "Jacob Schiff the New Money King," as the headline of one effusive 1903 article declared. It was a label applied not just to Jewish financiers but also to Christian moguls such as J. P. Morgan, John D. Rockefeller, and Edward H. Harriman. This name captured the titanic influence held by a relatively small cadre of investment bankers, industrial titans, and railroad barons, whose power, for a time, rivaled, and in some cases surpassed, that of the U.S. government, especially when it came to the still-unregulated realm of finance. The sobriquet "money king" was in some cases an expression of awe, crystallizing a new American obsession with corporate giants. In other contexts, it was a term of derision—an accusation of inordinate, unelected clout.

Wealth and power, and the myriad ways these German-Jewish dynasties left their mark on the modern world by expending both, are themes that run throughout this book—one that I initially hesitated to write. Like many Jews, I am sensitive to the antisemitic canards that have plagued our people for centuries, those that suggest our underlying traits are greed and avarice, that we control the media and the banking system, that we are party to a global plot to subjugate the planet.

The sudden and visible surge of antisemitism during the Trump era, when I began this project, alarmed me. Did exploring the epoch-shaping legacy of Schiff and his fellow "money kings" inadvertently risk arming bigots with fodder to weave into their conspiracy theories about Jewish bankers? It was these malign actors, I noticed, who seemed most committed to keeping Schiff's memory alive, for all the wrong reasons, in online ramblings filled with distortions and lies. But Schiff and his German-Jewish contemporaries—men who have been given far less than their historical due, considering their impact—deserve to be known, understood, in some cases celebrated. Their stories illuminate much about the past and present, and that includes the origins of modern antisemitism (and the forces behind it) and the fraudulent mythology, in which these German-Jewish bankers feature prominently, that was used to justify mass murder. Maybe, I concluded, there was no better way to counter the lies than to tell their stories in full.

Given the inauspicious beginnings of the patriarchs of New York's most prominent German-Jewish banking families, it was hard to imagine that they would ever grow notorious enough to be written into conspiracy theories. Most immigrated to the United States in their teens or early twenties, part of a swelling tide of German Jews seeking refuge from the oppressive conditions and discriminatory laws in their homeland. They arrived, after weeks-long voyages in squalid steerage conditions, with little more than their ambitions. Like many Jewish immigrants seeking a foothold in America, they found work as itinerant peddlers and merchants, vocations common back home in Germany, where Jews were prohibited from most other professions. Departing New York, they trundled off into the American heartland—men barely older than boys. Their paths, before long, would deposit them back in Manhattan, this time not as peons but as fledgling masters of finance.

Indeed, some of the world's greatest financial institutions, companies that would dominate Wall Street and power America's industrial transformation, were born out of rickety wooden carts and bulging canvas rucksacks.

PART I

ORIGINS

& BROS.

If Joseph Seligman seemed like a character lifted from the pages of a Horatio Alger novel, there was a good explanation for that. For about eight years spanning the late 1860s to the late '70s, the acclaimed author lived with the Seligman family in their Murray Hill home, where he tutored the banker's five sons and spent many evenings in Joseph's commodious library bantering with him about literature, philosophy, religion, and the latest scientific discoveries. Over the years, Alger soaked up Seligman's astonishing story.

"Horatio Alger had found in Joseph Seligman his prototype of the poor boy who, through courage and hard work, arrives at wealth and fame," recalled one of Joseph's grandsons. " 'Tattered Tom' and all those other miraculous heroes that follow the formula of the Alger books . . . are but other versions of Alger's employer."[1]

Joseph's journey to America began like those of many other immigrants of his generation. In July 1837 two horse-drawn carts steered away from the Bavarian farming town of Baiersdorf, beginning the trip that would carry Joseph and eighteen other would-be émigrés to the port city of Bremerhaven, on the North Sea. Joseph was seventeen and traveling alone. Sewn into the lining of his trousers was the equivalent of $100, which his mother had assiduously cobbled together to give her son a successful start in the United States.

Born in 1819, Joseph was Fanny Seligman's golden child, the oldest of a brood that eventually numbered eleven, eight of them boys.

Precocious and intellectual, Joseph, by the age of twelve, already displayed entrepreneurial instincts, offering his services as a money-changer—the German states had various currencies—to travelers transiting through his town of two thousand.[2]

The Seligmans operated a small shop in Baiersdorf's Jewish quarter—the family lived above it—where Fanny sold lace, linens, and ribbons, along with woolen goods produced by her husband, David, the town weaver. A reticent, world-weary man, David was eager to enlist his eldest son in the family trade, but Fanny insisted that Joseph continue his education after he completed primary school. At four-teen, he enrolled at the local university in nearby Erlangen, studying theology and medicine. He demonstrated a talent for languages—in addition to English, French, and Hebrew, he could discourse fluently in classical Greek.

The more he learned, the more he grew impatient of his surroundings and disdainful of the social order that shackled Jews with exclusionary laws that confined them to poverty and second-class status. For centuries in Europe, Jews had endured relentless persecution—expelled by monarchs and pontiffs, their property confiscated and their holy books incinerated. They had been massacred and burned at the stake; forcibly baptized; targeted with draconian edicts and extortionary taxes; banished to squalid ghettos. Attitudes had grown more enlightened, but only to a point. In Joseph's native Bavaria, Jews had only recently won the right to attend universities and own property.

At sixteen, he penned a treatise on the question of Jewish emancipation. Even though his sharp critique of German society angered university officials, he went on to give a forceful speech on this topic, in which he wondered why "my people" were "treated with little more consideration than that shown a negro slave."[3]

Like thousands of other young and ambitious men of his generation, enthralled by secondhand stories of what awaited industrious immigrants in *das Land der unbegrenzten Möglichkeiten* (the land of limitless possibilities), Joseph fixated on traveling to America. A cousin, Lewis Seligman, had settled in a town called Mauch Chunk (since renamed for the Olympian Jim Thorpe) in Pennsylvania coal country.[4] Joseph, who had yet to complete his university studies, pleaded with his parents to allow him to go. David initially protested, relenting only after Joseph secured a formal invitation from his cousin.

The trip to Bremerhaven took seventeen days. At night, Joseph and his fellow travelers camped on the roadside. This cramped and bumpy journey was luxurious compared to what awaited him aboard the *Telegraph*, where Joseph's forty-dollar steerage fare afforded him one meal a day and a dingy cabin he shared with five others.[5] The weather was stormy, the living conditions abysmal, and the voyage seemed endless—the *Telegraph* was at sea for forty-two days.[6] When he finally reached New York on September 25, he found the conditions on land no less turbulent than those at sea. He stepped ashore into the financial panic of 1837, one of the worst economic crises the nation had experienced since its founding.

The day of Joseph's arrival, the *New York Evening Post* carried a description of the origins of the banking crisis that sounded eerily similar to modern financial meltdowns:

> Confidence was extravagant, boundless; every body gave credit to every body . . . till at last the community began to see the folly of confidence without grounds, and they stopped short. Confidence was destroyed by its own excess. If the confidence of the people could have been kept up for ever, if the bill holders could have been prevented from ever calling to get their notes paid, the banks would have never stopped, bank paper would have become more and more abundant; prices would have risen indefinitely; speculation would have gone on without end.[7]

Across the country, banks toppled, spreading economic ruin from Vermont to Arkansas. The ensuing recession lasted well into the 1840s. During this traumatic period, eight states and the Florida territory declared bankruptcy.

Despite the tumultuous financial climate, Joseph found a job in Mauch Chunk working for Asa Packer, a self-made man then on his way to building a great fortune. Packer (who would go on to serve two terms in Congress and found Lehigh University) had established a handful of stores and a boatyard on the banks of the Lehigh Canal, where he operated a business transporting coal by barge from nearby mines. Packer hired Joseph as a cashier and clerk, but, impressed by his intellect, the businessman soon promoted Seligman to a $400-per-year position as his private secretary.

Perhaps inspired by Packer's bootstrapping tale, Joseph did not linger long in his employ. After about a year, he struck out on his own. Following a road map popular among young Jewish immigrants, he invested his savings (about $200) in merchandise that would appeal to the farmers and coal workers—and more important, to their wives— living in isolated locations outside town, gathered the goods into a pack, and then trudged off into the countryside.[8]

Pack peddling was arduous and lonely. A sort of boot camp for budding entrepreneurs, it necessitated a healthy reservoir of determination, charisma, and courage. Men like Joseph hauled back-crushing loads of one hundred pounds or more. Their profession required a fair bit of charm and rapport-building and not just to make sales, since they relied on the hospitality of their customers for food and lodging. Peddling was also dangerous. With their imperfect English and road-worn appearance, these roving salesmen were sometimes greeted with contempt, taunted with insults, and chased by rock-throwing locals. As foreigners and transients, they made easy scapegoats for various crimes. Traveling alone and carrying both merchandise and money, they were also attractive targets for criminals. In some cases, peddlers were robbed, beaten, stabbed, even murdered.[9]

Despite the perils and hardships of the road, Joseph thrived. Just as his cousin Lewis had provided glowing accounts of American life in letters home, Joseph's dispatches painted an enticing picture, and he included proof. He repaid the $100 his mother had given him when he set off for America and fronted the steerage fare for the second and third eldest Seligman brothers, Wolf and Jacob, to join him in Pennsylvania. In the spring of 1839, two more wagons departed Baiersdorf, carrying two more Seligmans, who thereafter would go by William and James. This was how chains of immigration often worked: a cousin, a brother, an uncle would serve as a magnet to other family members. In the case of the Seligmans, nearly the entire clan would soon join Joseph in America.[10]

For James, the journey across the Atlantic was unforgettable—in the worst imaginable way. "In the steerage large cots were placed close together, and seven of us slept on a cot," he recounted when he was well into his eighties. "During stormy weather we were crowded together in utter darkness for two or three days. It makes me sick to think of it, and the less said of it the better." On the miserable voyage, one passenger contracted smallpox, which spread quickly to dozens of others, including fifteen-year-old James, who was quarantined upon reaching New York. As he convalesced, James later recalled, a doctor administered "a dose of castor oil, which was so bad that I have tasted it ever since."[11]

The most handsome of the Seligman boys, James was a natural salesman, and Joseph staked his first foray into peddling, as he had William's. To get him started, Joseph bought him $300 worth of gold and silver jewelry—"rings, pins, chains, etc.," James recalled. He criss-crossed Pennsylvania, then ventured farther south in search of fertile new territory. Finally, he reached Alabama. He found the business opportunities so plentiful there that he excitedly returned north to persuade his brothers to relocate their peddling operations. To make his case, he needed to do little more than splash his profits in front of them. During his southward swing, he had pocketed around $1,000.[12]

In the summer of 1841, another Seligman, Jesse (born Isaias), then about fourteen, reunited with his brothers in Lancaster, Pennsylvania, where they had established a small store that served as a supply depot for their peddling excursions. "I remained in Lancaster a few weeks," Jesse remembered, "during which time I learned the English language to some extent, and, at the same time, mastered the science of smoking penny cigars."[13] That fall the four brothers sailed for Mobile with about $5,000 of merchandise.[14] They contemplated opening a store there, but the city was expensive and filled with competitors. "We therefore thought it advisable to go to some interior town," Jesse recalled.[15]

The Seligmans continued on to Selma, which James had touted from his previous trip. The community of about twelve hundred residents was a popular trading center, and the brothers established a makeshift shop there, arraying their goods beneath a tent, before eventually renting a storefront. Joseph stayed behind in Selma to run the store while his brothers embarked on what Jesse would describe as a monthlong "tour of inspection of the surrounding country."[16]

Perhaps the cause was a jibe about his foreignness—or his Jewishness—or maybe it was a dispute over merchandise, but while his brothers were on the road, Joseph quarreled with a local. Their argument turned violent, and Joseph was jailed as the instigator of the brawl. A local judge stood ready to impose a prison sentence, when a witness—the son of a prominent citizen—fingered the other man as the aggressor.

The tale in the Seligman family is that decades later, as Alabama struggled under the burden of its crushing Civil War debt, Joseph found a way to repay the favor. The witness who exonerated him,

now an Alabama judge, had traveled to New York in search of financing for the cash-strapped state. One by one bankers declined Alabama's business. The judge finally visited Joseph, not realizing that
the silver-haired banker was the young, battered merchant he had
once assisted. But Joseph recognized the Alabaman instantly. Without committing to a loan, he invited the judge to his home that evening for a dinner party celebrating the engagement of one of his
daughters. Midway through the evening Joseph silenced his guests
and told a story about an unjustly accused Jewish peddler who was
spared prison thanks to the unsolicited testimony of a young man. He
finally announced dramatically, "The youth is none other than the
illustrious Alabama jurist who honors our table tonight, the friend-
less Jew none other than my humble self." Addressing the surprised
judge, Joseph told him that the Seligman brothers would be pleased
to advance Alabama a loan of $1 million.[17]

Not long after the Seligman brothers relocated to the South, word
arrived from Bavaria that Fanny Seligman had died. She was forty-
two. Over the next two years the remaining Seligmans—sisters
Babette, Rosalie, and Sarah, and brothers Henry (born Hermann),
Leopold (Lippmann), Abraham, and Isaac—immigrated to the
United States. In 1842, James returned to New York briefly to meet
the first wave of Seligman siblings, who ranged in age from three
(Sarah) to twenty-one (Babette), and to set them up in a house at the
corner of Pitt and Grand streets. David Seligman, whose business
collapsed after Fanny's death, reluctantly left Baiersdorf in 1843. He
died just two years after reaching New York.

The brothers, meanwhile, continued to build their business in the
South, establishing stores in Eutaw, Clinton, and Greensboro. Their
shops carried a vast assortment of products: jewelry, fabric, clothing,
cookware, saddles, hardware, guns, sheet music, even pianos.

"The Ladies are respectfully invited to examine our beautiful
styles of Bareges, Balzarines, Polk-a Muslins, Thread Laces, Hosiery,
Bonnets and Ribbons, and a variety of Fancy Goods, which have been
selected with taste, and will be sold at prices to suit the times," the
brothers' Greensboro store advertised.[18] They called this shop Seligman's New York Cash Store—they often emphasized that their merchandise had been imported from New York—and boasted "quality
and low prices" that "cannot be surpassed by any establishment in
the South."[19]

Business was good, but by the late 1840s, Joseph and his brothers were eyeing new opportunities. Southern life had never really suited them. Uncomfortable with the slave-holding culture, the Seligmans gravitated toward the abolitionist politics of what would become the Republican Party. Jesse became an admirer of Henry Clay, the Kentucky statesman who denounced slavery's expansion into the new U.S. territories, when he visited Eutaw as the Whig Party's presidential nominee during the 1844 campaign.[20]

In 1848 the Seligmans decided to close their Alabama stores and return north. If slavery was part of the impetus for their departure, it was not the main cause, according to one of Joseph's grandsons, the writer and rare book dealer George S. Hellman (father of *The New Yorker*'s Geoffrey Hellman). "It would . . . be an exaggeration to suggest that their antipathy towards human subjection by reason of race or creed or color was their chief motivation in deciding upon the North as their future home," Hellman wrote in his unpublished history of Joseph and his brothers, "The Story of the Seligmans."[21] The decision to relocate to New York was mostly an economic one. "We thought that we might better our condition by coming North," Jesse maintained.[22]

As the Seligmans wrapped up their Alabama operations, they placed a notice in a Greensboro newspaper. "LAST CALL!" it announced. "All persons indebted to the late firm of J. Seligman & Bro's are earnestly requested to make payment, as longer indulgence cannot be given."[23]

Departing from the South marked a new phase in Joseph's life. In late 1848, as he was nearing thirty, he returned to Bavaria for the first time since he had left. To the townspeople of Baiersdorf, he personified America's promise. The teenager who'd left in the back of a crowded wooden cart had come back a prosperous businessman who sought out and paid his late father's creditors with interest. That wasn't the sole purpose of his visit, though. He also came to Germany, along with his brother James, to meet with local exporters—and to bring home a wife. In Munich, he married his nineteen-year-old first cousin, Babette Steinhardt.

As he sailed back to New York with his new bride, his days of peddling must have seemed deceptively distant. Seven years earlier the brothers had lacked the cash to open a business in Mobile, but now they had built enough capital to establish a beachhead in what was soon to be the nation's undisputed financial center. At 5 William Street in downtown Manhattan, James and Joseph formed J. Seligman & Brothers, Merchants, which was soon rebranded as J. Seligman & Brothers, Importers, in keeping with the brothers' growing business ambitions. Sixty years later, on that same corner lot, the Seligmans would erect an elegant eleven-story limestone tower befitting one of America's leading investment banks. A couple of decades later, when the Seligman firm had moved on to new premises, an ascendant Wall Street firm, established by another set of Bavarian brothers with Alabama roots, would claim the neo-Renaissance-style skyscraper as its own headquarters.

2

THE PEDDLERS' PROGRESS

As the Seligmans cleared out of Alabama, the Lehmans were just settling in.

"Not respectable"—that was how one representative of credit rating agency R.G. Dun & Co., assigned to assess Emanuel and Henry Lehman's business, described the brothers' operation in December 1849. The Lehmans, he noted, had sunk everything they owned into their Montgomery dry goods shop, located in a two-story wood-frame house at 17 Court Square, within earshot of the barking auctioneers at the city's slave market. The credit reporter provided no further information to support his conclusion. But subsequent entries hint at what he might have found objectionable about the Lehmans. "V[ery] little reliance is here placed in any descendants of the tribe," another correspondent commented a few years later. By this time a third brother, Mayer, had joined the business. "They are in fair cr[edit] here, but Jews seldom remain and make good citizens." Another note was even more pointed: "We think they are of that class to whom when goods are sold a strict watch sh[ould] be kept upon their movements."[1]

These early reports spoke less to the Lehmans' character than they did to the ingrained prejudices of the times. But in another respect, they did say a lot about the brothers—showing the obstacles they overcame as they established themselves as some of the South's leading businessmen in just a decade's time.

Henry Lehman, born in 1822, paved the way for the brothers' rise in Montgomery and, later, New York. The Lehmans hailed from the small Bavarian village of Rimpar, six miles north of Würzburg, where the family was part of a tight-knit Jewish community of 108. The family name had originally been not Lehman but Löw (lion). Following an 1813 edict requiring Jews to select new surnames and swear an oath of loyalty to the state, Abraham Löw, the patriarch, had chosen Lehmann. (After emigrating, the brothers dropped an *n* from Lehmann.)

Compared with other Jewish families, the Lehmanns were relatively prosperous. Abraham, a cattle merchant who had a sideline selling wine, owned a comfortable home near the fortified walls of a fourteenth-century castle, where Eva Lehmann gave birth to ten children. Only seven—four boys and three girls—survived until adulthood.

Henry was the second oldest of Abraham and Eva's sons, Emanuel the third, and Mayer the youngest, which meant they stood little chance of making a life for themselves in Rimpar or the surrounding villages. Abraham and other Jewish heads of household had to pay *Landesschutzgeld*, protection money, to live in Rimpar and other towns. Protected Jews were listed on a register known as a *Matrikelliste*— essentially, a quota system intended to limit the Jewish population. A Jewish family's oldest son typically received a place on the register (his brothers were out of luck), a privilege that went to Seligmann Lehmann, who joined his father in the cattle business. Little more is known about the oldest Lehman brother, though Mayer's youngest son, Herbert, a governor of New York and U.S. senator, once hinted at why this might be so. "I rather think he was the Lehman skeleton in the closet," he said, "as I have always understood that he was a very good, workman-like drinker."[2]

When Henry reached twenty-one, he faced an uncertain future in Bavaria. So like Joseph Seligman and thousands of other young men of their generation, he sailed for America. He arrived in New York on September 11, 1844, and soon boarded another ship to Mobile. Henry's itinerary suggested he already had friends or relatives in the South. He may have gravitated to Mobile based on family ties with the Goldschmidt family of Herbsdorf. Two Goldschmidts traveled to America aboard the same ship as Henry. And a Herbsdorf émigré named Lewis Goldschmidt (Goldsmith, after he reached the U.S.) operated a clothing store in Mobile.[3] If the Lehmans were not acquainted with the Goldsmiths before, then they would get to know them well. Mayer Lehman would later marry in the New Orleans home of one of Lewis Goldsmith's sons.[4]

Goldsmith's shop was a popular way station for young German-Jewish immigrants like Henry, who purchased all the merchandise they could carry and ventured out to peddle their wares, visiting farms, mining camps, and remote hamlets. Jews peddled throughout the United States, but they were often drawn toward developing regions where they faced little competition and could sell their merchandise at a premium. That was why budding businessmen such as the Seligmans migrated south, where the region's upstart communities were experiencing a surge in population growth.

Peddlers were like mobile department stores, and they tended to specialize in luxury items, extravagances, and "fancy" goods (decorative knickknacks and accessories). There often seemed to be no end to what a peddler could produce from his pack or excavate from his loaded cart: almanacs, mirrors, picture frames, china, cutlery, table linens, bedding, shawls, coats, shoes, lace, silk, embroidery patterns, watches, jewelry, sewing machines.

Peddling was the most popular start-up profession for the German-Jewish immigrants who came to the United States in the 1830s and '40s because it was a familiar one. It had been one of the few professions available to their fathers and grandfathers in the old country. In an America rapidly expanding south and west, peddling offered new arrivals a foothold on the economic ladder. "I call it the Harvard Business School for Jewish boys," said John Langeloth Loeb, Jr., a great-grandson of Mayer Lehman and onetime U.S. ambassador to Denmark.[5]

After gaining some experience, the next rung up for peddlers was opening a store. Within a year of arriving in Alabama, Henry Lehman had saved enough to take this step, choosing Montgomery as the place to hang his shingle.

Founded about twenty-five years earlier, Montgomery was a fast-growing outpost of about six thousand, a third of its population consisting of slaves whose toil turned the gears of southern commerce. Henry had good reason to see potential in the city, which became the state capital the year after he arrived. A railroad line was under construction that in the coming years would connect Montgomery to East Coast destinations. And the city sat at the northernmost navigable point for steamships traveling the Alabama River, making it an important commercial and transportation hub. Henry was far from the only merchant to glimpse Montgomery's promise—by the early 1850s, the city had more than thirty dry goods stores.[6]

Henry opened his first shop on Commerce Street—the move to more auspicious premises on Court Square would come a few years later—in a dilapidated house, where he tended to customers by day and retired each evening to the austere back room where he slept.[7] Much about Montgomery must have seemed alien to Henry, starting with the humid climate that made it ideal for cultivating cotton and other crops—but also for the spread of mosquito-borne illnesses such as yellow fever. "There is money to be made here," the young immigrant wrote home to his family at one point, "if the Fever doesn't get me first."[8]

The lack of an established religious community would have been another cause for culture shock. Henry was among the first Jews to settle in Montgomery: around the time he arrived, about a dozen other Jewish men lived there, enough at least for a minyan, the quorum of ten adult males required for public worship in the Jewish faith. The city had no temple, so they conducted religious services in the home of a local grocer.[9] In 1846, Henry joined other members of Montgomery's Jewish community to form a benevolent society, Chevra Mevacher Cholim, to tend to their sick and bury their dead in accordance with religious law. One of its first priorities was establishing a Jewish cemetery.[10]

In 1849, Henry and other members of Chevra Mevacher Cholim (Society for Relieving the Sick) organized the city's first Jewish congregation, Kahl Montgomery, and the twenty-seven-year-old merchant was elected vice-president of the fledgling organization of about thirty members. His twenty-two-year-old brother Emanuel, whom Henry had lured to Montgomery in 1847, was appointed the congregation's secretary.[11]

Kahl Montgomery was modeled on New York City's Temple Emanu-El, which had been founded a few years earlier. Emanu-El's congregants practiced a new, liberal form of Judaism that had been imported from Germany and that took a looser view of Jewish customs, including the dietary laws; Reform Jews saw their religion as a progressive one that should evolve with the times. Propelling this movement was the mass migration of Jews from the ghettos of Europe to the United States, where they settled among Christians and strove to blend into a society in which ancient prejudices, while present, typically did not abridge their rights as citizens.

A year after Emanuel's arrival, Henry moved his shop to Court Square, in the heart of Montgomery's bustling commercial district. And he hung a new sign above his door, signifying Emanuel's admission as a partner. It read, "H. Lehman & Bro."[12] Now in his late twenties, Henry had devoted himself single-mindedly to economic advancement. With his business steadily growing, he felt confident enough in his financial future to marry. On November 7, 1849, he wed twenty-four-year-old Rosa Wolf, who also hailed from Bavaria (and who was possibly a childhood sweetheart).[13] The following summer came two new Lehman arrivals—Henry and Rosa's firstborn, a son named David, and Mayer, who had come over from Germany.

It was not just the promise of economic opportunity but also the threat of political turmoil that delivered Mayer to the American South. Beginning in 1848, the year Karl Marx and Friedrich Engels published their *Communist Manifesto*, a series of bloody uprisings engulfed Europe. Like a lit fuse, the protests leaped from Italy to France to the independent states of Germany, to the Hapsburg Empire, until much of Western Europe was aflame with revolutionary fervor. The causes of the unrest, fueled in part by widespread economic hardships, differed from place to place, but a common thread running through the protest movements was a demand for democratic reforms and basic civil rights.

By some accounts, Mayer participated in the agitations in Bavaria and had links to a group of liberal revolutionaries that included Carl Schurz, who after fleeing Europe went on to political prominence in America as a U.S. senator and secretary of the interior during the administration of Rutherford B. Hayes.[14] Many Jews had joined in the demonstrations besieging the monarchies of pre-unification Germany, seeing a chance to liberate themselves from centuries of oppressive rule that had forced them to live as permanent outsiders.

In 1849 the Jews of Bavaria appeared to be on the cusp of a breakthrough. That December the lower house of the Bavarian *Landtag* approved a bill granting them the same rights as Christians. Jews rejoiced, but other citizens angrily denounced the measure. One incensed lawmaker argued that Jews would remain foreigners even if their Bavarian roots stretched back a millennium. Just as equality came within reach, it was snatched away: in February 1850 the upper chamber of parliament rejected Jewish emancipation.[15]

By May, Mayer had set off for America. He joined thousands of

"Forty-Eighters," as this wave of émigrés was known, who departed Europe in the aftermath of the revolutions of 1848 and 1849, many of them escaping reprisals or persecution for their revolutionary activities. Mayer traveled to the French port city of Le Havre—from which Henry had made the Atlantic crossing six years earlier—and boarded a three-masted ship dubbed the *Admiral*, cramming in with hundreds of other passengers in steerage. He arrived in New York on July 17.[16] Had the voyage lasted even twenty-four hours longer, the Lehman name might never have been etched into American financial history. Just as the *Admiral* docked, a hurricane was churning up the East Coast from the Caribbean. The storm made landfall in New York the day after Mayer's arrival, unleashing violent winds that peeled the tin roofs off buildings.[17]

After Mayer joined his brothers in business, an *s* was added to the firm's legend. The newly rechristened H. Lehman & Bros. advertised itself as "wholesale and retail dealers in dry goods, clothing" and stocked "groceries, hardware, boots, shoes, hats, caps, bonnets, cutlery, flowers, combs, etc., etc., etc."[18] There was much *et cetera* in the brothers' business dealings during this period. They also dealt extensively in real estate, buying and selling land and other properties, and they dipped a toe into the cotton business, the predominant local industry.

Cotton was the de facto currency of the South. There was plenty of paper money in circulation—that wasn't the problem. President Andrew Jackson's 1832 decision to pull the plug on the federally chartered Second Bank of the United States, which had kept the issuance of currency by state-chartered banks in check, had led to a proliferation of loosely regulated institutions, each churning out its own notes. Counterfeiters gleefully exploited this haphazard system, flooding the market with bogus bills. (The counterfeiting epidemic eventually led to the creation of the U.S. Secret Service in 1865, by which time about a third of all banknotes in circulation were thought to be fakes.)

Because paper currency was not always reliable, tangible commodities formed the backbone of American commerce, and in the South cotton reigned as the premier cash crop. In their general store, the Lehmans accepted payment for goods in cotton. "It was largely a barter arrangement," Herbert Lehman recalled of his family firm's business origins. "The farmers would come in with their cotton and trade it for shirts and shoes and fertilizer . . . and seed, and all the necessities. That's how they got started in the cotton business."[19]

The Lehmans also extended credit to farmers and plantation owners, advancing them merchandise and securing these loans with liens on the cotton harvest.

In contrast with the Seligmans, who opposed slavery and supported the Republican Party, the Lehmans, lifelong Democrats, grew accustomed to this practice as they acclimated to southern life. By 1850 they were buying slaves of their own, which they used for domestic help and to assist in their business. Eventually the brothers owned at least seven slaves. One was Martha, a girl of about fourteen at the time of her purchase, who was deemed "sound in body and mind, and a slave for life," according to the bill of sale. Her price: $900.[20]

How did the Lehmans rationalize owning slaves, given that one of the origin stories of their faith tells of the flight of the Jewish people from bondage and the harsh punishment meted out by God against the Egyptians who had enslaved them? Moreover, many Forty-Eighters naturally translated the values they had battled for in Germany into the struggle for abolition in the United States.

An unpublished Lehman Brothers–commissioned corporate history, titled "The Seed and the Tree" and authored by late Lehman partner Frank Manheim, notes dryly that the Lehmans "came to share the views and prejudices of their adopted community."[21] They were not alone. Many southern Jews came to accept, if not embrace, slavery—though the spiritual dissonance of this position, even at that time, was lost on no one. During one barbed congressional debate over slavery in the 1850s, an abolitionist senator inveighed against "Israelites with Egyptian principles"—a dart aimed at his slavery-defending colleague Judah Benjamin, the Jewish Democrat from Louisiana who would go on to serve in the cabinet of Confederate president Jefferson Davis during the Civil War.[22] For prosperous southern Jews, slaveholding was a rite of assimilation that placed them on equal footing with the white gentry. Indeed, for the Lehmans, owning slaves may have made them feel more "white" and southern.

In its ledger covering the businesses of Montgomery County, R.G. Dun & Co., year by year, recorded the Lehmans' progress. "Keep a large stock are d[oing] a g[oo]d bus[iness]. . . . Stand fair. Good for their contracts," the credit rating agency noted in December 1852. A couple of years later it described the Lehmans as "sober, indus[trious] & attentive bus. men" who were "d[oing] a v[ery] g[oo]d sort of bus." By 1855, R.G. Dun estimated the Lehmans' worth at about $50,000, 60 percent of which was "in real estate & negroes." And it noted that though the Lehmans were Jews, they "are consid[ered] almost as good as 'white men.' Are thought well of & consid[ered] as hon[est] and trustworthy as it is possible for Jews to be."[23]

The Lehmans, by now, were taking the next evolutionary step in their progression from merchants to bankers. Though they did not yet advertise themselves in these terms, they were becoming commission merchants—businessmen who brokered commodities such as tobacco, sugar, or, in the Lehmans' case, cotton. Local planters consigned their crop to the Lehmans, who arranged for its sale and for the logistics—including insuring the cargo against fire or maritime losses—of its transport. Such merchants, sometimes also known as cotton factors, collected a fee of about 2.5 percent on each transaction, plus expenses.[24]

As their business grew, so did the terrain the Lehmans covered. Emanuel traveled regularly to New York to meet with northern cotton buyers and exporters, purchase merchandise for their store, and manage their accounts in local banks. Henry, meanwhile, ventured often to New Orleans to visit business contacts in the busy port city, where ships ferrying cotton to New York and Europe were constantly coming and going. During his brothers' absences, Mayer minded the store in Montgomery and boned up on the cotton business. Outgoing and gregarious, he befriended local growers, who tutored him on their business, from the weather conditions that could affect the crop, to its growth cycles, to the elements that determined the commercial quality of a harvest.

During the summer of 1855, yellow fever outbreaks began flaring in the South. The virus manifested like a typical flu, causing fever, fatigue, muscle aches, and the chills. But then came bleeding in the eyes, mouth, and intestines, producing black vomit—a telltale symptom. Death often followed. Two years earlier the virus had wiped out as much as 10 percent of the population of New Orleans. In late September 1855 several cases of yellow fever were reported in Montgomery. "Many persons are already seeking safety in the country," a local newspaper reported.[25]

Sometime that fall Henry departed Montgomery on one of his periodic business trips to New Orleans. Various Lehman biographers have recounted the story of how, panicked by the outbreak in Montgomery, he left town at the urging of his brothers. But if so, New Orleans would hardly have qualified as a refuge. The city was experiencing its own full-blown yellow fever epidemic, with hundreds dying each week. During this outbreak, the fever eventually claimed nearly three thousand lives there—including Henry's. He died on November 17 and was buried in the city's only Jewish cemetery, leaving behind an estate of $42,000.[26]

The future of the business Henry founded now fell to Emanuel and Mayer. By appearance, it was easy to mistake the two brothers. Both stood about five foot six. Both had dark eyes and features. And both wore Vandyke beards, clean-shaven to the jawline, with whiskers that spilled over their shirt collars.

But temperamentally they were opposites. Mayer was energetic and amiable, the smiling outward face of their enterprise, who built relationships with members of the southern elite and slipped, with surprising grace, into prominent circles. He counted among his close friends Thomas Hill Watts, a Montgomery lawyer and plantation owner who would later serve as Alabama's governor, and Hilary Herbert, a future navy secretary. "It's an amazing thing how quickly my father apparently became integrated into the economic and social life of his community," Herbert Lehman, Hilary Herbert's namesake, once noted.[27]

One quality that served him well was his unusual ability to relate to people. "He could with ease and facility consider the feelings and emotions of other people and give due consideration to them," one friend remembered of Mayer and his "peculiar constitution of mind."[28] He relished the adrenaline rush of risk, and as the Lehmans edged further into the cotton trade, he drove this expansion.

Emanuel, by contrast, was reserved and a bit of a worrywart, averse to unnecessary hazard. He felt most comfortable handling the financial nuts and bolts of their business. A longtime employee recalled Emanuel as "mature already in his youth" and a "courteous" and supremely intelligent man to whom there was no artifice—"no sham, no glitter, no display."[29]

"My father was always very progressive," Herbert Lehman recalled, referring to Mayer. "My uncle Emanuel was conservative. . . . People used to joke about the firm's caution. They always said that when they came in, they'd ask my father's opinion of the cotton market, and my father would say, 'I would buy.' Then they would go to my uncle, and he would say, 'I would sell.'" The brothers provided a natural check on each other, with Mayer pushing the boundaries of their business and Emanuel serving as the voice of restraint. The story in the family was that Mayer made the money and Emanuel kept them from losing it—at least most of the time.[30]

Always close, the brothers pooled their resources and for decades shared a cash account, from which they paid their household expenses without concern for which brother was withdrawing more from the communal pot.[31] They shared this practice in common with the Seligmans, who kept "no account of private incomes or expenditure" and "trusted the other to spend just what was necessary to maintain his family in comfortable circumstances," according to Isaac, the youngest of the brothers.[32]

With Henry gone, Emanuel and Mayer changed the name of their firm a final time. From now on, they would go by Lehman Brothers.

3

MANIFEST DESTINY

During the mid-nineteenth century, the United States was expanding its frontiers in various directions. So, too, were the Seligmans. Soon after returning North, the brothers split up in search of new financial opportunities, a divide-and-conquer strategy they would employ throughout their careers. James and Joseph manned their Manhattan importing business, while William headed west to St. Louis to open a clothing store with his sister Babette's new husband, Max Stettheimer. Jesse and younger brother Henry, meanwhile, decamped hundreds of miles north to Watertown, New York, near the border of British North America (what would become Canada), where they established the New York City Dry Goods Store on a business-lined plaza known as Public Square.

One of their customers was a young army officer recently assigned to nearby Sackets Harbor, an important military outpost where American soldiers had repelled a British incursion during the War of 1812. First Lieutenant Ulysses S. Grant was fresh from his service in the Mexican-American War, where he had first seen combat. The two-year war, rooted in the doctrine of "manifest destiny," which placed the imprimatur of God on America's rapacious and bloody westward expansion, had resulted in the nation extending its borders still farther, swallowing 55 percent of Mexico's territory, including all or part of present-day Arizona, California, Colorado, Nevada, New Mexico, Texas, and Utah. Grant had no illusions about what he and his fellow soldiers had participated in, later calling the conflict "the most unjust ever waged by a stronger against a weaker nation."[1]

In Watertown, Grant grew friendly with the Seligmans. Over games of poker and checkers, they cemented a lifelong bond. "On our acquaintance we immediately became friends," Jesse recalled, "and from that hour until his death I know of no one who was entitled to greater love and respect from not only his own immediate friends, but from the people of the entire country."[2]

The brothers had not been in business a year when, early one Sunday morning in May 1849, a fire erupted in Watertown's main business district. The blaze leaped from one timber-frame building to the next. Banks, hotels, the post office, an Episcopal church—all succumbed to the flames. The fire incinerated one hundred structures, including Jesse and Henry's store.[3]

They worked quickly to rebuild, but barely had they reopened when Jesse grew restless. The north country, picturesque and profitable though it was, felt especially far from the action. To read the newspapers, the center of the universe was California, where, just days before Mexico signed away its claim to this territory, a sawmill operator discovered gold dust in a Coloma riverbed. A national stampede of fortune-seekers followed. The gold fever seemed to afflict a certain young swashbuckling type—Jesse, then twenty-three, caught the bug. But instead of following the horde into the Sierra Nevada foothills, he sought to stake a different sort of claim.

People were pouring into San Francisco by the thousands—and all these new arrivals were potential customers. Because of the logistical challenges of transporting merchandise to the West and the explosion in new wealth, Jesse wagered that in California he could sell goods imported from New York and Europe for many times their worth.

Whatever case he made to Joseph, the sober-minded paterfamilias, it was persuasive. Jesse not only secured his brother's permission to establish a new Seligman outpost in San Francisco, but he departed for California with a $20,000 trove of merchandise, representing a major investment by the brothers. While Henry remained in Watertown, Leopold accompanied Jesse west. At nineteen, Leopold had yet to contribute to the family enterprises—in California, Joseph hoped his artistic younger brother would gain some business sense.

No easy route to California existed, only marginally less dangerous ones. Many traveled overland in wagon trains, but the trip could take six months or more, if you survived a gauntlet of hazards. You could sail the entire way, but that required detouring around South America and rounding the continent's southernmost tip, Cape Horn, a perilous stretch of ocean known for its unpredictable weather patterns and towering swells. From New York, the trip was about sixteen thousand miles. The shortest journey, and the one Jesse and Leopold chose, entailed sailing to the Panamanian Isthmus, the narrowest stretch of land linking North and South America, where about fifty miles of rugged terrain separated the Atlantic and Pacific oceans. In Chagres, on the Atlantic side of the isthmus, goods and gear were off-loaded and lashed to mules; passengers caravanned through the jungle and over mountain passes to Panama City, where they boarded another ship to California.

The Panama route, which halved the length of the westward journey, came with its own risks. One of the biggest was contracting malaria, yellow fever, or any number of tropical illnesses endemic to the area. By the time the Seligmans boarded a paddle wheel steamship dubbed the *Northerner* for the second leg of their trip to California, Leopold and many of their fellow passengers had come down with a malarial fever. Anxious days passed as eight travelers died, their bodies heaved into the sea. But Leopold, to Jesse's great relief, slowly regained his strength.[4]

Sometime in the fall of 1850, the *Northerner* glided into San Francisco Bay and deposited the brothers and their brimming crates of merchandise into a freewheeling frontier outpost that had almost literally sprung up overnight. It was a city of vice and excess, populated by gamblers, rogues, and schemers of every description. Saloons and gambling houses lined the muddy, refuse-strewn streets. Street brawls and gun duels were a common sight.

Surveying the city's landscape of canvas tents and ramshackle structures, Jesse realized that San Francisco was at risk for the type of catastrophic blaze that had torn through Watertown. He managed to lease space in the city's only brick building, which adjoined a hotel called the Tehama House. Jesse's instinct was sound. Around eleven p.m. on May 3, 1851, a fire started in a paint store and spread with alarming speed, building to such cataclysmic proportions that an eerie glow was visible one hundred miles away.

Jesse rushed to his store. Next door the hotel's proprietor, Captain Joseph Folsom, had ordered his waiters to cover the roof with wet blankets. "I at once explained to Captain [Folsom]," Jesse recalled, "that if my house were to take fire, nothing could save his hotel from destruction, as it was built of wood, and I suggested that he transfer a number of his men to my roof, so that, in the event of my success in fighting the fire, his hotel would also be secure. He acted upon my suggestion; and it was well that he did so."[5] Jesse made a similar argument to the firemen of Howard Engine Company No. 3, the volunteer squad fighting the blaze in his neighborhood, convincing them to concentrate their efforts on saving his building.[6]

The fire destroyed three-quarters of San Francisco. But when the smoke cleared, Jesse's store and the Tehama House remained intact. The disaster proved lucrative for the Seligmans since it temporarily wiped out all of Jesse's competitors. "Of all the dealers in merchandise," he later said, "I was the only one whose house was saved, and as I had many articles that were needed at that time, I soon disposed of much of my stock, though I made no attempt to increase or reduce my prices."[7]

There was hardly a need for Jesse to mark up his merchandise. He already charged astronomical prices, as did other San Francisco merchants, due to the extreme hardships of transporting certain goods there. His store sold $5 blankets for $40. A quart of whiskey fetched as much as $30.[8]

The San Francisco store eventually overtook other Seligman enterprises as the family's biggest revenue generator. Ships slid into San Francisco Bay carrying cookware, clothing, stationery, liquor, cigars, and more for Jesse's shop, and they returned to Panama City loaded with strongboxes filled with gold dust and nuggets, the common tender in many San Francisco establishments. Local newspapers ran regular updates on the "shipment of treasure," and J. Seligman & Co.—not to be confused with Joseph's New York importing firm of the same name—often featured on this list of top gold exporters, named alongside the banking operation founded by Henry Wells and William G. Fargo and fellow merchants such as Bavarian immigrant Levi Strauss who, before inventing his famous riveted blue jeans, ran a San Francisco dry goods business supplied by his own set of New York–based brothers.

In 1852, Jesse and Leopold shipped at least $72,000 of gold to New York. By 1854, $159,000. The following year, $261,000. By decade's end more than $700,000 a year flowed to the New York operation. (Some of this gold may have belonged to customers.)

In the early 1850s, Henry shuttered the Watertown store and joined Jesse and Leopold in San Francisco. Soon Abraham, the second-youngest Seligman brother, headed there, too. Curious about the West and perhaps awed by Jesse's success, Joseph made the arduous trek to San Francisco to inspect the operation, a trip that would have kept him away from his young family in New York for the better part of a year or more.[9]

As the Seligmans gained prominence in the local business community, they also became active in city and community affairs, including those of the local Jewish population. At twenty-five, Henry served as president of the Reform congregation Temple Emanu-El, where he oversaw the construction of its first synagogue. (Meaning "God is with us," Emanu-El was a popular congregation name.) Described as "enthusiastic but undemonstrative, powerful in action, though always with gentle insistence," Henry ran the congregation's affairs with businesslike rigor, straightening out its finances and imposing fines on members who did not attend meetings.[10] Abraham, also an officer of the temple, served as the treasurer of the board that created Golden Gate Park.[11]

Following the 1851 blaze that destroyed much of San Francisco, Jesse joined Howard Engine Company No. 3. He also became a vigilante, one of the founding members of the Committee of Vigilance, a group of citizens who, lacking confidence in local government, took matters of crime and punishment into their own hands.

The influx of gold and the chaotic nature of the city's growth made it a hotbed for crime. For protection, Jesse carried a Colt revolver with a six-inch barrel. He nearly needed to use it one day when a bullet zipped by his head as he walked down the street. Jesse spun around to face his attacker, who, getting a better look at the young merchant, apologized for firing at him: "I mistook you for another man."[12]

The Vigilance Committee pledged in its charter that "no thief, burglar, incendiary, or assassin shall escape punishment either by the quibbles of the law, the insecurity of prisons, the carelessness or corruption of the police, or a laxity of those who pretend to administer justice."[13] Jesse and his fellow vigilantes operated a makeshift jail on Sacramento Street, where they corralled the accused in four-by-six-foot cells to await justice for their alleged crimes.[14] Their first prisoner was John Jenkins, an Australian ex-convict and member of a gang called the Sydney Ducks who had been caught robbing a safe from an office on Long Wharf. The vigilantes hastily convened a

trial. When members of the committee waffled over Jenkins's punishment, one vigilante spoke up: "Gentlemen, as I understand it, we
came here to hang somebody!"[15]

Pronounced guilty at midnight, Jenkins was marched in shackles
to Portsmouth Square.[16] The mob eventually strung Jenkins up from
a beam jutting from the porch of an adobe building. By that time, the
condemned man appeared to be already dead, killed by his execu-
tioners as they dragged him through the square by his neck. Along
with dozens of other San Franciscans, Jesse later signed his name
to a resolution claiming joint responsibility for the lynching.[17] He
recalled that he remained a member of the committee "until perfect
order was restored" to the city, via a controversial campaign of mob
justice that included multiple hangings, lashings, and the expulsion
of dozens of suspected criminals from the city limits.[18]

Jesse helped to channel the vigilantes' law and order aims into a
political organization that would enforce them. He joined with other
local merchants—and Vigilance Committee members—to form the
Committee of Twenty-One, which sought to root out political corruption in the city. The committee effectively overthrew the existing
political machine and replaced it with one of its own design, meeting
in secret to determine the slate of candidates who would represent
the People's Party, as their movement was known, in upcoming elections. The party would dominate local politics for a decade.[19]

Despite the difficulty of travel, Jesse and his brothers covered vast
distances with surprising frequency. During their lengthy absences,
their numbers gave them an advantage, since one brother could
step in for another. They moved between the East and West coasts
and increasingly ventured back to Europe to buy merchandise, to
exchange gold, and, as the brothers came of age, to embark on a
Brautschau, a bride search. The surge of Jewish immigration from the
German states during the 1840s more than tripled America's Jewish
population by the start of the next decade, yet by 1850 there were
still only about fifty thousand Jews scattered around the nation. To
find a suitable partner—someone who shared their language, their
culture, their religion, and who was committed to preserving their
heritage—Jewish men often had to return to the old country, as Jesse
did in the early 1850s. During this trip, he became engaged to Henriette Hellmann, who one relative described as "not especially good-

looking, but a cultured girl, aristocratic in bearing, and of superb courage throughout her life."[20]

Henriette's fearlessness would serve her well in still-gritty San Francisco, where she returned with Jesse after the couple married in 1854. They remained in the West for several years, before Joseph summoned Jesse to New York to join the eastern branch of the business, while Abraham, Henry, and Leopold managed the San Francisco operation. Jesse and his family—by now he had two young sons—arrived in late 1857, as another financial catastrophe paralyzed the nation's economy. For two months starting that October, New York banks ceased redeeming paper money for gold to protect themselves from a run on their vaults. As the crisis rippled across the country, thousands of businesses failed. In New York City, some nine hundred mercantile firms were wiped out, collectively leaving behind $120 million in debts.

The Seligmans evidently saw signs of a coming downturn before many of their fellow merchants. A sharp drop-off in gold shipments from the San Francisco business over the previous year may have tipped them off. Joseph always counseled caution, and he grew worried enough about the health of the economy to liquidate the family's speculative investments and convert their bank deposits into gold and silver while he still could.

A convergence of factors caused the Panic of 1857. Declining gold supplies spooked banks, leading them to raise interest rates and scale back credit, then take more drastic measures. Meanwhile reality began to dawn on investors who had engaged in an orgy of railroad and land speculation.

The Supreme Court's *Dred Scott* decision, in March 1857, also contributed to the downturn. The far-reaching verdict invalidated the Missouri Compromise, which had outlawed slavery in most of the western territories acquired by the Louisiana Purchase. The ruling, heralded in the South and pilloried in the North, injected into the fragile economy a dose of political uncertainty about the future of slavery and the Manifest Destiny–fueled western migration that had caused the speculative boom in land and railroad stocks. Then in late August 1857, the Ohio Life Insurance and Trust Company, its books bloated with bad investments, collapsed, triggering bank runs. The Cincinnati company's role in sparking the economic crisis is often likened to the effects of the 2008 implosion of one of America's best-known investment banks—Lehman Brothers.

. . .

While at his office five blocks away Joseph Seligman was sealing gold and silver in strongboxes to ride out the financial collapse he worried was imminent, Emanuel Lehman was attempting to launch a new northern venture to complement Lehman Brothers' southern operation.

After Henry died from yellow fever, his widow and their four children had relocated to New York City, and Emanuel joined them there in 1857, moving into their home at 120 Second Street.

Lehman Brothers increasingly required a northern presence to support the firm's expanding mercantile ambitions. From New York, Emanuel could purchase merchandise for their dry goods store and arrange its shipment to Montgomery. And he could attend to their growing cotton business. While the commodity itself was grown in the South, New York was now at the center of the industry. It was the primary shipping link to European ports such as Liverpool, through which much of Britain's cotton imports from the United States passed. As the nation's financial capital, New York was also home to the banks and insurance companies that handled the financing and mitigated the risks of the cotton trade.

Where one day Lehman Brothers would occupy a glittering thirty-two-floor skyscraper on Fifth Avenue (the headquarters it would inhabit starting in 1980), visitors to Emanuel Lehman's first place of business in New York, at 119 Liberty Street, would have found an unremarkable storefront advertising booze and cigars.

In the summer of 1857, Emanuel had formed a partnership with twenty-eight-year-old Bavarian immigrant Moses Ferst, who had been working for his father's cigar manufacturing business on Grand Street. Lehman & Ferst billed itself as an importer and manufacturer of fine cigars, and it also stocked wine and liquor. In addition to supplying the Lehmans' Montgomery store, the firm had customers throughout the South.

Emanuel's timing couldn't have been worse. The partners had just opened for business when the booming national economy entered a tailspin.

Emanuel initially sank $10,000 into Lehman & Ferst, which proceeded to lose money due to a series of "unfortunate transactions," R.G. Dun & Co. noted. The losses and the nation's tumultuous economic condition must have terrified the elder Lehman brother, who always saw financial ruin ahead. However, he held on, and the partners managed to rebound from their early losses, doubling the value of their business to about $25,000. "The house stands well," R.G. Dun & Co. reported in 1859, noting that Emanuel was planning a trip south "to form new acquaintances & to extend th[eir] bus[iness]."[21]

Down the block from Emanuel's office, at 89 Liberty Street, was a shop run by fellow German Jews that dealt in "fancy goods." But what caught Emanuel's eye wasn't the luxe merchandise but the teenage daughter of one of the partners, Louis Sondheim. Emanuel married Pauline Sondheim, who was about sixteen at the time, in May 1859, a couple of months after his thirty-second birthday. Mayer, meanwhile, had also settled down, marrying Babette Newgass, the daughter of family friends who hailed from a town near Würzburg.[22] Babette was the oldest of seven children, and two of her sisters would also go on to marry wealthy businessmen. One would become the wife of Abraham Stern, a Liverpool cotton merchant who did business with the Lehmans. Another would wed Isaias Hellman, a prominent California banker once considered one of the richest men in the western United States.

Babette had relatives in New Orleans, and her wedding to Mayer took place at the handsome St. Charles Avenue home of her cousin, Ferdinand Goldsmith, the son of the merchant who ran a store in Mobile when Henry Lehman first arrived there. In their union, Mayer gained not just a wife but a new, though unofficial, business partner. Herbert Lehman recalled, "I don't think my father ever took an important step in business without consultation with my mother." With her sharp mind and commanding presence, Babette inspired devotion and perhaps a twinge of fear. She was a quintessential matriarch, who ran her household with a firm hand; her children, who eventually numbered seven (an eighth child, a boy named Benjamin, died in infancy), knew better than to cross her. "I don't know any case where a woman, a person, could be so definitely the head of the family as was my mother," Herbert said.[23]

Mayer and his expanding family lived in a rambling house at 402 South Court Street.[24] It was located a short walk from the Lehmans' Montgomery store, and Mayer's employees would often eat meals there.[25] The home occupied the better part of a block, and, with the exception of its wraparound porch and plantation shutters, its features seemed more European than southern.

By 1860, the Lehmans' northern and southern operations were both thriving. In New York, Emanuel's partnership with Moses Ferst was doing a brisk trade in liquor and tobacco.[26] In Montgomery, Mayer had sealed his status as a member of the local business elite by joining the Masonic lodge. He was now the seventh richest man in Montgomery County, surpassed only by two bankers and a handful of plantation owners.[27] That year's census noted that Mayer owned real estate worth $28,000 and personal property valued at $75,000. R.G. Dun & Co. now considered Lehman Brothers "an old & well established house" that was worth at least $100,000.[28]

But from their vantage points in New York and Montgomery, the brothers could clearly see the political storm clouds gathering. The *Dred Scott* decision had only escalated the national debate over slavery, which dominated the 1860 presidential election. That spring the Alabama delegation to the Democratic National Convention in Charleston, South Carolina, stormed out in protest after northern Democrats blocked pro-slavery planks from the party platform. The delegations from Florida, Georgia, Louisiana, Mississippi, South Carolina, and Texas soon joined the walkout. The split could not be reconciled. The party's northern and southern blocs eventually nominated their own candidates to face Abraham Lincoln, even though dividing their vote ensured a Democratic defeat.

In December 1860, as Lincoln prepared to take office and the drumbeat for secession grew louder in Alabama and other southern states, R.G. Dun & Co. added to its ledger what turned out to be its last update on Lehman Brothers until the conclusion of the Civil War. "Jews," the entry noted, "but g[ood] as anybody."[29]

4

WAR'S FORTUNES

A lles ist beendet!"—It's all over!—Emanuel wrote despondently to his wife's relatives after the war began.[1] The shelves of his store on Liberty Street were barren. Once the hostilities commenced, he had hurriedly shipped his merchandise to Montgomery, unsure when he would have another opportunity.[2] Since then, trade between North and South had ground to a halt, and the Lehmans' New York and Montgomery operations were cut off from each other. Emanuel wondered how their business could survive. In dark moments, he feared it couldn't.

To Mayer, the charged atmosphere may have felt familiar. He had lived through similar tumult in Bavaria, when the revolutions of 1848 had swept across Europe. Now, more than a decade later, a bloody rebellion had come to his adopted homeland. Many Forty-Eighters, in keeping with the democratic principles they had fought to advance in Europe, strongly opposed slavery and supported the Union. Veterans of the '48 revolutions signed up in droves to serve in the northern armies, and German Americans formed the largest ethnic group fighting for the Union. Carl Schurz, the Prussian revolutionary with whom Mayer was said to be associated, commanded a division at the Battle of Gettysburg.

Even though the Confederacy sought to maintain and expand a system of subjugation to which the Lehmans surely could have related as members of an oppressed people, the brothers thoroughly identified with the southern cause. (Mayer would be described later in life as an "unreconstructed rebel.")[3] Like many southern enterprises, the Lehmans' business hinged on the slave economy. At stake in the war was their way of life, or at least it may have seemed that way at the time.

Sometime in the summer of 1861, as the armies of the North and South clashed in Virginia, Emanuel left New York and briefly returned to Alabama.[4] A vivacious city before the war, Montgomery, the Confederacy's initial capital, had become a center of military and political activity. Journalists, soldiers, politicians, and businessmen poured into the city, packing its saloons, theaters, and hotels. Jefferson Davis, the recently inaugurated Confederate president, lived and kept an office in a suite at the Exchange Hotel, across Court Square from the Lehmans' store. That February, after his election, Davis had ascended to the hotel's balcony and hoarsely declared to hundreds of cheering onlookers that "if we must again baptize in blood the principles for which our fathers bled in the Revolution, we shall show that we are not degenerate sons."[5]

Neither of the Lehmans marched off to war. But they did join a local militia unit known as the Fireman Guards, charged with the defense of Montgomery. Muster rolls list "E." and "M." Lehman as privates in this detachment.

The fate of the Union was at stake. But as would gradually become clear to Emanuel, all was certainly not over for the Lehmans.

Days after Confederate troops attacked Fort Sumter in April 1861, President Lincoln ordered a blockade of southern ports, tightening a noose around the Confederate economy. The South responded by imposing an embargo on cotton exports to Europe, a failed diplomatic strategy to pressure Britain and France, major importers of southern cotton, to ally themselves with the Confederacy. The flow of cotton initially dwindled to a trickle. With world markets starved for the commodity, prices spiked; at one point during the war, cotton sold for $1.89 per pound, up from about ten cents in 1860.

But by the war's second year, an active black market trade had commenced. Sailing in light, fast ships designed to outrun Union vessels, smugglers threaded the blockade, their holds brimming with cotton bales and military cargo. The risks to crew and cargo were great, but so was the potential for profit. In many cases, after reaching a European port a cotton shipment was transferred to another ship that headed straight back across the Atlantic to New York, a detour of thousands of miles to scrub the freight of its illicit origins.

A corporate history published by Lehman Brothers in 1950 to mark the firm's centennial sidesteps the question of whether Emanuel and Mayer dealt in black market cotton, but the considerably longer and more detailed unpublished version, "The Seed and the Tree," leaves little doubt that they were blockade runners. "The handsome reward stimulated daring and resourcefulness," Lehman veteran Frank Manheim wrote, reminding readers that "no moral obloquy . . . attached to blockade running."[6] To the brothers and other supporters of the Confederacy, thwarting the Union's economic sanctions would not just have been profitable but patriotic.

Ulysses Grant, of course, saw things differently. In mid-December 1862, Grant, recently promoted to major general, handed down a controversial order expelling "the Jews, as a class violating every regulation of trade established by the Treasury Department," from his military jurisdiction, which sprawled from northern Illinois to southern Mississippi. Known as General Order No. 11, this stunning act of official antisemitism—perhaps the most infamous in U.S. history—stemmed from Grant's belief that the black market trade in cotton, which helped finance the Confederate war effort, was carried out "mostly by Jews and other unprincipled traders," as the general wrote in one missive.[7]

As foreigners, with distinctive accents and dress, Jewish peddlers, merchants, and sutlers—who trailed the army, selling various provisions to the troops—were perhaps the most visible "class" of traders in the war zone, and there's no doubt that Jews took part in smuggling. But so did many Christian businessmen. Only a small percentage of illicit traders were actually Jewish, but that hardly seemed to matter. As had replayed through the ages in Europe—when Jews were confined to professions considered too lowly for other citizens, such as peddling, tax collecting, and moneylending, and then were despised even more for engaging in these trades—Jews shouldered disproportionate blame for black market activity and profiteering. Indeed, as the historian Jonathan Sarna has observed, in his book *When General Grant Expelled the Jews*, "common wartime practices" such as smuggling and speculation became "perniciously identified with Jews alone."[8] During that period, the term *Jew* itself became shorthand for anyone engaged in aggressive or potentially unsavory mercantile activities. "In the eyes of many Americans (including some in the military)," Sarna writes, "*all* traders, smugglers, sutlers, and wartime profiteers were 'sharp-nosed' Jews, whether they were actually Jewish or not."[9]

There was a subplot to Grant's order, involving the general's unscrupulous father, Jesse, who was never above using his son's rising station to leverage personal profit. The elder Grant had struck a deal with a trio of Jewish brothers from Cincinnati, the Macks, to exert his influence with his son to obtain a permit to transport southern cotton through the battle lines in exchange for a cut of the profits. Jesse and the Macks traveled to the general's headquarters in Mississippi, where Jesse Grant made his pitch. The scheme, and especially his father's role in it, infuriated General Grant. Shortly thereafter he issued his infamous directive.

After learning of Grant's order, Lincoln, then preparing to release his Emancipation Proclamation, quickly commanded his general to rescind it. The impact of the order, only in effect a few weeks, was largely psychological. But for Jewish immigrants, it reinforced that even in America they could not outrun the religious persecution they had fled from in Europe. The episode, for which Grant later apologized, haunted his career (though it apparently didn't affect his long and friendly association with the Seligman brothers). The controversy resurfaced during his presidential candidacy and deeply influenced his presidency, where, in moves largely viewed as acts of contrition, he appointed Jews to senior posts and strongly denounced anti-Jewish violence in Russia and Romania.

Even with an active black market trade, cotton piled up in the South, only a fraction of the harvest slipping through the North's tightening cordon. Around the time when Grant issued and revoked General Order No. 11, Mayer forged a new alliance with a fellow Montgomery merchant that would both expand the Lehmans' footprint in the cotton business and exploit the lucrative market for cotton storage. Five years younger than Mayer, John Wesley Durr was a twenty-seven-year-old Georgia native who had worked his way up from a grocery store clerk to a partner in M.E. Vaughn & Co., which owned Montgomery's largest cotton storage facility, known as the Alabama Warehouse. Mayer and Durr formed a company called Lehman, Durr & Co., and in March 1863, after a few months of negotiations, they bought the Alabama Warehouse for $100,000.

Until that February, Durr had served as the commissary of an

Alabama infantry regiment—in effect, a contracting officer who purchased all the necessary supplies for the unit—and he had seen combat in the Battle of Tazewell, Tennessee. But weeks before Lehman,
Durr & Co.'s founding, he abruptly resigned his commission, extri-
cating himself from military service by providing a replacement (who
deserted two days later).

Lehman Durr maintained close ties to Confederate officials, and
the firm did considerable business with the rebel government, which
was one of the biggest purchasers of cotton. The Confederacy bought
and stockpiled vast quantities of the crop, which it used to secure the
bonds it floated in Europe to finance the war effort. (Investors could
actually redeem their bonds for bales; the catch for overseas bond-
holders was that they were responsible for getting their cotton out of
the South.) The Confederate government parked thousands of cotton bales in the Alabama Warehouse, one year paying Lehman Durr
nearly $26,000 in storage fees.

Cotton formed just one aspect of Mayer's extensive business
dealings with the Southern government, which also contracted with
Lehman Brothers. The Lehmans supplied the Confederate States of
America with hundreds of pounds of rice and coffee, thousands of
woolen winter hats, and tens of thousands of yards of fabric—from
flannel to osnaburg, a coarse material used to line jackets—for use
in uniforms. All told, the brothers' Confederate contracts, and those
with the quartermasters of individual southern states, totaled more
than $200,000.[10]

While the Lehmans had always kept one foot planted in the general mercantile business founded by Henry, the formation of Lehman
Durr hastened their move into cotton. Around the time when Mayer
and John Durr joined forces, Emanuel terminated his partnership
with Moses Ferst.[11] Now the father of two young sons—Milton,
born in 1860, and Philip, who arrived the following year—Emanuel
and his young family spent most of the war years overseas. He traveled home to Bavaria and visited England. With communication
and commerce all but cut off between New York and Montgomery,
London and Liverpool, where the brothers had family connections,
became increasingly vital to Lehman Brothers' survival.

While tending to their cotton business in Europe, Emanuel also
tried to sell Confederate bonds. As he made the rounds in London,
stopping in at bank offices to market the southern notes, a fellow
New York merchant whom he would come to know well was hawk-
ing Union securities to British investors. For Joseph Seligman, like

his Confederate counterpart, the war years were turning out to be surprisingly profitable.

On April 20, 1861, New York City's Union Square was a sea of red, white, and blue. The United States flag flew from crowded rooftops and hung from the sills of windows filled with onlookers. Men pinned the national colors to their hats and lapels, while women fixed knotted ribbons to their bonnets. That afternoon more than one hundred thousand people flooded into the square and the surrounding streets.

Almost a week had passed since the capture of Fort Sumter by Confederate troops, and a group of prominent New Yorkers, including Joseph Seligman, had organized the massive rally in support of the Union. Major Robert Anderson, whose defense of the Union garrison while greatly outnumbered had turned him into a national celebrity, attended the event. He brought with him the bullet-strafed flag that had flown at the fort during the battle; it now fluttered from a bronze statue of George Washington in the center of the park. John Dix, the former U.S. senator who had recently taken command of the New York State militia, presided over the event. He denounced "these outrages on all we hold most dear" and directed the crowd's attention to the flag, declaring that "its tattered condition shows the desperate defense" undertaken by Anderson and the soldiers under his command.

"The time for action," he said, "has come."[12]

Five days later Joseph remained so intoxicated by pro-Union fervor that when his wife gave birth to their third son, he named the boy Edwin Robert Anderson in tribute to the military hero. (Joseph was in the habit of naming his sons after famous men, a practice followed by his brothers to a lesser extent. In addition to Edwin, Joseph's brood of nine children included a George Washington, an Isaac Newton, and an Alfred Lincoln.)

The war presented the Seligmans with a new set of challenges and opportunities. It disrupted business and roiled the markets for foreign exchange and gold, but the rapid military mobilization also provided the brothers with a big new customer: the federal government. When the war began, the U.S. Army consisted of about sixteen thousand career soldiers (some of whom joined the Confederate military). Heeding Lincoln's call for volunteers, hundreds of thousands of men flowed into its ranks in the ensuing months. Provisioning the ballooning military touched off its own variety of gold rush, as the northern government hurriedly and sometimes haphazardly handed out contracts for uniforms, food, weapons, and other supplies.

Through business and Republican Party circles, Joseph was reasonably well connected. But it was Isaac, the youngest of the brothers, who provided the Seligmans with a vital entrée at the onset of the war. Independent-minded and sometimes sharp-tongued, he had initially resisted joining the family business. At nineteen, he instead opened his own embroidery shop on Cedar Street in New York's financial district. Gradually, however, he was enlisted by his brothers to make purchasing trips to Europe and broker shipments of gold in London; by 1860, he had officially joined the family partnership. Though he was the most junior of the partners, his keen mind for business rivaled his eldest brother's.[13] Reflecting his trusted role within the family, Isaac maintained the clan's joint financial ledger.[14]

At the start of the war, Isaac had a well-placed friend working in Washington. Henry Gitterman was not a politician or a high-ranking official. He was an army sutler, responsible for outfitting soldiers headed into combat. Gitterman's unglamorous job suddenly thrust him into the center of a contracting bonanza. As the War Department inked millions in contracts, Joseph arranged for Isaac to serve as the beleaguered sutler's assistant—a mutually beneficial arrangement, to be sure. During the first year of the war, the Seligmans secured contracts worth $1.44 million to provide the military with uniforms and accessories.[15] Isaac, who attributed their success at winning business to Joseph's "great popularity in Washington," made the most of his time in the capital, once meeting Abraham Lincoln at the White House during a Friday evening reception. His main impression of the event was not shaking hands with the president, but his astonishment at the casual dress of the other guests. "Men appearing in their shirt sleeves!" he marveled. "What would be thought of such an occurrence at a Court reception in London?"[16]

The brothers quickly discovered that wartime contracting, while profitable, came with its own set of headaches. Along with manufacturing some of the uniforms themselves, at a clothing factory William had purchased, they subcontracted with other firms to fill their orders. In some cases, the army quartermaster rejected shipments of clothing for shoddy work or defects, and the Seligmans, unlike less scrupulous contractors, replaced the damaged items at their own expense.[17]

Additionally, doing business with the federal government carried substantial risk, requiring some confidence that the North would prevail in the war. With its gold reserves depleted, the U.S. Treasury financed the war effort by taking on vast amounts of debt (more than $2.5 billion by 1865), issuing high-interest bonds that broadcast the government's desperation to European investors, who initially favored the Confederacy's chances (and thus its debt) in the conflict. The federal government was so cash-strapped that in some cases Joseph accepted payment in Treasury bonds, which he in turn pledged to New York banks to cover payments to the brothers' subcontractors and other drafts on their accounts.

Squeezing payment out of the government, even in the form of bonds, could be a hair-raising experience, as evidenced by a panicked letter Joseph sent to a high-ranking Treasury official in late January 1862. "Your note just received," he wrote, "informing me that the appropriation for the clothing of the Army is exhausted, is a startling and an alarming announcement to me, for the United States are indebted to my firm a million of dollars." If the government did not honor its commitment, the indignant merchant warned, dire consequences would result not just for the Seligmans but for the daisy chain of contractors they employed. "I see no alternative but the suspension of our house, which will drag down 20 other houses, and throw 400 operatives out of employ. Do my dear sir, for God's sake see if you cannot make arrangements with the Secretary, by which this dreadful catastrophe can be avoided. This is really a question of life and death with me."[18]

Early the following month, Joseph traveled to Washington carrying a letter of introduction to Treasury secretary Salmon P. Chase. A remote and humorless man, Chase had challenged Lincoln for the Republican presidential nomination in 1860, and he did little to mask his belief that the wrong man had won the White House. So lofty was his self-regard that, around the time of Joseph's visit, he decided to decorate the one-dollar bill (the first federal currency) with a portrait of his own dour face. Joseph's letter, from the president of the National Shoe & Leather Bank, on whose board Joseph served, endorsed him as "one of our most intelligent, patriotic, and responsible citizens" and a man who has "always given his cordial support to the Government in putting down this unholy rebellion."[19]

During his visit to Washington, Joseph may have again pleaded his case for prompt payment, but he also delivered another pitch, offering to leverage his family's European business contacts to sell northern securities on the continent. Negotiations with Chase nearly broke down over the secretary's request that the Seligmans underwrite the portion of bonds they intended to sell. In other words, they would effectively have to agree to buy the bonds themselves, shouldering the risk if they couldn't off-load them. Joseph, wary after his previous dealings with the government, recoiled at the thought of getting stuck with a pile of unsalable bonds. But eventually he arranged to become a subagent of Jay Cooke, the Philadelphia financier overseeing a vast bond-selling network on behalf of the federal government. In this setup, the Seligmans assumed no responsibility for underwriting the securities and simply earned a small commission on each bond they sold. The work was only moderately lucrative, but, in addition to patriotic gratification, it offered a toehold in government finance, which in the decades to come would prove enormously profitable.[20]

Sometime in the spring or summer of 1862, Joseph sailed to Europe with Babette and their children. The family settled in Mainz, not far from Frankfurt, and took up residence in the Hôtel d'Angleterre, overlooking the Rhine. The medieval city was once home to Europe's largest Jewish population, and it was a target of some of the most gruesome acts of violence visited upon the Jews during the Middle Ages. In 1096, crusaders slaughtered hundreds of Jews in the city (some estimates place the figure at over a thousand) who refused conversion. In 1349, amid a wave of attacks throughout Europe by mobs who accused Jews of causing the plague epidemic, six thousand Mainz Jews burned to death in a single day. The city's proximity to Frankfurt and its bourse, one of Europe's most active stock exchanges, may have formed part of the reason why Joseph based himself there. Mainz was also a centrally located port city, from which he could visit other major European financial centers.

A certain mythology, encouraged in later years by some Seligman family members and their firm, rose around Joseph's bond-selling activities in Europe and his other contributions to the war effort. The legend grew to the point where he was credited with a singular role in swaying the outcome of the war itself. A corporate history published in 1964 recounts how through the sale of more than $200 million in war bonds, some "virtually forced on business friends" in the "difficult European market," Joseph raised desperately needed capital for the North. It was also said that Joseph and Jesse advised Abraham Lincoln himself to elevate their old family friend Ulysses Grant to the command of the Union Army, a decision that changed the course of the war.[21]

But the reality is more complicated. Joseph's grandson George

Hellman wrote in 1951 of finding "no evidence of any overwhelming financial contribution to the national cause."[22] Joseph's surviving letters to his brothers during the Civil War years show the Seligmans moving deeper into finance and trading in U.S. securities, but they don't reflect a massive bond-selling operation on behalf of the Lincoln administration.

From Europe, Joseph anxiously—and often pessimistically—tracked the war's developments. "The state of affairs in the U.S. begins to take on a very dark aspect," he wrote in early February 1863, the month after Lincoln issued his Emancipation Proclamation. He feared for

> the downfall of not only the Government, but of all law, order and society. It is a most serious thing, and reflecting men will do well to divest themselves of that accustomed feeling of ease & security and prepare for the evil day to come. Our want of success in Richmond & Vicksburg with daily expenditure of 2 million have of course had much to do to elate our enemies both North & South, while the Emancip. Proclamation has discouraged many who had hopes of the South soon coming back to the Union. As I have so often said, the wealth of the country is being decimated and people are rich in imagination only.[23]

Later that month, as Congress passed the Enrollment Act, instituting the nation's first wartime draft, Joseph wrote home to "advise Isaac to come to Europe soon before he be drafted." Isaac arrived in London in late April 1863, stepping off the boat to find another letter from Joseph. It warned his hot-tempered brother not to "argue politics" or discuss the war with their bankers in the city, who "have no particular love for the North."[24]

Like many wealthy men of that era, James, Jesse, and William avoided military service by availing themselves of a provision in the Enrollment Act allowing a draftee to pay a substitute $300 to serve in his place.[25] This policy contributed to a violent uprising in New York as the draft lottery got underway in July. Angry mobs, composed largely of poor Irish and German immigrants, tore paving stones from the streets and hurled them through windows and set dozens of buildings ablaze. "That 300-dollar law has made us nobodies, vagabonds and cast-outs of society," one rioter wrote at the time. "We are the poor rabble, and the rich rabble is our enemy by this law. There-fore we will give our enemy battle right here, and ask no quarter."[26]

Yet Blacks, not the rich, became the main targets of the rampag-ing mobs, who blamed them for the war and engaged in a terrifying spree of attacks and lynchings that killed more than one hundred Black people and injured thousands. (The riots led to an exodus of Black residents from Manhattan.)

Joseph, after learning of the upheaval, wrote home of the "heart sickening" events: "I am almost tempted to resell the U.S. stock which I bought and keep my hands clear of the present degenerated Ameri-can race. . . . The majority of the Americans and especially the for-eigners there are as unfit as they are unworthy to enjoy liberty. . . . I hope to hear that the riot has been put down and the leaders hung."[27]

Like many brothers—especially those effectively sharing the same bank account—the Seligmans often bickered. Joseph argued most frequently with William and James, the closest to him in age. Their disagreements typically centered on how much risk the brothers should take on as they edged further into finance. Joseph, always the voice of restraint, was happy to let their gold accrue in European accounts until the volatile economic conditions subsided, warning that the financial situation in the United States was "extremely dan-gerous."[28]

When William pointed out that their business friends in New York were making a killing while the Seligmans played it safe, Joseph erupted, "Bro. William wishes me to place implicit reliance in his statement that 19 out of 20 of our acquaintances have doubled & quadrupled their capital the past 15 or 18 mos. Well, it has either been made by 'our acquaintances' by smuggling goods to the Rebels or smuggling generally."[29]

James proposed investing in railroad securities, but Joseph nixed the plan. "Respecting R.R. stocks going up I consider this a specula-tion entirely out of our line, and as certainly none of us know enough of Erie, Central, etc. to keep them for an investment, we ought not buy them at all. Let the war once come to an end, and we can make money in a legitimate way without gambling or hazard."[30]

The eldest Seligman, more a father figure to his brothers than a peer, consistently cautioned against risky investments. James, who had married the beautiful but tempestuous Rosa Content, was a fre-

quent recipient of these admonitions. His aristocratic bride, whose
Sephardic family's roots in America stretched back before the Revolutionary War, enjoyed lording her pedigree over her husband, whose
clan she haughtily derided as "the peddlers."[31] Her unpredictable
temper was rivaled in size by the enormity of her spending habits,
and it was all that James could do to keep up with the expenses.

"I can very well imagine bro. James restiveness in not being
allowed to make money in stock or in exchange or gold operation,
like nearly all your neighbors, but I hope & trust he will be able to
restrain himself a short time yet," Joseph wrote in early 1863. He
pointed out that the brothers had so far "escaped" the "terrible" war
without losses. Moreover, they were comfortably rich.

> We have achieved the very thing which we had in view all
> our life viz.: a sufficient competency for all our large fami-
> lies, irrespective of the ups & downs of American currency
> & values, which is more than most our neighbors have got—
> besides if any of us have ambitions not only to be rich but to
> leave all our children rich, I am satisfied that as soon as mat-
> ters get settled, and not quite so dangerous as they seem to
> me at present, we can satisfy all our ambitions in rolling up
> more wealth.[32]

Despite Joseph's paternal vigilance, he sometimes engaged in
reckless transactions of his own, in one case risking $50,000 of the
family's capital on an unsecured loan; Isaac fumed that his brother
must have been "drunk or crazy" when he advanced the money with
no collateral.[33] Joseph was so self-conscious about the sloppy deal
that when his usual weekly letters from his brothers did not arrive as
expected, he interpreted their absence as an "act of revenge" (which
it may have been).[34]

The intra-Seligman squabbling ebbed and flowed with the pressures of business, with Joseph alternating between one day asking
warmly after the health of his New York–based brothers and another
upbraiding them for laziness and ineptitude.[35]

The brothers' disagreements intensified as their business hit
a fork in the road: Should they continue as merchants? Or should
they become bankers? William initially threatened that if the family abandoned importing and went entirely into investment banking,
he wanted no part of the business.[36] James, meanwhile, argued that
the financial returns of banking could not be ignored. Joseph was

conflicted. "I do not think I have shown myself a coward during my whole life," he wrote home in April 1863, "but the views I now take of the prospects of our country under the present hopeless circumstances are enough to make a hero a coward."[37]

But Joseph, careful but not timid, ultimately chose a bold course, reassured by favorable events in the war. In early July 1863 the Union triumphed at Gettysburg, and Ulysses Grant's forces captured Vicksburg, Mississippi. The following March, Lincoln promoted Grant to the command of the Union Army, and by May the general had embarked on the relentless military campaign that over the next year would bring the war to its conclusion. Joseph returned to New York that spring to start a new business—and a new chapter—for the family. On May 1, 1864, he established J. & W. Seligman & Co., Bankers, at 59 Exchange Place, down the street from the New York Stock Exchange. (The *W.* stood for William, who had come around on banking, perhaps because Joseph agreed not to phase out importing just yet.)

As he built their banking business, Joseph took inspiration from the world's most famous banking family, the Rothschilds. In the late 1700s, Mayer Amschel Rothschild, the founder of the dynasty, had served as court factor (or "Court Jew," as this position was often known) to the Crown Prince of Hesse. Due to Christian prohibitions on moneylending and usury, European royals often relied on Jewish bankers, who in exchange for their financial services enjoyed privileged status and were not subject to the same restrictions as others of their faith. But for its perks, royal banker was also a tenuous, even dangerous, position. Fall from favor or lose your patron, and exile, execution, or the confiscation of your property could follow. Mayer Rothschild built not just a fortune but a legacy by establishing a network of financial houses outside the jealous reach of any one monarch or noble. His sons fanned out across Europe, forming affiliated branches in London, Naples, Paris, and Vienna, with the original house located in Frankfurt.

Joseph coveted the Rothschilds' prestige. He took particular pleasure in obtaining insurance through the same firm that covered the Rothschild family's gold shipments—and he wanted the Seligman name to resound in banking circles with similar gravitas.[38] So he emulated the Rothschild model. He returned to Europe, where in the late fall of 1864 he formed the family's first foreign branch in London, the world's financial nerve center.[39] Located at 3 Angel Court, the offices of Seligman Brothers, as the new firm was known, were a short walk from the narrow, cobbled lane where N.M. Roth-schild & Sons had established its headquarters in a property known as New Court. Joseph placed Isaac, just over thirty and terrified by his new responsibilities, in charge of the operation.

"The chief business in the arbitrage of stocks and exchanges was transacted between New York and London, and, being alone, I had a great load on my young shoulders," Isaac recalled. "I remember being so excited by these daily transactions, involving so great a men-tal stress in sending and receiving telegrams every few minutes, that I got into a nervous condition; so much so that I had to give up walking home of an evening along the Thames Embankment for fear of tak-ing a sudden plunge into the river, thus ending my career."[40]

From London, Joseph visited Frankfurt, where he had tasked Henry with opening a German branch of their banking business. He would run this venture with Max Stettheimer, their sister Babette's husband. Sullen and stiff, Stettheimer preferred importing and had to be dragged into banking. Had it not been for his sense of family duty—*Familiengefühl*—Joseph would have eagerly cut his ties with Stettheimer.

In late 1864, as Joseph situated the family in banking, the news from the United States was more and more encouraging. That November, Lincoln won reelection in a landslide, and General Wil-liam T. Sherman and his troops had embarked on their famously ruthless March to the Sea, rampaging through Georgia. From Europe, Joseph could see the Civil War's end in sight. That reality was starting to dawn, albeit more forebodingly, in Mayer Lehman's Montgomery, too.

Mobile's vital port—a lifeline for military supplies and foreign trade—fell to the Union in August. By then, years of war and the Lincoln administration's campaign of economic starvation had deci-mated Alabama's treasury, and its soldiers were deserting in droves. The unhappy task of leading the state in one of its darkest hours had fallen to one of Mayer's close friends, Thomas Hill Watts, who before the war had been a prominent plantation owner and lawyer in Montgomery. (The Lehmans were clients.) Watts, who wore small oval spectacles and a distinctive neck beard, had served for more than a year as the Confederate attorney general before winning election as Alabama's governor in late 1863.

As the South's prospects grew bleaker, concerns mounted about the fate of captured Alabama soldiers. In December 1864 the state legislature authorized Watts to spend $500,000 to provide food, clothes, medicine, and other aid to Alabama's POWs. The governor had the option of contracting directly for these provisions or of shipping southern commodities north to purchase the necessary supplies. He chose the latter, much riskier option, resolving to send at least fifteen hundred bales of cotton through enemy lines. "The cost to the state will be trifling by adopting this mode," he reasoned.[41] In fact, Alabama might even realize a profit on the deal due to the high price of cotton in New York and Liverpool.

Watts turned to Mayer Lehman to arrange for the cotton shipment and its sale, which required the businessman to handle the logistics of transporting a few hundred tons of Confederate cotton (each bale weighing more than four hundred pounds) through the battle lines.

A few weeks before his thirty-fifth birthday, Mayer started out for Richmond accompanied by Isaac Tichenor, the pastor of Montgomery's First Baptist Church, whom Watts had appointed to assist him. Tichenor had served as the chaplain of a Confederate infantry regiment, and he liked to recount the story of the Battle of Shiloh—how, with the troops wounded and wavering, he ripped off his hat and waved it as he paced the front lines sermonizing and calling on his comrades to stand their ground. In Tichenor's telling, seized with patriotic zeal, he grabbed a rifle and ultimately picked off six Union soldiers.[42] Perhaps it was for his skill as a sharpshooter, rather than his gift for stirring oratory, that the "fighting chaplain" was chosen as Mayer's companion on his potentially dangerous trip to the Confederate capital.

Lehman and Tichenor reached Richmond shortly after the New Year in 1865, finding its streets slick with mud and low-lying areas of the city flooded by the St. James River.[43] A near-daily barrage of rain and snow had battered the region for weeks, tormenting the Confederate soldiers bivouacked in a thirty-seven-mile network of dank trenches protecting Richmond and nearby Petersburg from Union forces.[44] The weather compounded the dismal atmosphere, for it was clear to all but the most self-deluded that the South teetered on defeat.

In Richmond, Mayer and his companion secured an audience with Jefferson Davis, presenting a letter from Watts to the Confederate president. It introduced Mayer as "a business man of established character and one of the best Southern patriots. He is a foreigner, but has been here fifteen years and is thoroughly identified with us.

"It will be necessary for him to go through the lines," Watts noted. "I ask that he may be furnished with the proper passports and indorsed by you as the agent of the State of Alabama."[45]

Mayer's arrival in Richmond garnered enough notice that it elicited a brief entry in the diary of John Beauchamp Jones, a novelist of some renown before the war who was now serving as a senior clerk in the Confederate War Department:

> A Mr. Lehman, a burly Jew, about thirty-five years old, got a passport to-day on the recommendation of the Secretary of the Treasury, to arrange (as agent, no doubt) for the shipment of several thousand bales of cotton, for which sterling funds are to be paid. No doubt it is important to keep the government cotton out of the hands of the enemy; and this operation seems to indicate that some fear of its loss exists.[46]

During his stay in Richmond, Mayer discussed his plans with Robert Ould, the Confederate official in charge of negotiating with the North over POWs. Perhaps fearing Lehman would interfere with the prisoner exchange talks underway, Ould told him that securing passage to the United States was all but impossible. But this didn't deter Mayer from trying, evidently with the cooperation of Davis, who later reported to Watts that "efforts were made to pass Mr. L through the lines."[47]

On January 14, Mayer wrote directly to Ulysses Grant, proposing the shipment of cotton from Mobile Bay to New York aboard a "vessel of the United States." He stressed the humanitarian nature of his mission, appealing, somewhat obsequiously, to Grant's sense of chivalry. "We well know that a gallant soldier must feel for those brave men who by the fortunes of war are held prisoners, exposed to the rigors of a climate to which they are not accustomed, the severities of which are augmented by the privations necessarily attendant upon their condition," he wrote. "We ask this favor with confidence, assured that your sympathies with the unfortunate brave will lead you to do all in your power to promote the benevolent design entrusted to us by the State of Alabama."[48]

Two weeks passed with no reply. Mayer wrote to Grant again,

this time requesting an in-person meeting.[49] Again, he received no answer. When they returned to Montgomery later that winter, Tichenor regaled his congregation with news of their eventful though fruitless mission. He told of meeting Davis—whose intellect and patriotism had impressed Tichenor—and of their unsuccessful attempts to contact Grant. And he rallied congregants to follow the example of the besieged residents of Richmond, who he said refused to give up hope for victory. "In eloquent terms," the *Montgomery Advertiser* reported,

> he portrayed the loss of liberty and property, and self-respect, the abject servility and ignominy, involved in submission to Abraham Lincoln, and his black cohorts; and declared that, rather than submit, and experience the consequent self-degradation and witness the degradation of his wife and children, he would follow those dearest objects of his affection to their graves, and yield up his own life. He counselled continued and united resistance.[50]

Mayer continued trying to arrange for a large cotton shipment, but it's not clear whether he was operating on his firm's behalf or as Alabama's proxy. On February 6, five days after sending his second message to Grant, Lehman Brothers wrote to Confederate Treasury secretary George Trenholm seeking to buy five thousand bales of cotton, at twenty cents a pound.[51] This transaction would have cost the Lehmans close to $500,000—the amount the Alabama legislature had appropriated to aid its imprisoned soldiers—but the value of the cotton, in New York or in Europe, could have been more than $1.4 million. There is no record of whether this deal was consummated, but Trenholm wrote to another Confederate official that "such a transaction would be desirable to this department."[52]

Lehman Brothers requested delivery of the cotton in three installments, the last of which was to occur within ninety days, or sometime in early May. By that time, there was no longer a Confederate government.

Columns of black smoke rose into the sky, gathering into a hazy canopy that blotted out the late afternoon sun above Montgomery. On April 11, 1865, at five p.m., torch-wielding Confederate troops under the command of Brigadier General Daniel Adams set fire to Lehman Durr's warehouse, along with those of other cotton merchants.[53] Days earlier Adams had vowed to mount a "full defense of the city," but as federal troops advanced, he opted to retreat, giving the order to torch Montgomery's cotton stores and confiscate its liquor supplies, to ensure that neither fell into enemy hands.[54]

As flames spewed from the Alabama Warehouse, pandemonium consumed the city. Citizens darted through the streets, trying to save furniture from homes. Some took advantage of the chaos to plunder local stores. One intoxicated soldier was spotted lapping up whiskey that had been dumped into the gutter.[55]

When Union troops marched into Montgomery the next morning, hoisting the U.S. flag above the Alabama capitol, Lehman Durr's warehouse was a smoldering husk. All told, retreating Confederate soldiers had put some eighty-eight thousand bales of cotton to the torch. The Lehmans later estimated their losses at $400,000.[56] So greatly had the Lehmans strengthened their financial position during the war that the destruction of the Alabama Warehouse, which was insured along with its contents, was a surmountable setback. In fact, the brothers possessed enough spare capital at the close of the war to loan $100,000 to the government of Alabama, which had amassed millions in wartime debt.

"That the shrewd brothers had safeguarded sizable capital assets, presumably in English and New York banks, is evident from their post-war activities," Frank Manheim wrote in "The Seed and the Tree."[57] The brothers also stashed their assets in less conventional places, according to John Wesley Durr's granddaughter. Fearing the North's occupying forces might pillage the city, Durr's wife, Rebecca, initially secreted gold belonging to the Lehman Durr partners beneath the folds of her bustle.[58] This precaution was unnecessary. As the *Montgomery Daily Mail* reported, "With but few exceptions the troops behaved in a very exemplary manner, and their march evinced the highest order of discipline."[59]

After the war, Mayer and Emanuel petitioned Andrew Johnson, who had ascended to the presidency after Abraham Lincoln's assassination, for pardon and amnesty. Each maintained that he had not served in the army, though Emanuel acknowledged fielding a substitute to fight in his place—nor held any formal role in the Confederate government. In his application, Mayer said he had been against the war, writing he "was opposed, at the time it was passed, to the so called ordinance of secession." He said he "led a quiet business life" and had "never engaged in the business of office seeking or the activities of politics." During the war, he wrote, he had contributed "to the support of soldiers and their families, and other families made indigent by the calamities of war." Mayer stated he "was worth more in property" at the outset of the conflict than he was at its conclusion, though he acknowledged that his assets "may go beyond twenty thousand dollars." This was a significant admission since Johnson's initial amnesty proclamation excluded individuals who held property in excess of that amount, except under special circumstances. Emanuel, who had returned to New York from Europe, downplayed the extent of his holdings, writing he "was worth at the date of your excellency's proclamation twenty thousand dollars." In fact, he was worth perhaps ten times that. The brothers each signed an oath of allegiance to the United States, and with the backing of Alabama's governor, their pardon applications were granted.[60]

In the war's aftermath, Lehman Durr quickly rebuilt in Montgomery and soon acquired a textile factory in nearby Prattville. By the fall of 1865, the Lehmans had formed a new partnership in New Orleans with Mayer's rakish brother-in-law, Benjamin Newgass.[61] The new partnership of Lehman & Newgass was headquartered on the southern edge of the French Quarter.[62] Establishing a beachhead in New Orleans, which was second only to New York as a shipping hub for cotton, seemed a natural expansion of their burgeoning business. At the close of 1865, the trio of Lehman partnerships—New Orleans, Montgomery, and New York—were estimated to be worth $500,000, much of that capital belonging to Emanuel and Mayer.[63]

About the time that Lehman & Newgass formed, three blocks away, at 33 Carondelet Street, the firm of Seligman & Hellman opened for business. The resumption of cotton exports revived a lucrative market for exchange bills—financial instruments, similar to promissory notes, in which a buyer of cotton or other commodities agreed to pay a seller a fixed amount. Such bills were traded, like securities, on the secondary market. Jesse Seligman's lantern-jawed brother-in-law Max Hellman took charge of the new business, which, according to Joseph, soon gained the reputation of "having the choicest Southern bills."[64]

As Reconstruction dawned, the Seligmans presided over a small but growing international banking empire, emerging on the other side of the Civil War with more than $2 million in capital.[65] Not bad for "the peddlers."

The Civil War seeded vast fortunes that would grow vaster still during the Gilded Age to come, and it hastened the nation's transition from an agrarian economy to an industrial one. "An extraordinary nobility arose: oil kings, railroad barons, merchant princes, financial lords," wrote Manheim in "The Seed and the Tree." In the still-wet clay of the nation's financial future, they carved multigenerational fiefdoms. It was in New York, "the seat of empire" in the words of George Washington, that the tycoons of tomorrow converged to forge empires of their own.

PART II

ASCENT

5

CITY OF EMPIRES

Eighteen-year-old Jacob Heinrich Schiff arrived in New York on August 6, 1865—but not by way of steerage, like the earlier generation of bootstrapping German-Jewish immigrants who preceded him.

He hailed from a prominent Jewish family, whose roots in Frankfurt stretched back centuries.[1] Religious leaders, scholars, and prosperous merchants populated the Schiff family tree. One of his ancestors was Great Britain's chief rabbi. Another was a rabbinic prodigy whose Talmudic writings remain influential. During the eighteenth century, members of the Schiff clan occupied one of the finest homes in Frankfurt's Jewish quarter, at least by the shabby standards of the *Judengasse* (Jew Alley). Residents of that crowded street, gated off from the rest of the city, could leave only during daylight hours, and they were confined there on Sundays and Christian holidays.

The narrow, four-story house had close-set windows, spindly staircases, and a courtyard that featured its own well and water pump, a sign of the family's wealth and status. No. 148 Judengasse was home to two families. Etched into the sandstone archway above one entryway was a boat (*Schiff* in German). The other archway bore a red shield (*roten Schild*)—it led to the home of Mayer Rothschild, the patriarch of the financial dynasty, who bought one half of the twofamily dwelling in the 1780s and subsequently purchased the other side of the home from one of Jacob's ancestors.[2] (If the Schiffs and Rothschilds lived under one roof, it was not for long.)[3]

Both sides of Jacob's family were involved in finance. His paternal grandfather was a *Handelsmann*, or merchant. His mother's father was a *Wechselmakler*, an exchange broker.[4] That was also the profession of Jacob's father, Moses, who some sources suggest worked for the Rothschilds (though others make no mention of this affiliation).[5] Little is known about Moses, beyond the fact that he was relatively prosperous, rather strict, and exceedingly devout. "He is reputed as having valued highly the privilege of the family, which traces its descent to Aaron the high-priest, and to have proudly exercised this privilege by assisting, whenever he could, at the ceremony of the redemption of the first born son," wrote the Jewish scholar and historian Gotthard Deutsch.[6] In that Orthodox ritual, a father "redeems" his child by offering five silver coins to a member of the priestly class, descended from Aaron (elder brother of the Hebrew prophet Moses), to which the Schiffs claimed to belong.

Jacob, the third of Moses and Clara Schiff's five children, was born at five a.m. on January 10, 1847, entering the world as sociopolitical tensions were rising in his native Frankfurt and throughout Europe.[7] He was too young to remember the discord of 1848, but his eldest brother, Philipp, six years older, vividly recalled the revolutionary atmosphere. Philipp remembered fellow students at Frankfurt's Philanthropin, the Jewish grade school established by Mayer Rothschild, wearing the colors of the revolution (black, red, and gold) on their hats and how some classmates were "beaten by their parents" for this subversive display. He recalled the September 18, 1848, murder of two conservative parliamentarians by a mob of revolutionaries, and the execution of Robert Blum, a liberal politician and revolutionary figure whom Philipp and his peers revered.[8]

The clash between liberal and conservative political factions played out not just in Europe's streets but within its synagogues. Frankfurt, with its old and vibrant Jewish community, stood at the center of this struggle between traditionalists, who refused to waver from the rituals and practices that had guided their faith for centuries, and reformers, who believed their religious practice should evolve and modernize with the times. When the Reform movement prevailed in Frankfurt, Moses Schiff and a cadre of Orthodox separatists in 1853 founded a new congregation, the Israelitische Religionsgesellschaft (Jewish Religious Association). The group built its own synagogue and school, which Jacob attended until he was fourteen, when he left to apprentice for a mercantile firm and then entered the banking business of his brother-in-law Alfred Geiger.[9]

As an adult, Jacob's smothering religious piety elicited much eye-rolling within his family circle, but as a boy, he chafed under the religious strictures imposed by his father, which included thrice-daily visits to the synagogue.[10] Once, desperate to avoid a Hebrew lesson, he escaped through a window in his home and shimmied down a drainpipe to the street below.[11]

Relations between Moses and his second-born son were tense. What worried him about Jacob was not a lack of drive but a surplus of it. Even before the American Civil War ended, Jacob had lobbied him for permission to go to the United States, an alarming prospect to Moses, who feared that outside Frankfurt's religious community, his son would shed the trappings of his Orthodox faith (a fear that proved somewhat warranted). "My second son, now 17—Jacob—is quite a problem because he already feels that Frankfurt is too small for his ambition," Moses wrote to a relative in St. Louis, R. L. Strauss, testing the waters about the possibility of sending his son to live there. "I would like to hear from you if, whether I gave my per-mission, perhaps your brother-in-law would take him back with him, and he could continue to live the life of an orthodox Jew, which is of great importance to me."[12]

Jacob Schiff obtained a passport allowing him to travel outside the Free State of Frankfurt on March 3, 1865.[13] And on June 12 he followed up with a letter of his own to Strauss: "As my father told you some time ago, I have a strong desire to go to the United States, but before taking such a step I should like to find a permanent posi-tion in one of the large cities." Schiff continued, "I know my greatest difficulty will arise in connection with the Sabbath, but perhaps you will be able to procure a position which will leave me free on that day, because I am inclined by principle to devout religious observance."[14]

If a reply came, Jacob did not wait for it. Within weeks, he was bound for New York, carrying $500 given to him by Philipp and a bundle of kosher meats to see him through the voyage.[15] Schiff's close friend and biographer, Cyrus Adler, offered two differing accounts of Jacob's journey, but what's known is this: Jacob's stern father did not readily consent to his emigration. In his two-volume biography of Schiff, published in 1928, Adler recounted that even "when the car-riage was standing at the door," Moses had second thoughts about sending his son to the United States, finally giving his blessing due to "the combined pleas of the entire family." In an earlier telling, however, Adler implied that Jacob did not wait for his father's approval. He wrote that Schiff departed Frankfurt "ostensibly for England," but really with the intention of traveling to the United States. During a brief stopover in England, he penned a series of letters home and gave them to "a friend to be mailed at regular intervals, so that the mother should be spared the anxiety of his passage."[16]

When Jacob's ship arrived, a fellow Frankfurt émigré, William Bonn, greeted him.[17] The teenager who emerged into the humid New York summer was short and slender, with ethereal blue eyes and dark wavy hair. He had an erect, aristocratic bearing and an intensity of purpose that became apparent within moments of meeting him. As one longtime friend of Schiff remembered, "He had marked out for himself a map of life and he never diverged to a hair's breadth from the path that he had traced."[18]

A mutual friend had alerted Bonn to Schiff's arrival; though they'd never met, Bonn, also in the banking business, took it upon himself to get the young immigrant situated, remembering his own lonely debarkation in New York. He escorted Schiff to a small hotel, planning to deposit him at the front desk. But Schiff urged him to come up to his room so they could talk about the "new land and the old place." Each time Bonn rose to leave, Schiff urged him to stay a bit longer. Before he realized it, the sun was up.[19]

Schiff found employment as a clerk in the recently formed banking partnership of Frank & Gans, which dealt in gold, stocks, and government securities. Observing Schiff's energy, drive, and knack for attracting business, Adolf Gans, one of the firm's partners, noted that the young banker had the makings of "a born millionaire."[20]

As in Frankfurt, Schiff's aspirations quickly outgrew his surroundings. By 1866, he was making plans to open his own brokerage with two other Frankfurt natives, Leo Lehmann (no relation to the Lehmanns of Rimpar) and Henry Budge, both friends of William Bonn, who helped bring the partners together. On January 1, 1867, they formed Budge, Schiff & Co. in a basement room at 55 Exchange Place, across the street from the New York Stock Exchange. Schiff was not yet twenty.

Schiff arrived in the United States at a moment of profound social, political, and technological change. The Civil War had radically transformed the country, and with it the nation's fledgling financial system. Requiring both sides to mount large-scale efforts to market bonds to the public, the conflict hastened the financialization of American life, for good and ill.

The uncertain course of the war had caused huge price swings in securities and commodities based on battlefield developments, which in turn unleashed a wave of speculation. For the first time, average Americans began to wager their capital in the markets. In 1835, eighteen years after the formation of the New York Stock Exchange, 140,000 shares had changed hands, amounting to some $7 million in trading activity. By 1867, the annual churn surpassed 21 million shares, valued at $3 billion.[21]

The furious pace of the market would only quicken, thanks to a series of technological advances. In 1866 the successful laying of a transatlantic telegraph cable by financier Cyrus Field and his Atlantic Telegraph Company enabled the nineteenth-century version of high-speed trading between New York and London. The advent of near-instantaneous telegraph communication between the United States and Europe made it easier for traders on both sides of the Atlantic to engage in arbitrage transactions, exploiting price differences in securities, commodities, and foreign exchange to turn a profit by simultaneously buying in one market and selling in another.

On July 27, 1866, the day the cable went into service, Joseph Seligman was one of the first to use it, but he soon grew wary when his orders to his brother Isaac in London seemed to be delayed by hours. He wrote to Field demanding "fair play," suspecting their communications were being intentionally withheld—a reasonable assumption since bankers routinely bribed telegraph operators to gain an edge over their competitors. (Seeking his own information advantage, Joseph instructed Max Hellman to cultivate the "telegraphic people" in New Orleans.)[22]

The year after the transatlantic cable began operating, another technological revolution swept Wall Street in the form of Edward Calahan's stock ticker. Previously, young brokerage employees known as runners had sprinted between the floor of the stock exchange and their nearby offices to communicate the latest price quotations. Brokers could now monitor the action from their headquarters.

The financial markets were largely unregulated, leaving a gaping gray area for clever operators. Insider trading was routine, and capitalists engaged in a range of unscrupulous methods to manipulate the prices of stocks and bonds, in some cases tinkering with the very underpinnings of the economy as they sought to enrich themselves. "The Nabobs of Wall Street are continually forming new enterprises," one Wall Street guidebook reported in the 1870s. "They tighten money, lock up gold, and raise or depress the price of stocks at will; indeed their influence is felt in every financial community."[23]

It was during this ruthless and rollicking era that Schiff and many of the Wall Street icons who would shape investment banking for more than a century to come established themselves in New York, now the nation's undisputed capital city of finance.

The month after Budge, Schiff & Co. opened its offices, Solomon Loeb and his partner Abraham Kuhn formed the "general banking and commission business" of Kuhn, Loeb & Co. nearby.

Kuhn and Loeb, distant relatives, grew up in neighboring towns in the southwestern German state of Rhineland-Palatinate, and they were brothers-in-law twice over: Kuhn had married Loeb's sister Regina, and Loeb had subsequently wed Kuhn's sister Fanny.

A jowly man with thick, foreboding eyebrows, Kuhn emigrated in 1839 from Herxheim am Berg, and he had followed the typical trajectory of the German-Jewish immigrant: He started out peddling, eventually opening a dry goods business with his brothers Marx and Samuel in Lafayette, Indiana. In 1849, following Kuhn's marriage to Regina Loeb, twenty-year-old Solomon joined his new brother-in-law in business.

Loeb embarked for America during the last gasp of the revolution, which had limped on in the Rhineland into the summer of 1849. To preserve the soles of his boots for the long journey, Solomon wore them strapped to his back. Even after he had become wealthy, he treated his clothing reverentially. "As you honor your garments, so will they honor you," he once admonished one of his grandsons after witnessing the boy doff his overcoat haphazardly.[24]

In 1850 the Kuhns and Loebs moved to Cincinnati, a city dubbed "Porkopolis" for its role as the nation's hog-packing capital. It was also home to a large German-Jewish community and a booming textile industry. Solomon's 1852 marriage to Fanny Kuhn strengthened his position in the family firm, and he soon attained a partnership in Kuhn, Netter & Co., which operated a large clothing business in Cincinnati's main business district. (Netter was Jacob Netter, Samuel Kuhn's brother-in-law.) But tragedy soon struck. Fanny died shortly after giving birth to their first child, Therese. Nearly eight years passed before Solomon remarried. In 1862, as the Civil War intensified, he returned to Germany, where he wed Betty Gallenberg, the stout and vivacious twenty-eight-year-old daughter of a Mannheim violinist.

After honeymooning in Baden-Baden, Solomon whisked her back to Cincinnati, where she experienced profound culture shock due to her hog-choked surroundings and provincial new relations. To Betty, life in Cincinnati was drab and tedious. "She found everyone talking about nothing but business, and how to get rich quickly," according to a granddaughter.[25]

In personality and interests, Betty—a progressive sort who unapologetically and openly read the controversial work of French author Emile Zola—contrasted sharply with her sober- and money-minded husband, who practically had to be dragged to the theater. "In appearance, manner and habits, my grandmother was impractical, romantic and sentimental," the granddaughter remembered. "She never felt any need for money and did not let it play an important role in her life." She was also known for her hearty appetite and her unorthodox observance of Jewish holidays such as Yom Kippur, when Jews fast for twenty-four hours. "On that day she did not go near the dining table but had food brought to her . . . a cup of tea at eleven, a sandwich at one, and so on, eating more, I believe, than on any other day. But, since she was not sitting down at table, she felt she was fasting."[26]

Like the Lehmans and Seligmans, Kuhn Netter's partners bolstered their fortunes during the Civil War thanks to government contracts for military uniforms and blankets. In the words of one credit rating agency correspondent, the firm was considered one of Cincinnati's "most substantial houses."[27] By the war's end, Solomon was well on his way to becoming a millionaire, with a net worth of around $600,000.[28] Now Loeb and Abraham Kuhn decided it was time to move once again, this time to the more cosmopolitan environment of New York City.

Betty's disgust with Cincinnati influenced Solomon's decision to relocate, as did the sickly condition of their firstborn child, Morris, who in New York was joined by three more siblings: Guta, James, and Nina. Loeb had also resolved to exit the clothing trade, even though that business had made possible his family's comfortable new life in a simply furnished brownstone at 37 East 38th Street.[29] He would become a banker, a profession with which he'd grown familiar in Cincinnati. "Father's special task during the Civil War, and even before he had moved to New York, was to arrange for the financial requirements of his firm with New York banks," James Loeb remembered of his father's pivot to banking.

> It soon became clear to him that the enormous profits made by the clothing trade in its contracts with the Government would attract many newcomers to a branch of business which up to then had been in the hands of relatively few people. He saw that the "cream was off the business," and determined, for his own part, to abandon it and found a banking firm. His partners were slow to share his views, and still slower to join in the new venture.[30]

But they did join, at least initially. In partnership with Samuel Kuhn and Jacob Netter, who both remained in Cincinnati, Abraham Kuhn and Solomon Loeb established offices at 31 Nassau Street, and the young firm quickly struck up relationships with more established New York houses, including those of the Lehmans and Seligmans.[31] Banking suited Loeb better than the clothing business. The blue-eyed merchant, who wore a bushy mustache and muttonchops that framed his bald pate, was color blind.

After Kuhn, Loeb & Co. opened its offices, a fellow New York banker with whom Loeb had done business stopped in to offer his congratulations, telling Loeb he knew the firm would be a success.

"What makes you think I shall be successful?" Loeb replied suspiciously.

"Because," the banker said, "I have never known a man so young as you who was able to say 'No' as quickly as you can."

The comment stuck with Loeb. When decades later his son James entered the partnership, Solomon advised him: "Learn to say 'No.' You can then change your mind and say 'Yes' without breaking your word. But once you have said 'Yes' you are committed."[32]

Caution was a defining trait of another post–Civil War newcomer to New York, who in 1869 established offices, such as they were, around the corner from Kuhn Loeb. In the coal-choked basement of 42 Pine Street, forty-eight-year-old Marcus Goldman laid the cornerstone of an investment bank so massive and ubiquitous that today there is no need to say anything more than the surname of its founder. The financial goliath of Goldman Sachs, however, was very nearly known by the less stately moniker of Putzel & Goldman.

Marcus, like Solomon Loeb and Mayer Lehman, came over in the massive tide of German immigration caused by the revolutions of 1848 and 1849. And like the Lehmans, he was the son of a cattle dealer who emigrated from a small Bavarian town, Trappstadt, where he had been a teacher. Arriving in 1848 at the age of twenty-seven, Marcus sank his savings into a horse and wagon and began peddling, largely in New Jersey. Sometimes he ranged as far as Philadelphia, which is where he met a young woman, an eighteen-year-old German-Jewish immigrant also surnamed Goldman. During those times, when marriages between cousins and more distant relations were commonplace among German Jews, it was almost more unusual that Marcus and Bertha Goldman couldn't discern a common ancestor between them. Unable to afford a bouquet when he began courting her, Marcus gave Bertha a bunch of radishes.[33]

Bertha, whose family hailed from Darmstadt, was the daughter of a locksmith and jeweler; before marrying Marcus in 1851, she made a living as a hatmaker and doing needlework and embroidery. She was the independent, matriarchal sort. "She was consulted behind the scenes on many of the family problems," her grandson Walter Sachs remembered in his unpublished memoir, "and her views were always listened to with care and attention. She was intensely ambitious for her children and stressed all through her life the importance of a good home and a thorough education. Frequently, she was the one to settle family arguments." Sachs recalled of his grandfather, "He was always a man of dignity, of aristocratic manner, even though heavy and short-legged, typical of the entire Goldman clan."[34]

The couple settled in Philadelphia, and Marcus opened a small tailor shop. He eventually expanded his business into a wholesale clothing firm on Market Street, partnering with other local merchants to form Goldman, McComas & Co. (A noteworthy thing about this firm was that at least some—and possibly all—of his partners were not Jewish.) As with the Kuhns, Loebs, Lehmans, and Seligmans, the Civil War years were profitable ones for Marcus. Noting that his grandfather "was exempt from military service," Walter Sachs wrote in his memoir that Marcus "prospered . . . selling clothing to the Northern army."[35]

By the late 1860s, Marcus was well off. Since the war's end he had twice taken his family back to Europe to visit family, and during their second trip they encountered friends who owned a New York brownstone on 33rd Street near Fifth Avenue that they were trying to rent. Marcus, whose wife had been prodding him to expand the family's social and business horizons with a move to Manhattan, leased it on the spot. According to Sachs, after settling in New York, his grandparents quickly grew friendly with the Loebs, along with other prosperous German-Jewish clans. "Our friendship with the Kuhn Loeb people goes back to the year one," he recalled. "The family friendship is a very old one."[36]

When the Goldmans departed Philadelphia, Marcus left $40,000 in capital invested in the clothing business, where he remained a special partner. He sank $50,000 into a new partnership with Mayer Putzel, a longtime note broker who traveled the cobbled streets of the financial district making short-term loans to small businesses.[37] Putzel & Goldman dealt in what would later be known as commercial paper. Say a dry goods merchant sold $1,000 of merchandise but had not yet received payment. He might borrow against that sale to have funds available to immediately restock. The merchant would sign over a $1,000 promissory note to the note broker, who, if the annual interest rate was 10 percent and the debt was due in ninety days, would hand over $975. Such lenders were derisively known as "note shavers" because they excised a percentage from the face value of the notes.

Dressed in the banker's uniform of a black overcoat and tall silk top hat, Goldman spent his mornings visiting the jewelers of Maiden Lane and the tanners of Beekman Street, making small loans and collecting IOUs, which he slipped into the inner band of his hat. After making his rounds among the merchants, Goldman stopped in at various banks—the Chemical on Chambers Street, the Importers and Traders on Warren, perhaps the National Park Bank on John—to sell the promissory notes he had amassed.[38] There a version of the earlier process repeated. In this case, Goldman signed over the notes to the bank, which purchased them at a discount from their face value. This left Marcus with a slender profit (the difference between what he paid for the notes and what the bank offered) and his capital replenished for the next day's transactions. It was a volume business: during his first year on Wall Street, Goldman reportedly bought and sold $5 million in promissory notes, on which he likely netted 1 percent or less.

It's probable that Goldman partnered with the more experienced Putzel to learn the ropes of the new business, but their alliance didn't last long. They disbanded in late 1870, after less than a year, and Marcus opened a new office several doors down at 30 Pine Street. To his fellow Wall Street bankers, there was nothing to suggest this conservative-minded broker was making much money. That he would be the progenitor of the most powerful financial firm in modern history defied imagination. He was seen as exceedingly circumspect in his dealings, and he eschewed the speculative craze playing out around him. "Not inclined to take much risk," R.G. Dun & Co. mused in one ledger entry. Another noted: "Too timid to do much bus."[39]

A few blocks away, near Hanover Square, the city's commodities trading epicenter, Emanuel and Mayer Lehman, reunited after years apart, had opened new offices and were once again working shoulder to shoulder.

In 1868, Mayer had sold his Montgomery mansion, left Lehman Durr in the care of their business partners, and moved north with his family.[40] According to Herbert Lehman, some of the family's former slaves accompanied them to New York. "I know that they brought up at least two Negroes who had been slaves to New York when they moved up . . . and they remained with us a long time," he recalled. "I think one of them brought up several of my brothers and sisters."[41]

Mayer built a large brownstone for his family at 5 East 62nd Street, an area that remained so lightly developed at that time that the stoop offered a nearly unobstructed view of St. Patrick's Cathedral, then still under construction, around a half mile away.[42] Five stories high and one hundred feet deep, the home featured a long first-floor parlor—off-limits to the children—furnished with late Victorian furniture in gold satin. The Lehman children congregated in the second-floor library, which had a bowfront window and heavy walnut furniture upholstered in green and black brocade.[43]

While New York was the financial center of the Lehmans' enterprise—the place where cotton bills were brokered and futures contracts traded—they still did a largely southern business. Together, they maintained controlling interests of about 60 percent in Lehman Durr and in the New Orleans firm, which had been renamed Lehman, Stern & Co. They also served as financial agents for the State of Alabama, with the uphill task of placing the debt-riddled state's bonds in the North.

The brothers increasingly branched out into other commodities, including petroleum, coffee, and sugar. They traded extensively in gold, striking up a lifelong association (and doing $200,000 worth of business) with Kuhn Loeb during the first year of its founding.[44] But cotton remained at the core of their operations.

The fall of the Confederacy upended the cotton trade. No longer did slavery power the vast plantations of the South, but the labor system that replaced it was also highly exploitative. The plantation system gave way to tenant farming and sharecropping, whereby a landowner rented out tracts to emancipated Blacks and poor rural whites, furnishing them with all the necessities, including food, lodging, seed, and equipment; in return, the landowner claimed a share of the farmer's crop to cover these (often inflated) expenses. By the end of the harvest, the sharecropper received little or nothing for his toil; in fact, in many cases, he wound up in hock to his landlord when the sale of his cotton, tobacco, or wheat didn't cover the year's expenses. It was slavery by another name.

"With the general collapse of the great plantations in the debacle of defeat, the pre-war production and marketing system disintegrated," wrote Frank Manheim in "The Seed and the Tree," his unpublished corporate history. But the new mode of business, far from diminishing the brothers' prospects, "opened vast opportunities."[45] The brothers continued to broker cotton, but in the years after the Civil War, they also played a more direct role in the business, managing, through Lehman Durr, sixteen southern plantations.

"We rented a part out, and part we ran ourselves," a onetime Lehman Durr employee named Frederick Wolffe testified before a congressional committee probing a minor political scandal. Generally, he explained, "the land-owner, or the man who farms the land, is paying the negro off in provisions, and at the end of the year, in almost every instance, they come out behind. It is very seldom that they get any money."[46]

The Civil War also changed the financial dynamics of the cotton business. The market for futures took off during the conflict, when textile manufacturers sought to mitigate the risk of the uncertain cotton supply by entering contracts for the future delivery of the raw materials needed to produce uniforms and other clothing. By 1868, the Lehmans and other cotton merchants attempted to formalize the ad hoc marketplace in New York. Their first attempt, an organization known as the New York Board of Cotton Brokers, never got off the ground. But two years later, on a Monday in early September 1870, trading commenced with the strike of a gavel in a long, narrow, and dimly lit chamber at 142 Pearl Street, site of the newly formed New York Cotton Exchange, across from the offices of Lehman Brothers.

Mayer Lehman, now forty, was elected to the exchange's first board of directors, and he was a towering figure on the trading floor. In some cases, his very presence—and the vast resources he commanded—seemed to steady the market. As the *New York Herald* reported after one topsy-turvy day of trading, "The market acted rather as though it wanted to go down, but Mayer Lehman was there. He held it."[47]

Mayer was famous among his fellow traders for buying and selling contracts without making a single notation; when it came time to reconcile his contracts at day's end, he could recall every transaction by memory. He was also known for his generosity, particularly when fellow traders overextended themselves. "When failures took place on the Exchange he was always ready with his sympathy for the unfortunate if they were honest, and was a lenient creditor," one member of the exchange remembered.[48] Another recalled of Mayer and his brother, "Anyone who was unfortunate and got into their debt need only go to them, make a straightforward statement, and he would receive not only fair and honest, but very liberal treatment. This fair dealing and unwillingness to take advantage of a man was always, I believe, a marked characteristic of both brothers."[49]

The Lehmans, who resembled each other so closely they were hard to tell apart from a distance, were spotted together so frequently that friends called them the "Siamese Twins." Herman Baar, the superintendent of the Hebrew Orphan Asylum, of which both brothers were supporters, dubbed Emanuel and Mayer the "Cheeryble Brothers," a reference to the kindhearted twins, Charles and Ned Cheeryble, who employ the down-on-his-luck title character in Charles Dickens's *Nicholas Nickleby*.[50]

Like the gold and stock exchanges nearby, the cotton exchange was the scene of both legitimate transactions and unbridled gambling. And cotton futures were just as vulnerable to manipulation as any fly-by-night security. To the R.G. Dun & Co. representatives who rated their credit, the Lehmans insisted they took "no risks," traded purely on behalf of their clients, and never speculated for their own account. But close observers of their operation had their doubts, especially after Lehman Brothers represented a group of investors who drove up the price of cotton by artificially constricting the cotton supply. The Lehmans "acted as agent for the ring and made advances on a large amount of cotton, to be held out of this market," R.G. Dun reported. "It has been generally supposed that they were interested." A subsequent credit report stated: "They are considered by some . . . too speculative."

The Lehmans' financial wagers, nevertheless, appeared to be paying off. Their friends at Kuhn Loeb told the credit agency the Lehmans were easily worth more than a million dollars and their credit was "beyond a doubt."[51] If true, this meant that since the war's end, they had more than doubled their net worth.

The fledgling partnership of Budge, Schiff & Co. was also drawing notice on the Street, though not always in a favorable way.

In sharp contrast to Schiff's future image as a highly discerning and conservative banker, his first investment partnership immersed itself deeply in the speculative bacchanal that had overtaken Wall Street. It wagered heavily on the rise and fall of gold and brokered risky railroad securities.

Despite the youth of its partners, Schiff's firm had quickly become a significant Wall Street player thanks to its strong European banking connections. Henry Budge's father, Moritz, like Moses Schiff, was a Frankfurt broker, and Budge, Schiff & Co. gained a leg up in business by serving as his firm's U.S. financial agent, helping to place American railroad securities and government bonds with European investors, particularly in Germany.[52] According to Henry Budge, the new firm also did considerable business with Dabney, Morgan & Co., where thirty-year-old John Pierpont Morgan was developing a reputation as a gifted, if mercurial, financier.[53]

Budge, Schiff & Co. prospered, claiming to be worth as much as $400,000, but its early years were also marred by setbacks that seemed to betray the principals' inexperience. In one embarrassing episode, Schiff's firm unwittingly sold counterfeit Treasury bonds to a client—and then was forced into protracted litigation with the source of the fraudulent securities, which also happened to be Schiff's former employer, Frank & Gans. And in May 1869, Schiff and his partners suffered heavy losses speculating on gold when the thirty-four-year-old merchant banking house of Schepeler & Co.—which had accumulated a huge short position it could not cover—suddenly collapsed.

But these missteps were relatively minor compared with its part in a financial controversy that would cast a shadow over Schiff and his partners at home and abroad.

6

PANIC!

The scandal involved a railroad. They often seemed to in those days.

The industrial revolution touched off a railroad boom in the United States, as it had in Europe, and the country's westward expansion fanned the industry's explosive growth. By 1869, when the Central Pacific's Leland Stanford drove the ceremonial "golden spike" into the final railroad tie, knitting together the transcontinental railroad, tens of thousands of miles of track stretched across the nation, with the greatest concentrations in the North and the Upper Midwest. Conceived amid the chaos of capitalism, the rail system was the Frankenstein vision of dozens of industrialists, all competing for territory and traffic. As they parried for control of valuable terrain, rival tycoons built parallel roads, sometimes laying tracks within yards of a competitor's line, and disputes among railroad moguls occasionally spilled out of courtrooms and into armed clashes.

Fueled by a steady supply of Wall Street and European capital, the railroads were the nineteenth-century equivalent of the dot-com start-ups of the late 1990s and early 2000s, with investors showering money on new ventures regardless of merit or feasibility. Some lines, never built, existed solely on stock certificates sold to ravenous investors. To raise cash for construction, or just to line the pockets of unscrupulous railroad directors, these operations pumped a variety of debt-packed securities into the market. Frequently, these start-ups piled debt upon debt until they collapsed under the weight of their obligations. The line would fall into receivership and get sold off to new owners, who would issue new debt to cover the old. The speculative balloon would inflate once more, only to burst a few years later. Railroads were constantly being pulled out of bankruptcy and reorganized. It wasn't unusual for this same cycle to play out multiple times on the same godforsaken stretch of track. Bankers, brokers, and company insiders often seemed to be the only ones who turned a profit on these turnarounds.

On March 18, 1869, Moritz Budge, the father of Schiff's partner, inked a deal with Henry Boody, the treasurer of the recently formed Rockford, Rock Island & St. Louis Railroad, to sell $7.5 million of its bonds in the United States and Europe. Schiff and his partners handled the U.S. end of the business, and both Henry Budge and Leo Lehmann took seats on the company's board and on its finance committee. To whet the public's appetite for the road's securities, Boody employed a common tactic in the shady realm of railroad promotion: he bribed three reporters to hype the Rockford's bonds in their respective papers and vouch for the safety of the company's securities.[1]

Together, Moritz Budge and Budge, Schiff & Co. netted more than $1 million in commissions and fees from the Rockford, a hefty payout that came to light a few years later when the company defaulted on its interest payments and its supposedly rock-solid securities plummeted. As the railroad headed for insolvency, Boody was arrested for embezzling hundreds of thousands of dollars from the company. He subsequently pointed the finger at Budge, Schiff & Co.

Accusing the firm of fraud, he claimed Schiff and his partners had bilked the Rockford on a contract to supply eighteen thousand tons of rails and alleged they had billed the Rockford for a gold transaction it never executed. "I never believed there was any gold bought or any gold sold," Boody stated.[2]

Commenting on the Rockford's downward spiral, R.G. Dun & Co. noted charitably that Budge, Schiff & Co. had been "deceived in the character of the enterprise and the parties connected therewith."[3] Yet this explanation was less than satisfying to the investors holding worthless Rockford shares—while Schiff and his partners managed to profit handsomely.

In 1873, as evidence of Henry Boody's financial crimes came to light and the Rockford faltered, Budge, Schiff & Co. disbanded. Henry Budge attributed the firm's demise to his father's illness and subsequent death in May 1872, which brought Henry back to Frankfurt. Budge also cited Schiff's hardheaded and dictatorial nature. Even in his early twenties, the self-assured young banker insisted on control and did not brook dissent.[4]

But the Rockford debacle did notable harm to the young firm's standing, as well as to Schiff's personal image in the business world. Of Schiff, R.G. Dun & Co. commented:

> He is well regarded generally but there is a feeling among some of the foreign bankers that his old firm did not use the best of care in the selection of RR [railroad] securities, which they placed in Frankfurt and other markets and hence they do not speak very favorably about the business character of Schiff, while others speak quite favorably of him and blame Budge for the misfortune of the investors who lost their money in the poor class of RR bonds which B. S. & Co. induced them to purchase.[5]

The controversy seemed to teach Schiff an important lesson. Never again would he play fast and loose with his reputation, which he guarded zealously. He avoided publicity, trying to keep his name out of the papers even in connection with large philanthropic gifts and, when it worked to his favor, back-channeling with journalists to shape their coverage of him. He tried to steer clear of scandal, but in the circles of big money and immense power in which he traveled in later years, it found him nonetheless.

Schiff had planned to lay down roots in the United States. Not long after arriving, he had petitioned the government of Frankfurt to release him from his Prussian citizenship.[6] And in 1870 he officially became a U.S. citizen. But after Budge, Schiff & Co. dissolved, he too retreated to Germany.

The Rockford episode was emblematic of an era of unrestrained, smash-and-grab capitalism. Fueled by a speculative frenzy, the post–Civil War financial landscape was filled with unsound railroad ventures and unsavory operators like Henry Boody, including those who were hatching even grander financial shakedowns. One of the most spectacular involved an effort to corner the gold market by conning the president of the United States himself.

Boody was likened by one newspaper to a "Western Jim Fisk,"

but this wasn't entirely fair to Fisk, whose machinations, in partnership with the notorious Jay Gould, placed him in a different class of Wall Street hustler. Together with a cattle-driver-turned-Wall-Street-schemer named Daniel Drew, they controlled the Erie Railroad, brazenly manipulating its stock price and using the line as their private cash machine.

The Seligmans had close ties to Drew, Fisk, and Gould, serving as one of their brokers in New York and London. Joseph had once warned his brother James against getting involved with the railroads during the Civil War—it was an industry they didn't really understand, he said—but since then he had warmed up to the business. He still didn't quite get the ins and outs of railroading, but he knew it was lucrative, at least for some. In working with Drew et al., Joseph seemed willing to overlook his usual insistence that the brothers avoid lending their good name to any endeavor that might sully it, since he knew perfectly well who they were dealing with. At one point, the brothers had even guaranteed a $20,000 bail bond for Gould after his financial scheming landed him in jail. And Gould and Fisk, like a pair of cartoon villains, had once evaded arrest for fleecing railroad tycoon Cornelius Vanderbilt by escaping from New York in a lifeboat.

"Contrary to the experience of most people who came in contact with Drew, Gould, and Fisk, the Seligmans made money," recounted the journalist and onetime J. & W. Seligman & Co. employee Linton Wells in "The House of Seligman," a seven-hundred-page history that was commissioned by the firm but never published. "They had no illusions regarding them, and when their services were employed as brokers to buy or sell Erie, or other securities, they fulfilled their orders promptly at the usual rates of commission. But in addition they shrewdly engaged in a few transactions for their own account."[7] Put more directly: the Seligmans profited from their clients' financial shenanigans.

In 1869, around the time that Henry Boody was bribing journalists and pilfering a quarter-million dollars from the Rockford, Fisk and Gould were mounting the most audacious plot of their careers. They would secretly buy up the available supply of gold, run up the price of the commodity, then force short sellers to settle on their terms when the investors could not cover their positions—backing them into a "corner," in other words.

The gold exchange, situated in a cavernous hall with a large fountain at its center, was the scene of such wild speculation that it made the action at the New York Stock Exchange next door seem relatively tame. "Imagine a rat pit in full blast with twenty or thirty men ranged around the rat tragedy, each with a canine under his arm, all yelling and howling at once, and you have as good a comparison as can be found, in the outside world, of the aspect of the gold room as it strikes the beholder on his first entrance," Horace White, the editor in chief of the *Chicago Tribune*, wrote memorably of his 1866 visit to the gold exchange.[8]

The volatile gold market—prices could move 20 percent or more in the space of a day—was a vestige of the war. In 1862, for the first time in U.S. history, the federal government began printing its own currency, popularly known as greenbacks, to meet its mounting debts. Congress had established the dollar as the nation's monetary unit of measure in the late 1700s, pegging its value to a specific amount of gold or silver. It had previously left the issuing of money to banks, whose bills were redeemable in gold and silver coins (known as specie). But with skyrocketing wartime outlays and dwindling gold reserves, the U.S. Treasury printed cash that was not backed by precious metals but rather by the credit of the federal government—the belief that the government could cover its obligations.

With the dollar untethered from gold, their respective values diverged wildly, rising and falling on the latest battlefield news. Word of a Union defeat could send the price of gold soaring against the dollar, based on concerns about the very future of the U.S. government. At points during the war, gold traded at prices surpassing 200—meaning that one hundred dollars' worth of gold commanded two hundred greenbacks. It was this type of gambling—viewed as unseemly and unpatriotic, because it meant betting against the Union—that Joseph Seligman had warned his brothers against in his letters from Europe during the war. Gold speculators infuriated Abraham Lincoln, who once remarked that "for my part, I wish every one of them had his devilish head shot off."[9]

A gold corner was incredibly bold, but technically possible. The bullion supply was limited, with somewhere between $15 to $20 million in the New York market at any one time. But one thing stood in the way of Fisk and Gould controlling enough gold to execute their plan: the Treasury Department, specifically its policy of regularly selling gold to pay down the national debt. But what if they could convince the newly inaugurated president, Ulysses Grant, that it was in the national interest for the government to temporarily suspend gold sales?

Gould bribed Grant's brother-in-law Abel Corbin, who arranged for Gould to have several audiences with the president, where the financier made a pitch couched in populist rhetoric. He argued that halting government gold sales, causing its price to rise by constricting the supply, would benefit American farmers and exporters. Why? Since European countries were pegged to the gold standard, U.S. merchants could undercut foreign competitors by charging less for their products overseas, while reaping a hefty payout when they redeemed gold for greenbacks at home. (Think of it this way: If the gold premium was 130, a tobacco shipment that commanded $10,000 in gold in Liverpool would be worth $13,000 in greenbacks. That same shipment was worth $15,000 if the price of gold rose to 150.) Gould also paid off General Daniel Butterfield, the newly installed assistant Treasury secretary in the New York Sub Treasury, to feed him information on the agency's plans.

During the summer of 1869, Gould turned to Joseph Seligman, among other brokers, as he began hoovering up gold.[10] Butterfield was also a Seligman client. In addition to being Butterfield's personal broker, Joseph was one of the bankers that the assistant Treasury secretary relied on to sell gold on behalf of the federal government.

Joseph was a regular visitor to the New York Sub Treasury.[11] During his visits, Butterfield kept the banker apprised of the thinking of the Treasury Department—valuable intelligence—though Seligman already understood better than anyone the financial policies of the Grant administration: at Grant's request, he had worked with Treasury Secretary George Boutwell to design them. According to Seligman, Grant had even offered him Boutwell's job, but Joseph had declined, citing his obligations to his firm. "The bank needed him, and his brothers begged him to let politics and public office alone," his son Isaac Newton recalled.[12]

In early September 1869, Grant told Corbin that he had written to Boutwell suggesting that selling gold that month (which would have the effect of depressing the price) might harm farmers at the height of their harvest season. The Treasury secretary, in response, had delayed a planned gold sale.[13] Corbin hurriedly relayed this tip to Gould. This was their moment; Gould and his ring purchased gold furiously.

Even for the chaotic gold market, the buying by Gould and his conspirators caused an unusual price spike. Grant, once again taken advantage of by a close family member, eventually caught on to the scheme. But he had already placed his administration in a compromising position. He had allowed himself to be seen with Fisk and Gould, giving them a veneer of legitimacy, and he had accepted perks from the duo, including free transportation for his family aboard private Erie railcars.

According to Linton Wells, Grant met with Joseph Seligman in mid-September, aware of the banker's close association with Gould. Seligman and his brothers were top supporters of Grant's presidential campaign, and Joseph had been rewarded with a place of honor at the new president's inauguration, standing behind Grant as he took the oath of office and later attending the inaugural ball.[14]

The president asked Seligman pointedly about his role in purchasing gold on Gould's behalf; the banker admitted that his firm had bought a large amount for Gould and had also acquired gold for its own account. Perhaps because of his long friendship with the Seligmans, the usually tight-lipped president told Joseph "just enough to warn him that it would be wise to sever relations with Gould, at least temporarily, and to sell gold instead of buy it," Wells recounted.[15] Grant subsequently authorized Boutwell to sell $4 million in gold from the Treasury as its price topped 160.

On the morning of Friday, September 24, 1869, the day the Grant administration broke Gould's corner, the price of gold momentarily kissed 164. Wall Street reporters, accustomed to a certain level of daily bedlam, were stunned by the chaotic scene. "The shouts and cries of the hundreds of active operators seemed here like the outpourings of maniacs," *The New York Times* reported, "and for a short time a pallor seemed to overspread the faces, and a tremor to overcome the persons of the mass, which had been wrought up to a point beyond human endurance."[16]

Soon news of the Treasury Department's pending action rippled through the exchange.[17] In his office diagonally across the street from the gold room, outfitted with its own gold indicator, Joseph watched prices crater. "It ran down from [1]60 to [1]35 in ten, fifteen, or twenty minutes," he later recalled.[18] By five p.m., the price of gold had collapsed to 133. Yet the damage had been done. The wild swings in the market wiped out numerous brokerages, and the panic spilled over into the stock exchange, where shares declined by 20 percent. The "Black Friday" meltdown plagued the economy for months. Among those hurt the most were farmers, who saw commodity prices plunge.

When a few months after the gold panic Congress launched an investigation into its causes, Seligman was called as a witness. In the days before the panic, he had off-loaded $700,000 worth of gold on behalf of General Butterfield, who quietly resigned days after Black Friday. Seligman had also sold gold, worth hundreds of thousands of dollars, held in his firm's own accounts.

In late January 1870 the forty-nine-year-old banker, his silver hair combed back and his beard neatly trimmed, settled into his seat before the House Banking and Currency Committee, chaired by the Ohio Republican (and future president) James Garfield. After a few preliminary questions, Garfield went straight to the point: "For whom did you transact business during that week?"

"We sold chiefly for ourselves," Seligman replied. "I also sold some gold during the week for another gentleman." There was no sense being coy. Butterfield, after all, was scheduled to take his turn on the hot seat the following day. "I presume I might as well state what I suppose you refer to at once," he continued. "I sold gold that week for General Butterfield."[19]

Seligman testified that he had visited Butterfield at the Sub Treasury three or four times during the week leading up to Black Friday, but he denied having foreknowledge of the Treasury's plans to sell gold.[20]

Asked about the causes of the crisis, Joseph blamed it on a "combination of gamblers." Surprisingly, he was not questioned about— nor did he mention—his ties to its ringleaders.[21]

Even as the gold panic ballooned into a major political scandal for the Grant administration, Seligman managed to sidestep more pointed scrutiny for his murky role in Black Friday and emerged with his reputation unscathed. In addition to exposing the scoundrels in Grant's midst, the crisis highlighted the fragility of the nation's financial system and the ripple effects of speculation on the broader economy. It was a warning of more severe reckonings to come.

The memory of Black Friday was still fresh when panic again overtook Wall Street.

Shortly after noon on Thursday, September 18, 1873, the presiding officer of the New York Stock Exchange lowered his gavel and made a shocking announcement: "The firm of Jay Cooke & Co. have suspended!" A jostling mass of brokers hurtled out of the exchange to carry the unthinkable news back to their offices.[22] "Black Friday was nothing to this," one shell-shocked trader exclaimed that day.[23]

Jay Cooke & Co., in business twelve years, cemented its reputation as the nation's most venerable investment bank during the Civil War, when its founder had overseen the sale of hundreds of millions of dollars of government bonds on behalf of the Lincoln administration, financial reinforcements vital to the war effort. After the war, the company had plunged into railroad finance, and it had become the exclusive financial agent of the Northern Pacific Railway.

Chartered in 1864, the Northern Pacific was an ambitious venture. Congress had granted the company nearly 40 million acres of federal land to build a line stretching from Minnesota to Oregon, but the project had failed to gain traction until Jay Cooke, who had dreams of transforming Duluth into the next Chicago, took control of the financing. As with other railroad ventures, the success of the Northern Pacific hinged on the value of the surrounding land, which was used as collateral to secure the bonds that financed construction. The land was sold off to speculators and to settlers who typically paid inflated prices for a puffed-up vision of the American idyll. Many railroad companies were also, in effect, real estate companies—they even gave out mortgages.[24] Populating the route of a rail line was not only key to its financing but to its future viability, ensuring a certain level of traffic.

Real estate prices spiked along existing and proposed rail lines, and railroad promoters often made misleading and hyperbolic claims to drive demand. Major railroads opened offices in Europe to entice would-be immigrants to settle on their lands, selling them on fanciful visions of wide-open country and frontier outposts that were poised to become the next great American metropolises.

With the same zeal with which he had drummed up war bond sales, Cooke and his company aggressively marketed the Northern Pacific and touted the land it traversed as ideal for farming, with a "temperate, invigorating, and mild climate, similar to that of Virginia." Initial sales of the railway's bonds were strong, but demand weakened, particularly overseas, where Jay Cooke's London branch, Jay Cooke, McCulloch & Co., had little success placing the securities.

Here Jacob Schiff's young and soon-to-be-defunct firm entered the picture. In 1870, Moritz Budge and Budge, Schiff & Co. inked a contract with Jay Cooke & Co. to place the Northern Pacific's bonds in Europe, but later that year war broke out between France and Germany. The War of 1870 roiled European financial markets, and the Budges grew nervous. "Since the declaration of war Henry Budge has been like a child more than a man and in spite of their assertion to the contrary, I fear they may be hard up for money," one of Jay Cooke's associates informed him. Another colleague, faulting the Budges for the failure of the Northern Pacific bond-selling opera-tion in Europe, marveled that it was "the wonder of bankers that Jay Cooke and Company would entrust the loan to such people—a house, they say, who are just honest enough to keep out of the hands of the police." After more than a year, Jay Cooke severed his tense alliance with the Budges, but he had lost precious time in the pro-cess.[25]

Foreign investors, burned too many times by overhyped Ameri-can railroads, were growing skeptical, and the market for new bond offerings was drying up. Public confidence in the railroads was fur-ther shaken by the Crédit Mobilier scandal, which the *New York Sun* exposed shortly before the 1872 presidential election. Directors of the Union Pacific—which had received massive land grants and other financial incentives to build a line from the Missouri River to San Francisco—had orchestrated an elaborate fraud. They had renamed an existing company after a respected French banking firm (Crédit Mobilier) and then selected this supposedly independent outfit as the Union Pacific's construction contractor; Crédit Mobilier of America, as the firm was known, then overcharged the railroad for the work, enriching its shareholders.

To ensure favorable treatment in Washington, company directors doled out millions in bribes to politicians, in the form of cash and dis-counted Crédit Mobilier stock. Among those implicated: Schuyler Colfax, Ulysses Grant's vice president, and Congressman James Gar-field, who a couple of years earlier had led the Black Friday inquiry.

Congress launched a special investigation, and the hearings became a scandalous backdrop as Cooke tried to pitch a transconti-nental venture similar to the one that had been dubbed the "King of Frauds." Meanwhile, the European financial markets were increas-ingly shaky. Like the United States, Europe had experienced a surge of economic expansion in railroads and real estate. Banks handed out credit liberally. Speculation spiked. And then in May 1873 the bubble burst. Vienna's soaring stock market crashed, sending trem-ors throughout Europe's major financial centers. Credit tightened. Loans were called in. At first the European crisis did not affect the U.S. economy. But behind the scenes at Jay Cooke & Co., matters were growing desperate. Construction costs were mounting, and interest payments on the Northern Pacific's outstanding securities were coming due. Eventually Cooke ran out of road, and his firm was forced to reveal its deeply wounded condition. Police officers stood sentry outside its Philadelphia offices, and a notice was posted on its shuttered doors: "We regret to be obliged to announce that, owing to unexpected demands on us, our firm has been obliged to suspend payment."[26] Within a day, more than twenty other investment houses slid into oblivion, as credit froze up and banks defensively hoarded cash.[27] To contain the fallout, the New York Stock Exchange closed for ten days.

Following the September 18 crash, President Grant and his new Treasury secretary, William Richardson, hurried to New York, arriving that weekend and taking rooms at the Fifth Avenue Hotel, a frequent meeting ground for Wall Street eminences. On Sunday, September 21, anguished brokers and bankers packed every crevice of the hotel, excitedly swapping rumors about whether the Grant administration would take action to stabilize the market and hounding the desk clerks for an audience with the president. At one point, Jay Gould materialized, though after Black Friday there wasn't the slightest chance the president would agree to see him.

All day and into the evening, Grant and Richardson huddled with the city's leading financiers, including Cornelius Vanderbilt; Henry Clews, whose well-established banking firm was on the brink of collapse; and Joseph and Jesse Seligman.

The Seligmans had remained loyal to their old friend throughout his turbulent first term, and they threw their weight behind Grant even as a group of dissident Republicans, angered by the corruption plaguing his administration, broke away from their party and nominated the newspaper publisher Horace Greeley to challenge him. Shortly before the 1872 election, Joseph rallied New York's German vote behind Grant in a forceful speech at Cooper Union. He decried the "personal attacks and vituperation poured upon" the president but also acknowledged the shortcomings of Grant's administration. "That Grant has made mistakes we don't deny. . . . But that Grant tries to do his duty toward his country honestly and conscientiously, everyone who knows him well must concede, and I have known him well for a number of years."[28]

The Seligmans also helped Grant in other ways. When in 1871 their firm bankrolled a branch of the Missouri Pacific Railroad, stretching from the town of Kirkwood, outside St. Louis, to Carondelet, on the Mississippi River, Joseph stipulated that the route pass through a Missouri farm owned by the president, boosting the value of the land.[29]

Now, in a second-floor parlor at the Fifth Avenue Hotel, the Seligmans and their well-heeled peers pleaded with Grant to take bold action to stop the bloodletting. Their preferred method was for the Treasury Department to deposit federal funds with a New York bank to thaw the credit freeze. But Grant was wary of involving the government in Wall Street's mess—and was no doubt sensitive about being seen as in Wall Street's pocket. "We wanted more but the President would not agree to deposit his currency with Natl Bank as it was clearly illegal," Joseph wrote to his brother Isaac in London after spending "nearly all day Sunday with the President."[30]

As once-vaunted banking houses crumbled around them, the Seligmans faced another crisis: William was threatening to leave their firm and take his share of their assets, which now stood at about $6.6 million.[31] Tensions had been building for a while. In 1868 the brothers had opened a Paris branch, Seligman Frères & Cie, and William was dispatched to manage it—or rather, to co-manage it. Joseph, thinking his brother a bit lazy and profligate, also sent Theodore Hellman to Paris. Hellman, Jesse's brother-in-law, had up until then skillfully run the family's New Orleans branch. William hated the management arrangement, but he relished Parisian life, indulging his epicurean tastes and becoming a staple of the social scene; his wife threw parties that seemed over the top even by the extravagant standards of the Gilded Age. William increasingly came into conflict with Joseph over investment decisions. He was, perhaps wisely, worried about the partnership's large railroad holdings, where Joseph had sunk about a third of the family's capital.[32] Witnessing firsthand the shaky financial conditions in Europe during the summer of 1873 may have also convinced him to grab his share of the Seligman fortune—while it still existed.

But his request came at the very time when the family firm needed to marshal its resources to weather the panic. "It is criminal of Wm. to bother us now," Joseph fumed, "when all our intellect and energy are required in a crisis of unprecedented dimensions, making threats when he ought to be satisfied that we are fully cured of new investments and are bending all our nerves to get out of the old ones, which with God's help we shall do."[33]

In London, Isaac, for whom even the normal pressures of business brought thoughts of suicide, met both the panic and his brother's possible exit from their partnership with more than his usual level of acid-tongued excitability. When he learned that in the midst of the meltdown James, who had a hard time turning people down, had loaned nearly $200,000 to a railroad promoter, Isaac let loose. "I cannot conceive what insanity possessed your mind," he wrote to his brother. Now he could see why William wanted to exit their partnership. "He has good cause now in view of your extraordinary and inexcusable recklessness.

"It makes one's heart bleed to see a splendid fortune frittered away," he continued, predicting the loan would "end in our ruin." Isaac's mood gyrated with each cable and letter from New York. Two days later, after receiving a bit of positive news, he claimed breezily that the Seligmans were "as solvent as Rothschilds," and he maintained that he had never been "nervous" about their financial condition.[34]

The quarrelsome Seligman brothers fought their way through the panic—literally. By cable and post, fiery messages flew back and forth across the Atlantic. "While I shall invite that selfish bro. Wm. to carry out his threat and leave the concern on the 1st of Jan'y my self respect will impel me to tender the same invitation to you Bro. Isaac if you continue to vex us and bother us for an error of judgement," Joseph wrote to Isaac in late October. He continued,

> From Bro. Wm. I don't expect any consideration but from you, Bro. Ike, I did expect a less selfish and mean course. Now I shall not have time to write Bro. Wm. Please inform him that he is mistaken when he expects that we will buy him out and give him our obligations for his share. We shall do no such thing but want him to come here in Jan'y and take his ⅛th share of assets, consisting of railroad bonds and shares, mining shares, property, bad and good debts, and attend personally to collecting them and my word for it, he will find himself in better health than by eating heavy dinners, drinking heavy wines, writing heavy letters to us, and doing nothing else.[35]

Yet for all the Seligman infighting, their operation was in surprisingly strong shape. Unlike other New York firms, they were not overextended. And though they had substantial capital tied up in railroads, they maintained a healthy cushion of cash. "So far we are about the only flush house in N.Y.," Joseph noted the week after the panic hit.[36] The following month he wrote Isaac, "I don't believe we have lost a dollar. . . . We have not borrowed a dollar from a bank in the city of New York. . . . We have had large balances in bank every night during the panic, so as to be strong, and have . . . not offended anyone by cancelling running credits. We . . . shall come out of this with God's help better and stronger."[37]

While other firms struggled for survival, the Seligmans' solid financial footing presented them with opportunities. Joseph coveted the government business handled by Henry Clews and Jay Cooke, whose London-based branches served as the official financial agents for the State Department and the U.S. Navy, respectively. This business was attractive because both agencies maintained large balances and paid commissions on the millions in funds that were distributed annually. And it was useful for another reason: it broadcast to other clients that the firm had the confidence of the U.S. government.

Days after the suspension of Jay Cooke & Co., which was followed early the next week by the failure of Henry Clews's firm, Joseph aggressively pursued their business, taking the matter directly to President Grant. "We would respectfully offer our services to the Government in buying any drafts of our various departments in London, which by reason of the late suspensions may possibly not meet with prompt acceptance," he wrote Grant on September 25. In a separate letter to Grant, he offered up the London branch to "intervene for the honor of our Government" to handle State Department or navy transactions.[38]

Joseph's rivals, meanwhile, were just as strenuously working against him by circulating scurrilous rumors that the Seligmans had hastened Jay Cooke's downfall by suddenly demanding an outstanding payment from the wounded firm.[39] Nevertheless, by 1874, Joseph had won the navy's business.

That year the Seligmans rose to even greater heights in the financial pecking order when they partnered with N.M. Rothschild & Sons, the London branch of the Rothschild family's international banking juggernaut, on a U.S. government bond issue. But the deal did not go exactly as Joseph had planned.

The Seligmans had originally organized their own syndicate of U.S. and European bankers to bid for the bonds, but the Treasury Department conveyed its desire that they collaborate with the Rothschilds. The Seligmans, despite their recent successes and Joseph's considerable political influence, were still not on the same level as the Rothschilds, who made this clear when they dictated their terms: the Seligmans would get a mere 28 percent stake in the issue, with no say over how it was managed, and their firm's name would not appear in advertisements promoting sales of the bonds. The prestige

of working with the Rothschilds was worth suffering a certain number of indignities. But what good was it if the Seligmans received no
billing—and thus no bragging rights—on the deal? Joseph went to
the mat over this issue until the Rothschilds finally agreed to include
the Seligmans in the ads—beneath their own firm, of course, and in
much smaller typeface.

"Having now broken the ice, I wish you to cultivate this connection," Joseph instructed Isaac, who became a frequent visitor to New
Court, N.M. Rothschild's London headquarters.[40] Isaac recalled
once visiting Baron Lionel Nathan de Rothschild, the son of the
firm's founder, at his home on a Saturday, where he was observing
the Sabbath. Seated at a table covered with documents, the elderly
banker took the occasion to remind Isaac of his superiority not only
in financial matters but in spiritual ones, too: "I am a better Jew than
you. You go to business on Saturdays. I do not. My office is closed."

Isaac, always quick with a riposte, replied: "I think you do more
business in this little room on Saturdays than I do during the whole
week in my office!"[41] (Ultimately, Isaac was not diplomatic enough
to nurture the Rothschild connection. In the late 1870s, when Seligman Brothers worked together with N.M. Rothschild on another
U.S. bond issue, Isaac had a tense exchange with Baron Rothschild's
successor, his eldest son, Nathan. Isaac stormed out of their meeting and from that day forward "had no further personal contact
with N.M. Rothschild & Sons," according to Isaac's son, Sir Charles
Seligman.)[42]

Even though things looked up for the Seligmans in the months
after the panic, the crisis wrought economic devastation for years to
come. The U.S. economy—and those of some European nations—
entered a protracted depression. Unemployment climbed, factories
shuttered, and thousands of businesses went under. In the downturn,
financial tycoons vacuumed up railroad stocks and ailing businesses
for pennies on the dollar, cementing some of the vast monopolies
that would become the hallmark of the Gilded Age.

The Panic of 1873 was considered one of the first international
financial crises, and in certain ways, from the shaky mortgage-backed
securities underlying the railroad boom to the credit crunch that
exacerbated the situation, it bore a resemblance to the financial
meltdown of 2007–8 that drove Lehman Brothers into extinction
and imperiled Goldman Sachs and other long-established firms. In
1873 the crisis separated the wheat from the chaff on Wall Street,
and the Lehmans and Marcus Goldman were among the financiers

who emerged unscathed and who thrived during the postpanic years. Goldman continued his cautious business making loans to downtown merchants, underestimated by rivals as he quietly laid brick upon brick of his financial empire. As for the Lehmans, in October 1873, the month after the panic hit, they bragged to R.G. Dun & Co. that they "never were more easy in money matters than at present so much so that they have no indebtedness." This statement, of course, could have been bluster from an ailing firm eager to guard its credit rating. So the agency checked out the Lehmans' claims with their competitors. It was true: "We find their statement confirmed."[43]

At Kuhn Loeb, Solomon Loeb's instinct for saying no was also paying off. Like the Lehmans, the firm's partners claimed to be flush. By early 1874, they were arguing that R.G. Dun's valuation of the company—at under a million dollars—was far too low. Loeb alone, they insisted, possessed more than a million in cash.[44] The firm was in fact looking to expand and take on new partners. One prospect, a precocious young banker from Frankfurt, looked especially promising.

7

THE LITTLE GIANT

After the unraveling of Budge, Schiff & Co., Jacob Schiff's care-fully plotted life had taken an unexpected detour back to Germany, which had undergone sweeping changes in his absence. In 1862 the Prussian prime minister Otto von Bismarck had vowed to settle "the great questions of the time" through "iron and blood." Through a succession of wars with neighboring countries, culminating with Prussia's defeat of France in the war of 1870, Bismarck stoked German nationalism and, in early 1871, engineered the unification of the autonomous kingdoms, duchies, and principalities of Germany into a single nation-state under the rule of Kaiser Wilhelm I, previously the King of Prussia.

Schiff moved initially to Hamburg, the busy port city in northern Germany, where Moritz Warburg, of the long-established banking house of M.M. Warburg, had offered him a position. (Warburg would later become Schiff's in-law.) But Schiff did not remain long in his new post. In late August 1873, his father died, and he rushed home to Frankfurt to look after his mother.

Abraham Kuhn had settled in Frankfurt a few years earlier, returning to Germany from New York after the death of his wife. He remained a Kuhn Loeb partner but withdrew from the day-to-day running of the business. Their banking operation was now largely overseen by Solomon Loeb. Kuhn was likely already acquainted with Schiff from Wall Street banking circles, and in Frankfurt he offered

Jacob a position in Kuhn Loeb's New York office.[1] This time the
restless young financier was more hesitant to leave home, but his
widowed mother finally insisted he go. "You are made for America,"
she told him.[2]

Kuhn had floated the notion that Kuhn Loeb might found a
European branch and Schiff might one day run it, but after Schiff
returned to New York, that prospect quickly faded. "The opportunity is enormous here," he wrote his mother. "But the coming expansion of the United States, in railroading and all that, is so large that
I myself don't feel there will be a foreign branch for some time to
come, because there is more than enough to keep us busy here."[3]

In an agreement dated November 29, 1874, Schiff entered the
partnership of Kuhn Loeb, effective the first of the new year. (Also
joining the firm at that time were a Kuhn relative named Michael
Gernsheim and Loeb's cousin Abraham Wolff.) Schiff contributed
$50,000 of capital to the firm and received a 20 percent share of its
profits, second only to Loeb, who commanded a little over 33 percent. Abraham Kuhn received an 18 percent cut.[4]

Schiff made himself indispensable and not just in running the
business. The Loebs often entertained on Sundays at their home on
37th Street, and Schiff was a regular guest at these dinners, where the
table practically sagged under the weight of the spread. James Loeb,
the younger of Solomon's two sons, recalled that his family lived in
a "typical, unprepossessing twenty-five foot brownstone, high-stoop
house that made the streets of New York so hideous from the year
1860 on." The interior, in his estimation, was no less unsightly. "Our
furniture was as simple as, for the most part, it was ugly. . . . But the
spirit that dwelt in our home was of the finest," filled with "the tradition of an old culture, and music and poetry and aspiration were our
almost daily fare."[5]

While Solomon was so absorbed by his business that he once
absent-mindedly signed a letter to one of their sons, "Your Lov-
ing Kuhn Loeb & Company," Betty, who had trained in piano at a
Paris conservatory, nurtured her children's artistic and intellectual
instincts. She organized them into a quartet—Morris on the viola,
Guta playing piano, James the cello, and Nina on violin—and they
performed regular concerts for their father and other guests.[6]

It was not just the effervescent atmosphere that brought Schiff
to their doorstep Sunday after Sunday, but Loeb's twenty-year-old
daughter Therese, whom Schiff described in a letter to his mother as
"just sweetness itself." Petite, with her father's clear blue eyes and a

"virginal innocence," in the words of her daughter, she was the eldest of Loeb's five children and his only child by his late wife Fanny.[7] Betty had raised Therese as her own. And though born in America, Therese had been educated at home in the German style, and her old-world qualities appealed to Schiff. "I know that you haven't any clear conception of what an American girl is like," he reassured his mother, in a letter announcing their engagement. "You may think she is rather uncultured and uneducated and even a feminist—but don't imagine that of the girl I've selected. She might have been brought up in the best of German families."[8]

The couple married on May 6, 1875, with Marcus Goldman's youngest daughter, Louisa, serving as a bridesmaid.[9] Following the ceremony, the Loebs hosted a lavish reception. Catered by Delmonico's, the French-inspired seven-course dinner—excluding the sorbet palate cleanser—featured oysters and stewed terrapin, squab and capon, lamb and foie gras. Once guests had eaten themselves into a stupor, waiters brought out ten varieties of dessert, including pineapple gelée, rum cake, bonbons, and *napolitain*.

The congratulatory telegrams poured in from Cincinnati and Frankfurt. Clara Schiff—who might not have approved of the reception since the menu was not kosher—sent her "most heartfelt congratulations." Schiff's younger brother, Hermann, wired, "A long hurrah to the new pair." Henry Budge and Leo Lehmann, his old partners, telegrammed, "Hip hip hip hurrah." And a Cincinnati-based Loeb wrote, "May you be happy and the income of your bonds increase."[10]

Solomon Loeb presented the newlyweds with a home at 57 East 53rd Street, where their first child, a daughter named Frieda, was born on February 3, 1876, following an arduous three-day labor. "I can promise you neither mother nor child," the gaunt doctor told Schiff at one point during the tense delivery.[11] The timing of Frieda's birth—less than nine months after their wedding—led to some whispers about when the baby had been conceived. Schiff was not amused. "Shortly after my arrival," Frieda later recounted, "my father stopped in at my grandparents' house . . . and a friend of the Loebs', in an attempt at humor, said: 'I want to congratulate you on the appropriate name you have given your baby—Früh-Da,'" meaning "early arrival" in German. "My father never spoke to that man again."[12]

· · ·

Schiff could be kind, accommodating, and generous—indeed his compassionate philanthropy formed the bedrock of his legacy—but he was also quick-tempered and unyielding. He had a pathological desire for control, and he had no compunction about taking it. "Everyone was frightened of him," said David Schiff, Jacob's great-grandson. "He was austere and demanding."[13]

Both Schiff and Loeb were highly driven men, but there was no question who possessed the more dominant personality. Loeb commanded respect. Schiff inspired awe. He held a center of gravity stronger than those around him—people orbited him, whether they liked it or not. Due to his outsize presence and short stature, his daughter-in-law would later dub him "the Little Giant."[14]

The newly married twenty-eight-year-old came to dominate the family life of the Loeb clan, upon whom he imposed his conservative religious beliefs. Solomon was agnostic, and Betty practiced a highly liberal form of Judaism. But to please their son-in-law—and by extension their daughter—the Loebs went through the motions. Temple was attended, the Shabbat candles lit on Friday evenings. Even as his family members bowed to his demands, they resented what nephew James P. Warburg described as Schiff's "proselytizing religiosity."[15]

Schiff lectured his family members on their religious duties, but he also "seemed to have his own ground rules," according to his grandson Edward Warburg. He prayed each morning, partly in German and partly in Hebrew, concluding his daily worship by reverently kissing a pair of faded photographs of his parents (Clara Schiff died in 1877) that he kept in a small worn envelope in his wallet. Unlike his in-laws and many of their friends in New York's German-Jewish community, Schiff strictly observed the Sabbath.[16] "He avoided all secular business upon it," his friend Louis Marshall, the distinguished lawyer, once recalled. "He never so much as touched pen to paper on the day he thus held sacred, save on one occasion only, when it became necessary to write a cablegram intended to bring relief to the victims of a Russian pogrom."[17]

Yet though raised in Orthodox tradition in a kosher household, Schiff made a pretense of following the dietary laws, which he "observed . . . with some glaring exceptions—lobster and bacon somehow sneaked in under the wire," Edward Warburg remembered. Which is to say, Schiff did not keep kosher.[18]

On Friday evenings, the family gathered, holding hands around the Sabbath table, upon which were placed pictures of recently departed relatives, and Schiff said a grace of his own creation: *Our God and Father, thou givest food to every living being. Thou hast not only given us life, thou also givest our daily bread to sustain it. Continue to bless us with Thy mercy, so that we may be able to share our own plenty with those less fortunate than ourselves. Blessed be Thy name forevermore. Amen.*[19]

"As I recall," Warburg noted, "these observances dictated by my Grandfather bore little if any resemblance to the usual Jewish religious practices." And he said, "We were not trained in Jewish ritual compliance but in an inimitable Schiff-Warburg form of *Familiengefühl* (a sense of family) and ancestor worship."[20]

Schiff asserted his control not just in religious and family matters but in the affairs of Kuhn Loeb. Due to his influence, James Loeb said, "a new and more aggressive policy was pursued."[21] Picking up where he had left off a couple of years earlier, Schiff plunged Kuhn Loeb into the risky but profitable realm of railroad finance—to the palpable discomfort of his father-in-law, as well as Abraham Kuhn. The firm's new direction "scared the Kuhns, nearly to death," according to Samuel Kuhn's grandson.[22] Samuel Kuhn and Jacob Netter (who died in 1875) ultimately pulled out of the firm, and in the mid-1880s Abraham Kuhn withdrew his capital and formally retired from the partnership.

Loeb's conservative instincts clashed with Schiff's bold vision. And increasingly Loeb began to feel out of place within his own firm, a feeling Schiff seemed happy to fuel. Daily, Schiff peppered his father-in-law with ideas for new ventures and with memoranda laden with technical details that were all but inscrutable to the senior partner, who lacked Schiff's financial training.

Schiff surpassed Loeb in financial expertise but also in connections, which extended into the world's key financial centers: Amsterdam, Frankfurt, London, Paris, and beyond. Even in the early years of his association with Kuhn Loeb, Schiff's reputation, especially as a railroad financier, spanned both sides of the Atlantic. And if ill feelings among investors still lingered from the misadventures of his first partnership, they did not seem to hold back his ascent at Kuhn Loeb. European financiers such as Scotland's Robert Fleming, of Robert Fleming & Co., and Edouard Noetzlin, of the Banque de Paris et des Pays Bas, sought him out for his advice on the American market and wound up forming close business and personal ties to Schiff and Kuhn Loeb.

In 1879, Schiff forged one of his most important connections—and closest friendships—when he was introduced to Ernest Cassel.

The London-based financier occupied a similar role in Britain as
Schiff did in the United States—a rising young tycoon destined to
become a dominant force in investment banking. Born to a Jewish
family in Cologne, Cassel had moved to Liverpool as a teenager, then
to London, where he ascended the ranks at the firm of Bischoffs-
heim & Goldschmidt, before striking out on his own. But theirs was
a somewhat unlikely friendship, for philosophically Schiff and Cassel
disagreed on much. Schiff disliked overt displays of ostentation; Cassel's mansion in central London featured six kitchens and a dining
room that could comfortably seat one hundred people. Schiff's faith
was his lodestone; Cassel, fulfilling the dying wish of his British-born
wife Annette, converted to Catholicism, a secret revealed only many
years after the fact when he was sworn in to the Privy Council, whose
members advised the king, and requested a Christian Bible for the
ceremony. Yet when it came to business, Schiff and Cassel were usually simpatico, and their relationship was instrumental to Kuhn Loeb
deepening its British ties.

"If we could get into more intimate relations with London
through you, we should be highly gratified," Schiff wrote Cassel in
1882. The following year he sought Cassel's help forging a connection with a new brokerage firm to represent Kuhn Loeb at the London Stock Exchange. "What we have to stress especially is that our
brokers shall always be on the alert; understand the American market
well (which can after all be learned easily by a little practice); and
call our attention to possible transactions in London. Their responsibility and credit must be beyond question, so that we can entrust
them with large amounts of money." He added, "We should prefer
to establish connections with an English house, which is not too stiff,
which has no relations yet with New York, and which has very good
connections in England itself."[23]

In turn, Schiff offered the "loyal fellow" Kuhn Loeb's services,
writing, "we shall make advances to you at any time, even under
conditions of tight money; it will be our pleasure for us to put our
resources at your disposal." And he frequently counseled Cassel on
North American investments. "During the last few days I have had an
opportunity to investigate the position of the Erie more closely, and
I was surprised to find how sound the company was," Schiff wrote
Cassel of the perpetually troubled railroad that was once controlled
by Jay Gould and his cronies and where Schiff then held a seat on
the board. However, he advised, "the common stock is only trash."[24]
Over the years, their bond deepened, forming an important conduit

through which many millions in European investment capital flowed
to North America.

Not long after Schiff joined Kuhn Loeb, the firm's name started
appearing in the papers alongside those of New York's most vaunted
banking houses, including those of the Seligmans and J. P. Morgan,
and in connection with bigger and bigger deals.

It was a sign of Kuhn Loeb's stature—and of Schiff's—that in
1878 the banker received an invitation to consult with Treasury secretary John Sherman on a $100 million bond issue. Meeting with
Sherman alongside Schiff were New York's biggest financial heavyweights, including Joseph Seligman and August Belmont, the U.S.
representative of the Rothschilds, who like Schiff had grown up in
Frankfurt.[25] (One of the most powerful bankers of his era, as well as
a political eminence who for more than a decade helmed the Democratic National Committee, Belmont had taken pains to mask his
Jewish roots, converting to Christianity and changing his original
last name—Schönberg.) Seligman ultimately signed on for $20 mil-
lion of the bonds, while Schiff and Belmont subscribed their firms for
$10 million apiece.[26]

In 1880, hearing that negotiations had broken down between the
Pennsylvania Railroad and its bankers—J. P. Morgan and his partner
Anthony Drexel—over the flotation of a new loan, Schiff approached
the company's executives. Kuhn Loeb, he said, would be "delighted"
to handle the transaction.[27] Schiff arranged the loan, and increasingly the Pennsylvania shifted its banking business to Kuhn Loeb.
With some thirty thousand employees and $400 million in capital,
the Pennsy, as it was known, was then the world's largest corporation.
Winning its business was transformative. Over the next four decades,
Kuhn Loeb would handle more than $1 billion in stock and bond
offerings for the railroad.[28] Signifying the importance of the relationship, in Kuhn Loeb's offices hung two framed checks to the Pennsylvania Railroad, one for $49,098,000 and the other for $62,075,000.[29]

In 1885, Schiff moved his family into a four-story, Beaux Arts–
style townhouse in an Upper East Side neighborhood populated by
fellow moguls.[30] Nine-thirty-two Fifth Avenue sat a few blocks away
from Temple Beth-El, the other congregation Schiff belonged to in
addition to Temple Emanu-El and one to which he could easily walk
on the Sabbath (when Orthodox Jews don't ride in vehicles or perform any tasks that could be construed as work). The home, with

bowfront windows on the second floor, was long and narrow. The Schiffs' butler, an elderly Irishman named Thomas, found the 150-foot walk from the rear of the house to the front door so excruciating that he finally tendered his keys and resigned.[31]

At virtually the same time each weekday morning, Schiff exited his home with a freshly cut flower, often a rose, adorning the lapel of his coat. He employed a chauffeur named Neville, though he preferred to walk most of the way downtown, often reaching 14th Street before his driver picked him up, or he caught a trolley car the rest of the way.[32] He liked the exercise but also used these walks to discuss business, politics, and charitable work with a rotating group of friends and associates, including Louis Marshall, one of his closest allies and confidants. Schiff often preferred to converse in German, and his English was thickly accented. He suffered from hearing problems that progressively worsened as he grew older, though he seemed to compensate well for his impairment. An exacting man, Schiff hated waste. Instead of notepads, he used scraps of paper.[33] And he habitually saved newspapers and magazines, which he donated to hospital patients, bundled in twine he had also salvaged. Schiff was just as economical with his time and tried to make his daily walks as profitable as possible.

The year Jacob and family moved into their new abode, Solomon Loeb became a special partner in Kuhn Loeb and fully turned the reins over to his son-in-law, who in all but an official sense had already seized them. Schiff's brash style had made Loeb uneasy. He had steered the firm into unchartered waters, in some cases doing so without even consulting Loeb. According to James Loeb, a breaking point came for the elder banker when, "in the middle of the eighties, and while father was abroad with his family, heavy engagements in an ill-advised railroad enterprise had placed the firm in a rather precarious position. Father had ere then begun to realize that his views were little in accord with those of his younger associates and he decided to withdraw from further active participation." After his retirement, Loeb continued to putter around the office daily, though, his son said, "to his chagrin, he found that his counsel and experience were not being drawn upon as often or as freely as he thought his due."[34]

Loeb hoped that one of his sons would enter the firm, though neither displayed much interest in finance. Loeb's eldest son, Morris, was a shy, nervous man of austere and somewhat peculiar habits, including an obsession with the cleanliness of his food. His passion was chemistry. After Morris attended college at Harvard and earned a doctorate from the University of Berlin, Solomon stood ready to set his son up in business by investing in a synthetic dye factory that Morris would run. The contract was already drawn up when Morris informed his father that he could not "take the proffered post." But why? Solomon asked. "Because my nature will not permit me to ask more than I am willing to accept, nor to bid less than I'm willing to give."[35] Instead, he joined the faculty of New York University and forged a successful career as a chemist that was prematurely cut short when he contracted a fatal case of typhoid from a tainted oyster.

Like his older brother, James Loeb's interests lay in academia. Charming and handsome—"like a Greek god," in the words of his niece, Frieda Schiff—James studied Egyptology at Harvard, where a professor took an interest in him and offered him a program of continued study in London, Paris, and Egypt that would potentially lead to a professorship at Harvard and a curatorial role at the Boston Museum of Fine Arts.[36] Unlike Morris, James bowed to family obligation, joining Kuhn Loeb in 1888 and spending an agonizing thirteen years at the firm, his tenure marked by repeated mental breakdowns. Schiff, meanwhile, was grooming his own son, Mortimer, born in June 1877, to one day assume the leadership of Kuhn Loeb.

Elbowed out of his own firm, Solomon Loeb nevertheless remained active in business. He invested in Manhattan real estate and fastidiously looked after his properties, handling almost everything himself save for the collection of rent.[37] As a hobby, he took up drawing, making intricate pencil copies of pictures he enjoyed and later, as he grew more skilled, sketching nature scenes.[38]

Loeb was a serious man—he was sometimes mistaken for a former military officer, owing to his ramrod-straight posture—and his children viewed him as slightly unapproachable.[39] Few things made him laugh, but one thing reliably brought a smile to his lips: his youngest daughter Nina's spot-on impression of her imperious brother-in-law Jacob Schiff.[40]

8

THE GILDED GHETTO

Jacob Schiff was on the path to becoming one of the greatest financiers of his generation, but another mogul still towered above him. Joseph Seligman had realized his vision of becoming something like an American Rothschild, a banker whose firm was ubiquitous in major government and industrial transactions and who moved with ease in the elite financial and political circles where few Jews traveled. In New York, he and his brother Jesse numbered among the only Jewish members of the Union League Club, a stuffy clique of businessmen, politicians, and intellectuals formed during the Civil War to promote the northern cause, and Joseph served on various municipal boards and honorary committees, including the city's school commission, where he occupied the so-called "Jewish seat." But unlike Baron Lionel de Rothschild, the head of London's N.M. Rothschild & Sons who became the first Jew to serve in Parliament, Joseph stopped short of seeking elected office, despite the efforts of New York Republicans who twice tried to draft him to run for mayor.[1] (Jesse too was floated as a mayoral candidate.)[2]

Perhaps because the nation of his birth conveyed in countless ways that he was inferior and unwanted—that he was not a citizen but an interloper—Joseph strove consciously to blend into the fabric of the country that had welcomed him, and he raised his children to be thoroughly American. William, with his usual flair for making irritating propositions, once approached Joseph with the idea of changing their Jewish surname, pulling a Belmont as it were, to distance the family from the religious stigmas holding them back from unreserved acceptance in the gentile world. "An excellent idea," Joseph deadpanned, "but we might as well keep our initial letter, and for you I suggest the name 'Shlemiel.'"[3] Even though he shut William down with a thunderclap of sarcasm, Joseph seemed keenly aware of the social handicaps of their religion. When he wanted to honor Abraham Lincoln by naming his fifth-born son after the president, he opted to give the boy the similar though less Hebraic-sounding name of Alfred Lincoln.

There were limits to how far Joseph was willing to assimilate, and he drew a line at renouncing or concealing his Jewishness. And he embraced his role as one of the nation's most prominent Jews (some called him the "King of the Jews") even though he was by no means devout.[4] His interest in religion was largely intellectual. A well-read man who perused the pages of the Greek classics before bed—Horatio Alger, the family tutor, recalled Seligman closing each day "engrossed by business cares in the delightful companionship of the master spirits in the domain of literature and science"—Joseph enjoyed religious and philosophical debate.[5] On Sundays, when he and Babette entertained at their home on West 34th Street, Joseph liked inviting guests with divergent views to enliven the dinner table conversation. He counted as friends Henry Ward Beecher, the prominent congregationalist minister (and brother of Harriet Beecher Stowe), as well as Colonel Robert Ingersoll, a lawyer and popular orator known for his agnostic views. More than once, he hosted both men, strategically planting a provocative topic and sitting back from his place at the head of the table to take in the spirited rhetorical volley that ensued between his guests.[6]

Joseph's beliefs were closer to Ingersoll's than to Beecher's, his Judaism more cultural than spiritual, but he remained fiercely loyal to his people, using his political and social influence to garner support for Jewish causes and charities. For years he served as a trustee of Mount Sinai Hospital, originally called the Jews' Hospital when it was founded in 1852 to treat New York's Jewish population, who in some cases faced discrimination at the city's Christian-run wards. And he headed the German Hebrew Benevolent Society, as much a social outfit as a charitable one, which held banquets and galas to raise funds to distribute to various Jewish organizations. Among its charitable activities, the group provided coal to impoverished immigrant families and occasionally furnished them with the means to continue their migration to the lightly populated West and out of overcrowded New York, where the more established and assimilated Jews feared their newly arrived coreligionists—uneducated and penniless and packing into dilapidated Lower East Side tenements—might arouse antisemitic sentiments.[7]

Seligman's group had splintered off from an older charity, the Hebrew Benevolent Society. The split reflected larger divisions between the Germans and the rest of New York's Jewish community, especially the Sephardim (Jews tracing their ancestry to the Iberian Peninsula) who dominated the charity's leadership. The rift was based in part on religion and in part on class. The Germans had brought with them to America Reform Judaism, a controversial religious movement that had gotten its start in the temples of Berlin and Frankfurt. European Jews increasingly lived outside the ghettos into which they had been shunted for generations, residing more and more among Christians and in some cases losing touch with their faith or converting to Christianity. The Reform movement held that, if Judaism was to survive, the traditional observances needed to adapt to modern times. "Whatever makes us ridiculous before the world as it now is may safely be and should be abolished," noted one prominent Reform rabbi.[8] Reform Jews didn't cover their heads with yarmulkes. They didn't keep to the dietary laws. They held their services in German, not in Hebrew. In some cases, they didn't circumcise their sons. These practices were blasphemous to Orthodox Jews—men like Jacob Schiff's father—who believed that the reformers were watering down their religion beyond recognition. New York's Sephardic Jews, whose roots in the city extended back to when the island of Manhattan was still a Dutch colony, were bothered by the Germans' liberal religious practices. And they were equally put off by the ostentation of the German nouveaux riches. To them, Joseph Seligman would always be a mere pack peddler.[9]

When the Germans broke off to form their own benevolent society—announcing that this organization would serve only German Jews, not the community as a whole—they all but confirmed the Sephardim's low opinion of them. The rivalry reached outlandish proportions: in the 1850s, at a joint anniversary dinner attended by members of both groups, Orthodox Jews demanded that the Germans don yarmulkes during the closing benediction. When they refused, the Sephardim hurled handkerchiefs and napkins in an effort to forcibly cover the heads of the blasphemers. The evening ended ignominiously. During remarks by Samuel Adler, the rabbi of the

Reform congregation Temple Emanu-El who got up to address the religious controversy that had erupted, an Orthodox Jew stood up and whistled in protest. A mob of Germans descended, surrounding the man and delivering a fierce beating.[10]

Outside events gradually pushed these warring factions together. One factor was the financial crisis of 1857 and the ensuing depression: as donations dried up, it made even less sense to have two organizations with similar aims competing for resources. Another was an international controversy that united the world's Jews, even the bickering benevolent societies, in outrage. In 1858 papal authorities seized a six-year-old Jewish boy named Edgardo Mortara from his home in Bologna. As an infant, Mortara had fallen gravely ill, and a servant had secretly baptized him, believing the child was close to death. Years later, based on the servant's testimony, Bologna's inquisitor ordered Mortara removed from his home and placed under the protection of the church, where he was raised as a Catholic. Despite international protest and condemnation—not to mention pleas from Mortara's family to return their son—the pope did not relent.[11]

For Jews, the issue of conversion was a sensitive one, evoking both a painful past and an uncertain future. Jews were no longer forcibly converted at swordpoint or by royal decree, as they had been centuries earlier, but during the nineteenth century organized proselytizing targeting members of their faith was widespread and aggressive, both in the United States and in Europe. For Jewish leaders, it wasn't hard to envision a point at which their ancient traditions were slowly extinguished by attrition.

The benevolent societies coalesced around the creation of an orphanage for Jewish children, who were all but certain to be raised outside their faith if placed in Christian-run asylums. New York's Jews had been incredibly prolific in creating a philanthropic network to aid the neediest among them—between 1848 and 1860, they established no fewer than ninety Jewish aid organizations—but this was one institution the community lacked.[12]

In 1860 the groups merged, forming the Hebrew Benevolent and Orphan Asylum Society, which opened its first orphanage at 1 Lamartine Place (what is now West 29th Street). Joseph served as the organization's first president, though it was his brother Jesse who later spent nearly twenty years at the helm of the group. Jesse "felt himself greater and happier in this orphan home than in his bank," his friend Carl Schurz, the German-revolutionary-turned-American-statesman, once remarked.[13] And it was Jesse who suggested one of the group's most successful outreach and fundraising endeavors, the publication of a children's magazine, *Young Israel*. The illustrated monthly, printed in the orphan asylum's basement on equipment Jesse had donated, was an instant hit when it launched in 1871; it helped that Jesse recruited Horatio Alger as a regular contributor.[14]

Also active in the asylum's leadership were various members of the Seligmans' social set. Marcus Goldman's eldest son, Julius, a Columbia-trained lawyer, was a trustee. Emanuel Lehman served for seven years as its president, and he created a trust fund that handed out college scholarships to deserving orphans. Solomon Loeb was a generous financial backer. In the 1870s, when the asylum faced allegations that the religious schooling of its 173 residents was so paltry that "not one was able to recite correctly the ten commandments in English much less Hebrew," Loeb was a member of the committee that probed the charges. (In what may have been a whitewash, the businessman and his colleagues concluded the accusations were unfounded.)[15]

The needs of New York's growing Jewish population were great and growing by the day, and the newspapers carried regular reminders of the depredations motivating immigrants to seek refuge in America. In the late 1860s and early '70s, many of these harrowing stories—of synagogues desecrated, villages plundered, mobs out for blood—originated in the principalities of Romania, the scene of intense political debate over whether Jews should be granted citizenship. As one representative headline, in the *New York Herald*, reported: "Persecution of the Roumania Jews: Hundreds Wounded. Old Men and Helpless Children Beaten. Stores and Dwellings Broken Open and Robbed. Wanton Destruction of Property. The Police Encourage the Mob."[16] Another article told of a Romanian parliamentarian advocating that Jews be barred from owning property, while a colleague argued that perhaps they should simply be drowned in the Danube.[17]

In 1870, after news of horrific anti-Jewish massacres reached the United States, the Seligmans and other prominent Jews pressed Ulysses Grant to send Benjamin Franklin Peixotto, a Jewish lawyer living in San Francisco, to Bucharest to serve as U.S. consul. The post was unpaid; to raise funds to subsidize Peixotto's mission, Joseph and Jesse formed the American Roumanian Society, with Joseph serving as president. This money would allow the newly minted diplomat to "make the trial for a couple of years with those benighted and semi-civilized heathens, our co-religionists in Romania," Jesse explained.[18] Peixotto's appointment sent a strong message, and in case the symbolism of dispatching a Jew to Romania as the U.S. government's official representative wasn't clear enough, Grant provided his new consul with a letter spelling out his administration's position on the so-called "Jewish question." It read, "The United States, knowing no distinction of her own citizens on account of religion or nativity, naturally believes in a civilization the world over, which will secure the same universal rights."[19]

Joseph, though not religious, nevertheless took an active role in the leadership of Temple Emanu-El, the spiritual center of New York's German-Jewish elite, as did brothers James and Jesse, who each served terms as president of its board of trustees. Founded in 1845 by thirty-three German immigrants, Emanu-El was New York's first Reform congregation. Starting out from a rented meeting room on Clinton and Grand streets, Emanu-El now occupied a soaring edifice on 43rd Street and Fifth Avenue. Blending styles from Gothic to Norman to Arabesque, the temple, nearly one hundred feet tall and equally as wide, was built of red and yellow sandstone, featuring exotic minarets and spires, each topped by a Star of David. When the temple was dedicated in 1868, it was one of the city's most expensive religious structures, costing more than $650,000 to construct. "Of the many imposing edifices dedicated to sacred worship that line the sides of Fifth avenue and lift their delicate spires to the fleecy clouds none is so unique, so attractive and so captivating to the eye as this strangely constructed temple of Emanu-El," the *New York Herald* marveled. In addition to being an architectural wonder, it stood as an unmistakable monument to the economic ascendance of the German Jews.[20] (In 1927, Emanu-El, seeking a more residential location, moved farther up Fifth Avenue to new premises on 65th Street. The largest synagogue in the world at the time of its construction, its signature circular stained-glass window was gifted to the congregation by Herbert Lehman and his siblings in tribute to their parents, Mayer and Babette. Emanu-El's old location was purchased and demolished to make way for office towers by the real estate mogul Joseph Durst—grandfather of convicted killer Robert Durst.)

The congregation's Reform policies and practices reflected the assimilationist goals of its congregants. Traditionally, men and women worshipped separately, but Emanu-El introduced family pews where members of both sexes sat together. Services, eventually conducted largely in English, featured choir and organ music, borrowing from Christian worship, and the traditional bar mitzvah ceremony was modified into a confirmation. At one point, Emanu-El's congregants debated whether to begin holding Sunday services, in order to accommodate men who worked on the Sabbath.[21] Joseph and Emanuel Lehman served on a three-man committee that considered, and ultimately rejected, the idea.[22]

Many of the most significant reforms occurred during the tenure of Rabbi Samuel Adler, a prominent figure in European Reform Judaism who immigrated from Germany in 1857 to lead Emanu-El. Yet some Emanu-El congregants, including Joseph, found themselves more captivated by the religious philosophy of Adler's son Felix.

Felix had trained to become a rabbi, and it was widely expected that he would one day succeed his father. Yet his first Emanu-El sermon was also his last. In 1873 the twenty-three-year-old, fresh from studying for his Ph.D. in Germany, took the pulpit, stared out at the expectant faces of some of New York's foremost Jews, and launched into a radical treatise titled "The Judaism of the Future." It quickly became clear that the young rabbi, steeped in the teachings of the German philosopher Immanuel Kant, was advocating not a modern Judaism but a wholesale rethinking of religion itself.

He attacked the concept of the Jews as a "chosen people," calling on the congregation to "discard the narrow spirit of exclusion, and loudly proclaim that Judaism was not given to the Jews alone, but that its destiny is to embrace in one great moral state the whole family of men." The purpose of organized religion, Felix believed, was to propagate moral and compassionate behavior; in this sense Judaism was a worthy vessel for these teachings. But why prevent others from sharing in them? Religion, Felix told Emanu-El's congregants, should place its "greatest stress not on the believing but the acting out." He was preaching a religion—if that was what it could even be called—in which belief in God was optional.[23]

Adler's heretical sermon ensured that he would never attain Emanu-El's rabbinate, but it laid the groundwork for something bigger: a social movement that spread around the world. While scandalizing many Emanu-El congregants, Adler managed to win over Joseph Seligman and Marcus Goldman, whose son Julius was married to Felix's sister, Sarah. Emphasizing "deed over creed" and the belief that morality existed independent of religion, Adler's Society for Ethical Culture was founded in February 1877, with Seligman serving as president and Goldman as a trustee of the new organization.

Seligman maintained his Emanu-El membership, probably out of a sense of social obligation and to please his more observant brothers, even as he drifted further from the Judaism of his childhood. But as he would soon learn, it hardly mattered what he believed or what he had accomplished. To some, he would never be more than a Jew.

During the sweltering summer months, the townhouses of Murray Hill and the Upper East Side emptied as New York's wealthiest sought refuge from the heat. Some flocked to Staten Island or the New Jersey shore beach communities of Sea Bright and Long Branch, while others journeyed to the lakes of upstate New York, where tycoons built vast camps with wistful names like Wild Air.

In June 1877, Joseph departed with his large family for their annual pilgrimage to Saratoga Springs, the resort town on the southern edge of the Adirondacks, where the Seligmans had vacationed for the past decade.[24] Saratoga, with its racetrack and gambling parlors, its elegant hotels and curative waters, was at the height of its Gilded Age splendor, the summer playground of the robber barons, who arrived by private railcar toting armies of servants and mountains of baggage. Broadway, the fashionable downtown promenade, featured a number of luxury hotels, but the jewel of the bunch was the Grand Union. Built in the ornate style of the French Second Empire, the palatial, mansard-roofed resort formed a *U* that enclosed a shaded courtyard, where the Boston Symphony Orchestra performed regularly for the guests. It was the world's largest hotel, with a dining room that could accommodate at least twelve hundred people and 824 guest rooms, accessible via labyrinthine corridors spanning two miles. An acre of marble graced the hotel's polished floors and tabletops.[25]

The hotel had cycled through various owners over the years. Its latest proprietor was Alexander Turney Stewart—or rather, his estate. Stewart, an Irish immigrant who had built a retail empire through his chain of A.T. Stewart department stores, had died the previous year, leaving behind a fortune estimated at $50 million to his wife, Cornelia. Judge Henry Hilton, Stewart's longtime counsel and a relative by marriage, was the executor of Stewart's estate. A Tammany Hall denizen who had once served as New York City's parks commissioner, Hilton assumed a surprising amount of control over Stewart's holdings, raising eyebrows among the late businessman's friends and acquaintances and ultimately provoking lawsuits from his heirs. In exchange for $1 million, which Stewart had bequeathed to Hilton in his will, Cornelia signed over to the judge her late husband's valuable business. And Hilton, as the Stewart estate's executor, effectively ran the Grand Union.

The Seligmans arrived at the hotel on Thursday, June 14, 1877, crossing the expansive porch where guests lounged in wicker rocking chairs. Joseph's wife and children waited in the parlor, a row of large crystal chandeliers shimmering overhead, while he went to arrange for their rooms. Recognizing the renowned financier, a manager, a man named Wilkinson, ushered him to a private office. He had a pained look on his face.

"Mr. Seligman, I'm required to inform you that Mr. Hilton has given instructions that no Israelites shall be permitted in the future to stop at this hotel."[26]

Had he heard the man correctly? No Jews? His and other Jewish families had been staying there for years. Plus, he was not just any Jew. He was one of the nation's wealthiest and most powerful men, an adviser to presidents and Treasury secretaries, a pillar of Wall Street. An uncomfortable silence filled the room as Seligman, thunderstruck, conjured the words to respond.

"Do you mean to tell me that you will not entertain Jewish people?" Joseph demanded.

"That is our orders, sir."

"Are they dirty, do they misbehave themselves, or have they refused to pay their bills?" Seligman continued, his anger rising.

"Oh, no," the manager replied. "There is no fault to be found in that respect. The reason is simply this: Business at the hotel was not good last season, and we had a large number of Jews here. Mr. Hilton came to the conclusion that Christians did not like their company, and for that reason shunned the hotel. He resolved to run the Union on a different principle this season, and gave us instructions to admit no Jew."[27]

Embarrassed and indignant, Joseph channeled his outrage into a missive to Judge Hilton, which he sent from the Clarendon Hotel, down the street from the Grand Union. Written with a surface decorum characteristic of the times, Seligman offered "dear Judge" Hilton some "friendly and disinterested advice." The letter, of course, was neither friendly nor disinterested.

Now, permit me, dear Judge, in your own interest, and in the interest of Mr. Stewart's valuable estate, the lion's share of which you seem to have acquired, to say that you are adding to the many serious mistakes which you have committed since you inherited that estate by refusing admittance to the Union Hotel to a large class of people, irrespective of their respectability, wealth, and proper bearing, merely to pander to a vulgar prejudice, under the mistaken notion that by doing so you will fill the house with other nationalities. You will find yourself mistaken. You are no judge of American character. The civilized world is beginning to be more tolerant in matters of faith or creed or birth than you believe or would have them. They despise intolerance, low cunning, and vulgarity, and will not patronize a man who seeks to make money by pandering to the prejudices of the vulgar.

I regret that you are running the Union at a loss. I regret that you are making no headway in your wholesale departments in New-York and Chicago, and that even the Ninth-street retail store, so popular and prosperous under the management of the late Mr. Stewart, has lost its best patrons. A little reflection must show to you that the serious falling off in your business is not due to the patronage of any nationality, but to the want of patronage of all, and that you, dear Judge, are not big enough to keep a hotel, nor broad enough in your business views to run a dry goods store.[28]

A group of Joseph's friends in New York, led by his attorney Edward Lauterbach, briefed a *New York Times* reporter on the dispute, reading aloud Seligman's letter to Hilton.[29] By the following week, Seligman's Grand Union rebuff had become a national scandal. "A Sensation at Saratoga," the *Times* trumpeted in its front-page story, which included an interview with Hilton.

The judge claimed that Seligman had arrived "in an ostentatious manner," demanding the hotel's best accommodations. And he insisted that the Grand Union did not discriminate against all members of the Jewish faith—just a certain class of them. He drew a distinction between "Hebrews" and "Jews." The former category, which included such wealthy and long-established Sephardic clans as the Hendrickses and the Nathans (whose descendants included a founder of the New York Stock Exchange), he found upright and respectable. It was the latter group, the new-money sort, whom he

considered preening and flashy in their displays of wealth, that he
deemed objectionable. The *Times* reported:

> Mr. Seligman, Judge Hilton said, belongs to a class of, not
> Hebrews, but Jews, with whom this class of guests, especially
> the female portion of them, will not associate and whom they
> do not wish to be forced to meet, even under the etiquette of
> the dining-room and parlor of a public hotel. . . . It is the fault,
> continued Judge Hilton, of this class of "Jews" themselves
> that they are discriminated against. . . . They have brought
> the public opinion down on themselves by vulgar ostenta-
> tion, a puffed-up vanity, an overweening display of condition,
> a lack of those considerate civilities so much appreciated by
> good American society, and a general obtrusiveness that is
> frequently disgusting, and always repulsive to the well-bred.[30]

In a separate interview with the *Times*, which ran in the next day's
paper, Hilton unloaded on Seligman. He asserted that Seligman
"owes some of his most vaunted offices"—his memberships in exclusive clubs, bank directorships, and seats on prestigious municipal
boards—"to the practice of the veriest Shylockean meanness." He
alleged that the Seligmans had landed a role in a U.S. government
bond syndicate that included the Rothschilds and Drexel Morgan
(the predecessor firm of J.P. Morgan & Co.) by exercising "political influence not squarely secured" and contended that "the position
of the Seligmans in the syndicate is just as distasteful to the other
members of that organization as their presence is considered in the
Grand Union Hotel." The vaunted Rothschilds, he added, would
consent to meet with the brothers only "at second hand or through a
clerk."

Hilton went on, building up steam into a spectacular antisemitic
diatribe:

> Should the Seligman "Jew" be excluded from certain first
> class hotels? I say emphatically, yes. Not at all because he is a
> Hebrew, but because he is not wanted. . . . He is too obtuse
> or too mean to see his vulgarity, or to go where it may not
> be on public exhibition. He is shoddy—false—squeezing—
> unmanly; but financially he is successful, and that is the only
> token he has to push himself upon the polite. He is as auda-
> cious as he is vulgar; he is as fussy as he is worthless; he is

as vain as he is devoid of merit; and he is puffed out with as much importance as he is poor of any value. . . .

It is no wonder that Americans are down on the Seligman "Jew." The richness of this new country has tended to propagate the breed, and the breed has cursed the Hebrew race socially in this country. People won't go to hotels where the Seligman Jew is admitted. And hotels if they would thrive must keep out those who would ruin their existence.[31]

The Seligmans' partners in the loan syndicate signed a joint letter to the *Times* stating that "Judge Hilton is under a misapprehension as to the relations of Messrs. Seligman with their associates, which always have been and are of the most satisfactory character."[32] Meanwhile, Jesse Seligman, whom the *Times* had located at his firm's downtown offices, spoke out on his brother's behalf. "I am at a loss what to think concerning Judge Hilton," he said. "In view of his extraordinary statements . . . it would be charitable to suppose that the warm weather had affected his brain."[33]

The controversy snowballed in the days ahead, with stories appearing in newspapers as far away as Honolulu. Well-heeled Jews, who regularly summered in Saratoga, reported that they too had been turned away from the Grand Union that summer. That included Marcus Goldman, who said he had written seeking accommodations and had received a reply saying that his request could not be granted and offering no explanation why.[34] There was talk of organizing an "indignation" meeting to condemn Hilton's actions and of possible litigation. Jewish firms pulled their business from A.T. Stewart & Co., with one merchant informing the company he would no longer do business with a house that was "reviving the Middle Ages."[35]

The *Times* dispatched reporters to take the temperature of the hotel proprietors of New York City, Philadelphia, Newport, and Long Branch concerning their positions on Jewish clientele. Many were aghast at Hilton's policy; some knew Joseph Seligman personally and vouched for his character.[36]

Yet the paper also identified two Manhattan establishments with "substantially the same rules as those of the Grand Union" and unwritten policies in which Jewish families were charged more than other customers.[37] In Long Branch—where Joseph, along with brothers James and Jesse, kept summer homes—hoteliers seemed surprised that a high-flying tycoon like Seligman had been turned away from the Grand Union, while simultaneously grousing about the influx of

Jews marring their vacation paradise. "They have no grip here yet," one hotelkeeper told the paper, "and I hope they won't get one."[38]

A few days after Joseph and his family were barred from the Grand Union, his friend Henry Ward Beecher weighed in from the pulpit of his Brooklyn church, delivering what would become a famous sermon titled "Jew and Gentile."

"There are about seven million Jews in existence in all the nations of the earth," Beecher told his congregants. "They are living in almost every land under the sun. They excel all other people in being despised. There is not another race or people that is in such a sense a benefactor of the human race as they are, and have been. There is not another people under the sun that is treated so like despicable miscreants as they are, and have been."

Beecher condemned pernicious anti-Jewish tropes—"It is said that the Jews are crafty and cunning, and sometimes dishonest, in their dealings. Ah! what a phenomenon dishonesty must be in New York!"—and he walked his congregation through a brief history of the plight of the Jews over the previous two thousand years and the litany of medieval horrors that had befallen them. "Did a plague break out in Hungary? The Jews had poisoned the people, and a mob wreaked vengeance upon their households. Was there a black death in Germany? The whole country was in cruel riot to avenge their sufferings on the persecuted Jews. But this remarkable race, though fined, robbed, treated with the utmost injustice and cruelty, and kicked out from their abiding place again and again could not be destroyed."[39]

The Hilton-Seligman controversy made headlines for months, and there was some personal history to the feud that helped to explain the animus, particularly on the judge's behalf. Joseph had served on an anticorruption task force that had paved the way for the imprisonment of Hilton's ally and patron, William "Boss" Tweed, for looting the public coffers during his long reign as the kingpin of the Tammany Hall machine.[40] Another cause of Hilton's grudge against Seligman: the prestigious Union League Club (where Joseph was a vice-president) had rejected his application for membership.[41]

The scandal grew into something much bigger than Seligman or Hilton had ever imagined when they and their proxies began skirmishing in the nation's broadsheets. Some historians have pointed to the dustup as a singular episode that ushered in a new and overt

form of antisemitism in America. But Jews had experienced prejudice, in various forms, since they had first arrived in what would
become the United States. In 1654, when twenty-three Portuguese
Jews, among the first Jews to settle in North America, landed at New
Amsterdam, Peter Stuyvesant initially wanted to expel them from
his colony but was overruled by the Dutch East India Co. Allowed
to stay, they nevertheless faced prohibitions like those levied against
European Jews: they were barred from voting, holding public office,
and owning land. "Moreover," wrote the historian Leonard Dinnerstein, "although they were refused the right to stand guard with other
community dwellers, a special tax was levied on them because they
did not assume this task."[42]

Even decades after the nation's Founding Fathers declared that
"all men are created equal," some states still denied Jews voting rights
and prohibited them from practicing law. It wasn't until 1877—the
same year Joseph Seligman suffered his Grand Union humiliation—
that New Hampshire amended a colonial-era statute preventing
Jews from holding elected office.[43] Jewish peddlers had long been
the victims of ridicule and violence. In cities such as Baltimore and
Detroit, attacks on Jewish peddlers became so frequent that itinerant
merchants banded together to form their own self-defense groups.[44]
And as nineteenth-century credit reports show—like those assessing
the early business dealings of the Lehmans—Jewish merchants were
often viewed with suspicion based on ancient canards and stereotypes.[45] The year after the Civil War ended, seven insurance companies, including Aetna, formed a pact to cease doing business with
Jews, who they blamed for setting fires to collect the insurance proceeds.[46]

Stretching back centuries, Jews had been convenient culprits
during times of economic crisis—and recent financial meltdowns had
proven no different. In the aftermath of the Panic of 1873, European investors blamed Jews, and so did ruined midwestern American
farmers.[47] It said something about the way Jews were perceived in
America that Jay Gould, the widely reviled speculator, was regularly
described as either being Jewish or possessing Jewish traits. Henry
Adams, grandson of John Quincy Adams, called Gould, a Presbyte-
rian by birth, a "complex Jew." Gould biographer Trumbull White
noted, "Many who knew Mr. Gould intimately are in the habit of
asserting that his origin must have been Hebraic. . . . His habits of
thought and his extraordinary intellect were both Jewish, these people assert."[48]

Antisemitism had long simmered beneath the surface of American society, and occasionally it erupted into public view—as when Ulysses Grant levied his infamous General Order No. 11. But traditionally it had not impeded American Jews, in part because there weren't many American Jews to speak of. But that was starting to change. Between 1840, around the time Joseph arrived, and 1880, America's Jewish population soared from around 15,000 to about 230,000. The exodus from the Pale of Settlement—the western region of the Russian Empire—during the latter decades of the nineteenth century quickened the pace of immigration, as Jews fled poverty and persecution. By 1900, America's once-marginal Jewish population stood at a substantial 1.5 million.

The Grand Union episode did seem to form a kind of inflection point, and it deeply rattled American Jews who saw in Joseph Seligman the unlimited possibilities America offered. For them, it called into question everything they thought they knew about America.

"Can you, sir, fully appreciate this thing?" a Jewish businessman named Augustus Elfelt mused to a reporter.

> There stood Joseph Seligman, who had risen from a penniless youth up through all the grades of society and wealth, until he had reached the very top of both. . . . This man who had every right that any human being can have to feel proud of himself, and to expect the most considerate respect from at least every American—imagine him standing before a little hotel clerk and being refused the privilege of putting his signature—a signature which the great American Government had often found very useful to its very existence—upon the register before him, because he was a Jew.[49]

Two things happened in the wake of the Seligman-Hilton controversy, which enunciated something largely unspoken in American life. Discrimination against Jews appeared to grow more prevalent and acceptable, and American society grew more stratified. It wasn't just hotels: country clubs, college fraternities, private schools also excluded Jews.

Even before the Hilton episode, American Jews had begun to establish their own social institutions, such as the Progress Club and the Harmonie Club, which celebrated its twenty-fifth anniversary the same year as the Saratoga brouhaha. But in its wake, this trend seemed to accelerate, as Jews formed numerous social and athletic clubs, golf courses, and resorts. This was the heyday of the elite German-Jewish social scene in New York that the author Stephen Birmingham dubbed "our crowd"—a counterpart to the exclusive clique populated by the Astors, Morgans, Vanderbilts, and other A-list Manhattan dynasties.

The world of New York's German-Jewish aristocracy was as wealthy and privileged as it was insular and confining. And it was sometimes said these families inhabited "the gilded ghetto." Especially for the younger generations, born in America and with no memory of what life was like in Germany, where antisemitism had been enshrined in the laws of its kingdoms and duchies, it could be a stifling existence, one from which they increasingly struggled to break free.

The Hilton dustup came as Joseph Seligman reached his career's zenith. Ulysses Grant completed his second term in the winter of 1877, and Joseph and Jesse fêted him at Delmonico's before the outgoing president departed with his family for an extended trip in Europe, where he stopped in Frankfurt to visit Henry Seligman and spent time with Isaac Seligman and his family at their London estate.[50] But even with Grant out of office, Joseph had other close friends in Washington. Shortly after Rutherford B. Hayes settled into the White House, one of them, incoming Treasury secretary John Sherman, a longtime Republican senator from Ohio, invited Joseph to the capital to advise him on an urgent problem facing the administration.[51]

A couple of years earlier, the Republican Congress had passed a law calling for the Treasury, beginning January 1, 1879, to resume redeeming paper currency in gold coin, as it had done prior to the Civil War. This would effectively place the nation on the gold standard. (Controversially, earlier legislation, the Coinage Act of 1873, had all but removed silver as a form of legal tender.) But Congress, as was often the case, left the nitty-gritty details up to the executive branch—and the deadline was looming. Meanwhile, labor and farming interests had coalesced into a populist political movement dubbed the Greenback Party, which was agitating for "soft money" and arguing that linking currency to gold, which would have a deflationary impact, would harm the debtor class.

Along with Seligman, Sherman convened a handful of leading bankers to solicit their plans on how to refund the nation's Civil War debt and return to the gold standard. Sherman ultimately selected Joseph's proposal, which called for executing bond sales, mostly in Europe, to accrue a gold reserve of nearly $140 million, accounting for about 40 percent of the greenbacks in circulation. Joseph, meanwhile, advocated a series of new bond issues to retire old debts.

Over the next two years, the Treasury Department carried out his plan, and J. & W. Seligman & Co. teamed with Jacob Schiff's Kuhn Loeb and other firms to place hundreds of millions of dollars of U.S. bonds. On December 18, 1878, gold and greenbacks traded at par for the first time since the outbreak of the Civil War, signaling renewed confidence in the nation's creditworthiness. A couple of weeks later, the U.S. government resumed redeeming paper currency for gold. Joseph Seligman had helped to restore the nation's economic equilibrium—and his company netted enormous profits in the process.[52]

But even at the height of Seligman's professional acclaim, he couldn't seem to put the Grand Union episode behind him. In July 1879 the controversy was revived once more when a New Hampshire robber baron named Austin Corbin, the president of the Long Island Rail Road and the Manhattan Beach Co., declared he planned to follow Judge Hilton's lead by banning Jews from his Brooklyn resort. "We do not like the Jews, as a class," he stated. ". . . They make themselves offensive to the kind of people who principally patronize our road and hotel." New York's leading Jews, who had loudly condemned Hilton a couple of years earlier, thought it best to turn the other cheek to this offense, perhaps fearing that publicizing the Grand Union's "no Jews" policy two years earlier had only fueled antisemitism. When a reporter approached Jesse Seligman to ask about Corbin's comments, the banker responded tersely: "We have said all we have to say on this subject."[53] Joseph mustered a chuckle when a journalist cornered him, saying his family had no plans to visit Manhattan Beach.[54]

In November 1879, Joseph celebrated his sixtieth birthday. And the banker felt every bit of his age. He'd been suffering kidney problems, to which he'd recently added a heart ailment.[55] His family begged him to take a break from the stresses of business. His two eldest sons, David and Isaac Newton, had joined the firm, and the New York office would be in good hands with Jesse running things. James, meanwhile, occupied the brothers' seat on the New York Stock Exchange—so Joseph didn't have to worry about him spending too much time in the office, where he was prone to making rash loans.[56]

Joseph spent the winter of 1880 in Jacksonville, Florida, with his wife and their son George Washington, a lawyer and, like his father, an ethical culture devotee. George hunted alligators, and the family spent a week traveling with Ulysses Grant and his entourage, who were en route to Cuba. "From our parents in Jacksonville, Fla. we get excellent accounts. D[ear] Pa feels like a different man altogether which can be easily accounted for, because he needed rest," David Seligman wrote to one of his brothers.[57]

That spring, with Joseph feeling rejuvenated, the Seligmans stopped in New Orleans as they began their journey north. Their eldest daughter Frances, Joseph's favorite of their four girls, lived there with her husband, Theodore Hellman, who had taken over the running of Seligman, Hellman & Co. from his brother Max, now posted in Paris with William Seligman.[58] It wasn't merely a family visit—as usual, Joseph had business on his mind. Recently, the New Orleans operation had gotten hit with an embarrassing lawsuit by Kuhn Loeb, to which the Seligmans had strong business and personal ties, over the sale of allegedly forged bank drafts. Joseph wanted to investigate the matter personally.[59]

Joseph planned to leave New Orleans for New York on Saturday, April 24, 1880, but he postponed the trip, presumably because he felt unwell. The next day he ate a hearty lunch, then retired to an upstairs bedroom in the Hellmans' home to nap. He suffered a stroke that afternoon and died later that evening.[60]

The obituaries that filled the nation's papers in the coming days chronicled his dramatic rise, from Bavaria, to Mauch Chunk, to Selma, and finally to New York. They told of his service to the nation during the Civil War and of his recent feats of finance. But though it had been a mere blip in Joseph's accomplished life, few remembrances failed to mention the Hilton controversy, which was "still fresh in the public memory," in the words of *The New York Times*.[61]

Edwin Seligman received the tragic news in Heidelberg, where he was studying at the local university. Like his father, Edwin had a sharp mind and a talent for languages. (He spoke Dutch, French, German, Italian, Spanish, and Russian.)[62] Also like his father, he had enrolled in college at fourteen, graduating second in his class from Columbia in 1879. Afterward Joseph had tried to enlist Edwin to join the firm alongside his older brothers and cousins, but the intellectual son had persuaded his father to allow him to continue his academic career. At Heidelberg University, he was studying economics, philosophy, and, for good measure, the pandects (Roman law). He would go on to receive a law degree and a Ph.D. from Columbia, where he spent the rest of his career on the faculty as a professor of political economy.

"I suppose the shock must have been terrible to you, as it was to all of us, for, although we knew that father could live but a few years longer, we had no idea he would be taken from us so suddenly," Edwin's younger brother Alfred wrote him the day after their father's death.[63] In a letter dated the following day, Isaac Newton (whom everyone called "Ike") implored his brother to "bear up nobly" and sent words of comfort: "The general grief of both Jewish & Christian communities is the best evidence in what esteem our dear father was held. He has left to us dear brother a noble name & spotless reputation."[64]

Ike's letter also hinted at discord in the family over plans for their father's funeral. Joseph, who had made his intentions clear, wanted a simple secular service, free of pomp, officiated by Felix Adler. But his New York–based brothers, grieving the loss of not just a brother but a father figure, preferred a religious service. "I am considerably exercised over this matter as our uncles desire the Temple to have charge," Ike wrote.[65] Ultimately, a compromise was struck. Adler would give a sermon at the funeral service held at the Seligmans' home. Temple Emanu-El's Gustav Gottheil (who had taken over from Samuel Adler) and Max Lilienthal, a well-known Cincinnati rabbi whose son had married Joseph's daughter, Isabella, would preside at the gravesite.

On the morning of Sunday, May 3, Joseph's body lay in an open iron casket, illuminated by six flickering candles. Nearby stood his pallbearers, who included Noah Davis, the New York Supreme Court justice who presided over "Boss" Tweed's trial; J. P. Morgan's partner, Anthony Drexel; and the Seligmans' old pal Henry Gitterman, whose friendship had proved so useful during the Civil War.[66]

The parlor of the Seligmans' brownstone was filled with local and national eminences, including the financier Cyrus Field; Germany's former consul general Frederick Kuhne; the city's fire and police commissioners; and what seemed like every bank president in Manhattan.

At ten a.m., Felix Adler took his place at the head of the casket to eulogize his friend and patron. "He was one of those who believed that a gladder morning is about to dawn for mankind—that the time is nigh when, among the intelligent few, at least, if not yet among the ignorant many, the distinctions of race may be wiped out and the animosities founded on religious differences may be forgotten," Adler said solemnly. "He was not ashamed of his Jewish origin—all the less so because public scorn and insult are still at times attached to that origin. He was proud of the much-suffering, long and bitterly persecuted people from whom he had sprung." Adler told the mourners that Joseph "raised the Jewish race because his sympathies went beyond the limits of the Jewish race; because he had an ampler patriotism than race patriotism."[67]

More than 130 carriages accompanied Joseph's casket to Salem Fields, where Joseph had commissioned a palatial mausoleum. Situated on a wooded bluff, the structure was a hexagon of gray granite topped with a dome. Through a pair of brass gates, the burial chamber was finished in Italian marble. On the far wall was a stained-glass window, made in London, depicting an angel throwing off the shackles of mortality.[68]

"Joseph Seligman was without doubt the most prominent Hebrew in this city," a "well known Hebrew" told the *New-York Tribune* after his death. "He was the one who faced all the attacks of prejudice against the race. He did more for the Hebrews in this city than any other man. His death makes a gap which it will be hard to fill, and I know of no one who can assume the leadership as he did."[69]

The void of leadership, however, would not remain empty long.

9

AMERICAN MONTEFIORE

Joseph Seligman held a unique place in public life, occupying overlapping spheres of influence that reinforced one another. His business renown fed his political and civic clout. His religious background naturally made him an ambassador of the nation's small but growing Jewish community. None of his contemporaries, though well respected in financial and Jewish affairs, possessed commensurate gravitas.

The Lehmans oversaw a growing and successful concern and gave generously of their time and money to Jewish causes, but they lacked Seligman's political and social heft, and their Confederate history would not have made them logical allies of the four successive Republican administrations that spanned the late 1860s to the mid-1880s. Marcus Goldman remained a prosperous note broker, though not a particularly distinguished one, and his dealings with downtown merchants did not bring him into the same high-flying circles that fueled Joseph's ascent. Solomon Loeb, as he was fast discovering, was not even the most eminent member of the investment bank to which he had given his name.

Joseph Seligman's gregarious and well-connected brother Jesse, a beloved figure in the New York business world, rivaled his standing, though at fifty-three, he was entering his career's denouement. Joseph's mantle, as a Wall Street power and Jewish leader, would fall to a member of the next generation who was all too eager to claim it. Thirty-three years old when Joseph Seligman was interred, Jacob Schiff eased himself into the late financier's considerable footsteps. Even his rise as a civic leader followed a similar trajectory: in 1881, New York mayor William Russell Grace appointed Schiff to the city's board of education, a position Seligman held until a few years prior to his death. (Schiff approached the new post with trademark boldness: the year after taking the role, he roiled New York by successfully advancing a controversial resolution abolishing the city's "colored" schools, effectively integrating the public school system.)[1]

Schiff also picked up where Seligman left off in his fight against Tammany Hall. Though "Boss" Tweed perished in his Ludlow Street jail cell in 1878, his patronage machine lived on. Ahead of the 1882 elections, Schiff joined the Committee of Fifty, a bipartisan group of influential New Yorkers leading a citizens' uprising to "thoroughly purify and redeem the local Government, so long sapped by political leeches," in the words of *The New York Times*. (The Tammany crew, once again, proved resilient.)[2]

And like Seligman, Schiff took an active role in shaping what would become the New York City subway system. Seligman had chaired the city's Rapid Transit Committee, responsible for mapping the routes of what was initially envisioned as a series of elevated lines built by private enterprise; after Seligman's death, Schiff appeared before that panel to argue that the city should spearhead the construction of the system, lest New York's transit infrastructure "become the football of speculation."[3] Schiff also agitated against construction of more elevated train lines, in favor of an underground system. When city officials in one case contemplated plans to build an el line through the heart of the Lower East Side, Schiff lobbied against the plan, arguing that the tenement dwellers of Delancey Street—who already "get a scant supply of air and light"—should no more be subjected to the structure than the affluent residents of Fifth Avenue.[4]

In business, Schiff swam in similar circles as Seligman, and he maneuvered Kuhn Loeb into loan syndicates organized by J. & W. Seligman & Co. They also shared an interest in some of the same railroad enterprises: in 1881, Schiff became a director of the newly reorganized New York, Lake Erie, and Western Railway—previously known as the Erie, or the "Scarlet Woman of Wall Street" during the heyday of its abuse by Jay Gould and his compatriots.

As a budding philanthropist, Schiff donated to the Hebrew Orphan Asylum, and he gave to Seligman's beloved ethical culture movement to support some of its charitable work, but he stood firmly among the Temple Emanu-El congregants appalled by its rejection of organized religion and role in diverting more Jews from their faith.

The circle of wealthy Jewish philanthropists was small—and to be Jewish and rich at that time carried a certain social pressure to aid their growing community. The boards of the leading Jewish charities often included a representative from a familiar group of families—a Goldman, a Guggenheim, a Lehman, a Loeb, a Seligman, a Straus. Increasingly, the letterhead of these organizations included the name Jacob H. Schiff.

The year before Seligman's death, Schiff joined the board of Mount Sinai Hospital, signaling his rising station in New York's Jewish community. Over the years, the hospital's trustees had included members of some of the city's most prominent Jewish families. There were Nathans and Hendrickses—of the old Sephardic clans whom Judge Hilton had deemed acceptable as "Hebrews" and not "Jews"—and, of course, various Seligmans. Shortly after the hospital's founding in 1852, Joseph spent seven years on its board; his brother William replaced him, serving another five.[5]

During Schiff's board tenure, one of his fellow directors was DeWitt Seligman, James's eldest son. Named for former New York governor DeWitt Clinton, he held a law degree from Columbia and, before joining the family banking business, indulged literary aspirations. He wrote plays, never produced, that always seemed to conclude with an explosion, and for years he edited and published a weekly journal dubbed *The Epoch*.[6] Schiff also served alongside Mayer Lehman, who during his two decades as a trustee rarely missed a Sunday morning board meeting. Often one of his young sons—Irving or Arthur or the baby of the family, Herbert—accompanied him as he toured the wards and looked in on patients.[7]

In business and charitable affairs alike, Schiff was a forceful and often intimidating presence. While others viewed board positions as status symbols or sinecures, Schiff, whether helping to oversee the affairs of a railroad or a social welfare group, approached his role with signature intensity. Irving Lehman, who grew up to become a justice on the New York Supreme Court and worked closely with Schiff on various charitable campaigns, recalled the financier's unwavering approach to board deliberations. He believed "compromise was often required in regard to matters of detail and policy, but was dishonest and therefore intolerable on matters of principle."[8] Yet for Schiff, so much flowed from his inviolate ethical code and often black-and-white judgments of propriety.

During one Mount Sinai board meeting, Schiff learned that a fellow trustee, the forty-five-year-old coffee merchant Moses Hanauer, had declared bankruptcy due to some unwise speculation. Schiff was horrified. How could a man who was unable to manage his own financial affairs be trusted with the stewardship of a charitable institution? Schiff announced stiffly that he refused to serve on the same board as someone who was not good for his debts. He ultimately resigned from the board, as did his bankrupt colleague.[9]

Hanauer, financially ruined and despondent, later traveled far uptown to Fort Washington Point on the banks of the Hudson River, the site where the George Washington Bridge was later constructed overhead. The merchant pressed a pistol to his right temple and pulled the trigger.[10] Shocked by news of Hanauer's suicide and guilt-ridden by his possible role in pushing the fragile man over the edge, Schiff sought out Hanauer's sixteen-year-old son, Jerome, now the family's sole breadwinner. He took the teenager into Kuhn Loeb as an office boy, training him to become an investment banker. Decades later, in 1912, after performing every conceivable job at the firm, Jerome Hanauer was elevated to partner, the first in the firm's history who was not related to Kuhn Loeb's founders by blood or marriage.

It's not clear whether Hanauer, during all the decades he worked with Schiff, knew of his mentor's history with his late father. Schiff's granddaughter, Dorothy, only discovered this dark episode some fifty years later, when she was asked to become a Mount Sinai director and inquired of a long-serving doctor at the hospital "why there were no members of my family on the board." He replied by telling her the story of Moses Hanauer's suicide.[11]

In 1884, New York's Jewish community was preparing to celebrate the one-hundredth birthday of Sir Moses Montefiore, the British financier who was then the world's foremost Jewish leader and a figure of such renown that Jews throughout the world commemorated his centenary as a holiday. On February 4, Schiff joined a group of New York philanthropists and community leaders who convened in the vestry room of Shearith Israel, the Sephardic congregation founded in 1654, to consider plans for a fitting tribute to the self-styled Jewish ambassador.[12]

After retiring from business, Montefiore channeled his energy and fortune into defending Jewish rights around the world. No outrage or crisis seemed to escape his notice, and he embarked on many daring missions to assuage Jewish suffering. In 1840 he plunged into an international controversy known as the Damascus Affair, or the Damascus Blood Libel. False charges that Jews sacrificed Christians, especially children, in order to use their blood in religious ceremonies had long fueled anti-Jewish hysteria, forming the basis for executions and instigating massacres. In this case, Ottoman authorities accused a group of Syrian Jews of the ritual murder of a Franciscan monk, after torturing a confession out of a Jewish barber. Montefiore led a delegation to the Middle East where he negotiated the release of the nine prisoners who had managed to survive their draconian imprisonment and torture.

In subsequent years, Montefiore interceded on behalf of persecuted Jews in Morocco, Romania, and Russia; in 1858 he unsuccessfully lobbied the Vatican for the return of Edgardo Mortara, the Jewish boy seized from his family by papal authorities. As a Jewish statesman, he was a trailblazer not only because of his high-profile intercessions but because he was a fundraising pioneer, organizing relief efforts that united a global community of Jews in common purpose.

How best to celebrate Montefiore's lifetime of service? At the Shearith Israel meeting, Schiff spoke up: "There exists in the lower part of our city a population of Hebrews which socially stands as low and is no better than those of our race in Eastern Europe, Africa, and Asia," he commented, raising the idea of building a "new quarter of improved tenement houses" to be called the Montefiore Tenements.[13] Participants floated other proposals, but Schiff and his comrades finally zeroed in on the creation of a long-needed institution: a hospital for the long-term care of patients with chronic and incurable illnesses—tuberculosis, cancer, syphilis, infant paralysis, clinical depression. Schiff credited Mayer Lehman as "one of those who first agitated the necessity of the establishment of a home or hospital for the incurables, and he never rested until the noble ideal was carried out."[14]

The Montefiore Home for Chronic Invalids (later Montefiore Hospital) opened in October 1884 to coincide with Moses Montefiore's birthday on October 24. The twenty-six-bed facility, overseen by a single doctor, was housed in a thirty-five-dollar-per-month frame house on East 84th Street and Avenue A (later York Avenue).[15] It accepted five patients on the day it opened.[16] Mayer Lehman's eldest son, Sigmund, was a founding board member. But it was Schiff who would be most closely associated with the Montefiore Home, serving as president for some thirty-five years, up until the year before his death.

The hospital at first served only Jewish patients, but a few years after its founding, it opened to people of all faiths. Schiff considered the home a living "monument to Jewish benevolence."[17]

Of all the institutions Schiff helped to build up over the years—and there would be many—Montefiore was the first, and Schiff considered it his favorite. "I have reared it as I would my own child," he once said.[18] Under his nurturing yet stern leadership, the hospital grew steadily until, by the early 1920s, it could house eight hundred patients.

Schiff ruled Montefiore with the same authoritarian streak he brought to bear on his business and domestic life. When a Montefiore director once ribbed him about his tyrannical tendencies during a board meeting, Schiff responded unapologetically: "I did not know that it was considered that I acted the despot in the Presidency of Montefiore Home, but it is true that I am very jealous of the honor and dignity of the institution."[19]

Schiff, thin-skinned for a man often in the public eye, was rarely amused by jokes at his expense, unless he was the one making them. Once a board member proposed a new approach to fundraising, and Schiff replied with a tale that slyly poked fun at his own controlling nature. He told the story of a beggar who asked a Rothschild for a dole of two marks. The wealthy banker, having some fun with the man, said, "How is it you come to a Rothschild and ask for as small a sum as two marks?" The indignant beggar shot back: "*Willst Du mich mein Geschäft lehren?*" (Will you teach me my business?)[20]

Especially in the early days, Schiff was closely involved in the affairs of the hospital, personally investigating complaints about the food and making sure the coal bill got paid. He regularly inspected the premises (the hospital moved to larger quarters in West Harlem in 1889, then to its current location in the Bronx in 1913), always refusing the nervous employees who offered to escort him as he made his rounds. And he vetted every applicant seeking one of its coveted beds, explaining his verdict in detailed memos. "Nothing would influence him to change this decision if he felt it was a just one," remembered one Montefiore director. Nor was he swayed by lobbying efforts on behalf of specific applicants. "We cannot neglect the poor patient who has no one to speak for him," he would say. If anything, he seemed to display a bias in favor of patients who had no advocates.[21]

The board, like Mount Sinai's, met on Sunday mornings at the hospital, except in June and July, when the directors convened on Thursdays at Kuhn Loeb's downtown offices. This schedule accommodated Schiff, whose household relocated during those months to the Terrace, the fifty-acre estate he co-owned with Solomon Loeb on Rumson Road in Sea Bright. The New Jersey shore community and the surrounding towns of Elberon, Long Branch, and Rumson were a summer haven for Manhattan's wealthy German-Jewish families, including the Goldmans, Lehmans, and Seligmans. This windswept stretch of coastline earned the reputation of being a sort of "Jewish Newport," surely to the horror of the Jersey shore hoteliers who complained of Jewish encroachment in the wake of the Seligman-Hilton controversy. (In an antisemitic screed titled "Diamonds and Vulgarity" and published in *The New York Times*, a longtime Long Branch denizen lamented in 1887 that "the New Jerusalem has made its headquarters at Long Branch.")[22]

While staying at Rumson Road—or, "the Road," as Schiff's children called it—Schiff commuted to Wall Street during the week by ferry, catching up on correspondence and holding court in a private cabin during the hour-long trip.[23] When he returned home from the office, it was the family custom that his children—and later his grandchildren—would meet the patriarch when he debarked dressed in sailors' outfits, complete with white gloves and caps.[24]

On Sunday mornings, when Schiff often made his weekly visit to the Montefiore Home on foot, he was usually accompanied by his close friend Samuel Sachs, whom Schiff had recruited onto the hospital's board.[25] Like Schiff, Sachs had married into a burgeoning investment banking dynasty, becoming a partner in Marcus Goldman's firm. His wife was Louisa Goldman, the youngest of Marcus and Bertha Goldman's three daughters. The couple lived four blocks south of the Schiffs at 44 East 70th Street.[26]

The relationship between the Sachs and Goldman clans stretched back to the old country, where Marcus Goldman and Samuel's father, Joseph, received religious training at the same Würzburg synagogue.[27] The son of a saddle maker, Joseph Sachs was a rabbi and tutor who fell in love with one of his pupils, Sophia Baer, the daughter of a wealthy goldsmith. Fleeing Sophia's disapproving parents, the couple eloped to Rotterdam in 1847, then sailed for the United States. They settled in Baltimore, where Sam was born in 1851. According to Ann

Sachs, a great-granddaughter of Marcus Goldman and Joseph Sachs, the Goldman and Sachs families nearly struck a business alliance some three decades before Sam partnered with Marcus. When the Sachs family visited the Goldmans in Philadelphia in the late 1850s, Marcus tried to interest Joseph in joining his tailoring business, she noted. Joseph declined his offer, in order to pursue his dream of running his own school.[28]

According to an advertisement in *The Baltimore Sun*, Joseph tried to establish an "English, Hebrew, German, and Mathematical Institute" in the city.[29] But this venture did not take off. In the mid-1850s, Joseph moved his family to Boston, where he took a position as a cantor in the congregation of Ohabei Shalom. In 1861, as the Civil War broke out, the Sachses relocated again, this time to New York City.[30]

In 1864, Joseph purchased a large brownstone on 34th Street, across from where Nathan and Isidor Straus would later open the flagship location of the Macy's department store chain. He ran a boarding and day school for boys out of the building, where the Sachs family also lived. Joseph had finally become the headmaster of his own institution, but his health soon declined, and in 1867 the Sachses returned to Germany, intending to stay two years before returning to New York.[31] Joseph's condition worsened, and he died suddenly while visiting the popular spa town of Bad Kissingen.[32] Sophia Sachs died a few years later.

Before Joseph passed, Sam had already gone back to New York. "He felt he was destined for a business career and wanted to earn his own living and stand on his own feet," his younger brother Bernard wrote in his memoir.[33] Sam worked as a bookkeeper and later started a small dry goods business. In a family that placed a high premium on education and intellectual attainment, Sam's decision to forgo his schooling for business was tantamount to an act of rebellion. But striking out on his own kept the family afloat after the death of both parents. Though the second-born son, Sam possessed an air of confidence and authority, and he stepped into the role of father figure, taking charge of the family's affairs and ensuring his orphaned siblings could continue their schooling.

Bernard Sachs, who went by Barney, was eleven when his father died. He went on to attend Harvard Medical School, becoming a pioneer in neurology and co-discovering Tay-Sachs disease, the genetic disorder that disproportionately affects Ashkenazi Jews. A onetime president of the American Neurological Association, Barney consulted at Montefiore Hospital and for a time presided over its medical board. (Along with his more distinguished accomplishments, he was also Frieda Schiff's childhood physician.)[34]

The eldest Sachs brother, Julius, as theoretical as Sam was practical, pursued his graduate studies at Columbia and then at the University of Rostock, in northern Germany, where he received a Ph.D. An educator like his late father, Julius completed Joseph's unfinished legacy, founding Dr. Sachs' Collegiate Institute at 38 West 59th Street. It became the prep school of choice for New York's German-Jewish elite, attended by the scions of the Goldman, Lehman, Sachs, and Schiff families. "He was the kindliest man in the world, but had, as most Sachses had, a sharp temper on occasion, and he could come down on you like a ton of bricks," remembered Julius's nephew Walter, who attended Sachs' Collegiate along with his older brothers. Herbert Lehman, a classmate of Walter's brother Paul, remembered Julius as a fearsome headmaster who was "short-tempered and sharp" and "had us all pretty well scared."[35]

In 1874, Julius became the first member of the Sachs family to forge a marital bond with the Goldmans when he wed Marcus and Bertha's lively oldest daughter, Rosa, a talented actress who enjoyed putting on performances for the extended family.[36] In 1877, Sam's marriage to Louisa added still more sinews to the Goldman-Sachs family ties.

Sam's friendship with Jacob Schiff predated his marriage. They met in the early 1870s, prior to the disbandment of Budge, Schiff & Co., as both men sought to establish themselves in New York. Even then Schiff's charitable instincts impressed Sachs. "His active mind and intense energy in the way of movements for the amelioration of his fellow men's conditions were then already apparent," Sachs recalled. And he noted: "In all my acquaintance with Mr. Schiff and in regular walks on every Sunday morning to the Hospital, I never ceased to get the impression of a charitable citizen. . . . This applied not only to the care of the sick, but to the higher education of his co-religionists and to the improvement of the condition of the poor in various parts of the world."[37]

S. G. Rosenbaum, who took over the Montefiore's presidency from Schiff, marveled that "no man with whom I ever came in contact more thoroughly lived up to the principles of 'Noblesse Oblige.'"[38]

Schiff believed strongly that his privileged status gave him a responsibility to care for the less fortunate. "The surplus wealth we have gained, to some extent at least, belongs to our fellow-beings; we are only the temporary custodians of our fortunes," he once said. And he looked down on the millionaires who hoarded their wealth during their lifetimes and became philanthropists only in death. Nor did Schiff believe in passive giving, as his tight control over the organizations he supported made clear. "Charity and philanthropy, to become effective, should have personal supervision. . . . The heart being more readily touched than the head, charity abounds, while philanthropy is wanting."[39] He felt a responsibility not just to give but to lead. "Schiff never claimed leadership; he just naturally exercised it," remembered Morris Waldman, a social worker who worked closely with him.[40]

Schiff's upbringing in Frankfurt, where a philanthropic tradition was firmly ingrained within the Jewish community and where the Schiff clan had long assumed leadership, surely influenced his charitable convictions. But the intensity of his philanthropic work flowed from more than a sense of moral duty. He viewed his philanthropy through the Jewish concept of *tzedekah*. The term translated not to "charity"—a word Schiff disliked—but to "justice" or "fairness." Unlike charity, there was nothing voluntary about *tzedekah*. It was a religious requirement to help the poor and needy.

Schiff adhered to the traditional Jewish practice of tithing 10 percent of his income and required his children to donate a portion of their allowances to charities such as the Fresh Air Fund. On January 1 of each year, when Kuhn Loeb's balance sheet was drawn up, Schiff set aside one-tenth of his earnings in a separate account that he continued to supplement throughout the year.[41] Schiff's philanthropic fund ballooned in step with the profits of Kuhn Loeb, which under Schiff's leadership was earning a reputation as a shrewd operator in railroad finance.

As he grew in stature as a financier, Schiff never seemed to lack time for philanthropic business. If anything, he seemed to prioritize it. During one meeting at Kuhn Loeb's offices, a Montefiore director remembered, the board was reviewing the cases of various applicants when a clerk slipped into the room and handed Schiff a note alerting him that a client was waiting to see him. "He told him to tell the gentleman that he is at present engaged at a very important meeting and would be unable to see him for about twenty minutes." Only when the last application had been discussed did the banker rise to greet the man patiently waiting for an audience—not just any client but perhaps the firm's most important: the president of the Pennsylvania Railroad.[42]

Schiff's financial prowess was such that even the Reading Railroad, headed by Austin Corbin, the mogul who declared publicly that he planned to ban Jews from his Brooklyn resort, tried repeatedly to interest Kuhn Loeb in its business. Schiff refused, though he knew his firm could turn a quick profit. "Our self-respect forbids us to have anything to do with this man, able as he may be," Schiff told a business associate. And he noted that "I should be ashamed before myself and my children if I acted otherwise." Corbin had come to regret his antisemitic remarks, perhaps because of the negative press they had engendered. In 1886, to curry favor with New York's Jews—and maybe to suck up to Schiff specifically—Corbin cut a $10,000 check to the Montefiore Home. Once again, Schiff rebuffed him. He would not accept Corbin's money, but he also would not allow the hospital to lose out on the much-needed contribution. In lieu of Corbin's $10,000 check, Schiff substituted his own.[43]

Moses Montefiore died in 1885, shortly before reaching his 101st birthday. And in many ways, it was Montefiore's mantle—more than Joseph Seligman's—that Schiff claimed. *The Jewish World* dubbed Schiff the "American Montefiore," saying the nickname was "just" because he responded "in princely fashion to every call and need."[44] Joseph Buttenwieser, who met Schiff in 1883 and who worked closely with him on charitable endeavors, also drew a comparison to the British philanthropist: "No Jew in America, nor any one on the other side of the Atlantic since Moses Montefiore, has wrought as valiantly and as successfully for our people."[45]

Schiff soon became a legendary figure in his own right, presiding over a philanthropic era unparalleled in modern Jewish history. During this period, spanning more than three decades, "hardly any enterprise of a Jewish philanthropic or educational nature was launched, or any important policy adopted of local or nation-wide interest, without first consulting the dominant figure in the leadership of American Jewry" (that is, Schiff), Morris Waldman recalled.[46]

Once, during a joint interview with Louis Marshall and members of New York's press corps, Schiff offered a revealing perspective on his ascendance. A reporter had remarked to Marshall that "you speak in the name of all American Jewry," and the lawyer had retorted heatedly, "No one is elected to that throne!"

Schiff perked up. "You might talk to me about that," he interjected. "Jews do not elect their leaders. One becomes a leader among them."

"And how does that come about?" a journalist inquired.

Schiff replied, "One needs to have God in his heart. An ethical figure before whom the people stand in awe and to whom they will listen with deference even though they may not like what he has to say—such a person is naturally a leader."[47]

One of the most important philanthropic partnerships of Schiff's life-time came together via his mother-in-law, Betty Loeb. Like many women of her era, her accomplishments received less recognition than they deserved, though her grandson, James P. Warburg, cred-ited her as a guiding force, at least initially, behind the philanthropic projects of the Loeb and Schiff families. "She was the one who had a real humanitarian interest and this took many forms," he said.[48]

She served on the boards of various charitable groups and com-mittees, including those of the Hebrew Free School Association—an organization that provided religious and Hebrew instruction to Jew-ish children, an effort to counter the educational efforts of Chris-tian missionaries stealthily seeking converts—and the Mount Sinai Training School for Nurses. In the early 1890s, Loeb underwrote a home nursing and hygiene class for women on the Lower East Side, which was taught by a recent graduate of the New York Hospital for Nurses.

Lillian Wald had arrived in New York by way of Rochester, where she grew up in a relatively prosperous German-Jewish fam-ily. The Walds were not observant, and to the extent that the fam-ily practiced any form of Judaism at all, it was of a highly liberal, assimilationist strain, one that welcomed intermarriage as a means of integration with the white Christian society that predominated. Independent and idealistic, she fed the poor from the doorstep of her childhood home and, when Wald came of age, she rejected the path expected of her: marriage, children, homemaking. "This does not satisfy me now," she explained in her nursing school application. "I feel the need of serious, definite work."[49] This ambition led her to New York and to the overcrowded Lower East Side, where the plight of the urban poor confronted her for the first time.

One rainy March morning in 1893, after Wald completed a les-son, a small girl approached and pleaded with Wald to help her sick mother. "The child led me over broken roadways . . . over dirty mat-tresses and heaps of refuse . . . between tall, reeking houses whose laden fire escapes, useless for their appointed purpose, bulged with household goods of every description," Wald remembered. "All the maladjustments of our social and economic relations seemed epito-mized in this brief journey and what was found at the end of it."

Through the courtyard of a tenement and up mud-slick stairs, Wald discovered the girl's mother, who had recently given birth. Unable to afford a doctor, she lay on a bloody mattress in a two-room apartment occupied by nine people. "That morning's experience was a baptism of fire," Wald said. She emerged from it with a new purpose: she would live and work among the impoverished denizens of the Lower East Side.[50]

Wald was at the vanguard of the settlement movement, through which social reformers sought to narrow gaping class divides by embedding in poverty-stricken neighborhoods. Established in such cities as Boston, Chicago, and New York that had drawn an influx of immigrants, settlement houses offered education, health care, and other community services aimed at uplifting the poor.

In need of a benefactor, Wald secured an audience with Betty Loeb, to whom she pitched her plan to establish a settlement of visiting nurses on the Lower East Side. "I don't know if she is a genius, or whether she is mad," Loeb later confessed to her daughter, Nina. Inclined to believe Wald was the former, Loeb arranged another meeting, this time inviting her son-in-law, Jacob Schiff.[51] "Immediately did this busy banker respond," Wald recounted. "Money help was given and without conditions."[52]

At first, Wald's modest operation consisted of herself and a nursing school friend, Mary Brewster. They shared an apartment on Jefferson Street, a few blocks from the East River, and made house calls throughout the neighborhood. In 1895, Schiff purchased a Federal-style rowhouse at 265 Henry Street for Wald. More than a century later, it remains the headquarters of the Henry Street Settlement, which also spawned a sister organization, the Visiting Nurse Service of New York.

Henry Street was eye-opening for Schiff, exposing him to immigrants and sweatshop workers and giving the capitalist a new perspective on labor relations, among other issues. "I recall his visiting to our neighborhood one day when in answer to inquiries about industrial conditions, he learned of an impending strike in the garment trades," Wald remembered.

> Though protesting strikes as a method for settling labor difficulties, he readily agreed to bring the manufacturers to a conference—the Settlement to bring the workers and contractors. He left the conference convinced of the oppressive position in which the employees . . . had been placed, and all

through a long-fought struggle furnished money to relieve the needs of the families of the strikers until they, triumphant, were able to contract better terms for their labor.

In another instance, he arranged for a group of arrested picketers to be bailed out of prison.[53]

In addition to aiding immigrants and low-wage workers, Henry Street increasingly worked with New York's Black community, which drew Schiff into some of the earliest organizing efforts of the modern civil rights movement. He was a financial backer of Booker T. Washington and served on the general committee of the NAACP, which was founded at a conference convened at the Henry Street Settlement. "Race problems can be settled only by complete justice to the negro, and so long as this be not granted to the utmost this grave question . . . will come back to plague us and make us feel ashamed of ourselves," Schiff once declared.[54]

"His sense of justice offended repeatedly brought forth a gallant fighter for the oppressed, and his reverence for the sanctities of others was as marked," Wald recounted. "Devout and steadfast in his own faith, he could give generously to a visiting committee of women from Cuba who petitioned for the restoration of a Catholic shrine."[55]

Schiff's philanthropic interests were wide-ranging, and while Jewish causes remained at the core of his giving, he supported a variety of secular institutions. In some cases, these gifts were intended to build bridges with the gentile world and to obtain a seat at the table, literally, for Jewish interests.

He contributed generously to New York's cultural and academic mainstays—the Metropolitan Museum of Art, the American Museum of Natural History, Columbia University—even though their boards initially remained unofficially closed to Jews. Obtaining representation within these organizations was important to Schiff for reasons both symbolic and practical. As he explained in a letter to Columbia's president,

So long as . . . citizens of Jewish faith are, by a tacit understanding, kept out of the Government of Columbia University, the Metropolitan Museum of Art, the Museum of Natural History and other leading communal corporations, prejudice is being kept alive against the Jewish population, which those who lead public opinion should do everything in their power to eliminate. It cannot be expected that the stream run pure, so long as its source is contaminated.[56]

Bigotry, he believed, flowed down from above, not up from below; the people took their cues from the elites. Americans would not shed their prejudices until their leaders did.

Schiff's donations gave him entrée, and his entrée gave him a platform to press for Jewish leadership. When dollar diplomacy failed, he resorted to more aggressive tactics. George B. McClellan, Jr., a Democratic mayor of New York (and son of the Civil War general who challenged Abraham Lincoln in the 1864 election), remembered a visit from Schiff and Marshall who complained about the lack of a Jewish trustee at the Met. They said they had drafted a bill, which they hoped to get passed in the state legislature, that would give the mayor the power to appoint trustees to quasi-public institutions—such as the Met, the Natural History Museum, and the New York Public Library—that received taxpayer funding, and that would require two of the directors to be Jewish. Schiff and Marshall wanted McClellan's support, but he was noncommittal.

"As they were going out," McClellan recalled in his memoir,

> Marshall lagged behind and said to me, "Of course, Mr. Mayor, it is understood that if the bill becomes law you will appoint Mr. Schiff to one of the vacancies." I answered that I would make no pledges of any kind, whereupon he left my office and Schiff came back and said, "By the by, Mr. Mayor, of course it is understood that you will appoint Mr. Marshall to one of the vacancies." Whereupon I repeated what I had said to Marshall.

Once they had left, McClellan telephoned J. P. Morgan, the chairman of the Met's board, and told him, "The sooner you put a Jew on your board the better it will be." The following day, according to McLellan, Morgan called a meeting of the board, where he accepted the resignation of one trustee and appointed George Blumenthal, a Frankfurt-born Jew who was a senior partner in the banking house of Lazard Frères, to the vacancy.[57] Within Schiff's lifetime, the New York Public Library and the American Museum of Natural History also elected Jewish trustees. In the case of the museum, where Schiff had contributed not just funds but bankrolled archaeological digs to fill its galleries, its first Jewish director was his son-in-law, Felix Warburg.

Schiff pressed especially hard for a trusteeship at Columbia, if not for himself, then for a fellow Jew. When it never materialized despite more than a decade of strong-arming and cajoling, he sent an unmistakable message to the university's administrators. He donated $100,000 to form a Germanic studies department at Cornell, making clear he had done so because Columbia continued to exclude Jews from its boardroom.

While a Columbia board seat eluded him, Schiff did play a central role in the founding of its sister school, Barnard College. In 1888 twenty-one-year-old Annie Nathan Meyer—of the prominent Sephardic family—asked him to join a fundraising committee to form a women's college at Columbia. "I was frightfully nervous about approaching him," Meyer remembered. "Tales had reached me of his extreme arbitrariness. It was suggested that no one could hope to serve on a board with him unless prepared to agree with him in every respect." But beneath Schiff's "somewhat forbidding exterior," she found a warm and friendly man and, better still, one who took an interest in her plans. He became Barnard's first treasurer, which meant it was up to him in those lean first years to stretch the college's meager resources and energize its fundraising.[58] "Superbly loyal to his own people," Meyer later wrote, he "was particularly interested in helping Jewish students go through College." In some cases, his investment in students' futures continued after they left Barnard. Once, when the husband of a Jewish graduate of Barnard's first class was in jeopardy of losing his business, Schiff stepped in with a loan to help the man through a rocky stretch.[59]

He remained on Barnard's board a few years before handing over the financial reins to a friend, the publisher George Arthur Plimpton (grandfather of the journalist George Plimpton). Increasingly, his time and his money were being consumed by an unprecedented humanitarian crisis, one that New York's Jewish community could not have ignored even if it had wanted to.

10

EXODUS

On the morning of November 27, 1881, two hundred prominent Jews crammed into the Hebrew Orphan Asylum to debate the future of Eastern European Jewry. Though they didn't know that yet.

Earlier that fall, Jewish refugees fleeing the Russian Empire had begun to arrive at Castle Garden (the forerunner to Ellis Island). New York's Jewish community had responded by raising a relief fund, with DeWitt Seligman serving as treasurer, to care for the newcomers. Jacob Schiff provided the first contribution, $500, to the American Fund in Aid of Russian Emigrants.[1]

To some Jewish leaders, it had become clear that a temporary relief effort would not suffice. They had the resources to take charge of some five hundred refugees, but more than double that had already arrived, and hundreds more were coming each week. Some attendees of the November meeting were advocating for a permanent organization to assist the Russian immigrants.

The German Jews, who now dominated the social aid groups, were sympathetic to the plight of their Russian brothers and sisters but also wary. Would these impoverished immigrants from cloistered Jewish Podunks acclimate to American life as quickly as they had? What would it mean for their own fragile standing, fully assimilated but not always fully accepted, if the newcomers didn't adopt American ways and values? Such anxieties would create lasting animosity between the established Germans and the newer arrivals from Russia and its environs for years to come.

In later years, Jewish immigrants would find no more tireless champion than Schiff, but he initially spoke out against the proposal to establish an aid group. One newspaper, paraphrasing Schiff, said the financier denounced the notion as "smacking of sectarianism."[2] According to another account, he remarked that "the immigration was not such as was desired, and he asked whether any one had ever heard of any other race or nationality starting an emigration aid society." Members of the crowd grumbled at Schiff's remarks. Some shouted, "I have!"[3]

Finally, a lithographer named Julius Bien, who supported the creation of a new group, spoke up insistently: "Who is going over to Castle Island tomorrow morning to look after those 500 Russian Jews there?"[4]

The events that triggered the largest mass exodus of Jews since their expulsion from Spain in 1492, a migration that radically reordered Jewish life and brought nearly 2 million Jews to America in little more than three decades, began on March 13, 1881. Czar Alexander II was returning from his regular Sunday visit to review the changing of the guards at the Mikhailovsky Manège, a staging ground for the imperial cavalry in central St. Petersburg. As the Russian czar's bulletproof carriage bounced along the snowy street that ran alongside the Catherine canal, a short young man in a black overcoat approached carrying a package wrapped in a white handkerchief. He hesitated, then hurled the parcel under the carriage.

A massive blast, then an acrid plume of white smoke.

The lifeless body of a Cossack guard lay in the street at the rear of the carriage, where the bomb had detonated, but Alexander escaped the worst of the explosion. The sixty-two-year-old czar was by now accustomed to attempts on his life. Since ascending to the throne after the death of his father, Czar Nicholas I, more than twenty-five years earlier, he had survived five of them. The most recent had occurred the previous winter, when a revolutionary connected with a radical group known as Narodnaya Volya (People's Will) had planted more than one hundred pounds of dynamite beneath the dining room at his palace. By luck, Alexander had arrived late. The explosion killed eleven people.[5]

This latest bombing was also the work of Narodnaya Volya, an underground group that aimed to foment a socialist revolution. Alexander's guards quickly subdued the would-be assassin, as he tried to flee. Disoriented but unhurt, Alexander dismounted into the haze, ignoring the members of his entourage who implored him to return to the carriage. As he paced, a second Narodnaya Volya member threw another bomb. When the smoke dissipated, the czar lay mortally wounded in the blood-drenched snow. He died later that afternoon.[6]

Within weeks, the pogroms started.

On April 15, 1881, a few days after Easter, an anti-Jewish riot broke out in Elisavetgrad (now Kropyvnytskyi), a city of 43,000 in what is today Ukraine, where a trail of shattered glass, splintered furniture, and shredded bedding marked the path of the mob's rampage. Anti-Jewish violence was not unusual around Christian holidays, when carousing revelers sometimes vented their fury at the supposed Christ-killers living among them. But this uprising was different.

One of the conspirators arrested and hanged for the czar's murder was a young woman of Jewish descent. She had been a bit player in the scheme, but rumors spread—fanned to some degree by local newspapers—that Jews had killed the czar. Prior to the Elisavetgrad uprising, there were whispers of coming pogroms to avenge Alexander's death.

From Elisavetgrad, the mob violence spread. Less than two weeks later rioting began in Kyiv's Jewish quarter, lasting three days before order was restored. In the coming months, pogroms of varying severity flared up in hundreds of towns throughout the Pale of Settlement, a campaign of destruction, rape, and, in some cases, murder that both terrified the Jewish population and magnified their economic misfortunes.[7]

Jews had lived as an underclass in Russia ever since they had been permitted to live there at all. After Russia partitioned the territory of the Polish-Lithuanian Commonwealth in the late eighteenth century, the empire reluctantly gained a large Jewish population. Previously, Russian rulers had focused on keeping Jews outside their borders. But in 1791, Catherine the Great had dealt with the troublesome issue of Russia's new residents—citizens, they were not—by allowing Jews to live in a designated swath of territory in the southwestern corner of the empire. The Pale of Settlement would come to cover nearly 500,000 square miles, comprising all or part of present-day Belarus, Latvia, Lithuania, Moldova, and Ukraine, along with some areas of western Russia. At its peak, some 5 million Jews, nearly half of the world's Jewish population, lived within this territory. In the Pale, there were rules about where Jews could settle—initially, cities such as Kyiv and Sebastopol were off-limits. And Jews were also barred from creating new settlements within about thirty miles of the Pale's western border.

Alexander II's reign marked a slight improvement for Jews in the Russian Empire. His father, Nicholas I, had considered the Jews a threat to national unity—an "injurious element"—and took steps to forcibly Russify them.[8] His regime outlawed Jews from wearing traditional dress and censored certain Hebrew books. And he decreed that Jews, previously prohibited from military service, would now become subject to conscription. Boys as young as twelve were taken from their families and forced into military service for as long as twenty-five years. To the Jewish community, this seemed like nothing less than an effort to snuff out their faith by targeting its torchbearers, which was precisely what it was.

Alexander II, who embarked on a campaign to modernize Russia, had emancipated the empire's serfs, and he eased certain education, land ownership, and travel restrictions imposed on Jews. Under his rule, some Jews were permitted to live outside the Pale in areas previously forbidden.

Alexander III, who ascended to the throne after his father's assassination, despised Jews. "Deep in my soul I am very glad when they beat up Jews," he told Warsaw's governor-general, "but nevertheless it can't be allowed."[9] He organized a commission to investigate the causes of the pogroms that returned a report effectively blaming the Jews for provoking the violence against them through their "exploitation" of the populace. The report also faulted Alexander II's more liberal policies. Alexander III's solution was further repression. In 1882 he signed into law new regulations rolling back some of his father's reforms. Known as the May Laws, the rules barred Jews from settling outside existing towns and cities in the Pale, prohibited them from registering property or obtaining mortgages, and forbade them from doing business on Sundays and on Christian holidays, among other restrictions.[10]

Gripped by fear and uncertainty, the shtetls buzzed with tales of the magical freedoms available in America. And, as Irving Howe wrote in his seminal book about the Jewish exodus from Eastern Europe, *World of Our Fathers*, it was an "explosive mixture of mounting wretchedness and increasing hope" that wrenched open the floodgates. Within the Pale's terrorized communities, Jewish leaders heatedly debated whether immigration should be encouraged as official policy.[11]

In New York, meanwhile, proponents of establishing an organization to aid Jewish immigrants won out. The resulting outfit, called the Hebrew Emigrant Aid Society, had the mission of "aiding and advising Hebrew immigrants . . . in obtaining homes and employment, and otherwise providing means to prevent them from becoming burdens on the charity of the community." The group immediately set to work, including by forming relationships with the network of European relief organizations that had sprung up to handle the refugee crisis there. Schiff, despite his misgivings, joined the aid society's leadership. New York's Emigration Commission gave the new organization use of land and some rudimentary structures on Wards Island in upper Manhattan to house the Russian émigrés, who were arriving faster than they could be placed in jobs and homes. Schiff donated $10,000 to renovate the property, which was known as the Schiff Refuge; his firm contributed another $5,000, as did Jesse Seligman.[12]

From the start, the aid society struggled with the influx. "Too many immigrants are coming at once," an aid society official groused in June 1882. "It was all very well so long as the number was limited. Now it is different. Over 1,300 arrived last week, and during Saturday and Sunday about 3,000 more."[13]

Tensions flared between the immigrants and their wardens, as the new arrivals began to wonder why they had crossed an ocean for the privilege of living in conditions not much improved from those they had fled. The residents of the Schiff Refuge, who lived in a collection of four wooden barracks, complained of being served rotten food and of being beaten by the shelter's superintendent and his deputy.[14] Finally, in October 1882, they rioted, laying siege to the superintendent's home and showering it with stones as he and his assistant cowered inside.[15]

The revolt was pacified, but ill feelings continued between the Russians and their American benefactors. Some disillusioned immigrants asked to be sent back; frustrated officers of the aid society were resigning by the day, and the group burned through three presidents and four secretaries in a year.[16] One of those secretaries, after parting ways with the group, grumbled that "only disgrace and a lowering of the opinion in which American Israelites are held . . . can result from the continued residence among us . . . of these wretches."[17]

Meanwhile, the officers of the Hebrew Emigrant Aid Society bickered with their European counterparts over financial resources and over the quality of the immigrants being foisted upon them. The European relief groups were supposedly vetting the refugees to ensure that only the healthiest and most employable were sent on to America, but the Hebrew Emigrant Aid Society complained in a cable to its European representative that most of the newcomers were "incapable of supporting themselves" and would be a "permanent burden."[18]

The society established an employment bureau at 35 East Broadway and issued each immigrant starting a new work assignment a twelve-dollar set of clothes.[19] But the hope, at the outset, was to divert many of the Russian Jews away from New York, lest they stoke antisemitism or damage by association the stature of their German brethren. The leadership also believed that the immigrants might Americanize more quickly if placed in communities where few Jews resided. With financial assistance from the HEAS, agricultural colonies were established in locations including Cotopaxi, Colorado; Beersheba, Kansas; Sicily Island, Louisiana; and Vineland, New Jersey. Through a group called the Montefiore Agricultural Aid Society, Schiff and Jesse Seligman personally bankrolled the creation of a farming commune in Oregon dubbed New Odessa.[20]

The HEAS dispatched Julius Goldman to the West to investigate possible locations for Jewish settlement. The sharp young attorney, who was Schiff's personal lawyer in addition to handling legal matters for his father's banking firm, had no farming experience, though he dutifully toured sites in Minnesota and the Dakota territories. On his return, he tendered a pessimistic report: "To settle the refugees in lands in the West in masses . . . is entirely unfeasible," he wrote.[21]

Indeed, most of the farming colonies collapsed. One of the few marginally successful ventures was Vineland, where seventy-two families eventually settled, raising chickens and growing corn, sweet potatoes, and strawberries.[22]

In 1883, the Hebrew Emigrant Aid Society itself shut down, after clearing the Schiff Refuge of the remaining immigrants in its charge. The demise of the beleaguered group was in some ways inevitable. New York's established Jewish community had stepped up admirably to fund the organization—which expended $250,000 in its first year alone—but there remained a great deal of ambivalence, if not open hostility, toward the new wave of immigrants suddenly thrust upon them.[23]

By the time the HEAS disbanded, the spasm of violence that had caused the initial flood of refugees had largely subsided, and in 1883 the number of Jewish immigrants seeking refuge in the United States dropped by a third.[24] To New York's Jewish leaders, it seemed the worst had passed. In fact, the diaspora was only getting underway.

More than eleven thousand in 1884. The next year, nearly seventeen thousand. Twenty-one thousand the year after.[25] When the Hebrew Emigrant Aid Society closed its doors, it turned over the remainder of its funds—all of $10,000—to United Hebrew Charities, which attempted to fill the void.[26] But the crushing need was beyond what any one organization could handle. Week after week boatloads of needy immigrants arrived, requiring shelter, food, jobs, medical care, education, and more.

For Schiff, the years after the HEAS dissolved were a time of furious philanthropic activity and institution-building. He joined the board of the New York chapter of the Young Men's Hebrew Association, which offered citizenship classes and educational programs for immigrants, and he accepted the presidency of the Home for Aged and Infirm Hebrews. Cordial yet insistent, he constantly pressed his friends and associates to open their wallets ever wider to the variety of causes to which he devoted his time and money. In 1886 he launched a fundraising drive to build a new headquarters for the Montefiore Home on 138th Street and Broadway, and two years later, after amassing $160,000 in contributions, he reverently spread mortar on the building's cornerstone. "May the stone which we here lay become the foundation of a house in which the true Spirit of God, the spirit of charity, dwelleth," he said.[27]

With construction of the Montefiore's new edifice underway, Schiff joined his brother-in-law Morris Loeb, Joseph Seligman's son Edwin, and others to raise $125,000 to build a headquarters for the Educational Alliance, which Schiff had helped to establish by brokering a partnership between three existing groups, including the YMHA and the Hebrew Free School Association. Schiff became the founding president of the alliance, whose aim, *The New York Times* reported in an article about the dedication of its new building on East Broadway, was the "Americanizing, as far as possible, of the large mass of foreign-born Jews in this city."[28] Over the next two decades, so many immigrants flowed through the building that its marble stairs, worn thin by foot traffic, had to be replaced.[29]

Schiff's philanthropy, always aimed at improving the lives of his fellow Jews, sometimes took an indirect path. Such was the case in 1889, when he provided $10,000 in seed funding to establish a museum of Semitic history at Harvard. His goal in preserving ancient Hebrew texts, artwork, and other relics was in fact rooted in present concerns. As he explained during the opening ceremony:

> Antisemitism in Europe, social prejudice and ostracism in free America, may for a time be rampant; posterity will with shame and disgust repudiate these passions. To combat in the meantime these unsound currents in an efficient manner, opportunities should be created for a more thorough study and a better knowledge of Semitic history and civilization, so that the world shall better understand and acknowledge the debt it owes the Semitic people.[30]

In the summer of 1890, the Russian crisis flared once more. Reports circulated that the Russian government planned to begin enforcing the May Laws, which until then had been only lightly applied. New York's philanthropic stewards braced for a new crush of immigrants, which, thanks in part to Schiff, they were now in a better position to manage. A couple of years earlier, Schiff had reached out, through his close friend Ernest Cassel, the British financier, to Baron Maurice de Hirsch, a Munich-born mogul who had amassed his fortune through European railway ventures. Hirsch's only son, Lucien, had recently died. "My son I have lost, but not my heir; humanity is my heir," Hirsch declared at the time.[31] Like Moses Montefiore, Hirsch, after making his millions, began pouring his fortune into Jewish relief work.

Hirsch had focused on trying to improve economic conditions for Jews living in the Pale of Settlement through farming and education programs. In 1887 he offered the Russian government 50 million francs to establish elementary and agricultural schools throughout the Pale, but negotiations broke down when it became clear to Hirsch that Russia's leaders had little desire to improve the lives of their Jewish subjects and perhaps even preferred for them to live in a perpetual state of poverty and subjugation.[32]

"[Hirsch] has tried to make large donations in Russia and Galicia [a region covering parts of present-day Ukraine and Poland], but they were not feasible," Schiff told Cassel in December 1888. The baron's money could be far better used to settle the "Jews who are constantly pouring into this country." Cassel knew Hirsch well, so Schiff asked his friend to recommend to the baron that he "donate a considerable sum" in the United States.[33]

Hirsch, meanwhile, had come to his own realization that the problems of Russia's Jews could not be solved in Russia; though he had previously viewed wide-scale emigration as unrealistic, he now saw it as the only path. In July 1890, as reports of the Russian government's coming crackdown on the Jews began to surface, Schiff met with Hirsch in London, where he struck the mustachioed noble as a "quiet, thoughtful man" with a deep commitment to helping "our unhappy co-religionists." A few weeks later Hirsch wrote to Schiff of the "horrible decrees" the Russians were reportedly enacting against the Jews. "The time has arrived when we men of property must stand by the breach," he stated. And he enclosed a copy of a letter announcing that he was contributing $2.4 million to establish a charitable fund to assist America's Jewish immigrants. Early the following year the Baron de Hirsch Fund officially launched, with Schiff, Jesse Seligman, Julius Goldman, and Oscar Straus, until recently the U.S. envoy to the Ottoman Empire, serving among its officers. (Emanuel Lehman later joined as the organization's treasurer.)[34]

Despite early failures, a focus remained on turning the arriving Jewish immigrants into farmers, which served the dual purpose of steering them out of New York's overcrowded downtown ghettos and providing them with a vocation that could make them self-sufficient. Among the Hirsch Fund's first projects was a new farming colony and agricultural school in Woodbine, New Jersey. The organization also assisted Jews in purchasing farmland in Connecticut and supported existing agricultural collectives formed years earlier with the backing of the Hebrew Emigrant Aid Society. But such efforts managed to divert just a trickle of the immigrants deluging New York, where the Hirsch Fund, thanks to its vast resources and the prominent men on its board, fast became a central player within the city's Jewish community.

Hirsch dollars flowed to existing groups working with Jewish émigrés, such as the United Hebrew Charities, which trained immigrants in the needle trades, and the Educational Alliance, which provided free English classes—part of a program of "Americanization" that was central to the Hirsch Fund's mission. Often these initiatives had to adapt to suit the various needs of the newcomers: an immigrant training in metal- or woodworking at the Hirsch-funded Hebrew Technical Institute, for instance, also needed English instruction to learn the names of his tools. He required trolley fare to and from his classes and arrived so hungry that a small meal of bread, cheese, and coffee was served before classes commenced.

The Hirsch Fund built free public baths on Henry Street for use by Lower East Siders whose tenement buildings lacked bathing facilities. And it provided loans to business owners, often in the garment industry, who agreed to train and employ immigrant workers. At the prodding of Julius Goldman, a separate loan program was created to assist members of the immigrant intellectual class—typically those who had received some training in Europe—to continue their education in the United States. Along with Goldman, this program was administered by Morris Loeb, Solomon's brilliant yet eccentric son who had just been appointed a professor of chemistry at New York University, and Edwin Seligman, the Columbia economist.[35]

Seligman also served on a Hirsch Fund committee tasked with recommending new programs, where he studied the question of how the immigrants could establish their economic footing. He lamented in one memo that many Jewish newcomers were being swept into unskilled trades, such as rolling cigars or finishing garments, where they scratched out a living "by inordinately long hours of work at inadequate pay, huddled together amid filthy and foul air, necessarily shut out from the joys of life, and begetting a progeny which if exposed to the same influences, must necessarily develop only the baser instincts of mankind."

"What is needed for the unfortunate horde of unskilled immigrants is opportunity," he mused. "And this opportunity can be acquired only by such an education as will enable them to escape the necessity of being driven into these soul-destroying vocations. What is needed is industrial training for adults on a vast scale."

But he also worried that a new class of skilled immigrant workers might stir up anti-Jewish feeling among Americans whose livelihoods they were encroaching on. "Every nerve," he wrote, "must be strained to check the growth among the workmen of race prejudice, for that would mark the beginning of the end, of the commencement of a serious concerted action against the Jews, of which the present social ostracism in the higher classes is but the faintest premonition."[36]

Schiff, too, worried about image. He had initially approached the baron with an initiative more limited in scope, perhaps the creation of an agricultural credit bank to seed Jewish farming projects and finance the settlement of the Jewish refugees.[37] While he welcomed

Hirsch's generous investment—indeed, he had solicited it—he also knew that the wide-ranging activities of the fund, created by a German who lived in Paris and London, might foster the impression that the organization was facilitating immigration and serving as an American proxy for Europeans seeking to thrust their immigrant problem on the United States. "He expressed to me his grave doubts as to the wisdom of accepting large sums of money for philanthropic work in the United States from European sources," Julius Goldman remembered. "Above all, he feared that the public, and more particularly, the public authorities, might ascribe to those organizations, the function of furthering and assisting immigration to the United States." Indeed, according to Goldman, immigration authorities at one point did investigate the Hirsch Fund to ensure that it was not actively encouraging immigration.[38]

The new Russian exodus predictably led to public alarm and resentment, and in Washington it fueled efforts to restrict immigration. In 1882, during the initial mass migration from the Pale, Congress had passed some of the nation's first immigration measures. One targeted the influx of Chinese workers, barring all immigration from China for a decade. The Chinese Exclusion Act was followed a few months later by the Immigration Act of 1882, which blocked convicts, "lunatics," and those likely to become public charges. The Immigration Act of 1891, enacted just as the work of the Hirsch Fund got underway, strengthened the general restrictions imposed nearly a decade earlier and specifically outlawed "assisted" immigration. Significantly, it brought immigration firmly under the control of the federal government, creating a bureau of inspectors posted at every major port.

Supervision of immigration, including the outfitting of Ellis Island to serve as a new processing center, fell to an assistant Treasury secretary named Alvred Bayard Nettleton. A retired brigadier general and former Northern Pacific Railway executive, he pushed for strict enforcement of the law and made no secret of his belief that America's Anglo-Saxon heritage was at stake. During one speech, according to a summary of his remarks, he declared that "a Government established by Anglo-Saxons did not gain by too great an admixture of Latin races" and that "something must be done now to check immigration."[39]

Nettleton aggressively policed for assisted immigrants. In July 1891, four months after the immigration law passed, he instructed immigration officials in New York to "closely question" Russian Jews to see if they had been "diverted from their original destination" by foreign officials. The result was that some Jewish immigrants were making the harrowing trip to the United States only to be turned around—or, as Schiff put it, "sent back to hell."[40]

In late July 1891, American-Jewish leaders, led by former diplomat Simon Wolf, the chairman of the Union of American Hebrew Congregations, advocated a more lenient approach to the new law in a letter to Treasury secretary Charles Foster, arguing that Russian immigrants should not be classified as paupers or assisted immigrants so long as members of the American-Jewish community ensured they would not become a drain on public resources.[41] Schiff and a group of other prominent Jews subsequently met with Foster, where they received his assurance that New York immigration officials had been instructed to ease up on their clampdown. But to Schiff, this wasn't sufficient. According to Max Kohler, a New York lawyer and Hirsch Fund trustee, Schiff "pointed out very dramatically" that since the policy had come from the top, the situation could be remedied only by Nettleton's firing.[42] Before long, Nettleton's responsibilities were handed to another Treasury official, and the general announced his retirement.[43] A representative of the American Federation of Labor, serving on a government commission on immigration, would subsequently warn of the Hirsch Fund's "hypnotic influences" over the nation's immigration policy.[44]

While Schiff and his colleagues attempted to ease immigration restrictions, they also pressed the presidential administration of Republican Benjamin Harrison to apply diplomatic pressure on Russia. Along with Jesse Seligman, whose firm represented the navy, and Oscar Straus, the former diplomat, Schiff formed part of an influential triumvirate, each man using his contacts and cachet to advance their cause.

In response to inquiries from the U.S. minister in St. Petersburg, Russia denied imposing any anti-Jewish measures, despite mounting reports of Jews being driven from their homes in the dead of night, of businesses looted and seized, of attacks and riots ignored or egged on by local authorities, and of the enforcement of laws designed to starve the Jews commercially and thus physically. Schiff, Seligman, and Straus concentrated on mustering evidence of Jewish persecution and getting it into the hands of both the State Department and the media. Schiff preferred to keep his name out of the press, but he enjoyed friendly relationships with journalists including Horace White, editor of the *Chicago Tribune* and later the *New York Evening Post*, and he reported "trying to win over the daily press . . . and other periodicals which have great influence on the thinking public." In a letter to Ernest Cassel, he said that he and his colleagues were "working very effectively here through the press and the Department of State to exert wholesome influence."[45]

To publicize Russia's repression, Schiff, along with Straus and Emanuel Lehman, also provided modest financial backing to *Free Russia*, a journal devoted to covering the abuses of the autocratic regime and laying bare "all the actions of the authorities in suppressing all aspirations for freedom" of the Russian people.[46] The Society of Friends of Russian Freedom, a group founded in 1890 by British opponents of the czarist regime, published the journal. An American branch of the organization, whose founding members included prominent literary figures such as Samuel Clemens (aka Mark Twain) and James Russell Lowell, formed the following year. This nascent movement supporting the revolutionary cause in Russia was inspired in part by the explorer and journalist George Kennan, a society member who had traveled extensively through the region since 1864, when he had been hired to survey the possible route of an overland telegraph line between Russia and the United States, via Siberia and the Bering Strait. (Kennan was the great-uncle of the diplomat George Frost Kennan, a onetime ambassador to the Soviet Union and architect of the Cold War–era policy of "containment.") His travels through Russia had gradually turned him into an ardent foe of the czar's government, and during the mid-1880s his dispatches from Siberia, exposing the labor camps where political prisoners were banished, caused a national sensation. Schiff's support for *Free Russia* brought him into Kennan's orbit, and they struck up a long friendship based on a mutual disdain for the Russian Empire.

Together and separately, the trio of Schiff, Seligman, and Straus met repeatedly with Secretary of State James Blaine both to apprise him of new developments on the ground and to vent their frustration that the U.S. envoy in St. Petersburg, Charles Emory Smith, wasn't doing more to convey to his Russian counterparts that the Harrison administration would not tolerate the regime's ongoing persecution of the Jews. Indeed, they complained that Smith was being taken in by Russia's lies concerning the plight of its Jewish citizens.

U.S. administrations had generally been reticent to meddle in the internal affairs of friendly foreign nations, but Schiff and the others argued convincingly that Russia's harsh treatment of the Jews was having a direct and profound impact on the United States by unleashing a stampede of immigration. The Harrison administration seemed to agree, and during one meeting Secretary of State Blaine told Schiff and Straus that he had instructed Smith to "exercise a friendly influence upon the Russian Government in favor of its Jewish subjects."[47] Such entreaties, however, seemed to have little effect. In late March 1891, several months after the meeting with Blaine, police in Moscow began systematically expelling the city's Jewish population, composed largely of artisans and other skilled workers who had special permission to live there. The authorities presented Jewish residents with documents stating that they would agree to leave the city within one year and demanded that they sign them. These agreements were voluntary only in the sense that if they declined to sign, they would be expelled from the city within forty-eight hours. Jewish families were forced to sell their property and possessions for a fraction of their worth. People who had spent years building up prosperous businesses were abruptly robbed of their livelihoods, compelled to leave behind factories and storefronts. Uprooted from their homes, these Jews faced a choice: return to the bleak existence of the Pale or emigrate to one of the relatively few countries that would accept them.

On July 1, 1891, Schiff, Seligman, and Straus met with President Harrison, who listened sympathetically as they advocated for a firm diplomatic rebuke. According to Straus, Harrison agreed action was warranted "but suggested that our Government ought to have before it an official report or statement of facts."[48] Harrison had recently appointed a five-member commission to study the causes of emigration from Europe; its members were scheduled to embark in days on a three-month fact-finding mission. This delegation was headed by the U.S. immigration commissioner for the port of New York, Colonel John B. Weber, who oversaw Ellis Island, and Harrison instructed the commission to visit Russia to investigate conditions there. A friend to marginalized groups, Weber had elected to command a Black infantry unit during the Civil War; Straus, pleased with Weber's selection, gushed that the colonel was "entirely in sympathy with us."[49]

Weber and another commission member, Walter Kempster, a well-known physician who was an expert on mental illness, crossed into the Russian Empire in mid-August 1891, conducting dozens of interviews as they traveled throughout the region, from Warsaw to Moscow. They heard harrowing tales of businesses shuttered and property confiscated, of arbitrary imprisonments, of pregnant women forced from their homes in winter weather. They met a gaunt Jewish seamstress with sunken eyes who told of subsisting on "two meals a day, of black bread, watered with tears"; a peasant who wondered "will it finally become necessary to drown ourselves?"; a once successful soap maker soon to be jettisoned from Moscow. "I am ruined," he said, "and nothing but misery stares me in the face."

Weber's commission encountered "want and misery such as we had never seen." After its members returned to the United States in October 1891, they delivered a report, spanning more than three hundred pages, that included a stinging critique of the Russian government:

> We gave more time to the investigation of, and more space to, Jewish immigration than to any other, as in every other country visited, except Russia, the movement is due almost entirely to normal causes. In Russia, however, emigration is incited by causes within the control of the authorities. There is a propulsive force behind it which can be stopped by an imperial edict, or by an intimation to cease the persecutions.

The report continued:

> While the principle of non-intervention in the regulation and management of the domestic affairs of foreign countries is recognized and generally observed by all nations, especially by the United States, it can not in respect of the Russian government be regarded as a friendly act to strip these persons of their substance and force them to our land impoverished in means and crushed in spirit. . . . To push these people upon us in a condition which makes our duty of self-protection war against the spirit of our institutions and the ordinary instincts of humanity calls for a protest so emphatic that it will be both heard and heeded.[50]

The report was significant because it documented, for the first time and in official form, Russia's campaign of repression against Jews. Schiff reveled in its findings, believing it would "go far towards bringing about an exertion of the influence of the United States Government with the Russian Government in favor of our persecuted brethren."[51]

Later that year, during his State of the Union address, President Harrison, using language honed with the help of Straus, raised the situation in Russia.[52]

> This Government has found occasion to express in a friendly spirit, but with much earnestness, to the Government of the Czar, its serious concern because of the harsh measures now being enforced against the Hebrews in Russia. By the revival of anti-Semitic laws, long in abeyance, great numbers of those unfortunate people have been constrained to abandon their homes and leave the Empire by reason of the impossibility of finding subsistence within the pale to which it is sought to confine them. The immigration of these people to the United States—many other countries being closed to them—is largely increasing and is likely to assume proportions which may make it difficult to find homes and employment for them here and to seriously affect the labor market. It is estimated that over 1,000,000 will be forced from Russia within a few years. The Hebrew is never a beggar; he has always kept the law—life by toil—often under severe and oppressive civil restrictions. It is also true that no race, sect, or class has more fully cared for its own than the Hebrew race. But the sudden transfer of such a multitude under conditions that tend to strip them of their small accumulations and to depress their energies and courage, is neither good for them nor for us.[53]

A little over a month later, a 340-foot steamer dubbed the *Massilia* docked in New York Harbor, carrying 268 Russian Jews and 470 Italian immigrants. Colonel Weber happened to see its passengers disembark, and he was stunned by the "emaciated, worn condition" of the Jewish refugees, some of whom appeared as if they should be "sent directly to a suitable hospital for treatment and care."[54] Soon cases of typhus cropped up on the Lower East Side, and the epidemic was quickly traced to the *Massilia*. New York authorities launched a panicked search for the ship's passengers, rounding them up and placing them in quarantine, and breathless headlines—"DISEASE WAS HER CARGO"—filled the front pages of newspapers.[55]

Senator William Eaton Chandler, a New Hampshire Republican and former navy secretary, seized on the outbreak to push for new immigration restrictions. A die-hard nativist, Chandler chaired the Senate Immigration Committee and played an important part in the passage of the Immigration Act of 1891, a law that he nonetheless felt didn't go far enough to prevent "undesirable classes"—which he defined as "southern Italians and Russian, Polish, and Hungarian Jews"—from entering the United States.[56] With the House Immigration Committee, he launched a joint investigation into the typhoid epidemic, holding hearings in New York. The panel called Colonel Weber as its first witness, and during his testimony, Chandler chided the immigration commissioner for being blinded by his "sympathies" for "pauper Russian Hebrews."[57]

Cloaking his agenda in public health concerns, he pushed for new hurdles to immigration, including literacy tests and asset requirements (not less than $100 per head of household).

A few days after Chandler held his hearings in New York, Schiff wrote a forceful letter to Harrison warning of the "unjustified and great hardships" that would occur "should existing laws be construed in an extreme manner." Severe immigration restrictions would be both "narrow and un-American."

He asked, "Would it be just and fair to now throw obstacles in the way of an unhappy people, solely because of the demand of a handful of demagogues, who not very many years ago themselves sought the hospitality of our country, or because of an unfortunate and largely magnified outbreak of an illness among a single shipload of emigrants?"[58]

Following a cholera outbreak later that year, Chandler, emboldened, introduced a bill calling for a one-year suspension of immigration. The measure failed, but President Harrison did impose a mandatory twenty-day quarantine on steerage passengers arriving from France, Germany, and Russia. The order referred to immigrants from these "infected districts" as a "direct menace to public health."[59]

The Russia crisis ushered in a new phase of political engagement for Jewish leaders, who had never before worked in such a concerted way to influence the nation's immigration policy or its diplomatic stance toward a foreign ally. It presaged future battles to come over immigration and U.S. foreign policy that went to the core of America's national identity. Was the United States a refuge for the oppressed, and would it use its growing international clout for humanitarian ends outside its borders? Or should the nation turn its back and close its door to foreign problems and influences, whether cholera or anarchism?

For the next three decades Schiff stood at the center of these fights, no longer ambivalent about the role of American Jews in helping their oppressed brothers and sisters. This was about survival. He viewed the Jewish exodus from Russia in biblical terms, comparing it to the flight of the Israelites from Egyptian bondage. And in this modern-day story, he may have seen himself as a Moses figure, using his capital and his clout to part the waters of injustice and lead his people to freedom.

This tumultuous age, in which America's Jewish lobby was born, had a name. Some called it "the Schiff era."[60]

11

END OF AN ERA

A n ovation greeted Jesse Seligman as he entered the dining room
of Delmonico's with Jacob Schiff, the older banker leaning
on the arm of the younger. It was eight p.m. on October 1, 1891,
a Thursday, and some two hundred men stood in applause beside
long rows of tables decorated with roses and smilax, while Seligman's
three daughters, Alice, Emma, and Madeleine, looked on from a balcony overhead. Familiar faces populated the crowd: ex-mayor Abram
Hewitt; Columbia University president (and future New York City
mayor) Seth Low; Marcus Goldman, with sons Julius and Henry and
son-in-law Sam Sachs; Solomon Loeb; and Emanuel Lehman, who
with Schiff, the master of ceremonies, had helped to arrange this
banquet honoring Seligman for his lifetime of charitable and patriotic service.[1]

The following day Jesse would sail for Europe on the first leg of
a yearlong trip, during which he would undertake a diplomatic mission, before heading to Egypt to spend the winter. President Harrison had tasked the well-connected banker with visiting European
finance officials to test the waters about forging an international
compromise on a monetary standard based on both gold and silver.[2]

The United States had operated on the bimetallic standard
prior to the Civil War, when the cash-strapped Lincoln administration began printing greenbacks. But when Ulysses Grant signed the
Coinage Act of 1873, drastically limiting the minting of silver-based

currency, he had placed the nation on the path to adopting the gold standard alone, as many European nations had already done and as others would do in the years to follow.

Decried as the "Crime of '73" by its detractors, the law touched off decades of acrimonious political debate, pitting the East Coast financial establishment, whose constituents argued for "sound money" backed by gold, against midwestern farmers and the citizens of western mining outposts, who pushed for a vast expansion of silver-based currency. Ballooning the money supply was attractive to debtors struggling to repay their loans, and farmers hoped it would increase the price of their crops; for the miners of Montana and Nevada, where the Comstock Lode had been discovered in 1859, it would almost literally give them the ability to mint money.

But bankers such as Seligman warned that unilaterally returning to bimetallism could have disastrous economic results, crippling international trade and causing precious gold to flee across the Atlantic while Europe dumped its silver on the U.S. Treasury. "A standard different from that of the commercial world would affect the vast mass of our imports and exports," Jesse cautioned in an essay published in *The North American Review*, "and but little less directly every other industry touching these at any point."[3] One possible solution to America's monetary impasse was convincing key European trading partners—such as Britain, France, and Germany—to adopt international bimetallism and establish a commonly accepted ratio between gold and silver. Seligman's mission was to gauge European attitudes and pave the way for an international conference where the silver question might finally be settled.

After dinner, as servers passed around cigars, Schiff rose to speak. He began by praising Seligman as "the truest and best exponent of the type of a man and Jew whom only a country like our own can produce—a representative Hebrew-American." Such men, he said, were needed now more than ever.

> Tens of thousands of our unfortunate co-religionists are being driven to our shores, expatriated by an intolerant mother country, which would even deny them the right of existence. The scenes of the Middle Ages repeat themselves, and the days of Ferdinand and Isabella are again upon us at the very moment when, after the lapse of four centuries, we prepare to commemorate the discovery of that continent which alone has become a safe asylum for the oppressed of all nations.

But, my friends, history too repeats itself. The exiles of the fifteenth century have in no small degree aided in creating the prosperity of the countries which gave them shelter, while Spain, then the dictator of Europe, has degenerated and lost its power and influence. For the moment, as of yore, intolerance may again appear to triumph; but who would now even dare to picture the greatness and mightiness our beloved country shall have attained in coming centuries, while the Russian colossus will have crumbled to pieces.

With so many wealthy men in the room, Schiff did not waste the opportunity to fundraise. Before the evening was out, he had distributed subscription papers throughout the hall that netted $30,000 in pledges for the Hirsch Fund.

The toasting went on throughout the evening. One of the final speechmakers was Colonel Elliott Shepard, the owner of New York's *Mail and Express* newspaper, who professed to "know more things about Jesse Seligman and his celebrated firm than he has forgotten." Shepard then proceeded to raise an episode that Jesse probably wished to forget. "They undertook the construction of the Panama Canal," Shepard said, "and they are entitled to the greatest credit that, while they so managed things no American investors lost a cent, but, to the contrary, made plenty of money out of the scheme, yet the scheme in the end became a total failure and has been abandoned."[4]

Seligman may have winced at the mention of the project and the international controversy it had sparked, and his fellow bankers in the room may have cocked an eyebrow at Shepard's contention that shareholders had profited. Indeed, the bankruptcy of the Panama Canal Co. had wiped out thousands of investors, particularly in France.

After Joseph's death, Jesse had taken the helm of J. & W. Seligman & Co. James was technically the eldest New York partner, though his brothers had long questioned his judgment. During Joseph's lifetime, Jesse had matched his brother in prestige and may have surpassed him in popularity on the social circuit. He too was a confidant of presidents and cabinet members, often summoned to Washington for his advice or input, and he held memberships in various of New York's exclusive clubs. The coveted guest list at Friday night dinners at his home on East 46th Street, in addition to friends such as the Schiffs and the Loebs, often included distinguished generals and politicos, along with rising artists, musicians, and writers. The opera singer Adelina Patti, a frequent guest, often serenaded her dinner companions.[5]

Five foot six and stoutly built, Jesse wore his silver hair short and his sideburns long. On most mornings, he rose early, selected a horse from his stable, and trotted through Central Park before heading to his office downtown. He was outgoing, charismatic, supremely loyal to his friends, and possessed a serene temperament. "His 'No' was so kindly pronounced that it sounded like a 'Yes' in disguise," a friend once recalled.[6]

In 1880, shortly after stepping into his brother Joseph's considerable shoes, Jesse promptly steered the firm into a business debacle from which the company never really recovered. His fearlessness had brought him to California during the Gold Rush, a decision that fueled the growth of the Seligman empire. This same swashbuckling quality propelled him headlong into one of the firm's biggest disasters. Both paths, ironically, led through the same place: Panama.

Ferdinand de Lesseps, the French diplomat and businessman, had spearheaded the construction of the Suez Canal, a decade-long project that carved a 120-mile pathway through Egypt that linked the Mediterranean and Red seas, reducing by thousands of miles the journey between Europe and Asia. This feat turned him into an international celebrity, and by the late 1870s he turned his attention to undertaking a similar project to join the Atlantic and Pacific via the Panamanian Isthmus. An organization formed by the Geographical Society of Paris and headed by De Lesseps, now in his seventies, negotiated exclusive rights to build the canal through Panama from the government of Colombia. William Seligman, based in Paris, suggested to Jesse that their firm back the De Lesseps venture.

In France, Seligman Frères & Cie formed a syndicate with the Banque de Paris to sell shares of the recently formed Panama Canal Company; in the United States, J. & W. Seligman & Co. joined with investment banks Drexel Morgan and Winslow Lanier. But from the start, the function of the American syndicate seemed to be largely public relations.

The French-led project was deeply unpopular in the United States. President Rutherford B. Hayes and members of Congress viewed it as a violation of the Monroe Doctrine and opposed any canal in the region that was not firmly under American control. It would be hard to attract European investors if they believed the U.S. government might try to thwart the effort; an attempt to sell shares in De Lesseps's Panama Canal Company in 1879 had drawn underwhelming interest for that reason. So De Lesseps needed either to change American attitudes—or to manufacture the illusion of support. The backing of J. & W. Seligman & Co., a prominent American bank that was known to do business on behalf of the U.S. government, would go a long way toward creating that perception. "The object of this is perfectly clear," a congressional select committee would later conclude. "It was to give a widespread public impression that American capital, in the persons of some of its most respectable agencies . . . was backing the enterprise, and that Americans intended to become shareholders in the canal."[7]

The role of the American syndicate—what De Lesseps called his Comité Américain—centered largely on promoting the project in the United States and advocating against a separate proposal, popular with some American politicians, to build a canal through Nicaragua. Ulysses Grant was a prominent backer of the Nicaragua route, and that is perhaps why Jesse approached his old friend to serve as the chairman of the Comité Américain, in order to both nullify the former president's backing for the rival plan and to leverage Grant's political contacts. The position paid a salary of $25,000 per year for life, but Grant wisely turned it down. "While I would like to have my name associated with the successful completion of a ship canal between the two oceans," Grant confided to a childhood friend, "I was not willing to connect it with a failure and one I believe subscribers would lose all they put in."[8] So Jesse recruited navy secretary Richard Wigginton Thompson, whom he knew well. Thompson promptly resigned from Hayes's cabinet to begin promoting a project at odds with the foreign policy of the administration he had just served.

In October 1880, Jesse responded to the naysayers in a newspaper interview. "It is a private undertaking altogether, and we have every confidence in its success," he said. "The Suez Canal is sufficient evidence that an enterprise of this kind will pay. Naturally the United States will receive the largest share of the benefit from it, all the machinery to be used in the work of construction will be bought here. When the scheme is fully understood and appreciated there will be many eager to subscribe to it."[9]

When shares in the Panama Canal Company were again offered to the public in December 1880, the response was beyond what De Lesseps and his bankers had dreamed of. More than one hundred thousand people clamored for stock in the company, which easily raised the 400 million francs required to get the project underway. Most of the shares were sold in France, where Seligman Frères earned hefty commissions. The stock issue, however, drew little interest in the United States, where investors purchased only about $8 million worth of shares. The Seligman-Drexel-Lanier syndicate made out handsomely nonetheless. De Lesseps's company paid each of the firms $400,000 for doing little more than lending their names to the enterprise.[10]

From the outset, the canal project was plagued by technical setbacks, tropical disease outbreaks, and rampant fraud and corruption. As Duncan McKinlay, a former Republican congressman from California, recounted in his 1912 book on the project, "The old timers on the Isthmus will tell the inquirer that of the enormous sum of money raised by the French Canal Company, one-third was wasted, one-third was grafted and one third probably used in actual work."[11] In fact, by the late 1880s, De Lesseps had completed barely a third of the canal but had blown through the project's entire proposed budget.

In 1889, with funding dried up, work ground to a halt, and the Panama Canal Company collapsed into bankruptcy. The expression *quel Panama*—meaning "what a hopeless morass"—soon entered the French lexicon.[12] Shock at the company's downfall turned to rage, as the depth of the scandal slowly came to light. To hide the project's deteriorating financial condition from the public, it turned out, the Panama Canal Company had liberally doled out bribes to French parliamentarians, who in 1888 authorized the outfit to issue an additional 600 million francs of bonds.[13] A French government inquiry commenced, and Ferdinand de Lesseps and his son Charles, who was also connected to the project, stood trial for corruption. Both were sentenced to five years in prison. (His health failing, the elderly engineer avoided serving prison time; his son spent a year behind bars.)

The scandal's ramifications extended beyond squandered millions, ruined investors, and jailed executives and bureaucrats. Three of the men implicated in bribing French politicians were Jewish, and the controversy rapidly took on an antisemitic flavor, with polemicists such as Edouard Drumont warning darkly of the unscrupulous Jewish influences secretly controlling French institutions and fortunes.[14] The flare-up paved the way for another controversy in 1894, when Alfred Dreyfus, a young Jewish artillery officer in the French Army, was convicted of treason for supposedly passing military secrets to the German embassy in Paris. Dreyfus was ultimately exonerated, but the twelve-year struggle for his freedom divided France and became a damaging flashpoint, fueling anti-Jewish sentiments despite his innocence.

Jesse arrived home in New York in the fall of 1892, having failed to make headway on international bimetallism with America's European allies, whom he found only too happy to continue foisting their surplus silver on the U.S. Treasury. During his stay in Europe, the canal scandal was roiling France, and he returned to find articles about the failed project filling the pages of America's newspapers as well—and to discover an old and dear friend, Jay Gould, in declining health.

Gould and Seligman lived a block from each other, and Jesse was a regular guest at the tycoon's Fifth Avenue mansion. Gould was Wall Street's most infamous buccaneer, the most reviled robber baron of the Gilded Age. But his public image contrasted sharply with his private life, in which he was a devoted family man who lovingly tended to a greenhouse full of rare plants and flowers. Few knew him well, but Jesse was among those who had penetrated the mogul's enigmatic exterior.[15]

A few years earlier Gould and Seligman had found themselves on opposite sides of a bitter business dispute from which few friendships would have recovered. The Seligmans held a large stake in the St. Louis–San Francisco Railway, which was constructing a line linking Waldron, Arkansas, to Little Rock, on the southern side of the Arkansas River. Gould, who owned a line running along the river's northern bank, fiercely opposed the Frisco's expansion. Gould's business skirmish with the Seligman-backed line escalated into actual warfare. Gould deployed gangs of armed men who sabotaged the Frisco's tracks and ambushed its workmen. "The Seligmans naturally retaliated and fought fire with fire, and for a time, seldom a day passed that one or more men was not killed," Linton Wells wrote in "The House of Seligman." The bloodshed lasted weeks, until a truce was brokered.[16]

Gould and Seligman's friendship evidently survived the clash. When Gould, suffering secretly with tuberculosis, died in early December 1892, Seligman was spotted weeping at his wake. A couple of weeks later Jesse told a reporter that Gould was "the most misunderstood, most important, and most complex entrepreneur of this century." Despite Gould's famous transgressions, Jesse mused, he had gotten a bad rap. "I can't say that Mr. Gould was, in his moral nature, much better, much worse, or much different than any other shrewd or sharp player of his generation," he said. "I've known them all. I've known Jay Gould better than most. And I can tell you he deserves no more notoriety than those against which, and with which, he played." After all, Jesse wondered, what separated Gould from other hard-charging business titans, such as Cornelius Vanderbilt and John D. Rockefeller? What separated him, for that matter, from Jesse Seligman?[17]

Jesse soon got a small taste of the controversy that Gould courted throughout his business career. In late December 1892, Joseph Pulitzer's *New York World* reported that "there is an American end to the Panama scandal," alleging that more than $2 million in unexplained funds had flowed through the American committee, overseen by the Seligman syndicate, and charging that bribes had been paid to members of Congress to pacify objections to the canal project.[18] The next month the House of Representatives launched a select committee to investigate the Panama scandal. In February 1893, Jesse was among the first witnesses summoned to testify.

Pressed repeatedly about the American committee's opaque role in advancing the canal project, Jesse replied vaguely that its purpose had been "for protecting the interests and neutrality of the company" and for "the harmonizing of controversies and removing the objections to the enterprise."[19]

Jesse was also questioned about his job offer to Ulysses Grant, who one lawmaker pointed out was "neither a great financier nor a great statesman."

"General Grant was a bosom friend of mine," Jesse responded unapologetically, "and I always look out for my friends."[20] Indeed, the ex-president, who had died of cancer in 1885, might have spent his final days in poverty if not for his bosom friend. After leaving office, Grant had gone into business with a suave, smooth-talking financier named Ferdinand Ward, who turned out to be a con man. The swindler's Ponzi scheme unraveled spectacularly in 1884, swallowing Grant's modest fortune. Jesse had provided the ex-president—yet again taken advantage of by someone close to him—and his family with financial assistance as Grant completed his memoirs, which were published to widespread acclaim shortly after his death, and their sales replenished the ex-president's depleted estate.[21]

Other than some uncomfortable hours in a congressional hearing room, little came of the select committee probe. Allegations of bribery by the American committee were never proven, and Seligman denied any impropriety, though a general whiff of it clung around the whole affair.

The scandal might have continued to generate uncomfortable attention for Jesse had the economic world not been beset by yet another panic. The cause was, in part, the unresolved currency question involving silver.

In 1890, to appease the backers of "free silver"—the unlimited coinage of the precious metal—Congress passed legislation requiring the government to purchase 4.5 million ounces of silver per month, payable in new Treasury notes redeemable in either gold or silver. European investors, concerned by the uncertain currency situation in the United States, sold American securities, causing gold exports to increase. Meanwhile Americans converted silver to gold, the more stable commodity. Gradually, the nation's gold reserve dwindled, until in April 1893 it fell below $100 million, the minimum threshold required by congressional mandate to meet the government's obligations. Weeks later the stock market plummeted. In the depression that followed, hundreds of banks and thousands of businesses went under, among them numerous railroads, including the once mighty Union Pacific.

The crisis struck as Jesse was reeling from a more personal blow.

On April 13, 1893, he arrived at the Union League Club, a sprawling Queen Anne–style building that occupied the northeastern corner of Fifth Avenue and 39th Street, for what was to be a momentous occasion. The club was voting on the applications of new members, including Jesse's eldest son Theodore, a well-liked young attorney whom a friend of Jesse's described as a "second edition of the father." Given his pedigree, Theodore was viewed as highly "clubable." The club had been founded in 1863, during the height of the Civil War, by well-heeled Republicans as a patriotic organization to support the Union and the policies of Abraham Lincoln. Its criteria for membership, along with Republican Party affiliation, included "absolute and unqualified loyalty to the Government of the United States." Jesse and his late brother Joseph were early and faithful members, and Jesse had served for fourteen years as a vice-president of the club. Just up the block from his mansion, the elegant clubhouse, with its

Pompeian library and oak-paneled dining room, was like a second home.

Naturally, he wanted to pass the torch to his son; this was how it worked among the elite, who sought to bequeath to their children not only a financial legacy but a social one. Jesse lobbied for his son's admission, getting all the club's officers on board. When Theodore's name came to a vote, a parade of high-profile members, including future secretary of state Elihu Root; William Strong, who the following year was elected New York's mayor; and banker Cornelius Bliss gave speeches in favor of his admission. But when the votes were cast, Theodore was rejected as his dumbfounded father looked on.

Jesse, trembling, got to his feet. He had tears in his eyes and his voice quavered as he asked his fellow members to accept his resignation. "What is good enough for the father is good enough for the son."[22] There was no anger in his voice, just defeat.

Cries of "Shame!" rose from Jesse's supporters in the crowd. But the club's members had spoken. The reason for Theodore's rejection soon became clear. His opponents weren't even particularly coy about their rationale. He was a Jew. And though in addition to Jesse the club had one other Jewish member, former New York congressman Edwin Einstein, the group's newer members were not inclined to admit more. (Einstein, who took Theodore's rejection personally, also resigned.)

"I think that a majority of the men who frequent the club habitually are opposed to the admission of Hebrews," a club member told *The New York Times*. "Their opposition is not based upon any dislike of particular individuals, but upon the general belief that men of the Jewish race and religion do not readily affiliate in a social way with persons not of their own persuasion."[23]

Like Joseph's banishment from the Grand Union Hotel more than a decade earlier, Theodore Seligman's blackballing received front-page treatment. A reporter visited J. & W. Seligman & Co.'s offices the next day, where Jesse was reticent to discuss the previous evening's events. "It is a private club matter," he said. Though when pressed he admitted his son had been a victim of "unfortunate religious prejudice."

James, sitting nearby, was all too happy to comment. "You may tell them that this won't do the Republican party any good," he remarked, while Jesse shook his head, hoping that his older brother would stop talking. But he went on. "What has religion to do with a club? One would think that we did not live in a free country. In fact,

I don't believe this is a free country when such prejudice can prevail, and against the son of a man who has done the party such service as Mr. Seligman has. You will find that this will hurt the Republican party."[24] Indeed, the local Republican Party was so concerned Theodore's rejection might diminish the GOP's support among Jews that it voted to censure the Union League Club and to repudiate any other organization that engaged in discrimination.[25]

But it was Jesse who seemed to suffer most. Friends noticed that in the wake of this episode, he grew progressively frailer and weaker. "That weight . . . never seemed to be lifted from his heart," remembered Noah Davis, who was beside Jesse during the Union League vote and who witnessed his friend's "paternal agony."[26]

In April 1894, almost a year to the day after the Union League vote, Jesse, his wife Henriette, and their daughter Emma boarded a private railcar and embarked on a cross-country trip, rumbling along stretches of track that Jesse and his brothers had helped to finance. Where once the trip to California had taken months, now it took days. Jesse was suffering from kidney disease, and his family thought spending some time in a warmer climate might do him some good. But his condition worsened on the trip. Along the way he contracted pneumonia, and by the time the family reached the Hotel del Coronado, a beachfront resort overlooking San Diego Bay, Jesse was in grave condition. At around nine a.m. on Sunday, April 23, he died. The next day the offices of J. & W. Seligman & Co. closed to mourn another fallen leader.[27]

The railroad titan Collis Huntington gave the Seligmans use of a three-car train to carry Jesse's body back to New York. James met the train in Albany and continued with Jesse's family to Grand Central Station, where the board of trustees of the Hebrew Orphan Asylum stood waiting to console the mourners.

A few days later, on the morning of Jesse's funeral, a sixty-man contingent from the Union League Club marched in formation up Fifth Avenue from their clubhouse to Temple Emanu-El to pay their respects.[28]

Within the temple, a chorus composed of 150 children from the Hebrew Orphan Asylum sang a mournful hymn. Emanuel Lehman, an old friend of Jesse's who lived a few doors down from him on East 46th Street, was one of the pallbearers. Lehman and Seligman had worked closely together on charitable projects and shared a passion for the Hebrew Orphan Asylum, where the pair arrived for board meetings "linked together as if they were a bridal couple of cheering benevolence and humanity," the asylum's superintendent Herman Baar recalled.

"To me, who have known him so many years, the loss seems irreparable," Lehman said of his friend's death. He would go on to succeed Jesse as president of the asylum.

Jacob Schiff, Seligman's other philanthropic brother-in-arms, could not attend Jesse's funeral. He received word of Jesse's death in Frankfurt and cabled his regrets, calling Jesse "the most worthy Hebrew American of this generation."[29]

After the services, the funeral cortege proceeded to the ferry depot at 23rd Street, where it took three boats to convey the mourners across the East River, on the way to the Seligman family mausoleum at Salem Fields. The surviving brothers—Abraham had died in Frankfurt in 1885—lived into their eighties and nineties. Isaac, the last of them, would survive to ninety-three and die the year before the 1929 crash. But Jesse's death closed a chapter in the story of the Seligmans; with him departed some of J. & W. Seligman & Co.'s considerable prestige, and as it lost ground, Schiff's Kuhn Loeb surpassed it in international banking circles.

Leadership of the firm fell to the second generation, who "did not take the fullest opportunity that their fathers had bequeathed," according to Joseph's grandson, George Hellman. The sons of James, Jesse, and Joseph had grown up comfortably rich and lacked the drive of their fathers. They were already living the American success story, so why bother writing a new one?

The Seligman cousins were generally happy to cede the "lion's share of financial work," Hellman said, to the Strauss brothers, Albert and Frederick, who were the first nonfamily members to be made partners of the firm. "The Seligmans themselves took considerable leisure for travel and sports and their cultural tastes."[30]

After Jesse's death, Joseph's son Isaac Newton (Ike) effectively took over management of the family firm. (Ike's oldest brother, David, also a partner in the business, had died suddenly in 1897, at the age of forty-seven, following an appendectomy. The youngest of Joseph's sons, Alfred Lincoln, also died young, when a collision catapulted him from his car headfirst into a curb.)[31] In 1883, Ike had married Solomon Loeb's beautiful but emotionally fragile daughter Guta, making him Jacob Schiff's brother-in-law and strengthening the Seligmans' ties with Kuhn Loeb. Trim and handsome, with a distinctive bushy beard he wore parted on his chin, Ike was athletic, civic-minded, and, like his late father, a good governance crusader and Ethical Culture Society member. He rowed crew at Columbia and served on numerous committees and charitable boards, championing causes ranging from the regulation of child labor to the decriminalization of prostitution. Charming and well liked, Ike also had a reputation for cheating at golf, slyly kicking an errant ball out of the rough and shaving off a stroke here and there. However, his golf partners found his subterfuge tolerable, if not endearing, because he was not selfish about it. George Hellman recounted: "If the ball of his adversary—especially if it was a woman's—had a bad lie, he would examine it with the query: 'Is this yours or mine?' Then, after stating that it wasn't his, he would replace it in a position which made possible a good shot for his opponent."[32]

Jesse's son Henry, a horse-racing enthusiast, and James's son Jefferson were also senior partners in the firm. Jeff inherited his father's seat at the New York Stock Exchange. He was a man of eccentric habits who routinely handed out fruit and ginger to the partners and employees of J. & W. Seligman & Co., on the belief these foods would boost their mental acuity. He espoused the theory that kissing was more hygienic than shaking hands and lived in an Upper East Side hotel suite, where his closets were crammed with women's dresses, which he distributed to his retinue of mistresses.[33]

Quirkiness was a defining trait among most of James's offspring. James's granddaughter Peggy Guggenheim wrote that her Seligman aunts and uncles "were peculiar, if not mad," with the exception of DeWitt, the unpublished playwright, whom she deemed "nearly normal." Her uncle Washington, she wrote, "lived on charcoal"—which he ate to settle his stomach—"and as a result his teeth were black. In a zinc-lined pocket he carried cracked ice which he sucked all the time. He drank whiskey before breakfast and ate almost no food. He gambled heavily, as did most of my aunts and uncles, and when he was without funds he threatened to commit suicide to get more money out of my grandfather."[34]

These were more than mere threats. In 1887 his family forced Washington to break off a relationship with a young woman who was likely a prostitute—a newspaper described her as hailing from a provincial town and noted euphemistically that "her rustic bloom had not yet been worn away by the somewhat dissipated life she had followed since her arrival in the city."[35] Washington shot himself with a Smith & Wesson revolver in a St. Augustine, Florida, hotel room.

He survived, but years later he made a second attempt. He was discovered in another hotel with a deep self-inflicted gash to his throat. Once again he lived, telling a police officer, "I have been suffering from a nervous ailment for the past twenty years and only a few days ago I noticed that it was getting much worse and I was afraid to face it. Besides I have been having a whole lot of trouble on Wall Street lately, and so I determined to end it all."[36] In 1912, Washington once more attempted suicide, and this time he succeeded. He shot himself in the head in his apartment at New York's Hotel Gerard, leaving a one-line note scrawled on an envelope: "I'm tired of being sick all my life."[37]

Mental illness afflicted other branches of the Seligman family. A few years after Washington's suicide, the media would report news of another dramatic Seligman death, when Jesse's grandson and namesake, Jesse L. Seligman, shot his wife and then himself while their three-year-old daughter was in a nearby room. "This is the only way," he scrawled in his cryptic suicide note.[38] Decades later Joseph L. Seligman, Ike's son, named for his grandfather, also took his own life.[39]

Joseph, and later Jesse, had held the family partnership together through years of bickering and acrimony, but Ike, after his uncle's death, sought to dismantle it. He was often at odds with the family members running the European branches of the business, as his father had been. William was "too greedy," he thought, and Henry "too cautious." Uncle Isaac, meanwhile, he labeled "the London Shylock."[40]

Bad investments in Frankfurt and Paris threatened the capital of the New York firm, and Ike saw his uncles as out of step with the times. Their generation had financed the construction of the railroads and bankrolled utilities and large industrial concerns. His generation specialized in reorganizing these debt-laden enterprises, forging mergers, and consolidating industries through vast combinations—what was popularly known as Morganization, in a nod to the monopoly-building technique that Pierpont Morgan perfected to an art form. Meanwhile the balance of banking power was beginning to shift to the United States.

Ike and his New York–based cousins had designs on a reorganization of their own, and in the spring of 1897, he sailed to Europe for a series of contentious meetings with his uncles on dissolving the "family arrangement." On July 1, 1897, the Seligmans—and the executors for their departed brothers—signed an agreement unwinding their long-standing partnership. The capital to be divided among them came to $7,831,175.64, more than half of it tied up in a maze of investments. The task of liquidating this tangle of assets—a process that lasted five years—was assigned to DeWitt Seligman, James's "nearly normal" son. The Seligmans didn't cut their business ties entirely, however. After more than a half century, how could they bear to? The European firms invested in J. & W. Seligman & Co., and the New York firm likewise took stakes in its European affiliates. But the age of the "American Rothschilds" was over.[41]

On June 21, 1897, as Ike and his uncles dickered over the final details of disentangling their respective firms, another half-century-old partnership, that of two inseparable brothers from Rimpar, came to a different sort of end with the sudden death of Mayer Lehman, following an operation for gangrene. On the morning of his funeral later that week, the Cotton Exchange closed in tribute. Once again, the pews of Temple Emanu-El, where Mayer had been a longtime board member, filled with mourners. And then he too went to Salem Fields, his casket carried by Jacob Schiff and other family friends.[42]

When Mayer died, Lehman Brothers' ledger showed the firm's worth at about $8 million, up from a little over $2 million in 1879. Lehman partner Frank Manheim, in his corporate history of the firm, noted that the company's steady growth was admirable but by no means noteworthy by the high-flying standards of the times. "In the context of that epoch of fabulous fortune-making that was not in any sense a spectacular achievement. Hundreds of the Lehmans' Wall Street neighbors and colleagues had made a lot more, made it faster and made it more showily."[43] Still others had lost fortunes with just as much spectacle. The Lehmans weathered successive financial panics because they were generally conservative and highly discerning of their business partners. "We used to say that the firm had to know your grandfather before it condescended to take your business," remembered Alice Brenner, Mayer and Emanuel's senior secretary.[44]

The Lehmans largely ignored the railroad mania that had both enriched and eviscerated their Wall Street colleagues; what little in the way of railroad interests they held were mostly concentrated in the South. But they did participate in the consolidation craze of the late nineteenth century. The brothers aided in the organization of the Cottonseed Oil Trust, as it was known, when dozens of companies—including one the Lehmans held a large stake in—were combined into the American Cotton Oil Co. The Lehmans also joined the so-called Cotton Duck Trust, merging a 76,000-spindle cotton mill they owned in Alabama into a textile conglomerate that controlled 85 percent of the market for cotton duck (a heavy woven fabric).[45]

Commodities remained the crux of their business, but the Lehmans also dabbled in a range of other industries, from mining and manufacturing to real estate and insurance. The brothers helped to found or direct a series of New York City banks, and Emanuel invested in utility companies, becoming a director of the East River Gas Company and vice-president of Consolidated Gas of New Jersey. The brothers additionally held large interests in ferry lines.

In 1892, Lehman Brothers moved to more spacious premises at 16 William Street, where the firm had its own floor. The partners occupied offices that opened into a large room, where around fourteen employees buzzed throughout the day. The office had a single phone, which connected the firm via private wires to commodities trading hubs including Chicago and New Orleans. Alice Brenner remembered an intimate environment in which the firm's staff were often invited to family occasions, and "we felt ourselves part of the Lehman clan."[46]

Various financial eminences routinely passed through the office to confer with the brothers, including Julius Rosenwald, co-owner of Sears Roebuck. And Southern politicians occasionally stopped in to see the Lehmans, who, unlike many of their Wall Street colleagues, remained die-hard Democrats, owing to their Alabama roots.[47]

Mayer's children grew up hearing their father complain bitterly about the election of 1876, when New York's Democratic governor Samuel Tilden had lost to Rutherford B. Hayes in one of the most contentious elections in American history—the second time since the nation's founding in which the losing candidate won the popular vote. The Republicans, Mayer insisted, had stolen the presidency. In the 1884 election, the Lehmans backed Grover Cleveland, another New York governor, who after winning the White House went on to appoint Mayer's old Confederate friend Colonel Hilary Herbert as his secretary of the navy.[48]

In the final presidential election of his lifetime, Mayer faced a difficult choice. With the U.S. economy still wallowing in the depression it had entered after the Panic of 1893, the race effectively became a referendum on silver. Like his fellow bankers, Mayer was a "sound money" man. Yet his cherished Democratic Party had chosen as its standard-bearer the populist firebrand William Jennings Bryan, one of the nation's most outspoken proponents of "free silver," who had built his political career on bashing the Wall Street elite. The two-term congressman from Nebraska went into the Democratic Party's convention a dark horse candidate. He emerged its nominee based largely on a masterful speech on the currency question that he delivered during the party's platform debate.

"You come to us and tell us that the great cities are in favor of the gold standard; we reply that the great cities rest upon our broad and fertile prairies," he bellowed. "Burn down your cities and leave our farms, and your cities will spring up again as if by magic; but destroy our farms and the grass will grow in the streets of every city in the country." Some delegates stood on chairs, while others stamped their feet as Bryan expertly whipped the audience into a frenzy. "You shall not press down upon the brow of labor this crown of thorns. You shall not crucify mankind upon a cross of gold," he concluded.[49]

The prospect of a Bryan presidency terrified Wall Street; Mayer and his financial world friends were convinced that the inflationary monetary policies Bryan espoused would be catastrophic. So Mayer held his nose and voted for the Republican nominee, William McKinley. A few months into McKinley's presidency, in 1897, Mayer died, so he did not see the Republican president finally lay to rest the silver question: in 1900 McKinley signed legislation formally placing the United States on the gold standard.

The year Mayer died, Emanuel celebrated his seventieth birthday, commemorating the occasion with the establishment of a $100,000 trust fund to aid graduates of the Hebrew Orphan Asylum. Over the next couple of years, he gradually withdrew from the firm to focus on philanthropic work, turning its day-to-day operations over to a new generation of Lehman partners.

Meyer H. Lehman, the youngest son of Mayer and Emanuel's late brother Henry, went to work for the family business in 1870, and by 1880 he was named a junior partner. Like his uncle Mayer, he was a cotton expert who was a frequent presence at the cotton exchange. A couple of years later, in 1882, Mayer's eldest son, Sigmund, made partner, and in 1887 the firm purchased a seat on the New York Stock Exchange in his name.[50] After graduating from Harvard in 1894, another of Mayer's sons, Arthur, joined Lehman Brothers.

Mayer intended for only his two eldest sons to work for the firm; he had other plans for the two youngest, Irving and Herbert. Since boyhood, Irving had dazzled his parents and teachers with his intellect. He was studious and reserved, and he took an interest in Jewish history and scholarship.[51] Groomed for a career in law, he ascended to the top of his profession. He was elected the youngest-ever justice of the New York Supreme Court and rose to become the chief justice of the state's appeals court.

Herbert's path seemed more uncertain, and no one figured his trajectory would lead to the New York governor's mansion and then the U.S. Senate. As a child, he had been so nervous that his worried parents, at one point, pulled him out of school for a year.[52] Herbert's friend and Sachs' Collegiate classmate, Paul Sachs, remembered Lehman as a "very serious boy who always had ink on his fingers."[53]

For reasons that were never clear to Herbert, Mayer thought his youngest son, always a mediocre student, should become an engineer. Fortunately, Herbert's favorite teacher at Sachs' Collegiate, Frank Erwin, dissuaded Mayer from sending his son to engineering school. "He told my father that he was spoiling what might be a reasonably good businessman and instead would make a very poor engineer," Herbert recalled.[54] Erwin recommended Williams College, the liberal arts school in northwestern Massachusetts that he had attended; Mayer took the teacher's advice.[55]

Shortly after Herbert enrolled at Williams, Mayer sent him a brief letter containing a few lines of fatherly counsel. "Only one thing I urge you to do," Mayer wrote, "use your time advantageously, the few years pass quickly and don't come back. Don't do anything of which you have to be ashamed. Should you however with or without your fault get into trouble call on me as your best intimate friend and don't hide anything from me."[56] After Williams, where Herbert earned largely Bs and Cs, he joined J. Spencer Turner & Co., a New York commission house that did business with Lehman Brothers; he spent almost ten years there before joining the family company in 1908.[57]

Emanuel, whose wife Pauline died at the age of twenty-eight, had two sons. Little is known of his elder son, Milton, who attended Columbia and received a Ph.D. from the University of Heidelberg. In Columbia's alumni directory, he listed his address at Lehman Brothers' offices, though there is no sign he ever attained a partnership. There are hints, however, that Milton suffered from some type of debilitating physical or mental illness. In a letter to his children outlining his final wishes, written six months after Mayer's passing, Emanuel noted that he had created a $100,000 trust fund to support his son. "Unfortunately," he wrote, "my son Milton will never be well again."[58]

Emanuel's younger son, Philip, joined the partnership in 1885, and his initial responsibilities largely centered on representing the firm at the New York Coffee Exchange.[59] Philip was intelligent, regal, and fiercely competitive. He exuded a patrician quality, and one colleague remembered that he would not allow so much as the word *hell* to be uttered around the office and was scandalized when one of his partners displayed a copy of *Esquire*.[60]

At thirty-six, Philip became the firm's unofficial leader after his uncle's death. Steeped in Wall Street from childhood, he was more "banking minded" than his father and uncle, wrote Frank Manheim, nudging Emanuel into investment banking syndicates. Philip was enthralled by technology, especially the new "horseless carriages" that were starting to appear on American roads. His father was one of the first New Yorkers to own one of these early automobiles, in which Emanuel regularly rode home after work, though not without a bit of embarrassment at this showy contraption that elicited stares from passersby. In 1897, Philip and Sigmund helped to launch one of the nation's first automobile companies, the Electric Vehicle Company. The cousins also made a related bet on an Ohio-based business called the Rubber Tire Wheel Company, which manufactured the pneumatic tire used by 90 percent of vehicles on the road at the time.[61]

The Electric Vehicle Company had grand plans of establishing electric taxicab monopolies in America's biggest cities, and it held a broad patent that also covered gasoline-powered vehicles, enabling it to extract lucrative royalties from other fledgling automakers. But the taxicab fleets never materialized, and the company's aggressive defense of its patent led it into a protracted legal confrontation with a young, upstart automaker named Henry Ford. The Detroit industrialist ultimately prevailed, and the Electric Vehicle Company became a footnote in America's automotive history, declaring bankruptcy in 1907.

The public was both beguiled by and wary of the first automobiles; due to the initial lack of traffic regulations or licensing requirements for drivers, they were viewed by some as a menace to public safety. Citizens and city officials alike raised concerns that "horseless carriages" might spook the real horses that pulled the carriages and trolleys on which many New Yorkers traveled.

Bankers, among the few people wealthy enough to own automobiles, were often getting embroiled in vehicle-related controversies. Jeff Seligman, who sold his horses and purchased a stable of three electric vehicles, publicly sparred with New York's parks commissioner after he was prohibited from driving his brougham through Central Park, accusing the official of trying to "halt the march of progress." And in 1902 his chauffeur was arrested for driving over the recently established speed limit—twelve miles per hour.[62]

Philip Lehman was later involved in a more serious automobile-related episode. On New Year's Day in 1906, he was driving on Fifth Avenue when a man darted into the street in front of him in pursuit of his hat. Lehman swerved but could not avoid the pedestrian, a fifty-five-year-old eyeglass merchant named Orlando Peck. The impact hurled Peck twenty feet, and Lehman's car skidded to a halt on top of him. Police pulled Peck's body from beneath the car and carried him into a nearby hotel, where Lehman, in a state of panic, exhorted the unconscious man to speak. A crowd gathered "denouncing and threatening Lehman," the *New York Sun* reported, while the banker tried to explain that the collision was not his fault. A police officer on the scene arrested Philip, who was charged with criminal negligence. A week later Peck died of his injuries. An inquest subsequently deemed Peck's death accidental and cleared Lehman of charges.[63]

After taking the helm of Lehman Brothers and becoming, as Mayer had been, the firm's suave front man, Philip commissioned a new home for his family at 7 West 54th Street. In 1885 he had married the daughter of a prominent merchant banker with roots in Cincinnati, and the couple had two children, Pauline (after Philip's late mother) and Robert. Philip hired the architect who had designed Grant's Tomb to construct his five-story limestone townhouse, which featured three copper-trimmed oculi that looked out from its mansard roof. The ornate, Beaux Arts–style mansion fit the ambitions of no mere millionaire—the neighborhood was full of them—but a mogul. The address was notable, too. It placed Lehman directly across the street from America's richest man, John D. Rockefeller, who presided over the colossal Standard Oil monopoly.

Other scions were content to coast off their fathers' fortunes, but Philip was determined to make his mark. With his cousins, he led Lehman Brothers into a new phase that marked the firm's transition from a commission house that also did some investment banking into an investment bank that also traded commodities. Unlike their friends the Seligmans, whose banking heyday had passed, the Lehmans' best days were still ahead.

PART III

GOLDEN AGE

12

MERGERS AND ACQUISITIONS

O ne of the most consequential deals in Kuhn Loeb's history was consummated on March 19, 1895. The merger occurred not in the boardroom but at the altar, where nineteen-year-old Frieda Schiff married twenty-four-year-old Felix Moritz Warburg, the rakish fourth-born son of a Hamburg banking dynasty.

The Warburgs were old acquaintances of Jacob Schiff. After the unraveling of Budge, Schiff & Co. in 1873, Felix's father, Moritz, had hired the young banker to manage the Hamburg branch of the London & Hanseatic Bank, an institution that Moritz's firm, M.M. Warburg & Co., had recently helped to found. During Schiff's short stay in Hamburg, he visited Moritz, his wife Charlotte, and their family at their lively home at Mittelweg 17, where music and poetry always seemed to echo through the halls. Felix, born in January 1871, would have been a little over two at the time, toddling among a gaggle of siblings. Schiff presented the Warburg children with a toy fort.[1]

In Hamburg, Moritz and Charlotte were jestingly referred to as *"das Paar das nicht sitzen kann"* (the couple that can't sit), because Moritz preferred to recline and Charlotte had the habit of sitting ramrod straight on the edge of her chair. She was as determined as he was easygoing. As a hobby, she wrote poetry and prose, sometimes publishing short articles in German newspapers. Good humored and a bit vain, Moritz masked his baldness using one of three toupees, each a different length. Once, after one of his grandsons walked in on him without his customary hairpiece, Moritz divulged the mysteries of his wigs: "This one I wear when I need a haircut. This one I wear when I've had a haircut. And this one is for in-between."[2]

By the time of Felix and Frieda's marriage, M.M. Warburg & Co. had been in business for nearly a century. It was a venerable bank, situated in a bustling port city, though lacking the lofty international reputation enjoyed by Kuhn Loeb or the Rothschilds, with whom the Warburgs did business. M.M. Warburg considered its relationship with the Rothschilds so important that it maintained a separate supply of stationery for exclusive use when corresponding with them and their representatives.[3] Conservative and steadily profitable, the Warburg bank did an energetic business brokering exchange bills, and it had cautiously branched out into more adventurous forms of finance, participating modestly in sovereign loans and share offerings of railroads and commercial banks.

Brothers Moses and Gerson Warburg, who had taken over their father's money-changing business, founded M.M. Warburg in 1798. But the family's roots in finance stretched back to at least the sixteenth century, when Simon von Cassel, from whom the clan was descended, settled in the Westphalian city of Warburg. Prohibited from taking surnames, Jews were often known by the towns where they were allowed residence. Simon from Cassel, after obtaining a protection agreement permitting him to live in Warburg, became Simon from Warburg. The town register described Simon as a "money changer, pawnbroker, and lender of funds against grain." In 1773, Simon Warburg's descendants settled in Hamburg, a city with a more enlightened attitude toward Jews, where people of their faith were not penned in by ghettos and enjoyed freedoms unavailable to their brethren in other German states.[4]

M.M. Warburg's founding brothers made the disputatious Seligmans seem almost harmonious by comparison. Moses, sober and strait-laced, and Gerson, irreverent and carefree, quarreled constantly. According to one family story, the brothers, who held back-to-back seats at the Hamburg Bourse, once stopped speaking for nearly a year. According to another, in 1812, when Napoleon's armies occupied Hamburg and took some of the city's wealthiest men hostage, including Gerson, Moses initially balked at paying the ransom for his brother's release. When Gerson was ultimately freed, Moses seemed mildly disappointed. "Why don't they keep him for good!" he was said to have exclaimed.[5]

A generation later, a different pair of feuding Warburg brothers controlled the bank: Siegmund and Moritz, the grandsons of Moses, who died in 1831. Without a male heir, Moses had married off his only daughter, Sara, to her second cousin Abraham (Aby) S. Warburg, who was neither attractive nor particularly ambitious. His main asset appeared to be that he was a Warburg. Though her husband technically ran the bank, Sara, formal and intimidating, was the hidden hand behind it. Each evening Aby gingerly handed over the bank's ledger for his wife to review. This ritual continued when Sara's sons ran the bank, following their father's death in 1856, with the brothers presenting themselves to their mother after the close of the bourse for her daily audit. Like Moses and Gerson, Siegmund and Moritz had divergent personalities. Siegmund, who was older, was hard-charging and high-tempered, with a gruff, world-weary mien. Moritz, who stood out among his homely siblings for his handsome features, had the charm his brother lacked though half the drive. The bank's small oil-lamp-lit offices, which featured a large green couch where Moritz sometimes napped, often reverberated with the din of the brothers' ear-ringing shouting matches.[6]

And then, suddenly, there was no one to argue with.

In May 1889, Siegmund died of a heart attack. Their mother had passed five years earlier. This left Moritz to helm M.M. Warburg alone as it neared the first centennial of its existence. Fortunately for Moritz, a competent banker but not an enterprising one, he didn't face the same problem as his grandfather: he had sons to spare.

Moritz and Charlotte, a strong matriarch in the mold of her mother-in-law, raised seven children. The Warburg siblings—Aby, Max, Paul, Felix, Olga, and fraternal twins Louise and Fritz—formed a close-knit confederacy. When apart, they looked up at the seven stars of the Big Dipper, a constellation the Warburgs imbued with special significance and through which they believed they could cosmically commune with one another.[7]

In banking clans, the eldest son traditionally received a partnership in the family firm in preparation for one day taking leadership of the company. Banking held no interest for Aby, the eldest Warburg son, who possessed a towering intellect and a tempestuous streak; his genius was of that frenetic type that disposed itself to madness. As a teenager, Aby struck a deal with his younger brother Max, the second eldest of the Warburg sons and an impulsive, swashbuckling type. "When I was twelve years old Aby put to me that I should buy from him his birthright, not indeed for a mess of pottage but against my pledge that I would always pay for his book purchases," Max recalled. "I was a child, but the bargain seemed to me splendid."[8]

Freed of his primogenitary duty, Aby became a pioneering art and cultural historian, his career interrupted by bouts of psychosis and stays in psychiatric wards. Max, who initially thought he got the better end of the deal, upheld his part of their bargain even as his brother voraciously assembled a sprawling library that spanned some sixty thousand volumes, now housed at the Warburg Institute in London.

Paul, the third of Moritz's five sons, also became a partner in the firm. He was a banking prodigy, who like his brothers wore a bushy, drooping mustache, and who betrayed a hint of melancholy even—or perhaps especially—when he smiled. Paul was introspective and reserved, but like his brothers he also had something of a puckish streak. Printed in Hebrew on one of his calling cards was the German phrase *Leck mich im arsch*—"Kiss my ass."[9]

Before taking their places at the family bank, Max and later Paul cycled through banking apprenticeships in Europe's major financial centers. Moritz dispatched Max to Frankfurt, Amsterdam, Paris, and London, where he completed his training in 1890 at N.M. Rothschild. During this period, Max also performed a stint in the Third Bavarian Light Cavalry, briefly considering a career as a military officer.[10] (When Max floated this plan to his father, Moritz replied that he was "*meschugge*"—crazy—and his military dreams appear to have died there.)[11]

Paul, meanwhile, apprenticed at Samuel Montagu & Co. in London and at the Paris branch of the Banque Russe pour le Commerce Étranger, part of the banking operation of a wealthy Russian clan and one of the rare Jewish families ennobled by the empire's ruling family, the Romanovs. Both brothers used their time away from Hamburg to sow their oats. When Max visited Paris later in life, he liked to joke of recognizing past lovers on the Champs-Élysées: "Ah, there is Philippina. Oh, how well I knew her!"[12] Paul, for his part, contracted gonorrhea during one of his assignations. "To hell with women who want to have sex," he wrote despondently to his brother Aby, praying that he had finally shaken the venereal disease after five months.[13]

Paul capped his banking training by taking a round-the-world trip that brought him first to Egypt, India, Japan, and China. In Macau, then a Portuguese colony, he showed traces of his future banking brilliance. In his diary, he calculated how much the Portuguese government would save annually if it relinquished the colony, tabulating the cost of the policemen, soldiers, bureaucrats, and others required to keep Macau under its control.[14]

Unlike previous generations of Warburg brothers, Max and Paul worked well together. "Their temperaments had admirably complemented each other," recalled Paul's son, James. "Max supplied the initiative and Paul the careful analysis of new projects."[15]

Moritz and his wife chose a different path for their next youngest son, Felix, nicknamed "Fizzie," both for the soda water he was always drinking and for his effervescent personality. Handsome and stylish, with a good singing voice and a love of frivolity in all its forms, Felix had many fine qualities, but Moritz didn't think he had a mind for finance. "My father was considered too stupid to be taken into the bank," Felix's son Edward once said.[16] There was no small irony in this, because Felix was destined to join the banking partnership of one of the world's foremost financiers, Jacob Schiff, forging a connection between M.M. Warburg and Kuhn Loeb that would prove more vital to his family firm's prosperity than even its early association with the Rothschilds. Schiff's son, Mortimer, recalled: "M.M. Warburg became eventually in effect the official continental European representative of Kuhn, Loeb & Co., at which they rendered most excellent service, while at the same time making large financial profits and gains in prestige for themselves."[17]

While his brothers settled into their banking careers—and Aby researched his doctoral thesis on two mythological masterpieces by Sandro Botticelli, *The Birth of Venus* and *Spring*—Felix, at sixteen, decamped to Frankfurt to live with his maternal grandparents and apprentice with his grandfather, Nathan Oppenheim, who dealt in diamonds and precious stones. Oppenheim loved art and languages (he spoke seven) and encouraged Felix to take up English, French, and Italian. "The influence that that wonderful grandfather had on me I feel every day," Felix later mused, noting that Oppenheim's "knowledge and understanding of art, be it painting, wood-carvings or other fields, laid the foundation for the little that I have acquired since."[18] His grandfather's imprint manifested in other ways too, such as in Felix's lifelong habit of sitting with his arms tightly folded across his chest. This was an unshakable vestige of his years working for Oppenheim, when Felix, traveling to visit customers with gemstones sewn into the lining of his jacket, adopted this pose as a defense against pickpockets when he dozed off on night trains.[19]

Felix had lived in Frankfurt for about six years when, in May 1894, the Schiffs arrived on one of their periodic visits. With his wife and daughter, Jacob had embarked on a whirlwind tour of Europe that had already taken them to Athens, Budapest, Constantinople, Prague, and Vienna. Frieda turned eighteen that February, and the trip was as much in honor of that milestone as it was Jacob's sly way of delaying Frieda's formal debut to New York society—signifying she was now of marriageable age.[20]

During their stay in Frankfurt, Isaac Dreyfus, Philipp Schiff's brother-in-law, held a reception in their honor. He invited Moritz and Charlotte Warburg, who happened to be visiting the city, along with Felix, who grumbled about attending. "You know they give the dullest parties in Frankfurt," he complained. At dinner, Frieda sat between Felix and another young man, whom she found "neurotic and tiresome." So she struck up a conversation with Felix. "I don't think I flirted," Frieda said later; her upbringing was so sheltered that she had no concept of the rituals of courtship. Felix, by the end of the night, had reconsidered his position on Isaac Dreyfus's soirées. Well after midnight, he rapped excitedly on his parents' bedroom door. "I have met the girl I'm going to marry," he announced.[21]

When the Schiffs attended the horse races in Frankfurt, Felix showed up, lingering by Frieda's side, while her father's blood boiled. From Frankfurt, the Schiffs went to Paris, then to London, and eventually to the Austrian spa town Bad Gastein. Desperate to see Frieda again, Felix racked his brain for a pretext to turn up there. He tried to rope Aby into an elaborate plan in which his brother would feign an illness requiring him to convalesce in Gastein. Then—oh what a coincidence—Felix would arrive a few days into Aby's stay to look after his supposedly ailing brother. Aby, however, had no interest in participating in what Felix called a "pious fraud." He bristled at his brother's American love interest—why not marry a jeweler's daughter in Frankfurt, he told Felix.[22]

Felix found another way, wrangling an invitation to join Morti Schiff and his cousin on a hiking expedition in the Alps that would culminate in Gastein. (Morti, then a sophomore at Amherst, had joined his family in London.) Felix disliked mountain climbing, but he endured the trek because ultimately it got him a few minutes alone with Frieda. As they strolled one day, Felix asked her if she could see herself living in Germany. Frieda was white-faced when she joined her mother later in the day. "I think that fellow proposed!" she stammered. Mother and daughter stayed up until three a.m. rehashing what had transpired—and weighing how to break the news to Frieda's father.[23]

Predictably, Jacob didn't take it well. On paper, the match between Frieda and Felix seemed perfect. Both were the children of well-to-do banking families, and the connection with M.M. Warburg would strengthen Kuhn Loeb's already robust network of European affiliates. Felix was raised in an Orthodox home with a strong philanthropic tradition; his father was considered a leader among Hamburg's Jewish community. Yet initially Schiff raged against the match, in part because he had played no role in orchestrating it and in part because it had occurred out of sync with his rigid timetable—twenty, he believed, was the appropriate age for his daughter's betrothal.

Schiff was an exacting man. This made him formidable in business, because he overlooked no details, in some cases personally inspecting the companies his firm underwrote down to the railroad tie. This same quality also made him a high-handed and unyielding patriarch. For Frieda, this meant spending her formative years living a cloistered, highly chaperoned existence. Schiff believed strongly, almost religiously, in guarding the virtue of the female members of his family. His granddaughter Dorothy (who went by "Dolly"), later the owner and publisher of the *New York Post*, recalled visiting her grandfather as a girl and showing off her makeup. He asked to see her compact. When she handed it over, he promptly threw it out the window.[24]

To Schiff, his daughter's blossoming relationship with Moritz Warburg's dandyish son—who had not even been deemed worthy of a partnership in the family bank!—was a crisis. Ernest Cassel, the British banker who was among Schiff's closest friends, was traveling with the family, and he took Jacob for a long walk. "I took her to Europe to get her out of the way of temptation, and this happens!" Schiff vented.

"Don't carry on so!" Cassel replied. "Two years sooner than you expected—but what do you want in a son-in-law?"[25]

Schiff began to come around. By the time Felix departed Gastein, he and Frieda were all but engaged—though Schiff would not allow him to so much as write to his daughter directly.[26] Because the news was not yet official, Moritz and Charlotte decided against sending the Schiffs their formal congratulations but instead proposed a meeting in the Belgian coastal city of Ostend, where they were vacationing.

In this letter, they also made clear they would not stand in the way of their son moving to New York—removing one possible obstacle to the marriage, since Schiff, who wanted to keep his daughter close, wouldn't countenance her living in Germany.[27]

In September 1894, the Schiffs hosted a luncheon for the Warburgs in Ostend. It got off to a tense start. The Warburgs kept kosher, so Schiff had instructed the headwaiter to serve filet of sole instead of lobster. "When we sat down, there was non-kosher *écrevisse* (crayfish) at every place," Frieda remembered. "My father was quite upset, but my father-in-law-to-be took it all in good humor."[28]

Charlotte found Jacob strict and rigid, but she was nevertheless pleased that the Schiffs were not "showy," as one might have expected of the family of one of Wall Street's preeminent financiers. They "behaved very well," she later wrote her son Aby.[29]

During the summit, the Schiffs and Warburgs reached an understanding concerning their children's courtship. Felix and Frieda's engagement was to be kept under wraps for the time being; he would sail to the United States that November to make the news official. In the interim, though, Schiff still wouldn't allow Felix to write to Frieda, as if even a letter from her suitor might corrupt her innocence. Instead, Frieda recalled, "my father would write weekly letters to him with news of me, and I would write to his mother."[30]

That fall Felix, as planned, boarded a steamer for New York. Before he departed, his father soberly pulled him aside. "I have just one request to make of you." Felix braced for a lecture about keeping kosher—something he had no intention of doing, though why tell his father that? Moritz, however, had another concern in mind: "Do not take the iced drinks that spoil Americans' digestions and force them to go to Carlsbad for annual cures."[31]

Frieda's long-planned coming-out reception turned into an engagement party, where several hundred guests toasted the young couple. In honor of their engagement, Schiff cut a $25,000 check to the Montefiore Home.[32] And to his future son-in-law, he handed the most valuable prize he had to offer, next to his daughter's hand in marriage: a Kuhn Loeb partnership. This ensured Felix could keep his daughter living in the style to which she was accustomed. Schiff also bought the couple a five-story limestone townhouse at 18 East 72nd Street, a short two-block stroll from his own home.

Frieda grew increasingly anxious during her engagement, due

both to the barrage of social events where she and Felix were paraded but also because of her cluelessness about sex—of which her father ensured she was completely in the dark. "I got to the point where I would burst into tears if anyone looked at me," Frieda wrote. Felix, meanwhile, gamely navigated his new surroundings. He had yet to master English, so had a habit of mumbling into his mustache to mask his grammatical blunders.[33] The distance from his family he no doubt felt keenly, and one imagines him looking often to the Big Dipper during his early days in New York.

On a gusty March evening, Felix and Frieda married at the Schiffs' Fifth Avenue townhouse. The ceremony was officiated by two rabbis, one from each of the temples the Schiffs attended, Emanu-El and Beth-El. At the altar, Frieda, petite and almost doll-like, practically sagged under the weight of her satin gown.[34]

Moritz and Charlotte did not make the trip to New York—Moritz was terrified of sailing long distances: "*Das Wasser hat keine Balken!*" (Water isn't very solid.)[35] Olga and Paul came over as the Warburg family's emissaries, with Olga serving as one of Frieda's bridesmaids and Paul as Felix's best man. The reception was catered by Sherry's, a popular midtown haven for New York's upper crust, and 125 guests crowded into the lower level of the Schiffs' home, where fifteen tables had been set up. The guest list, which drew heavily from Jacob's financial and philanthropic circles, featured various Goldmans, Sachses, and Seligmans, including Jesse and Ike, who with his wife Guta sat at the bridal table with the newly married couple.[36]

Flirtatious young bachelors and bachelorettes, members of the bridal party, filled the next table over. Along with Paul and Olga sat Frieda's brother Morti; Paul Kohn-Speyer, a successful London metal trader and old pal of the Warburg brothers; Nina Loeb, the maid of honor; and Addie Wolff, a close friend of Frieda's and the youngest daughter of Schiff's Kuhn Loeb partner Abraham Wolff. Also at the table was a well-dressed young banker who wore a waxed mustache and spoke with a German-inflected British accent. Born in Mannheim, Otto Hermann Kahn had recently moved to New York from London to take a job with the investment bank Speyer & Co. He rivaled Felix as a bon vivant and a blade, though in contrast to the groom, later one of his close friends, he was also a formidable financier.

Before honeymooning in Europe, Felix and Frieda stayed at the Plaza. Therese Schiff visited her daughter and son-in-law there the day before their departure. Jacob did not join her, Frieda suspected, "because he could not bring himself to . . . ask for me under my new name." Later that evening, while dining with her parents at their home, Jacob erupted when his daughter asked his opinion on some trivial matter. "Why do you ask me? You now have your husband to turn to!"[37]

When Frieda and Felix sailed for Italy the next day, Schiff sent his wife's maid, Hermine Steinmetz, to accompany them. The newlyweds spent a queasy voyage under her vigilant gaze. Felix felt as if he had been transported back into childhood, once again under the care of a governess.

During her honeymoon, innocent Frieda figured out the facts of life. In Hamburg, she felt the first stirrings of a pregnancy, their daughter Carola. She confided her suspicions to Oma Loeb, who was also visiting Hamburg: "Don't you think I'm going to have a baby?"

"Such things have happened on honeymoons before," her grandmother knowingly replied.[38]

One day in the spring of 1895, shortly after returning home from Felix and Frieda's wedding, Paul Warburg hurtled down the steps of his Hamburg office. He nearly careened into his mother, on her way up to see her husband. "I am engaged to Nina Loeb!" he exclaimed.

"And you break the news to me on the stairs?" Charlotte curtly replied.[39]

Paul and Nina first met in 1892, when he passed through New York during his globetrotting *Wanderjahr*.[40] When they met again three years later as best man and maid of honor at Felix and Frieda's wedding, the attraction between them was undeniable.

Nina, whom relatives called "Puss" or "Pussy," was the youngest of Solomon and Betty's children. Five years older than Frieda, she was technically her aunt, though their relationship was more akin to that of especially close cousins. Slim and pretty, Nina walked with a pronounced limp, the result of a broken hip caused by a childhood fall from a goat-drawn cart. "Since there were then no X-rays, the injury was improperly treated and the bone never knit," her son James remembered. "This caused her to be bedridden in traction for a year and an invalid for much of her childhood."[41] The accident shattered Nina's girlhood dream of becoming a ballet dancer, though her handicap never clouded her cheerful nature. Nor did she suffer from the nervous ailments and melancholia that afflicted her other siblings, including Guta, whose adult life was punctuated by break-downs and sanitarium stays.

When Paul and Olga returned to Germany after Felix and Frie-da's wedding, Nina accompanied them. Lovestruck, Paul proposed during the voyage. Before she could answer, she had to confer with her parents, who were vacationing in Carlsbad. In Hamburg, Paul anxiously awaited her wire, and when it finally came, he could barely contain his excitement. His mother's sharp response to his announce-ment became an inside joke within the Loeb, Schiff, and Warburg families whose members liked to deploy this line—*and you break the news to me on the stairs!*—when they received surprising news.[42]

During their visit to New York, Olga fell for Nina's brother, James, whom Frieda Schiff described as having the "most vivid, bril-liant personality" of all her Loeb aunts and uncles. "He charmed everyone, was an excellent scholar, a fine musician and an esthete in the best sense of the word."[43] James wasn't a banker, though he forced himself to be one to please his father and spent fifteen miser-able years regretting it.

In his biography of the Warburg clan, Ron Chernow wrote that "the Loebs and Warburgs reacted vehemently against a match between Jim and Olga." He posited that one reason the relationship never progressed to marriage may have been Nina, who placed her brother on a pedestal and adored him to a near-incestuous degree. James and Olga's lives would each take a dark turn in the years to follow. He experienced repeated breakdowns during his Kuhn Loeb tenure, and, in 1901, when his fragile psyche could no longer take it, he retired from the firm. Soon thereafter he moved to Germany, where he sought treatment for depression and epilepsy. He lived quietly on an estate outside Munich, surrounded by leather-bound volumes of Greek classics and antiquities, never again setting foot in New York. He channeled his fortune into philanthropy, bankroll-ing what would become New York's Juilliard School, Harvard's Loeb Classical Library (James's effort to make the great literary works of the Greeks and Romans accessible to the masses), and a world-renowned psychiatric research institute in Munich. (In a disturbing twist, the institute was turned into a eugenics research center during the reign of Adolf Hitler.)

Olga's fate was more tragic still. Though holding a flame for James, she agreed to marry her brothers' friend Paul Kohn-Speyer, a solemn, undemonstrative, and business-minded fellow who could not have been more unlike the man she fell in love with. In 1904, not long after giving birth to her fourth child, she leaped to her death from the third-floor window of a Swiss hotel.[44]

On October 1, 1895, Paul and Nina were married at Sunset Hill, Solomon and Betty Loeb's flower-bedecked country home, located on the Schiff and Loeb families' New Jersey shore estate. By joining in matrimony, they added a complicated new branch to an already convoluted family tree. Frieda's aunt now became her sister-in-law. Paul, meanwhile, became a brother-in-law to his brother's father-in-law.

This time Aby, the diminutive and dark-featured eldest Warburg brother, represented the family. An iconoclast and a maverick, he had chosen to pursue an academic life, even though his Jewish roots made it unlikely he would ever attain a professorship in Germany, where antisemitism was particularly pronounced within the academy. With his sharp mind, always perceiving hidden meaning in the world around him, Aby could be delightfully engaging and bitingly funny. But his moods also oscillated unpredictably between levity and rage. The family enfant terrible, he had a lofty sense of entitlement, especially when it came to new acquisitions for his beloved library, for which he didn't so much ask for money from his brothers as demand it.[45]

Aby combined his social visit to the United States with a research trip to study Native American art and culture. Fascinated by the American West since boyhood, he roamed the East Coast visiting museums and consulting leading anthropologists and archaeologists. Because they shared similar interests, Aby forged a close bond with James Loeb, who brought him to Cambridge to tour Harvard's Peabody Museum, whose collection contained artifacts from North America's prehistoric past.[46] Then, wearing a flat-topped cowboy hat and a bandana tied around his neck, Aby ventured into the field. He traveled as far as he could by rail and then set out in a two-horse buggy to visit the remote Hopi villages of southwestern Arizona. He witnessed ancient rites and ceremonies, including a snake dance involving live serpents, and carefully documented his trip, taking photographs, jotting copious notes in his diary, and sketching maps and pictures of traditional dress.

A letter Aby received, while still traveling in the West, suggests his fieldwork also took a troubling turn. In March 1896, Ike Seligman—

Paul's new brother-in-law—alerted Aby that he had "just received news from the Postmaster in Santa Fe that a family of Indians (by name of Ra-ba that is 'red eyes') propose bringing a suit against you for damages, and that the young squaw Minnemōsā . . . alleges serious charges—the nature of which I do not venture to put on paper!" Without spelling out the accusations, Seligman strongly implied some type of sexual impropriety, joking that he didn't think "it will be necessary to send the papouse"—a term for a Native American baby—"to you for your birthday present." (Aby was then a few weeks away from turning thirty.) Seligman noted that the case could be "compromised for 2 horses a lock of hair & payment of 150 dollars" and he pledged to settle the matter discreetly. "I shall try to avoid all publicity."[47]

While Aby continued his travels (and maybe his mischief), Paul returned to Germany with Nina, following a short honeymoon in Atlanta, where they attended the Cotton States and International Exposition, a World's Fair–like extravaganza showcasing the South's postwar economic progress.[48] Paul and Nina—who in Warburg shorthand would become Panina, just as Felix and Frieda were known by the portmanteau Friedaflix and Max and his wife Alice as Malice—set up house on Fontenay Avenue, a block from Outer Alster Lake, where Paul and his brothers had sculled their small rowboat as children.[49] In August 1897, ten months after their wedding, Panina welcomed a baby boy. They named him James, after Nina's beloved brother. ("There was a great psychological confusion in my youth because my mother was over-attached to her brother Jim and I can remember her saying on various occasions that there were two men she loved—my uncle Jim and my father," James recalled. "I was never quite sure who came first. Of course, my father did, but it was a confusing kind of thing for a kid.")[50]

Nina desperately missed her family, but that fall, as she settled into Hamburg among the inimitable Warburgs and raised her infant son, a visitor from New York helped to relieve some of her pangs of homesickness. On October 25 her nineteen-year-old nephew Morti Schiff showed up to begin a nine-month apprenticeship at M.M. Warburg. Upon arriving, he reported to his parents that "Puss is looking very fine and has grown quite a bit stouter." And of his new cousin: "Her boy is a darling, no beauty but a very healthy looking bit of humanity."[51]

Morti, the younger of Schiff's two children, was a handsome, if slightly plump, pale-eyed young man, color blind like his grandfather. He always seemed desperate to please his father and just as routinely fell short of the mark. During Morti's boyhood, as Jacob scrutinized his son for imperfections, father and son often clashed. "As a youngster, my brother was always being punished for various misdemeanors," Frieda recalled. "Morti was often sent from the table, denied dessert for a week, or otherwise made to do penance."[52] Their father was particularly obsessed with his son's deportment—a category on which students were graded at Julius Sachs's prep school. When Morti received demerits in this area, Schiff furiously exorcised him of his bad habits in what Frieda euphemistically described as "seances." After one of these spanking sessions, she remembered her brother hollering, "I can't sit down! I can't sit down!"[53]

A gifted student, Morti graduated from Sachs' Collegiate at fifteen. The school was a pipeline to Harvard, where many of Morti's classmates were headed in the fall. Morti wanted to go there too, but this became another source of father-son conflict. Schiff fretted about "the many temptations a young man is subject to with so many students around."[54] According to Frieda, "my father said that Harvard was too large, that many wealthy boys attended it, that Morti was inclined toward extravagance and would become more extravagant there."[55]

So Jacob sent Morti to Amherst, the small liberal arts college in western Massachusetts, where his classmates included future president Calvin Coolidge and Dwight Morrow, later an influential J.P. Morgan & Co. partner and ambassador to Mexico. Once there, Morti still managed to earn his father's opprobrium when he purchased a flashy new bicycle. His parents also upbraided him after he reported, in one of his regular letters home, making a weekend visit to Mount Holyoke, the nearby women's college.[56]

Morti joined the basketball team and pledged the Beta Theta Pi fraternity.[57] Morrow, who hailed from a poor family, was one of Morti's frat brothers; Morti kept his friend supplied with hand-me-downs. His well-tailored shirts were monogrammed with his initials—MLS—which Morrow joked stood for "Morrow's Little Shirts."[58]

Morti earned high marks and took an interest, like his father, in the plight of Russian immigrants. "Although I am in favor of a restricted immigration I do not see what right, for I mean a moral right, to deny admittance to our country to those who crave admittance. . . . Is this not a fair country and should it not be a home of refugees driven from their homes by the persecuting land of a tyrant?" he wrote in one essay, titled "Plea for the Immigrant."[59]

Morti's studiousness earned him occasional teasing and harassment from his peers. During French lessons, one of his classmates recalled, "a favorite pastime in my particular class was to eject Mortimer Schiff from the room. Schiff was probably the only serious student in the group, and his recitations, whenever he was allowed to finish them, were all that could be asked for. Scarcely ever though was he allowed to finish." Often, as he read aloud, several classmates would rise from their seats and, as their professor pounded his desk for order, carry Schiff from the classroom. They returned "quietly to their seats, while Schiff, when he had had time to gather his breath, would sneak back to his place."[60]

After completing freshman year, Morti asked to transfer to Harvard—and his father quashed the idea. "You've proved my point," Schiff told his son, according to Frieda. "You're extravagant at Amherst, and you're not ready to go to Harvard."[61] Morti spent another year at Amherst and then asked once more to attend Harvard. This time Schiff agreed that Morti was ready to begin the next phase of his education, but instead of Cambridge, he dispatched his son to St. Paul, Minnesota, to learn the railroad business from his friend James J. Hill, head of the Great Northern Railway, where Schiff served on the board.

Morti made the best of his apprenticeship, circulating through the Great Northern's various departments, from accounting to operations to the repair depot. The experience was valuable, though so too was the intelligence Morti gathered on Hill's operation. "I keep my eyes and ears open and so pick up many things," he told his father in one letter.[62] In another he reported, "The unpopularity of the Great Northern out here is something marvelous. Nobody has a good word for it. . . . Its unpopularity is, however, greatest among its employees whom it underpays and overworks. There is no other railway out here which has such long office hours. Then it also has the reputation of having the worst equipment of any of the transcontinental lines. I write you these facts not out of any spirit of hostility to the road, but because I have found them out and think it is due to you, dear Father, to know them."[63]

During his off hours, Morti rode his bicycle around St. Paul, went duck hunting with Hill's son, Louis, and attempted to penetrate the local social scene. He applied and was rebuffed for membership at St. Paul's exclusive Town & Country Club, likely on account of his Jewish background.[64]

By May 1896, Morti had rotated through virtually every key office in the company, and Hill felt he had no more to teach him. "I think you will agree with me that he has acquitted himself very creditably," Hill wrote to Schiff. "He has done better than I expected, even while I expected he would do well."[65]

Soon it was on to Hamburg for the next stage of Morti's training—banking. Morti took rooms at Eichenallee 33, a quaint one-bedroom with a balcony overlooking the street, and reported for duty at M.M. Warburg on a Wednesday morning in late October 1896. Max and Paul placed Morti in the bank's exchange department. "Business is handled differently here than it is with us; especially the hours are quite curious," he wrote home after his first day in the office. "I come down at about nine and stay until one. Then I have nothing to do until three, then I start work again until six or seven."[66] One day Morti accompanied the Warburg brothers to the Hamburg Bourse, where the laid-back atmosphere surprised him. "They seem to gather there only to gossip and . . . it seemed rather curious to see them all sitting around chatting and taking it easy," he reported to his father.[67]

In Hamburg, Morti got a front-row seat not just to the Warburg family business but also to the Warburg family drama. At the time, Aby, who had returned from his travels in the United States, had scandalized the family by announcing his intention to marry Mary Hertz, the daughter of a Hamburg shipper. A talented artist, she was sweet-tempered, patient, and pretty, and best of all, she put up with Aby's turbulent moods. But she was not Jewish. Moritz, despondent that his future grandchildren might be raised outside of their faith, begged his son to change his mind, even resorting to bribery. If Aby came to his senses, his anguished father said, he would double his allowance.[68] But Aby could not be swayed.

"Matters are in a very bad shape just now, but we hope that they may clear up soon," Morti wrote home. "Miss Hertz is perfectly charming and just the wife for Aby to make a man of him. It is very unfortunate that the religious question stands in the way and I can well understand how Mr. Warburg feels about it. . . . Max, for Aby is useless, is doing his best to smooth matters over and I hope he will be successful but at present the sky is very dark."[69]

Moritz couldn't bring himself to be present when the engagement was formally announced, and he and Charlotte didn't attend the wedding, even requesting that it not take place in Hamburg, but they subsequently came to accept the marriage.[70]

On weekends Morti bicycled out to Kösterberg, the Warburg family's summer retreat in Blankenese, located on a hilltop overlooking the Elbe River.[71] He often dined with Nina and Paul, spending long hours with his aunt lounging in the smoking room of her comfortable home and reminiscing about their "dear ones" back in New York.[72] During the final weeks of his stay in Hamburg, Morti received a surprise visit from his friend Arthur Lehman. Together they toured the city, and over cigars, Morti pumped Arthur for information about family and friends back home.[73] Less than a month later, while still traveling overseas, Arthur would receive word that his father, Mayer, had died.[74]

In late July 1897, Morti completed his training at M.M. Warburg, with the members of the firm sending him off with a black pearl scarf pin as a memento of his time there.[75] From Hamburg, he sailed to London to begin a series of jobs arranged by his father. He rented a posh flat at 12 Park Lane, once again arousing the displeasure of his parents with his profligacy.[76]

Like Paul before him, Morti was posted to Samuel Montagu & Co., where he complained that he was constantly "pumped for information" about Kuhn Loeb and M.M. Warburg.[77] Eventually Morti apprenticed with his father's old friend Ernest Cassel, who became something of a mentor. Cassel, then on the verge of attaining knighthood, moved in the highest circles of British society and was among the closest confidants to Edward VII, who ascended to the throne in 1901. Stout, bearded, and bald, Cassel looked as if he could be Edward's brother, a resemblance the banker accentuated by grooming his beard in the same style as the king's. Cassel managed Edward's money under an unusual setup, in which he shouldered all investment losses. Such was the price of preserving his access to power.

While schooling him in the genteel ways of continental banking, Cassel also nurtured Morti's spendthrift tendencies. As Cassel later told Frieda, "I don't think your father was too well pleased with what I did for your brother; I rather encouraged his spending money, because I believe a gentleman must learn how to spend gracefully but not showily. Your father, you know, didn't usually hold with many of my ideas."[78]

Morti took to the life of the English gentry, playing tennis and golf and attending balls with members of the aristocracy.[79] His cousin

Otto Schiff squired him around town. And he spent time with the London-based Seligmans, particularly Isaac's son Charles, who was around Morti's age. Ensconced in London for three decades by then, Isaac and his family were well on their way to reaching the uppermost rungs of English society. Both Charles and his brother Richard were eventually knighted.

Weekends often found Morti at Dalby Hall in Leicestershire, one of Cassel's two country estates. He wrote home so often of spending lazy weekends in the country, or of hitting the links with Charlie Seligman, or of hunting excursions, that his parents began to wonder how he was finding the time for work. "I was sorry to see . . . you are displeased with me for going to the country so much," he wrote in reply to one presumably irate letter from his father, explaining that he had "very little real work to do."[80]

During his stay in London, a diplomatic crisis developed between the United States and Spain over Cuba, then under Spanish control and roiled by an ongoing revolt by the populace against their colonial overlords. In February 1898, the mysterious sinking of the USS *Maine*, the naval cruiser that President McKinley had dispatched to Havana Harbor to protect U.S. interests on the island, paved the way for the Spanish-American War. Eager to measure up in his father's eyes, Morti offered to enlist: "If at any time you think it my duty as an American citizen to volunteer, for you can judge that much better over there, please let me know and I will come home immediately."[81] Jacob agreed it was time for his son to return home, but he had different plans for him.

It was time to join the partnership.

13

PARTNERS AND RIVALS

Goldman and Sachs. In the history of modern finance, there was no alliance more consequential than the one that forged the world's most powerful investment bank. But the business partnership that resulted from Sam Sachs's 1877 marriage to Louisa Goldman sowed bitter resentment that eventually drove the Goldman and Sachs families apart. The more the bank flourished, the more the family relationship suffered.

In 1881, Marcus turned sixty. His business had progressively grown, to the point where he now placed about $30 million worth of commercial paper annually. His daughter Rosa and her husband Julius Sachs threw him a birthday celebration, and during the festivities he rose to say a few words. Marcus spoke of the fortuitous path his life had taken, from peddler to banker, and then he surprised the assembled Goldmans and Sachses by turning to Sam and offering him a partnership. The company would henceforth be known as M. Goldman & Sachs—not, notably, M. Goldman & Son.[1]

Marcus advanced Sachs $15,000 to cover his capital contribution to the newly rechristened company. The loan came due in three installments, though Marcus waived the final payment in honor of the birth of his grandson Walter, the youngest of Sam and Louisa's three boys. "It would appear that on the very first day of my entrance into this world, I concluded my first business deal for Goldman, Sachs," Walter liked to joke.[2]

Surely, Marcus had glimpsed a hint of himself in dependable and industrious Sam Sachs. But it was lost on no one in the room, during that birthday dinner, that when Marcus had selected his first partner, he had passed over his son Henry, who was eagerly waiting to join his father in business. (The elder Goldman son, Julius, had already embarked on a successful legal career and was busying himself with charitable work in the Jewish community.)

To Henry, who wore thick glasses to correct his nearsighted vision and who as a young man was already balding, his father's snub may have brought painful childhood memories flooding back. His relationship with Louisa, two years older, had always been troubled. He felt she was her parents' favorite (an impression that was probably correct), brooded when they sided with her in childhood squabbles, and lashed out in fits of jealousy.[3] Now his father was handing Louisa's husband *his* birthright. If Henry ever needed confirmation of his second-class status within the family, this was it.

Despite his poor eyesight, which made it difficult to read, Henry excelled in school, and at sixteen, he followed his older brother Julius to Harvard. But halfway through freshman year, Henry dropped out, blaming his vision for his inability to keep up with his studies. Marcus, worried for Henry's future, did not mask his disappointment, and his decision to bypass his son and award a partnership to his son-in-law was likely rooted in his belief that Henry was not up to the task. "I've always believed that Henry was seen by his father as unable to manage such a role because of his physical ailments," recalled Henry's granddaughter, June Breton Fisher, in her biography of her grandfather. "While Marcus's decision was based on what he thought was common sense and not emotion, it was a crushing blow for Henry."[4]

After getting passed over, Henry went to work as a salesman for Dreyfus, Willer & Co., the dry goods firm part-owned by the family of his brother-in-law, Ludwig Dreyfuss, the elegant and sharply dressed husband of Henry's eldest sister, Rebecca. He spent the next three years exiled to rattling railcars, as he traveled the country lugging textile samples. Evidently, he showed some initiative as a traveling salesman. In 1885, Marcus admitted Henry and Ludwig Dreyfuss into his firm, which was renamed Goldman, Sachs & Co. The pecking order remained clear, however: Henry entered the firm in a junior position to Sam Sachs, and the brothers-in-law would not reach equal footing until 1904, when Marcus died and elevated Henry to a senior partnership in his will.

The company, by the time Henry entered the firm, had graduated from its basement premises to a two-room office on the second floor of 9 Pine Street, where the company's name was printed in gilded lettering across plate glass windows. The partners sat in the front office, while the rear was occupied by the aptly named stenographer Ms. Schreiber ("scribe" in German), a handful of messengers, and eight to ten clerks working with "their shirt sleeves hitched up by rubber bands, green shades over their eyes, standing at high desks, laboriously posting entries into fat ledgers," recalled Walter Sachs, who as a teenager occasionally tagged along with his father when he went in to work on Saturday mornings.[5]

In 1894, Sam took his younger brother Harry into the firm, and over the next decade, as each of his three sons graduated from Harvard, they too entered Goldman Sachs. This added to Henry Goldman's grudge against his brother-in-law, who was stacking his father's firm with Sachses. It also irked Henry that, because Sam had entered the partnership earlier and held a senior role, his fortune surpassed his own. The financial disparity was brought home to Goldman when his brother-in-law commissioned a palatial home, which he dubbed Ellencourt (after his daughter Ella), in the New Jersey shore town of Long Branch, near the summer homes of Wall Street friends such as the Schiffs. (Walter likened the property to "Versailles on a very small scale.")[6]

"He viewed the imbalance of power and money between the two branches of the family as thoroughly unjust," according to Henry's granddaughter.[7]

Blood and money were always a volatile mixture. For Jewish businessmen who experienced a certain amount of prejudice, building business networks through family relationships made sense, especially when carrying out inherently risky transatlantic transactions. Who better to trust than a relative? For Kuhn Loeb and M.M. Warburg, intermarriage strengthened both firms. But mingling family and finance also tended to magnify disputes, foment rivalries, and create complications totally apart from the already complex conduct of business over vast distances by letter and short (often coded) telegraph messages. It set the stage for disputes over the admission of new partners and over succession, and it injected sentimentality and emotion into business decisions where such feelings were better set aside.

With family involved, business was never just business.

Marital ties brought the Seligmans into partnership with the dynamic Munich-born Hellman brothers: Max, who ran the New Orleans and later Paris branches of the business, was Jesse's brother-in-law; his younger brother Theodore, who took over the New Orleans firm, married Joseph Seligman's daughter Frances. Yet marriage also impelled Joseph and his brothers into business with their sister Babette's husband, Max Stettheimer, and his brother, Jacob, both of whom the Seligmans viewed as a drag on their operation. The Stettheimers, who clung to the importing business as the Seligmans moved into banking, were a constant source of annoyance to Joseph, who wanted desperately to jettison Max from the partnership but worried about alienating his sister. (Max's untimely death in 1873 at the age of fifty-five solved the problem without raising family tensions.) Of Max's brother, Joseph once complained that their family had been "wronged out of many thousands of dollars, all owing to our folly in keeping Jacob Stettheimer as partner as long as we did."[8]

The Lehmans were somewhat unique among their friends in New York's German-Jewish banking world because Lehman Brothers (in contrast with their New Orleans firm) did not admit in-laws as partners. For decades, all the partners were Lehmans, a tradition broken somewhat dramatically in 1924, when the firm brought on John Hancock, a former naval officer who was neither a Lehman nor a Jew. Mayer and Emanuel took steps to ensure that their families and their business partnership would remain closely bound in the next generation by arranging a marriage between their eldest children, Sigmund and Harriet. (As a wedding present, Mayer gave his son $30,000, while Emanuel gifted his daughter $50,000—the modern-day equivalent of handing their kids around $2 million.)[9]

But this measure did not prevent family drama from erupting over business. One of Mayer's brothers-in-law was Isaias Hellman, who had made the leap from dry goods into banking, rising to become one of California's wealthiest financiers. Hellman and the Lehmans frequently did business together, circulating investment capital between New York and Los Angeles, the frontier city that Isaias would help to transform into an American metropolis.

Isaias and Mayer were also personally close. When Hellman married Babette's sister Esther in New York, the Lehmans hosted their wedding party at their home, and as Isaias built his fortune in California, he often turned to Mayer as a confidant. Yet it took just one transaction to drive a deep wedge between them.[10]

Commercial banks—like Hellman's Nevada National Bank,

which he later merged into Wells Fargo—operated through a network of correspondent banks, allowing their customers to clear drafts and make withdrawals in different cities throughout the United States as well as overseas. In New York, Hellman kept a large balance on deposit with Lehman Brothers to cover his customers' transactions. The Lehmans paid modest interest on Hellman's funds, about 3 percent. He could have obtained better rates elsewhere, but family was family.

In 1891, with the money market growing tight in California, the Nevada Bank's cash balance dipped too low for Hellman's comfort. Panicked, he wired Lehman Brothers requesting to withdraw his cash to shore up his reserves. The Lehmans read his telegram in disbelief. They too were experiencing a cash crunch, and Hellman's sudden request came at exactly the wrong moment.

Hellman's wire led to a heated exchange of messages between Mayer and Isaias until the brothers-in-law were no longer speaking. In a fit of pique, the Lehmans off-loaded their shares in Hellman's bank. Isaias, meanwhile, ordered his wife to steer clear of her sister and brother-in-law.

"The truth of the matter is the Lehmans have had for years past many favors from me," Isaias wrote to Benjamin Newgass, Babette and Esther's brother.

> They have had hundreds of thousands of my money, without even the acknowledgement of a promissory note or an acceptance and without collateral they have allowed me whatever rate of interest they saw fit (never any too much). . . . I have *never* received a favor from their hands, they always found an excuse when I even intimated I *might* want something, but I have, on the contrary, never tired to be of service to them.

The chill in their relationship lasted two years, thawing only after Mayer and Babette sent news of their daughter Clara's engagement. Isaias replied with a conciliatory note, writing that "this happy event paves the way to reconciliation and good feeling between us."[11]

Around the office, relations between Henry Goldman and Sam Sachs were tense. In style and temperament, the partners clashed, never mind the personal baggage festering between them. Henry was creative, energetic, and outspoken—often infuriatingly so—with a healthy appetite for risk and a combative streak. He became expert at trading railroad securities and had ambitions of turning his father's conservative business into a house of issue—a firm that handled stock and bond offerings. In the summer, Henry worked with his shirt-sleeves rolled up, a halo of smoke swirling above his head from one of his ubiquitous Cuban cigars. Sam, courtly and dignified, insisted on wearing formal attire around the office, though on the most swel-tering days he allowed himself a thin alpaca coat. He lacked Henry's originality, though he, too, had a greater vision for Goldman Sachs.

"My father was the great conservative commercial banker who inspired confidence," Walter Sachs remembered.

> People only had to look at him to see what a wonderful type of man he was. And Henry Goldman was the great dynamic imaginative person. There was this check and balance between these two men. Perhaps, in a sense, there was a certain rivalry between them. They were partners and brothers-in-law, and maybe they rubbed each other, because they had diametri-cally opposed views on many subjects, important and unim-portant.[12]

The brothers-in-law argued over major business decisions but also over things as petty as who paid the boy who delivered their lunch from the nearby deli. Obstinate and opinionated, Henry had a special talent for triggering Sam's red-faced rage—Sachses were known for their volcanic tempers—but Sachs also knew how to get under his brother-in-law's skin. He took special pleasure in remind-ing Henry, when his brother-in-law griped that Sachs's sons were too inexperienced for sales calls, that his boys were "Harvard *gradu-ates.*"[13]

The friction within the firm didn't seem to impair its perfor-mance. Its commercial paper sales continued to climb, reaching $67 million in 1894.[14] By that year, Goldman Sachs had working capital of $585,000, up from $100,000 when Sam Sachs joined the firm; after expenses, the partners cleared $200,000 in profit. "With no income tax, this was a set-up that lent itself to the rapid building up of capital in the succeeding twenty years," Walter recalled.[15]

As Henry and Sam strove to build the business, their efforts seemed complementary, at least for a time. Henry, accustomed to long stints on the road from his days as a traveling salesman, can-vassed the Midwest—Chicago, St. Paul, Kansas City—to broaden the firm's commercial paper business. More commercial paper accounts required more outlets to sell the short-term loans, so he and his partners ventured up and down the Eastern Seaboard forming new banking relationships in cities such as Boston, Hartford, and Philadelphia. Henry, meanwhile, never lost sight of his goal of navigating Goldman Sachs into railroad finance, the exclusive terrain of Wall Street's heaviest hitters. And in the years after the Panic of 1893, he shrewdly hoovered up railroad securities at recession-battered prices.[16]

Sam, for his part, pursued a mission to internationalize Goldman's business. If he had any hopes of taking the company's business global, London, the world's financial capital, was the place to start. He envisioned providing Goldman's growing roster of clients with commercial letters of credit and foreign exchange services to facilitate their overseas transactions, and he foresaw arbitrage opportunities to exploit in London's typically lower interest rates, allowing Goldman to borrow in London and lend in New York at a narrow profit. But first, he needed a reliable partner.

In the late 1890s, Sam pitched Herman and Alexander Kleinwort, the brothers running Kleinwort, Sons & Co., one of London's top merchant banks, on his vision of forming a transatlantic alliance. He happened to make his case at just the right moment. The Kleinworts were looking to replace their New York–based financial agent, which was continually missing lucrative business opportunities in the U.S. market. They had never heard of Goldman Sachs, but after their inquiries into the firm's business standing turned up no red flags, they took a gamble on doing business with an unknown house.[17]

It said something about the trust that existed between bankers at the time—really, trust undergirded the whole of the global credit system—that when Kleinwort Sons and Goldman Sachs made their partnership official by opening a joint account, they did so without so much as a written agreement.[18]

Marcus Goldman was by now well into his seventies and pondering retirement. He had recently purchased, for $15,000, a seat at the New York Stock Exchange, signifying his firm's arrival as a bona fide financial player. It now appeared that the credit reporters who years earlier had dismissed the banker as too cautious to prosper had misjudged him. Perhaps he wasn't as timid as they thought.

As he reached his fifties, Jacob Schiff began to muse about stepping back from business. His own father, after all, had died at sixty-two.

He felt pulled in too many directions, stretched between Kuhn Loeb, the various charities to which he devoted considerable time and money, and the ongoing Russian refugee crisis, each shipload of immigrants adding to the weight of obligation Schiff and his fellow philanthropists had shouldered to take care of their own. He began thinking of succession.

Starting in 1894, Kuhn Loeb had begun admitting a new crop of partners: James Loeb; his cousin, Louis Heinsheimer, who had started clerking for the firm some twenty years earlier; and Felix Warburg, who could not have turned down his partnership even if he had wanted to. Presently, Morti Schiff, fresh from three years of training in banking and railroading, would take his rightful place in the firm, whose command his father intended for him to inherit one day.

And to Jacob Schiff's annoyance, there was a fifth new partner who had joined the firm: Otto Kahn, who in January 1896 had married Abraham Wolff's petite, fair-skinned daughter, Addie. Kahn hailed from a prosperous German family that, by Otto's boyhood, had risen from provincial roots to a comfortable position within Mannheim's bourgeoisie. His paternal grandfather had started a small featherbed business from his rural home in nearby Stebbach, eventually opening a factory in Mannheim and then a small bank.

Otto's father Bernhard was politically minded and, like many young men of his day, believed ardently in the liberal doctrine of equality and self-rule that ignited the 1848 rebellions within the German states and elsewhere in Europe. A young man of about twenty-one when the uprisings began in his southwestern German province, Bernhard fell in with the revolutionaries and then fled for his life when Prussian forces brutally crushed the revolt. He spent the next decade in the United States, where he found work as a bank clerk in Albany, New York, and became an American citizen, before finally returning home to Germany in 1860. Still committed to the liberal principles that the revolutionaries of '48 had spilled blood over, Bernhard was elected to the Mannheim city council, where he would serve for more than twenty-five years. Now in his early thirties, he married the striking and vivacious Emma Eberstadt, who bore eight children—though "only every other child was Bernhard's," according to a "waggish kinsman" quoted by one of Kahn's biographers.[19]

The Kahns were Jewish by ancestry, though, as far as religion went, they sought their spiritual fulfillment at the National Theater, within walking distance of their home in Mannheim's most desirable neighborhood, and at gatherings of the local Brahms Club, where the composer's works were analyzed and performed. Otto and his siblings, who were tutored largely at home, were raised to revere art and music. By the time he was a teenager, Otto played piano, cello, and violin. He wrote poetry and plays, though his mother, who could be severely critical of the children who were not her favorites (and Otto fell into this category), apparently didn't think much of his dramatic work. She advised him to incinerate the plays.

Though no expense was spared and no connection untapped to launch his older brother Robert's musical career as a composer and conductor, a profession in which he would earn distinction if not renown, young Otto was destined for a more pragmatic vocation. At sixteen, Bernhard dispatched his son to Karlsruhe to apprentice for a small bank, in preparation for him one day joining the family banking business, and where he spent his days fetching sausages and beers for the partners, scrubbing inkwells, and handling other menial tasks. It may have been drudge work, but Otto performed it well. He earned his first promotion after his boss took notice of his uncanny speed at licking the stamps placed on the firm's voluminous correspondence. "One must learn to obey before he is fit to command," Kahn rhapsodized later of his formative years.[20]

At nineteen, he paused his banking training to serve with the Mainz hussars, opting to volunteer for one year of military service rather than be forced into three if he were conscripted.[21] He took away from the experience a lasting distaste for Prussian militarism, though he rather liked his hussar mustache. He returned to banking, spending a year with a Berlin-based firm before striking out for London. In 1888 he landed a job in Deutsche Bank's London office, eventually rising to a junior management position. His early years in London overlapped with Paul Warburg's training at Samuel Montagu & Co., and for a time the future partners, both destined for Kuhn Loeb, were flatmates.[22] The connection was surely more than a strange coincidence and may have come through one of Paul's maternal cousins, a friend of Kahn's.

In London, Otto fell into a routine that he would carry on throughout his life: he spent his days in the buttoned-down world of international banking and his nights among artists, musicians, and writers, floating through literary salons and ravenously consuming theater and opera. His entrée into London's most rarefied artistic circles came through his maternal aunt Elizabeth, who had married Sir George Lewis, a prominent lawyer. The Lewises' Portland Place mansion was a gathering ground for creative types and intellectuals, including Oscar Wilde, then approaching the peak of his fame. It was a heady time, and Otto, enchanted with his London life, became a British subject. He seemed to have every intention of putting down roots—but he didn't.

In 1893 he accepted a job as an arbitrage clerk in the New York office of Speyer & Co., then run by Jacob Schiff's old friend William Bonn, the Frankfurt native who had greeted Schiff at the docks when he first set foot in America. Speyer was a formidable investment bank that competed (and collaborated) with top-tier Wall Street firms including Kuhn Loeb and J.P. Morgan, and this may have been why Kahn accepted the position, which was technically a step down in responsibility. Still, it was not his move to Speyer & Co. but his marriage to Addie Wolff that ultimately secured Kahn the promotion he desired.

A widower, Abraham Wolff had no male heirs, and he pushed Jacob Schiff to admit Kahn to their partnership. It was hard to say no, given that Schiff had recently promised a partnership to his own son-in-law. Yet Schiff was still reluctant. He found something off-putting about Kahn.

There was something unserious about the dandyish young man who palled around with artists and poets and sometimes spontaneously burst into arias. And then there was his attitude toward Judaism. Kahn seemed to regard his heritage less as a point of pride and more as a vexing handicap to his lofty social ambitions. Another count against him may have been his association with Speyer—Schiff disliked James Speyer, the son of the firm's late founder. Speyer was a prickly fellow who was then attempting to assert his claim to run the New York branch of the company, eventually succeeding in driving Schiff's friend Bonn from the business.[23] But there may have been still another cause for Schiff's initial distaste for Kahn: in the smooth young banker, he glimpsed a rival, if not for himself, then for his inexperienced son, Morti.

"As conditions now stand I probably must follow Wolff's wishes and agree that his son-in-law, Mr. Kahn, shall enter our firm, unpleasant as it may be to me," Schiff confided to Ernest Cassel in April 1896, while the newly married Kahns were off on their yearlong honeymoon. "I do not want to have Wolff feel badly about it as he has always been a very good friend to me. He told me he would be very unhappy if his eldest son-in-law should not become his successor. As soon as Morti will be a few years older I hope to be able to retire from active work and than [sic] I also hope that Morti will get the whole business in his hands."[24] In a separate letter sent the following year, Schiff told Cassel: "I . . . owe it to Morti to keep the name of the firm high until he can take over the leadership."[25] Schiff grudgingly withheld his objections to Kahn who, along with Felix Warburg, joined Kuhn Loeb as a junior partner in 1897.

No doubt aware of Schiff's misgivings, Kahn treated Kuhn Loeb's elder statesman with courtly deference, even as he rose to become a financial and cultural icon in his own right. "I remember seeing him quickly rise whenever Jacob Schiff came to his desk to speak to him," recalled Benjamin Buttenwieser, who joined Kuhn Loeb in 1918. "He never remained seated."[26]

Despite Schiff's initial reticence, Kahn, a financial maestro who would orchestrate some of Kuhn Loeb's biggest deals in the years ahead, earned his respect, even if he didn't always approve of Kahn's extracurricular activities. An arts patron who reveled in publicity (he eventually retained the PR guru Ivy Lee to polish his image), Kahn scoured the newspapers for his name and collected the clippings into a dozen bound volumes, each spanning more than a hundred pages. He was as often in the news for a railroad deal or industrial stock offering as he was in connection with the financially troubled Metropolitan Opera, which he rescued from oblivion, becoming its long-serving chairman and guiding force. He relished the role of impresario, leveraging it to court young starlets eager to further their careers in show business. It was rumored that his New York mansion featured a hidden stairway, accessed through his library, that he used to squire his conquests discreetly to his bedroom.

Kahn possessed virtuosic powers of suasion and boardroom diplomacy. Buttenwieser recalled witnessing the financier at work one Saturday morning when he conducted four meetings simultaneously. Kahn had stashed his visitors in the small offices encircling the large partners' room in Kuhn Loeb's downtown headquarters. Two of the rooms contained the presidents of rival railroads, both Kuhn Loeb clients, locked in a contentious territorial dispute. Another was occupied by Giulio Gatti-Casazza, the Metropolitan's general manager, who Kahn had poached from Milan's La Scala. In Felix Warburg's office, which included a back door leading directly to an elevator, sat one of the Metropolitan's prima donnas, "but Gatti-Casazza did not know she was there," remembered Buttenwieser. For more than two hours, Kahn traveled between the offices. "And I must say, he satisfied all four, I guess, for the lady in question left seemingly quite happy," Buttenwieser said. "She was shown out as she had been shown in by the Warburg office rear door. . . . How he accomplished all he did was a source of great wonder and admiration to me."[27]

Abraham Wolff anointed Kahn as his successor at just the right time. On October 1, 1900, he was struck down by a fatal heart attack at his Morris Township, New Jersey, estate. Wolff and Schiff had entered Kuhn Loeb at the same time twenty-five years earlier, and after Solomon Loeb relinquished day-to-day control of the business in 1885, they ran the firm virtually on their own. "No one can understand how much I have lost," Schiff told James Stillman, president of the National City Bank, shortly after his partner's death.[28] He expressed similar sentiments to Ernest Cassel: "What Wolff has been to me, nobody can know, and what the firm and I have lost in him, hardly anyone can imagine." And he confided: "Mr. Wolff was such an important factor in our business life that we shall be forced to change many things. It will especially be necessary now that the younger partners shall assume greater responsibility and become used to getting along without me."[29] Kahn, it turned out, would make a formidable replacement for his father-in-law.

Wolff's Wall Street friends and colleagues were astonished to learn of the tremendous estate the unassuming banker left behind, estimated by some at $20 million. The size of his fortune spoke to Kuhn Loeb's rise from a small merchant bank to a Wall Street juggernaut with few equals. "It is now plain that Mr. Wolff is another 'Silent Man of Wall Street,' and the mystery of his vast estate is interesting the financiers no little," one newspaper commented. "In every large railroad corporation in America he had shares. In many of the mines that have had great outputs of wealth he was a shareholder; in city, state and government bonds he could count several fortunes among his holdings."[30]

Some of his vast fortune had lately come from Kuhn Loeb's audacious maneuvers in the railroad industry, and in particular Schiff's rescue of the bankrupt Union Pacific Railroad, a feat that elevated him to the very peak of banking renown, a place he occupied with just one other financier, the man nicknamed "Jupiter" for his godlike reign over the financial world: John Pierpont Morgan.

14

JUPITER'S SHADOW

Winslow Pierce poked his head into Jacob Schiff's private state-room as their ferry churned toward the New Jersey shore.[1] It was the fall of 1895, and Schiff was commuting from Wall Street to his Sea Bright estate, where his family lived throughout the summer and into early autumn, save for a monthlong interlude in Bar Harbor.

Pierce was a young railroad lawyer who had worked for Jay Gould and was now advising the late tycoon's eldest son, George, who had recently inherited his father's empire. They had a proposition for Schiff: Would Kuhn Loeb undertake the reorganization of the Union Pacific? The Gould family held a large interest in the legendary rail-road, which Jay Gould had run at various points over the years. Prior to his death, he had been engaged in an unsuccessful effort to avert the struggling company's financial collapse.

The Lincoln administration had approved the Union Pacific's charter in 1862 as it sought to stitch together the far-flung states of the fraying republic. In doing so, it had helped the nation achieve the long-held dream of a transcontinental rail line, but since then finan-cial hardships and scandal had plagued the railroad.

Like many of its rivals, the Union Pacific had vastly over-expanded, taking on more and more debt as it laid mile after mile of track in a race to claim territory and assert its dominance. Its network eventually swelled to more than eight thousand miles.[2] Then came the Panic of 1893, which hit the railroad industry especially hard, toppling many overleveraged lines, including the Union Pacific, into receivership.

Immersed in railroad finance almost since the moment he stepped off the boat as an eighteen-year-old immigrant, Jacob Schiff had earned a reputation as a turnaround artist whose feats of financial alchemy had set right numerous failing ventures. The complex process of reorganization required more than financial acumen. It called for diplomacy and political savvy, a person with a certain gravitas to restore confidence to skittish investors. Reorganization entailed not only devising a path to profitability but selling major shareholders—often with their own ideas about how a railroad should be plucked from insolvency—on the plan. In the case of the Union Pacific, there was an additional complication. A massive infusion of federal subsidies had funded the company. That meant a turnaround effort would necessitate navigating a gauntlet of government obstacles.

The purpose of any reorganization was reducing fixed costs to the point where these recurring expenses were easily covered by revenues. The process required pruning unprofitable branch and feeder lines and streamlining bloated back offices. It helped to understand not just the financial details of railroading but the technical ones—for instance, that a wider gauge of water pipe at each station would more quickly cool down a locomotive's engine, lessening the time at each stop.[3]

Schiff understood this well, and it was one reason why he had dispatched his son Morti to St. Paul to learn from James Hill, who surveyed his company with such microscopic intensity that he even noticed unused railroad spikes lying by the side of the tracks, no minor offense in the eyes of the waste-obsessed mogul.[4] Jacob often made it a point to closely inspect a railroad's financial and physical operations, and this was one thing that set him apart from other railroad financiers, who tended to have little on-the-ground knowledge of the operations they backed.

Schiff heard Pierce out but was dubious. A committee had already formed to revitalize the Union Pacific, and Pierpont Morgan had joined the effort. For nearly two years, this group had labored to concoct a reorganization plan that would satisfy the company's creditors, most importantly the U.S. government, which had bankrolled the construction of the Union Pacific and its sister lines, the Central Pacific and Northern Pacific, by issuing millions in bonds that were now starting to mature. "But that is J. P. Morgan's affair," Schiff told

Pierce when he laid out his proposal. "I don't want to interfere with anything that he is trying to do."[5]

Still, he was intrigued. And not long after his meeting with Pierce, Schiff paid a visit to 23 Wall Street, Morgan's marble and mahogany sanctum.

Morgan and Schiff were the undisputed heads of two distinct Wall Street factions—Morgan the leader of the patrician "Yankee" bankers with New England roots, and Schiff the chieftain of the ascendant German Jews, whose mighty houses had often risen from modest mercantile origins.

Morgan was tall, broad-shouldered, and girthy, though it was his nose that overwhelmed his other features—craggy and pockmarked, it screamed out like a fire-red beacon above the financier's shaggy walrus mustache. Gruff and volatile, Morgan's temperament matched his imposing visage. Perhaps slightly intimidated by the titan whom some called "Jupiter" or "the Colossus of Wall Street," Schiff acted somewhat deferentially toward Morgan. It was Schiff who usually called on Morgan and not the other way around.

In person, Morgan and Schiff treated each other with a kind of exaggerated courtesy that belied a hint of mutual suspicion. Behind Schiff's back, Morgan referred to the German émigré derisively as "that foreigner." And he held a general disdain for the growing power of German-Jewish banking firms—and for Jews in general. At one point he groused to the representative of another bank, also run by Protestants, that their firms "were the only two composed of white men in New York."[6]

Whatever Morgan's opinion of Jewish bankers, his firm and Kuhn Loeb had a close and somewhat symbiotic working relationship, each house holding a healthy respect for the power and influence of the other. When one firm organized a loan syndicate for a railroad, industrial, or sovereign client, it frequently offered the other participation in the venture. Morgan and Schiff generally found competition to be counterproductive and undesirable—it was more profitable to be allies than enemies. Particularly in the rough-and-tumble early years of the railroad industry, companies had battled each other into insolvency through destructive rate wars, with rival outfits slashing their fees for freight and passengers to the point of unprofitability to undercut their competitors.

Morgan and Schiff preferred forming "communities of interest"—a rosy euphemism for monopolistic and occasionally illegal alliances in which rivals agreed to work together, or at least to refrain from working against each other, to prevent unnecessary corporate warfare. Usually, these arrangements involved joint stock ownership, with companies owning shares in their competitors to incentivize cooperation. As Schiff once explained the concept, "if I held stock of 'A' company and you held stock in 'B' company, and my shares were depressed in value because you were competing with me—each of us cutting the rates of the other—our interests would evidently be better served if you owned some of the stock in my company and I owned some of the stock in your company. In other words, if we had a community of interest."[7] These communities of interest were governed—and refereed—by bankers such as Schiff and Morgan, who along with their partners held board directorships in a maze of closely associated railroad, bank, and trust companies.

Turn-of-the-century bankers generally hewed to an unwritten gentlemen's code, one that seems quaint by modern standards: Moving in on another banker's business or poaching a client was typically considered out of bounds; aggressively pursuing business was viewed as unbecoming, even vulgar. As Kuhn Loeb had haughtily announced when it advertised its formation, "We do not chase after business. . . . We do business with people who come to us."[8] Decades earlier, when Schiff had won the lucrative business of the Pennsylvania Railroad, he had arguably transgressed the genteel etiquette of banking by approaching a disgruntled client of Drexel Morgan (the predecessor firm of J.P. Morgan & Co.). Older, wiser, and solidly established, Schiff now thought it best to seek out Morgan after hearing Pierce's proposal.

Morgan, it turned out, had abandoned the reorganization. The political morass in Washington—where some lawmakers were trying to pass a bill to relieve the Pacific roads of their crushing debt burden, and others were denouncing the effort as a corporate giveaway at taxpayer expense—was too confounding even for Morgan to navigate. Finally, he had thrown up his hands. The turnaround of the Union Pacific, which Morgan now condemned as "two streaks of iron rust across the plains," was all Schiff's, if he wanted the nuisance.[9] Morgan was busy enough orchestrating the revival of the Northern Pacific.

Schiff's subsequent decision to take up the project spoke to his supreme confidence. If the great J. P. Morgan had walked away from the politically fraught reorganization, what made Schiff think he would succeed?

In November 1895, Schiff canceled a planned trip to Mexico to devote himself to the monumental task before him.[10] Knowing most investors believed, as Morgan did, that the Union Pacific was hardly worth saving, Schiff carefully curated his reorganization committee, recruiting, among others, Marvin Hughitt, president of the Chicago & Northwestern Railroad, and Chauncey Depew of the New York Central. Both men were considered lieutenants of the Vanderbilt family, and their selection spurred newspaper chatter that the Vanderbilts, in a bid to extend their railroad empire to the West Coast, were behind the reorganization—an impression Schiff happily allowed to linger, since it generated interest in the financial community.[11]

The political situation complicated Schiff's effort from the start. His reorganization played out during a presidential election year, one in which William Jennings Bryan stoked populist sentiments with fiery oratory about how the elite monied interests of the East Coast controlled the economic destinies of midwestern farmers. Still, Schiff's committee began to make progress.

They rolled out a plan to recapitalize the road by issuing more than $200 million in new securities to retire old debts, fund repairs and improvements, and provide for the road's ongoing operating needs. Under the plan, existing bondholders would exchange their holdings for a combination of new bonds and preferred stock; stockholders would swap their old shares for new ones and pay in fifteen dollars for every share they owned in order to help fund the reorganization, receiving an equal value of preferred stock for their contribution. Slowly, investors began to deposit their holdings.[12]

Then there was the matter of the Union Pacific's substantial government debts. Collectively, the Pacific roads owed the U.S. Treasury more than $100 million. For years, as revenues slumped and the railroads struggled to make interest payments, Congress had fruitlessly tried to pass legislation to reduce their debt loads to manageable proportions. In April 1896, Representative H. Henry Powers, the Vermont Republican who chaired the congressional Pacific Railroads Committee, made another attempt. He introduced a bill to extend by decades the government's loans to the Union Pacific and the other federally backed roads. The measure appeared to gain traction, and there was cautious optimism about its passage.[13]

But just as Schiff's effort gained momentum, it began meeting puzzling pushback from various quarters, including among some lawmakers and Union Pacific investors. The opposition was subtle but worrisome. Word reached Schiff that Morgan had experienced a change of heart and was secretly orchestrating the resistance. Finally, Schiff paid him another visit. Morgan assured him that he still had no interest in the Union Pacific and offered to discreetly investigate the mysterious forces hindering the reorganization committee's progress. Several weeks later Morgan produced a name that was familiar but surprising. "It's that little fellow Harriman," he told Schiff, "and you want to look out for him."[14]

E. H. Harriman, Ned to his friends, of whom he didn't seem to have many, was a director of the Illinois Central Railroad, which from Chicago ran west to Sioux City, South Dakota, and south to New Orleans. Schiff knew him, though not well. Recently, he had met with Harriman several times to hash out the possibility of building a connection between the Illinois Central and the Union Pacific, which terminated in Omaha, a little under one hundred miles from Sioux City.[15] During these meetings, Harriman hadn't mentioned an interest in the reorganization.

Though Harriman would later be a major figure in American railroading, he was not that man yet. Diminutive and frail, with a bedraggled mustache that he sometimes chewed nervously when deep in thought, Harriman was a little-known investor—a "two-dollar broker," in the words of people who knew him during his early years—and it seemed hard to fathom that he possessed the gumption to take on Kuhn Loeb.[16] Harriman was frequently plagued by various ailments, and he developed a knack for conducting business by telephone. At Arden, Harriman's estate in New York's Hudson River Valley, he had a hundred of them. "What the brush is to the artist, what the chisel is to the sculptor, the telephone was to Harriman," commented one turn-of-the-century journalist.[17]

Harriman's skill was neither diplomacy nor savoir faire; he seemed physically unable to flatter, cajole, or ingratiate. Rather, it was his iron determination, his immovable obstinacy, that he wielded like a sledgehammer—even when a more delicate instrument would do—against any foe or obstacle that crossed his path.

Schiff summoned Harriman to a meeting and got right to the point. "For a long time we have been making good progress, but now we are meeting everywhere with opposition, and I understand this opposition is being directed by you. What have you to say about it?" he inquired.

"I am the man," Harriman admitted.

"But why are you doing it?"

"Because I intend to reorganize the Union Pacific myself."

The man's arrogance amused Schiff. But his confidence was also disquieting. Schiff flashed a smile. "How do you propose to do it, Mr. Harriman?" he asked. "Most of the securities of the company are in our possession. What means have you of reorganizing the Union Pacific?"

"The Illinois Central ought to have that road and we are going to take charge of the reorganization. We have the best credit in the country. I am going to issue $100,000,000 in three per cent bonds of the Illinois Central Railroad Company and am going to get close to par for them. You, at the best, can't get money for less than four and a half percent. In that respect I am stronger than you are."

"You'll have a good time doing it, Mr. Harriman," Schiff replied, "but meanwhile, what is your price?"

"There is no price. I am determined to get possession of the road."

Were there no terms under which they could work together? Schiff asked again.

"If you'll make me chairman of the executive committee of the reorganized road, I'll consider the expediency of joining forces with you."

"That is out of the question," Schiff retorted. The reorganization committee had already promised that role to Winslow Pierce.

"Very well, Mr. Schiff. Go ahead and see what you can do."[18]

In early January 1897, Congress took up the Powers bill, but its passage now seemed anything but assured. When debate opened, lawmakers squabbled bitterly over the fate of the Pacific railroads, with some now arguing that the government should assert its control over the lines. Denouncing the past management of the Pacific roads as a "labyrinth of frauds and rascalities," Senator John Tyler Morgan, Democrat of Alabama, introduced a new bill under which a government commission would run them.[19] Harriman's Illinois Central, meanwhile, mounted a lobbying campaign in support of yet another plan, stirring the pot of dissension. On January 11, when the measure came to a vote, a bipartisan coalition came together to soundly reject the Powers bill.[20]

Schiff, who had closely monitored the bill's progress, had prepared for its defeat. His committee had been pressing the Cleveland administration to quickly authorize a foreclosure sale if the bill failed. In some ways, this option was preferable, since it would allow the reorganization committee to cleanly sever the government's ties to the Union Pacific, though it also required raising a large amount of cash in a still-depressed economy. On the eve of the vote, Schiff wrote to Pierce, who was in Washington monitoring the legislative wrangling, telling him that Kuhn Loeb had in three days assembled commitments of nearly $40 million should the Union Pacific go to foreclosure—a feat, he boasted, that "I believe has never been done before in financial history."[21]

Less than two weeks after the defeat of the Powers bill, the outgoing Cleveland administration initiated foreclosure proceedings, as Schiff had hoped. By late April 1897, the banker seemed so confident of the sale's imminence that his committee commissioned a new bond plate so they could immediately begin printing up new securities when the transaction closed.[22]

Then came more setbacks. In May a group of creditors materialized and petitioned to intervene in the foreclosure action.[23] And in July, Senator Morgan began agitating to block the foreclosure, arguing the sale couldn't go forward without congressional consent and claiming the minimum bid ($45.8 million) Schiff's committee negotiated with the government amounted to robbery.[24] "There has been some agitation in the Senate on the part of the Populistic element to put obstacles into the sale of the property," Schiff wearily reported to his friend Robert Fleming, the Scottish banker. "We strongly suspect that behind these efforts is a small clique of parties who are disappointed because they have been unsuccessful in getting their finger in the pie, and having failed in other blackmail, they are now using the ever-ready Populistic element in the Senate in an endeavor to secure their ends."[25] Meanwhile the press had become increasingly hostile to Schiff's reorganization plan.

What role, Schiff had to wonder, was Ned Harriman playing in antagonizing his plans? As he struggled to keep the reorganization on track, he arranged another meeting with Harriman, where he laid out a proposition: "If you will cooperate with us, I'll see that you are made a director of the reorganized company and a member of the executive committee. Then, if you prove to be the strongest man in that committee, you'll probably get the chairmanship in the end."

This was precisely the type of challenge Harriman thrived on. "All right," he replied, "I'm with you."[26]

Thirty-year-old Otto Kahn, upon joining the Kuhn Loeb partnership, was thrust directly into one of the biggest deals it—and certainly he—had ever undertaken. Harriman beguiled him, and his fascination perhaps stemmed from the fact that Harriman eschewed the qualities—tact, style, charm—the young banker had so carefully cultivated.

Harriman was a dynamo who operated through the sheer force of his nature. "All the opportunity I ask is to be one among fifteen men around a table," he once told Kahn. Once Harriman got his seat at the table, Kahn later recalled, "over and over again did I observe him bending men and events to his determination, by the exercise of the truly wonderful powers of his brain and will."

Harriman wasn't cowed by a fight; in fact, he was pugilistic to a fault. "When there was an easy way to accomplish a thing, and also a difficult way, Mr. Harriman's inclination would be to take the latter," Kahn remembered. "I once told him I suspected him of purposely creating difficulties and obstacles for himself for the mere sport of overcoming them."[27]

By brokering an alliance with Harriman, Schiff removed one impediment to the reorganization, though others remained. In September 1897, news reports suggested that William McKinley's attorney general, Joseph McKenna, was considering appealing the foreclosure sale in order to modify its terms to better protect the government's interests.[28] Later that month, Schiff vented his frustrations to his son, who was just then completing his apprenticeship in London:

> We have not reached any understanding yet with the Attorney General in Union Pacific matters & have notified him today that he must finally decide whether he is going to let us go on with the sale of the road or whether he will appeal, & that in the latter case we shall withdraw certain concessions we have lately made to the government in order to remove obstructions. We must bring matters to a head now.

He worried that "if we cannot get through with the foreclosure before Congress meets in December," his plans might be shredded in a volley of "populistic attacks."[29]

Eager to speed things along, Schiff's committee agreed to boost its opening bid for the Union Pacific to $50 million, and the McKinley administration dropped its threat of an appeal. The sale was scheduled for November 1, and in the weeks leading up, it was all Schiff could do to keep his plans from unraveling. Joseph Pulitzer's *New York World* newspaper launched a full-scale assault on the deal—or rather the "steal," as the paper dubbed it—reporting that the Union Pacific was poised to fall to a "gang of robber speculators."[30] Meanwhile rumors surfaced that rival syndicates were forming to challenge Schiff's group for the railroad. Suddenly, less than a week before the auction, Attorney General McKenna informed the reorganization committee that he planned to postpone the sale until mid-December. It seemed clear he wanted to provide more time for rival bidders to emerge.

Desperate to salvage the deal, Schiff's committee raised its bid by another $8 million, and McKenna agreed to proceed with the foreclosure. But even as Schiff boarded his private railcar, bound for Omaha, where the auction would occur, he had no way of knowing if another shoe was about to drop.

On the evening of October 31, the night before the auction, Schiff paced his hotel room nervously. He worried not just about whether everything would proceed as planned but also about what would happen when his syndicate finally did have control of the railroad.[31] He had taken one of the biggest gambles of his career, and the gravity of it was finally sinking in.

At eleven a.m. the following day, hundreds gathered outside the Union Pacific's Omaha freight depot for what the *Nebraska State Journal* called "the greatest auction sale in the history of the world."[32] Spectators whispered about whether a rival syndicate would emerge to battle for control of the road. But when the time came, the auction proceeded without drama. The only bidder was Schiff's group, which ultimately offered a little over $58 million.

Now, after two years of arduous political and financial wrangling, came the hard part: turning around the Union Pacific.

True to his word, Schiff saw to it that Harriman was named a director of the Union Pacific and was appointed to the board's executive committee, the body with decision-making and spending authority over the road. Harriman's inclusion within the elite club of bankers and railroad executives spearheading the reorganization sparked a mix of puzzlement and consternation. Who was this intense, abrasive little man who spoke in rapid-fire bursts of thought, as if his mouth were struggling to keep pace with his mind? "He was looked at askance, somewhat in the light of an intruder," remembered Kahn, who with Schiff also served on the Union Pacific's board. "His ways and manners jarred upon several of his new colleagues, and he was considered by some as not quite belonging in their class, from the point of view of business position, achievements or financial standing, a free lance, neither a railroad man nor a banker nor a merchant." In other words, in the eyes of some of his colleagues, he remained nothing more than a "two-dollar broker."

That image did not remain long. Through the clarity of his vision, the boundlessness of his confidence, and the keenness of his intellect, Harriman won over his fellow board members. His dynamism even surprised Schiff, who by engineering Harriman's board appointment thought he was merely neutering an enemy.[33]

Winslow Pierce had started out as chairman of the board and of its executive committee. By May 1898, with Pierce's responsibilities in the legal arena mounting, the board elevated Harriman to the spot he coveted, the executive committee chairmanship, a perch that effectively gave him management authority over the railroad. Soon afterward Harriman decamped on a twenty-three-day expedition to inspect the "streaks of rust" the company had to work with. "Going on an inspection trip with him was an ordeal," one Harriman colleague recalled. "He noticed everything; he asked you about everything."[34]

What he noticed was that despite the Union Pacific's reputation for decrepitude, it was in reasonably good shape. Outdated? Yes. In need of repairs and improvements? Sure. But it had a solid foundation to build upon. Moreover, as his private train car rumbled west, he saw the blossoming of industry and commercial activity all over. He realized that a modern railroad stood to reap a traffic bonanza in the coming years. Harriman excitedly wired the executive committee for approval to spend $25 million on new equipment and upgrades. In New York, Harriman's wire was met with shock, and a tense meeting of the committee took place when he returned to the city in July 1898 to forcefully argue his case for the expenditures.[35] He came away with his $25 million, which he promptly poured into new, more powerful locomotives that could haul more tonnage and into efforts to make the Union Pacific's trains run faster and smoother by straightening sections of track that snaked inefficiently—shaving off miles in some cases—and lessening the grade in the steepest sections.

Rehabilitating the railroad was just one piece of the puzzle. Harriman, Schiff, and their colleagues also faced the challenge of reassembling it. During its receivership, as creditors lobbed lawsuit after lawsuit, the Union Pacific had been dismembered of many of its branch and connecting lines, with separate receivers taking responsibility for the assorted assets. The "Union Pacific" that they purchased consisted of a fraction of the original system—1,038 miles of track that stretched from Council Bluffs, Iowa, to Ogden, Utah. With its most "important branches, feeders, and outlets" stripped away, Kahn recalled, "nothing was left of the old Union Pacific System but the bare trunk stem."[36]

The Union Pacific, in other words, was no longer a transcontinental railroad. Returning it to profitability—and capturing the spike in western traffic Harriman knew was on the horizon—would necessitate reacquiring some of its old appendages or buying new ones. Within months of emerging from foreclosure, the Union Pacific absorbed the Kansas Pacific (running from Kansas City to Denver) and the Denver Pacific (stretching from Denver to Cheyenne, Wyoming). Schiff and Harriman also had their eyes on the Oregon Short Line, once a Union Pacific subsidiary, and the Oregon Railway and Navigation Company, in which the short line held a large (but not controlling) stake. Together these lines had once provided the Union Pacific with a path to the West Coast, branching off from the main line in Wyoming and continuing on a northward slant through Idaho and into Oregon, ending in Portland.

Harriman and Kuhn Loeb began discreetly buying up shares in the Oregon Short Line. By mid-February 1898, they had amassed enough stock that Kahn informed the Union Pacific's newly anointed president, a pompous engineer named Horace Burt, that they had secured "practical control of the property."[37] Schiff followed up five days later with an enthusiastic letter to Burt declaring that "with the control of the Oregon Short Line practically assured to us, it appears to me that we shall have in the new Union Pacific System everything which in the old system was of real earning capacity, and that in consequence the reorganized Company will not have the drawback of any unprofitable mileage whatsoever."[38] Soon the Union Pacific's control of the Oregon Short Line would be total, and it would also assert its dominion over the Oregon Railway and Navigation Company.

The Union Pacific's new leadership pushed the company to squeeze more profit out of its holdings. Along with the railroad itself, the reorganization committee had also acquired millions of acres of land granted to the company by the federal government. Schiff reminded Burt that the "Union Pacific lands" needed "more careful and vigorous management than they had heretofore, so that land sales be pushed. Aside from the funds which prompter sales would bring into the Company's treasury, it is a better policy to get the lands under cultivation and bring new business than to hold them and pay taxes on them."[39]

The Spanish-American War began several months into the reorganization. It was a conflict, Schiff told Robert Fleming, that "had to come . . . after all, this is simply a war of civilization against barbarism, and of methods of the end of the nineteenth century against those yet surviving from the sixteenth century."[40] The War Department quickly mobilized men and matériel, and America's leading railroads were vital to this effort. For the Union Pacific, the conflict offered a chance to showcase the railroad's rebirth, demonstrate its patriotism, and obtain lucrative government contracts.

Schiff and Kahn wanted the Union Pacific to play a significant role in the deployment. The bankers were incensed when they learned the company had lost out on the business of the Astor Battery, a detachment funded and equipped by Colonel John Jacob Astor IV, scion of the wealthy New York family, who had volunteered his services to the War Department at the outset of the war. Rival roads had conveyed the battery to the West Coast, where the soldiers would deploy to the Philippines, then a Spanish colony.[41]

Kahn communicated their dismay to Horace Burt, writing:

Mr. Schiff and myself have been struck with the fact—and we have heard it commented upon a good deal—that . . . the Union Pacific has not had its proper share of that traffic. Thus, to quote only one instance, the Astor Battery a few days ago went to San Francisco over the Missouri Pacific, Denver & Rio Grande and Rio Grande Western. Of course, the newspaper reports may have been incomplete and the Union Pacific may have obtained all that it had a right to expect but the impression prevailing certainly is, that it did not, and people are asking the reason why and thinking that somebody must have been remiss in having allowed the U.P.'s competitors to get ahead of it.[42]

It turned out the bankers' ire was misplaced. The Union Pacific had in fact moved a large number of troops—more than ten thousand as of late June 1898. And as Burt explained in his patient reply to Kahn, the railroad lost the Astor business because the federal government had waived competitive bidding. "The Union Pacific has been on the alert and has secured a large and satisfactory share of the business, especially so in view of the very sharp competition," Burt wrote.[43]

The market sensed major things afoot within the Union Pacific. By the end of 1898, shares of its preferred stock had surged by 60 percent; its common stock had nearly tripled.[44] And this reflected more than just Wall Street hype—the turnaround was working. Within a few years, the railroad would boast annual revenues of $8,167 per mile of track, up from $5,621 in 1892, the year before the Union Pacific collapsed into receivership.

So great was Harriman's faith in the company's prospects—in his own ability to revitalize the railroad—that he had amassed thousands of shares of Union Pacific stock at rock-bottom prices, even though they were initially considered to hold "little intrinsic value," Otto Kahn recalled.[45] His Union Pacific holdings helped transform a modest fortune into a formidable one, and a two-dollar broker into a magnate.

Harriman turned fifty in 1898, and he entered what would be the final decade of his life at a full-tilt sprint, propelled by a type of ravenous ambition usually reserved for younger men. With Schiff, Kahn, and the resources of Kuhn Loeb at his disposal, he went on a spree of reorganization and acquisition, bringing tens of thousands of miles of track under his complete or de facto control.

"Everybody that goes in with Harriman makes money," Schiff would later comment.[46] The same, of course, could have been said of Schiff, who had done the financial spadework from which the rejuvenated Union Pacific, among other Harriman ventures, had bloomed. Schiff's Union Pacific gamble had turned out to be highly lucrative. His firm received $6 million in preferred shares alone for its role in putting together the underwriting syndicate.[47] Schiff had also won a less tangible but equally valuable prize. In undertaking the Union Pacific reorganization, he had shown himself to be every inch J. P. Morgan's equal.

Yet stepping out of Morgan's shadow placed Schiff directly in his path.

15

A PERFECT PEACE

The only suggestion I have to offer," Schiff told Horace Burt, after the engineer took charge of the Union Pacific, "is that you try to keep harmony with and among your neighbors, for I believe, as a rule, the Railroad Companies themselves have been their own worst enemies as to rates &c."[1]

Harmony: all the railroad bigs—Schiff, Morgan, Harriman, Hill—spoke of it, while keeping a close watch on their flanks for signs of ambush or incursion. Sure, they wanted peace, so long as it came about on their terms. A maze of alliances maintained a façade of order, but the truces, voting trusts, and traffic agreements preventing the industry from slipping back to the violent anarchy of old were always at risk of coming undone. Communities of interest worked, until the interests of one party diverged.

The trouble began in the Northwest, where in 1899 the Union Pacific, led by Harriman, had gained control of the Oregon Railway and Navigation Company, its access point to Portland and the Pacific coast. Three competing companies—the Union Pacific, the Northern Pacific, and James Hill's Great Northern—had previously controlled the line, forming a pact to keep it neutral in order to avoid the unnecessary and costly construction of new lines. Hill had been negotiating to maintain the railroad's neutrality, and he warned Harriman in a letter that his hand would be forced if an agreement was not reached. "I think that with five million dollars I could build a much better line from our road into Portland; and with, say, two million more, reach the most productive sections of the Navigation Company."[2] Hill was threatening to move in on the Union Pacific's territory. Talks continued half-heartedly, but the fragile detente had clearly broken down.

"Who the hell is Harriman?" James Hill had wondered just a few years earlier when he spotted Harriman's name on a roster of the Union Pacific's newly appointed directors.[3] The answer had fast become clear: Harriman was a dangerous rival.

Schiff increasingly found himself in an awkward spot, caught between two indomitable railroad titans: his old friend Hill, who had mentored his son Morti in the railroad business, and his new ally Harriman, the unlikely juggernaut, with whom he had joined in a series of railroad ventures. Harriman and Hill were on a collision course, which also placed their respective bankers, Schiff and J. P. Morgan, on an inexorable path to confrontation.

Both sides had much to lose and to gain in the epic clash to come over who controlled the main arteries of transcontinental rail traffic. Their struggle vividly showcased the unbounded financial clout these titans had amassed. It rattled Wall Street so fiercely that Harriman, Hill, Morgan, and Schiff would end up inadvertently making the case for restricting and regulating the outsize power they had exercised so freely in the past, permanently altering the relationship between corporations and the U.S. government.

Hill was as hardy as Harriman was sickly, a stout bear of a man who once, when a fire broke out in his St. Paul offices, muscled a three-hundred-pound rolltop desk out a second-floor window to save its contents. Blind in his right eye from a childhood accident with a bow and arrow, Hill had a legendary temper and a rugged, salt-of-the-earth quality. Beneath his gruff mien was a surprisingly cultured man who quoted Shakespeare and whose mansion on St. Paul's Summit Avenue featured a two-floor art gallery filled with landscapes by nineteenth-century French masters. (After visiting Hill's massive home, which had twenty-two fireplaces, sixteen bathrooms, and a three-story pipe organ, Morti reported to his father that it was "very stiff" and rife with "those enormous cut glass chandeliers" that "disfigure every room in which they are placed.")[4]

Born in Ontario, Hill came to St. Paul at eighteen, working as a clerk for a steamship company, then managing a wharf. Steeped in the shipping business, he scraped together the money to construct a warehouse on the banks of St. Paul's Mississippi River levee. Soon he formed a small steamboat line on the Red River, running cargo between Moorhead, on Minnesota's western border, and Winnipeg. In the late 1870s, he staked his growing fortune on the St. Paul and Pacific Railroad, a 437-mile line running through the Minnesota hinterlands. Where others saw a lost cause, Hill, an evangelist for the economic potential of the Northwest, glimpsed the cornerstone of the transportation empire that would become the Great Northern Railway. For fifteen years, Hill stabbed westward, laying mile after mile of track across the northern fringe of the United States, across rivers, over plains, and through mountain passes, until the Great Northern reached Seattle. (A branch at Spokane linked the line to Portland, via the Oregon Railway.) The achievement was all the more significant because Hill completed his transcontinental line without a dollar of federal assistance.

A transportation visionary, Hill foresaw not only an economic boom in the Northwest but the possibility of using his line as a conduit to ship American goods to Asia. On his railroad, cars laden with timber rumbled east; they returned west brimming with grain bound for China and Japan.

Hill completed his transcontinental line in 1893—just as the economy cratered. Hill's railroad (notwithstanding Morti's report to his father about the low morale of his employees) was perhaps the nation's soundest and best constructed. While other tycoons had looted their lines for quick profits, Hill built a system that withstood the financial maelstroms that had swamped his overcapitalized competitors. Now he watched as his rivals slipped one by one into receivership. As with most financial catastrophes, this one brought an opportunity.

Hill had long had his eye on taking over the Northern Pacific, which ran roughly parallel to the Great Northern, spanning the Great Lakes to Puget Sound. Like the Union Pacific, the Northern Pacific was a congressionally chartered road conceived during the Civil War. A poorly managed and debt-ridden line, it had just gone bankrupt for the second time. Its first collapse had come twenty years earlier, in 1873, when Jay Cooke's disastrous financial stewardship contributed to a national economic crisis. By early 1895, Hill was writing to Schiff excitedly about the potential of acquiring the Northern Pacific. "A very large saving could be made in (Northern Pacific) operating expenses and waste of revenue, and further by reducing all unnecessary train mileage. The net result would be so great as to astonish you," he wrote Schiff that January.[5] In another missive, Hill told the Kuhn Loeb banker, "Every day shows the great advantage control of the Northern Pacific would give us in matters of rates, and particularly in controlling unnecessary train service and cost of handling the business of both Companies."[6]

Just as the revival of the Union Pacific had pulled Harriman into Schiff's orbit, Hill's pursuit of the Northern Pacific had thrust him into an alliance with Pierpont Morgan, who was spearheading its reorganization. In May 1895, at Morgan's London mansion, Hill inked an agreement with Deutsche Bank, the Northern Pacific's largest investor, for the Great Northern to acquire the railroad. But the deal, stoking fears of a railroad monopoly in the Northwest, soon fell apart, becoming the subject of a lawsuit that rose to the United States Supreme Court, which ultimately blocked the merger. Morgan and Hill had anticipated an adverse ruling, so the Minnesota railroad titan personally acquired a large minority stake in the Northern Pacific, a move that gave him a say in the management of the railroad and sidestepped state and federal antimonopoly laws. In the spring of 1896, days after the Supreme Court's decision, Hill returned to England to meet with Morgan, who spent part of each year there rotating between his Kensington mansion and Dover House, his country estate southwest of London. They struck a new deal forming a "permanent alliance" between the Great Northern and Northern Pacific that was "defensive and in case of need offensive, with a view of avoiding competition and aggressive policy and of generally protecting the common interests of both Companies."[7] For the next four years, Morgan operated the Northern Pacific through a trust that he controlled. Finally, in the fall of 1900, he turned the reins over to Hill.

While Hill waited impatiently and, at times, irritably for his chance to control the Northern Pacific, Harriman scoured the country for lines to fortify and bolster his burgeoning empire. The era of small independent railroad systems had ended. The industry was rapidly consolidating through mergers and more creative alliances brokered to avoid government scrutiny under new antitrust laws, dividing the nation's railroad system into regional fiefdoms controlled by a handful of moguls. It was a trend occurring in other sectors of the American economy, as independent industrial concerns combined to withstand larger competitors. The wave of consolidation and reorganization, requiring financiers to mobilize capital on

a massive scale, was making bankers such as Schiff and Morgan outrageously wealthy. Some of these same trends were fomenting widespread labor strife and fueling an anarchist underground, imported
by European immigrants, whose members in some cases lashed out
at their capitalist foes with violence.

After strengthening the Union Pacific's position in the Northwest,
Harriman shifted his focus east. He zeroed in on the Chicago, Burlington & Quincy, a midsize railroad system with lines that coursed
through the midwestern heartland, stretching from Chicago as far
west as Denver, Colorado, and Billings, Montana. Its extensive network included the line formerly known as the Rockford, Rock Island
& St. Louis Railroad, the company whose controversial downfall
appeared to have contributed to the abrupt dissolution of Schiff's first
investment partnership, Budge, Schiff & Co.

By acquiring the Burlington—or the Q, as the line was sometimes
known—the Union Pacific would eliminate a possible threat to its
transcontinental hegemony. From its western outposts, the Burlington could at any moment decide to continue building to the Pacific
Coast. As Schiff later explained, "It was felt that, with a comparatively small expenditure," the Burlington "could, and in time probably would, construct a series of branches to tap many of the most
important traffic-producing districts along the line of the Union
Pacific Railroad, and that ultimately the Chicago, Burlington &
Quincy would in all likelihood extend its lines into Ogden and Salt
Lake City, if not to San Francisco."[8] Indeed, rumors spread that the
Burlington planned an expansion.[9] One paper reported the "partly
authenticated" scuttlebutt that Burlington executives contemplated
constructing a line all the way to Portland—the heart of the Union
Pacific's newly reclaimed territory.[10] This turned out to be groundless
gossip, but it hardly mattered. If the Burlington didn't build its own
line to the coast, it was ripe for a takeover by one of the larger systems.

In January 1900, Harriman approached Charles Elliott Perkins,
the Burlington's president of nearly two decades, to feel him out
about an acquisition. Perkins recognized as well as anyone that the
railroad industry was undergoing a vast transformation and that the
"days of small things," as he would later put it, were ending.[11] Ensuring his company's survival, he knew, would mean eventually marrying
it to a larger competitor. But as a potential buyer, he disliked Harriman, whom he found pushy, arrogant, and charmless.

The Burlington was not on the market, Perkins told Harriman coolly. Though he left the door open just a crack, noting that if it were for sale, the price would be a minimum of $200 per share.[12] (The Burlington's common stock was then trading at around $122.) Harriman took several more runs at Perkins throughout the spring and summer, but he wouldn't budge.[13] Getting nowhere, Schiff and Harriman spent a couple of months quietly buying up shares in the company to surreptitiously gain control of the Burlington, but eventually abandoned the plan after it became evident they could not amass a controlling interest.[14]

Harriman and Schiff weren't the only suitors circling the Burlington. Hill and Morgan had decided they needed an outlet in Chicago for their railroads. By early 1901, Hill had quietly commenced negotiations with Perkins, who stuck to his $200-per-share price but now seemed more open to cutting a deal. In part this was because Perkins believed Hill's Great Northern was the proper partner for the Burlington; the fact that Hill was also bringing to the table Morgan and the Northern Pacific only sweetened the pot.

As Hill moved in, Harriman and Schiff were distracted by a separate set of talks. In August the death of seventy-eight-year-old Collis P. Huntington, the railroad magnate who owned the Southern Pacific Railroad (which also included the Central Pacific system), had put his vast holdings in play. If the Union Pacific could gain control of Huntington's railroads, it would not only dominate rail traffic in the southern United States but secure a direct link to San Francisco over the Central Pacific. Harriman had wasted no time in plunging into negotiations with Huntington's bankers to acquire a controlling stake in the Southern Pacific.

Initially, Schiff did not recognize Hill as an adversary, though the coming conflict between them would be obvious to anyone who could read a railroad map. Still, he sensed a growing distance between them. In their correspondence, Hill grew increasingly circumspect and cryptic. During a visit to New York in late December 1900, Hill paid a social call to Schiff at his Fifth Avenue home, and the pair danced awkwardly around the reason for his trip east, which Schiff assumed involved meetings with Morgan, but he was never able to pry the truth from his friend. (It was around this time that Hill made his first approach to the Burlington's executive committee.)[15]

On February 4, 1901, after Kuhn Loeb successfully negotiated the purchase of a 37.5 percent interest in Huntington's company on behalf of the Union Pacific, Schiff sent Hill a breezy note. "We have finally landed the Southern Pacific bird, and I am sure this has your approval," he wrote.[16] But for Hill, what was there to celebrate? The deal, giving the Union Pacific a virtual lock on traffic to and from San Francisco and a valuable rail network through the cotton belt, only confirmed Hill's belief that the Union Pacific posed an imminent threat to his empire. If Harriman also gained control of the Burlington, Hill later explained, "both the Northern Pacific and Great Northern would be largely shut out of the states of Nebraska, Kansas, Missouri, South Dakota, Iowa, Illinois, and Wisconsin, except by using other lines of railway, some of which were in the market for sale and might at any time pass under the control of or be combined with the Union Pacific interests."[17]

Days after sealing the Southern Pacific deal, which *The New York Times* described in its front-page story as "one of the largest" transactions "in the railroad and financial history of this country," Harriman turned his focus back to the Burlington.[18] On February 10 he met again with Perkins, this time proposing acquiring half of the Burlington's stock. Perkins dismissed the offer. The following day, unknown to Harriman, Perkins sat down with another visitor with an offer to present. It was Hill.

Thinly sourced reports of an impending takeover floated in and out of the nation's financial pages, sending the Burlington's stock surging.[19] It climbed past 140, past 150, past 160, past 170. By early April, it would break 180. Schiff grew concerned by what he later described as "the large and continuous buying, irrespective of price," of the company's shares, suspecting Hill and Morgan might be behind it. Finally, Schiff decided to confront Hill. In mid- or late March, he and Harriman met with Hill, and Schiff asked him directly if he was angling for control of the Burlington. Hill, as he had when reporters posed the same question, denied having any interest in the railroad.[20] "I accepted this statement on Mr. Hill's part," Schiff would later say, "for I could not believe that a man whom I had known and with whom I had closely associated for some fifteen years, whom I had never wronged, but whom I had shown friendship without reserve, and whom I believed to be my friend, would willingly mislead or deceive me."[21] Hill had apparently done just that. In truth, he and Morgan were closing in on a deal to acquire the Burlington. By the end of March, newspapers reported that the transaction was imminent.[22]

Given the pervasive rumors of the Burlington's consolidation with the Great Northern and Northern Pacific, there is reason to suspect that Schiff saw through Hill's denial from the start. But he unquestionably felt deeply betrayed by his friend's deception. Hot-tempered Harriman was ready to do combat.

Aiming to avoid a ruinous clash between Harriman and Hill, Schiff sought out Morgan in early April 1901. He hoped that the Union Pacific could potentially join the Great Northern and Northern Pacific in the Burlington deal, eliminating concerns that the railroad would be used to mount an incursion into the Union Pacific's territory. Morgan, who was about to sail for Europe, wasn't interested in talking, telling Schiff to forward whatever plan he had in mind to London. Schiff then appealed to one of Morgan's partners, Robert Bacon, offering on the spot to bankroll a third of the transaction. Bacon replied that it was too late. Schiff warned that the Union Pacific was being forced into an "intolerable" position "against which it would have to protect itself."[23]

On April 7, Easter Sunday, Schiff and Harriman again confronted Hill, who was dining at the Murray Hill mansion of George F. Baker, the president of the First National Bank. Hill and Baker were scheduled to take an overnight train to Boston, where they planned to meet Perkins and other Burlington officials to finalize the buyout.

Still wounded by Hill's deception, Schiff asked him straight off why he had lied to his face. Hill apologized. Schiff's connection to the Union Pacific, he said, had left him no choice.

Schiff and Harriman argued strenuously for Hill to delay the Burlington deal until they could thrash out an agreement under which the Union Pacific "could and would be protected against aggressions in its legitimate territory," as Schiff later recounted.[24] And they asked again to finance a third of the Burlington purchase. Hill refused, saying later that cutting them in on the deal would have "defeated our purpose in buying the Burlington."[25]

According to one account, the heated conversation continued in Baker's carriage on the way to Grand Central and lasted until Baker and Hill's train pulled away from the station.[26] "Very well," Harriman declared finally, with both sides at loggerheads, "it is a hostile act and you must take the consequences."[27]

The consequences? What did Harriman mean by this? Schiff understood all too well, and the prospect made him queasy. While Schiff had been trying to broker peace, he and Harriman had simultaneously prepared for battle. Harriman had devised a plan so audacious that it recalled Jay Gould's attempted corner of the gold market some thirty years earlier. They would steal the Northern Pacific away from Hill and Morgan, giving them 50 percent control of the Burlington. In essence, Harriman was proposing to broker a community of interest with brute force.

Tussles for corporate control involving surreptitious buying were not uncommon in the railroad industry—Cornelius Vanderbilt had once secretly bought up Erie stock, only to have Daniel Drew and his confederates flood the market with new shares, diluting ownership. But what made Harriman's scheme especially bold was both the size of the company he was targeting, and who he was going up against in the process—namely Morgan.

Unlike Harriman and Schiff's abortive effort to seize the Burlington, it seemed technically possible to buy majority control of the Northern Pacific. Morgan and Hill held less than half of the Northern's preferred and common shares. Large blocks of Northern stock changed hands regularly. But the question was not only could it be done, but should it.

Schiff, at first, recoiled at the idea, which seemed no less underhanded than Hill's deceit. He fretted over irreparably rupturing their friendship; moreover, he worried about arousing Morgan's legendary wrath. "Mr. Harriman is a very remarkable man," he confided to Otto Kahn, "but I frankly don't feel that I am called upon to pay for his friendship with the loss of Mr. Hill's friendship and with the jeopardizing of the goodwill, esteem, and regard, which for so long have prevailed between Mr. Morgan and myself."[28]

Kahn, who had grown close with Harriman, backed his plan; Schiff reluctantly came around. He rationalized that the "aim of the proposed transaction was not to harm or antagonize the Northern Pacific–Great Northern interests, but to establish fair and friendly and mutually advantageous working relations between them and the Union Pacific interests," as Kahn later recounted.[29] According to Schiff's junior partner, Schiff also determined it was his duty as a Union Pacific board member to protect the railroad. But if that was the case, Schiff did not display the same loyalty to the Great Northern, where he remained a director even as he plotted to undercut its president.[30]

The day after the contentious meeting at Baker's home, Schiff penned a heartfelt letter to Hill, knowing what he had to do but fearful of the repercussions. It seemed written as much to reassure Schiff as Hill over the strength of their friendship. "Wherever our business interests may place us, I feel it is too late in our lives to personally go apart. Friendships have little value, if they are only determined by personal interest and go to pieces on the first clashing of interest." And he noted, "As to the Union Pacific, it must take care of itself, as it will be able to do, but in any event, I want to feel that nothing has come between us."

Hill replied that "no act or thought of mine can ever knowingly destroy or impair the feeling of affectionate friendship which I hold to both yourself and those who are nearest you."[31]

After the tender expressions of friendship, each mogul retreated to his corner for the battle that Schiff knew was coming and that would shortly reach Hill's doorstep.

Schiff and his Kuhn Loeb partners skillfully executed Harriman's plan. The firm engaged a far-flung network of brokers to discreetly canvass the globe for Northern Pacific shares. Meanwhile, in a sly twist, Kuhn Loeb conspicuously sold just enough Northern Pacific stock to camouflage the scheme. Throughout April and into early May, the company's stock price rose steadily due to the large-scale buying. Morgan, off on a European art-buying spree, didn't seem to notice anything amiss. Hill thought little of it, too. The market was experiencing record churn for railroad and other securities amid constant rumors of various mergers, and the Northern Pacific was hardly alone in seeing big gains.

On April 30, the trading volume on the New York Stock Exchange demolished the record high set just the previous day, with more than 3.2 million shares changing hands.[32] That same day Morti Schiff married Adele Neustadt, the daughter of family friends.[33] Jacob and his wife gifted the newlyweds 932 Fifth Avenue as a wedding present and moved into an even more stately townhouse just up the block at 965 Fifth Avenue. "It's wonderful to be the master of the house where you had so many spankings," Morti joked of the gift.[34]

Harriman and his wife attended Morti and Adele's lavish wedding. But there was no sign of Hill. One apocryphal account placed him in Seattle on that day, where, as the story goes, a "dark-complected angel" appeared to him in a dream; taking this as an omen that his railroad empire was in trouble, he raced across the country to New York in his private railroad car, setting a transcontinental record. But in fact on April 30, Hill was already in New York seeing his daughters off as they sailed for Europe. It would be another few days before he discovered, to his shock, what Harriman had meant when he threatened "consequences."

On the morning of Friday, May 3, Hill visited Schiff at Kuhn Loeb's offices, then located at 27 Pine Street (where Hill also kept an office on a different floor).[35] It's not clear who called the meeting or what Hill may have suspected about recent purchases of Northern Pacific shares, but Schiff, apparently believing control of the Northern Pacific was a fait accompli, revealed to his old friend what he and Harriman had been up to over the previous month.

Hill didn't believe him at first. "But you can't get control," he blurted. Together he, Morgan, and their allies controlled some $35 to $40 million of Northern Pacific stock. But what he did not realize was that some of his allies had sold off chunks of stock as the company's shares reached record highs; at one point the previous month, J.P. Morgan & Co. itself had parted with $1 million of Northern stock to capitalize on the rise in its value.[36]

At a cost of $60 million, Schiff had managed to scoop up 420,000 of the Northern Pacific's 750,000 preferred shares and 370,000 of its 800,000 common shares. Combined, this constituted a majority of the company's outstanding stock.

"What was your purpose in doing this?" Hill stammered.

"To enforce peace in the Northwest," Schiff replied, explaining that he intended to broker the "community of interest" that Hill had previously rebuffed. Schiff wanted at least some Union Pacific influence over the affairs of the Northern Pacific and ideally representation on the board of the Burlington.

Hill would later say that Schiff and Harriman, who he said was also present for part of the meeting, laid out a grandiose plan to consolidate the Union Pacific with the Northern Pacific, Great Northern, and Burlington and offered to allow Hill to run this behemoth. Implicit in such a plan was that Morgan would be pushed out of the management. Hill also claimed that Harriman and his allies had at one point during the Northern Pacific drama "boasted how they would show the world that Morgan & Co. were not the only financial house in America."[37] But there is reason to doubt whether Schiff and Harriman had really contemplated such an audacious frontal assault on Morgan, who held it within his power to clap back with equal, if not greater, force. Over the years, Hill told various, sometimes conflicting accounts of the battle; nor was he above dissembling when it suited his purposes.

Whatever else may have transpired during the meeting, Hill

departed fully aware that his plans were in jeopardy. He also appeared to have given some indication that he was willing to deal, for he accepted an invitation to join the Schiffs that evening for their Sabbath dinner, after which Hill and Schiff stayed up past midnight discussing how to bring harmony to their competing fiefdoms. According to Schiff, Hill "repeatedly assured" him they could come to terms.[38]

Earlier that day, Schiff had confided to Kahn his relief that he had come clean with Hill. But Kahn and Harriman didn't share his sangfroid. With their plan now out in the open, they felt deeply anxious about how the Hill-Morgan interests would respond. And they didn't trust Hill. That, it turned out, was wise.

After meeting with Schiff and before attending dinner at his home, Hill rushed over to 23 Wall Street. Along with Morgan partners and clerks, he pored over account books to determine how many shares each side held. And he realized the game was not yet up. A provision within the Northern Pacific's charter allowed the company to retire its preferred shares as of January 1, 1902, vesting control of the company in whomever held a majority of the common stock. Schiff and Harriman were more than 30,000 shares short of that amount. If the Hill-Morgan-dominated board could cobble together a majority of the common stock and then postpone the company's annual meeting that fall, where Harriman and Schiff would surely install their allies, they would have a shot at preserving control. Hill's assurances to Schiff had been an act—a stall tactic. He was about to set his own secret plan in motion.

On the morning of Saturday, May 4, Harriman was in bed nursing another of his frequent colds. He and Schiff knew about the preferred stock provision. Their lawyers had advised them that it would not interfere with their control of the company; they could exercise their voting rights, forming a new board, before the New Year. Still, he couldn't shake a feeling of disquiet. The issue nagged at him. He picked up the phone at his bedside and called Louis Heinsheimer, one of Schiff's junior partners and the firm's trading specialist. Buy 40,000 shares of Northern Pacific common on my account, he croaked into the receiver. "All right," Heinsheimer replied.[39]

To execute Harriman's order before the close of the market at noon that day, Heinsheimer needed to first clear it with Schiff, who was at temple, as he was almost every Saturday morning. Heinsheimer managed to locate Schiff and convey Harriman's directive.

Schiff countermanded Harriman's order—he would only be wasting his money. They already possessed control, Schiff reasoned.

As Schiff was waving Heinsheimer off, Morgan partner Robert Bacon dispatched a coded cable to J. P. Morgan, who was making his annual visit to the French spa town of Aix-les-Bains, explaining Harriman and Schiff's gambit and requesting permission to purchase 150,000 shares of Northern Pacific. Morgan, wide-eyed with rage, quickly replied, giving Bacon carte blanche to buy at any price.[40]

Harriman did not learn that Schiff had overruled his order until Monday morning, after an army of traders working on behalf of J.P. Morgan & Co. swarmed London and then New York, frantically buying Northern Pacific. Nervous that he had received no confirmation of the trade he had placed over the weekend, Harriman rang Heinsheimer, who broke the news. Harriman worried they had made a fatal error. "I then knew that the whole object of our work might be lost," he later recalled. He rushed downtown to strategize with—and probably berate—Schiff.[41] Together, they watched Northern Pacific—or the "Nipper," as it was sometimes known, due to its ticker symbol, NPPR—leap as high as 133 from its previous close of 110.

Why did Schiff refuse to fortify their position when he had the chance? In part, it was due to his friendship with Hill. Though Hill had already lied to him once, Schiff refused to believe he had been duped again. "He felt that buying on our part of additional Common Stock after his conversation with Mr. Hill would have indicated a lack of confidence in Mr. Hill's professions, and he did not want to put himself into that attitude," Kahn recalled. Moreover, he remained confident in his analysis that they held enough shares to achieve their objective—a say in the management of the Burlington. According to Kahn, Schiff held firm even after the frenzied buying began.

He foresaw that if the other side was really determined to go ahead and buy every obtainable share of Northern Pacific Common, an alarming, if not critical, situation would be created, and he wanted to be able to say, if such a situation did come, that he and those with and for whom he acted had had no hand in bringing it about and had not bought a share of Common Stock from the day on which his conversation with Mr. Hill occurred.[42]

Indeed, a calamity soon unfolded. By Tuesday, May 7, the Hill-Morgan group had largely wrapped up its buying, believing it now controlled a majority of Northern Pacific's common stock. Together, the Hill-Morgan and Harriman-Schiff factions now held nearly all the company's stock. But the massive buying had unintended consequences. Shares of Northern Pacific became so hard to locate that short sellers found themselves in increasingly desperate straits.

Even under the best conditions, short selling was a risky proposition. It entailed selling shares you did not yet own on the gamble that the stock price would fall, allowing you to buy the shares at a lower price, fulfill your contract, and realize a profit. For instance, if you shorted one share of Northern Pacific at $125 and were later able to purchase the stock at $110, you would net $15. Alternately, if shares rose to $140, you could be forced to cover your position at a $15 loss. It was the latter scenario that began playing out as the scarcity of Northern Pacific shares caused their price to spike. What transpired was sometimes known as a short squeeze, a version of which famously played out more than a century later, when retail investors drove up the price of GameStop by more than 1,400 percent, forcing hedge funds and other traders, whose accumulated short positions surpassed the number of public shares in circulation, to stem their losses by covering at eye-popping prices.

Traders bid Northern Pacific ever higher: On Tuesday, it nearly hit 150, before ending the day at 143½.[43] Meanwhile, as Northern Pacific soared, other stocks on the list plunged, the result of traders selling off securities to cover their short positions (that is, buy the shares they had already sold) in the Nipper.

That night reporters tracked down Hill at the Hotel Netherland, where he was staying, and asked him about the rumors, now widespread, that he and Morgan were locked in a titanic struggle with Harriman over the Northern Pacific. Hill feigned ignorance. "I have not bought a share of Northern Pacific in six months," he said. "I'm president of the Great Northern, you know, and I'm not interested in the Northern Pacific. I don't know anything about Mr. Morgan's relations to the road—we are two separate individuals."[44]

The speculative wheels of Wall Street were spinning off the wagon, and control of the Northern Pacific was at stake. It was perhaps the most tense and high-stakes period of Schiff's career. Yet remarkably, he still made time for his philanthropic commitments, even during the height of the battle. He and Julius Goldman had planned a trip to visit Woodbine, the agricultural commune the Baron de Hirsch Fund had helped to establish outside Philadelphia. Shortly before they were scheduled to leave, Schiff told Goldman that he would have to take a later train to attend to some pressing business in New York. In Philadelphia, Goldman bumped into a mutual friend who filled him in on the Wall Street intrigue. "Mr. Schiff will not meet you tonight nor tomorrow morning because he is deeply interested in the Northern Pacific contest," the friend said confidently. But the next morning Goldman found Schiff waiting for him in the lobby. Throughout the day, Schiff seemed distracted, placing frequent calls to his office, and as they rode home together that evening, Goldman alluded to the Northern Pacific fight. "I am afraid we picked a rather inauspicious moment for our visit," he said. Schiff smiled. The timing, he said, was unfortunate, but he had not wanted to break their plans.[45]

On Wednesday, May 8, Northern Pacific shares gyrated wildly, leaping as high as 180 and diving as low as the 140s. In the moments it took to place a buy order, the Nipper could be up or down by 20 points. To calm the stormy market, the Harriman and Hill contingents began lending some of their shares to the shorts. A young broker named Al Stern, who had orchestrated some of the Northern Pacific purchases for Kuhn Loeb, was nearly mauled in the process. Wading onto the exchange floor, he announced loudly, "Who wants to borrow Northern Pacific? I have a block to lend."

A "deafening shout" rose from the crowd, and then a jostling mob encircled Stern, recalled the financier Bernard Baruch, who witnessed the scene. "They were like thirst-crazed men battling for water, with the biggest, strongest, and loudest faring best." One frantic broker snatched Stern's hat and began aggressively rapping him on the head with it to get his attention. After lending out all the shares he had to offer, Stern, white-faced and disheveled, finally slunk away.[46]

Efforts to pacify the roiling market had little effect. After the exchange opened on Thursday, the first shares of Northern Pacific sold at 170. Then pandemonium erupted. Shares jumped in leaps of 100, 200, 300 points between trades. Shortly after eleven a.m., 300 shares of Northern Pacific sold for an astounding $1,000 a share. Anguished short sellers, unwittingly caught in a clash between railroad giants, could no longer buy or borrow the shares needed to cover their positions. They were forced to watch helplessly as the ticker tape spelled out their financial ruin.

"The thing was so sudden that conservative men lost their heads, and language was heard from reputable churchgoing members of society that would not bear repetition under ordinary circumstances in a barroom of even the second class," one broker told a reporter. For the first time anyone could remember, the exchange's viewing galleries were shuttered to the public.[47]

As the stock market spun out of control, Otto Kahn proposed to Schiff that they take advantage of the situation to hoover up securities at panic-battered prices. Schiff shot him a withering glance. "If you want to buy stocks personally, you are free to do so," he replied. "But Kuhn, Loeb & Co. will not, with my consent, make one dollar's worth of profit out of this calamity."[48]

Only the moguls who had caused the market to go haywire could bring the chaos to an end. Harriman, Hill, and their bankers were ultimately forced to the bargaining table by a lawsuit seeking to enjoin them from demanding the delivery of shares owed to them by short sellers.[49] Both sides—each convinced that they held control of Northern Pacific—huddled throughout the day, conferring late into the afternoon at the offices of J.P. Morgan & Co. The question of who controlled Northern Pacific would have to wait. Now they had to jointly hammer out a solution to the immediate crisis. Finally, Schiff emerged from the Morgan offices, and both firms announced that they would settle open contracts with short sellers for $150 a share, a reasonable deal considering that Northern Pacific shares had recently traded at multiples of that. But this price would have also yielded a healthy profit for the Harriman and Hill factions, marking a nearly 60 percent advance in the value of the company's shares in the space of a month.

Given the chaotic situation on Wall Street, no one would have blamed Schiff for canceling his plans for that evening. But to the surprise of Lillian Wald, who had been reading the newspaper coverage of the Northern Pacific struggle, her patron and his wife showed up, as scheduled, for dinner with her at the Henry Street Settlement House.[50]

The corner broken, next came the backlash.

In a blistering editorial on Friday, May 10, *The New York Times* condemned Harriman, Hill, and their respective backers for their display "of vast power for private ends unrestrained by any sense of public responsibility. Possessing the strength of Titans, they have behaved like cowboys on a spree, mad with rum, and shooting wildly at each other in entire disregard of the safety of the bystanders." By one estimate, "the bystanders" had sustained some $10 million in losses during the Northern Pacific fight.[51] One distraught investor reportedly drowned himself in a vat of hot beer.[52] The fire-breathing op-ed closed with apt lines from Shakespeare's *Measure for Measure*. "Oh, it is excellent to have a giant's strength; but it is tyrannous to use it like a giant."[53]

The key players in the drama expressed varying levels of public and private remorse, ranging from mild contrition to none at all. A couple of days after the panic, a reporter located J. P. Morgan outside his hotel in Paris, where he had hurried earlier that week to monitor the Northern Pacific struggle from the offices of his firm's French affiliate, Morgan, Harjes & Co. The financier had been spotted earlier that day pacing, wringing his hands, and muttering to himself. "Don't you think that since you are being blamed for a panic that ruined thousands of people and disturbed a whole nation, some statement is due to the public?" the reporter inquired. Morgan's notorious reply would come to define a rapacious era of unrestrained capitalism. "I owe the public nothing," Morgan growled.[54]

In his own comments to the press, Hill accused his rivals of "wicked work" and said—in what seemed a clear jab at Harriman and Schiff—that "there are men who have come to believe that money can do anything in this country. If we have reached that point, then money must be shorn of its power to do harm. . . . I have no wish to have that kind of power, and in my opinion, the events of Thursday will do much to bring about legislation that will make them impossible in the future."[55]

Otto Kahn provided his firm's first extended comments about the panic. "We have been accused of bringing about the corner, and Mr. Morgan has been accused of the same thing. We had nothing to do with cornering the stock: or, rather, any blame for the corner must not be laid at our doors." He faulted Hill for forcing a showdown. "None of us expected that that which did happen would happen, and I have not any doubt that we are all a little ashamed of ourselves."[56]

Beneath Schiff's mask of calm and command he was deeply rattled by his bout with Hill and Morgan and the financial disaster that had resulted from their clash. "The worry, strain and regret resulted in a serious impairment of his health, from which it took him quite some time to recover," Kahn recalled.[57] In the immediate aftermath, Schiff seemed most concerned with explaining himself not to the public but to Morgan. He penned him a kowtowing letter stating that the

"Union Pacific interests" had never meant to be "antagonistic to you or your firm" and that he and his partners "have at all times wished, as we continue to do, to be permitted to aid in maintaining your personal prestige, so well deserved."[58]

Schiff ventured that perhaps the panic had served a positive purpose since it burst a speculative bubble that had been building for months:

> While it is always to be deplored when the public must suffer, it is my own opinion that if this had not come and the mad speculation had run its course for a month or two longer, something else would have happened which would have brought about much more serious disaster, of a character which possibly might have inflicted lasting injury upon the entire country.[59]

Notwithstanding his olive branch, taking on Morgan did have the result Schiff had feared, straining the long-standing cooperative relationship between their firms and likely confirming Morgan's already prejudiced view of Jewish bankers.

Schiff would have to contend with the public, too—at least to some degree. Two weeks after the market meltdown, the U.S. Industrial Commission, a panel appointed by President William McKinley to probe railroad industry consolidation and pricing, summoned him to a hearing at the Fifth Avenue Hotel. Given the gravity of what had just occurred, Schiff's questioning was relatively friendly—he was treated more as an industry expert than a central player in an unfolding financial scandal. A member of the commission later contended that the McKinley administration had instructed the panel to tread lightly: "The Commission received orders from Washington to apply the soft pedal, and instead of examining him in the open, he was questioned in a back room."[60]

"Will you receive the oath," queried the commission's chairman, a New England newspaper publisher and railroad executive named Albert Clarke, as the proceedings got underway on the morning of May 22.

"Am I compelled to?" Schiff demurred. "I never like to swear, because I think my word is good enough."

"Then you make a solemn affirmation, do you?"[61]

Clarke began by asking Schiff about the "great movements" taking place among the major railroads, a reference to the wave of mergers and acquisitions concentrating control of the industry among a handful of magnates.

"The movements to which you refer I assume are those that are generally understood as coming under the expression 'community of interest,'" Schiff replied, explaining that destructive competition had

> brought about a gradual coming together of the railroad interests and induced them to buy into one another's properties. . . . That is, in simple words, the process which has been going on on a large scale among the railroads, and which, in my opinion, while it is not completed yet, will naturally bring about some protection, as the way to perfect peace is always through war.[62]

When the topic finally came to the Northern Pacific "contest," Schiff was circumspect, denying that a "contest" had even taken place. "There may have been some Wall Street speculation, of which I know nothing," he said, "but I am not aware that there has been any contest."[63] (In a separate hearing, Harriman would make a similar contention: "We made no contest for the Northern Pacific. We purchased a majority of the capital stock. We purchased prior to the supposed contest and no stock was acquired during the panic in May.")[64]

Commission member John Farquhar, a former Republican congressman from Buffalo, pressed: "How would you, as a financier, explain the fact of a single share of Northern Pacific stock going up to $1,000 cash?"

"Gamblers who sold things they did not have and tried to get back what they had not possessed, found it was not there," Schiff responded.[65]

In the "Battle of the Giants," as newspapers dubbed the Northern Pacific struggle, the combatants had fought to a stalemate. Continuing their skirmish in the courts would only arouse more public opprobrium. They had to negotiate an armistice. A little over a week after the industrial commission hearing, Hill and Harriman scrawled their names on an agreement designed to quell uncertainty about the future of the Northern Pacific; it stated that both sides were working together to devise a plan for "complete and permanent harmony."[66]

With Morgan and Schiff nudging the strong-willed railroad moguls along, a deal gradually came together. On November 12, 1901, Hill and Morgan formed the Northern Securities Company under the permissive corporate laws of New Jersey. Into this gargantuan holding company, capitalized at $200 million, went shares of the Great Northern and Northern Pacific, and investors received stock in the new company in exchange for their holdings. It was a community of interest on a nearly unprecedented scale, in which, in addition to the Hill and Harriman interests, representatives of the Gould, Rockefeller, and Vanderbilt systems also had a seat at the table.

Outwardly, the deal seemed like an unqualified victory for Hill and Morgan. Elected chairman of the new corporation, Hill retained control of the railroads; Morgan held the power to appoint its board. With Harriman's shares safely locked up within the new company, they didn't have to worry about him mounting another takeover. The corporation was so massive that it was virtually impervious to a stock raid from other quarters as well. Hill described the company proudly as a "strong fortress, where in peace or war, those who had seen the work of their hands grow great might establish it against all assaults and for all time to come."[67]

But if it appeared that Morgan and Hill came out on top, Schiff and Harriman also achieved what they had set out to. Morgan named them and several of their allies to Northern Securities' fifteen-member board, giving them a voice in the new company. And they neutralized the threat posed by the Burlington, their original objective. A separate holding company was established to lease the Burlington for 999 years, with the Union Pacific and Northern Pacific each receiving a 50 percent interest. To sweeten the overall deal, Hill and Morgan paid the Harriman contingent a $9 million premium for trading in their Northern Pacific shares for Northern Securities stock.[68]

"Although the Union Pacific is in the minority in this holding company," Schiff explained in a letter to Ernest Cassel,

> it will nevertheless exercise a potent influence upon the management of the two Northern lines, on the strength of its rather large holdings. In addition, the Union Pacific has made territorial agreement with the two companies which protects it against any invasion and gives it the extensive use of important lines on the northern Pacific Coast. I believe the whole arrangement is of the greatest importance and advantage to the Union Pacific, and justifies in every way our attempt last spring to preserve the Union Pacific from damage.[69]

Corporate harmony was finally at hand. Or so everyone thought.

. . .

Late in the afternoon of September 6, 1901, President William McKinley, six months into his second term, was gladhanding supporters at the Pan-American Exhibition in Buffalo, New York. A man approached with a white handkerchief covering his right hand and fired two bullets into the president's abdomen. It initially appeared that McKinley might survive the attack, carried out by an anarchist named Leon Czolgosz. On September 10, Schiff cabled Vice President Theodore Roosevelt to express his "deep gratification" at reports that the president's health was improving.[70] But McKinley's wounds were gangrenous, and his condition deteriorated. He died in the early morning hours of September 14; Roosevelt took the oath of office that afternoon.

Wall Street had flourished under McKinley, a reliable friend of big business who had settled the acrimonious silver question by signing into law the Gold Standard Act. He took a hands-off approach to the collusive trusts and monopolistic combinations proliferating across the industrial landscape. But within two months of taking office, McKinley's successor signaled a sharp departure from the laissez-faire policies of the previous administration.

On December 3, in his first annual address to Congress, Roosevelt began to articulate the new corporate doctrine that would define his presidency. "It should be as much the aim of those who seek for social betterment to rid the business world of crimes of cunning as to rid the entire body politic of crimes of violence," he said. "Great corporations exist only because they are created and safeguarded by our institutions; and it is therefore our right and our duty to see that they work in harmony with these institutions." He asserted that because large corporations "do business in many States, often doing very little business in the State where they are incorporated," the federal government should assume "power of supervision and regulation over all corporations doing an interstate business."[71]

Despite Roosevelt's ominous remarks about reining in corporate excesses, Harriman and Hill were blindsided by what came next. On February 19, 1902, Teddy Roosevelt's attorney general Philander Knox, a diminutive lawyer who had grown wealthy representing robber barons and their corporate trusts, announced the Justice Department was filing suit to dismantle Northern Securities under the Sherman Antitrust Act, an 1890 law that until then had rarely been wielded against a corporate conglomerate. Roosevelt, with growing concern about the concentration of corporate power and an eye on the upcoming 1904 election, had decided to use Northern Securities as a test case as he flexed the federal government's regulatory muscles.

J. P. Morgan hurried to Washington, where he met with Roosevelt and Knox on Saturday, February 22. Morgan seemed genuinely befuddled about why Roosevelt had targeted Northern Securities without warning. Why hadn't he first consulted with Morgan on the parts of the arrangement the government found objectionable? There was still time to settle matters without resorting to a legal circus.

"If we have done anything wrong, send your man to my man and they can fix it up," Morgan said.

"That can't be done," Roosevelt replied.

"We don't want to fix it up," Knox added. "We want to stop it."[72]

If it wasn't plain to Morgan before, it was now: a new corporate era was dawning—one that he and Schiff, in their market-quaking bout for the Northern Pacific, had played a pivotal role in ushering in.

Schiff also tried to appeal to Roosevelt. On February 25, when both men attended the christening of German emperor Wilhelm II's new racing yacht on an island off New York City, Schiff pulled the president aside to express his concerns about the Northern Securities suit. He even sought to influence him through Roosevelt's friend and former Harvard roommate Lucius Littauer, then serving as a Republican congressman from New York. "The more I think about the situation, which has now been created, the more I have become filled with apprehension and anxious foreboding," Schiff wrote Littauer on March 24. He said that while he believed Roosevelt was operating from the "highest and purest" motives, a court decision against the Northern Securities Company could have far-reaching ramifications.

> The decision sought by the Administration against the Northern Securities Company will, if rendered, strike with vehemence at almost every Railroad Company in this country. . . . It will call forth a disorganization and a chaos such as have never been known before in our history, and it will shake the structure, upon which our existing prosperity rests, to its very foundations.[73]

A few days later, after Littauer showed him Schiff's letter, Roosevelt invited Schiff to Washington to "go over the situation" with him and

Knox.[74] At their subsequent meeting, Schiff warned Roosevelt he was "entering upon a thorny path, which would finally lead to radicalism becoming rampant."[75]

Schiff also used the opportunity to appeal to Roosevelt concerning Romania's persecuted Jewish population, which faced harsh educational and economic restrictions, including a 1902 law barring them from practicing most trades. Like Russian Jews, Romanian Jews were fleeing in droves. Roosevelt was sympathetic to their plight; in response to lobbying by Schiff, Oscar Straus, and others, his secretary of state, John Hay, issued a diplomatic rebuke to the Romanian government later that summer.[76] But Roosevelt did not budge on Northern Securities. Over the next two years, the case traveled all the way to the Supreme Court, which, on March 14, 1904, sided with the Roosevelt administration in a 5–4 decision.

The process of unwinding the holding company inevitably reawakened the Harriman-Hill feud. The moguls disagreed on how to disband the company. Harriman wanted to extract the Northern Pacific shares he had originally deposited in the holding company; Hill had other ideas. He wanted to compensate investors, regardless of what they had initially exchanged, in a combination of Northern Pacific and Great Northern stock. It was the difference between Harriman walking away with a large, if not controlling, interest in the Northern Pacific or as a minority investor in both companies. The board of directors, largely loyal to Hill and Morgan, sided with Hill. When Harriman lost in the boardroom, he took his fight to the courtroom, suing, ultimately unsuccessfully, to halt the distribution of any stock. Once again Harriman and Hill were locked in combat.

In the wake of the Northern Pacific fight, Schiff attained a certain mythical status. "There is no banker in the country who is more closely identified with great corporate interests, especially railroads, than Jacob H. Schiff," the *Wall Street Journal* reported.[77] One publication called him the "uncrowned king of transatlantic finance." Another coronated him officially.[78] Calling him "the New Money King," the *Philadelphia Press* boldly asserted that Schiff had eclipsed Jupiter himself:

> Both Mr. Morgan and Mr. Schiff have financed very large propositions, but it has been observed by the more powerful banking interests in Wall Street, that, gradually, little by

little, the authority of Mr. Schiff, from the financial point of view, over the railroads of the United States has been equaling and then surpassing that obtained by Mr. Morgan, until at last it is acknowledged that there is none other here who can match in the extent or strength of his power that which Mr. Schiff has obtained.[79]

In November 1904, Schiff invited his friends Robert Fleming and Ernest Cassel—both major investors in the Union Pacific and other Kuhn Loeb–financed ventures—on a cross-country tour of his railroad kingdom. A private three-car train carried the financiers from New York to California, over the Pennsylvania and Union Pacific lines. "The aggregate wealth of the party is sufficient to buy up the whole State of Louisiana at its own valuation," one newspaper marveled.[80]

The press tracked their travels closely, speculating that the financiers were hatching a new railroad combination. "Is there any truth in the statement that you are making this tour with a view to bringing about a railroad merger?" a reporter asked Schiff, as he checked his party into their ten-room suite at the Van Nuys Hotel in Los Angeles. Schiff tugged at his beard with one hand and clutched a large bundle of mail and telegrams in the other. "Nothing in that, I assure you," he replied. "We are here for pleasure, nothing but pleasure. I have nothing to say and must beg to be excused."[81]

The financiers returned east over the Southern Pacific system, stopping in Washington for an audience with Teddy Roosevelt, who had just been elected to his first full term. During the race, as Roosevelt worried about a possible challenge for the Republican nomination from Senator Mark Hanna of Ohio, rumors had reached Roosevelt that Harriman—and perhaps Schiff—were working against him. Nicholas Murray Butler, then president of Columbia University, warned Roosevelt that "the conspirators against you are as active as ever." And he reported a "particularly juicy item" concerning Harriman, who had been named a delegate to the upcoming Republican National Convention:

Mr. Harriman has just returned from a trip through the West and reports that you are surely defeated, as the West is now in revolt against you. He thinks that he himself has managed to lay the basis for either antagonistic or indifferent delegations from Iowa, Nebraska, and California. Mr. Schiff on hearing this at a private meeting remarked philosophically that it might be so, but he himself feared that when September came they would all be throwing up their hats for you and giving money besides.[82]

Reading the tea leaves, Schiff quickly fell in behind Roosevelt, pledging in a January 31, 1904, letter to "do anything, in my limited power, to help bring about" his election.[83] By now it looked increasingly unlikely that Hanna would challenge Roosevelt. A day before Schiff wrote his letter to Roosevelt, Hanna, in declining health and looking poorly, had been asked about his condition at a Gridiron Club dinner. "Not good," he replied. Two weeks later he was dead.[84]

In addition to generous financial backing for Roosevelt's candidacy, Schiff was outspoken in his support for him, praising the president in newspaper interviews and declaring that "the Jewish citizen should and will consider it a duty to his race to cast his vote for the continuance in office of President Roosevelt" because "of the President's intense patriotism and of his fearless courage in behalf of the oppressed and persecuted."[85] Schiff even admitted publicly that he had been wrong to predict catastrophic results from Roosevelt's effort to dismantle Northern Securities. "When, at the insistence of President Roosevelt, the litigation against Northern Securities Company was begun, I thought an error in judgement had been committed," he said. "But the course of events has borne out the wisdom of, and given justification to the President's course in this important instance."[86]

Despite Roosevelt's trust-busting, Schiff had found him an ally in other areas, receptive if not always fully cooperative to the pleas of the Jewish community concerning their persecuted brethren in Eastern Europe and Russia, where Jews faced a new wave of violence that would make the pogroms of the 1880s seem mild. The battle for Jewish emancipation, to Schiff's mind, was simply bigger than the power struggle of two headstrong railroad titans.

The first of this new round of attacks came around Easter, as they often did, in 1903. For two days bloodthirsty marauders terrorized the Jewish populace of Kishinev (the capital of present-day Moldova, today known as Chişinău). Wielding clubs, crowbars, and axes—anything that could be used to bludgeon, pummel, impale—the rioters plundered hundreds of Jewish homes and businesses; gang-raped numerous women, sometimes in front of their husbands and children; and savagely murdered forty-nine men, women, and children, decapitating some and mutilating the bodies of others beyond recognition. During the pogrom, along with cries of "Death to Jews," rioters also shouted the name of Pavel Krushevan. He was the founder of *Bessarabets*, a popular and rabidly antisemitic daily newspaper that had helped to incite the massacre by repeatedly airing allegations that Jews killed two Christian children in nearby villages so their blood could be used to make Passover matzo.[87] (Months after Kishinev, Krushevan would deliver another—and in its future ramifications, far more lethal—wound to Jewry, publishing, in serialized form, parts of the *Protocols of the Elders of Zion*, the forged tract that purported to be the secret Jewish blueprint for global domination.)

The massacre, graphically recounted in the world's newspapers, sparked international outrage. American Jews, as they had in the past, mobilized quickly to fundraise for the victims and publicize the atrocities, organizing a protest rally that filled Carnegie Hall and featured prominent speakers including New York City mayor Seth Low and former president Grover Cleveland. And they pushed for a diplomatic response.

At the urging of Jewish leaders, Roosevelt ordered his State Department to forward to the Russian czar a petition, organized by the Jewish fraternal organization B'nai B'rith, strongly condemning the attacks and pleading for "religious liberty and tolerance."[88] The czar, through his foreign minister, refused to accept the document. Even so, the act of sending it and the widespread publicity it generated broadcast the message that America would not ignore the anti-Jewish violence within Russia's borders. During an era in which the default American foreign policy stance was isolationism, this was a bold statement, in part because it invited Russia and other nations to critique the internal politics of the United States, which had its own troubling history of violence against minorities. One prominent St. Petersburg paper explicitly made this point in an article titled "Pogroms in the United States," noting the lynching of southern Blacks.[89]

Schiff believed that a diplomatic protest was the wrong course. Because the Kishinev attack did not technically involve U.S. interests and because the regime could easily disclaim responsibility for the mob violence, he preferred a more aggressive strategy. He wanted Roosevelt to pressure Russia over another matter vexing American Jews—the so-called "passport question." The Russian Empire had been denying Jewish-American passport holders access to its territory without special permission, violating the terms of an 1832 treaty outlining "a reciprocal liberty of commerce and navigation" between citizens of the United States and Russia. In some ways, the passport issue was a small matter; few American Jews had any desire to set foot in Russia or its territories. But Schiff considered it crucial for symbolic reasons. "Indeed," he wrote to Roosevelt in June 1903, "the time has come to insist that the American passport is as good in the hands of any American citizen, and if this be not recognized friendly intercourse with the offender must cease." If what he was proposing seemed radical, that was because "nothing but extreme measures will bring Russia to the understanding that to be considered a civilized government, she must also act like a civilized government."[90]

Roosevelt declined to take up Schiff's hard-nosed tactics—which amounted to severing diplomatic ties with Russia if it would not recognize the passports of American Jews—but he understood the importance of keeping Schiff close to the fold. The banker was among a trio of prominent Jews whom the president invited to Oyster Bay, the Long Island enclave where he had his summer home, in July 1904 to see him officially notified that he had received the Republican nomination.[91] ("It seems to me that if we could have one or two of our good Jewish friends out here to see me notified, it would be all right. . . . Would three be too many?" Roosevelt wrote to Cornelius Bliss, treasurer of the Republican Party, prior to inviting Schiff to the event.)[92] And, in a letter accepting the nomination, Roosevelt raised the passport matter: "One of the chief difficulties arises in connection with certain American citizens of foreign birth, or of particular creed, who desire to travel abroad. Russia, for instance, refuses to admit and protect Jews. . . . This government has consistently demanded equal protection abroad for all American citizens."

Schiff's blunt persistence and his deluge of letters and cables seeking action to protect Russia's Jews at times chafed the president and members of his cabinet. Following one volley of "hysterical" cables, Roosevelt fumed, "Does he want me to go to war with Russia?"[93] Schiff, by this point, had decided to do exactly that.

16

THE SINEWS OF WAR

S chiff rapped his knuckles on the table, and his guests, midconversation, fell silent.

On the evening of February 6, 1904, an elite clique of New York Jews who called themselves the Wanderers were meeting at Schiff's Fifth Avenue manse. The group, which included a handful of financiers, lawyers, journalists, and academics, gathered monthly to puff cigars and debate the issues of the day.[1] Present that Saturday night were Schiff's brothers-in-law Morris Loeb and Ike Seligman; Oscar Straus, then serving as Roosevelt's minister to the Hague; lawyer Louis Marshall; Jewish communal leader and scholar Cyrus Adler; and *New York Times* owner and publisher Adolph Ochs.

Adler, Ochs, and Straus were discussing the mounting tensions between Japan and Russia, whose expansionist ambitions had brought these nations to the brink of war. The roots of the conflict stretched back more than a decade to when Russia unnerved Japan by embarking on the construction of the Trans-Siberian Railway, which would eventually snake nearly six thousand miles, linking Moscow to the port city of Vladivostok, located on the Sea of Japan and bordering Korea and Manchuria.

Japan, just coming into its own as a modern power, grew more wary of Russian encroachment following the Sino-Japanese war of 1894 and 1895. During that conflict, Japan seized from China Manchuria's Liaodong Peninsula and the strategic jewel at its tip, the heavily fortified naval base known as Port Arthur; facing diplomatic pressure from Russia and its European allies, Japan relinquished the peninsula under the terms of its peace treaty with China. No sooner had it done so than Russia stepped in to lease this valuable territory from China, also brokering a deal with Japan's recently vanquished rival to extend the Trans-Siberian Railway into Manchuria via a line called the Chinese-Eastern Railway.

Then, in 1900, came the Boxer Rebellion, a nationalist uprising in northern China aimed at purging foreign colonists and influences. Russia deployed troops to Manchuria, ostensibly to protect its commercial interests, but it left a hundred-thousand-man detachment in the region after the rebellion was brutally extinguished. Years of diplomatic wrangling ensued.

But now a deadline for Russia to withdraw its troops had passed, and talks between the nations over dividing up territory in Korea and Manchuria had stalled. On the same day the Wanderers met, Japan formally severed diplomatic ties with Russia, escalating the standoff.

"Gentlemen, I have something very serious to say to you," Schiff said gravely as the room went quiet. Unlike Ochs and Straus, who thought the conflict could be defused, Schiff was certain war was imminent; he had been approached about financing it. "The question has been presented to me of undertaking a loan for Japan," he said. "I would like to get your views as to what effect my undertaking this would have upon the fortunes of the Jewish people in Russia."[2]

Cyrus Adler recalled this episode nearly two decades later in a letter to Schiff's son, as Adler compiled material for his two-volume biography of Schiff. Adler didn't record what ensued after Schiff broached the topic of bankrolling Japan, but surely the discussion was animated, as the group debated the possible consequences of going to war with the czar. Would he retaliate against his Jewish subjects, worsening their already bleak existence?

While the Wanderers debated, a flotilla of Japanese destroyers secretly cruised toward Port Arthur. Just after midnight on February 9, the warships slipped into the mouth of the harbor, took aim at the anchored Russian fleet, and loosed a salvo of Whitehead torpedoes.

The eighteen-month war that followed, in which Schiff played a decisive financial role, formed one of the most fascinating chapters of his storied career. It contributed to his legend as a fearless titan with few equals, undaunted by deploying his financial resources in righteous battle. But this period was also the tinder from which numerous conspiracy theories later erupted—including some that formed part of the Nazi canon—concerning Schiff's part in the eventual overthrow of the House of Romanov and the supposed monolithic financial power of the Jews. His decision to intervene would shape the destinies of Russia and of Japan, of Schiff himself and of the Jewish people, in ways he scarcely could have imagined.

Three months after the start of the war, Schiff stopped off in London as he returned to New York from a visit to Germany.[3] On May 3 he attended a gathering at the home of banker Arthur Hill, a partner in the Speyers' London banking operation. When dinner was served, Schiff took his seat beside Takahashi Korekiyo, the fifty-year-old vice-governor of the Bank of Japan, who was scouring the West for loans to finance his country's costly war.

Short, bearded, and round of face and physique, Takahashi was nicknamed "Daruma" because of his likeness to the traditional Japanese dolls representing the fifth-century Buddhist monk Bodhidharma and considered a good luck symbol. Takahashi, who would later serve as Japan's prime minister, had climbed from humble origins to the top of his country's financial and political elite. Born the illegitimate son of a Kano school artist in the court of the shogun and a teenage maid, Takahashi had learned English as a boy from missionaries. His peripatetic formative years had included a period of indentured servitude in northern California, where he had traveled to continue his language studies.[4] His English fluency enabled him to rise through a series of bureaucratic posts, including a stint as head of Japan's fledgling patent bureau, and it made him an ideal candidate for his vital financial mission to secure war funding—though his assignment was proving frustratingly difficult.

Before traveling to London, Takahashi spent five dispiriting days meeting with top bankers in New York, where he found plenty of sympathy for Japan's cause but no interest in floating its bonds. Partly this was because U.S. bankers were at that time more focused on channeling capital into American industry and had little experience handling foreign loans. But it was also because American financiers, like their counterparts elsewhere in the world, believed Japan stood little chance of defeating the powerful Russian Empire.

Takahashi had higher hopes of drumming up financing in London, since a couple of years earlier, the British had entered an alliance with Japan. But there too he found support for Japan's military struggle and reticence about bankrolling it. "During my pourparlers with

British bankers, Japan was often likened to a promising young man who had chances of success as well as of collapse, while it was thought that Russia was like a landlord whose mortgage would remain safe irrespective of momentary vicissitudes," Takahashi said.[5] Through pluck, persistence, and personal connections, he eventually cajoled a few banks into coming on board, including the Hongkong and Shanghai Bank Corporation (HSBC) and Parr's Bank, where Alexander Allan Shand, who had once employed Takahashi as a houseboy in Yokohama, managed the Lombard Street branch.[6] The British bankers, however, were initially willing to underwrite just half of the £10 million bond issue Takahashi's government desired. They also wanted American involvement, so that the war loan didn't seem like a purely British endeavor.

At Hill's dinner, attended by representatives of various banks, Takahashi explained his predicament to Schiff, who he recalled had been introduced to him simply as "an American financier on his way home from a visit to the Continent." Takahashi found the American banker "uncommonly interested in the war as well as in the affairs of Japan," and Schiff peppered him with questions about Japan's economy and the morale of its people.[7] Schiff's interest in the country, in fact, dated back to at least 1872, when as a twenty-five-year-old banker with Budge, Schiff & Co., he had chased a share of a Japanese bond issue. He believed this business might open the door to broader opportunities in the empire, which had just emerged from centuries of feudal reign, perhaps even enabling him to secure for his friend and client James H. Wilson, the Civil War general who had hunted down Jefferson Davis, "a hand in the laying out of a system & building of the railroads of the Japanese Empire," as he wrote at the time.[8] Nothing came of the Japanese business back then, but now, three decades later, another opportunity had materialized.

The day after meeting Schiff, Takahashi received word that the Kuhn Loeb banker had offered to take up the other half of Japan's bond issue, the equivalent of $25 million. Takahashi would later say he was "dumbfounded" by Schiff's unexpected offer, which he attributed to "good fortune . . . because of an accidental meeting."[9] But their meeting was almost certainly not serendipitous, even if Takahashi was not aware of that fact.

Takahashi later speculated that, through Schiff's plugged-in friend Ernest Cassel, he "must have been especially well posted in all aspects and bearings of Japan's conflict" and "must have been aware that American participation in the Japanese loan was ardently desired in England." Indeed, Cassel likely had a hand in the match-making between Takahashi and Schiff. As Cassel later told Taka-hashi, "I wanted to bring the American and British people closer together. . . . I helped bring about the issuance of Japanese bonds in the two countries to unify their sympathy for Japan and to create inti-macy between the United States and Great Britain."[10] Two days after Kuhn Loeb officially signed on to the Japanese loan, Cassel escorted Schiff to an audience with King Edward VII, who expressed his gratitude to the banker and said he was "glad that his country alone was not to supply money to Japan," as Takahashi recounted in his diary.[11]

In many accounts of how the loan came together, Schiff is said to have decided on the spot to underwrite Japan after meeting Taka-hashi. That's a myth. Schiff had carefully contemplated backing Japan for weeks if not months—nearly three months, according to Cyrus Adler. The deal also came together far too quickly to have been spon-taneous, and it seemed no accident that Schiff's young partner, Otto Kahn, was also conveniently in London at that time to help work out the particulars of the bond issue.[12] By May 10 the loan syndicate cir-culated a prospectus to investors.[13] A day later subscriptions opened in London and New York. By then, just over a week had elapsed since Schiff and Takahashi had dined together at Arthur Hill's—a meeting that was likely just a formality since Schiff had already made up his mind to back the Japanese issue.

Investors on both sides of the ocean clamored for the bonds—in the United States, demand outstripped the supply by five times over.[14] The terms were enticing. The bonds paid 6 percent interest and were secured to Japan's customs duties in case of default. And the timing helped: earlier that month Japan had notched a victory in the first major land campaign of the war, the Battle of the Yalu River, dispelling any notion that Japan would be easily defeated.

The loan's success also owed to the fact that Japan had aroused significant support in the United States—among those rooting for the country was President Roosevelt, though officially his adminis-tration remained neutral—while Russia increasingly evoked enmity. The United States had traditionally enjoyed close diplomatic ties with Russia, but Kishinev and news of other anti-Jewish attacks had gradually turned the tide of public opinion. By working to make sure such assaults and oppression received widespread publicity, Schiff and his allies helped to transform a mostly Jewish affront into an American one.

. . .

The huge demand for the bonds caught Kuhn Loeb off guard. Most of the firm's partners had already scattered to their summer homes or to European spas, so the tedious job of countersigning the securities, to confirm their authenticity, fell largely to Kuhn Loeb's newest partner, Paul Warburg. "There were thousands and thousands of bonds to be countersigned, and the bulk of the work had to be done when only three of us were left on the job," he remembered.[15]

Paul had joined the firm two years prior, filling an opening created by Abraham Wolff's sudden death. Unlike his brother Felix, whose only qualification for a partnership was his marriage to Frieda, Paul was a brilliant banker and financial theorist. "He will prove a great acquisition," Morti Schiff remarked to his father when Paul came aboard.[16]

Leaving Hamburg had pained Paul. As he decided on his future, he had been virtually drawn and quartered by the opposing pressures of his parents and siblings, on the one side, and his wife, on the other. Nina, who had given birth to another child, a daughter named Bettina, did not hide her misery in Hamburg. She seemed to perk up mainly when relatives came to visit from New York, bringing news of other "dear ones." Her sense of isolation became more acute as her mother's health declined and as her brother, Jim, battled mental demons that increasingly made it impossible for him to carry on as a banker. Nina pushed Paul to accept the Kuhn Loeb partnership, and out of a sense of duty, he finally bowed to her wishes, even though it meant abandoning his recently won seat on the Hamburg city council.

But what would M.M. Warburg do without Paul? Aby, as usual, was his brother's harshest critic. Felix, well acquainted with his father-in-law's domineering tendencies, also worried that Paul was making a mistake.[17] Filled with guilt and angst, Paul entered a mental tailspin, checking himself into a clinic run by the Swiss psychiatrist Otto Binswanger, who had once treated Friedrich Nietzsche. Mental illness was prevalent in the Warburg family. Paul's daughter, Bettina, influenced by the struggles of her uncles Aby Warburg and James Loeb, would grow up to become an accomplished psychiatrist; she annotated a Warburg family tree with the afflictions of its members—manic depression, epilepsy, mania, schizophrenia. "Idiot," she scrawled next to the name of one relative.[18]

Suspicious of Binswanger's methods, Max nevertheless hoped the treatment would restore his brother to health. "Paul suffers from too many worries that he makes himself and that are brought by him, which with his temperament is too much to handle," Max confided in a letter to Aby, also a Binswanger patient.[19]

Max viewed his brother's departure in more pragmatic terms, placing only one condition upon him: that he remain a M.M. Warburg partner. The reason for this was two-fold, Morti Schiff explained: "His partners . . . desired the continuation of his capital contribution and wanted this concrete evidence of the intimacy of the relations between the two firms." The arrangement "further cemented" the Kuhn Loeb–M.M. Warburg alliance, Morti said, and in the years to follow, each firm rarely left the other out of any significant business undertaking.[20] This included the Japanese bonds, which M.M. Warburg helped to place in the German market.

Panina arrived in New York in October 1902, a month after Betty Loeb died during a visit to Fish Rock Camp, the Adirondack retreat on Upper Saranac Lake belonging to her son-in-law Ike Seligman. The Loeb matriarch's death "was in keeping with her colorful life," her granddaughter Frieda recalled. Confined to a strict diet to control her diabetes, Betty disregarded her doctor's orders one evening and, to her husband's alarm, said she planned to eat a second helping of dessert even "if it costs me ten years of my life." Within twenty-four hours, she was dead.[21] A fatal heart attack claimed Solomon Loeb the next year.

As Paul got his bearings in New York, he settled into the morning routine of accompanying Schiff on his daily walk downtown. Paul disliked this showy ritual but performed it without complaint in the interest of family and business harmony.[22] He did, however, permit himself to peel off after about forty blocks, while Schiff continued on foot for another twenty blocks or more.[23] Because he saw Paul as a peer, if perhaps not an equal, Schiff seemed to prefer his company to Felix's—though Felix too had been roped into his father-in-law's downtown marches.[24]

For Paul, new to the ways of U.S. banking, their daily strolls served as a sort of master class on American finance, though their conversations, at least early on, were also the source of considerable anxiety. "It was my constant dread that Mr. Schiff would ask me about some detail with which I was not familiar," Paul said. "Knowing that the moment would come when the unexpected question would be asked, not for the purpose of embarrassing me, but simply because he wanted to know, I kept myself posted as well as I could."

Schiff schooled Warburg in other areas, too. One morning, when he met Schiff for their walk, Paul noticed his partner's eyes linger on his black bowler hat with a squint of disapproval. "I was promptly reprimanded and told that it was becoming for a promising member of the banking fraternity, and partner of his firm, to wear a silk [top] hat," Paul said. Though somewhat intimidated by his powerful new partner, Paul observed him with a sense of awe, describing him as "the most systematic of all men I ever knew." He recalled, "The Japanese have a rare gift of drawing in daring outlines, and not spoiling the boldness of the picture even though they add to it the minutest detail. Mr. Schiff's business genius was very much of this type. He could conceive financial transactions on gigantic lines, but at the same time, no business detail escaped his attention."

Schiff, Warburg noted, habitually carried in his pocket a silver notepad with two ivory tablets, on which he scribbled a to-do list throughout the day, striking a line through each item as he completed it. "Business thoughts of the greatest importance would find their first origin registered on these little tablets just as much as the most trivial things," Paul recalled. "All the thousands of little attentions that Mr. Schiff had for people, high and low, were noted in advance, and attended to in the course of the day. It was extraordinary how he could find time to attend to these small matters with the big ones."

Working alongside Schiff, Paul glimpsed the financier's infamous wrath—"people who became the object of his criticism would not easily forget it"—but also the kindness for which he was also renowned. Inundated with Japanese bonds during the summer of 1904, Paul remembered lugging bags full of the certificates aboard the ferry to Sea Bright, where he and Schiff commuted each evening. "He never could see me sign bonds without sitting down at the other end of the small cabin table and joining me in my task, in spite of my protests," Warburg recalled. "And so in the evening when after dinner I used to sit down at the desk in his writing room in order to continue my boresome work, it never lasted long before he came in to share my tortures in spite of the heat, and in spite of his age."

Perhaps more impressive to Warburg was Schiff's decision to take up the Japanese bond issue in the first place. Though he shared his brother-in-law's disdain for the czar, he also recognized Schiff had assumed considerable risk to his firm's finances and its reputation if the loan did not gain traction in the United States. "It was . . . one of the characteristics of Mr. Schiff that where his sense of justice and pride was aroused, his courage and energy knew no bounds," he said.[25]

· · ·

Takahashi was pleased—but initially puzzled—by Schiff's eagerness to assist his country, when other financiers recoiled. "Schiff's investment in Japan seemed a bit too adventurous for other bankers," he recalled in his memoir.[26] As Takahashi came to know Schiff better—struck by his "keen sense of justice which . . . went to the verge of severity"—he eventually understood why Schiff had taken a gamble on Japan. "He had a grudge against Russia on account of his race," Takahashi said. Schiff, he noted, wanted to "admonish the ruling class of Russia by an object lesson," and the country's war with Japan offered an opportunity to do so. "He felt sure that, if defeated, Russia would be led in the path of betterment, whether it be revolution or reformation."[27]

Over the years, many historians have scrutinized Schiff's reasons for aiding Japan, questioning whether he was driven by moral outrage or a baser instinct: profit motive. His letters from that period unequivocally reflect his desire to deliver the czar his comeuppance—creating the conditions for regime change—but backing Japan was also a sound, though certainly bold, business move. A. J. Sherman, a former Kuhn Loeb banker and the firm's resident historian, assessed Schiff's motivations in a 1983 article, concluding:

> punishing the Tsar for ill-treating the Jews was only one of the factors he as a prudent banker had to take into account. Japanese credit was a risk; but one that a banker could measure, weigh against potential advantage, secure to some degree. Investors' money was not to be tossed away for political ends. In short, the war loans made eminent sense on purely business grounds. Daring they may have been; imprudent or merely vindictive, certainly not.[28]

Schiff did more than supply what Takahashi called the "sinews of war" (borrowing a phrase coined by Cicero, who once wrote that "a limitless supply of money" forms the "sinews of war"). He also exerted his influence in the opposite direction—starving Russia of the international financing it needed to prosecute the war. Early in the conflict, Schiff wrote a long, blunt letter to Lord Nathaniel Rothschild, grandson of the founder of N.M. Rothschild & Sons, who occupied a similar role in England as Schiff did in the United States as a business and communal leader. Predicting that "troubled times are still in store for our unfortunate co-religionists in the Czar's dominion," he wrote of his hope, for their sake and Russia's, that the war would "lead to such an upheaval in basic conditions upon which Russia is now governed that the elements in Russia which seek to bring their country under constitutional government shall at last triumph." The work would be plodding, "but meantime we can all help it on by making it, each as far as is in his power, impossible for the Russian Government as presently constituted to strengthen itself."[29]

Dating back at least to 1892, when Schiff turned down an opportunity to finance the Trans-Siberian Railway, he had refused all Russian business.[30] But only more recently had he taken active steps to block Russia's access to American capital. Around 1900, Russia's then finance minister, Count Sergei Witte, dispatched a St. Petersburg banker to confer with Schiff about an issue of Russian Treasury notes. The banker, a baptized Jew named Adolph Rothstein, pledged Witte's cooperation in seeking to repeal Russia's anti-Jewish May Laws. Schiff rebuffed the offer, telling Rothstein that "promises were cheap." Until he saw evidence of reform, he vowed to "bring all the influence we could command to bear against Russia getting a foothold in the American money markets."[31] And he had done just that.

Schiff told Rothschild that he prided himself that "all the efforts, which at various times during the past four or five years have been made by Russia to gain the favor of the American markets for its loans, I have been able to bring to naught." And he sought Rothschild's commitment to apply similar pressure in Europe, where Russia had in the past raised financing from its allies France and Germany.

> When the Russian Government again applies to the European money markets, as it before long must do and to a large extent, may we not hope that Jewish bankers of influence will not again be satisfied with promises on the part of the Russian Government as to its good behavior toward its unfortunate Jewish subjects—promises as readily broken as made—and not only decline cooperation, but work with all their might against any Russian loans so long as existing conditions continue.[32]

Rothschild replied, "There is absolutely no chance of Russia getting a loan in England, either from Jewish or non-Jewish houses, and I am equally convinced that Messieurs de Rothschild Frères in Paris could not and would not bring out a loan for Russia under present conditions."[33]

Going into the war, Russia justifiably believed it held the financial upper hand. "The Japanese cannot resist our finances," Witte boldly asserted. "I have nothing to say of the two other factors—the army and the navy. Perhaps the Japanese can carry on the war one and a half, two, at the most two and half years. Considering the finances alone, we can keep it up for four years. Other factors being left out of account, the Japanese can therefore be brought to sue for peace by their financial ruin."[34] But it was Russia, not Japan, that soon found itself in worrisome financial condition, burning through its treasury, as it flailed for financing. Meanwhile the Russian Empire faced growing social unrest and waning morale due to mounting military defeats by the Japanese.

Recognizing Schiff's hand in its declining fortunes, the Russian government, as it had before, sought to mollify him. In June 1904, weeks after Kuhn Loeb spearheaded the New York end of Japan's bond offering, the Russian interior minister Vyacheslav von Plehve, the enforcer of the czar's anti-Jewish policies, contacted Schiff via an intermediary with the offer of a meeting to discuss measures to improve the lot of Russia's Jews. Schiff replied that he would happily sit down with Plehve—and could be in St. Petersburg as soon as that fall—if the Russian government would meet several conditions. Refusing to appear before Plehve as a "suppliant," he requested a direct invitation from the interior minister. And he also declined to enter Russia by special permission—the government would have to abolish its restrictions on Jewish-American passport holders before Schiff would consider setting foot in the country.

The negotiations never progressed further. The following month a socialist revolutionary tossed a bomb into Plehve's carriage as he returned from a weekly meeting with the czar. Schiff called Plehve's assassination a lesson that "even the greatest and most powerful, whether an individual or a whole empire, cannot sin and go unpunished, and that sooner or later justice from on High will overtake even the mightiest of nations."[35]

The Russian government tried other avenues to win the cooperation of Schiff and Jewish bankers in his orbit. Around the time Plehve made his back-channel overture, Russia deployed Gregory Wilenkin to Washington as its financial envoy. A member of an old and wealthy Jewish family in St. Petersburg, Wilenkin had been plucked from the bureaucratic ranks in 1895 by Witte, who dispatched him to London in pursuit of financing to aid Russia's industrial development. Beyond his Jewish pedigree, Wilenkin held an additional credential useful to his Russian paymasters. He was a Seligman in-law—married to Abraham Seligman's daughter, Irma.

Tempting Schiff with generous financial offers proved futile—the financier remained steadfast in his demand that Russia take concrete steps to reform its anti-Jewish policies before he would consider rendering his aid. Until then, Schiff explained bluntly in a letter to Wilenkin, "My own firm, which is more or less leading in finance in the United States, has deemed it its duty to discourage favorable reception to Russian overtures so long as Russia persisted in its harsh attitude toward its Jewish subjects and in its mortifying discrimination against foreign Jews."[36]

Wilenkin pumped the partners of J. & W. Seligman & Co. for information about Kuhn Loeb, including about its relationship with J.P. Morgan & Co. (which was sympathetic to Russia). "I would say that Messrs. J.P. Morgan & Co. and Messrs. Kuhn, Loeb & Co. had not been friendly in years, and their differences were rendered particularly acute by the incident in connection with the corner in Northern Pacific stock and the contest for control of that company," Seligman partner Albert Strauss told Wilenkin. He added that "much to the astonishment of Wall Street," the two companies had joined forces in recent bond issues, indicating "that the proper business being offered, these two houses can now be induced to work together."[37]

Like Kuhn Loeb, J. & W. Seligman & Co. refused to participate in a Russian loan, but it was eager to do business with Wilenkin on other war-related matters. Having cut their teeth in government contracting by manufacturing uniforms for the U.S. Army during the Civil War, the Seligmans now held a large stake in William Cramp & Sons, a Philadelphia shipbuilding company that supplied the naval fleets of the United States and various foreign powers, including Japan and Russia. While Russian and Japanese battleships clashed in the waters surrounding the Korean Peninsula, representatives of J. & W. Seligman & Co. pursued Russian naval contracts on behalf of Cramp & Sons. Wilenkin—"Greisha" to the Seligmans—and the Russian military official Baron Pyotr Wrangel served as intermediaries to their government; in what appeared like kickbacks, J. & W. Seligman

THE SINEWS OF WAR

& Co. offered the Russians "a commission of two and one-half per cent on the purchase price of vessels so placed through you."[38]

Even as the firm sought the Russian business—also expressing interest in contracts with Japan—Albert Strauss worried about the legality of supplying warships to the belligerents in a conflict in which the United States had not taken sides. In early December 1904, he wrote to Henry Grove, president of Cramp & Sons, wondering if it might be "necessary to protect ourselves in the contract" from "any act" that might violate the "neutrality laws of the United States." Strauss continued:

> I am not familiar with what these requirements are, possibly the sending of a war ship to a port of the purchasing country unequipped with ammunition and not in charge of its own crew, is not in contravention of our laws. We do not wish to insert any troublesome clauses, unless this should be absolutely necessary to save us from getting into trouble. . . . It is needless to say that it should be as short as possible and as innocently worded as circumstances will permit.[39]

Grove departed for St. Petersburg early the following year, where he discovered another American competitor circling—steel tycoon Charles Schwab. Strauss learned that Schwab had offered to accept Treasury notes in payment from the cash-pinched Russian government, and he advised Grove to be prepared to negotiate on a similar basis.[40]

When Grove arrived in Russia, the country was in the early stages of a revolution. Weeks earlier the czar's imperial guard had opened fire on demonstrators who marched on his St. Petersburg palace to deliver a petition calling for an end to the war and better wages and working conditions. The episode, in which hundreds were killed, lit the fuse on a powder keg of discontent. In the ensuing months, peasants rioted and millions of workers went on strike, bringing Russian industry to a standstill and leaving beleaguered Czar Nicholas II to battle for control of his empire while prosecuting an increasingly unpopular foreign war.

In early March, as Grove's negotiations continued, Japan was driving the Russian Army out of southern Manchuria in the culmination of a three-week battle, one of the bloodiest in history. More than 160,000 troops from both sides perished in the Battle of Mukden, which presaged the ultimate defeat of the Russian military that came a couple of months later when Japan destroyed or captured much of its naval fleet in the Battle of Tsushima. Its military in shambles, treasury barren, and populace in revolt, Russia was no longer able to buy new ships—and both Schwab and the Seligmans came away without the lucrative contracts they sought.

Russia's credit was ruined, but Japan's had never been stronger. Weeks after Japan's victory at Mukden, Kuhn Loeb floated another tranche of bonds. The response was manic. Arriving for work on March 29, 1905, Kuhn Loeb's employees fought their way through a thick scrum surrounding the entrance to 52 William Street, the twenty-story building the firm had erected two years earlier and where its gleaming new offices occupied the entire ground floor.[41] The chaotic scene resembled a classic bank run—only, in this case, the anxious mob was clamoring not to withdraw their money but to hand it over to Kuhn Loeb's dazed clerks.[42]

Schiff gloried in Japan's military victories, tracking the war so closely that he cabled Takahashi about Russia's defeat at Tsushima before the Japanese banker had even learned this news from his own government.[43] "Mr. Schiff was gleeing with joy over the substantial successes of our arms," Takahashi said.[44]

Over the course of the war and in its immediate aftermath, Kuhn Loeb underwrote five Japanese loans, totaling $180 million. This amounted to more than 20 percent of Japan's wartime expenditures.[45] The governments of both sides recognized Schiff's pivotal role. Before the war had concluded, Japan's emperor awarded him the Second Order of the Sacred Treasure, conferred on those who had provided distinguished service to the empire. Schiff, meanwhile, earned the special scorn the czar's government reserved for its most reviled enemies. "Our government will never forgive or forget what that Jew, Schiff, did to us," Russia's finance minister during the conflict, Vladimir Kokovtsov, seethed six years after the war. "He dealt us a terrible blow by helping our enemy, Japan, at the most critical moment of our war against Japan. He alone made possible for Japan to secure a loan in America. He was one of the most dangerous men we had against us abroad."[46]

In March 1905, as Japan completed its rout of the Russian Army at Mukden, President Roosevelt quietly offered to mediate between the warring nations, though initially neither side appeared ready to come to the table. Late that month, before disappearing into the Colorado wilderness for a poorly timed, six-week bear hunting expedition, Roosevelt invited his old Harvard classmate Kaneko Kentarō to lunch. Kaneko, now a Japanese diplomat, had been deployed to Washington during the war because of his long friendship with the president. Kaneko couldn't help remarking on the unintended symbolism of Roosevelt's upcoming hunting trip. "If you should kill a bear," he commented, "this will be an augury of victory for the Japanese fleet."[47] During his trip, Roosevelt felled not one but three bears.[48] Japan's fleet, for its part, went on to eviscerate the Russian Navy in the Strait of Tsushima in the war's culminating battle.

Days after this victory, Japan signaled that it was prepared to accept Roosevelt's offer. The country, spending money as fast as it could raise it, could not continue to finance the conflict much longer. Russia's financial position was even more precarious. "We had exhausted all our means and had lost our credit abroad," Witte recalled in his memoir. "There was not the slightest hope of floating either a domestic or a foreign loan. We could continue the war only by resorting to new issues of paper money, that is, by preparing the way for a complete financial and consequently economic collapse."[49] In early June 1905, Czar Nicholas II, much of his fleet sunk or scuttled off the coast of Korea and beset by revolution at home, informed America's ambassador to Russia that he too was amenable to peace talks.[50] By July, the plenipotentiaries from both sides had settled on Portsmouth, New Hampshire, as the venue for their talks, scheduled to commence that August. (The negotiations were in fact held not in Portsmouth but at a naval base across the Piscataqua River in Kittery, Maine.)

Czar Nicholas II appointed Witte to head Russia's peace delegation. A hulking six foot seven inches, Witte was not only physically imposing but a towering political figure in Russia, known for dispensing blunt, unvarnished counsel. This outspoken quality endeared him to Alexander III but irritated his son. Witte's vocal opposition to the Russian Empire's imperialist policies in Manchuria had, in 1903, cost him his job as finance minister, from which he was "promoted" into a role with little real authority, as the chairman of Nicholas's council of ministers. There was only one reason why Nicholas chose Witte as Russia's peace envoy: his top candidates refused the post.

Witte, whose second wife converted from Judaism, held a more sympathetic view of Jews than many top Russian officials. Ike Seligman viewed Witte's appointment as a "hopeful sign"—not only for the establishment of peace but because he was "friendly to a more liberal policy toward Russian people and Jews."[51] Seligman, Schiff, Oscar Straus, and two other prominent American Jews arranged to meet with Witte during the peace conference to advocate for their Russian brethren, whose situation had grown even more dire during the war. With increasing frequency, Russian Jews faced violent flare-ups, including pogroms incited by the false charge that they had allied themselves with Japan. (In fact, more than thirty thousand Jews fought for Russia during the conflict.)[52]

Outwardly, this high-profile sit-down would focus on human rights, but there was also an inescapable financial subtext. Part of Witte's mission in the United States entailed negotiating a loan to stabilize the Russian Empire's economic tailspin. Facing financial collapse, Witte's government was desperate to break the blockade Schiff, Seligman, and other bankers had imposed on Russia's access to American capital. Schiff and Seligman, meanwhile, remained adamant about holding the line until Russia changed its policies toward Jews.

Gregory Wilenkin served as Witte's deputy at Portsmouth. In early July, prior to Witte's arrival in the United States, he met with Schiff and Seligman to test the waters for a Russian loan if the peace talks succeeded, proposing that J.P. Morgan & Co., Kuhn Loeb, and J. & W. Seligman & Co. spearhead the bond issue. Later that month Wilenkin invited Ike Seligman and Oscar Straus to a dinner party he hosted for Russia's new ambassador to the United States, Baron Roman Rosen, where the topic of a loan again came up. During their discussion with the ambassador, Seligman said, they aimed to "prepare Rosen's mind—in advance of Witte's arrival—on the Jewish question which is so inseparably linked with the financial question on this side." In Portsmouth, he noted, they intended to "impress [Witte] with the absolute necessity of according a more liberal treatment to the Russian Jews abroad as a *sine qua non* of opening our markets to Russian securities."[53]

When the peace conference commenced, Schiff was already in New England. Each August the Schiff clan and their retinue of domestic help laboriously relocated from Sea Bright to Bar Harbor, Maine; even their horses made the journey. Few if any Jews vacationed in this seaside enclave, where New England Brahmins, including Schiff's friend Charles Eliot, the president of Harvard University, had their summer cottages. It said something about Schiff's stature—and his confidence—that he glided over social barriers that would have repelled others of his faith.

In Bar Harbor, Schiff enjoyed hiking the coastal trails and summiting the peaks of Mount Desert Island in what would become Acadia National Park. He was always trying to rope one of his grandchildren into accompanying him, and it was on one of these treks that Edward Warburg recalled the "shocking revelation" of seeing his aristocratic grandfather, an otherworldly figure in his mind, urinate in the woods. "He, too, had to perform such earthly functions: and I had thought him above all that!"[54]

As the meeting with Witte approached, Schiff confessed misgivings in a letter to Philip Cowen, editor of *The American Hebrew* newspaper. "Firstly," he explained, "because I know it can do no good—and secondly, because I do not wish to have it said, that I went to discuss Russian finance with Mr. Witte." He continued, "There is only one thing we can do, to give as hard knocks to Russia as we can, whenever opportunity offers, to accept no promises in return for our aid as bankers, when this is asked for, and to do nothing for Russia until she has actually given civil rights to her Jewish subjects."[55]

Nevertheless, on August 14, Schiff departed Bar Harbor for the Hotel Wentworth, the sprawling resort outside Portsmouth where the Russian and Japanese delegations occupied opposite wings. At eight-thirty p.m., after another strenuous day of negotiations had concluded, Witte welcomed Schiff and his fellow Jewish emissaries into his two-room suite, where Wilenkin, acting as Witte's interpreter, and Baron Rosen were also present.

Schiff, the group's de facto leader, entered first. The Jewish delegation raised the massacre at Kishinev, how the attack had outraged the "civilized world," and said that Russia would not regain the goodwill of the American people or tamp down the discord within its own borders until it afforded equal rights to its Jewish citizens. Even while his colleagues attempted to temper his remarks, Schiff did not hold back. Jabbing a finger at Wilenkin, he pointedly asked Witte, "Will you please tell me why you, as a Russian, have full rights in your country while he, also a Russian, has none?"

Witte did not bother to defend his government's anti-Jewish policies but also said that "the horrors of the Jewish situation in Russia had been presented to the world in a somewhat exaggerated light." He agreed that anti-Jewish restrictions should be removed, but he felt this should happen gradually. Moving too quickly, he said, might fuel the Russian Empire's internal upheaval. He claimed that Jews were leaders of the revolution and that the czar could scarcely be expected to ameliorate conditions for Russian Jews while his throne was under siege. He suggested to Schiff and his colleagues that they exert their influence to convince young Jews to remain loyal to the czar, who would then be more likely to help the Jews.[56]

"We have no such influence," Schiff scoffed. "The influence must come from within, not without. And is it not probable that the young men became revolutionists in the hope that a republic will grant them just laws which are denied under the rule of the Emperor?"

"The revolutionists cannot succeed," Witte retorted. "Some day a republic may be established, but we will not live to see the day, for the Romanovs will rule Russia for at least another hundred years."[57] Witte, who died in 1915, would not live to see the fall of the House of Romanov, though it would come far sooner than he predicted.

The Jewish delegation emerged from Witte's suite close to midnight. Their discussion had lasted more than three hours. Schiff provided a canned statement to members of the press, who eagerly awaited a debrief: "While the discussion in its nature could not well lead to any immediate practical results, the gentlemen present at the conference . . . believe that in the course of time, and indirectly the mutually frank exchange of opinions and views which have been had, cannot but bear beneficial consequences."[58]

Schiff cabled a fuller account to *The American Hebrew*'s Philip Cowen. "Please do not use my name as informant," he instructed the journalist.

> Witte most liberal and sympathetic but fears anything but gradual removal disabilities impracticable. We honestly sought to impress him with necessity prompt granting full civil rights and stated without reserve that unless this granted the steadily growing Jewish influence in America would be thrown against Russia. . . . We feel we have made an impression on Witte personally. Whether this will have any affect on Russian government future must show.[59]

As Schiff had feared, newspapers speculated that his much-publicized meeting with Witte would surely involve discussion of a Russian bond issue. But both Schiff and Seligman sharply denied that any discussion of finance had taken place. "There was no allusion whatever to the question of financing any loans," Seligman wrote to President Roosevelt a few days after meeting with Witte. "The papers manufactured that matter out of whole cloth, and there's not a particle of truth in such published reports."[60]

But if the topic of financing Russia was not discussed in detail, it did come up in a general way. According to Witte, Schiff repeated his warning that unless Russia changed its ways, he would work with all his might to deny the empire American capital. The Russian could not help marveling at Schiff's bravado, even while he considered the banker's behavior at times antagonistic, even belligerent. "I have never before met just such a Jew as Schiff," Witte recounted years later.

> Proud, dignified, conscious of his power, he declared to me solemnly that so long as the Tsar's government would continue its anti-Jewish policy he would exert every effort to make it impossible for Russia to get a copeck in the United States. He banged the table with his fist and declared that a government which indulged in massacres and inhuman persecution on religious grounds was not to be trusted, that such a government was a blot upon civilization and could not last long, for it carried within itself the seeds of destruction.[61]

Schiff returned to Bar Harbor to the news that a bomb, intended for him, had been delivered to Kuhn Loeb's Manhattan offices. It had arrived with the morning mail, concealed in a package wrapped in olive-green paper. The purported sender, whose name was typewritten on the exterior of the parcel, immediately caught the attention of a clerk: King Edward VII. Inside was a pine box with a sliding cover, like a pencil case. The box was also marked in gilt lettering with King Edward's name. Suspicious, the clerk pried the lid up, instead of sliding it, perhaps saving his life in the process. The would-be bomber had rigged the crude device to detonate when its cover was slipped off, striking matchsticks and lighting a cylinder of gunpowder that would, in turn, ignite a payload of .38 caliber bullets and lead slugs. By pulling the lid upward, the clerk unwittingly defused the makeshift bomb.

When reporters descended on Kuhn Loeb's offices seeking comment, Otto Kahn downplayed the letter bomb as a prank. "In the first place," he said,

> anybody who knows anything would know that Mr. Schiff does not open his mail. If the thing were really dangerous and

exploded, the one to suffer would be the clerk whose duty it is to open the mail. Besides, Mr. Schiff is at Bar Harbor. Also if any one sent it with malice he must have been a strange person not to know that the fact that the name King Edward VII was inscribed on the box would draw attention and suspicion to it. I think, though, that it was some practical joker who did this. Of course I can't see much of a joke in such a thing, but then jokes are queer and some jokers are queerer.[62]

In Bar Harbor, Schiff took the attempt on his life—ham-handed as it had been—seriously enough to post guards outside of Ban-y-Bryn, the cottage where his family was residing.[63]

Who was behind the bomb? The New York police detective assigned to the case theorized it was "the work of some crank who had lost in Wall Street speculation." But the timing was odd, coming directly after Schiff's meeting with Witte. Some press reports suggested Schiff had been targeted because of his financial blockade against Russia. Schiff had thought little of it at the time, but a few months earlier he had received a death threat from a man who called himself Zantis Parozitz (an apparently fictitious name) and purported to be Russian. Parozitz claimed to represent a group he dubbed the "Secret Society of the Oppressors of the Selfish, Greedy Jews of the Western Hemisphere," and he claimed its mission was "to kill any Jew who is prominent or rich . . . in North or South America."

The police never found the culprit in the bomb plot. Nor did they discover who was behind another letter bomb, designed to look like a present for the Jewish New Year, that was intercepted the following year before it reached Schiff. *The New York Times* reported the device contained "enough powder, guncotton, and nitroglycerine to blow up a house."[64]

At four p.m. on August 29, a cacophony of church bells, factory whistles, and sirens sounded throughout Portsmouth. The sound of peace. After nearly a month of intense negotiations, the Japanese delegation announced it would accept Russia's terms. To Witte's surprise, Japan backed down from its demand for reparations, one of the final sticking points. Under the terms of the treaty, Russia relinquished the Liaodong Peninsula and its railroad interests there, and both countries split the contested island of Sakhalin, with the southern half going to Japan. That afternoon Witte, looking drained but elated, was spotted embracing Baron Rosen and kissing the ambassador on both cheeks.[65]

Four days earlier Schiff had sent a forthright letter to the Japanese plenipotentiary, Baron Komura, nudging his government to strike a deal with Russia. He assured Komura that Kuhn Loeb stood ready to assist Japan whatever the outcome of the talks, but he warned that other bankers would not look favorably on a decision to resume the war and that the "money markets of the United States, England, and Germany will . . . no longer be prepared to finance Japan's requirements to any great extent."[66]

After learning peace was at hand, Schiff sent a congratulatory cable to Takahashi: "Banzai."[67] Schiff also fired off another message that day, this one to James Stillman, president of the National City Bank, where Schiff held a board seat. The rumor on Wall Street was that Stillman was mulling joining a Russian loan syndicate organized by J.P. Morgan & Co. Politely but firmly, Schiff made clear where he stood. "While I wish in no way to interfere with what may be considered the interests of your stockholders," he wrote, "it is but right that I should say to you if the report is correct, self-respect will necessitate my withdrawal from the board."[68] So adamant was Schiff against financing Russia that when the topic came up at a meeting of top New York bankers, he rose from his chair and announced that he had forbidden his firm to have any dealings with Russia not just during his lifetime but in perpetuity, so long as its anti-Jewish policies persisted.[69]

Japan's war with Russia had concluded, but Schiff's continued. When during their meeting in Portsmouth, Witte had asked Schiff to use his influence to help pacify the revolution roiling his country, and Schiff had demurred, what Schiff didn't say was that he had taken direct steps to fuel the uprising threatening to bring down the Russian autocracy. In the months leading up to and after the Portsmouth peace conference, he bankrolled a propaganda campaign aimed at sowing anticzarist sentiment among Russian prisoners of war in the hopes that those soldiers would join the revolutionary ranks when they eventually returned home.

The effort was the brainchild of George Kennan, the journalist whom Schiff had befriended through their mutual involvement in the Society of Friends of Russian Freedom and its journal, *Free Russia*. After the war broke out, Kennan traveled to Japan to cover the conflict for *Outlook* magazine. Early on he toured the prison camp at Matsuyama with other foreign correspondents, a visit arranged by the Japanese government, which wanted to show the world that it was treating Russian POWs humanely. Kennan interviewed some of the prisoners, who expressed one main complaint: the crushing boredom. They had nothing to do, nothing to read. "I'm ready to read even cook books and arithmetics, if they're only in Russian," one inmate told him.[70]

An idea formed. Kennan saw an opportunity to bring comfort to the Russian soldiers, while simultaneously enlightening them about the czar's despotic ways. He secured permission from Japan's Ministry of War to distribute subversive Russian literature, including the liberal journal *Osvobozhdenie* (Liberation), among Russian POWs. Then he wrote to the New York chapter of the Friends of Russian Freedom asking the group to send him all the Russian-language material it could gather.

In June 1905 the requested literature arrived in Tokyo along with Dr. Nicholas Russel, whom the Friends of Russian Freedom had dispatched to oversee the propaganda campaign. Russel's real name was Nikolai Konstantinovich Sudzilovsky. A veteran socialist organizer, his revolutionary activities had forced him to flee Russia in the 1870s. Russel was in his mid-fifties, gray-bearded, and had most recently been living in Hawaii. Though he grew up in western Russia and attended medical school in Kyiv and Bucharest, he spoke flawless English.[71]

By the war's end, Japan had captured some seventy thousand Russian soldiers, and Russel immediately set to work disseminating anti-czarist pamphlets widely throughout the prison camps. The Japanese allowed the charismatic doctor to convene mass meetings, where he held forth before large groups of prisoners.

Russel also convinced the Japanese to release into his custody political prisoners held in the Russian penal colony on Sakhalin Island. By enlisting these dissidents to help him organize Russian POWs, Russel magnified his efforts. "Most of them had no money and no suitable clothes," Kennan remembered of the political prisoners, "but, thanks to the powerful and wealthy friend in New York who was financing our enterprise, we were able to supply them with everything that they needed." That wealthy benefactor was Schiff, who funded most if not all of Kennan and Russel's work, though his role in stoking revolutionary fervor among Russian soldiers would remain secret for more than a decade.

By some accounts, the Schiff-funded propaganda blitz was

remarkably effective. In late 1905, *The New York Times* reported (with some apparent exaggeration) that Russel

> succeeded beyond all expectation, as is shown by the fact that he organized under the banner of Socialism nearly all of the Russian soldiers taken prisoners by the Japanese, who are now in detention camps in Japan awaiting transportation to their homes. . . . Wherever they go, it is to be expected that the men from Japan will act as leaven and that, hard as authorities may try, they will be unable to eradicate the effect of the awakening which the prisoners have undergone.[72]

In a private letter to Schiff, written shortly after the Russian Revolution of 1917 finally toppled Czar Nicholas II from power, Kennan commended him for the

> very great service which you rendered to the cause of human liberty when you financed the propaganda among the Russian officers and soldiers in the prison camps of Japan. . . . Not only did you make it possible to sow the seeds of freedom in perhaps a hundred different regiments of the Russian army, but you enabled Dr. Russel and me to take care of all the Russian political convicts whom the Japanese released when they took possession of the island of Sakhalin. . . . All of these men helped us in our revolutionary propaganda, and then returned either to Russia or to the United States.[73]

In the hands of conspiracy theorists, Schiff's wartime activities—helping to finance the conflict and bankrolling revolutionary propaganda and proselytizing—formed the raw molding clay for a grotesque mythology of the supposedly all-powerful banker. In this version, with shards of truth cherry-picked to make believable a portrait filled in with falsehoods and conjecture, Schiff, sometimes identified as an Illuminati member or perhaps a thirty-third-degree Mason, was the ruthless godfather of the Russian Revolution; he was the secret financial angel of Leon Trotsky and Vladimir Lenin who not only orchestrated the Communist takeover of Russia but personally gave the order for the execution of the Russian royal family, held hostage as the second Russian Revolution unfolded during World War I. Echoed from decade to decade, the conspiracy's details vary, but the dangerous lie at its center remained unchanged: a Jewish banker was the secret choreographer of world-altering events.

The Schiff conspiracy theories echoed the themes of the *Protocols of the Elders of Zion*, the hoax text that purported to detail the Jewish program for world control, including by whipping up various forms of civil and economic unrest. It was no accident that the first full versions of the *Protocols*—portions were printed in 1903—were published in 1905 and 1906, as allies of the Russian monarchy sought to blame Jews for the Empire's humiliating defeat in the Russo-Japanese War and the internal chaos that resulted from it.

By the fall of 1905, the revolution had placed enough pressure on Czar Nicholas II that he finally acceded to demands for a constitutional government. On October 17 he issued the October Manifesto, a document heavily influenced by Witte, that pledged political reforms, including the establishment of a constitution that would protect the civil rights of all Russians (Jews included) and the creation of a parliament, the Duma, that would approve all new laws. Nicholas appointed Witte Russia's first prime minister, with the task of managing this transition and pacifying Russia's internal discord.

Barely had Russia taken its first steps toward political reform when blood again spilled on the streets of Jewish enclaves. The war-depleted economy, coupled with the promise of equal rights for the Jews and the misguided belief they had caused Russia's hardships, sparked a wildfire of anti-Jewish violence that swept across the Pale of Settlement. Members of the Black Hundreds, an ultranationalist group that emerged during the revolution to defend the Russian monarchy, often incited the attacks, using the phony *Protocols* to justify anti-Jewish rampages. The day after the czar issued the October Manifesto, a terrifying four-day orgy of violence erupted in Odessa, the port city on the Black Sea where Jews formed more than a quarter of the population. Some estimates placed the number of dead as high as eight hundred. The wounded numbered in the thousands.

"The American people stand aghast at atrocities in Odessa and elsewhere," Schiff cabled Witte. "No government should expect the moral support of other nations which under any conditions permits such a situation to continue."

Witte replied that his government was "horrified at these outrages," but he noted that with the country in such an "excited state the local authorities are often powerless."[74]

Anxious cables zipped between New York, London, St. Petersburg, and Berlin as Schiff, Lord Rothschild, and other Jewish leaders conferred on how to address the crisis and coordinated their response. On the afternoon of November 7, 1905, Schiff and Oscar Straus convened a mass meeting at Temple Emanu-El, where all the disparate factions of New York Jewry were represented: the Lower East Side socialists, the Zionist crowd agitating for the creation of a sovereign Jewish state, and, of course, the uptown elite. Schiff read aloud from the harrowing cables he had received from Russia. "The cablegrams speak louder than words," Schiff declared. "This is the time for doing."[75]

With Straus and Cyrus Sulzberger, the Philadelphia merchant and philanthropist, Schiff established the Committee for the Relief of Sufferers by Russian Massacres and plunged into doing what he did best, whether on Wall Street or in communal affairs: raising money. He immediately put up $50,000 toward the relief fund—which he insisted should benefit not just Jews but all Russian victims—and the committee dispatched more than fourteen hundred telegrams across the country soliciting donations.[76] Within weeks, the fund swelled beyond a million dollars.

But was money enough? Brimming with indignation and despair, Schiff once again directed an impassioned plea to President Roosevelt, this time going so far as to advise that the United States intervene directly to halt the Russian violence and calling for the president to seek congressional approval "to take such measures as may become advisable." He argued that if the United States had been justified in coming to the aid of oppressed Cubans during the Spanish-American War, "is it not in the face of the horrors now occurring in Russia, and which its very Government declares it is powerless to prevent, the duty of the civilized world to intervene?"[77]

Barely containing his exasperation with the hotheaded banker, Roosevelt told Schiff that his recommendation "would make the United States Government ridiculous" and was likely to backfire, harming not just the Jews of Russia but those in the United States. "I thoroughly believe," Roosevelt told Schiff, "that in national affairs we should act in accordance with the plains adage when I was in the ranch business: 'Never to draw unless you mean to shoot.'"[78]

The Russian Revolution peaked during the fall of 1905, then it began slowly to subside. In its wake, the czar maintained his hold on power and the situation for Russian Jews—despite pledges of equality—remained as tenuous as ever. Bursts of violence continued, ultimately leaving thousands dead, wounded, and dispossessed. As the political status quo returned to Russia, Schiff and his allies began to rethink their tactics. The Jewish community's past approach to crises—protest meetings, fundraising drives, the intercession of well-connected Jews with political leaders—no longer seemed adequate.

When the Wanderers convened in December 1905, members of the group discussed establishing a new organization devoted to the defense of Jewish rights wherever they came under threat. The group would harmonize aid and advocacy efforts across the far-flung network of Jewish relief groups, and it would speak for the whole of American Jewry. A few weeks later, in the pages of *The American Hebrew*, Cyrus Adler articulated their vision, writing that "the affairs of the Jew throughout the world are so important to make it necessary and desirable that there should be a national Jewish organization in the United States which can, in cases of necessity, cooperate with similar bodies in other countries for the welfare of the Jews elsewhere."[79]

On the evening of February 3, 1906, Jewish leaders from across the country convened in the conference room of the Hebrew Charities building on Second Avenue to debate the proposition. Along with Schiff and members of the Upper East Side elite, the attendees included Julian Mack, a circuit court judge from Chicago; the Zionist rabbi Judah Magnes; Adolf Kraus of B'nai B'rith; and Cyrus Sulzberger (whose son, Arthur Hays, would go on to become publisher of *The New York Times*, following his marriage to Adolph Ochs's only daughter).

The concept of creating a committee to represent America's factionalized Jewish community was controversial. Some worried that forming what amounted to a Jewish lobby risked fueling the long-standing and pernicious charge that Jews existed as a state within a state, loyal not to the countries where they lived but to their own people. They worried about raising a "Jewish question" in their own backyard. But the ongoing crisis in Russia ultimately outweighed fears of stoking antisemitism.

Schiff strongly backed the creation of a central committee, in part because he believed it might relieve some of the obligations on him. The fundraising effort following the Odessa pogrom, largely undertaken by Schiff and two others, had left him feeling bitter. For his toil, he had received little appreciation but many complaints about how and where the funds were spent.

The organization that emerged from this meeting, and other discussions in the months ahead, was dubbed the American Jewish Committee. Arriving on the scene as the Jewish people faced a gauntlet of threats to their very survival in the decades ahead, it would become a singular force in combating Jewish persecution—and Schiff, far from relieving himself of the burden of leadership, would become a singular force within it.

In the war's aftermath, as the dark clouds of crisis spread abroad, Schiff also glimpsed troubling portents closer to home. The national economy, following a yearslong boom fueled by a frenzy of industrialization and railroad building and restructuring, showed signs of faltering. And a populist sentiment was building across the nation, arraying the public against the corporate titans with whom so much wealth and unaccountable power seemed to vest.

Following the 1904 election, Roosevelt had claimed a mandate to aggressively pursue the corporate reforms he had begun during the partial term he inherited from McKinley. He was asserting a muscular agenda aimed at dismantling monopolistic combinations and eradicating corporate abuses, a crusade that could no longer be dismissed or ignored. In early 1906, during the same speech in which he coined the term *muckraker*, Roosevelt declared that "the national government must in some form exercise supervision over corporations engaged in interstate business." And in a passage that struck an ominous chord on the mansion-lined stretch of Fifth Avenue known as Millionaire's Row, Roosevelt said, "We should discriminate in the sharpest way between fortunes well won and fortunes ill won; between those gained as an incident to performing great services to the community as a whole and those gained in evil fashion by keeping just within the limits of mere law honesty. Of course, no amount of charity in spending such fortunes in any way compensates for misconduct in making them."

Schiff, who believed corporate excesses should be curbed but worried how far the Roosevelt administration might go, knew better than to dismiss the president's rhetoric. The same cowboy wisdom that guided Roosevelt to steer clear of the robust response to Russian barbarism that Schiff desired also suggested that he was not making idle threats against corporations.

17

THE HARRIMAN EXTERMINATION LEAGUE

In January 1907, Ike Seligman sat for a long interview with the *Los Angeles Times*, rhapsodizing with surprising candor about the rigged nature of Wall Street and the tenuous state of American fortunes. He wore a black coat, striped pants, and lemon-colored spats. Appearing reed thin and older than his fifty-one years, he only faintly resembled the college athlete he had once been.

"Has the man who is without information concerning the purposes of important speculators an opportunity to make money in Wall Street?" the reporter asked.

Seligman considered the question. "There's one chance for him to win against four or five chances for him to lose," he replied.

> A widely celebrated stock operator, a maker of the markets on more than one occasion, has said that with all his knowledge of the intentions of his competitors in the streets, he counts himself fortunate if he wins four times out of seven. The "lamb," as he is called, who knows nothing and is a beggar among kings, can figure out his own future from that hypothesis.

"The struggle for wealth is becoming almost alarming," he mused. "Wealthy men are no longer satisfied with horses. They must have automobiles. . . . Men have got to make money to keep up with the parade, and the savage pursuit of it by the rich and the manner of their living have quickened the step of the whole nation until everybody, almost, is on the run."[1]

Increasingly, congressional inquisitors and state investigative panels were chasing the corporate giants leading the financial footrace. Goldman Sachs and Lehman Brothers, not yet among the top tier of American investment banks, for now remained outside the political storm front surrounding some of their friends and competitors. Ike Seligman's firm, slipping behind as a Wall Street leader, was landing too little major business to generate much scandal. But Kuhn Loeb, in the wake of the Northern Pacific struggle, had become an emblem of the wayward financial power Roosevelt and other politicians deemed so dangerous. Harriman, now one of the partnership's most important clients, was a magnet for controversy. Indeed, he seemed to run into it headlong. Thanks in part to their close association with Harriman, Jacob Schiff and Kuhn Loeb would undergo a turbulent period of scrutiny and scandal.

On February 26, 1906, the typically tight-lipped Kuhn Loeb issued a surprise statement. The firm's partners had resigned en masse from their railroad directorships.[2] Reporters who visited 52 William Street seeking additional comment from the firm's senior partner on this head-turning development would have found Schiff unavailable for interviews. He was, at that moment, thousands of miles from New York, plowing westward across the snow-swept plains of Utah aboard a private train supplied by the Union Pacific (whose board he had just resigned from); to ensure that no comfort or culinary detail was overlooked during his cross-country journey, the railroad also dispatched its assistant superintendent of dining room service to personally attend to Schiff and his party, which included his wife, Therese; their nephew Ernst Schiff; their in-laws, the Neustadts; and Jacob's old business partner Henry Budge, accompanied by his wife, Emma. They were on the way to San Francisco, where they would board a steamer to their ultimate destination: Japan.[3]

Kuhn Loeb explained its sudden exit from the management of more than a dozen railroads by citing "the steadily increasing difficulty which the members of the firm have been experiencing in meeting the demands of their own business." Yet this rationale seemed curious, given that Kuhn Loeb partners did not relinquish their directorships of various banks, trust companies, and other concerns. They had merely retreated from the railroads. The timing was also suspect: this drastic step came in the wake of a scandal that had dogged Schiff and his top client, E. H. Harriman, for the past year.

The contretemps began with a battle for corporate control of the nation's largest insurer, Equitable Life Assurance Society, where both Schiff and Harriman held board seats. James Alexander, the company's president, ignited the conflict when he attempted to oust from its management James Hazen Hyde, the dilettante son and heir of Equitable's late founder and majority shareholder, Henry B. Hyde. Factions formed behind each of the combatants, and the controversy quickly spilled from the boardroom onto the front pages of New York's dailies, with each side shoveling dirt about the corporate abuses of the other to eager journalists. By inadvertently exposing questionable practices in the mostly unregulated insurance industry, the feuding board members wound up sparking an investigation by a special committee impaneled by the New York legislature and led by Republican state senator William W. Armstrong of Rochester.

Because insurers controlled vast wells of capital—Equitable's assets totaled nearly $380 million—they had increasingly formed cozy relationships with investment banks.[4] Firms such as Kuhn Loeb and J.P. Morgan relied on insurance company capital to finance some of their biggest deals, and they also counted insurers among their best customers for large blocks of corporate securities. Insurance company officers and directors, meanwhile, often used corporate resources to gamble on stock speculations and fund personal investments—risking policyholders' deposits in the process.

Equitable's Henry Hyde had used the capital under his command to dispense sweetheart loans that he and his allies channeled into investment syndicates. In some cases, they sold securities purchased with Equitable cash back to the insurance company at a premium.[5] These practices continued after Hyde's death, though his son reputedly took the graft a step farther by raiding the corporate coffers to fund lavish soirées.

Prior to the showdown between Alexander and James Hyde, Harriman had little to do with Equitable beyond attending board meetings, but by the time the dust cleared, he had emerged as one of the scandal's primary villains. Otto Kahn would later shake his head at Harriman's decision to plunge into the fight. "There was no earthly reason why he should have been drawn into the fierce and bitter contest . . . but in he jumped with both feet and laid about with such vigor that in the end he became almost the principal and probably the most attacked figure of the conflict."[6]

Harriman opposed Alexander's power grab, though he didn't exactly side with Hyde either. He decided the best way to straighten out the company was by taking the reins himself. And he pursued this goal in a distinctly Harriman-esque fashion—that is, lacking all finesse. During the Armstrong committee's hearings, the investor Thomas Fortune Ryan, who had quietly swooped in to buy Hyde's Equitable shares when the insurance scion finally realized maintaining control of the firm was futile, testified about one memorable meeting with Harriman, in which the mogul all but commanded him to hand over half of his stock. When Ryan refused, Harriman threatened to muster all his political influence against him unless he acquiesced. The papers depicted Harriman as a ruthless corporate barbarian intent on gaining a stranglehold over Equitable, perhaps as a first step toward asserting his control over the insurance industry as he had over the railroads.[7]

The Equitable fight also proved bruising for Schiff, though for different reasons. He faced accusations that his firm improperly profited from the sale of bonds to Equitable, acting as both buyer and seller due to his role as a Kuhn Loeb partner and a finance committee member of the insurance firm. Deepening the ethical morass, Schiff and his partners had been the directors of railroad companies whose stock Kuhn Loeb had sold to Equitable. Due to Schiff's conflicts of interest, a Republican state senator from Saratoga, Edgar T. Brackett, petitioned New York's attorney general to remove Schiff from Equitable's board.[8]

As he came under fire, Schiff wrote to Teddy Roosevelt, who was keeping tabs on the scandal, seeking to assure the president that "far from having done anything which should subject my firm or me to criticism, the true record of our dealings with the Equitable Society is such, that we have every reason to be proud of it."[9]

Schiff also contacted *The New York Times*'s Adolph Ochs seeking his paper's help in refuting the charges of financial impropriety leveled against him. Nearly a decade earlier, Schiff, an investor in the paper, had helped Ochs gain control of the *Times* by recommending him as a possible buyer for the struggling broadsheet.[10] Since then Ochs had grown accustomed to Schiff's frequent missives, scrawled in hurried cursive, providing unsolicited feedback on the paper's coverage. Most often these notes pressed for the *Times* to do more to spotlight the tragedies befalling their people in Russia and Romania, though sometimes Schiff provided Ochs with off-the-record context on his own high-profile dealings. (After completing the Union Pacific purchase, Schiff privately gave Ochs a detailed financial rundown of the deal and remarked that "the magnitude of this operation justifies an editorial comment for I believe no similar transaction is on record in this country.")[11]

Relations between the publisher and the banker, whose name appeared frequently in the pages of the *Times*, were sometimes fraught. And in October 1904, as the Equitable affair simmered on, they had a bitter falling-out over an article concerning a railroad transaction brokered by Kuhn Loeb. "Not for a long time has Wall Street been so disappointed by the outcome of any deal," the *Times* reported, noting that certain shareholders had been cut out of concessions they had been promised during the negotiations. Perhaps because he felt his integrity was already under attack due to the Equitable mess, Schiff took extreme umbrage at the story, though it didn't even name his firm. He furiously clipped the article from the morning paper and sent it to Ochs along with an irate note denouncing the story as a "wanton and entirely unjustified, if not libelous, attack upon the good faith of my firm." And he answered with an attack of his own, writing that "it is a matter of common knowledge that whoever has shown you personally good will has in return at some time been maligned in the N.Y. Times." Indignant, Ochs replied the same day, writing that he was "shocked, amazed beyond expression, that even in anger you should so far forget yourself as to write me as you do."[12]

For the next few months, the men all but ignored each other in social settings, until finally Schiff offered an olive branch. "I believe it is as unpleasant to you, as it is painful to me, that when we meet from time to time, it need be as strangers to each other, and while it can be of no avail to review the cause, which has led to our estrangement, I am quite willing, if you are, that we should reestablish our former relations," he wrote Ochs.[13]

Only a month had passed since their rapprochement when Schiff wrote Ochs, somewhat acerbically, about the Equitable scandal. "Is the Times not going to say anything in my defense against the attacks made upon me . . . ?" Schiff wondered. "I think it is very generally understood that these charges are unjustified and frivolous, but I am not going to say anything in my own defense & if the respected press permits the character of one, who is trying to lead a righteous life, to be besmirched . . . the worse for the press & the public opinion it represents."[14] The following day a favorable editorial appeared stating that excluding "Schiff from all part or influence in the management of the Equitable would seem to be unwarranted. That, it strikes us, is going too far.

"Mr. Schiff is one of the first financiers in this great money centre," the editorial went on. "His experience, his ability, his knowledge of the investment market, and his probity would make him we should suppose, a somewhat desirable addition to the Directorate of any financial corporation."[15]

Nevertheless, Schiff soon withdrew from the Equitable board, as the drumbeat of scandal grew louder. Harriman soon followed.

In late September 1905, Schiff appeared before the Armstrong committee and was questioned by its counsel, Charles Evans Hughes, whose role in the high-profile investigation formed the launchpad for his political career, propelling him to the governorship of New York, to secretary of state, and to the bench of the U.S. Supreme Court. "I am not conscious of ever having done as director of the Equitable Life Assurance Society any wrong of commission," Schiff testified. "I may have done something of omission. It is a case of hindsight and not of foresight, but my conscience frees me from any wrong." He acknowledged selling the Equitable $33 million worth of stocks and bonds over the previous five years, which amounted to about one-sixth of the securities the company had purchased. And, to place this figure in context, he disclosed another number that revealed the stunning breadth of his business. Between 1900 and 1905, Kuhn Loeb marketed nearly $1.4 billion in securities.[16]

The committee released a report early the next year calling for a sweeping overhaul of the insurance industry. It recommended sharp limits on the types of investments insurance companies and their corporate directors could make and prohibiting their participation in investment syndicates. News of the committee's conclusions was reported in the morning papers on February 22, 1906, which was also the day that the Schiff grandchildren and their parents ceremoniously gathered at 965 Fifth Avenue to see Jacob and Therese off on their Far Eastern journey.[17] Four days later came Kuhn Loeb's announcement that its partners would no longer serve on railroad boards. No doubt this was in part a reaction to the Equitable affair—in which the railroad entanglements of Schiff and his partners had become an issue—but the move also appeared forward-looking, a preemptive effort to defuse conflict-of-interest questions bound to arise during a fledgling regulatory effort by the Roosevelt administration targeting the wayward railroads. Lord Nathaniel Rothschild commented on the impeccable timing of Schiff's trip in a snide letter to his Parisian cousins, noting that his "well earned holiday" also had the benefit of allowing him "to be absent from New York pending the railroad inquiries President Roosevelt was making."[18]

Determined to rein in the recalcitrant railroad titans, Roosevelt had turned to the Interstate Commerce Commission, a once tooth-less regulatory body whose authority his administration had worked to bolster. In early 1906, the ICC was beginning to hold hearings on railroad rates, mergers, and other industry practices—an inquiry that would eventually narrow its focus to Schiff's partner in railroad hegemony: Harriman.

Oblivious to the perils multiplying around him, Harriman was pre-occupied with a plan more ambitious than any he had hatched during his career. He controlled the largest railroad network in the United States—twenty-five thousand miles of track spiderwebbing across the nation. But he envisioned a kingdom that was larger still: a trans-portation network that encircled the globe.

Japan's victory in the Russo-Japanese War, and the close ties Schiff had forged with its grateful government, gave him an open-ing to make his move. As a result of the Portsmouth talks, Japan had acquired from Russia (with some strings attached) the southern branch of the Chinese Eastern Railway, stretching from the city of Harbin, in China's far northeastern corner, to Port Arthur, at the southern tip of the Liaodong Peninsula. Harriman viewed gaining control of the railroad, which Japan renamed the South Manchu-ria Railway, as the first step in achieving his vision. As he explained to the wide-eyed U.S. minister to Japan, Lloyd Griscom, "If I can secure control of the South Manchuria Railroad from Japan, I'll buy the Chinese Eastern from Russia, acquire trackage over the Trans-Siberian to the Baltic, and establish a line of steamers to the United States. Then I can connect to the American transcontinental lines, and join up the Pacific Mail and Japanese Transpacific Steamers. It'll be the most marvelous transportation system in the world. We'll gir-dle the earth."[19]

Harriman wasted no time attempting to carry out his vision. In mid-August 1905, while the Russian and Japanese peace delega-tions were still finalizing the terms of their armistice, he sailed for Yokohama. His relationship with Schiff opened doors to key Japanese officials, and Harriman began his voyage home that fall having secured a tentative agreement for joint ownership of the South Manchuria Railway with the government of Japan. But this preliminary deal soon unraveled. Returning to Japan a few days after Harriman departed, Foreign Minister Baron Komura, who had negotiated the Portsmouth Treaty, pointed out that partnering with Harriman was at best premature because the details of the railroad transfer still needed to be hashed out with China, whose territory the railroad traversed. The deal with Harriman also seemed unwise for political reasons. Japan's failure to secure reparations at Portsmouth inflamed the public to the point where riots had erupted in Tokyo. Cutting an American railroad magnate in on the railroad—one of the few tangible concessions Japan had won—risked further angering the populace. While Harriman steamed toward San Francisco, his mind playing out the corporate chess moves that would make him a global transportation titan, he received a cable telling him the deal was on hold.

A few months later, Schiff departed on his own trip to Japan, an extended vacation the banker also used to strengthen the business connections he had cultivated over the previous two years. He and his party docked in Yokohama on March 25, 1906, following a seventeen-day voyage aboard the SS *Manchuria*.

Schiff was welcomed in Japan as a celebrity, and throughout his six-week trip the local newspapers carried near-daily articles about his comings and goings.[20] Every day brought a new gala or dinner party in his honor, as Schiff was fêted by diplomats and dignitaries, financiers and government ministers, and whisked from one high-level meeting to the next. On Harriman's behalf, Schiff tried to get the South Manchuria Railway talks back on track. Accompanied by Takahashi Korekiyo, he met for two hours with the country's prime minister to discuss the railroad and other Japanese financial matters. The prime minister, Schiff recorded in his diary, "assures me that the views to which I give expression will go far to mold his own—particularly in regard to the financing of the Manchurian Railway and the manner of its control by Japan and China."[21] Yet he made little progress in rescuing the deal from bureaucratic limbo.

During his visit, Schiff mingled with practically every political figure who was—or would be—central to the rise of modern Japan, strengthening Kuhn Loeb's ties to the country as it experienced a major industrial awakening. Schiff's friend Takahashi would in the years to follow go on to become Japan's finance minister and twice serve as prime minister. But Schiff's most important audience came several days into his trip, when he was escorted through the gates of the imperial palace to meet with Emperor Meiji, who had overseen the dramatic transformation of Japan from an isolated shogunate to a budding capitalist superpower.

"The Emperor extends his hand and bids me welcome to Japan, saying that he has heard of the important assistance I have given the nation at a critical time, and that he is pleased to have an opportunity to thank me in person for it," Schiff recounted of their meeting. "I reply that my services have been overestimated, but from the start my associates and I, believing in the righteousness of the cause of Japan, when we had the opportunity practically to prove our sympathy, gladly embraced it." The emperor awarded Schiff the Order of the Rising Sun, upgrading the lesser decoration the financier had received the previous year to one of the highest honors conferred by the Japanese government.

Japanese gratitude toward Schiff extended beyond the country's ruling class, as he discovered one day when he visited a dentist in Tokyo. After fitting Schiff with a temporary filling, the dentist initially refused to accept payment. "I have found all over Japan that people who have heard of me are anxious to render me any service they can; it is really touching—the appreciation and gratitude of these people," Schiff wrote in his diary.[22]

Schiff's legend seared itself deeply into Japan's national consciousness, to the point where some seventy years later, Kuhn Loeb partners were still treated reverentially by Japanese bankers, who were well versed in Schiff's legacy.[23] In 1972 a U.S. Air Force chaplain posted in Japan wrote to Dolly Schiff of the magical effect that her grandfather's name had in the country. "It is difficult to describe how much Jacob Schiff has meant to me during my four years in Japan," he wrote.

> Like a talisman, the name opened doors and hearts to me from Wakkanai in the uttermost frigid north to the southern tip of Kyushu. Three years ago, while visiting an Ainu (aborigine) village in Hokkaido, a group of Japanese students made disparaging remarks pointing at my Air Force uniform. I walked up to the group and said: "Watakushi wa Yudaya jin desu"—"I am a Jew." That stopped them cold. Then I added that I am of the same people as Jacob Schiff. The next response was a spirited set of three banzais. Next, I was

treated to a soda pop and a grand tour around the village and museum—all expenses paid.[24]

In 2012, David Schiff, Jacob's great-grandson, was surprised to receive a letter from Japan's deputy chief of mission in New York introducing himself and asking for a meeting: "Japan has never forgotten the kindness shown by your great-grandfather to the people of Japan during the height of the Russo-Japanese War. At an hour of gravest national peril your great-grandfather took a great risk by showing confidence in our people and government, and we shall remain forever grateful."[25]

Schiff's fame in Japan shaped how its people viewed Jews in profound and unexpected ways, including by reinforcing stereotypes about Jewish financial power, such as those contained in the debunked and discredited *Protocols of the Elders of Zion*. His complicated legacy in the country was never on clearer display than during the run-up to World War II, when Japan saved thousands of Jewish lives by providing temporary sanctuary to refugees fleeing from Europe. The country's favorable policy toward the Jews flowed from Japanese officials—considered "Jewish experts"—who bought into conspiratorial myths about Jewish aims for world dominance. By taking in Jewish refugees, they sought to ingratiate Japan with the supposed international financial cabal that controlled the levers of world finance and harness Jewish power to serve their nation's own empire-building ambitions.[26]

On May 18, 1906, when the Schiffs boarded their steamer home, their party had grown by four. The new additions included Takahashi's fifteen-year-old daughter, Wakiko; the teenager's governess; and a pair of playful Japanese spaniels named Fuji and Kittie. Earlier in their trip, during a visit with Takahashi and his family, Schiff had innocently asked Wakiko, "How would you like to come to America one day?" Takahashi and his daughter, however, took the pro forma invitation more seriously than Schiff realized. As Frieda Schiff recounted in her memoir, Takahashi appeared at Schiff's hotel the following day, telling his friend: "My wife and I talked about your wonderful invitation to Wakiko. It is not customary for Japanese girls to leave home. But this is such an unusual chance, that we will be glad to let her visit you for two years." Schiff must have concealed his shock well, perhaps feeling it best to make good on his promise rather than cause embarrassment on either side by reneging. Therese, however, was initially apoplectic that her husband had committed them to raising a teenager who spoke no English and had no clue about American customs. Wakiko would go on to become a cherished member of the Schiff family, calling Jacob and Therese "uncle" and "auntie" and living with them for nearly three years before returning to Japan.[27]

Following his triumphant tour of Japan, Schiff's homecoming may have been jarring. From 1600 Pennsylvania Avenue to the midwestern main streets, a populist revolt was building against the nation's corporate titans. Upton Sinclair had recently published his novel *The Jungle*, portraying in visceral detail the lives of exploited immigrant workers in Chicago's meatpacking industry. The book became a national sensation. Meanwhile the labor movement, now millions strong, was beginning to exercise political power as never before, with Samuel Gompers, president of the American Federation of Labor, exhorting his members to "reward friends" and "punish enemies" at the ballot box during the 1906 elections and "carry the war for justice . . . deeper into politics."[28] Congress was considering a raft of measures to curb corporate abuses. On June 9, 1906, the day after Schiff returned home, the Senate passed the Tillman Act, which would ban corporate contributions to political campaigns. Weeks later, Roosevelt signed into law two seminal regulatory measures: the Pure Food and Drug Act, inspired by Sinclair's novel, which led to the creation of the Food and Drug Administration; and the Hepburn Act, which bolstered the Interstate Commerce Commission's regulatory authority and gave it the power to set railroad shipping prices.

Schiff's ally, Harriman, quickly found himself in the crosshairs of the newly strengthened agency. "True to his fatal gift of getting into trouble, he managed to become the storm-centre around which the agitation for reform in railroad laws raged most violently," Otto Kahn recalled.[29] The timing of the ICC's intensive scrutiny seemed no coincidence to Harriman and his friends, coming after a bitter falling-out between the railroad mogul and President Roosevelt. They had been on friendly terms dating back to Roosevelt's governorship in New York, their relationship even managing to survive the strain of the Roosevelt administration's regulatory assault on Northern Securities. The president seemed to have a special talent for courting the wealthy businessmen he needed to fuel his political ambitions, while simultaneously clubbing them with anticorporate rhetoric and actions. Harriman, meanwhile, recognized the utility of having a friend, even a somewhat unreliable one, in the Oval Office.

The source of their eventual rupture traced back to the final weeks of the 1904 election, when Roosevelt learned that the campaign coffers of New York's Republican state committee had run dry, imperiling a slate of GOP candidates. Roosevelt worried that he might suffer a humiliating defeat even in his home state.[30] He summoned Harriman, who agreed to help dig the state committee out of its hole. Harriman ultimately raised $250,000—contributing $50,000 of his own money—to save the Republican ticket in New York. In exchange for his help, Harriman asked Roosevelt to appoint his friend Chauncey Depew, then completing his first term as a U.S. senator, ambassador to France. Roosevelt agreed, but according to Harriman, the president later reneged. Roosevelt stoked Harriman's fury further through his aggressive push to regulate railroad pricing via the Hepburn Act. Harriman stewed in silence until, during the 1906 campaign, the chairman of the Republican Congressional Committee, Representative James Sherman of New York, approached Harriman to see if he might reprise his role as GOP financial savior. Harriman responded by bitterly recounting Roosevelt's betrayal—and refusing to give a penny to the Republican Party.

Sherman relayed his encounter with Harriman to Roosevelt, who in turn memorialized his conversation with Sherman in a six-page letter that he authorized the congressman to show to Harriman. In it, Roosevelt denied asking Harriman to raise funds to bail out New York's Republican Party and accused him of "deep-seated corruption." Harriman, Roosevelt wrote, was "at least as undesirable a citizen" as the nation's most radical leftist agitator, Eugene Debs, head of the Socialist Party. "The real trouble with Harriman and his associates," Roosevelt confided to one Republican senator, "is that they have found themselves absolutely powerless to control any action by the National Government. There is no form of mendacity or bribery or corruption that they will not resort to in the effort to take vengeance."[31]

A difficult man, Harriman had accrued many enemies. Kahn, one of the few Wall Street financiers who not only knew Harriman well but seemed to understand him, dubbed the magnate's detractors the "Harriman Extermination League." Members of this anti-Harriman clique, Kahn contended, were responsible for "poisoning President Roosevelt's mind against Mr. Harriman," causing him to "see in Mr. Harriman the embodiment of everything which his own moral sense most abhorred and the archetype of a class whose exposure and destruction he looked upon as a solemn patriotic duty."[32]

Three days after the 1906 elections, newspapers reported that the ICC planned to launch a federal inquiry into Harriman's railroad operations—one that would inevitably drag Kuhn Loeb into the fray.[33] By early the next year, the investigation had begun in earnest. And with it came what Kahn called "the crisis in Mr. Harriman's career." Kahn reflected that Harriman, whether because of his colossal ambition or a rare lapse in judgment, committed "one serious mistake" in his management of the Union Pacific, which had helped to fuel the regulatory onslaught against him. After the Supreme Court ordered the dissolution of Northern Securities, Harriman had eventually decided to sell the Union Pacific's holdings in the Great Northern and Northern Pacific, whose share prices had risen considerably since he and Schiff had executed their takeover attempt. With the proceeds, he acquired, on the Union Pacific's behalf, large stakes in seven other railroad companies. In addition to providing the Union Pacific a large and steady stream of dividend income, the move gave Harriman a voice in the management of these lines, though it also seemed like a flagrant example of the type of collusive behavior the Roosevelt administration was trying to root out.[34]

In late February 1907, Kahn and Harriman appeared before the ICC, where Kahn's testimony was as genial and polished as Harriman's was feisty and defiant. The commission interrogated Harriman about his spree of railroad acquisitions. Where would it stop? What was enough?

If the ICC wasn't standing in his way, Harriman testified bluntly, "I would go on as long as I lived."

Commissioner Franklin Lane prodded him further. "And your power, which you have, would gradually increase as you took one road after another, so that you might spread not only over the Pacific coast, but spread out over the Atlantic coast?"

"Yes," Harriman replied, "but hasn't your organization increased its power?"[35]

Harriman subsequently griped to a *Wall Street Journal* reporter, "I prefer the penitentiary, if that is the reward for the upbuilding of the railroad properties of this country, rather than the poorhouse, which is the reward of unprogressive railway management."[36]

The ICC probe played out against the backdrop of a worsening financial climate. During the previous few years, the country had experienced an adrenaline boost of prosperity. Stock prices soared and, in the space of two years, between 1904 and 1906, the Dow Jones Industrial Average doubled. A speculative fever had once again infected Wall Street.

It wouldn't end well. It never did.

The speculative churn on Wall Street placed mounting strain on America's financial system. For more than a year, Schiff had seen worrying signs. In early 1906, a month before his departure for the Far East, he had sounded a dire warning about the state of the economy during a meeting of the New York Chamber of Commerce. He pointed to "conditions in the New York money market which are nothing less than a disgrace to any civilized country." Interest rates had gyrated wildly, reaching as high as 125 percent. The cause of this turbulence, he said, was the nation's "inelastic" currency—the amount of money in circulation remained fixed. This made the United States unique among the world's major financial powers, which relied on government-run central banks to contract or expand their supply of currency based on present economic needs. If Roosevelt channeled only part of the energy he had devoted to regulating railroad rates to currency reform, Schiff said, "the material interests of this country can be safeguarded for a very long time to come."

"I don't like to play the role of Cassandra, but mark what I say," he warned. "If this condition of affairs is not changed, and changed soon, we will get a panic in this country compared with which the three which have preceded it would only be child's play."

Delivered an hour before the closing bell on Wall Street, Schiff's call for currency reform—or else—sent stocks tumbling for the day.[37]

He returned from Japan to worsening financial conditions. During the first half of 1906, stocks declined in value by nearly 20 percent. Then came the passage of the Hepburn Act, which battered railroad securities. Schiff cautioned his partners to steer clear of new deals. "I am very much opposed to tying ourselves up in any way at all at present, because monetary conditions everywhere are so uncertain, and here in particular so much agitation is going on against all corporations that no one knows what the morrow will bring forth," he told Paul Warburg.[38]

Now Schiff watched Harriman's public evisceration with mounting alarm. The antipathy toward the railroads, exacerbated by Roosevelt's crescendoing attacks on corporations, worried the banker. He complained to Ernest Cassel that under the Roosevelt administration "large fortunes are prohibited, and . . . the influence and power which wealth brings are considered dangerous to the state and are therefore constantly open to attack."[39] The government had recently claimed the right to set railroad prices. Where would the regulatory onslaught ultimately lead?

In February 1907, around the time that Harriman and Kahn testified before the ICC, Schiff met privately with Roosevelt. "Mr. Schiff," the president assured him, "I have nothing to avenge, but I wish to make certain that we are protected in the future against the abuses of the past."[40]

During March 1907, U.S. stock prices slid precipitously, and the market declined by nearly 10 percent. On one harrowing day of trading, shares of the Union Pacific—a target, along with Harriman, of the ICC's probe—plunged more than 20 points. Dubbed a "silent crash" or "rich man's panic," the financial shock was thought to be confined to Wall Street, and some bankers predicted it would not spill over into the rest of the economy.

Schiff, however, was skeptical. "We are dealing no longer with a theory but a condition," he wrote Roosevelt late that month. "Events have travelled fast. We are confronted by a situation not only serious, but which, unless promptly taken in hand and prudently treated, is certain to bring great suffering upon the country."[41]

In July the ICC released the results of its investigation into Harriman and the Union Pacific. The scathing report portrayed Harriman as a piratical "railway dictator," in the words of *The Saturday Evening Post*. Harriman's railroad industry enemies could barely contain their glee; one railroad president pronounced himself "dee-lighted" at Harriman's public drubbing.[42]

During the ICC's wide-ranging probe, it zeroed in on one deal the railroad magnate had put together in conjunction with Kuhn Loeb: the 1899 takeover of the Chicago & Alton Railroad, a midsize midwestern line with a record of steady profitability but in need of modernization. The commission highlighted the deal as a case study in "indefensible financing" and pointed to Harriman as the main culprit behind the railroad's "exploitation."[43] Specifically, it accused Harriman and his allies of looting a once financially strong railroad, including by using a tactic familiar to modern-day corporate raiders. After taking over the Alton, Harriman's syndicate hiked its stock dividend more than threefold, to 30 percent, extracting $7 million from the company's coffers. Harriman's group, the commission charged, had also paid themselves with bonds at below-market rates and had generally overcapitalized the railroad, which foundered as the Harriman interests profited.

The Alton deal tainted Harriman's legacy more so than any other hard-nosed venture he spearheaded during the final years of his career, including the Northern Pacific corner, rendering him as a rapacious robber baron of cartoonish proportions, his generation's Jay Gould. George Kennan, Harriman's authorized biographer, would later undertake a strenuous defense of the Alton buyout with the assistance of Otto Kahn, writing a lengthy treatise on the "misunderstood" transaction in which he argued, in part, that Harriman and his fellow investors had reaped a modest profit and that bonds had been sold to certain investors at low prices to spur a market for them.[44] But Kennan's plodding, methodical analysis failed to dispel Harriman's nefarious image.

Roosevelt, whose feud with the railroad baron had gone public, fanned the anti-Harriman sentiment. During a speech in late August 1907, he decried the "malefactors of great wealth," who he blamed for orchestrating the "financial stress" the nation was undergoing in a cynical bid to discredit his policies. Roosevelt didn't name names, but it was clear Harriman was chief among the "predatory capitalists" he had in mind.[45]

"A kind of hysteria of fury against him swept over the land," Kahn remembered. "He was denounced and anathematized as a horrible example of capitalistic greed, iniquity and lawlessness."[46]

Two months after Roosevelt's speech, following a stretch of relative financial calm, the stock market entered the tailspin Schiff predicted. A failed scheme to corner the stock of the United Copper Company triggered the crash, causing a domino effect of financial mayhem. Depositors stampeded to withdraw their money from banks and trust companies, including the Knickerbocker Trust Company, which was forced to suspend operations after burning through its cash reserves. The contagion spread to other banks and trusts, as panicked customers lined up to safeguard their savings. In a familiar scenario, financially strong institutions—bracing for a run on their vaults—refused to lend to weaker ones.

J. P. Morgan, who was attending an Episcopal convention in Richmond, raced home as the crisis snowballed. At seventy, Morgan was now partly retired, with his only son, John Pierpont, Jr. ("Jack"), handling the day-to-day running of the firm, but he played an extraordinary role in saving the U.S. financial system from collapse. Stepping into the part of central banker in an era when the

United States still lacked a central bank, he oversaw the rescue effort from his library, a magisterial, Italian Renaissance–style structure adjacent to his mansion on East 36th Street. Designed by the famed architect Charles McKim, the sumptuous and soaring space featured three tiers of walnut and bronze bookcases containing Morgan's collection of rare medieval and Renaissance manuscripts. Overhead were richly painted apses and lunettes inspired by the artistic oeuvre of Raphael and Pinturicchio. And above a massive marble fireplace hung a sixteenth-century Flemish tapestry, one of a series depicting the seven deadly sins. Dubbed "The Triumph of Avarice," it bore a Latin inscription: "As Tantalus is ever thirsty in the midst of water, so is the miser always desirous of riches."

Chain-smoking eight-inch-long Havana cigars—on doctor's orders, he limited himself to no more than twenty a day—Morgan presided over marathon meetings attended by New York's leading financial minds, including Schiff, Ike Seligman, and even Morgan's old nemesis, Harriman. Using a tactic he had employed in the past, Morgan in one case locked a group of squabbling trust company presidents inside his library until they agreed to chip in to bail out weaker competitors. When the president of the New York Stock Exchange informed Morgan that dozens of brokerages risked collapse unless $25 million could be raised immediately, the banker conjured that amount in an afternoon. Before the crisis was over, Morgan would even rescue the City of New York from insolvency.[47]

Exercising remarkable authority for a private citizen, he decided which institutions warranted rescue and which were beyond saving. Just as a century later, during the financial crisis of 2007–8, Federal Reserve chairman Ben Bernanke and Treasury secretary Henry Paulson wrote off Lehman Brothers, Morgan deemed the Knickerbocker too far gone to resuscitate, even refusing to see its president, Charles T. Barney, when the banker nervously visited Morgan's library to beg for help. The disgraced executive soon jabbed a revolver into his abdomen and took his life.

Schiff, meanwhile, dispensed soothing statements to the public, pronouncing that "the situation is well in hand"—even though he harbored private doubts that the crisis was under control.[48] Knowing the working class would be hardest hit, he rallied New York's philanthropic community to ensure a financial calamity didn't turn into a humanitarian one. "I say to the wealthy that the man who has an income beyond that which he needs, before he adds anything to his capital in such a crisis as this, should make it a point to see that there exists no great suffering in our midst that can be alleviated," he declared during one speech. "Let us be more liberal in adversity than we have ever been in prosperity—for that is the true charity."[49]

That winter, once the worst of the panic passed, Schiff departed on another globetrotting trip, bound for Palestine and Egypt. Schiff's visit to the Holy Land was something of a surprise. He had clashed sharply with the Zionist movement, whose adherents sought to establish a Jewish homeland there. He believed the future of the Jewish people was in the United States and spoke of an "American Israel" composed of "the children's children of the men and women who, in this generation, have come from all parts of the globe to these blessed shores."[50] Moreover, he believed Zionism conflicted with "true Americanism" and risked lending credence to antisemitic canards that had been used for centuries to marginalize Jews—that Jews were a nation unto themselves and thus could not evince true loyalty to any state.[51] As a result of his outspoken views, Zionists denounced Schiff as a "traitor," though his Zionist critics were heartened when Schiff turned up in Jerusalem to tour Jewish settlements.[52]

Schiff spent part of his vacation on a cruise down the Nile, accompanied by Ernest Cassel. As he drifted past the sand-strafed remnants of an ancient civilization, his thoughts turned to Harriman, whose railroad empire, like the kingdoms of the pharaohs, would one day be ground to dust. The scenery placed him in a reflective mood, and he sat down to write Harriman a brief letter: "The imposing ruins on the shore remind me how hollow everything earthly is; how we strive so often for naught; how short a time we live and how long we are then dead. Take my advice, my good friend, do not work so constantly." He urged Harriman to step down from the various railroad presidencies he held and reduce his business commitments.[53]

Harriman largely ignored the advice, even as his frail, pain-racked body began to visibly weaken, sparking rumors about his health that wreaked havoc on shares of Harriman-connected companies.[54] During the final year of his life, the onslaught against him lifted as rapidly as it had materialized. Roosevelt completed his final term in office and would soon be succeeded by his secretary of war, William Howard Taft. The attacks let up. Kahn wrote Harriman a tender letter congratulating him for standing firm through the maelstrom. "I saw you close by in the hours of your many successes and triumphs as well as in those of disappointment and worry, and finally last year in the period of trial and storm and stress," Kahn wrote. "Envy, jealousy, hatred & misunderstanding had combined into an unholy alliance to destroy you, financial panic added its nerve wearing strain—but you stood calmly, resolutely, unflinchingly, amidst weakening friends and powerful enemies . . . boldly facing and fighting and finally overcoming an onslaught formidable enough to have unnerved almost any one but yourself."[55]

Harriman's global ambitions even seemed within reach. Schiff learned from Gregory Wilenkin, now serving as Russia's financial agent in Japan, that Russia would consider parting with the Chinese-Eastern Railroad if Japan sold its interest in the South Manchuria Railway.[56] China, eager for foreign capital, supported a plan for an international syndicate composed of British, French, German, and U.S. banking interests to acquire both lines—a proposal enthusiastically backed by the State Department, as it sought to establish an American commercial foothold in the region. Kuhn Loeb and J.P. Morgan & Co. formed part of what would be known as the American Group. Max Warburg entered the negotiations on the part of Germany.[57]

As Harriman worked to push the deal forward, one of his doctors delivered grave health news. He had stomach cancer, inoperable. He hid the diagnosis even as his gaunt, waxy countenance betrayed his worsening condition. In late August 1909, Schiff visited Harriman at Arden, the titan's sprawling country estate, situated on a ridge overlooking the Ramapo River Valley. Harriman spoke so convincingly of his future plans that he fooled Schiff into thinking he would bounce back.[58] He died two weeks later.

Reflecting on Harriman's life, Kahn saw his passing as the closing of a chapter of America's financial history. Harriman would have no successor, Kahn contended, because never again would one man hold such great power over the railroads. "For better or worse—personally I believe for the better unless we go too far and too fast—the people appear determined to put limits and restraints upon the exercise of economic power and overlordship, just as in former days they put limits and restraints upon the absolutism of rulers."[59]

The end of anything is the start of something else. And as the age of the railroad barons closed, new frontiers opened. If the previous decades had been dominated by giants of industry, the coming years would be defined by upstarts and by an investment banking alliance that would alter the course of modern finance.

18

"THE GOLD IN GOLDMAN SACHS"

W hen the Panic of 1907 struck, Walter Sachs, the youngest of Sam's three sons, was in London completing his banking training before joining the family firm. Like his brothers, he had attended Harvard, graduating in 1904 in the same class as Franklin Delano Roosevelt. Though he moved in different social circles than "Frank," he got to know FDR while they worked together on *The Harvard Crimson*, which Walter tried out for during his freshman year after receiving assurances that his Jewish background would not pose an obstacle.[1]

At Harvard, Walter pursued his passion for theater, even considering a career on the stage. "Then I thought better on it and decided on banking," he recalled.[2] His father and brothers, however, tried to steer him in a different direction, perhaps concerned about causing more strife with Henry Goldman by admitting another Sachs to a partnership that was now more Sachs than Goldman. Why not study law? Walter resisted, but to placate them he spent a couple of unhappy semesters at Harvard Law. "I passed my examinations, but I didn't do very well, because my heart wasn't really in it," he said, "and I told my father that what I really wanted to do was to go into business." Sam relented, tapping his European banking contacts to line up a series of apprenticeships for Walter.[3]

He was posted first to Paris, where he learned currency arbitrage while working for the private banking house of Louis Hirsch. Then he moved on to Berlin, receiving a crash course in the securities business at the Direction der Disconto-Gesellschaft. At the German bank, Walter shared an office with another young banker named Franz von Rintelen, later an infamous World War I spy. Operating covertly in the United States, Rintelen sabotaged munitions shipments to the allies by planting time-delayed bombs in the holds of merchant ships and by fomenting labor strikes at arms factories to slow down production. After his capture, Rintelen spent the final years of the war in an Atlanta penitentiary.

Walter completed the final phase of his training in London working for the banking house of S. Japhet & Co. The firm with which Sam Sachs had previously established a transatlantic banking partnership, Kleinwort, Sons & Co., had politely declined to take Walter on as a trainee—"they didn't want any American, I suppose, to know too much about their business," he speculated—though he socialized frequently with the firm's partners.

His first encounter with the Kleinwort family, years earlier, still mortified him. When he was fifteen, his parents had taken him to a dinner party at Sir Alexander Kleinwort's Victorian estate in South London. To everyone's embarrassment, Walter introduced himself to the butler, mistaking the tuxedoed servant for the ennobled banker his father was working so hard to cultivate. During his London apprenticeship, while striving to put his best foot forward, Walter inadvertently made another faux pas. Over dinner, a London banker told Walter of some recent chatter in financial circles about the quantity of Kleinwort-Goldman finance bills flooding the market, a sign that both firms might be financially vulnerable. Walter dutifully reported these rumors to Alexander Kleinwort, who listened stone-faced. Only later did Walter learn that he had offended the banker. "A youngster simply did not intimate to one of the great merchant bankers of London that anyone had questioned his credit standing," Walter said.[4]

The influx of salmon-colored bills circulating in London (reflecting loans Kleinwort Sons had made to Goldman Sachs and was now trying to sell on the secondary market) evinced the broader economic concerns that preceded the Panic of 1907. Due to the tumultuous American money market, banks such as Goldman were attempting to raise large amounts of cash overseas, which was in turn heightening anxieties in London. In the summer of 1907, the Bank of England defensively placed a temporary moratorium on American finance bills—a move that may have contributed to the crisis that struck that fall by placing further strain on the U.S. credit system.[5]

As harrowing reports reached London about bank runs in New York and the stunning collapse of the Knickerbocker, Walter was preparing to pack up his Jermyn Street flat and depart on an around-the-world voyage, a trip his father had promised him as a reward for completing his training. But with panic paralyzing Wall Street, this was not the time for a *Wanderjahr*. "My boy," Sam wrote to his son, "you had better come home and go to work."[6]

On January 1, 1908, Walter formally joined Goldman Sachs at a salary of $1,800 a year. On January 2 his older brother Arthur—a somewhat cold and haughty man, with a thunderous temper like many of the other males of his clan—dispatched the neophyte banker to Hartford on the seven a.m. train to call at the local banks and find buyers for Goldman's commercial paper.[7] Training was over. He returned to New York that evening having sold exactly nothing—not completely unforeseen, due to the depressed state of the economy— and with his ears still ringing from a tongue-lashing delivered by the cantankerous president of the Hartford National Bank, who flew into a rage when Walter could not supply a satisfactory answer about the relationship between two commercial paper clients with similar names.[8]

Marcus Goldman had died four years earlier at the age of eighty-three. And the partnership Walter entered, now firmly in the hands of his father and uncle, had already taken on a different flavor from the steady, conservative business his grandfather had built up from nothing. For years, Sam had worked to internationalize Goldman Sachs by forging connections with a network of correspondent banks throughout Europe. Henry, meanwhile, pushed the firm to become a player in the securities and underwriting business—and not always successfully. For instance, he had steered the company into what the partners ruefully described as "that unfortunate Alton deal." This was the very same transaction for which Harriman had been accused of pillaging a healthy company to extract undue profits—though somehow it had wound up a money-loser for Goldman Sachs. "No transaction was perhaps more dramatic or fraught with more problems," Walter recalled. Harriman's syndicate, led by Kuhn Loeb, had recapitalized the railroad with an issue of $45 million worth of bonds.

Goldman Sachs had purchased $10 million of the new issue, splitting its allotment with the New York Life Insurance Company. The firm divvied its share up among various investment houses, including Lehman Brothers, which took a modest $100,000 participation, and retained nearly $1 million of the bonds for its own account. "The bond market soon became 'sticky' and the Alton deal from a money-market point-of-view became fraught with difficulty," Walter remembered. "Most of the bonds remained unsold." The deal resulted in a "considerable loss."[9]

But Henry persevered, fixated on breaking into the elite investment banking club that held a virtual lock on the issue of new railroad securities, one dominated by Schiff, Morgan, and James Speyer. Much as Harriman had done during the early years of his career, Goldman tried to elbow his way into the action by buying up large blocks of railroad securities and making himself a factor who could not be ignored. "I recall as a youngster the story of how he began to buy shares of a certain railroad in order to secure a position in the picture, and thus enable the firm to become the railroad's banker," Walter remembered. "One day Jimmy Speyer, who had discovered the source of the buying, summoned my uncle to his office on Pine Street, told him to quit buying and offered to take off his hands all the shares purchased at cost plus 6 percent interest." Kuhn Loeb, J.P. Morgan & Co., and his own Speyer & Co. controlled the railroad underwriting business, the banker told Henry bluntly. "Newcomers were not wanted."

Henry and Sam clashed over their next move. Goldman wanted to hang on and fight. Sachs was just as adamant that they sell, realize a quick and painless profit, and avoid a confrontation with their more powerful rivals. Henry's older brother Julius, the firm's coolheaded lawyer, was finally called in to mediate the bitter dispute. He sided with Sachs, pointing out that antagonizing the nation's top bankers could place their father's firm at risk. "It became apparent that to break into the railroad business at that time was hopeless," Walter said. "Henry Goldman's imaginative mind turned in another direction."

His focus shifted to the industries neglected by the leading investment banks. Largely ignored by the capital markets were the retailers and wholesalers, the dry goods merchants and department store mavericks, the manufacturers and consumer goods entrepreneurs. Few of these types of businesses had been taken public and listed on the New York Stock Exchange.

Traditionally, companies were valued based on their physical property, which backed the issue of stocks and bonds. Railroads were popular with investors because their balance sheets were loaded with capital assets. But what about the tire manufacturer that had landed contracts with the nation's top automakers or the department store rapidly turning over inventory and opening new locations? They were often short on hard assets, their ledgers failing to reflect valuable, yet intangible factors, such as their brands, their customer bases, their future prospects, and their earning power. These hard-to-value assets were known as goodwill, and the most successful consumer and mercantile businesses possessed a surplus of it. Goldman wagered he could capitalize goodwill as never before, enticing the public to invest in a new class of companies based largely on their earning potential. His timing couldn't have been better. Theodore Roosevelt's crackdown on the railroads and other monopolies caused investors to seek out new outlets for their capital, ones that might be safe from a president's antitrust crusading. This provided an opening for mid-level financiers previously squeezed out of major industrial transactions, such as Henry Goldman, and to a generation of businesses that benefited from an influx of investment capital and blossomed into household names.

Goldman has often been mythologized as the godfather of the modern IPO. That's an exaggeration. There was no questioning his genius—his mastery of the financial and marketing alchemy required for a successful flotation—but he was less a pioneer than an early entrant into a wide-open new market for corporate underwriting. In early 1906, when Goldman entered talks with his friend Fred Wertheim about taking his United Cigar Manufacturers Company public, the Lehmans and Seligmans had already dabbled in this field. In 1899, J. & W. Seligman & Co. issued shares in the American Hide & Leather Company. The same year Lehman Brothers spearheaded the stock offering of the International Steam Pump Company. For the Lehmans at least, this solo foray into underwriting—they had previously been participants in numerous syndicates—was "neither a brilliant success nor a failure," noted Lehman partner Frank Manheim in his unpublished corporate history of the firm. Seven years passed before the firm, now under Philip Lehman's command, took the lead in another stock offering. And this time it would do so in partnership with Henry Goldman and Goldman Sachs.[10]

. . .

Henry and Philip were boyhood friends, raised within the tight-knit community of New York's German-Jewish financial elite. Each was ambitious and competitive; each eager to step out of his father's shadow. The banking scions shared, in addition to similar backgrounds, a passion for collecting art.

The friends would often convene for lunch at Delmonico's on South William Street, usually settling in at a table near the back of the second-floor dining room, where they were less likely to be overheard by Wall Street competitors. Perhaps it was during one of these visits when, in early 1906, Henry broached the topic of jointly underwriting the United Cigar Manufacturers offering. Philip and Henry initially considered striking out on their own to pursue the underwriting business, but they instead forged a partnership between their family firms.[11]

That June, Goldman Sachs and Lehman Brothers floated United Cigar's shares, the start of a long and immensely profitable accord that launched both firms to new heights within the investment banking brotherhood. The underwriting partnership made good sense. Not only were they already linked by strong personal ties—Arthur Sachs and Arthur Lehman were also close friends—but they complemented each other well. Through its commercial paper dealings, Goldman Sachs already had long-standing relationships with companies it could approach as underwriting clients. The Lehmans, meanwhile, had a well-established name and capital to spare.[12] The partners of both firms additionally had close friendships, and in some cases family connections, with other German-Jewish entrepreneurs who would eventually join their growing roster of clients, such as the Gimbels, founders of the famous department store chain; the Guggenheims, who made their fortune in mining and smelting and owned a large stake in Gimbels; and the Strauses, owners of the Macy's and Abraham & Straus retail empires.

Walter Sachs attributed his firm's underwriting success to its adventurous approach: "Our firm was bolder and more imaginative; and bolder still was the capitalization. To justify this capitalization required a degree of optimism almost beyond the dictates of conservatism." In other words, Goldman Sachs was willing to push the financial envelope to justify large stock offerings pegged to very rosy predictions of future performance.[13]

In retrospect, Sachs marveled at "the simplicity of these early transactions," crafted with no government oversight, decades before regulators such as the Securities and Exchange Commission appeared on the scene. He recalled his uncle sketching out the particulars of an IPO on a single sheet of a yellow notepad. A contract between the parties was signed. And on the agreed-upon date, Goldman and Lehman purchased the company's shares and then marketed them, through a network of banks and brokerages, to investors.

Sachs recalled the United Cigar offering as "a prolonged affair." But if placing the company's shares dragged on, this did not seem to deter Henry Goldman and Philip Lehman. Two months after United Cigar hit the market, their firms spearheaded an even more ambitious IPO: Sears Roebuck.

Founded in the early 1890s by Richard Sears and Alvah Roebuck, the company had started out as a small mail-order business selling watches. The firm took advantage of the nation's burgeoning railroad system to market and distribute its goods—at prices far lower than those of local stores—to a clientele composed largely of farmers. The demand was enormous, and the company was continuously adding new products to its inventory: sewing machines, farm equipment, hardware, furniture, buggies, clothing. Its catalog ballooned from thirty-two pages in 1891 to 322 by 1894.[14]

Sears bought Roebuck out of the company early on, and in need of more capital, he took on a new partner, a young businessman named Julius Rosenwald. The son of German-Jewish forty-eighters who settled in Springfield, Illinois, Rosenwald was a distant relation of the Sachs family—Rosenwald's maternal uncle, Samuel Hammerslough, had married Sam Sachs's sister Emelia. After their parents died, Sam Sachs had lived for a time with the Hammersloughs, where he met Rosenwald, who was boarding in their home while he apprenticed for his uncles' garment business. Rosenwald, J.R. to his friends, eventually returned to Illinois, settling in Chicago and partnering with Sears in 1895.

Together, over the next decade, Sears and Rosenwald built the business into a retail juggernaut that was doing nearly $50 million in annual sales. The company was growing so rapidly that by 1906, Sears and Rosenwald decided to build a sprawling new headquarters and distribution center to keep pace with the orders pouring in. But they required a large loan to undertake the project. Rosenwald, the company's vice-president and treasurer, had in the past turned to Goldman Sachs to raise relatively modest sums of short-term capital through sales of commercial paper. Now Rosenwald and his partner approached the investment bank seeking $5 million. After hearing them out, Henry Goldman countered with a bolder proposal—a $40 million public offering that would net Sears and Rosenwald $4.5 million apiece.

A thrifty man, Rosenwald had booked himself into a small, inexpensive hotel room during his stay in New York, and as negotiations commenced, some of the talks occurred in his cramped chambers, with the participants forced to sit awkwardly on the edge of his bed.[15] By August 1906, Sears was a public company. There was skepticism, if not outright hostility, to the stock issue in some quarters, particularly farming communities, where there were already concerns that Sears was displacing small-town stores. "Farmers Betrayed to Wall Street," editorialized Kansas's *Hanover Democrat and Enterprise*, describing the stock offering as a blatant money grab. "The plan now seems to be to let Wall Street have the farmer's money and finance a gigantic mail order trust. In other words, the farmer foots the bill."[16]

For investors, the offering was enormously profitable—at least over the long term. An initial investment of $1,000, representing twenty shares of common stock in 1906, was worth more than $62,000 two decades later, factoring in dividends.[17] Over the short term, however, there were perhaps some sleepless nights for Richard Sears and Julius Rosenwald, as well as their bankers. Sears Roebuck shares hit the market during the tumultuous year before the Panic of 1907 and proceeded to get battered, along with other industrial securities.

Vacationing in Paris in July 1907, Henry Goldman gave an interview to a *New York Times* correspondent concerning the bleak economic picture at home. He blamed the volatility on a "debauch of speculation." But the investing public, having "burned their fingers sufficiently," was returning to its senses. He predicted optimistically that "the altered conditions will show themselves before the end of the year in a decidedly easy money market." In fact, several months later, exactly the opposite happened; the credit system seized up. During the worst of the panic, shares of Sears common stock, originally offered at $50, slid into the thirties; preferred shares, initially valued at $100, dipped into the sixties.

The financial crisis struck a significant, though not crippling, blow to Goldman Sachs, claiming nearly 17 percent of the firm's capital. "Owing to the fall in securities," the firm breezily reported to Kleinwort Sons in one communiqué, "instead of being able to say that we have 4½ millions we knock off $750,000."[18] Goldman would have fared even worse if not for its ties to the British bank; amid the market tumult, Alexander Kleinwort gave Sam Sachs free rein to draw on his bank as needed—giving rise to those pesky rumors in London about the financial condition of both companies. That Kleinwort was willing to risk injury to its standing spoke to its deepening relationship with Goldman Sachs. Their transatlantic partnership had recently entered a new phase when Kleinwort had joined Goldman and Lehman Brothers in the Sears offering, handling the London end of the business and placing shares in Europe through a network of brokers on the continent. Since Europe formed the largest market for American industrial securities, the Kleinwort alliance formed an essential (though often overlooked) ingredient in the rise of Goldman Sachs and Lehman Brothers.

The Panic of 1907 and recession that followed forced the budding triumvirate to pause their underwriting activities. After the Sears offering, nearly three years passed before the Trio—as the firms referred to their partnership—cautiously attempted another public offering. In June 1909 they floated shares in the National Enameling & Stamping Company, followed in short order by a succession of IPOs: Underwood Typewriter, May Department Stores, Stern Brothers (another department store chain), Studebaker, Knickerbocker Ice Company, and B.F. Goodrich.

The firms established dedicated cable addresses for their joint business—Kleingold for London-bound traffic, and Goldwortco for missives sent to New York—and communicated in code to prevent rivals from gaining insight into their plans. Occasionally, when especially sensitive business needed to be discussed, Henry Goldman boarded a steamer for London to meet in person with the Kleinwort partners.

More conservative than their American counterparts, the British bankers occasionally worried the deals that Goldman Sachs and Lehman Brothers were putting together were too intrepid, and they warned of "several mistakes in valuing Common Stocks"—which, unlike preferred shares, pegged to hard assets, were based on the far less scientific assessment of a company's goodwill and earning power. This resulted in securities that could be bought below their offering price within weeks of their issue, as was the case with shares of Stern Brothers and tire maker B.F. Goodrich.[19]

Frustrations ran in the other direction, too. "You can well appreciate that this was very embarrassing to us," Goldman Sachs wrote to Kleinwort after learning that shares of the Stern Brothers issue had been sold in France, at discounted rates, through unauthorized brokers.[20]

Despite occasional hiccups and tensions, the Goldman-Lehman-Kleinwort partnership was highly successful. "We are overrun with underwriting applications beyond any precedent," Goldman reported to its London partners.[21] And as Paul Sachs boasted to Herman Andreae, one of the British firm's newest partners, "There is a daily procession of people of importance who are knocking on our door with a view to doing business with us sooner or later."[22]

The underwriting business was so lucrative that, by the time Paul Sachs reached his mid-thirties, he felt secure enough to retire from the partnership to pursue his real passion: art and antiquities. Like James Loeb, Paul, the eldest Sachs son, entered the family business reluctantly. At Harvard, he studied under Charles Herbert Moore, an art historian who was the founding director of the university's Fogg Museum; when Paul graduated, Moore offered him a position as an assistant. Sam Sachs, however, refused to augment the meager $750 salary the job offered, forcing Paul to choose between an austere life in the arts or an indulgent one in investment banking.[23] Paul joined the partnership, though, as he later recounted in his memoir, "I vowed never to give up the thought of an ultimate professional career in art."[24]

In 1911, Edward Waldo Forbes, a grandson of Ralph Waldo Emerson, who was now leading the Fogg, invited Paul to serve on the museum's visiting committee. The opportunity thrilled him, and he viewed the invitation as "an opening wedge" to the academic life he had dreamed of.[25] When Forbes later offered Sachs a job as the museum's assistant director, he didn't hesitate to accept it. He later cited James Loeb as an inspiration behind his decision to leave banking. Loeb's departure from Kuhn Loeb, in order to pursue his real passions, "had the effect of strengthening my determination to emulate his example some day. . . . He illustrated my idea of what a scholarly patron of the arts might be."[26]

The Fogg position came with no salary. But Sachs didn't need the money. He had amassed an ample fortune on Wall Street, thanks in no small part to the string of IPOs engineered by Henry Goldman and Philip Lehman. He relocated to Cambridge, along with his wife, Meta, and their three daughters. The family moved into Shady Hill, the imposing mansion on the edge of Harvard's campus that Paul's college dorm room had once overlooked.

"A great many people on 'the Street' thought I was a damn fool and couldn't understand it," Sachs recalled.[27] His Wall Street contacts, however, proved valuable in his new vocation, serving as deep-pocketed contributors to the museum. Among the donors Sachs recruited was his friend Felix Warburg, himself an art connoisseur. Warburg's massive new C.P.H. Gilbert–designed mansion at 1109 Fifth Avenue, overlooking the Central Park reservoir, was a museum unto itself, filled with Baroque and Renaissance-era woodcuts, etchings, tapestries, and other objets d'art collected during the Warburgs' travels. (The six-floor French Gothic–style manse, which boasted a squash court, was extravagant even by Gilded Age standards. Jacob Schiff was appalled by his son-in-law's ostentatious château—perhaps more so due to the timing of its construction. It was completed in 1908 amid the recession left in the wake of the prior year's Wall Street panic.) Warburg became one of the museum's most generous patrons, at one point contributing $500,000 toward the construction of its new home.

Five foot two and pudgy, Sachs emitted an air of self-importance. He had an imperious streak and was prone to rages. Henry Goldman considered his nephew an "irritating little bantam cock," and his exit from the firm presumably pleased him.[28]

"His passion and his knowledge was much more oriented to art than it was toward banking," said Ernest Paul Sachs, who goes by Rusty and whose middle name is an homage to "Uncle Paul." (Rusty's grandfather, also named Ernest and a pioneering neurosurgeon, was Paul's cousin.) "What a wonderful character he was."[29]

Paul wasn't much of a banker—he frequently slipped away from the office for hours at a time to browse New York's antiquarian bookstores and galleries—but he did make a lasting contribution to the firm's future when he spotted a glimmer of raw talent in a high school dropout from Brooklyn working for Goldman Sachs, for three dollars a week, as a janitor's assistant. Impressed by the personable young man, Sachs promoted him to the mailroom and, to polish the teenager's rough edges, paid for him to attend classes at Browne's Business College in Brooklyn. Decades later Sidney Weinberg would be running Goldman Sachs. Perhaps the firm's most iconic CEO, the scrappy banker, with scars on his back from boyhood knife fights, led the firm out of the financial wreckage of the Great Depression and, over the next forty years, established Goldman Sachs as a global investment banking powerhouse.

Freed of his obligations to the firm, Paul carved out a significant legacy of his own. Rising eventually to the directorship of the Fogg and earning a Harvard professorship, he taught a yearlong class in museum stewardship, grooming a generation of curators who dispersed to some of the nation's most prominent institutions and, in some cases, formed their own. His acolytes included the founders of New York's Museum of Modern Art, and Sachs both recommended MoMA's first director and helped to shape its mission as a founding trustee. During World War II, Sachs helped to establish the Allied task force known as the Monuments Men, and his protégés featured prominently among this squad of curators, art historians, and architects who recovered works pilfered by the Nazis.

Edward Warburg, Felix and Frieda's youngest son, who studied under Sachs, recalled him as "a humorless little cannonball of energy." Eddie's friend and classmate Lincoln Kirstein, another Sachs pupil, remembered him as "a small and nervous man who hated being a Jew."[30] If not universally beloved by his students, he nevertheless stamped his mark, through his trainees, on the evolution of artistic taste. His influence was so profound and pervasive that it even affected the way art was displayed. The diminutive curator hung pictures horizontally at eye level, presumably so he could see them better, a departure from the European style of positioning art vertically and in dense clusters. Sachs's method, carried forth by his students, became dominant in American museums and galleries.[31]

Flush from their underwriting successes, Henry Goldman and Philip Lehman also indulged their artistic interests. In 1911, Lehman made his first significant purchase, Rembrandt's *Portrait of a Man Seated in an Armchair*. It was the cornerstone of a collection, expanded by his son Bobbie and comprising some 2,600 works, that now fills a wing at the Metropolitan Museum of Art.

The year after Philip purchased his Rembrandt, Henry Goldman paid $100,000 for the Dutch master's *Saint Bartholomew*; though he had been collecting since college, it too was his first major acquisition. He followed it with Renaissance and Baroque masterworks by Rubens, Van Dyck, and Donatello.

The art historian Wilhelm Valentiner said Goldman possessed "one of the best American private collections." In contrast to major collectors such as J. P. Morgan, who hoovered up "masterpieces of all periods and schools," Valentiner noted, Goldman took a more intellectually curious approach, eschewing the fashionable works of the Barbizon School and of the eighteenth-century English and

French masters and gravitating toward their antecedents. He pointed to Goldman's Rembrandt as evidence of his sharp eye and maverick nature. The Dutch artist painted *Saint Bartholomew* during the rocky final years of his life, after he had gone bankrupt and experienced a series of personal misfortunes, a period overlooked by many collectors but during which "the artist disclosed the inmost secrets of his soul," Valentiner said.[32]

Goldman's purchase of *Saint Bartholomew* came on the heels of one of his most successful IPOs: F.W. Woolworth & Co.

Frank Winfield Woolworth had pioneered the concept of the five-and-dime store, which sold a smorgasbord of discount products. From a single shop in Lancaster, Pennsylvania, he built a retail kingdom of more than three hundred Woolworth's locations. In 1911 he persuaded his four largest competitors—who between them controlled another three hundred stores—to merge their businesses into an empire. Tall and stout, with a silver mustache and blazing blue eyes, Woolworth sought an investment banking house that would float shares in the merged company, which would bear his name. Goldman Sachs aggressively pursued the business, but one of Woolworth's friends, Lewis Pierson, who ran a small bank, recommended J.P. Morgan & Co. instead. Pierson proposed the deal to a Morgan partner, who laughed off the idea that his firm would underwrite a chain of discount stores. A few days later the Morgan partner telephoned Pierson, saying that his firm might in fact be amenable to the business. Perhaps he had heard that Woolworth and his fellow five-and-ten operators were pulling in some $50 million in annual sales. By then, Goldman Sachs had locked down the deal. "That is how Mr. Morgan failed to float our securities and Goldman Sachs & Co. took it up," Woolworth recalled.[33]

In early 1912, the Trio—with Kuhn Loeb joining the syndicate—underwrote Woolworth's $65 million offering. Such a frenzy of buzz built up about the IPO that shares of the company's preferred and common stock hit the market at ten and twenty-one points over their offering prices, respectively.[34]

The following year, as if signaling his ascendance, Frank Woolworth achieved what had become his obsession: erecting the world's tallest building. Rising 792 feet in Lower Manhattan, the sixty-story Woolworth Building, built to accommodate thousands of tenants, towered nearly a hundred feet over the Metropolitan Building, the skyscraper that had previously held the distinction of world's tallest.[35] (At nearly one thousand feet, the Eiffel Tower remained the world's tallest *structure*.) The building cost $13.5 million. Woolworth paid for it in cash.

On the evening of April 24, 1913, eight hundred guests gathered on the twenty-seventh floor of the tower to fête Woolworth and the building's designer, C.P.H. "Cass" Gilbert, New York's most sought-after architect (who had also built Felix and Frieda Warburg's palatial new home). Members of the nation's political, financial, and cultural elite filled immense banquet tables. Eighty members of Congress traveled from Washington to attend. Otto Kahn, for whom Gilbert would later design a mansion, was there. So was Charles Schwab. The best-selling novelist F. Hopkinson Smith served as master of ceremonies. At seven-thirty p.m., the lights dimmed, and at the push of a button, eighty thousand bulbs illuminated the building. The orchestra played the national anthem, competing to be heard over cheers and applause.[36]

According to Walter Sachs, during the speechmaking that followed, Woolworth, exuberant at the fulfillment of his dreams, clapped one hand on Henry Goldman's back and the other on Cass Gilbert's, exclaiming, "These are the two men who have made this wonderful building possible."[37]

The tale, perhaps apocryphal, did speak to a broader truth about Henry Goldman and his legend. Of all the issues Goldman Sachs had brought out up to this point, no deal "added more to the reputation of the firm than that of the Woolworth business," Sachs recalled.[38] The same bankers who had denied him a place on their railroad boards and in their syndicates now wondered what he and Philip Lehman would do next. As Lehman would later say, "Henry Goldman put the gold in Goldman-Sachs!"[39]

Together, Henry and Philip shaped not just the destinies of their firms and those of their clients, companies that became fundamental to American life during the twentieth century. They also profoundly influenced Wall Street's trajectory. Nothing would ever be the same again.

left: Eldest of the eight Seligman brothers, Joseph rose from peddler to pater-familias of one of America's preeminent banking dynasties. His up-from-nothing tale, according to a grandson, inspired Horatio Alger's bootstrapping protagonists.

right: Jesse Seligman's San Francisco dry goods store became the family's biggest moneymaker. He would later lead J. & W. Seligman & Co. into the damaging Panama Canal scandal.

On foot or by wagon, peddlers traveled deep into the American countryside, visiting farms, mining camps, and rural towns far from the nearest shops. Peddling was often a first rung on the economic ladder for recently arrived Jewish immigrants.

Home of Mayer Lehman, Montgomery, Alabama
Father of Herbert H. Lehman, U.S. Senator, New York

left: Months before the Civil War ended, Mayer Lehman, pictured here in 1866, undertook a mission on behalf of Confederate POWs.

right: Mayer and Babette Lehman's sprawling home on South Court Street in Montgomery, Alabama.

The Lehmans' businesses were headquartered on Court Square, Montgomery's main commercial hub.

Mayer and Babette Lehman, center, with their children and grandchildren in Tarrytown, New York, circa 1888. Herbert (*left*) and Irving are seated in the front row. Sigmund (*center*) and Arthur (*far right*) are standing in back.

left: Emanuel, who established Lehman Brothers' beachhead in New York, was more cautious than his adventurous younger brother. The joke in the family was that Mayer made the money and Emanuel ensured they didn't lose it.

right: Herbert Lehman, pictured in his army uniform during World War I, left his Lehman Brothers partnership for a career in politics. He replaced FDR as New York's governor in 1932 and later served in the U.S. Senate.

top left: The son of a prominent Jewish family in Frankfurt, Jacob Schiff joined the partnership of Kuhn Loeb in 1875 and established himself as one of the nation's preeminent investment bankers.

top right: The Haus zum Grünen Schild, located in Frankfurt's Jewish ghetto, was occupied in the seventeenth and eighteenth centuries by members of the Schiff family. Mayer Amschel Rothschild, patriarch of the Rothschild banking dynasty, purchased the home in the late 1700s.

left: "She might have been brought up in the best of German families," Jacob wrote to his mother of his future bride, Therese Loeb, eldest daughter of Kuhn Loeb cofounder Solomon Loeb.

top left: Solomon Loeb cofounded Kuhn Loeb in 1867, following a successful career in Cincinnati in the clothing business.

top center: Solomon Loeb's second wife, Betty, was a classically trained pianist and a guiding force behind her family's philanthropic endeavors.

top right: Abraham Kuhn, Loeb's brother-in-law, returned to Germany shortly after establishing Kuhn Loeb. In Frankfurt, he recruited Jacob Schiff as the firm's newest partner.

Members of the Schiff and Loeb families at their cottage Far View, in Bar Harbor, Maine, where the Schiffs vacationed each August. Pictured in the front row, right to left, are James Loeb, Betty Loeb, Jacob Schiff, Mortimer Schiff, Therese Schiff, and Solomon Loeb. Also pictured: Isaac Newton and Guta Seligman (*second row, right*); Felix and Frieda Warburg (*second row, center*); and Otto and Addie Kahn (*balcony, right*).

Children play in the back-yard of the Henry Street Settlement. The photograph was taken by muckraker Jacob Riis, author of *How the Other Half Lives*, which documented the plight of the urban poor.

Lillian Wald's vision of creating a visiting nurse service on the Lower East Side blossomed into the Henry Street Settlement with support from Jacob Schiff, who gifted the social welfare group its headquarters at 265 Henry Street.

Founded in 1845, Temple Emanu-El was New York's first Reform congregation. Expanding from a rented room on the Lower East Side to a towering synagogue on Fifth Avenue, Emanu-El was the spiritual center of Manhattan's German-Jewish elite.

left: The youngest of Samuel and Louisa Sachs's three sons, Walter joined Goldman Sachs in 1908 and remained a partner until his death in 1980.

right: Marcus Goldman got his start in banking by making small, short-term loans to businesses in New York's financial district. The credit rating agency R.G. Dun & Co. initially considered him "too timid to do much bus[iness]."

Marcus and Bertha Goldman celebrated their fiftieth anniversary at Ellencourt, Samuel and Louisa Sachs's New Jersey shore estate, surrounded by assorted Goldmans and Sachs. Henry Goldman is pictured at far right in the third row.

A SENSATION AT SARATOGA.

NEW RULES FOR THE GRAND UNION.

NO JEWS TO BE ADMITTED—MR. SELIGMAN, THE BANKER, AND HIS FAMILY SENT AWAY—HIS LETTER TO MR. HILTON—GATHERING OF MR. SELIGMAN'S FRIENDS—AN INDIGNATION MEETING TO BE HELD.

On Wednesday last Joseph Seligman, the well-known banker of this City, and member of the syndicate to place the Government loan, visited Saratoga with his wife and family. For 10 years past he has spent the Summer at the Grand Union Hotel. His family entered the parlors, and Mr. Seligman went to the manager to make arrangements for rooms. That gentleman seemed somewhat confused, and said : " Mr. Seligman, I am required to inform you that Mr. Hilton has given instructions that no Israelites shall be permitted in future to stop at this hotel."

Mr. Seligman was so astonished that for some time he could make no reply. Then he said: " Do you mean to tell me that you will not entertain Jewish people !" " That is our orders, Sir," was the reply.

top: This caricature of the anti-Jewish policies at the Grand Union Hotel in Saratoga, New York, appeared in an 1877 edition of *Puck*.

bottom left: Once the world's largest hotel, the Grand Union served an elite and wealthy clientele of vacationers during the summer months. It was demolished in 1953.

bottom right: Joseph Seligman's expulsion from the Grand Union dominated headlines for weeks, becoming one of the most notorious episodes of antisemitism in U.S. history.

19

AND STILL THEY COME

The landscape was changing—and not just on Wall Street. The very premise of the United States as a refuge for immigrants—a "mother of exiles," as the poet Emma Lazarus dubbed the Statue of Liberty, the ultimate symbol of the American ethos—seemed in question. Between 1880 and 1910, more than 17 million immigrants poured into the country, the majority of them from Northern and Western Europe. Jews, many fleeing Russia and its environs, accounted for more than 1.5 million of the new arrivals. They settled in large numbers in New York, gravitating toward Manhattan's primary Jewish enclave, the Lower East Side.

"It is said that nowhere in the world are so many people crowded together on a square mile as here," the journalist Jacob Riis wrote of the neighborhood, which he called "Jewtown," in his famous turn-of-the-century study of tenement life, *How the Other Half Lives*. It was a breeding ground of disease and despair—half a million Jewish immigrants crammed into dilapidated, dreary apartments that lacked electricity and plumbing and were situated so closely together that natural light and ventilation were rare luxuries. It was not uncommon for twenty people to share two small rooms.

"Life here means the hardest kind of work almost from the cradle," Riis wrote, noting that "the homes of the Hebrew quarter are its workshops also. . . . You are made fully aware of it before you have travelled the length of a single block in any of these East Side streets, by the whir of a thousand sewing-machines, worked at high pressure from earliest dawn till mind and muscle give out together. Every member of the family, from the youngest to the oldest, bears a hand, shut in the qualmy rooms, where meals are cooked and clothing washed and dried besides, the live-long day."[1]

Beyond religion, these immigrants shared little in common with the wealthy uptown Jews whose daily lives were as comfortable as theirs were burdensome. But as religious minorities living in a society that did not fully embrace them as equals, circumstances had thrown them together. Rich or poor, German or Russian, investment banker or pushcart peddler, they represented their community to the broader public. It was not the spirit of charity alone that caused the German-Jewish elite to grow preoccupied by the living conditions on the Lower East Side. They also had an image to uphold. The more that image was threatened, the more aggressively the Jewish upper crust sought to shape it through muscular philanthropy.

The jarring demographic changes that resulted from large-scale immigration and fears that low-paid foreign workers (such as the legion of Jews hunched over sewing machines in downtown sweatshops) would crowd out Americans in the job market prompted an upsurge of nativism. Groups such as the Immigration Restriction League, founded by a trio of Harvard alums, emerged to beat back the flood of foreigners, contending they imported disease, crime, and moral decay to American soil; stole jobs from American citizens; and became a burden on public resources. Careful not to portray themselves as anti-immigrant, the group's members contended they merely wanted to prevent "undesirable" émigrés from taking root in the United States. Many of these undesirables, in the view of the Immigration Restriction League's founders, which included a climatologist who dabbled in eugenics, were the supposedly racially inferior Jewish immigrants hailing from Russia and Eastern Europe.

Making common cause with trade unions, patriotic societies, and farmers' associations, the Immigration Restriction League lobbied aggressively for stringent measures to curb immigration, including a literacy test and deportation for foreigners who had become a "public charge." Fierce debate over immigration raged in Congress, which year after year edged closer to passing sweeping legislation. Restrictionists found a powerful ally in Senator William P. Dillingham, a Vermont Republican who chaired the immigration committee. In 1906 he introduced a controversial bill, denounced as "un-American" by opponents, that amounted to an Immigration Restriction League wish list. It raised the existing "head tax" on arriving immigrants from two dollars to five dollars; imposed a literacy test; and barred "imbeciles," "feeble-minded persons," and others whose physical or mental handicaps might prevent them from holding steady employment.[2]

The legislation cleared the Senate, but House lawmakers drastically watered it down, stripping out the literacy test and lowering the head tax. Lucius Littauer, a Jewish congressman from New York and Schiff ally, slipped into the final bill an amendment specifically designed to protect Russian refugees from deportation. Outraged the bill had been blunted, Republican congressman Augustus Gardner of Massachusetts, its sponsor in the lower chamber, paced the House floor muttering cryptically about "certain influences"—that is, Jewish influences—which he claimed succeeded in weakening the measure, and he implied that his colleagues had removed the bill's most stringent provisions to appease Jewish voters.[3] Though immigration opponents lost this round, the legislation did create a commission, chaired by Dillingham, to make a thorough study of the issue. Eventually, this panel paved the way for some of the harshest immigration restrictions of the twentieth century.

Dating back to the 1880s, Jacob Schiff and other Jewish leaders had fended off attempts to restrict Jewish immigration, including successive efforts to impose literacy requirements. But by the early 1900s, nativism had gone mainstream.

The problem of immigration nagged at Schiff, who sometimes lay awake in the early morning hours turning the question over in his mind. "Who would have imagined in the early eighties, when the wholesale Jewish emigration from the land of the Czar first began, that in less than three decades the Jewish population in this country would increase because of this influx, from two hundred thousand to two millions: that in the city of New York alone the number of our coreligionists would rise to a million?" Schiff marveled during a 1909 speech. "Such, however, is the fact, and still they come!"[4]

And still they come.

For decades, American-Jewish leaders believed the "Jewish question" in Russia could be resolved through diplomatic pressure and other means. Schiff, through his financial and propaganda activities during the Russo-Japanese War, had even supported the more aggressive strategy of regime change. But in the wake of the failed revolution, the czar's personal antipathy toward the Jews, whom he faulted as the chief source of the revolutionary agitation against him, only hardened, and Schiff feared Nicholas II could never be made to see reason. He oscillated between hope that the "mighty forces of liberty . . . will further and successfully assert themselves," and despair that if conditions worsened, "then the time will have arrived for [Jews] to leave Russia as our forefathers have left Egypt and Spain."[5]

Schiff also believed New York could no longer absorb the large numbers of Russian and Eastern European refugees arriving daily. His periodic visits to the Lower East Side, to visit his friend Lillian Wald at the Henry Street Settlement and review other charitable projects he backed, made that clear to him. The charitable network Schiff and other Jewish philanthropists supported, impressively robust though it was, strained under the escalating demand. And the crime and squalor of the Lower East Side was now a vivid case study that restrictionists could point to when they argued to cut off the flow of immigrants.

If the foreign influx continued unabated, the Jewish community might risk its hard-won standing in the American social hierarchy. And Schiff and other Jewish leaders worried about antisemitism. "New York and the North Atlantic seaports . . . are getting in a state of super-saturation with regard to the Jewish population," Schiff declared in one interview. "I am certainly not a Restrictionist, but as far as New York is concerned, I will gladly welcome any legitimate measure which would prevent the settlement of further large numbers in New York itself. . . . The problems to which the existing congestion gives rise—social, economic, even moral—are, I feel, getting beyond our control."[6]

The solution, Schiff believed, was not halting immigration—but diverting it.

When the first waves of Russian immigrants landed in the United States during the 1880s, New York's established Jewish community initially sought to disperse some of them to the American heartland. Such was the idea behind the Jewish farming communes supported by the Baron de Hirsch Fund. In the 1890s, Schiff attempted to settle Russian immigrants in Minnesota on land owned by James J. Hill's Great Northern Railway. Promising Hill that "only the best of Russians will be sent" and that the Hirsch Fund would ensure each family would arrive with at least $500, Schiff convinced the railroad mogul the arrangement would prove mutually beneficial: "not only would a considerable number of unfortunate homeless people be thus provided for, but moreover your road would in the end be considerably benefited by these proposed settlements." But only about a dozen families settled there, the equivalent of a raindrop in a downpour.[7] When Jewish immigrants arrived in New York, they found a thriving if impoverished community. And they seldom wanted to leave after that, even for the promise of a forty-acre homestead in Milaca, Minnesota, and $500.

In 1901, to systematize the dispersion of immigrants, Schiff and other Jewish leaders founded the Industrial Removal Office, its mission to find jobs for unemployed Jewish immigrants across the United States and assist them in relocating. The organization placed thousands of immigrants in hundreds of towns and cities throughout the country. But with boatloads of immigrants arriving daily, even this effort barely made a dent.

Public opinion, meanwhile, was shifting sharply in favor of restriction. During his annual address to Congress in December 1905, President Roosevelt made clear he favored more regulation. "The laws now existing for the exclusion of undesirable immigrants should be strengthened," he said.[8] By early the next month, Dillingham was drafting his bill. Around this time, Schiff had an alarming conversation with Frank Sargent, the U.S. immigration commissioner, who told the financier bluntly that the Atlantic port cities were nearing a point where they could no longer "digest the foreign elements."[9]

During Roosevelt's recent address, he suggested that the "right kind of immigration" should be directed "away from the congested tenement-house districts of the great cities" and "properly distributed in this country." In his conversation with Schiff, Sargent raised a similar proposition, though instead of relocating immigrants after they arrived on the East Coast, he advised routing them directly from Europe to southern ports.

This conversation planted the seed for what would become one of Schiff's most monumental, if quixotic, philanthropic undertakings. By August 1906, Schiff was sketching the outlines of his plan to redirect the flow of immigration in a letter to the British author and activist Israel Zangwill, whose work, focusing on immigrant life, earned him the nickname "the Dickens of the ghetto." The son of Russian immigrants and an acolyte of Theodor Herzl, the father of modern Zionism, Zangwill had broken with the Zionist movement following its leader's death in 1904, forming an organization called the Jewish Territorial Organization (ITO). Where Zionist die-hards pushed for the creation of a Jewish homeland in Palestine—to the exclusion of other options, including an offer by the British government of land in East Africa—Zangwill and his ITO, reacting to the ongoing crisis in Russia, were open to exploring alternative territories for the mass settlement of Jewish immigrants.

At their core, both Zionism and territorialism turned on an ideology of Jewish nationalism Schiff found distasteful, if not dangerous. "Political Zionism places a lien upon citizenship," he said, noting that the establishment of a Jewish state "creates a separateness which is fatal."[10] He contended that Zionists "by their very movement are furnishing the Anti-Semites one of the strongest arguments for their nefarious attacks upon our race."[11]

Setting aside his philosophical differences with Zangwill, Schiff sought the ITO's help in carrying out his plan to route immigration away from New York. "It appears to me that in this existing emergency the Jewish Territorial Organization, if for the time being it will occupy itself with something which is immediately practicable and sidetrack its cherished project of finding a separate land of refuge where the Jew can live under autonomous conditions, can be of very great service to the momentous and pressing cause which we all have so very much at heart," Schiff wrote Zangwill, who after some wrangling agreed to join the effort.[12] The author, whom Schiff found "brusque" and difficult, would later call the operation "the only constructive idea my dear friend Schiff ever had."[13]

Schiff initially favored New Orleans as the port of arrival for the diverted immigrants, but he and his compatriots finally settled on Galveston, because it was located farther west, was already served by a Bremen-based shipping line, and was a railroad hub, making it a simple matter to transport the newcomers to their new homes. They also picked Galveston because, unlike New Orleans, it was not a major city where immigrants would be tempted to settle. The idea was that Galveston would serve not as a destination but as a transfer point, funneling Jews to towns and cities west of the Mississippi where employment had been prearranged for them.

Along with Zangwill's ITO, Schiff also enlisted the Hilfsverein der Deutschen Juden, a Berlin-based Jewish relief group cofounded by Moritz Warburg. With Jewish refugees swamping Germany, where the primary transatlantic ports were located, the Hilfsverein had worked to facilitate their immigration to the United States and other locales. Encouraged by his father, Max Warburg played a significant role in the group and in the Galveston movement itself. Negotiating with contacts in the shipping industry, "he succeeded in reducing passage to the United States to about $20—and in introducing better sanitary arrangements and in providing better general care for these emigrants," Bernhard Kahn, the Hilfsverein's onetime secretary general, remembered. "In the ten years from 1904 to 1914 about 1,250,000 Jews migrated to the United States. By his emigration work Max Warburg, in a sense, helped to build up the present powerful Jewish community in the United States."[14]

Under Schiff's plan, the ITO, which had an existing presence in Russia, would spearhead operations in that region, promoting the benefits of the American West to the populace and carefully selecting immigrants to take part in the Galveston program. The ITO would arrange their transportation to Germany, where they would come under the care of the Hilfsverein, which would place them on ships bound for Galveston. The Industrial Removal Office, through a newly formed offshoot dubbed the Jewish Immigrant Information Bureau, would receive the immigrants in Galveston, provide them with some money, and send them on to one of nineteen cities—including Des Moines, Denver, and Kansas City—where local committees had formed to sponsor the immigrants and place them in jobs. The Information Bureau made clear to Zangwill's ITO that it sought only the most employable immigrants—laborers and tradesmen, preferably under forty. Controversially, the organization requested the ITO send no immigrants who kept the Sabbath (and would be unwilling to work on Saturdays).[15]

Schiff pledged $500,000 toward the Galveston movement. Crucially, the project had the support of President Roosevelt, who, Schiff reported, following a visit to Washington in early 1907, "was particularly happy that we are making this effort."[16] Schiff additionally won the backing of Oscar Straus, whom Roosevelt had named his secretary of commerce and labor and whose agency had jurisdiction over immigration. With Straus's help, Schiff secured passage of legislation establishing a new immigration hub at Galveston.

At eight a.m. on July 1, 1907, the first group of Jewish refugees trudged down the gangway at the Port of Galveston. The Galveston movement's inaugural party consisted of eighty-seven people, the bulk of them men between the ages of eighteen and forty-two. One by one the immigrants were examined by a doctor, grilled by immigration inspectors, and scrutinized by customs officers who riffled through their baggage. Then they climbed into wagons that carried them the half mile to the Jewish Immigrant Information Bureau's spacious processing center. After a hot meal and a bath, most boarded trains that evening for their new homes; others departed the following day. A second party of twenty-six immigrants arrived two weeks later, and the process repeated. Seventy more came in early August, and eighty-nine followed at the end of that month. By the end of the year, nine hundred immigrants had passed through Galveston.[17]

But soon outside circumstances halted the movement's momentum—the Panic of 1907 and the recession that came in its aftermath made it difficult to find jobs for the immigrants. The flow of Russian immigrants, via Galveston, slowed to a trickle. The Russian government, meanwhile, cracked down on the ITO's recruitment activities, shutting down most of the emigration bureaus it had established. While Schiff's Galveston project flailed and the economy wallowed, a crisis struck that forced Schiff and other Jewish leaders to take more concrete steps to get a handle on the immigration problem in their own backyard.

On September 1, 1908, *The North American Review*, a respected literary journal cofounded in 1815 by Nathan Hale, published a treatise by New York's police commissioner, Theodore Bingham, a retired Army brigadier general who hobbled on a wooden leg following an engineering accident. Titled "Foreign Criminals in New York," Bingham's article included the shocking—and false—claim that Jews comprised 50 percent of the city's criminal element. "The crimes committed by the Russian Hebrews are generally those against property," Bingham wrote. "They are burglars, firebugs, pickpockets and highway robbers—when they have the courage; but though all crime is their province, pocket-picking is the one to which they take most naturally. . . . Among the most expert of all street thieves are Hebrew boys under sixteen who are being brought up to lives of crime."[18]

Bingham's explosive essay drew widespread condemnation, sparking a volley of fiery editorials from the Jewish dailies and a round of protest meetings. Downtown leaders directed their fury not just at the peg-legged commissioner but at the uptown Jews, Schiff in particular, who were slow to speak out. "When someone refused to allow a [Jewish] aristocrat into a Gentile hotel, the Jewish four hundred did not rest until the guilty party had been dismissed; and now, they are quiet!" the Yiddish daily *Tageblatt* fumed. The paper declared in a subsequent editorial, "We cannot be dependent on our grand moguls."[19]

In theory, the Bingham situation was the very type of controversy the fledgling American Jewish Committee had been formed to address. But the committee, a creation of the Jewish elite, was silent. When the scandal blew up, Schiff was on his annual vacation in Bar Harbor. He confided to a member of the Educational Alliance, one of the charitable organizations that he funded, that he had no desire to engage in a "public discussion of the question of Jewish criminality in New York," which he considered "unwise for obvious reasons." But finally, after more than a week and with the controversy showing no signs of abating, Schiff weighed in. Declaring himself "shocked and astonished" by Bingham's "reckless statements," he asked, "What is Commissioner Bingham driving at? Does he wish to add to the unfortunate prejudice which already exists against the foreigner in general and the Jew in particular, and is he in favor of restricting immigration illegitimately using his official position to further his ends?"[20]

Soon Bingham retracted his comments, claiming that the statistics he cited in his article—"furnished to me by others"—were "unreliable." He managed to hang on to his job for another nine months before New York mayor George McClellan fired him for insubordination, a move cheered by the Yiddish press.

The scandal faded from the front pages, but resentments between uptown and downtown lingered. If any consensus emerged from the traumatic Bingham drama, it was the need for some form of unity among New York's factionalized Jewish community, which was deeply riven along religious and ideological lines. After Bingham repudiated his comments about Jewish crime, Judah Magnes, a charismatic thirty-one-year-old associate rabbi at Temple Emanu-El, gave voice to these sentiments in a statement to *The New York Times*: "The one million of Jews of New York . . . should draw proper deductions from this incident. They need a permanent and representative organization that may speak in their behalf, that may defend their rights and liberty, and that may also cope with the problems of criminality just as Jewish charitable organizations are effectively coping with the problems of destitution and disease."[21]

Magnes, a founding member of the American Jewish Committee, was an ideal figure to bridge uptown and downtown. His position at Emanu-El and recent marriage to Beatrice Lowenstein, making him a brother-in-law of the prominent lawyer and Schiff confederate Louis Marshall, meant that he moved in the same circles as the uptown upper crust. Yet Magnes had also forged close ties with the Lower East Side intelligentsia, and he served as an officer of the Federation of American Zionists.[22] Adroitly navigating the indignation of downtown leaders and the class anxieties of his uptown patrons, Magnes led the movement to form a kehillah, a central body to oversee and organize the communal affairs of New York Jewry.

Any serious effort required buy-in from Schiff and his allies, who dominated Jewish charities and composed the New York–based leadership of the American Jewish Committee. So Magnes shrewdly pitched the Kehillah as a sort of local auxiliary of the group, one that would focus on issues in New York while leaving national and international affairs to the AJC. Months of tedious negotiations among the various stakeholders led to a convention, held in late February 1909, where the representatives of more than two hundred Jewish organizations unanimously approved the formation of a kehillah to "further the cause of Judaism" and "represent the Jews of this city." This step toward democratizing Jewish life in New York did not seem to diminish Schiff's position of authority. A spontaneous round of applause greeted the banker when he rose to speak in favor of the Kehillah. When the delegates selected the group's twenty-five-member governing body, Schiff received more votes than any other candidate.[23] In subsequent years, Julius Goldman and Herbert Lehman would take a leading role in guiding this body.

From the start, Schiff was the Kehillah's largest benefactor, joined by his son-in-law, Felix Warburg, who served on its executive committee and, later, as its first president.[24] Though a Kuhn Loeb partner, Felix spent little of his time on banking matters, devoting the majority of his days to an expanding roster of charitable groups, which he kept track of with a custom-built cabinet in his office that had compartments for each of the organizations he supported—fifty-seven in all.

Shortly after moving to New York to marry Frieda, Felix, with the encouragement of the Schiff and Loeb families, began supporting the work of Lillian Wald and the Henry Street Settlement. It was the gateway to a frenetic life of charitable service, as he threw his time and money behind a head-spinning array of Jewish and secular causes. He served as president of the Young Men's Hebrew Association, helping to build and sustain, along with his father-in-law, its iconic 92nd Street location, and joined the boards of organizations including the Educational Alliance, the Jewish Theological Seminary, the Welfare Council of New York, the New York Association for the Blind, the Metropolitan Museum of Art, and the American Museum of Natural History. Thanks to his rising philanthropic profile, he was also tapped for various municipal posts, including seats on the city's board of education (a position once held by Schiff), the state probation commission, and the Westchester County Parks Commission. Felix, along with Schiff and other members of Kuhn Loeb, also became a notable backer of W.E.B. Du Bois's National Association for the Advancement of Colored People and Booker T. Washington's Tuskegee Institute.

He was always getting roped into new philanthropic schemes and hounded for handouts by hard-luck cases. "He became the clearing house for almost every pet plan that germinated in the brains of social workers or of other communal-minded citizens," one of Felix's children remembered.[25] He kept a quotation on his desk that summed up his charitable philosophy:

> *I shall pass through this world but once*
> *Any good thing, therefore, that I can do,*
> *Any kindness I can show, to any human being*
> *Let me do it now.*
> *Let me not defer it nor neglect it,*
> *For I shall not pass this way again.*

Felix's philanthropic obligations grew so immense that even Schiff—the greatest Jewish philanthropist of the twentieth century—thought it a bit much. "Felix," he cautioned, "one can be overgenerous even in charity."[26] More than Schiff's son, Morti, Felix emerged as heir to the financier's charitable legacy, likened, as Jacob had been, to the great British philanthropist Moses Montefiore.

"Father was thought of and spoken of as a great Jew," recalled Felix's second-born son, Gerald,

> but paradoxically he disliked almost everything about the Jews except their problems. He couldn't bear the sound of Jewish music, or of Yiddish, or of most of the rabbis he had to listen to. He ate what he pleased and he was a terrible squirmer at any synagogue. He was also far from convincing at some of our Jewish festivities and just seemed to go through the motions of blessings and candle lightings and "seder" services with a rather pained and must-I look on his face.[27]

Gerald, an accomplished cellist who married the daughter of publisher Condé Nast, recalled his father as "a most delightful and quixotic character, and in case you do not know this, not such an angel besides."[28] Far from pious in his personal life, Felix carried on numerous affairs throughout his marriage to Frieda. His buxom mistresses, some of them (like Otto Kahn's) plucked from the talent pool at the Metropolitan Opera, were an open secret, and his thin cover story for his assignations—that he was headed out for a bike ride—became a family joke. "Are you going out to ride your bicycle, Father?" his sons would deadpan when Felix departed for what they suspected was another of his liaisons.[29]

Felix, who constantly whistled arias and jingles, possessed an "almost terrifying joie de vivre," Gerald remembered. Invariably "dressed to the teeth" in a tailored suit with a white carnation tucked in his buttonhole, Felix "looked at times like a French actor in a Guitry play." Like his sharply attired partner Otto Kahn, he was a bon vivant who imbibed art and music like an addictive drug, sometimes attending three concerts in one day. But he lacked Kahn's innate banking talent and ambition. When Felix joined Kuhn Loeb, his partners were initially unsure what to make of him. And his ebullient, carefree nature clashed with the tense office atmosphere. "There were ambitions, jealousies, and bickerings," his friend Sol Stroock remembered, noting that "his spirit could not flourish in the atmosphere of [Kuhn Loeb] in the early days."[30]

For a man who earned an enormous fortune as a banker, Felix sometimes seemed clueless about finance basics. "Father's vagueness concerning financial matters showed itself even in the trivial matter of supplying me one summer with funds to take along on my trip to camp," Felix's youngest son Edward recalled. "He countersigned some of his American Express checks which he had left over from a previous trip and which he had already signed when they had first been issued to him; it never occurred to him that while they might be valid as cash for him, they were useless to me. But who was I to question a partner in Kuhn, Loeb?" According to Edward, Felix's primary banking feat at Kuhn Loeb was landing "one large flotation" of Kodak stock.[31]

Despite a lack of financial acumen, Felix possessed a personal magnetism that served him well in business and philanthropy. He could "draw the honey even from the sour flower," as he put it.[32] Newcomb Carlton, the president of Western Union, recalled one meeting with Kuhn Loeb's partners during which Schiff appeared to nod off as the executive presented his plan to spin his company off from its parent firm, the New York Telephone Company. Schiff awoke suddenly as Carlton concluded, hastily pledging Kuhn Loeb's support for the project. Felix caught Newcomb's eye and shot him a wink, turning an awkward moment into an amusing one. It was a small gesture, but Felix instantly endeared himself to the Western Union president.[33]

"Business came to him rather than his having to seek it, for everyone admired and implicitly trusted him, as well they could for he couldn't have pulled a dirty trick even if someone gave him a blueprint and specifications on how to do it," said Kuhn Loeb partner Benjamin Buttenwieser.[34]

Felix "had a tidy mind," Gerald remembered, and a knack for organization and planning. "When he came into a hotel room on some foreign visit, his first task before going to bed was to rearrange the furniture." Woodlands, Felix and Frieda's country estate in Westchester, was the blank canvas where he indulged his instincts as an amateur architect. A mile-and-a-half-long driveway snaked to a sprawling Tudor-style manse, surrounded by hundreds of bucolic acres. The estate, which Felix was constantly expanding as he bought up adjoining parcels (what he referred to as "squaring off the property"), featured a polo field, seven miles of bridle paths, and an indoor pool that doubled as a hothouse (where his signature boutonnieres were cultivated).[35] A herd of prizewinning Guernsey cows roamed the premises. Felix was always dreaming up new ways to beautify the grounds. Sometimes the superintendent of the estate built Felix wooden platforms in the treetops, where he could survey the scenic possibilities and concoct plans to clear trees and shrubbery to reveal new scenic vistas.

Felix's passion for improvement and talent for hatching grand schemes spilled over into his communal work. Late at night, he sketched plans for organizing or re-organizing this or that charitable group on the backs of manila folders. His instinct as a planner may have been one reason he gravitated toward the kehillah concept, which provided a mechanism for coordinating a collection of sometimes competing efforts, each drawing from a finite pool of donor funds.

Together with Schiff, Felix underwrote the first major Kehillah initiative, the Bureau of Education, which focused on professionalizing Jewish education by opening schools, creating textbooks, training teachers, and offering loans to students who planned to pursue Jewish teaching. A succession of targeted initiatives followed, including a Bureau of Industry, to mediate labor disputes and bring order to the chaotic state of industrial relations largely in the garment trades; and a Bureau of Philanthropic Research, devoted to systematically studying the Jewish community's charitable needs.

With Jewish leaders still traumatized by the Bingham controversy, a major thrust of the Kehillah's early activities focused on rooting out Jewish vice and crime, an ongoing problem, if not one of the magnitude the police commissioner had asserted. Prostitution, gambling, drugs, and petty theft pervaded the Lower East Side. The Kehillah devoted two separate offices—the bureaus of Social Hygiene and Social Morals—to rooting out Jewish crime and "white slavery," as prostitution was sometimes called at the time, launching what amounted to a shadow law enforcement apparatus.

With substantial contributions from Schiff and Warburg, the Kehillah hired a young detective named Abe Shoenfeld, who by his early twenties had already established a reputation as an authority on the downtown underworld. Posing as a writer, Shoenfeld went undercover to catalog the panoply of gambling parlors, brothels, pool joints, saloons, and other "disorderly houses."

Shoenfeld and a team of investigators working under his command compiled files on downtown criminals, tracking their associates and hangouts and including detailed descriptions of their physical features and alleged crimes. Their targets included Hymie Hundred ("an ex-pimp" and "a dealer in drugs"); Waxey Gordon (a "gangster and a tough man" who "broke many a poor Jew's head"); Desperate Little Yudel ("the number of his crimes will never be known"); and Stiff Rifka (a "booster" and "a very clever one," who often found her marks at crowded synagogue services).[36]

The Kehillah needed more than intelligence to bust up the gangs and shut down the drug dens blighting the Lower East Side. Its anticrime efforts required the cooperation of New York's notoriously corrupt police department. A group of Kehillah members, including Schiff, approached New York mayor William Gaynor with the prospect of a partnership. Shoenfeld and his investigators would supply dossiers on Lower East Side crime; the police would execute raids based on this information.

Gaynor, a former New York Supreme Court justice, was a Tammany Hall–connected Democrat, though once in office he had dismayed his political overlords by displaying a surprising independent streak. Among other anticorruption reforms, he placed cleaning up the Tammany-dominated police department at the center of his agenda. His efforts to reform city government nearly cost him his life. Not long into his first term, a fired municipal dockworker shot Gaynor in the neck, where the bullet remained lodged for the rest of his life.

Popular among New York's Jews, Gaynor, prior to taking office, had sparred so viciously with Theodore Bingham over his policing tactics that the soon-to-be-ousted commissioner sued for defamation. (Bingham later dropped the case.) And he eagerly embraced the joint crime-fighting effort.[37] With the mayor applying pressure on the police behind the scenes and Shoenfeld and his investigators supplying a steady flow of intelligence, the crackdown commenced. The police shuttered dozens of pool halls, gambling parlors, drug fronts, and brothels, arresting scores of mobsters and thieves or driving them out of the Lower East Side and into the virgin neighborhoods of the outer boroughs. The Kehillah supplied lawyers to the city to make sure the police department's cases against downtown scofflaws stuck.

In 1913, electoral politics threatened the Kehillah's alliance with Gaynor. When the mayor sought another four-year term, Tammany Hall blocked his renomination, putting up a candidate less likely to stray from the wishes of the Democratic political machine. Schiff, as a stalwart Republican and longtime Tammany foe, opposed Gaynor during his first campaign. Now he took action to rescue the candidacy of an important ally. Bucking both political parties and risking his reputation as a political reformer to aid a pol who owed his rise to Tammany, Schiff backed an independent run by Gaynor and pledged his financial support. "You . . . go right ahead with the campaign and do not give a thought to finances. All of the money that will be needed will be forthcoming," he told the mayor's executive secretary, Robert Adamson, who later described Schiff as one of Gaynor's "closest and most trusted advisers."[38]

That September, as Gaynor sailed for Europe on what was supposed to be a restorative getaway before the bruising election battle to come, he died suddenly while reclining in a deck chair. Because of the loss of its most important champion and the indifference of the incoming administration, the Kehillah's law enforcement activities slowed and, within a couple of years, faded away entirely, followed in 1922 by the Kehillah itself.

A change in administrations also doomed the struggling Galveston movement, which Schiff and his allies attempted to resurrect when the economy recovered from the 1907 panic. After leaving office, Roosevelt disappeared for the better part of a year on an extended safari in East Africa (an expedition Schiff helped to underwrite with a contribution of $5,000). His secretary of war and political protégé, William Howard Taft, succeeded him to the presidency, easily vanquishing William Jennings Bryan, who was then making his third attempt on the White House. Schiff supported Taft's candidacy, and the politician showed promising signs that he would be an important friend of the Jews. As Taft ran for president, Schiff urged him to take a firm position on an issue he described as an "open sore with my coreligionists."[39]

Schiff was referring to the "passport question" that he had pressed so strenuously with Taft's predecessor. American Jews had long protested that Russia was flouting its 1832 treaty with the United States—promising "reciprocal" rights for citizens to trade and travel freely—by treating Jewish passport holders differently than other U.S. citizens. But by 1907, exasperated by years of inaction, the newly formed American Jewish Committee had begun ratcheting up political pressure to annul the treaty if Russia refused to uphold its side.

"You can count on my giving special attention to the passport business should I be entrusted with the mandate of power," Taft told Schiff. And he referenced the controversy, though without singling Russia out by name, both in his letter accepting the Republican presidential nomination and during his inaugural address, in which Taft declared, "We should make every effort to prevent humiliating and degrading prohibition against any of our citizens wishing temporarily to sojourn in foreign nations because of race or religion."[40]

But months into Taft's presidency, Schiff began to doubt whether the new president was the ally he professed to be. The passport issue didn't seem to be going anywhere, and the Taft administration was cracking down on immigration, especially at Galveston.

Unlike Oscar Straus, the new commerce secretary, a corporate lawyer from St. Louis named Charles Nagel, held no special sympathy for the Jews. His deputy, Benjamin Cable, seemed outright hostile to the Galveston cause. This may have owed to a personal grudge against Schiff, whose firm had recently refused a request for financial assistance from his father's overextended railroad company. Daniel Keefe, a longtime labor leader and proponent of tighter immigration restrictions, replaced Frank Sargent, the immigration commissioner who had encouraged Schiff's immigration deflection efforts.

For the previous two years, the immigration inspector at Galveston, E. B. Holman, had worked closely with officials of the Jewish Immigrant Information Bureau. Rarely did he deport immigrants under its care. But in the new administration, it was clear that changes were coming from the top in Washington. Keefe, Holman confided to a JIIB manager, was "not very much in favor of increased immigration, Jewish particularly."[41] In November 1909, Holman was suddenly suspended and later fired for improperly enforcing the nation's immigration laws. A hard-liner replaced him.

The deportations soon commenced.

Mirroring a trend taking place at ports of entry around the country, inspectors seemed to look for any excuse to turn immigrants away and disregarded, when making determinations about whether a person was likely to become a "public charge," the considerable support networks they had in place through the JIIB and other Jewish charities. When shiploads of Jewish immigrants arrived at Galveston, many of the refugees were turned back. "The entire future of the movement was in jeopardy," recalled Max Kohler, an immigration lawyer who worked closely with the JIIB.[42]

The Commerce Department mounted an investigation into immigration at Galveston and the JIIB itself, on the suspicion that it was actively promoting and facilitating immigration. In August 1910 newspapers reported that the investigation had found immigration regulations had been laxly enforced at Galveston and that immigration officials planned to more closely regulate the influx of Russian Jews. "Assistant Secretary Cable is determined that the immigration standards at Galveston shall come up to those required at all other ports. He is convinced that the admission there has been too easy, and that fact, known in Europe, has stimulated immigration to the port," *The Baltimore Sun* recounted. Referring to the work of the JIIB, which the paper referred to as the "Jacob H. Schiff Society," the *Sun* reported that the "Department retains some doubts about its legality."[43]

Barely containing his rage, Schiff wrote Cable, reminding him that the Galveston project had been instigated at the suggestion of the previous immigration commissioner. "Surely in an endeavor to promote such a movement, which has already proven beneficial alike to the immigrant, to the section in which he settled, and to the overcrowded centers from which he is kept, those behind the so-called Galveston movement had every right to expect the good will of the authorities, and, until recently, this appears not to have been withheld," the financier wrote. "Of late, however, and for no satisfactory reason, the Department of Commerce and Labor has changed its attitude, and is now throwing needless difficulties in the way of the admission of those who arrive in Galveston, a course which, if persisted in, is certain to break down the Galveston movement." Schiff also insisted that "our work can in no wise be described as inducing or illegally assisting immigration."[44]

Schiff forwarded his letter to Taft, and, after Cable stridently replied by inviting Schiff to do battle in court if he did not like the agency's immigration policies, the outraged banker followed up with a letter to the president's secretary, in which he called for Cable's "retirement" from the Commerce Department.[45] Schiff also issued a thinly veiled political threat. Referring to Taft's unmet promise to take action on the passport issue, he wrote:

> We have in other respects experienced keen disappointment because of the non-fulfillment thus far of platform pledges and personal promises made during the last presidential campaign, and if I now write so unreservedly it is partly because I do not wish to see the President, whose loyal supporter I have been ever since he was nominated, placed into a false position, or lose the good will of the important section of the American people for whom I venture to speak in this.[46]

The political pressure seemed to have some effect, for soon the Taft administration brokered a meeting between members of the committee overseeing the Galveston movement and senior officials, including commerce secretary Nagel, assistant secretary Cable, and attorney general George Wickersham. The two sides met on December 11, 1910, with Schiff and Max Kohler, the immigration lawyer, doing much of the talking on behalf of the Galveston movement. Over the course of the two-hour meeting, Schiff grew increasingly frustrated. Finally, he erupted, as he had in the past during similar conferences concerning the fate of his people. The banker jumped to his feet, wagging a finger at Nagel: "You act as if my organization and I were on trial! You, Mr. Secretary, and your department are on trial, and the country will rue it if this undertaking—so conducive to promoting the best interests of our country, as well as humanity—is throttled by your Department's unreasonable obstacles!"

Schiff's outburst angered Nagel, and Wickersham pulled the banker aside to defuse the tensions. "Mr. Schiff," the attorney general said, "try not to make them antagonistic here; I will help you if I can." Once Schiff and Nagel had calmed down, the commerce secretary assured the Galveston representatives he would do what he could, within the parameters of the law, to aid their work. In a display of good faith, he ordered the release of a group of Jewish immigrants detained at Galveston for possible deportation.[47]

The movement now had the qualified support of the Taft administration, but it struggled to gain traction. Hobbled by its stop-and-start nature and plagued by internal squabbling among its European partners, Schiff's project limped along for a few more years before finally shutting down in 1914. During its seven-year existence, the Galveston movement settled some ten thousand Jewish refugees, less than half of the twenty-five thousand immigrants Schiff hoped to support with his initial $500,000 pledge. Still, Schiff refused to concede failure. "I believe we have a right to feel that we have in a measure succeeded," he told Felix, a member of the committee overseeing the work at Galveston. Each of the immigrants settled "in the vast hinterland of the United States" would attract others, and he noted, "we have acquired experience which is certain to be most useful in further efforts, which must come to deflect immigration into and through the overcrowded cities of the North Atlantic to ports where it can be more practically distributed over sections of the United States where the immigrant is actually needed."[48]

As Schiff and his colleagues struggled to address the immigration crisis at home—and to outmaneuver the restrictionists trying to cut off the flow of Jewish refugees and other undesirables—they never lost sight of the foreign roots of the problem. In fact, their efforts to see the czar and his empire rebuked and chastened, and to force Russia to recognize the equal rights of its Jews, only intensified. This campaign, calling forth an unprecedented display of unified Jewish power, culminated in another high-profile clash with the Taft administration—one that would leave Taft a one-term president. But the political wrangling and controversies of this era would also inflict deep scars on Jacob Schiff and his family.

20

THE PASSPORT QUESTION

On February 15, 1911, two months after Schiff's combative meeting with the commerce secretary and the attorney general over the fate of the Galveston movement, President Taft summoned the financier and a small group of Jewish leaders to the White House to discuss another matter that had become a political flashpoint: the Russo-American Treaty of 1832.

With Taft's first term nearing its end, the passport question had gone unanswered, though the president seemed to be leaning toward the position of his ambassador to Russia, William Rockhill, and secretary of state, Philander Knox, who pointed out the economic and foreign policy perils of treaty brinkmanship. To them, the passport matter seemed minor when compared with the possible consequences, since few American Jews had any desire to travel to Russia. But the issue had broader significance, Schiff and other emissaries of the American Jewish Committee had stressed in multiple meetings with Taft and members of his administration. "Our anxiety to see our Government take action should not be misunderstood," Schiff explained in a letter to *New York Times* publisher Adolph Ochs.

> It is not because the Jews of the United States lay stress upon the admittance into Russia of a few hundred of their number who may annually wish to go there, but because of the conviction that the moment Russia is compelled to live up to its

treaties and admit the foreign Jew into its dominion upon a basis of equality with other citizens of foreign countries, the Russian Government will not be able to maintain the pale of settlement against its own Jews. You see, it is a large question, involving the most sacred of human rights.[1]

By January 1911, the American Jewish Committee had noticeably swapped its tactics of patient, though persistent, advocacy for a more aggressive and public posture. Schiff and other Jewish leaders had resolved, in the banker's words, to "build a fire in the rear of the president."[2] If their private lobbying efforts failed to move the president, perhaps stoking popular opinion would influence him. Schiff encouraged Louis Marshall to take their case public, which the lawyer did on January 19, 1911, delivering a forceful and well-publicized speech at a meeting of the Union of American Hebrew Congregations in which he all but called Taft cowardly for his inaction. "Unless the virtue of manhood has deserted this Republic," Marshall declared, "its citizens will no longer patiently witness the mockery of diplomatic procedure but will insist on a complete abrogation of every treaty now existing between the United States and Russia."

Following Marshall's address, the members of the UAHC unanimously approved a resolution he had drafted urging the president to "take immediate measures" to break off treaty relations with Russia.[3] Upping the pressure on Taft, Congressman Herbert Parsons, a Republican who represented New York City, introduced a resolution the following month to sever the 1832 treaty.

Less than a week later, apparently feeling the heat, Taft extended his White House invitation to Schiff and his allies. The president and his guests—who in addition to Schiff included Marshall, Representative Henry Mayer Goldfogle of New York, and the former diplomat Simon Wolf—exchanged small talk over lunch. Then they adjourned to the White House library to discuss the topic at hand. Schiff and the others sat in a circle facing the president, prepared to argue once more why the United States should terminate its treaty with Russia. But before anyone could speak, Taft plucked a sheaf of papers from a desk drawer and began to read aloud. It soon became clear that the president hadn't brought them to the White House to hear them out, but rather to deliver his decision.

"I would be willing to take this drastic step and sacrifice the interests that it certainly will sacrifice if I was not convinced from everything I had seen and heard . . . that instead of benefiting anybody, and especially benefiting those persons in whose interests and for the preservation of whose rights the step would be taken, it would accomplish nothing at all," Taft announced.

Schiff's pale blue eyes flickered with indignation as Taft erased any hope that his administration would punish Russia's intransigence. "I think perhaps that if I had the same justifiable pride of race that you have and the same sense of outrageous injustice that comes home to a man of that race much more than it can to a man who is not of the race, I should feel as you do," Taft went on. "But I am the President of the whole country, and I feel that in exercising a responsibility affecting everybody I have to try to look at the subject from all sides."

The mood in the room was dark as Taft concluded his remarks. Wolf was the first to speak. "Please do not give to the press such conclusions, for it would prove highly injurious to our people in Russia," he sputtered.

Schiff interjected. "I want it published," he said. "I want the whole world to know the president's attitude." Here, once again, was the side of the financier his compatriots worried about, the impetuous, quick-to-anger mogul who thought nothing of browbeating the most powerful man in the country, even if it set back their cause in the process.

The president gave his guests a few minutes to confer in an adjoining room, and when they emerged, Schiff resumed his dressing-down of Taft. "We feel deeply mortified, that in this instance, Mr. President, you have failed us and there is nothing left to us now but to put our case before the American people directly, who are certain to do us justice."

Wolf recalled that as the dejected Jewish leaders exited, all shook Taft's outstretched hand—except for Schiff, who brusquely strode out. (Schiff remembered the episode slightly differently. "I know I was very angry at the manner in which the delegation was treated by President Taft . . . but the President did not give me an opportunity to shake hands with him and I likewise did not seek it," he said.)[4]

"This means war," Schiff seethed as he left the White House. And he pledged $25,000 on the spot toward a publicity campaign targeting the treaty.[5]

"Wasn't Mr. Schiff angry yesterday?" Taft remarked to Wolf when he saw him at the White House the following day. Taft's tone was lighthearted, but privately he denounced the imperious banker. "He has been consumed by fury because he could not control the Administration and sacrifice all national interests to the gratification of his vanity and that of some wealthy Hebrews," Taft told one confidant. "Schiff is truculent and was rather disposed to threaten me with political destruction."[6] In a letter to another ally, Taft complained that "Jake Schiff is engaged in spending money to rouse" the "formidable" Jewish vote against him—"but he can't frighten me into a useless injury to our National interests."[7]

Engaging in political combat with Taft was risky for Schiff and the American Jewish Committee. Losing this fight would confirm the critique of the committee's detractors, who already derided it as ineffectual. And a high-profile campaign, win or lose, might stir up antisemitic sentiment at home and abroad. But to Schiff there was no turning back.

By the spring of 1911, the AJC had launched a full-scale campaign to mobilize public opinion behind a legislative effort to invalidate the treaty. The committee's goal was to make such a massive public relations splash that abrogation would become a campaign issue in the upcoming presidential election.

Parsons's resolution expired without coming to a vote at the end of the congressional session that March, but once the new Congress convened in April, New York's William Sulzer, the incoming chairman of the House Foreign Affairs Committee, introduced a similar measure to void the treaty. Senator Charles Culberson of Texas filed a version of the bill in the upper chamber.

Meanwhile the AJC blanketed legislative offices and newsrooms with Marshall's speech on the passport question, distributing thirty thousand copies. It pressed state legislatures to adopt symbolic pro-abrogation resolutions and drafted language denouncing the treaty for use in state party platforms. And it deployed a lobbying campaign targeting key members of Congress in both parties.

Building momentum behind the issue, the AJC and its allies convened rallies across the country. The largest took place at Carnegie Hall on December 6, 1911, days before the Sulzer resolution was scheduled for debate in the House. The protest meeting, attended by some 4,500 people, was held by the National Citizens' Committee, a newly formed group chaired by William McAdoo, a railroad president who had earned notoriety for completing a long-stalled project to build a train tunnel beneath the Hudson River. The committee,

McAdoo noted in his memoir, was "composed largely of gentiles" so that the antitreaty movement "could not be regarded as a narrow racial Jewish protest."[8]

The featured speakers at the event, organized with the help of Schiff and Oscar Straus, included New Jersey governor Woodrow Wilson, a front-runner for the Democratic presidential nomination. McAdoo, who would later marry Wilson's daughter Eleanor, was helping to guide Wilson's campaign. Wilson discarded his prepared remarks and spoke extemporaneously, as cries of "our next president" rose from the audience. "This is not their cause," Wilson said of the Jews, "it is America's." And he framed the issue as a test of the American principles that "underlie the very structure of our government." When it was Schiff's turn to speak, he confidently declared, "In my opinion, this resolution is as sure of becoming a law as the sun is sure to rise tomorrow morning. Then Russia will ask us for a treaty. We will beg no more; we will wait for Russia to come to us."[9]

The following week Schiff, McAdoo, and other abrogation advocates traveled to Washington to testify in support of the Sulzer resolution, which the House approved on December 13 by a vote of 301 to 1. With the measure's passage all but assured in the Senate, Taft's hand was forced. He directed his ambassador to Russia to notify the country that the United States planned to pull out of the treaty, effective January 1, 1912.

Returning home from Washington by train, Schiff sat beside McAdoo in the parlor car. Their discussion turned to Wilson, whose Carnegie Hall speech impressed Schiff. By the time they pulled in to Pennsylvania Station, the banker, a lifelong Republican, had resolved to throw his support behind the New Jersey Democrat in the upcoming election. A few days later McAdoo opened the mail to find a $2,500 campaign contribution from Schiff.[10] It wasn't just Schiff. The 1912 election marked the beginning of a transition by Jewish voters away from Republicans and toward Democrats, a trend that accelerated in the 1920s.

Reveling in the treaty victory, Schiff declared that Russia had finally "received a slap in the face from a great nation," positing that this rebuke "must be of the greatest consequence in the history of civilization." And he deemed the treaty fight "of greater importance than anything that has happened, since civil rights were granted Jews under the first Napoleon, or since English Jews were admitted to parliament."[11] Schiff was equally pleased that the battle had validated the American Jewish Committee's raison d'être. "It has heretofore been frequently asked, what is the reason for the existence of this committee. We think after the recent American Jewish passport episode . . . this query is answered," he wrote to Felix Warburg.[12]

After declaring war on Taft, Schiff now sought to make peace, at one point sending the president a box of pills and a radium pad to relieve a flare-up of gout. But Taft remained bitter that Schiff and his "circumcised brothers" had hijacked his foreign policy and convinced of the folly of severing the treaty, which he believed was borne out when Russia neither came groveling to broker a new accord nor changed its hostile attitude toward Jews.[13] Taft, however, had bigger problems than "Jake" Schiff: Teddy Roosevelt, his onetime political mentor, was positioning himself to reclaim the presidency, eventually launching a campaign on the independent Bull Moose Party ticket. Roosevelt's entrance into the race split the Republican vote, all but assuring Woodrow Wilson the White House.

Before turning over the Oval Office to Wilson, in one of the final major acts of his presidency, Taft did prove his friendship to the Jews— and to immigrants of all nationalities. In 1911, following more than three years of investigation, the immigration commission headed by Senator William Dillingham released the findings of its inquiry, all forty-one volumes. The exhaustive study—examining topics including "Fecundity of Immigrant Women," "Immigration and Crime," and "Changes in Bodily Form of Descendants of Immigrants"— fueled another legislative volley. Once again Dillingham introduced legislation to restrict immigration by imposing a literacy test. The measure, which garnered widespread support, passed the Senate. A House version of the bill also passed overwhelmingly, but it fell five votes short of the two-thirds majority necessary to shield the legislation from a presidential veto. Taft struck down the legislation, saying, "I cannot approve that test."[14] The victory was temporary, for the ground on immigration had shifted inalterably. Four years later, over President Wilson's veto, Congress enacted sweeping immigration restrictions, including a literacy test.

During the final years of Taft's presidency, a bizarre and embarrassing scandal ensnared the Schiff family, playing out on the front pages in the weeks after the passport battle concluded. It involved one of Morti and Adele's former footmen, who was serving a long prison sentence for burglarizing their property.

On March 8, 1907, according to Morti's account, the couple

returned home to 932 Fifth Avenue around ten p.m. after an evening out with Paul and Nina Warburg. Adele retired to her bedroom.
Morti stayed up reading in the second-floor sitting room for another
forty minutes. Then he wandered down the hall to his dressing room,
located at the rear of the townhouse. The hallway was dark when he
stepped into his dressing room. Before he could turn on the lights, he
received a sharp blow to the head. Injured but still conscious, Morti
flipped on the light to find a man he knew as Lawrence de Foulke
clutching a tenpin from the bowling alley Morti's father had installed
in the basement.

Morti had fired the twenty-one-year-old footman the previous
month after the servant had slipped his wife a love letter. It read in
part: "I am a poor fellow but I have a heart which I would part with
to a Lady which I love dearest on earth ('it is you dearest Lady.'). . . .
I do not know if you are interest or like my person, but I do know
that am awfly fond of you, in every respect I like and admire you. . . .
My feelings towards you dear Lady has grown every day in larger
circumferenc [sic]."[15]

A few days after his firing, De Foulke, a handsome young Swede
whose real name was Folke Engelbrecht Brandt, contacted Adele
seeking a job reference; Morti refused. Nearly a month had passed
with no sign of Brandt—but now there he was, wild-eyed and shoe-
less and brandishing a bowling pin. His head throbbing, Morti lit a
cigarette—he thought this nonchalant gesture might convey that he
had no fear of Brandt—and began trying to talk his assailant down.

"He told me a long story about being out of work, being dis-
charged, and all that sort of business," Morti later recounted before
a grand jury. "I said, 'I will help you.'"[16] Morti eventually convinced
Brandt to leave peacefully, telling him to drop by Kuhn Loeb's offices
the following Monday, where he would assist him in making a fresh
start. Morti gave Brandt fifty dollars and showed him out.

Brandt showed up on Monday as directed, where he found Schiff
with his lawyer, Howard Gans, and a Pinkerton detective, who took
Brandt's confession. Later that day Morti filed criminal charges
against his former servant. The following month Brandt pleaded
guilty to first-degree burglary for stealing two diamond scarf pins
from the Schiff residence on the night of the assault and received a
harsh sentence of thirty years in prison.[17]

Locked away in upstate New York's Dannemora prison, Brandt
had no intention of accepting his fate quietly. He began contacting

politicians and others he thought could secure his release, including Senator Knute Nelson, a Minnesota Republican of Scandinavian background, who had pressed for parole reform in federal penitentiaries. In early 1909, Brandt wrote to Nelson of his "inhuman sentence," telling the senator he was "entirely without friends on God's earth."[18] In a subsequent letter to Nelson, the prisoner recanted his previous confession and recounted a salacious and convoluted tale.

After going to work for the Schiffs, he claimed, "Mrs. Schiff began to shower upon me such extravagant favors and forced her affections upon me, then an inexperienced youth of 20 years, in such a manner that I was absolutely unable to account for her behavior towards me." He said that "affectionate epistles" often passed between them and that Morti had discovered one of these notes. He wrote that Adele had later given him a key to her home and had instructed him to meet her there at eight p.m. on the evening of Friday, March 8. But when he arrived, she wasn't there. So, he said, he retrieved a bowling pin to defend himself if any of the household servants discovered him in the house and waited. When Adele returned with her husband, Brandt claimed, he spoke with her furtively in her dressing room. "My mind was in a very excited state, my only thought of the unhappy woman who had induced me to call upon her. In my haste I picked up two diamond pins from the chiffonier with the intention that, should I be discovered, it would appear as I had come with the purpose of stealing." As he tried to escape from the house undetected, Brandt contended, he collided violently with Morti Schiff. "To make it short, Mr. Schiff and I had a talk of two hours duration and I left at one o'clock with the promise of the gentleman . . . that he would make no trouble for me." Instead, Brandt was apprehended. He claimed he was subsequently duped by his attorney, who promised he would face a short prison sentence of perhaps a year if he pleaded guilty.[19]

After learning Nelson was looking into the Brandt case, Morti wrote to him and offered to have his attorney brief the senator: "This man has caused Mrs. Schiff and me a great deal of annoyance and unpleasantness, and it was really by the merest chance and good-luck that his attempt to kill me was unsuccessful. I feel certain that you would not wish to give any encouragement to this really dangerous man, if you were conversant with all the facts in this case."[20] Apparently satisfied in Brandt's guilt, Nelson dropped the issue, but the imprisoned footman continued to seek his release. In late 1911, Brandt petitioned New York's Democratic governor John Dix for clemency. And on December 12, while in Washington Jacob Schiff testified in favor of the Sulzer resolution, Morti's lawyer hurried to Albany in a bid to "clinch the matter."[21]

This time the case did not go away quietly. Stoked by the media empire of William Randolph Hearst, the scandal came roaring back. Soon the Brandt controversy, with its embarrassing allegations of infidelity, was plastered on the front pages of the nation's newspapers, where it remained for weeks. The narrative emerged of a poor young immigrant railroaded by the justice system at the hands of a powerful family. The storyline was bolstered when allegations surfaced that Otto Rosalsky, the judge who presided over Brandt's case, had conferred secretly with Morti and his lawyer Howard Gans at the Criterion Club days before he handed down his sentence.[22] By late February 1912, not only did it appear that Brandt might win his release, but New York's district attorney, Charles Whitman, who had his eye on the mayoralty, was now threatening to indict Morti and Gans on charges of conspiracy and had impaneled a grand jury to investigate.

"I must decline to discuss that," Jacob Schiff told reporters who approached him for comment on the Brandt affair, locating him at the docks as he boarded a steamer to Bermuda with his wife, Therese.[23] Privately he confided to a journalist that "the liberation of Brandt would be a calamity" for his family.[24]

As the scandal snowballed, letters from friends and well-wishers poured in. "I want to send just a line to let you know that the sensible people of the country sympathize with you very deeply in what you are passing through, and that exaggerated and sensational newspaper reports do not deceive as many persons as some people are inclined to believe," read one note to Morti, from Booker T. Washington, whose Tuskegee Institute the Schiffs supported. "More and more, I think that the people in this country are beginning to see that in proportion as a man succeeds in acquiring wealth or is making himself prominent or useful in any direction, he becomes a target. You and your family have done so much for this country, that sensible people cannot be deceived."[25]

After years of trying to keep the whole mess under wraps, Morti, besieged by bad press and under investigation by the DA, released a lengthy public statement that included Brandt's letter to Adele and other evidence in the case. Sprawling over the better part of six columns in *The New York Times*, it read in part:

I have reached the decision to make this statement very reluctantly, because I naturally shrink from making public my private affairs. But for a month some newspapers of the city have been full of false charges, insinuations, innuendos, and accusations of almost every conceivable character, from almost every conceivable source. Mr. Gans and I have been accused of conspiring to defeat the ends of justice, of dishonestly influencing an upright Judge, of "railroading" an innocent young man to State prison to serve a long sentence, of inducing Brandt by false promises of leniency to plead guilty of a crime which he did not commit, and, finally, of seeking by improper methods to keep an innocent man in prison after his innocence had been proved.[26]

On a Tuesday afternoon in late March 1912, Adele Schiff, appearing slightly nervous, arrived at the Criminal Courts Building at Centre Street. She told a reporter as she entered the courthouse she was appearing before the grand jury "at my own request." During her testimony, she refuted Brandt's claims of an affair and said she had not given him a key to their home.[27] Later that week the grand jury, after hearing from forty-one witnesses, including Brandt, concluded its investigation, finding no grounds to charge Morti or his lawyer. But the jury also concluded that Brandt should have been indicted on the lesser charge of grand larceny.[28]

In April, another front-page story overshadowed the sensational Brandt case: the sinking of the *Titanic* on its maiden voyage. The luxury ocean liner was filled with prominent passengers (aristocrats, bankers, entertainers, railroad executives), including one of the world's richest men, John Jacob Astor IV. And the tragedy struck particularly close to the German-Jewish crowd. Aboard was Benjamin Guggenheim, son of mining mogul Meyer Guggenheim, who valiantly helped to rescue passengers, then dressed in formal wear and tucked a rose into his lapel to await his fate like a gentleman; and Macy's co-owner Isidor Straus and his wife Ida. The Strauses were a staple of the uptown Jewish social and philanthropic set. Isidor had worked closely with Jacob Schiff on charitable projects over the years. Together, they had helped to cofound the Educational Alliance, and Isidor was a director of the Montefiore Home. As passengers evacuated the *Titanic*, Isidor refused to board a lifeboat while women and children remained on the ship; Ida refused to leave her husband's side. They were last seen wrapped in each other's arms. At their memorial service, held at Carnegie Hall and attended by thousands, Schiff praised Ida for upholding "the oath that she had given at the altar, 'Until death do us part,'" and he declared, "The world has been inspired by the manner of death of those two noble souls."[29]

The Brandt matter, meanwhile, continued to generate news coverage. Governor Dix ultimately declined Brandt's appeal for clemency, lambasting the convict for his "accusation against the purity of a woman," but the controversy still did not dissipate, even becoming a campaign issue in the 1912 gubernatorial election.[30] Though his friend Oscar Straus (one of Isidor's younger brothers) had launched a campaign for governor, Jacob Schiff threw his backing behind Representative William Sulzer, his ally in the treaty fight (he "saved the day for us," Schiff said), who was challenging Dix for the Democratic nomination.[31] At a banquet for Sulzer, Schiff raised eyebrows when, instead of extolling the man of the hour, he gave a short speech lashing out at the press for its coverage of the Brandt case. "I have devoted most of my life to the upbuilding and the good of New York," he said, "but now in the evening of my life I see an infamous and vicious attack made on the reputation and good name of my family. Pity the community whose disreputable newspaper publishers can band together to attack the good name of decent citizens and virtuous women."[32]

Sulzer narrowly defeated Dix and went on to win the election. Within days of his swearing-in on January 1, 1913, he faced questions about Brandt, who New York's attorney general had recommended for a pardon. After first declaring he was not ready to take up the matter, Sulzer reversed himself, agreeing to Brandt's release and calling his sentence "excessive." Sulzer's pardon came with a couple of stipulations, including that Brandt confess he had concocted his tale of an affair with Adele Schiff and that he never attempt to profit commercially from his tale.[33]

Senator Nelson, to whom Brandt had initially appealed for help, agreed to sponsor the Swede in Minnesota. By late January 1913, Brandt was on his way to a new life in Bemidji. For months after Brandt settled there, Pinkerton detectives shadowed his every movement, reporting back to Morti.[34] When a Minnesota official complained to Sulzer about the operatives surveilling Brandt, Sulzer forwarded his letter to Kuhn Loeb's offices at 52 William Street. "Of course," Sulzer wrote slyly to Morti, "I feel confident you have nothing to do with this."[35]

A year after his release, in February 1914, Brandt returned to Europe. A few years later newspapers reported that the notorious footman had been killed in battle during World War I.[36] But in 1927 letters arrived at Morti and Adele's home written in Brandt's familiar script. He was alive, if not altogether well, and living outside London, where he had worked as the manager of a sawmill, manufactured knife handles, and patented a handful of inventions. All his ventures ended in failure, and he told Morti and Adele that he had turned to God for spiritual redemption. "With a penitent heart I pray for a pardon from you both and may the cloud of ill will be lifted from above our heads that freedom and peace may be felt," he wrote. "I committed my error at the age of 21. It's now 21 years ago and I have suffered much. Sin begets sin."[37]

Morti deliberated over a reply, finally writing back, via his secretary, that "Mr. and Mrs. Schiff forgive you for the pain and anguish they suffered because of your misdeeds."[38] It turned out Brandt was seeking not just forgiveness but financial assistance for a new business scheme. And over his correspondence, in which he noted ominously that he had turned down offers over the years to tell his story, hung the whiff of extortion. Alarmed, Morti wrote to his cousin Ernst in London, who had contacts in the British government. Ernst replied that his friend, who ran the Home Office's immigration department, had advised him "that it would be quite easy to counteract any move of Brandt's at once in case he molests you at all."[39]

The scandal hovered disconcertingly over the Schiff family for decades, and in 1954 the conservative newspaper columnist Westbrook Pegler dredged it up once more, using the tale to attack Morti and Adele's daughter, Dolly, then a prominent Manhattan socialite and the publisher of the *New York Post*. "N.Y. Publisher's Family Had Swede Railroaded to Prison," Pegler's broadside was titled.

Dolly dismissed the possibility that her mother, who she remembered as a cold and distant woman who disliked being touched by her children, would have carried on an affair with the footman, and not because she had any illusions that her parents were faithful to each other. "The insinuation was ridiculous," she told her biographer. "Anyone who knew my mother was aware that her set offered more interesting possibilities. Brandt may have been handsome, but everyone engaged footmen in those days with an eye for how their calves would look in knee breeches."[40]

The reality was that Morti and Adele were locked in a deeply unhappy marriage brokered by their parents. He wasn't her first choice of husband or perhaps even her second—but as the scion of one of America's most prominent banking families, his proposal was impossible to turn down. During their courtship, Frieda remembered, "Adele was very elusive, and Morti never knew from one day to the next whether they were still engaged. Poor darling, not that it hurt him much, he lost thirty pounds during the engagement because he never knew where he stood!"[41]

Morti was constantly presenting his wife with expensive jewelry— only for her to hold him at arm's length. Recalled Wendy Gray, Morti and Adele's great-granddaughter, "I remember my mom saying in an off-handed way, 'Oh yeah, he was always trying to buy her love. He gave her this, but she still didn't love him.' "[42]

After giving Morti a male heir—John, born seventeen months after his sister, in August 1904—"the husband-wife relationship, to put it the old fashioned way, ended," Dolly said, "and they lived largely separate lives."[43] As was common for men of his financial means and social station, Morti had mistresses, including one he stashed in the Hôtel de Paris in Monaco. He nevertheless strove to project an image of family harmony. "It seems so sad how hard my father tried to show *his* father what a happy family we were, just to please him," Dolly remembered. "We weren't, and the whole thing was untrue."[44]

His marital problems were just one aspect of his life that Morti hid from his father. The patriarch, always wary of his son's profligacy, was also in the dark about Morti's ownership of French racing stables. It was better this way, since Morti knew his father disapproved of gambling. On one occasion, when Morti and Adele were returning from their European honeymoon, the newly married banker's name ended up in a *New York Times* squib about "heavy gambling" during the voyage. Morti and his fellow first-class passengers were laying down large bets on how many nautical miles the ship would log each day. "Mortimer Schiff was the lucky man in the smoke saloon," the paper reported, noting he had won $1,700.[45] Jacob spotted the story, harshly berating Morti for his conduct.[46] "He was terrified his father would hear about his racehorses, gambling and women," Dolly recalled.[47]

Lewis Strauss, who joined Kuhn Loeb as a clerk after World War I, recalled an episode emblematic of the father-son dynamic. One morning Morti called Strauss into his office, asking him to represent the firm at a dinner for a delegation of Japanese businessmen that J.P. Morgan partner Thomas Lamont was hosting at the Uni-

top left: Jacob and Therese Schiff out for a stroll.

top center: In 1901, the Schiffs gifted their home at 932 Fifth Avenue to their newly married son and his wife as a wedding present and moved up the street to the newly completed 965 Fifth Avenue, pictured here, and described as an "epoch-making mansion."

top right: The drawing room of 965 Fifth Avenue, which *The Architectural Record* described as "a room belonging almost exclusively to the Louis XV period, both in the design of the walls and in the character of the furnishing."

bottom right: Located in the New Jersey shore enclave of Elberon, near the summer residences of Jacob Schiff, Philip Lehman, and other German-Jewish banking titans, the Sachs' Ellencourt was named for Samuel and Louisa's daughter Ella. Walter Sachs said his family's property evoked "Versailles on a very small scale."

bottom left: Mortimer and Adele Schiff were locked in a troubled marriage, living largely separate lives after the birth of their children Dorothy and John.

left: Max Warburg (*right*) and his M.M. Warburg partner Carl Melchior, pictured in 1919 at Versailles, became the targets of antisemitic vitriol in Germany due to the punitive peace terms imposed on their country.

right: The Warburg brothers in August 1929 after the first board meeting of Aby's Kulturwissenschaftliche Bibliothek (Culture and Science Library). Clockwise from top left: Felix, Fritz, Aby, Max, and Paul.

Representatives of the Joint Distribution Committee and the American Jewish Relief Committee meet in Kuhn Loeb's offices on July 10, 1918. Felix Warburg and Jacob Schiff are seated at the head of the table. Arthur Lehman and Cyrus Adler are directly behind Schiff.

Felix and Frieda's C.P.H. Gilbert–designed mansion at 1109 Fifth Avenue, completed in 1908, is now the Jewish Museum.

Felix, Frieda, and Edward Warburg pictured with Simon W. Rosendale, who served briefly as New York's attorney general.

Felix Warburg, in typically ebullient form, in Cortina, Italy, in August 1922.

John Pierpont Morgan, center, circa 1907. His epic battle against Harriman and Schiff for control of the Northern Pacific sent Wall Street into a tailspin.

left: Great Northern Railway president James J. Hill, circa 1913, deceived his old friend Jacob Schiff about his intentions for the Northern Pacific.

right: Railroad titan Edward H. Harriman would become a focus of Teddy Roosevelt's trust-busting wrath.

An inspiration for the Monopoly man, Otto Kahn owned palatial homes on Fifth Avenue, on Palm Beach's South Ocean Boulevard, and on the North Shore of Long Island, site of the 127-room Oheka Castle.

left: An arts patron and impresario, Kahn helped to rescue the Metropolitan Opera and was an early Hollywood financier.

bottom: The partners of Kuhn Loeb in 1932. Clockwise from center: Otto Kahn, Jerome Hanauer, Lewis Strauss, John Schiff, Felix Warburg, Benjamin Buttenwieser, Frederick Warburg, and William Wiseman. On the far wall is a portrait of Mortimer Schiff, who had died the previous year.

top left: Bobbie Lehman, who took the helm of Lehman Brothers in the 1920s, was "obviously more interested in art than banking," said one of his partners. His art collection fills a wing at the Metropolitan Museum.

top right: Jeff Seligman (son of James and Rosa), an early car enthusiast, at the start of the 22,000-mile "Great Race" in 1908.

bottom right: Morti Schiff departs the White House in December 1923 after meeting with President Calvin Coolidge.

bottom center: Philip Lehman, Emanuel's second-born son, led Lehman Brothers into an underwriting partnership with Goldman Sachs that dramatically shaped the futures of both firms—and of Wall Street itself.

bottom left: Tensions flared between Samuel Sachs (pictured) and his brother-in-law Henry Goldman, eventually leading to sharp divisions within the family and Henry's departure from the company his father, Marcus, founded.

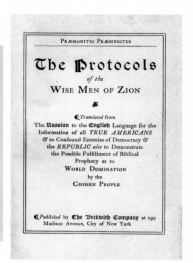

The article that signaled the beginning of Henry Ford's seven-year hate campaign against the Jews. (COLLECTIONS OF THE HENRY FORD MUSEUM, GREENFIELD VILLAGE)

left: Henry Ford purchased the struggling *Dearborn Independent* in 1919. It would soon launch a seven-year anti-Jewish campaign spanning ninety-two issues, becoming a wellspring of modern antisemitism.

center: The *Independent*'s antisemitic screeds were published widely in Germany, influencing Adolf Hitler and other rising Nazi leaders, who considered Henry Ford an inspiration.

right: The fraudulent *Protocols of the Elders of Zion*, first printed in Russia in the early 1900s, received little attention until it was published in the United States in 1920 by Romanov loyalist Boris Brasol.

left: Max Warburg, center, is pictured in a Nazi propaganda image titled, "Jews as rulers of the money markets. 4 Jews in the directorate of the German banking industry."

right: A Nazi propaganda image, circa 1936, titled "The Jew avoids work, he lets others do the work for him," featuring pictures of Felix Warburg and Jacob Schiff in the top right corner.

top left: The inaugural board of the Federal of Reserve, clockwise from top left: Paul Warburg, John Skelton Williams, William Harding, Adolph Miller, Charles Hamlin, William McAdoo, Jr., and Frederic Delano II.

top right: The author's grandmother, Lena, immigrated to New York in the early 1900s from a small town in what is today western Ukraine. She is pictured with sons Raymond, Marvin, and Bernard (center, the author's father).

bottom right: Schiff stands beside New York mayor William Gaynor on September 3, 1913, as Gaynor is nominated for reelection.

bottom left: On July 1, 1907, the first group of Jewish immigrants arrived in Texas via Jacob Schiff's Galveston movement.

versity Club. Strauss (later a pivotal figure in the U.S. atomic energy program) said that he had already declined an invitation to this gathering, and he explained why. Like other social clubs, the University Club did not admit Jewish members. On principle, Strauss chose not to attend. Morti grew irate.

"What I had not known," Strauss recalled, "was that he paid no attention to this particular peculiarity of the institution, many of its members were his friends," and he attended a regular Saturday afternoon poker game at the club. "The fact that I would not go when he did irritated him to the extent that he gave me a dressing down, and his voice was raised," Strauss remembered. Suddenly Morti stopped speaking midsentence and rose from his desk. His father was standing in the doorway. "Morti, I could not help but hear your voice," Jacob said. "What is the trouble?" Morti explained the disagreement, according to Strauss, "whereupon the old man laid him out, concluding by saying, 'I never expected to live to see the day when a new clerk in my office would have to tell my son how to behave!' "[48]

Jacob Schiff, model of propriety and high-minded dignity that he was, surely must have resented being dragged into the humiliating Brandt scandal. And on the heels of Brandt's pardon, the banker featured in another controversy tied indirectly to the Swede's case. Shortly into Sulzer's gubernatorial tenure, the New York State Assembly initiated impeachment proceedings against him, the product of a feud between the governor and the Tammany political apparatus from which Sulzer was struggling to free himself. The wide-ranging probe centered partly on unreported political donations Sulzer had allegedly misappropriated, including a $2,500 check from Schiff. Called to testify during Sulzer's impeachment trial, Schiff contradicted the governor's account that he was unaware of Schiff's contribution, saying the politician had in fact personally solicited it. In doing so, Schiff helped to put a nail in the coffin of Sulzer's governorship. Allies of the governor, who left office in disgrace less than a year after his swearing-in, contended Schiff intentionally provided damaging testimony as payback for Sulzer's decision to pardon the man who had tormented his family.[49]

In the twilight of his career, controversy stalked Schiff, his name a fixture in the press as one conflict overlapped with the next. A product of the Gilded Age, Schiff had earned his reputation and his fortune during a bacchanalian period when a relatively small group of capi-

talists exercised enormous sway over the financial system and used
questionable methods to bring order to the economic cannibalism
playing out in the marketplace, forming monopolistic arrangements
that further consolidated power in the hands of a few. But times were
changing.

The age of unfettered capitalism that had, in often ugly and bru-
tal ways, powered the industrial revolution gave rise to a backlash
against the so-called robber barons, paving the way for a Progressive
Era that sought to redress the economic, political, and social ills of
the past and that turned on the issue of control, particularly government's role in regulating industry. During the presidency of Woodrow Wilson, the upheaval of the Progressive Era would culminate
in a raft of sweeping labor and financial reforms. Among the most
dramatic changes were those to the foundation of the American economic system. Prominent in the early battles of Wilson's presidency
were Schiff and the German-Jewish banking families who composed
his social circle. Together they helped originate and usher in some of
the most transformative reforms of the twentieth century.

21

THE HUNTING PARTY

I t was a Thursday afternoon in mid-January 1913, and Jacob Schiff was in a now-familiar setting: on a witness stand. As the Brandt debacle played out in New York, he was summoned to Washington to answer for another alleged conspiracy, this one involving control over the national banking system.

The trust-busting fervor of the Progressive Era catalyzed congressional debate over what some lawmakers considered the most pernicious monopoly of all—a "money trust" of bankers who held undue influence over the economic fortunes of the United States. Representative Charles Lindbergh of Minnesota, the father of the famous aviator and a Republican known for his insurgent tendencies and quixotic crusades, stood at the vanguard of a populist faction that was pushing to probe this alleged cabal. Lindbergh accused New York bankers of manufacturing the 1907 panic in a crafty bid to conduct mergers and other deals that would have been off-limits in a normal economic climate and, he contended, to fuel the case for currency reforms that would only tighten the money trust's financial stranglehold.[1] In 1911, Lindbergh began pushing a resolution to open a broad probe into the banking system. A version of this measure eventually passed early the following year, kicking off an inquiry by a subcommittee of the House Committee on Banking and Currency led by the banking panel's chairman, Arsène Pujo.

Capping Pujo's mostly unremarkable five-term congressional

career, the headline-grabbing investigation came to define his legacy. Yet the committee's most pivotal figure was not Pujo but its mustachioed general counsel, Samuel Untermyer. The son of German Jews and a law partner of Louis Marshall, Untermyer had left his lucrative practice to guide the investigation. A smooth dealmaker and courtroom virtuoso, he built his career, and a multimillion-dollar fortune, working for corporations and creating the very type of monopolies he was now tasked with exposing. His appointment struck fear into the hearts of the nation's bankers because for years he had worked alongside them.

"He was instrumental in forming a good many of the so-called trusts, and made a great deal of money out of it," remembered Herbert Lehman, whose family firm had been one of Untermyer's clients. Lehman recalled that the lawyer "had one of the keenest minds that I've ever known, and was one of the best cross-examiners that I've ever heard. Ruthless. Perfectly ruthless."[2]

Untermyer's inside view of the business world had gradually transformed him into a crusader for reform who called for "stringent federal regulation of the trusts" and for curbing the "concentration of the money power." Few men were as familiar with the schemes and tactics of the nation's financial barons, who now, one by one, presented themselves before the Pujo Committee, where they experienced for themselves one of the lawyer's infamous inquisitions. Before the committee came a parade of the nation's most powerful moguls, including Frank Vanderlip and James Stillman of the National City Bank and First National Bank's George Baker, the portly and muttonchopped dean of the U.S. financial establishment who, at his death, ranked among the top three richest Americans. (William Rockefeller, Jr., younger brother of John D. and a cofounder of Standard Oil, went to elaborate lengths to dodge a congressional subpoena.) But no banker's appearance was more closely watched than the testimony of the money trust's purported kingpin: John Pierpont Morgan.

Morgan testified over portions of two days on December 18 and 19, 1912. Seventy-five and in flagging health, the lion of American finance seemed almost docile. Hunched in a flimsy rattan chair, he spoke in a low monotone, his eyes occasionally wandering over the crowd of hundreds who had massed to see him testify. Instead of the brusque and impetuous robber baron of popular legend, Morgan displayed an "almost extravagant politeness," one newspaper reported.[3]

Gently parrying with Untermyer, Morgan dismissed the notion of a banking conspiracy and downplayed his own legendary financial clout, as the lawyer tried repeatedly to get him to confess to holding boundless power.

"When a man has got a vast power, such as you have—you admit you have, do you not?" Untermyer probed in one exchange.

"I do not know it, sir," the banker replied.

"You admit you have, do you not?"

"I do not think I have."

"You do not feel it at all?"

"No, I do not feel it at all."[4]

As Morgan testified, Untermyer displayed charts that told a somewhat different story. They showed the overlapping relationships between eighteen firms, including J.P. Morgan & Co. and Kuhn Loeb, that possessed, if not outright control, then vast influence over numerous banks, trust companies, insurers, utilities, railroads, and other corporations. The partners of these outfits, the Pujo Committee determined, held 746 directorships in 134 corporations that collectively had resources or capitalization of more than $25 billion.[5]

A month after Morgan's grilling, Schiff's turn came. The timing was terrible. Back in New York, Folke Brandt was poised to be released from prison, and the matter was once again bringing great strain and turmoil to Schiff's family. But in Washington he presented a serene façade. Like Morgan, Schiff gave little ground, demurring when Untermyer quizzed him about Kuhn Loeb's banking "alliances."

"I cannot call them alliances," he said. "We have correspondents and friends that cooperate with us, but we are not allied to anybody."

Schiff denounced monopolies as "odious" and said he did not believe in concentrating corporate power through holding companies (though this is precisely what he and Morgan had done years earlier through the formation of Northern Securities), but he also said, "I would not limit the individual by law to buy whatever he pleases."

"Even if it amounted to a monopoly?" Untermyer asked.

"Even if it amounted to a monopoly," Schiff answered.

Untermyer dug further. "I want to know where you would draw the line with respect to the license you would give to individuals to get control of any industry or any line of business?"

"I would let nature take its course," Schiff said. "The first monopoly attempted was in the building of the Tower of Babel. They wanted to make a monopoly of language. And it broke down by its own weight. Anything that goes too far will break down by its own weight." In a remark much quoted in the newspaper coverage of Schiff's testimony, the banker declared, "I would not limit, in any instance, individual freedom in anything, because I believe the law of nature governs that better than any law of man."[6]

The Pujo Committee released its findings in late February. If the panel fell short of proving a "money trust" in a literal sense, it succeeded in showing in stark terms how consolidated corporate power had become. A handful of firms held a lock on the issue of major securities in the United States, as Henry Goldman had discovered as he tried to break into this market. Their representatives served on the boards of a dizzying assortment of corporations and wielded immense financial power, including the ability to stifle competition and starve would-be rivals of credit. The panel determined that

> there is an established and well-defined identity and community of interest between a few leaders of finance, created and held together through stock ownership, interlocking directorates, partnership and joint account transactions, and other forms of domination over banks, trust companies, railroads, and public-service and industrial corporations, which has resulted in great and rapidly growing concentration of the control of money and credit in the hands of these few men.

The committee's report identified Kuhn Loeb as one of six primary "agents of concentration," noting that it had marketed $1 billion worth of securities since 1905 in partnership with J.P. Morgan, the First National Bank, or the National City Bank (sometimes all three). Kuhn Loeb had what "virtually amounts to an understanding not to compete" with certain firms and had, together with its allies, "preempted the banking business of the important railways of the country," the committee concluded.[7]

A month after the money trust probe concluded, word came from Rome that J. P. Morgan had died, expiring in a $500-a-night hotel suite in the city's Grand Hotel. The financier's son, Jack, blamed his father's rapid decline on the strain of the investigation and his public interrogation by Untermyer, whom the younger Morgan dubbed "the Beast."

Schiff was visiting Sicily when Morgan passed, and in his absence Kuhn Loeb issued an effusive tribute to the late banker: "The financial community mourns in him the greatest leader it has ever had whose influence and power were based no more upon his commanding ability than upon the universal confidence in the loftiness of his motives, in his loyalty, fair-mindedness and the ever splendid qualities of his character."[8] A few days later, Schiff cabled a more muted statement to *The New York Times* from the Ionian coast, and one must wonder how he felt about his firm lauding his rival as the financial world's "greatest leader."

"Mr. Morgan's leading characteristic was to be helpful and to do right," Schiff's statement read. "His worth as a good and great citizen will, now that he is no more, be even more fully appreciated, and we shall not soon see his like again."[9]

The newspapers speculated on "Who Will Wear Morgan's Mantle," and the names floated, in addition to Jack Morgan, included Morti Schiff and Otto Kahn.[10] But no banker would again fill Morgan's singular role in American finance. This had as much to do with the man himself as it did with the times. Public opinion had now tacked sharply in favor of government regulation to curb corporate excesses. His death—and the money trust investigation that plagued his final days—formed a coda to the Gilded Age. In the months and years ahead, Progressive reforms, some fueled by the Pujo Committee's work, would dramatically remake America's financial system.

One of the most monumental changes occurred during Morgan's final weeks, when the Sixteenth Amendment, authorizing a federal income tax, was officially appended to the Constitution. This followed nearly two decades of debate and legislative wrangling, culminating with a constitutional amendment, first introduced in 1909, that was eventually ratified by more than three-fourths of the states (the threshold required to amend the Constitution). Few men played a greater role in ushering in the progressive income tax than Joseph Seligman's son, Edwin.

A professor of political economy at Columbia University, Edwin had devoted himself to the study of public finance, spending nineteen years researching and writing an influential 750-page history of the income tax. But he was no mere theorist. Edwin became one of the leading voices calling for a direct tax on income—up until that point, tariffs formed the main source of government revenues—that would be graduated based on a citizen's ability to pay, with the wealthy contributing a higher percentage than the poor.

When, in 1910, the New York legislature began debating the constitutional amendment, Seligman joined the fight to secure its passage, which was considered especially vital there since the state was home to many of the nation's wealthiest citizens. He testified twice before the state senate in favor of the amendment, and in the pages of *Political Science Quarterly*, a journal Seligman edited, he rebutted the arguments of critics who contended a federal income tax bestowed too much power on the state—power the drafters of the Constitution never envisioned—and steered the nation dangerously into socialistic territory and away from its founding values of self-determination. "The conditions which existed when the constitution was framed are no longer existent," Seligman wrote. "During the last century . . . the development of the underlying economic and social forces has created a nation, and this development calls for uniform national regulation of many matters which were not dreamed of by the founders." He noted, "Let us not make a fetich of 'self-government,' and let us not oppose central authority in those cases where self-government means retrogression rather than progress."[11]

The Republican-dominated legislature voted down the amendment three times in 1910. But elections that year brought a national reckoning for the GOP; in New York, the Republicans were swept out of power in the governor's office and the legislature. A loyal Republican, Seligman blamed the state party's comeuppance on its refusal to advance the amendment, which the Democratic-controlled legislature passed the following year, making New York the thirty-first state to ratify the income tax.[12]

That a son of one of the nation's leading banking dynasties played such a visible role in ushering in the Sixteenth Amendment carried a certain irony. And some members of the Seligman clan seemed less than appreciative of Edwin's pioneering work. His acerbic uncle Isaac, who had lived in London for decades, as well as his cousin David Albert (one of Abraham's sons), reportedly renounced their U.S. citizenship to avoid paying the new income tax.[13]

Yet other members of his family and social circle approved of an income tax, believing it was the only way to fund the government without the nation taking on dangerous levels of debt. Edwin's older brother Ike, head of the Seligman family's U.S. banking business, called the income tax "the most ideal sort of tax ever devised." The civic-minded banker, who made curbing child labor a focus of his philanthropy, noted, "Hitherto the people of this country have considered an income tax as too inquisitional and as savoring a little of socialism, and therefore been opposed to it. But in time, I think, they will come to see the justice and benefit to be derived from it."[14] Jacob

Schiff also backed an income tax, and in 1909 he proposed levying a tax on "income or revenue derived from business and especially inter-state commerce. . . . So far as the banking business is concerned such an income tax would yield a very large revenue to the Government, and this is even truer, of course, in many other forms of commercial and industrial enterprise."[15]

On the heels of the Sixteenth Amendment, legislative momentum built for other financial and corporate reforms. By 1914, Congress had passed the Clayton Anti-Trust Act (strengthening its predecessor, the Sherman Anti-Trust Act) and created the Federal Trade Commission to crack down on monopolistic business practices. Late that year the Federal Reserve opened its doors. The product of years of political skirmishing, the institution ushered in a new era of American banking and brought Wall Street into partnership with the federal government as never before.

That August, shortly after they were confirmed by the Senate, the Fed's inaugural board of governors posed rigidly for a photograph in front of the granite columns of the U.S. Treasury building on Pennsylvania Avenue, where the Federal Reserve was initially headquartered. From right to left stood the railroad executive Frederic Delano (uncle of FDR); Adolph Miller, a prominent economics professor; Charles Hamlin, a Boston lawyer who had until recently served as an assistant Treasury secretary; and, clutching his black homburg with both hands, Paul Warburg, one of the most pivotal figures in the Fed's creation.

One day in 1907, during the height of the financial panic, Paul Warburg glanced up from his desk in Kuhn Loeb's offices to see National City Bank's James Stillman squinting down at him through heavy-lidded eyes. "Warburg," Stillman asked, "where is your paper?"[16]

The document in question was a memo Warburg had drafted shortly after moving to New York in the fall of 1902, in which he outlined the many flaws in the American banking system. Stillman had read it at the time and was none too impressed. To Warburg, accustomed to the European model of central banking—in which a single institution regulated the flow of credit and currency, empowered to expand or contract the monetary supply based on market conditions and to purchase or discount commercial paper to bolster the cash reserves of national banks—America's decentralized system was confounding. "There existed as many disconnected banking systems as there were States," Warburg later recalled, "and even among the banks of a single State there was no machinery for mutual protection except the 'clearing-house associations'"—independent financial institutions that settled trades and made sure that buyers and sellers lived up to their contracts.[17]

Moreover, the amount of currency in circulation remained fixed, or "inelastic," making the nation particularly vulnerable to financial shocks. "When heavy demands for gold from abroad, or excessive domestic demands for circulation, or an abnormal increase of bank loans and bank deposits had brought excess reserves down to or below the legal requirements, financial conditions became at once critical," Warburg recounted.[18] The disconnected nature of the American banking system caused financial institutions to act for self-preservation during times of crisis, calling in loans and hoarding cash at the expense of their competitors and clients—and ultimately, at the expense of the American financial system, which seized up like the gears of an engine run dry of oil.

The last major effort at banking reform had occurred during the Civil War, when Congress passed the National Bank Act, establishing a system of federally chartered banks authorized to issue notes backed by U.S. government bonds deposited with the comptroller of the currency (a new office created by the law). The law imposed strict reserve requirements on national banks—those in New York, for instance, had to keep 25 percent of their deposits on the sidelines. The National Bank Act had uniformized the monetary system (though various types of legal tender, including greenbacks, the bills printed by the Treasury in the early days of the war, remained in circulation), but it had done little to stabilize the volatile U.S. financial system.

Paul initially shared his critique of American banking with Jacob Schiff, who told his young partner that he largely agreed with him. But, Schiff noted, Warburg did not yet understand the national psychology; Americans, with their inborn skepticism of government power, would never accept a European-style central bank. At least, not again.

During its infancy, the nation had experimented with central banking. In 1791, Alexander Hamilton had championed the creation of the First Bank of the United States, modeled on the Bank of England. The bank was a political lightning rod, and its twenty-year charter was not renewed by Congress. In 1816, James Madison chartered the Second Bank of the United States, but it was later dismantled under the administration of Andrew Jackson, who called the institution a "hydra of corruption." (The demise of the bank, which had helped to stabilize the nation's haphazard monetary system, contributed to the financial panic of 1837.) By the time Warburg arrived in the United States, America's last experience with central banking was nearly seventy years in the past.

Schiff cautioned Warburg against airing his views too widely; doing so might alienate him from the American banking fraternity. But he agreed to show Warburg's memo to a couple of trusted friends for their feedback. One was James Stillman, banker to the Rockefellers and Standard Oil, who presided over America's largest bank.

Stillman, predictably skeptical, had sought Paul out at Kuhn Loeb's offices after reviewing his treatise.

"Warburg, don't you think the City Bank has done pretty well?" Stillman asked, looming over his desk.

"Yes, Mr. Stillman, extraordinarily well," Warburg replied.

"Why not leave things alone?"

Warburg hesitated. Finally, he said, "Your bank is so big and so powerful, Mr. Stillman, that, when the next panic comes, you will wish your responsibilities were smaller."[19]

When, just a handful of years later, that panic came, forcing Stillman and other top financiers to play the role of central bankers to halt the economic tailspin, the National City Bank's chairman once again appeared at Warburg's desk, now more receptive to the ideas he had previously dismissed, and asked after that bygone memo.

By now, Warburg had already dipped a toe in the stormy political waters of banking reform, with the encouragement of Edwin Seligman. In 1906, Warburg had attended a dinner party at Seligman's West 86th Street townhouse, where he entranced the Columbia professor with his lucid diagnosis of the American banking system's defects.

"You ought to write. You ought to publish," Seligman blurted excitedly.

"Impossible," Warburg demurred. He was still mastering English, which he spoke with a British, not a German, accent, though certain words, such as *iron*, which he pronounced "i-ron," always confounded him. And he was insecure about his written English.[20] "I can't write English yet—not well enough for publication."

"The English can be arranged," Seligman said, volunteering his services as editor. "It's your duty to get your ideas before the country."[21]

Early the next year Warburg published a lengthy article in *The New York Times*—based in part on his original memorandum—outlining the primitive nature of American monetary policy. "The United States is in fact at about the same point that had been reached by Europe at the time of the Medicis, and by Asia, in all likelihood, at the time of Hammurabi," he wrote. And he stated plainly: "That a central bank is the ideal solution of the difficulty and that it must finally come—though, perhaps we may not live to see it—is my firm belief."[22]

"It certainly was a very carefully worked out expose," Schiff wrote to *Times* publisher Adolph Ochs after Warburg's article appeared.[23] Indeed, Schiff had recommended that Ochs publish it. Over the years, during their morning walks downtown, Warburg had waged a relentless campaign to convince Schiff that Americans could—and must—adopt a central banking system.[24] Evidently, Warburg was persuasive. So were the traumatic events of the Panic of 1907, which injected new urgency into the case for reform. In late 1907, when Schiff spoke at the American Academy of Political and Social Science, Warburg's influence was apparent. "There is needed a central authority," Schiff declared. Speaking at the same event, Ike Seligman endorsed the idea of a central bank more strongly still: "There is no doubt in my mind that if we had a modified central banking system the forced closing of the Knickerbocker Trust Company of New York could have been avoided," averting the bank runs and trust company collapses that followed.[25]

In 1908, Edwin Seligman organized a lecture series at Columbia focused on banking and currency reform, inviting Warburg to participate. Congress had reacted to the panic with a flurry of reform legislation, including a pair of rival bills advanced by the chairmen of the House and Senate banking committees. Representative Charles Fowler, a New Jersey Republican, dusted off an old plan for an asset-based currency, in which national banks could issue notes backed by their general assets, not just by government bonds. Senator Nelson Aldrich, the Rhode Island Republican who had presided over the upper chamber's banking panel since 1898, floated a separate measure aimed at expanding the currency supply during times of crisis by allowing national banks to form currency associations empowered to issue emergency banknotes backed by their collective holdings of bonds and certain other securities. During Warburg's speech at Seligman's symposium, he sharply criticized the Fowler and Aldrich bills, saying neither "can be deemed a step in the right direction. Every measure is bad which accentuates decentralization of note issue and of reserves."[26]

Warburg had recently met Aldrich when the senator visited Kuhn Loeb's offices. Known as the "General Manager of the Nation," Aldrich, who stood about six feet and sported a bushy white mustache, was among the most powerful men in Congress. Also among the wealthiest, he was at the time constructing a rambling, seventy-room château situated on 254 bucolic acres overlooking Narragansett Bay. Aldrich wasn't born into wealth and spent most of his career in public service—first the Rhode Island legislature, then the House, then the Senate. Rather, his fortune had come in part through the type of casual corruption endemic during the Gilded Age: he reaped millions through an investment in an electric streetcar enterprise arranged by a political benefactor and financed in part by the Sugar Trust, whose bidding Aldrich reliably did in the Senate.

Aldrich was not an inspired public speaker, a deficit he made up for as a deft backroom operator. A persistent foe of progressive reforms (such as the "communistic" income tax), he was depicted in a political cartoon from that era as a spider whose web had hopelessly ensnared progressive legislation, trapping the measures in committee. As he devised his currency reform bill in the aftermath of the 1907 panic, Aldrich consulted with Jacob Schiff on his plan. Aldrich was curious about the workings of the German monetary system, and Schiff had sent for Paul Warburg, the resident expert. Paul provided Aldrich with the information he sought, and after Aldrich departed Schiff's private office, Warburg muttered to himself, "There goes currency reform." Warburg asked Schiff if he could send Aldrich a letter outlining his views. Schiff, appearing somewhat bemused, replied: "If you do, he will never look at you again."[27]

Paul, now on a nearly religious mission to spread the gospel of central banking, ignored Schiff's advice. "Did not the last panic show that we are suffering from too much decentralization of our banking system and from the absolute impossibility of securing any concerted action as to the free use of our reserves, instead of competitive hoarding of currency by the financial institutions?" he wrote Aldrich. He pitched the senator on the creation of a "central clearing house"—in essence, a watered-down central bank, which he believed was the most that Americans would be willing to accept.[28]

Aldrich did not reply, and Paul had little reason to think he had made much of an impression.[29] Aldrich navigated his bill to passage in the spring of 1908. In addition to creating a mechanism for

emergency currency, the legislation established a National Monetary
Commission, chaired by Aldrich, that would undertake a comprehen-
sive study of U.S. and European banking laws. That August, armed
with letters of introduction supplied by bankers including Schiff and
J. P. Morgan, Aldrich led a fact-finding delegation through the major
European banking capitals of Berlin, London, and Paris.[30] Conducting interviews with officials at the Bank of England, the Banque de
France, and the Reichsbank, Aldrich received a humbling education
in modern banking practices. He returned home that October converted to the idea of an American central bank.

That November, Aldrich summoned Warburg to a National
Monetary Commission hearing convened at the Metropolitan Club,
the Stanford White–designed refuge of New York's banking elite
located on the northeast corner of Fifth Avenue and 60th Street.

Warburg testified before a sleepy panel of commissioners. After
the hearing concluded, Aldrich pulled him aside. "Mr. Warburg," he
said, "I like your ideas. I have only one fault to find with them."

What fault was that? Warburg inquired.

"You are too timid about it," he said.

Warburg replied that he was virtually the only banking reform
advocate calling for bold action, even if his plan envisioned a modified central banking system tailored to American sensibilities.

"Yes, but you say we cannot have a central bank, and I say we
can," Aldrich said, as Warburg tried to mask his mounting elation.
The stunned banker departed the Metropolitan Club "confident that
genuine banking reform was within grasp of the United States," he
later wrote.[31]

Over the next two years, as the National Monetary Commission completed its work, eventually issuing some thirty reports on all
aspects of the international banking system, Warburg corresponded
sporadically with Aldrich. He traded letters more frequently with
A. Piatt Andrew, a Harvard economist serving as a special assistant
to the commission, whom Warburg supplied with financial data and
peppered with his latest articles.

In April 1910, Aldrich, increasingly under attack by progressives
as a mascot of political corruption, announced his plans to retire
from the Senate at the conclusion of his term the following year. He
intended to make banking reform the cornerstone of his legacy in
public service—but he was running out of time. The 1910 election
complicated his plans. Democrats took control of the House for the
first time in sixteen years and progressives in both parties substan-

tially increased their numbers, diminishing Aldrich's power. Nevertheless, he remained committed to overhauling the banking system.

The week after the election a J.P. Morgan & Co. partner named Henry P. Davison called on Warburg at Kuhn Loeb's offices, bearing an invitation from Aldrich. Davison, who had been quietly assisting Aldrich and his commission, asked Warburg if he could disappear from work for a week or two to accompany the senator and four other men on a secret expedition to plot the future of banking reform. Their destination: Jekyll Island. Located off the coast of Georgia, the secluded island housed what was perhaps America's most exclusive club, whose members included J. P. Morgan; Joseph Pulitzer; William Rockefeller, Jr.; and other millionaires.

Davison told Warburg that attendees of the confab would travel to the island under the guise of a duck-hunting trip. The prospect of Warburg on a hunting expedition would have amused his friends and family. He didn't hunt. Nor did he own a gun.

On the evening of November 18, 1910, toting a rifle and ammunition he had purchased earlier that day to make his cover story passably believable, Warburg boarded Aldrich's private railroad car at New Jersey's Pennsylvania Station.[32] He found the National City Bank's Frank Vanderlip waiting inside.

"On what kind of an errand are we going, anyhow?" Vanderlip asked.

"It may be a wild goose chase instead of a duck hunt," Warburg quipped. "And it may be the biggest thing you or I ever did." The comment reflected Paul's lingering suspicion of Aldrich. He wondered if he was being taken "into the fold in order to make him a fellow conspirator and thereby to muzzle him."[33]

The rest of their party soon arrived one by one, as Aldrich had instructed: Aldrich; his secretary, Arthur Shelton; A. Piatt Andrew; and Davison. The train jerked forward, and the hunting party traveled south through the night, arriving in Brunswick, Georgia, the following day. Taking pains to keep their mission sub rosa, the group had agreed to refer to one another only by their first names—Aldrich, for instance, was Mr. Nelson. And when the stationmaster greeted Warburg and his colleagues, he found them loudly discussing their hunting plans. He broke in with some bad news: "Now gentlemen, this is all very pretty, but I must tell you that we know who you are and the reporters are waiting outside."

Davison took the stationmaster by the arm. "Come out, old man, I will tell you a story," he said. He returned a little while later, with a gleam in his eye. "That's all right, they won't give us away." It wasn't clear how he had mollified the press, but the trip remained secret until 1916, when the journalist B. C. Forbes, founder of *Forbes* magazine, revealed the Jekyll Island confab in a little-noticed article. The participants in the meeting, however, did not acknowledge its existence for decades.

The reason for the vow of omertà was clear: if discovered, the role of representatives of three of the nation's leading financial institutions in crafting national banking policy, convening no less at an island resort accessible only to America's most elite moguls, would have rendered any legislation dead on arrival. Indeed, when later revealed, the Jekyll Island conclave fueled assorted conspiracy theories about the creation of the Federal Reserve that have metastasized for a century. Some contend that the meeting's true purpose was establishing a banking monopoly and asserting control over the nation's financial resources. The myths emanating from this secret retreat in some cases assumed an antisemitic tone. In 1952, for instance, the Holocaust denier Eustace Mullins wrote a widely read book that attempted to link the Jekyll Island conference to the Rothschild family, a clan that has become a byword for a supposed international Jewish banking conspiracy.

Jekyll Island Club member J. P. Morgan arranged for the resort to be deserted, save for two Black servants, around whom Warburg and his colleagues continued to shield their identities. Settling into a conference room in the island's turreted clubhouse, the group sequestered themselves for eight days. Working in marathon spurts of discussion and debate, the group paused only when the servants entered at mealtimes, bearing sumptuous spreads of wild game—deer, turkey, quail—and trays of freshly shucked oysters.[34] On Thanksgiving, which fell during their stay on the island, the men feasted and then went right back to work.[35]

The participants agreed in principle on the creation of a central banking system, but the thorniest details still needed to be worked out, such as who would run the bank and what authorities it would possess. Warburg had developed a plan for what he called a "United Reserve Bank of the United States," composed of regional banking associations operating in twenty commercial centers, each with its own board of directors. The system would be overseen by a central body in Washington whose leadership would be named by a combination of banking and political officials to ensure all interests were represented. Members of the banking associations would deposit their reserves with the central reserve bank, which would have the power to discount commercial paper—in other words, banks could sell their loans to this body to raise cash—and issue currency.

Of all the Jekyll Island participants, Warburg was the most adroit financial theorist and had spent the most time considering the mechanics of an American central banking system. So the plan they formulated hewed closely to Warburg's blueprint. Opinionated and at times argumentative, Warburg dominated the discussions, pressing his points so forcefully that he at times angered Aldrich. At one point, he clashed fiercely with the senator over how reserves would be defined.

When the group broke for the evening, Davison took Warburg for a stroll in the crisp evening air among oak trees draped with Spanish moss. "Paul, you must not do that," he said in his deep, even voice. "You can not force Mr. Nelson. If you try to, you will lose him. Drop the matter for the time being, and see whether you can not take it up again later on." Warburg later credited Davison with an important contribution to the "human side" of the meeting. In addition to helping select the attendees, Davison played the role of peacemaker, redirecting the conversation when tensions flared and lightening the mood with his jocular personality. "Always he could be counted on to crack a joke just at the right moment to ease a strain," Vanderlip recalled.[36] Paul took Davison's advice and eventually his position won out.

When the main issues were ironed out, the men allowed themselves a day of recreation, venturing out with their rifles. At least now they could say with straight faces they had gone duck hunting.

On November 28 the group returned north with a plan for a central banking system outlined in Vanderlip's neat scrawl. In New Jersey, Warburg and his compatriots parted as furtively as they had arrived.

Emphatic about secrecy, Aldrich warned that the Taft administration, including the president himself, should not be taken into their confidence. Back home, Warburg began carefully laying the groundwork so the forthcoming Aldrich Plan would debut to an enthusiastic reception. He was in a tricky spot since he could divulge neither the contents of the plan nor his outsize role in drafting it. But working through a trio of powerful business groups, including the Chamber of Commerce, he nudged his fellow bankers and businessmen in the right direction. Skillfully steering these groups in favor of some of the key tenets agreed upon by the Jekyll Island conferees, he took command of a joint committee charged with drafting a single resolution that would effectively place the imprimatur of the New York business world on a central banking organization along the lines of the one Aldrich would soon propose.

Also part of this committee was Sam Sachs, who wanted to ensure that private banking houses such as his—and not just commercial banks—would be allowed to have direct dealings with the central bank. In a letter to Sachs the day after this point was debated at a Chamber of Commerce meeting, Warburg worried about opening "the door for the criticism that private interests might enjoy undue favoritism with the Central Bank." To appease Sachs, he agreed to vague language in the resolution raising the possibility that private banks might be included. "I hope that our critics will not discover our weak point," Warburg told the Goldman Sachs partner.[37]

The New Year came and went with no sign of the Aldrich Plan and, for that matter, little sign of Aldrich himself. Newspapers reported he had fallen ill, possibly with tonsillitis. In fact, after returning from Jekyll Island and as his retirement from the Senate neared, he had fallen into a depressive episode, racked by self-doubt and tortured by insomnia. Still, with considerable help from A. Piatt Andrew, Aldrich finally managed to release a draft of his proposal on January 17, 1911. That day Paul Warburg sent a lengthy statement to *The New York Times* declaring himself "delighted" by the plan. He conspicuously omitted his own role in authoring it.[38]

Aldrich remained out of the public eye as his plan generated headlines and heated debate. On the advice of his doctors, he had returned to the luxurious solitude of Jekyll Island to convalesce.

The Aldrich Plan landed as Democrats prepared to take control of the House that spring (at that time, new congressional sessions commenced in March), as an anti–Wall Street mood infected members of both parties, and as a presidential election loomed. Politicians waxed conspiratorially about the "money trust," and Representative Charles Lindbergh mounted his successful push for an investigation. Lindbergh, predictably, eyed the Aldrich proposal with suspicion, glimpsing behind it a Wall Street effort to further consolidate its power. Not only had Wall Street "brought on the 1907 panic and got people to demand currency reform," Lindbergh warned, but "if it dares will produce another panic to pass the Aldrich central bank plan."[39]

His health restored—and not fully aware of how profoundly the political winds had shifted—Aldrich emerged from seclusion that spring ready to begin courting endorsements for his plan. The now-retired senator remained the head of the National Monetary Commission, which was scheduled to deliver a final version of his proposal to Congress the following January. Aldrich met personally with reluctant bankers, and he embarked on a speaking tour of the West, a stronghold of populism where the citizens and their congressional representatives were naturally disposed to view his initiative with skepticism. Warburg, meanwhile, helped to organize an advocacy group, the National Citizens' League for the Promotion of a Sound Banking System, to build national support for the Aldrich Plan. At its peak, this organization had thirty local chapters.

By the end of 1911, their movement had secured the backing of the powerful American Bankers Association and twenty-nine other influential interest groups. President Taft voiced his support for the Aldrich Plan—though his political future now seemed increasingly uncertain as he faced a two-pronged challenge to his incumbency: from his onetime political mentor, Theodore Roosevelt, who was intent on reclaiming the Oval Office, and from New Jersey governor Woodrow Wilson.

On the campaign trail, Wilson offered a sharp critique of Wall Street, sounding at times almost Lindberghian. During one 1911 speech, he declared that "the great monopoly in this country is the money monopoly." The nation's economic "activities are in the hands of a few men who . . . chill and check and destroy genuine economic freedom," Wilson added. "This is the greatest question of all."[40]

Wilson's position on the Aldrich Plan was more difficult to decipher. Chasing the endorsement of William Jennings Bryan—the three-time Democratic nominee who had all but made opposition to the Aldrich Plan a litmus test for his support—he denounced any "plan that would concentrate control in the hands of the bankers." Yet word reached Paul Warburg, through a journalist acquaintance, that Wilson was largely "in sympathy" with the Aldrich effort. Throughout the campaign, Wilson pulled off the politician's trick of leading both sides to believe he was in their corner. Publicly, Wilson seemed to voice hostility toward a central bank—at one point, he stated plainly that "I am myself opposed to the idea of a central bank"—while privately sending signals that Warburg and his allies interpreted favorably.[41]

The partners of Kuhn Loeb were as divided as the rest of the nation on the upcoming presidential election. Paul's brother Felix backed Taft. Otto Kahn, meanwhile, worked to resurrect Roosevelt, whose views on regulating corporate power the banker had come to respect. ("The Bourbons of corporate finance have no place in the present scheme of things," Kahn declared in 1910.)[42] Jacob Schiff and Paul Warburg leaped across party lines entirely, supporting Wilson.[43] His sharp oratory on the Russian passport issue had deeply impressed Schiff, but that wasn't the only reason Wilson's candidacy appealed. Schiff opposed the protectionist trade policies embraced by Roosevelt and Taft, faulting the "tariff such as we have" for the nation's "social ills." Wilson, on the other hand, pledged tariff reform. As the presidential campaign wore on, it became clear Taft had little chance of reelection—"It will be either Wilson or Roosevelt," Schiff told his friend Louis Marshall, in a letter explaining his support for the Democrat.[44]

A similar political fissure erupted at Goldman Sachs, where Henry Goldman outraged Sam Sachs by defecting from the Republican Party to back the Democratic nominee. In the months before the election, Goldman wrote a $10,000 check to Wilson's campaign fund and signed on to lead a Democratic National Committee fundraising effort targeting New York bankers and brokers.[45]

The final months of the campaign played out against the backdrop of the Pujo Committee's money trust probe, an investigation that stoked public distrust of Wall Street to new levels of intensity. In this climate, the Aldrich Plan, which the monetary commission had formally submitted to Congress in January 1912, struggled to gain traction. In part, the legislation suffered because of its namesake, an old guard politician who to the public represented cronyism and the status quo during a moment of great social upheaval—and who refused to distance himself from his plan even if that meant smothering it.

During their respective conventions that summer, the parties staked out their positions on banking reform. Penned largely by Bryan, the Democratic Party platform declared: "We oppose the so-called Aldrich bill or the establishment of a central bank." The Republicans, riven by an internecine conflict between backers of Taft and supporters of Roosevelt, mustered the most tepid of statements, affirming their commitment to the "progressive development of our banking and currency systems"—but making no mention of the Aldrich Plan. The Progressive Party, formed after Roosevelt was denied the nomination at the Republican convention in Chicago, followed the Democrats in opposing the Aldrich bill, saying it "would place our currency and credit system in private hands, not subject to effective public control."

The Aldrich Plan was dead—that was clear even before Wilson won a landslide victory and the Democrats swept both chambers of Congress. Yet in the incoming Wilson administration, its spirit miraculously lived on, thanks in part to its most relentless advocate, Paul Warburg.

On January 7, 1913, Warburg appeared before a House subcommittee that was impaneled to operate in parallel with the money trust probe, its role to formulate new banking reform legislation. The panel was led by Carter Glass, a Virginia Democrat and onetime newspaper publisher who would soon succeed Arsène Pujo as chairman of the House Banking and Currency Committee on his way to an eventual cabinet post as Treasury secretary. Glass was known for his sharp pen and tongue; *The New York Times* once likened him to "a compact high explosive which may go off at any moment."

Glass faced a difficult challenge. The Democratic Party's unequivocal Bryan-authored platform statement circumscribed his effort, and during the hearing he stated plainly that he and his colleagues felt they were "precluded" from considering anything that resembled the Aldrich bill or a central bank. "Well, do not forget that the Aldrich plan contains some things which are simply fundamental rules of banking," Warburg cautioned. "Those you will have to include in every plan, and I think that the Democratic Party would make a great mistake, if I may say so, to say, 'Because Senator Aldrich ate his soup with a spoon we are not going to eat with spoons but must use forks.'"[46]

Though for political reasons he refused to admit it, the plan Glass was crafting drew heavily from the Aldrich bill. It envisioned a network of as many as twenty reserve banks scattered strategically around the country, with regional banks holding shares in their nearest reserve institutions. Yet when Glass presented his views to the president-elect that winter at Wilson's home in Princeton, Wilson quickly homed in on what the plan lacked, wondering how his proposal would address "centralization." The system, Wilson said, needed a "capstone"—a central governing body in Washington. In essence, Wilson wanted a centralized system with a regional character that would appeal to progressives. The president "had found the only way of reconciling the progressive demand for decentralization with the practical necessity for centralized control," Wilson's biographer, Arthur Link, later wrote. Departing Wilson's Tudor-style home on Cleveland Lane, a blanket of fresh snow covering the ground, Glass had cause to wonder if Warburg had gotten to the incoming commander in chief.[47]

Indeed, behind the scenes Warburg worked diligently to shape the reform effort. The month after the election he outlined a revised plan for a centralized banking system. He supplied copies to two Wilson confidants: Henry Morgenthau, Sr., a New York lawyer and real estate investor of German-Jewish extraction whom Wilson had rewarded for his work during the campaign with an ambassadorship to the Ottoman Empire; and Edward House, a sphinxlike political operative who possessed a special knack for stroking Wilson's ego. Known as "Colonel" House, a nickname that stuck after he was given an honorary rank in the Texas militia, he held enormous sway over Wilson, rising to become his most trusted adviser.

As the bill that would become the Federal Reserve Act took shape, House served as a frequent Warburg back channel to the Wilson administration. In late April 1913, after obtaining a summary of the legislation Glass was drafting, House promptly supplied the document to Warburg, asking him to quickly provide feedback. Warburg feverishly dissected the proposal, which notably included the "capstone" Wilson requested, a Washington, D.C.–based Federal Reserve Board to oversee the system. Believing he had only twenty-four hours to work, Warburg dashed off what he called a "short resume of my criticism." The critique spanned twenty pages.[48]

A copy of Warburg's unsigned memo made it back to Glass and H. Parker Willis, the finance expert advising the Virginia Democrat and drafting the bill's language. Willis suspected its source, and though he was incensed by the "vicious" commentary, the final Federal Reserve legislation incorporated many of Warburg's suggestions.[49]

Complicating matters, a second banking plan began taking shape that spring under the guidance of Senator Robert Owen of Oklahoma, a Bryan acolyte who was Glass's counterpart on the Senate Banking Committee. In May, days before departing with his family on their customary trip to Europe, Warburg met with Owen for seven hours. They spent much of that time debating Owen's position that the U.S. government—not the reserve banks—should issue currency. The notion horrified Warburg, who worried that making money an obligation of the federal government risked harming the nation's credit.

Over the next month, Owen and Glass thrashed out the differences in their respective bills and crafted similar legislation for introduction in each chamber. From abroad, Warburg anxiously monitored the latest developments. "Is there anything I can do in the currency situation," he cabled House from Hamburg, "it looks to me as if they were bungling it most terribly."[50] In a separate missive to Wilson's adviser, he vented, "if this child of mine is to be turned into a mongrel I want to protest."[51]

The House version of the Federal Reserve Act passed easily on September 18, 1913. The next month, as the battle over the legislation heated up in the Senate, Warburg returned home aboard the newly completed German ocean liner, *Imperator.* While at sea, eager to join the legislative fray, he sketched out fifteen pages of proposed amendments, which he sent to Owen and William McAdoo, whom Wilson had tapped as his Treasury secretary. In the weeks ahead, Warburg traveled repeatedly to Washington to press for changes to the bill, conferring frequently with Glass, Owen, and McAdoo. During one meeting, Glass stunned Warburg—with whom he had a sometimes antagonistic relationship—by asking him if he would consider serving on the Federal Reserve Board. Warburg assumed he was joking. Appointing a partner in a Wall Street firm accused of being part of a "money trust"? Congressional populists would go berserk. But Glass pressed, and Warburg realized he was serious. If the president asked, he replied, the honor would be hard to refuse.

Wrangling over the bill continued into December, until finally, on December 18, 1913, the Senate passed its version of the Federal Reserve Act. Populists fumed. "When the President signs this act, the invisible government by the money power, proven to exist by the Money Trust investigation, will be legalized," Charles Lindbergh, Sr., declared.[52]

Alternating between four gold pens, Wilson signed the Federal Reserve Act into law shortly after six p.m. on December 23. Warburg was jubilant, even though he viewed the final product of the legislative sausage-making as flawed. In the end, the number of Reserve Banks was capped at twelve, which Warburg viewed as unwieldy but considered a victory when compared with the twenty originally proposed. Despite Warburg's fierce arguments against doing so, the law made Federal Reserve notes—U.S. currency—"obligations of the United States."

"The law, as it has been enacted, contains quite a number of serious defects," Warburg wrote to the president of the Dutch central bank in late December, noting he had "no doubt that it will not last long until this law will gradually have been brought into a satisfactory shape." He added, "A great deal will depend now upon the personnel of the Federal Reserve Board."[53]

In later years, many would claim credit for bringing the Federal Reserve into existence, among them Glass, Owen, and even Samuel Untermyer, who contended that the disclosures of the Pujo Committee probe led to the law's passage.[54] "I really don't know who was the baby's father, but, judging from the number of men who claim the honor, all I can say is that its mother must have been a most immoral woman," Paul Warburg later joked of the Fed's parentage.[55] Though Warburg, too, would eventually assert his own claim of paternity. After Glass penned an aggrandizing memoir that all but erased the Aldrich bill from the Federal Reserve's lineage, Warburg published an eight-hundred-page, two-volume tome on the origins of America's central bank and his role in its creation. One section of the book juxtaposed passages of the Aldrich legislation with the Federal Reserve Act, revealing nearly identical language.

President Wilson recognized Warburg's vital contribution to the banking reform effort when, on April 30, 1914, he formally asked the banker to join the Federal Reserve board.[56] Up until then, many on Wall Street believed Jacob Schiff would chair the board, thanks to an erroneous report that came over the Dow Jones news ticker. "The only offer of the position I have had has come through the newspapers," Schiff told one friend.[57] But according to McAdoo, Schiff did play a part in Warburg's selection. "It was at Mr. Schiff's suggestion that Paul M. Warburg was made a member of the Federal Reserve Board," he recalled.[58] Warburg's name also reached Wilson through other prominent citizens, including Edwin Seligman, who wrote the president on March 10, 1914, emphasizing that it would take a banker of Paul's knowledge and skill to navigate the Federal Reserve Act's "defects" and "utilize the present provisions with effectiveness."[59]

The afternoon after receiving Wilson's offer, Warburg visited Colonel House in New York, his eyes moist as he expressed gratitude for his selection. "I never saw anyone so appreciative as he is," House wrote Wilson later that day.[60] Paul's nomination was a high honor, especially for an immigrant who had only recently become a naturalized citizen. However, accepting the job would require him to resign his partnerships with Kuhn Loeb and M.M. Warburg, step down from various corporate directorships, and relocate to Washington. "It is a great sacrifice for him, for the firm, and the family, and his experiences in this important public position will probably not always give him pleasure," Schiff wrote to Sir Ernest Cassel. "Nevertheless Paul, as a Jew, a foreign-born citizen, and the only Eastern banker nominated, could not possibly shirk this patriotic duty."[61]

Warburg's nomination predictably drew suspicion among the populist element in Congress, who appeared eager to seize the moment to relitigate past controversies involving Kuhn Loeb. "The Banking and Currency Committee desire to have a statement concerning your alleged connection with the Chicago & Alton transaction" and other controversial railroad deals, McAdoo told Warburg that June.[62] The Alton deal—in which Warburg's partners, along with Edward H. Harriman, had been accused of overcapitalizing the railroad and reaping large profits while driving the company into the ground—had taken place before Warburg joined Kuhn Loeb. Warburg explained as much in his reply to McAdoo.[63] Atlee Pomerene, chairman of a Senate committee that oversaw federal appointments, soon wrote to Warburg directly to convey questions posed by an unnamed Senate Banking Committee member. This senator inquired again about the Alton. He asked what Warburg's "views are upon the methods of financing railroads and industrial enterprises" and queried Warburg on his past political donations and whether Kuhn Loeb had ever loaned money to McAdoo or his business associates.[64] It was a fishing expedition, but Warburg grudgingly answered many of the questions. His replies to the committee were promptly leaked to the press.[65]

In early July 1914, the banking committee favorably reported three of his fellow nominees—paving the way for their confirmation—while withholding its seal of approval from Warburg. Soon he received a request to appear for questioning before the panel. On July 3, Warburg asked Wilson to withdraw his name from consideration, citing the "suspicion and doubt" cast upon his nomination.[66] In a telegram four days later, Wilson urged Warburg to reconsider, saying there "can be no bad effect and should be no mortification in your appearing before the Senate committee." The following day a note of encouragement arrived from Carter Glass. "While I appreciate your feeling of disgust at the sort of opposition which you have encountered," the congressman wrote, "I am thoroughly persuaded that it would be a tremendous mistake to surrender to such demagogism."[67]

Warburg relented, and after meeting with members of the banking committee, where "mutual misunderstandings were cleared up," he agreed to testify before the full panel. At the hearing, he pledged not just to cut his ties with Kuhn Loeb and M.M. Warburg and to step down from his corporate directorships, but to ensure he was "above suspicion," to resign from all charitable boards on which he served.

On August 7 the Senate confirmed his appointment. It was that day or the following that Warburg, wearing a somber expression, posed in front of the Treasury with his fellow Federal Reserve appointees. A new epoch in America's financial evolution had begun, but news from abroad overshadowed the momentous occasion. Earlier that summer, a Bosnian-Serb nationalist assassinated Archduke Franz Ferdinand, considered the likely heir to the Austro-Hungarian throne, as his motorcade traveled through Sarajevo, setting ablaze regional tensions. By August, the major European powers were at war. On the day the Senate voted to confirm Warburg, 120,000 British troops deployed to France.

The war would profoundly shape the modern world—culturally, demographically, financially, geographically, psychologically—upending the global order in ways that continue to reverberate through the twenty-first century. For America's German Jews, especially those who had risen to stations of political or financial prominence, the conflict was a traumatic crucible. It divided families and firms. It strained friendships and business alliances. It challenged their very identities as Germans, as Americans, and as Jews.

PART IV

GÖTTERDÄMMERUNG

22

RAMPARTS BETWEEN US

The meeting lasted all Sunday afternoon and through the evening, as the partners of Goldman Sachs planned for a possible crisis when the financial markets reopened on Monday. A day earlier, on August 1, 1914, Germany had declared war against Russia. "A fateful hour has fallen for Germany. . . . The sword has been forced into our hands," Kaiser Wilhelm II told a crowd of fifty thousand people that day from the balcony of his palace in Berlin. Germany soon threw down the gauntlet with France, launching a surprise invasion of Belgium in a bid to capture Paris—and in the process drawing the British into the battle.

Walter Sachs and other members of the firm were vacationing at their summer homes on the New Jersey coast when the hostilities began. They piled into a car that Sunday and drove to New York to convene at the St. Regis Hotel, where Henry Goldman lived at the time in a palatial apartment.[1] The only partner absent was Sam Sachs, who was returning from Europe with his daughter, Ella, aboard the *Mauretania*, part of an exodus of Americans fleeing the war zone. Once at sea, the ocean liner traveled at high speed through dense fog. One day, in the distance, passengers thought they glimpsed the lights of German warships in pursuit. Some would later claim two shots were fired in their direction, though after safely disembarking, Sam dismissed reports of panic aboard, telling a local paper, "It was a very interesting experience all through, and I really enjoyed it."[2]

In Goldman's apartment, the partners combed over a list of maturing contracts involving foreign currency. Through its British partner, Kleinwort Sons, Goldman Sachs provided its American clients with sterling credits. (With London then at the center of the banking universe, such instruments were the primary method of financing international trade.) If exchange rates spiked—and the partners believed they would—the firm and its clients would need to put up additional funds to cover the increase.

"Our clients and we ourselves had large amounts of foreign exchange to cover," Walter Sachs recalled. "These bills of exchange were coming due." On Monday, as the partners feared, the British pound rose sharply.[3] "We had to take a position with our clients that as their maturities came along, they had to buy the pounds to meet their obligations in London," Walter said. The partners anxiously conveyed the news to their customers, unsure how they would react. Two clients objected, but the rest agreed to pay. "It was a remarkable record," Walter recounted—and one that saved Goldman Sachs from steep, if not catastrophic, losses.

But with one disaster averted, another began to materialize. Henry Goldman and Sam Sachs seemed to find themselves at loggerheads on most every issue. So it was with the war. Both were first-generation Americans, but while Sam held little sentimentality for his ancestral homeland, Henry felt a strong kinship to Germany, cultivated during frequent visits to the country that began during his childhood.

From the outset of the war, Sachs, his sons, and his brother Harry, also a partner in the firm, staunchly supported the Allies, a conviction strengthened when reports reached the United States of atrocities committed by German soldiers during their rampage through Belgium. Henry's loyalties, however, remained steadfastly with Germany.

"It's rather difficult to understand at the present time, after the advent and destruction of Hitler's Germany, that a division of opinion could exist in American minds, at the time of the first World War," Walter wrote in his unpublished autobiography. "This was true, however, of a good many people of German origin who admired German culture. Henry Goldman, intense man that he was, was more outspoken than most, and this intensified the rift between him and my father and the other partners."[4]

. . .

The politics of the war similarly, though more evenly, divided the partners of Kuhn Loeb. Felix and Paul Warburg, who would soon leave the firm for his Fed post, reflexively backed Germany, though early in the war Felix at one point felt it necessary to reassure their brother Max of his loyalty, writing in one letter "how ridiculous it is to assume that my sympathies even for a moment can be elsewhere."[5]

A painful period for the Warburgs, the European conflict made communication between the Hamburg and New York branches of the family increasingly difficult; when the United States finally entered the war, the only contact that Felix and Paul had with their mother and siblings came through occasional letters smuggled past government censors.[6] After the war, Paul lamented to Max that "temporarily so many ramparts were erected between us, as only a wayward world can erect."[7] Though Paul became a naturalized U.S. citizen in 1911, "I think he still lived emotionally on two sides of the ocean until 1914," his son James said.[8]

Jacob Schiff had family in Frankfurt and London and nephews fighting on both sides of the conflict. Though a critic of German imperialism, he nevertheless felt a powerful attachment to the country of his birth. His perspective, like those of other American Jews, was also colored by his long-standing animosity toward Russia.

"My sympathies are naturally altogether with Germany, as I would think as little to side against my own country as I would against my own parents," Schiff confided to a friend during the first months of the conflict.[9]

Prior to the war, Schiff often spoke proudly of the "trinity" of his heritage. "I have three nationalities embodied in me," he explained in 1913, during a speech at Cornell University, where he had just donated $100,000 to endow a foundation for the study of German culture. "My strongest nationality is that which I selected for myself, for which I am responsible. First, I am an American, a member of the nation I selected for myself many years ago. Then, my truest attachment is to my religion. I am not a national Jew, for the Jewish nation ceased to exist 900 years ago. But I am a Jew in religion. And I am proud of my German nationality."[10]

On another occasion, before an audience of Jewish communal workers and activists, Schiff similarly declared: "I am divided into three parts. I am an American, I am a German, and I am a Jew." A Zionist agitator named Shmarya Levin rose from the audience and asked Schiff whether he divided himself horizontally or vertically. And if the former, which section belonged to the Jewish people?[11]

The episode was prophetic, for during the war the three parts of Schiff's identity came increasingly into bitter conflict.

Germany declared war as Schiff arrived in Bar Harbor for his regular August sojourn. He raced back to New York, determined to be at his "post" as the "hideous European war"—with all its political and financial unknowns—commenced.[12] August was peak season for well-heeled Americans on extended European holiday. The conflict exploded so quickly that some travelers found themselves stranded amid a mass military mobilization, with trains and passenger ships repurposed for the transport of troops and matériel. Such was the case for Morti and his family, who were vacationing in France when Germany invaded Belgium.

The Schiffs spent eleven anxious days marooned in Aix-les-Bains along with about three hundred other Americans. Finally, the French government arranged for a train to transport the Americans to Paris and from there to the coastal city of Boulogne, where they crossed the English Channel by ferry. Fifty-one hours later Morti and family were safely ensconced at Claridge's, the luxury hotel in London's posh Mayfair neighborhood, where he wrote to his parents of their journey. "France is deserted," he reported. "Practically no men are to be seen as they have all been called to the colours. . . . All the best young men are going and many, I fear, will not come back."[13]

A Francophile, Morti collected medieval French sculptures and illustrated texts. He would later own a home on Paris's Rue de la Tour. Though typically deferential to his father, Morti did not share Jacob's German leanings. "I am frank to say that my sympathies are absolutely on the side of the French and English and that I hope Germany, or rather its rulers, will be taught a good lesson," he wrote home from London.[14] He mused in another letter, "While I, of course, regret that Russia should be on what will probably be the winning side, I think that even we of German descent, must in this instance hope for a thorough chastisement of Germany, who have forced this awful catastrophe upon the world."[15]

Jerome Hanauer, Kuhn Loeb's newest partner, whom Jacob Schiff had taken into the firm as a teenager after Hanauer's father committed suicide, also sympathized with the Allies, as did Otto Kahn.[16] Though born in Mannheim, Kahn was a British subject and faulted Germany's aggressive militarism for starting the conflict. Until shortly before the war, Kahn had been carefully laying the groundwork to relocate to London and run for Parliament. He ultimately abandoned these plans at the last minute, deciding to maintain his lucrative Kuhn Loeb partnership and to officially become a U.S. citizen. But during his flirtation with political office, Kahn had leased a fifteen-acre estate in Regent's Park that now sat mostly idle. During the war, he loaned the rambling property to a charity that cared for soldiers blinded in battle—a shrewd public relations move that earned the financier goodwill both in England and in the United States, where anti-German sentiment was building.

Schiff watched in horror as the conflict escalated and more nations marched to war, drawn into the fight by a tangle of international alliances. "The world will never be the same again," he told friends wearily.[17] In late August, as Japan, a British ally, prepared to declare war on Germany, Schiff exerted what influence he could to keep the Empire out of the battle. "Fearful involvement in conflict may end in bankruptcy," Schiff cabled his friend Takahashi Korekiyo, now Japan's finance minister.[18] Coming from Japan's most important international banker, who had placed hundreds of millions of dollars of the Empire's debt, this may have seemed like more than merely friendly concern. When Japan nevertheless entered the war on the same side as Russia—once their common enemy—Schiff took it as almost a personal betrayal. He registered his outrage by tendering his resignation as a member of the Japan Society, an organization established to promote friendly U.S.-Japanese relations.[19]

In late November 1914, the banker gave a rare interview to *The New York Times* that covered nearly a full page and ran under the headline "Jacob H. Schiff Points a Way to European Peace." He openly declared his "pro-German" allegiance, saying he believed war had been "forced upon Germany against her will," but also remarked that it was "impossible for me to say that I am anti-English." He told the paper he worried about the geopolitical consequences of either side claiming a decisive victory. Should Britain triumph resoundingly, he argued, it would assert its control over Europe and, due to its naval dominance, over the seas, forcing "every nation in the world to . . . do the British bidding." Yet should Germany prevail, he said, the country would likewise become a "menace not only to her immediate neighbors, but to the entire world." The solution, from Schiff's perspective, was a negotiated peace and, afterward, "some means"—on this point, he was vague—to ensure this detente marked "not the ending of this war alone but the ending of all war."[20]

His fence-straddling interview succeeded only in uniting the warring parties in outrage. The London *Globe* decried Schiff's "insidious moderation," while *The Times* of London described his interview as a "brief for Germany."[21] A German paper, meanwhile, commented, "Such peace talk impresses us as entirely frivolous. We are convinced that today no German diplomatist or soldier thinks of making worthless peace with Powers whom we have already totally defeated, and amongst which we confidently hope again to hold the chief place."[22]

"I know very well that on account of what I have said, openly and honorably, I have been bitterly attacked, not only in England and France, but even more so in Germany," Schiff complained to Max Warburg, with whom he frequently swapped political and financial news. "He who attempts the role of peacemaker where passions have been unloosed as they have been in Europe must needs be misunderstood, and must expose himself to vile attacks; nevertheless, I shall continue, with others, to labor unflaggingly in this direction, because I am convinced that that is my duty."[23]

Max complimented Schiff on the *Times* interview, even if he could not fully endorse his friend's reticent position. By now, Max occupied powerful political circles, becoming a trusted adviser to the Kaiser and steering his firm into close partnership with the German Empire by financing its ravenous colonial ambitions in Africa. Germany's bid for influence on the African continent, placing it in fierce competition with England and France, formed some of the smoldering tinder that ignited the European conflagration.

With Germany at war, typical commercial activity largely ceased for Max's firm. More than forty of M.M. Warburg's employees were called to military service, and the firm and its partners were enlisted as virtual adjuncts of the German government.

"Our financial fate was ever more closely linked with the political destiny of Germany," Max later recounted. "The fiction that an individual firm could maintain itself in wartime independent of the economic and political institutions of the Empire was clearly revealed. There was probably no German private banking firm that issued guarantees on behalf of the German Empire to as great an extent as we did. To that degree it is certainly true that we partially co-financed the war."[24]

A fellow Hamburg businessman described Max during the war as a "rock amid the surf," exuding stoicism as the world fell to pieces around him and indefatigably working on behalf of the Fatherland.[25] Chaim Weizmann, the Zionist leader (and later the first president of Israel), assessed Max's German patriotism more unsparingly. He called Max and the banker's close friend Albert Ballin—head of the colossal Hamburg-American shipping line and another vital cog in the German war machine—"the usual type of Kaiser-Juden . . . more German than the Germans, obsequious, superpatriotic, eagerly anticipating the wishes and plans of the masters of Germany."[26]

During the war years, Max straddled a role between financier and statesman. He and his deputy Carl Melchior (the first nonfamily member to attain a partnership in M.M. Warburg) helped to organize a central purchasing agency for the importation of critical food supplies, and they negotiated contracts for war matériel on behalf of the German government. Due to M.M. Warburg's business ties in Scandinavia, the German foreign ministry dispatched Max repeatedly to Sweden in an effort to get the country to budge from its pledged neutrality. (His brother Fritz relocated to Stockholm for much of the war, where he worked closely with the German embassy.)[27] At one point, Max was offered the ambassadorship in Washington, a position he turned down, possibly to shield Paul from uncomfortable questions about his loyalties.[28]

Though the Wilson administration planted itself on the sidelines of the war for nearly three years, the United States from the beginning formed a shadow front of the conflict. Since money greased the gears of war, an early German priority was raising Wall Street capital to finance the purchase of American supplies and fuel a robust U.S. espionage and propaganda operation, which began taking form within weeks of the war's outbreak. Here, too, the German government turned to Max Warburg, who gave initial assurances that he could help secure a $100 million loan via Kuhn Loeb.

In late August 1914, an old friend of Max's named Bernhard Dernburg deployed to New York to conduct secret negotiations with banks considered sympathetic to Germany. Of Jewish descent on his father's side, Dernburg was a heavyset and thick-bearded banker-turned-bureaucrat who had previously served as a cabinet minister overseeing Germany's colonial portfolio. Officially, Dernburg represented the German Red Cross, his job was to raise funds from German Americans for the care of soldiers wounded in battle. But that was a cover for his true mission.

Obtaining financing from American banks, however, proved largely futile, because the Wilson administration had warned Wall Street that it would consider loans to the belligerent countries a violation of U.S. neutrality. The administration, though, did permit U.S. firms to extend short-term credit to the warring nations to avoid a breakdown in international commerce. Far from the $100 million loan Warburg dangled, Dernburg managed to secure from Kuhn Loeb an advance of just $400,000—and under highly unfavorable terms that required the German government to deposit 25 million marks' (equivalent to about $6 million) worth of Treasury bonds with M.M. Warburg in Hamburg.[29] Out of sympathy to his homeland, Jacob Schiff personally made a subscription of 5 million marks (or nearly $1.2 million) to a German war loan.[30]

Flailing in his financial mission, Dernburg took charge of another covert German project: a propaganda campaign aimed at softening American public opinion toward Germany. From a first-floor office at 1153 Broadway—ostensibly, the headquarters of the German Red Cross delegation—he oversaw a small team of German operatives who flooded newspapers with pro-German articles and editorials. Dernburg authored many himself, and he also hit the speaking circuit to flog the German perspective. His "name now appears more frequently in American newspapers than that of any other German alive," one magazine reported.[31]

Working closely with the German ambassador in Washington, Count Johann Heinrich von Bernstorff, Dernburg and other German officials quietly bankrolled a collection of news outlets. One of them was *The Fatherland*, a nakedly pro-German weekly headquartered a floor above Dernburg's propaganda shop and edited by George Sylvester Viereck, who would later reprise his role as Germany's American press agent on behalf of the Nazis.

Badly losing the public opinion battle, the Germans took desperate measures to sway American minds, secretly arranging the purchase of the *New York Evening Mail* (which remained under German control until 1917). Bernstorff even came close to orchestrating the acquisition of the *New York Sun* and *The Washington Post*.[32]

Especially early in the war, Schiff and the Warburg brothers interacted regularly with Bernstorff and Dernburg, as well as with other German officials and emissaries. In Washington, Paul and Nina socialized frequently with the German ambassador and his American-born wife. Dernburg occasionally dropped by Kuhn Loeb's offices, and Felix routinely updated Max on the German official's activities.[33] Dernburg "has certainly made an impression, although the audience here, which is really getting the best reports from all sides . . . gets a little propaganda-tired," he reported in one missive.[34] In another, Felix wrote of hosting Dernburg at his Westchester estate on a weekend that Paul and Nina, who had their own house on the rambling property, were visiting from Washington. "He continues to work with great vigor and has attained a collection of money that is quite astonishing," Felix informed Max, referring to Dernburg's fundraising under the banner of the German Red Cross.[35] (These funds, while eventually credited to the Red Cross in Germany, were first deposited into accounts controlled by Bernstorff and a German financial attaché named Heinrich Albert, who served as the paymaster for Germany's covert operations in America. Contributions to Dernburg's Red Cross campaign were in fact helping to finance propaganda efforts.)[36]

Though Kuhn Loeb declined to help Dernburg in his financial mission, at least to the extent he desired, there is evidence to suggest that before the United States entered the war, the firm and its pro-German partners assisted Dernburg in other ways, including by serving as an intermediary for coded messages that passed between Dernburg and the German foreign office. In one of its first acts of war, England had moved swiftly to isolate Germany by severing the undersea cables linking it to North America. This forced Dernburg to devise more creative means to communicate with his government. A top-secret memo, dated two weeks after the start of the war, explained the system he established. Secret messages from Dernburg in New York were routed to an M.M. Warburg representative in Amsterdam, who in turn sent them to Max in Hamburg. Max then forwarded these communiqués to Berlin. The memo listed Kuhn Loeb as one of the "transmitters" in this communications chain.[37] In at least one case, Felix forwarded a message to Dernburg that was concealed within correspondence from Max's wife, Alice.[38]

Felix's association with Dernburg stirred some controversy in late 1914, when he invited the German official to be the guest of honor at a dinner held by the Young Men's Hebrew Association. "Dr. Dernburg is de facto, and I believe also de jure, an official representative of the German government, charged with the mission of presenting before the American public the German case in the war quarrel," a New York rabbi named David de Sola Pool wrote Felix disapprovingly. "The invitation to any such man would be an invasion of our neutrality. As Americans, and especially as American Jews, it is of world wide importance that we preserve our neutrality free from all suspicion."[39] Louis Marshall appealed directly to Schiff, asking the banker to speak with his son-in-law over the Dernburg invitation.[40]

That same day Felix told Dernburg the dinner was off, writing, "I am so sorry that young people will not have the advantage of listening to you."[41]

The British ambassador to the United States, Cecil Spring Rice, eyed Dernburg warily, suspicious of his ties to leading Jewish bankers, especially Schiff and Kuhn Loeb. "Dernburg and his crew are continually at work, and the German Jewish Bankers are toiling in a solid phalanx to compass our destruction. One by one they are getting hold of the principal New York papers," he complained to a fellow diplomat, going on to float a false rumor that Schiff—"the arch-Jew and special protege of the Emperor"—had "practically acquired" *The New York Times*. The German-Jewish cabal, Spring Rice claimed, extended to Washington, where Paul Warburg "practically controls the financial policy of the Administration." Dealing with Warburg, he wrote, was "exactly like negotiating with Germany."[42]

Antisemitic canards polluted Spring Rice's appraisal, but there was no question that Germany was expending considerable energy to manipulate American-Jewish public opinion, particularly by trying to exploit a collective disdain for Russia. In September 1914 a trio of Zionists arrived in New York to spearhead this branch of the influence operation, their mission "to spread a favorable opinion of Germany in the Jewish press of North America and in financial circles," according to a memo that circulated to a senior official in the German foreign office.[43] The leader of this delegation was Isaac Strauss, who hailed from a Munich banking family. "Gossip clothed him with romance and mystery," one acquaintance recalled. "He was reported to be a German magnate of some sort, as one might well have believed, seeing his lavish spending. An attractive gentleman he was, and one who soon endeared himself to every Zionist in New York, for he himself was a most ardent one."[44] Strauss's companions were Arthur Meyerowitz, an employee of Albert Ballin's North German Lloyd steamship line (which provided cover to German agents operating in America), and Samuel Melamed, a Russian-born journalist.

By mid-October, Strauss reported to Heinrich Albert, the German financial attaché, that "the manipulation of the Jewish press in America, formerly casual, has now been changed by me into a regularly systematic information service and organized on a firm basis."[45] During the years Strauss operated in the United States, Albert provided him with a hefty budget of as much as $5 million to bankroll his work. Some of these funds were likely used to make secret investments in Jewish publications, possibly including *Der Tog* (The Day), an influential Yiddish daily newspaper formed during the fall of 1914 under the editorship of the Jewish journalist Herman Bernstein. In one missive to Bernstein, Strauss referred to *Der Tog* as "our paper."[46] Later, Strauss formed his own weekly magazine called *The American Jewish Chronicle*. Edited by Melamed, the periodical was a frequent source of Zionist agitprop.

During the early months of his American propaganda work, Strauss outlined his strategy in a lengthy memo, in which he explained:

> The influence for the German cause among the Jews of America has to begin from a separate position for the emigrated Eastern Jews and the "German" Jews. The first have an extensive press which alone in New York has a circulation of about a million as well as numerous periodicals of all kinds. This press is for the most part in Yiddish . . . and is even in the Hebrew language. Due to the high level of education among the Eastern Jews, the press reaches even the poorest people and has a great influence. The "German" Jews also have a number of periodical magazines that appear in English but in general it can be said the influence of the press in their circles is not very high due to the differentiated individual interests for the higher classes, and their closer ties with the American environment. . . . In order to influence Eastern Jewry the primary focus would be on the press, and in order to influence the "German" Jews one would prefer a more personal contact with individual influential persons and organizations.[47]

No man possessed more clout with American Jews than Jacob Schiff. And Strauss and Meyerowitz—who arrived in the United States bearing a letter of introduction from Jacob's older brother, Philipp—wasted no time making inroads with the financier. "After several conferences that we had with Mr. Schiff," Strauss reported, the banker agreed to arrange an audience for him with the leaders of the American Jewish Committee, who assembled on October 8, 1914, at Kuhn Loeb's offices. Once the floor was his, Strauss recalled, "I pointed out that the war had created entirely new conditions under which the Jewish question had now to be considered." He told Schiff and the other AJC members that "in Germany there is the firm intention since the beginning of the war to solve a large number of historic social wrongs," and he said the German government now gave "highest priority" to Jewish equality, both within its borders and in Russian-held territory to the east, in what is present-day Poland, which Germany hoped to conquer. The essence of his message: supporting Germany was supporting the cause of Jewish human rights.

Shortly after this meeting, Schiff penned a long letter to Arthur Zimmermann, the German foreign secretary (and the author of an infamous 1917 telegram proposing a German alliance with Mexico if the United States entered the war). Strauss and Meyerowitz, Schiff wrote, "have explained to me that their coming here is intended to awaken the full sympathy of the German Jews for Germany, by pointing out what Germany has become for its own citizens of Jewish faith."[48]

Schiff noted that while, legally speaking, Jews possessed equal rights in Germany, in practice they remained an underclass, denied civil service jobs, professorships, judicial appointments, and high-ranking military positions. And he emphasized the divided nature of American-Jewish public opinion on the war. True, many Russian-born Jews supported Germany. But, he added, "a great number of Jews, especially those born in this country, whose parents came here from Germany many years ago, do not share this sympathy, because members of this younger generation, very much convinced of their human dignity, cannot forget that Germany has been the breeding ground of anti-Semitism and that this irresponsible movement has spread out further from Germany." It would not be enough to appoint a few token Jews to academic, government, or military posts. American Jews, Schiff wrote, would need to be convinced that "the harm which anti-Semitism has wrought will first of all be completely banned and, in the course of time, the virus which in this connection has gone into the blood of the German people will be completely eradicated."[49]

Throughout the fall of 1914, Strauss courted Schiff and his influential friends. And he could point to at least one instance in which he had persuaded Schiff to take action to aid the German cause. U.S. arms sales to the European belligerents had become a source of fierce public and congressional debate, with some lawmakers floating legislation to ban American munitions manufacturers from doing business with the warring parties. The Germans highly favored the U.S. government extending its neutrality to weapons exports, because, due to a suffocating naval blockade imposed by the British, the Allies were the primary importers of American weaponry. Strauss approached Schiff to ask him to contact President Wilson on the subject. "Con-

sidering the prominent importance of Mr. Schiff in American economic life, I believed that I could assume that his private influence
at this point would not remain without attention," Strauss told the
German foreign office.[50]

In mid-November, Schiff penned a letter urging Wilson to ban
weapons exports to Europe, arguing that America's role in furnishing the arms fueling the conflict was "immoral and obnoxious to a
large majority of our people."[51] Strauss reported to Berlin that he had
helped craft Schiff's letter to the president.

Schiff's appeal received special attention from Wilson, as Strauss
predicted. The president wrestled with the issue for more than two
weeks, before finally replying that he would not intervene: "The
precedents of international law are so clear, the sales proceed from
so many sources, and my lack of power is so evident, that I have felt
that I could do nothing else than leave the matter to settle itself."[52]

Strauss's relationship with Schiff frayed as the war progressed—
and as the German agent immersed himself in the unruly world of
Jewish communal politics, where the old squabbles and rivalries
raged with new intensity on account of the conflict, its unprecedented
demands, and the existential questions it posed for world Jewry.

For the Jews of Eastern Europe and their American stewards, the war
sparked a crisis within a crisis. The eastern theater of combat was the
backyard of millions of Jews, who lived in the borderlands between
the warring empires of Austria, Germany, and Russia. Their suffering, already profound, worsened as the advancing armies displaced
and dispossessed hundreds of thousands of people.

Less than a month into the war, in late August 1914, Schiff
received the first of what would become a constant stream of appeals
for aid from every corner of the war zone. It came not on behalf
of the Jews of Eastern Europe, but those living in Palestine, home
to about sixty thousand Jewish settlers who were largely reliant on
foreign aid and imports—and who suddenly found themselves cut
off from the Western world. The cable, sent by the newly appointed
ambassador to Turkey, Henry Morgenthau, Sr., read in part:

PALESTINIAN JEWS FACING TERRIBLE CRISIS BELLIGER-
ENT COUNTRIES STOPPING THEIR ASSISTANCE SERIOUS
DESTRUCTION THREATENS THRIVING COLONIES FIFTY
THOUSAND DOLLARS NEEDED[53]

Schiff and his allies marshaled the funds within forty-eight hours, with the American Jewish Committee kicking in $25,000, Schiff contributing $12,500, and the remainder coming from the Provisional Executive Committee for General Zionist Affairs, chaired by the "people's lawyer" and future Supreme Court justice Louis Brandeis.[54] The logistics of getting the money to Palestine proved trickier. Morgenthau enlisted Standard Oil, which had a presence in Turkey. The relief funds raised in the United States were directed to the oil company's New York office, and Standard's representatives in Constantinople (now Istanbul) in turn paid over $50,000 in gold to Morgenthau. Toting a loaded revolver, the ambassador's son-in-law, the banker Maurice Wertheim, personally escorted the gold to Palestine.[55]

By the fall of 1914, American-Jewish organizations had begun actively fundraising for war relief along factional lines. A group of Orthodox congregations established the Central Committee for the Relief of Jews Suffering Through the War. American Zionists organized their own aid efforts, largely focused on Palestine. As the enormity of the humanitarian crisis became clear, Schiff pushed for a coordinated response, bringing together the often-feuding camps.

On Sunday, October 25, at the invitation of the American Jewish Committee, delegates representing more than forty organizations convened at Temple Emanu-El. "All differences should be laid aside and forgotten," the letter announcing the meeting stated. "Nothing counts now but harmonious and effective action."[56]

This confab eventually led to the formation of a Joint Distribution Committee to coordinate relief work across the main troika of Jewish interests—the American Jewish Relief Committee led by Schiff and his allies; the Orthodox community's Central Committee; and the People's Relief Committee, representing labor, socialist, and Zionist elements.

Felix Warburg was appointed to chair the JDC, a position he held for the next eighteen years. His bonhomie and organizational prowess made him well suited for the taxing role. Brothers Arthur and Herbert Lehman served in the group's leadership. Almost as fast as donations entered the Joint's coffers, the money flowed to local Jewish groups provisioning aid throughout the expanding war zone. Within a few short years, the Joint raised and spent $15 million, maturing into a sprawling and well-oiled humanitarian aid operation.

Behind the veneer of unity, battles raged between the various orbits represented by the Joint. The rivalry was particularly fierce between the monied German Jews, led by Schiff, and the ascendant Zionists, represented by Louis Brandeis. When, in 1916, Wilson appointed Brandeis to the Supreme Court, rumors circulated that Schiff had spitefully attempted to torpedo the nomination. The gossip grew so loud that Schiff wrote to Brandeis disclaiming any role in opposing his appointment.[57]

A flashpoint between the Schiff and Brandeis camps came over the timeworn question of who spoke for America's Jews. The American Jewish Committee had tried to claim that mantle, but the war renewed old calls, now championed by the Zionist and socialist contingents, for an American Jewish Congress, elected by the nation's Jews, to fill that role. The idea horrified Schiff for the same reason he recoiled at Zionism—it seemed to lend credence to the "nation within a nation" charge at the poisonous root of antisemitism. "The holding of a Jewish Congress means nothing less than a decision in the affirmative, that we are Jews first, and Americans second," Schiff fumed.[58]

When it became clear that calls for a Congress could not be stifled, Schiff and fellow American Jewish Committee members grudgingly participated, in a bid to exert a moderating influence. Instead of a permanent governing body, they succeeded in ensuring that the resulting organization had the limited mandate to consider "the Jewish question as it affects our brethren in belligerent lands."[59]

Schiff's opposition to Zionism and the creation of an American Jewish Congress made him a target of an ongoing fusillade of criticism from Jewish activists and newspapers. His enemies made particular hay out of his comments during a 1916 speech in which he spoke out against Jewish nationalism and appeared to fault Russian Jews for provoking the persecution against them by holding themselves apart.[60]

A little over a week later, after facing days of attacks in the Yiddish press, Schiff addressed his detractors at the seventh annual convention of the Kehillah. His voice trembled, and he held back tears as he spoke. "Now, just think, to accuse me of such a crime," he said. "Think of it! I, who have for twenty-five years single-handed struggled against the invasion of the Russian Government into American money markets, and to this day stave them off. Think of it! Who, as I, have been foremost in the past for agitation and insisted to the President of the United States—as some of you must know—that our treaty with Russia must be abrogated."

"I have been hurt to the core," he declared finally, "and hereafter Zionism, nationalism, the Congress movement and Jewish politics in whatever form they may come up will be a sealed book to me."[61]

One of Schiff's chief antagonists was Isaac Strauss, the German operative who had aligned himself firmly with the Zionists. Strauss's *American Jewish Chronicle* often lobbed grenades at Schiff, while also sharply critiquing the work of Felix Warburg and the Joint. "We find that the attitude of men of Mr. Schiff's type is lacking in one fundamental thing: These men are entirely out of touch with the actual life of the Jewish people. . . . Nevertheless they persist in applying their own conception of Judaism to Jewry at large," read one characteristic barb in Strauss's journal.[62]

Strauss's broadsides infuriated Schiff and Warburg, since the German government was effectively subsidizing a smear campaign against them and, through Strauss, stirring up dissension at the very moment they were striving for Jewish unity. Schiff told Ambassador Bernstorff that he felt personally insulted by Strauss's activities in the United States.[63]

Felix, meanwhile, griped to Max, "The Zionist people here have caused the greatest disturbance," identifying Strauss as "one of the main liars and agitators." He fumed that Strauss was operating a "hate paper"—presumably *The American Jewish Chronicle*—"at German expense."[64]

Max reported Felix's concerns to his government contacts. "As you will see, a 'palace revolution' has broken out over there which I have foreseen for some time and I have to admit we are not completely innocent regarding this development," he wrote to Arthur Zimmermann, requesting that the foreign secretary instruct Bernstorff to cut off support to Strauss.[65] Nevertheless, Strauss remained on the payroll of the Reich—that is, until he was arrested in 1918 by military investigators, who accused him of operating a Brooklyn chemical company that illegally stockpiled the components of high explosives and of obtaining under false pretenses the formula for the gas masks issued to U.S. troops, intending to pass this information to Berlin.[66] Branded a "dangerous enemy alien," Strauss spent the remainder of the war interned with other suspected German agents, including his fellow propagandist Arthur Meyerowitz, at Georgia's Camp Oglethorpe.[67]

.   .   .

While Schiff and his milieu clashed with the Zionists, the once-distant battlefields of the European war crept unmistakably closer to America, and, for the Wilson administration, maintaining neutrality became an increasingly tricky tightrope walk. In the first months of 1915, Germany began waging its campaign of unrestricted submarine warfare, challenging England's command over the seas by mastering the ocean depths with its submarine fleet.

On the afternoon of May 7, 1915, Ambassador Bernstorff was traveling by train from Washington to New York, where he planned to attend a performance of the operetta *Die Fledermaus* (The Bat) benefiting the German Red Cross. Bernstorff was accompanied by Paul Warburg. During a stopover in Philadelphia, the ambassador bought a copy of the evening paper. Stunned, he read the front-page news to Warburg: earlier that day a German submarine had torpedoed the *Lusitania*, sister ship of the *Mauretania* and the jewel of the Cunard Line's fleet.

Carrying nearly two thousand passengers and crew, the British steamer was completing a weeklong voyage from New York to Liverpool when the U-boat attacked it eleven miles off the southern coast of Ireland, in a swath of the Atlantic where the Germans had declared open season on military and merchant ships alike. The ocean swallowed the 787-foot vessel in less than twenty minutes.

It couldn't be true, Warburg protested. But when he and Bernstorff disembarked in New York, they found Jacob Schiff waiting for them. He was so alarmed by the news, he had rushed to the station to meet their train.

The attack, in which 124 U.S. citizens were among the twelve hundred dead, had a profound psychological impact on the American public. "The *Lusitania* incident first brought home to the United States the horrors of war, and convinced all her people that a flagrant injury had been done them," Bernstorff recalled in his memoir.[68]

The sinking of the *Lusitania* rattled Schiff, marking the beginning of his disillusionment with Germany. The day after, as bodies were still being hauled ashore in the Irish seaport of Queenstown (later Cobh), Schiff paid an unannounced visit to the offices of J.P. Morgan & Co. It was a Saturday, when the pious banker would typically be found in the pews of Temple Emanu-El intoning his Shabbat devotionals, but the news had shaken him so thoroughly that he set aside his routine and went downtown to find Jack Morgan.

The month after Pierpont's death, the firm's old building at 23

Wall Street was demolished to make way for a new Trowbridge and Livingston–designed headquarters, a squat, triangular edifice requiring so much Tennessee marble that the partners at J.P. Morgan purchased a quarry to ensure a ready supply. The imposing, unmarked doors of the Corner, as the iconic building was known, opened to the intersection of Wall and Grand streets. Encased in the building's cornerstone was a copper box that contained the firm's partnership articles, Pierpont's will, and a copy of the late banker's testimony before the Pujo Committee.[69]

Schiff located Jack Morgan in the wood-paneled partners' room. Jack was tall and broad like his father. He was also an anglophile who owned an estate in the English countryside. J.P. Morgan & Co. had partnerships in London and Paris—Morgan Grenfell and Morgan Harjes, respectively—and, from the war's very first bombardment, the firm closely aligned with the Allies, even stepping into the role of purchasing agents for the British and French governments.

Jack shared his father's suspicion of Jewish bankers, and the pro-German leanings of Schiff and other Jews in Wall Street circles contributed to his antisemitic beliefs. He told one of his partners that he blamed the "German Jew element, which is very close to the German Ambassador," for fomenting the peace movement and thwarting the United States from picking a side in the conflict.[70]

The strained relationship between Kuhn Loeb and J.P. Morgan & Co. dated back to their tussle over the Northern Pacific, yet the firms still partnered on large bond offerings. For the sake of their joint business, Jack had to maintain genial relations with Schiff, as his father had. And it was for this same reason that Schiff, keenly aware of Morgan's allegiances, visited his counterpart to personally express his dismay over the tragedy and condemn Germany for "this most unfortunate outrage."

But Schiff's words of sympathy, spoken in his thick German accent, stirred Morgan's anger, and his mask of collegiality momentarily slipped. Morgan turned his back to Schiff, refusing to speak with him. Once Schiff departed, noticeably deflated, Morgan regained his composure. "I suppose that I went a little far," he remarked to one of his partners, Dwight Morrow, who had watched the encounter in stunned silence. "I suppose I ought to apologize." Morrow scrawled a verse from Ezekiel on a piece of paper and handed it to Morgan: "Not for thy sake, but for thy name's sake, O House of Israel!" Morgan retrieved his hat and took off after Schiff.[71]

Relations were smoothed over, but the episode highlighted how

Kuhn Loeb's association with Germany was becoming a liability. For J.P. Morgan & Co. and other blue-blooded investment houses, the war was a bonanza. But Schiff's insistence on neutrality meant his firm was forgoing lucrative business opportunities. Long neck and neck with J.P. Morgan in terms of prestige, Kuhn Loeb was now falling behind, at risk of losing its status as a first-class investment bank.

Schiff recognized that the tide had turned. Strolling through Bar Harbor one summer during the war, he was conversing with Frieda in German, as he typically did. "Father, we can't do this anymore," she said, suddenly self-conscious.[72] Schiff's Cornell endowment, promoting German culture, now seemed comically ill timed. At his suggestion, the university broadened its focus to the study of "human civilization."[73] The already publicity-shy financier tried to maintain an even lower profile, trading his box at the Metropolitan Opera for less conspicuous orchestra seats. "When I asked him if he enjoyed the opera as well from those seats as he had from his accustomed place," one friend remembered, "he replied that it was not a question of enjoyment but rather that in the dreadful times through which we were then passing, it was better that we should all be as unseen as circumstances would permit."[74]

This wasn't as evident to Bernhard Dernburg, the German propaganda chief, who instead of lying low (as was Bernstorff's strategy) gave an inflammatory speech arguing that the *Lusitania* had all but brought the attack on itself by transporting munitions. Schiff wrote to Dernburg, enclosing a letter he had received from a friend begging him to intercede. "Perhaps you can say to Dr. Dernburg: 'Keep quiet. Do not express *any* opinions. Do not talk to the newspapermen. Say absolutely nothing.' He can think as hard as he likes, but he should not talk."[75]

A German operative working in the United States complained that Dernburg was an "imbecile" whose propaganda work had harmed the German cause.[76] Dernburg's comments provoked such an uproar that Bernstorff advised him to return to Germany at once. The day before he sailed that June, Dernburg held court at the German Club on Central Park South. Schiff, perhaps relieved by Dernburg's departure, dropped by to bid him and his wife farewell.[77]

Heinrich Albert, the punctilious German financial attaché, took over Dernburg's portfolio. Within two months he had caused a stunning diplomatic debacle of his own.

.   .   .

On the afternoon of July 24, 1915, Heinrich Albert and George Viereck, publisher of *The Fatherland*, were riding the Sixth Avenue elevated train line uptown, oblivious to the two Secret Service agents shadowing them. Viereck disembarked at 23rd Street, and one of the operatives followed him off the train. The other, an agent named Frank Burke, who headed a Secret Service counterintelligence unit tracking suspected German spies, kept watch over Albert, who was seated beside a bulging leather briefcase. Albert was so engrossed in a book that he nearly missed his stop at 50th Street. He leaped up and hurried off the train; he was on the platform before he realized he'd left his briefcase inside.

Thinking quickly, Burke swiped the bag and slipped out another train exit, concealing the valise beneath his jacket as he rushed out of the station and hopped onto the running board of a passing trolley. Glancing behind him, he could see Albert in the street frantically scanning passersby.[78] A few days later an ad appeared in the *New York Evening Telegram*: "Lost on Saturday. On 3:30 Harlem Elevated Train, at 50th St. Station, Brown Leather Bag Containing Documents." Albert offered a twenty-dollar reward for the return of the bag, a measly price considering the invaluable records it contained, providing a road map of German covert operations in the United States by way of the financial attaché's meticulous bookkeeping.

The Wilson administration shared some of Albert's documents with the *New York World*, which published a series of exposés revealing a wide range of German subterfuge and sabotage aimed at disrupting the production and shipment of arms to the Allies. Coming after the torpedoing of the *Lusitania*, the revelations further hardened American public opinion against Germany.

Among the operations that Albert's files revealed were those orchestrated by one of the most prolific German saboteurs operating in the United States—Franz von Rintelen, Walter Sachs's old officemate at the Direction der Disconto-Gesellschaft in Berlin. Debonair and handsome, with pale blue eyes and sandy hair that he combed straight back, Rintelen spoke English with barely a trace of an accent. He received his banking training in London and New York, where he had apprenticed at Goldman Sachs. According to one account, Rintelen also worked for Kuhn Loeb.[79]

A naval reserve officer, Captain Rintelen was called to active duty at the start of the war, and in the first months of the conflict he put his banking expertise to use by arranging the (often complicated) transactions required to supply the far-flung German fleet. "My work in providing money for our cruisers abroad had gradually earned me the reputation of a man who knew his way about the world in the matter of financial transactions," Rintelen recounted in his memoir, *Dark Invader.* "I knew America, had numerous connections there . . . and the authorities became convinced that I was the man to go to the United States and take action against the shipment of munitions."

"*Ich kaufe, was ich kann; alles andere schlage ich kaput!*" the brash officer told his superiors before departing for America. "I'll buy up what I can and blow up what I can't."[80] He arrived in New York in early April 1915, traveling under a counterfeit Swiss passport in the name of Emile Victor Gaché, one of a handful of aliases he adopted during his U.S. mission. He quickly set about doing as he told his higher-ups he would, managing to stir up considerable havoc during his brief stay in the United States.

With Heinrich Albert, he set up the Bridgeport Projectile Company, a front operation that existed for the sole purpose of buying up mass quantities of gunpowder and shell casings to tie up munitions production. And Rintelen poured nearly $400,000 into the creation of an organization called Labor's National Peace Council, which he used to stoke unrest among munitions plant workers and longshoremen in a bid to cause strikes that would delay arms shipments. His network of operatives also planted incendiary devices known as pencil bombs in the cargo holds of ships transporting weapons to England and France, with the goal of causing fires on these vessels. Meanwhile the German agent was plotting with Victoriano Huerta, the exiled former president of Mexico, who agreed to launch a war against the United States in exchange for German assistance in restoring him to power.

One day, amid Rintelen's sabotage campaign, Walter Sachs spotted his former colleague at the Bankers Club, where both men were having lunch. Walter, unaware of Rintelen's covert mission in the United States, tried to make eye contact with him from across the room, but the German didn't seem to notice him.

Finally, Sachs strolled over. "Aren't you Franz Rintelen?" he asked.

"Oh yes, how are you?" Rintelen said, jumping up from his chair.

"I didn't know you were over here," Walter said. "I hope you'll come in to see us, see my father, he'll be delighted to see you."

Rintelen agreed to drop by Goldman Sachs's offices.

Soon Walter would learn the truth about why Rintelen was back in New York, when in early December 1915 newspapers reported that the German spy was apprehended by the British government as he attempted to return to Berlin. The Germans disavowed him, claiming he was just a purchasing agent who had gone rogue. Rintelen was later extradited to the United States, where he spent nearly three years in a federal penitentiary.

Shortly after his release in 1920, Rintelen showed up at Goldman Sachs looking for Walter. Pale and rail thin, the German was a ghost of the regal man Walter once knew.

"Mr. Sachs, I want to get back to Europe," Rintelen explained. "You won't believe this, but I need three hundred dollars to get back."

Despite Rintelen's past, Walter didn't hesitate to aid his old acquaintance. "Certainly," Walter replied. After reaching Germany, Rintelen repaid the loan. Walter never heard from him again.[81]

23

ALLIES

On the morning of September 10, 1915, Jack Morgan and his partner Henry Davison waited at a downtown pier for the *Lapland*, which had sailed from Southampton, to disgorge its most important cargo—a six-member contingent of British and French officials who had come to New York seeking to raise a half-billion-dollar loan.

The Wilson administration's policy of strict neutrality by now had started to crumble. Under pressure from his State and Treasury secretaries, Wilson lifted his moratorium on American banks making loans to the combatants, convinced that the nation risked a financial calamity if the Allies could not raise American capital to cover their expenditures on U.S. exports.

The travel plans of the Anglo-French Financial Commission were a closely guarded secret, and a pair of British destroyers escorted the ship through the war zone to ward off a possible German attack.[1] Packed away in his trunk, the head of this delegation, Lord Reading, chief justice of England, carried the inflatable waistcoat his wife had foisted on him before he sailed.[2]

Rufus Isaacs, as the British official was known before his elevation to the peerage, was the son of a successful fruit importer who had rapidly ascended to the heights of the British political class, his rise all the more impressive because his Jewish faith seemed to pose no obstacle.

Morgan squired Reading and his fellow commissioners to his late father's library uptown, where he had assembled some of the nation's top bankers, who stood ready to commence the loan negotiations. Absent from the talks were representatives of Kuhn Loeb, typically at the table for any deal of this magnitude, who were excluded due to the firm's perceived pro-German bias. Jacob Schiff nevertheless contacted Reading shortly after his arrival, offering him a seat in the Schiff family pew at Temple Emanu-El during upcoming Yom Kippur services. Schiff made no mention of the loan negotiations but wrote, "I shall be much gratified to meet you during your visit to our country."[3]

The Minnesota railroad magnate James J. Hill was working closely with the Morgan syndicate and attempted to bring his old friend into the fold on the massive transaction, visiting Schiff at Kuhn Loeb's offices on September 14 to discuss participating in the deal. Conflicting rumors spread on Wall Street, one version holding that Kuhn Loeb would welcome the opportunity to join the Allied loan syndicate, the other stating that the firm would refuse an offer to participate.[4]

On Friday, September 17, Otto Kahn met confidentially with Reading, who wanted to sound him out privately on whether Kuhn Loeb would join the loan syndicate before making a formal invitation that might cause embarrassment to both parties if it were rebuffed.

"You mean on an absolute parity with Morgans?" Kahn asked.

"Yes, I so take it," Reading replied.

"And that position of parity with Morgans would apply to future Anglo-French transactions?"

"I feel sure that can be arranged."[5]

Kahn was ready to enter the deal then and there. Not only would the business be lucrative, but along with Morti, he wanted nothing more than to remove the pro-German stain from Kuhn Loeb's reputation by playing a high-profile role in the Allied financing. But there was a problem, he explained to Reading: Kuhn Loeb's senior partner. Even if Jacob Schiff could be persuaded to finance Britian and France, it was unlikely he would support any transaction that would benefit their ally, Russia.

Kahn returned to his office, where he briefed his partners. Schiff seemed distressed by Reading's offer, and according to Kahn, he said, "Let us all consider the matter for twenty-four hours and reach a conclusion at a partners' conference tomorrow."[6] It seems unlikely that this meeting was held the following day, which was Yom Kippur,

the Jewish Day of Atonement. But the partners did convene sometime between then and Monday to thrash out the loan question.

When they met, Schiff opened the discussion with a grave pro-
nouncement: "Before asking your opinions, I want to tell you that my
mind is made up, unalterably," he said.

> I realize fully what is at stake for the firm of Kuhn, Loeb &
> Co. in the decision we are going to make. But come what may
> I cannot run contrary to my conscience; I cannot sacrifice
> my profoundest convictions for the sake of whatever business
> advantage; I cannot stultify myself by aiding those, who in
> bitter enmity, have tortured my people and will continue to
> do so whatever fine professions they may make in their hour
> of need. I ought not to be asked to do so. It is not fair to put
> me in this dilemma.

Schiff said that there was one condition under which he would consider participating in the Allied loan: if the Anglo-French commission stated in writing that "not one cent of the proceeds of the loan
will be given to Russia." If the other partners disagreed with him and
wanted to proceed without preconditions, Schiff said, "I shall, in that
case, withdraw from the firm."[7]

After Schiff's dramatic speech, there was little point in further
discussion. On Monday morning, Kahn and Morti Schiff visited
Reading to lay out Kuhn Loeb's position—that is, Schiff's. According to a memo of their conversation, initialed by both partners and
dated that same day, they included an additional stipulation when
they outlined their terms. For the firm to participate in the transaction, not only would the commission have to formally guarantee that
none of the proceeds would flow to Russia but also that the money
would not be used for the direct purchase of "death-dealing instruments of warfare." As they undoubtedly knew before carrying this
proposition to Reading, the loan commission could not accede to
these demands. Though these talks were supposed to be confidential,
word that Kuhn Loeb would not take part in the Allied financing
leaked almost immediately, resulting in headlines such as this one in
Philadelphia's *Evening Public Ledger* the following day: "Kuhn Loeb
& Co., Pro-German Bankers, May Not Aid in Loan."[8]

In a dispatch to Berlin, the German consul general in New York,
Erich Hossenfelder, noted that he had worked behind the scenes

to keep Kuhn Loeb out of the deal. "When the negotiations began and in the knowledge that it would be of great importance if the bank Kuhn Loeb would refuse to support the loan, I have tried to take an influence on Schiff," Hossenfelder wrote. At his direction, the German official noted, "Schiff was approached by Jewish religious representatives"—Hossenfelder didn't specify whom. He also implied he had played a role in stirring up a Jewish protest against the loan.[9]

Newspapers reported that Morti Schiff and Otto Kahn had personally subscribed to the Allied loan in a show of solidarity with England and France. Certainly, Kahn and Schiff did nothing to dispel these rumors. But Paul Warburg told Ambassador Bernstorff they weren't true. "I was assured by my dear friend Paul Warburg that such a signature had never happened," Bernstorff reported to Theobald von Bethmann-Hollweg, the chancellor of the German Empire. "And Mr. Max Warburg is said to have been informed by Otto Kahn. But neither Mr. Kahn nor Mr. Mortimer Schiff had the courage to repudiate that they had signed such a loan. Such behavior would discredit them with Mr. Morgan and his people."[10]

Bernstorff complained of an increasingly hostile climate in the United States—the newspapers were fiercely anti-German, and his activities and those of his associates were closely monitored by American operatives. (Unbeknownst to Bernstorff, military intelligence officials had tapped the phones at the German embassy and were listening in on his calls.) "Detectives and agents provocateurs are always on the qui vive. The same terror is exerted against anyone who is on friendly terms with us, so it's often not easy for our friends to remain faithful to us." He raised Kuhn Loeb as a prime example of a fair-weather friend. "Regardless of the efforts of their German relatives, none of the partners had the courage to openly declare that they wanted to have nothing to do with a loan hostile to us."[11] In a frustrated missive of his own, Heinrich Albert described Kuhn Loeb as an "unreliable" partner that in the past had "let us down" with "unusual and unnecessary ruthlessness."[12]

While Kuhn Loeb's apparent willingness to finance the Allies—if not for the Russia sticking point—angered German officials, the British also looked askance at the firm's decision to forgo this vital transaction. It fell to Otto Kahn to explain his firm's tortured position to his British friends. "The controlling consideration consisted not in Mr. Jacob H. Schiff's pro-German leanings, which are by no means pronounced and have become steadily weaker as the real spirit of the

German ruling classes became manifested in the conduct of the war and in various incidents, but in the circumstances that he can only see Russia in this war, and in her he can see only the ruthless oppression of his coreligionists, responsible for the blood of many thousands of innocent Jews," Kahn confided to Sir Max Aitken, the egomaniacal British press baron and politician later known as Lord Beaverbrook. (In a strange twist of fate, Beaverbrook would later carry on a brief affair with Dolly Schiff, Morti's daughter.) Kahn spun Kuhn Loeb's neutral position as favorable to Britain, pointing out that his firm had declined to take up any financing on behalf of Austria or Germany—"for which . . . we could have obtained pretty nearly any compensation"—and in doing so had "rendered a very great" service to the Allies.

There was no question, however, that Kuhn Loeb's stance came at considerable expense to the firm, further branding it as sympathetic to German interests. As Kahn acknowledged, "The attitude of strict financial neutrality which we imposed on ourselves has cost us much, as we knew before it necessarily would, for it kept us from many a profitable transaction and it led to the aggrandizement of other firms."[13]

The year after the Anglo-French loan closed, the subject of wartime financing again roiled the Kuhn Loeb partnership. Morti and Otto Kahn had managed to engineer a piece of Allied business that satisfied Jacob Schiff's strict terms—a $50 million loan to the city of Paris. It would be used solely for municipal purposes, and there was no danger that any of the funds would benefit Russia. Kuhn Loeb followed this deal with loans to three other French cities. When Max Warburg learned of the Paris deal, he immediately wrote Schiff proposing that Kuhn Loeb conduct a similar transaction on behalf of the German cities of Berlin, Frankfurt, and Hamburg. Schiff replied favorably, but the issue caused discontent among Kuhn Loeb's partners, with Kahn, Jerome Hanauer, and Morti Schiff strongly opposed to doing any German business.

Kahn enumerated his objections in a forceful letter to Jacob Schiff, writing: "I am frank to say that I cannot quite see why we should undertake to swim against the stream, antagonize our friends and neighbors, facilitate the way of our rivals and ill-wishers, and isolate ourselves by being the one and only important house to assume sponsorship for German financial business on a large scale, especially as long as the *Lusitania* crime against American citizens is unatoned for."[14]

Schiff responded with a forthright letter of his own. He began by commenting on Kahn's decision to write his letter in English, since they typically communicated in German. Had the public-relations-savvy Kahn done so because he anticipated a wider audience for his letter, perhaps planning to share it with English friends or even members of the press, to show he had registered strong objections to the German business? "Felix, for motives which I am sure we all can understand, would much like to have a way found in which the proposition which has been made to us could be accepted and carried into effect," Schiff wrote.[15]

As usual, Schiff had the final word, and the negotiations proceeded. Meanwhile Kahn and Morti worked to close another French loan ($60 million for the cities of Bordeaux, Lyons, and Marseilles), a deal that Jack Morgan and his partners attempted to sabotage. Threatened by Kuhn Loeb's sudden reentry into European finance, the Morgan partners informed France's finance minister of their competitor's German talks. The official was predictably outraged, and the deal nearly fell apart.

Ultimately, two events in late November 1916 doomed the German loan. First, Wilson, through his closest adviser, Colonel House, conveyed to Schiff that the "unsatisfactory and doubtful state" of U.S.-German relations made it "most unwise at this time to risk a loan."[16] Then, on November 28, the Federal Reserve warned its member banks against tying up their funds in foreign Treasury bills, a move that depressed the market for foreign bonds and made a new German issue untenable.

The announcement enraged Morgan, whose firm had bet heavily on foreign securities and was the de facto American banker for the Allies. He and his partners saw the machinations of Paul Warburg behind the warning. Henry Davison waxed conspiratorially that his erstwhile traveling companion to Jekyll Island was "doing everything he can to thwart the financial endeavors of the Allies." Morgan responded, "It may be necessary to come out in public attack on the German-Jews and their influence with the Government." Davison, always the cooler head, advised restraint. But their dark suspicions reflected a rising tide of American antisemitism, as old stereotypes that imbued Jews with outsize power, suspect allegiances, and devious motives gained new oxygen. To the Morgan partners, even the loyalties of Morti Schiff and Otto Kahn, vocal supporters of the Allies, were in doubt. Who knew where they *really* stood?[17]

By early 1917, any possibility of German business was fully off the table. On February 1, after pausing its ruthless campaign of U-boat warfare following the *Lusitania* attack, Germany once again unleashed its submarine fleet; the Wilson administration responded by severing diplomatic ties. The British government, meanwhile, intercepted and decoded German foreign secretary Zimmermann's telegram to Mexico proposing an alliance against the United States, which it shared with the Wilson administration and which the president released to the public on March 1. America's entry into the fight was now inevitable.

As the United States prepared to go to war, political upheaval consumed the Russian Empire. Over the previous three years, Russia's military forces had suffered staggering losses. Nearly 2 million soldiers had died in battle. Millions more were wounded, captured, or missing. Inflation spiked, and food and fuel shortages sowed misery throughout the country. While women and children starved, soldiers were being sent to battle without rifles and ammunition, expected to forage for their own weapons among the corpses littering the Eastern Front. On March 8, 1917, International Women's Day, striking textile workers demonstrated in the streets of Petrograd (now St. Petersburg); within days, protests enveloped the city. When Czar Nicholas II ordered troops to quell the unrest by force, soldiers revolted. Powerless, this time, to halt the revolution, he abdicated his throne on March 15. The three-century reign of the Romanovs was over.

Though Schiff had long prayed for the fall of the czar, its abrupt arrival surprised the financier. He was en route that day with Therese to the Greenbrier Resort in White Sulphur Springs, West Virginia, for three weeks of respite following a taxing winter of Jewish relief fundraising and business commitments.[18] That January he had celebrated his seventieth birthday, and two days before their departure, the Schiffs had welcomed their first great-grandchild, Carol, born to Felix and Frieda's daughter Carola.

"Praised be God on High!" Schiff cabled *The New York Times* from the Greenbrier, exalting in news of the Russian Revolution.[19] And he sent a congratulatory telegram to Pavel Milyukov, the new foreign minister of Russia's hastily assembled provisional government.[20] In a letter to his brother Philipp, Schiff marveled at the miraculous and "sudden deliverance" of Russia's Jews, writing, "It is almost greater than the freeing of our forefathers from Egyptian slavery."[21] Later events in Russia, including the rise of the Bolsheviks, would temper his jubilation.

On March 23, at a celebratory rally organized by the Friends of Russian Freedom and held at Carnegie Hall, the journalist George Kennan, speaking from a podium adorned with a pair of unlocked leg-irons from a Siberian prison, linked his Russo-Japanese propaganda work more than a decade earlier to the revolution, noting the role of the military in the recent uprising. And Kennan revealed Schiff's part in planting the seeds of revolution among Russian POWs. "The movement was financed by a New York banker you all know and love," he announced. In Schiff's absence, he sent a short note that was read to the audience, in which he expressed regret that he was not there in person to celebrate "the actual reward of what we had hoped and striven for these long years."[22]

In light of the revolution and impending war with Germany, Schiff reconsidered his opposition to Allied financing, cabling his son, "If partners wish to join in . . . future Allies loans I shall have no longer any objection."[23] After long blocking Russia's access to American money markets, Schiff also signaled his willingness to finance the new regime, personally making a one-million-ruble investment in a Russian loan organized that spring.

Morti quickly conveyed Kuhn Loeb's new position to Jack Morgan and to their friend Sir Ernest Cassel, who would be sure to broadcast the news in the right British quarters.[24] Relieved that Kuhn Loeb had finally picked a side, Morti advised his father to make a public statement to clarify the firm's stance. But Jacob declined, saying such an announcement "would be sure to be misunderstood and belittled."

"Neither I nor the firm have done anything that needs explanation," he continued, "and even in this moment of . . . passion and jingoism a good many things are done and said, which may hurt, that will pass, while manliness and self-respect are certain to last."[25]

Schiff underestimated the damage to his firm's standing. The partnership still had many lucrative years ahead, but its long run of Wall Street dominance was ending, and it would not reclaim the mighty reputation it had possessed at the start of the war.

If the question of wartime loans stirred conflict at Kuhn Loeb, it sparked an existential crisis at Goldman Sachs. Even after the sinking of the *Lusitania*, Henry Goldman continued his pro-German pronouncements. And he enraged his partners by vetoing the firm's participation in the Anglo-French loan, invoking a partnership rule stating that underwriting decisions needed to be unanimous. "So as to go on record where we stood," Walter Sachs recalled, his father visited the Corner to personally subscribe to the loan spearheaded by J.P. Morgan & Co. on behalf of himself and his brother, Harry.[26] Sam Sachs—as Otto Kahn and Morti Schiff had done—also visited Lord Reading to explain his firm's position.

The Henry Goldman situation was particularly embarrassing because of Goldman Sachs's close relationship with London's Kleinwort Sons, a member, along with Lehman Brothers, of the Trio underwriting partnership. Indeed, the British firm warned Goldman Sachs that it faced blacklisting in England. "It is natural that views and opinions on such matters differ," Kleinwort's Herman Andreae wrote to Arthur Sachs, "and I for my part always treat Mr. Goldman's opinions with special respect. It was the publicity given to the matter which alarmed us. I am very glad your father called upon Reading and have no doubt that if no active steps have been taken, it is due to the explanations given at this interview."[27]

Yet there were consequences. During the fall of 1915, the Bank of England blocked Kleinwort Sons from joining with Goldman Sachs and Lehman Brothers in the IPO of the Jewel Tea Company.[28]

The following summer, in July 1916, the Ministry of Blockade, a bureaucratic contrivance that policed trade with Britain's enemies, abruptly summoned Kleinwort representatives to a meeting where, to their shock, British officials confronted them with a stack of intercepted cables between Goldman Sachs and Austrian and German banks. The correspondence, Kleinwort subsequently told its American partner, made it "clearly evident that you are doing an active exchange business with the countries with which we are at war. We were frankly astonished at the evident importance of these operations." The British government forced Kleinwort to close its joint account with Goldman Sachs to avoid the possibility that, even in an indirect way, British currency might support foreign exchange transactions with its enemies.[29]

It's not clear how much intelligence the British government possessed about Goldman Sachs's business associations with the Central Powers, but the Bureau of Investigation, the forerunner to the FBI, later intercepted a letter suggesting that German operatives in New York viewed Henry Goldman as an important ally. In the missive, dated January 27, 1917—a little more than two months before the United States entered the war—Richard A. Timmerscheidt, a German-born banker working clandestinely with Heinrich Albert's operation, wrote to Berlin of "our friend Henry Goldman"—"an energetic and highly experienced banker" who has "proved himself to be highly reliable as to his sentiments."[30] (In July 1917, after being questioned by federal agents, Timmerscheidt slit his wrist with a safety razor and hurled himself from the window of his tenth-floor apartment on Central Park South.)[31]

The Bureau of Investigation's case files show that a member of the American Protective League, a government-sanctioned network of citizen-spies who hunted for German sympathizers and suspected radicals, reported Henry Goldman to the agency: "He and his wife associate almost entirely with people whose views are unpatriotic, and they are especially friendly with certain very pro-German musicians, among them Bodansky"—a reference to Artur Bodanzky, the Viennese conductor who oversaw German repertory at the Metropolitan Opera.[32]

Among the Goldmans' closest German musician friends was the mezzo-soprano Elena Gerhardt. When the United States declared war on Germany on April 6, 1917, Henry and his wife, Babette, were in San Francisco with the singer, whom they had accompanied to the West Coast for a series of recitals. The news "broke on us with the suddenness of a storm cloud," Gerhardt wrote in her memoir, recalling that the Goldmans were "in tears" over America's entrance into the conflict.[33]

Less than a year earlier, Woodrow Wilson had narrowly won reelection under the campaign slogan "He kept us out of war." But now a wave of patriotic exuberance swept the country, as citizens joined Loyalty Day parades, Wall Street bankers mobilized behind an issue of Liberty bonds, and young men packed recruiting offices. "I can recall my grandmother Dora [Sachs, daughter of Julius and Rosa] saying how when the U.S. entered World War I in 1917, lots of families smashed their German Christmas tree decorations," said Sir Stephen Barrett, who served as the British ambassador to Czechoslovakia and Poland.[34]

Henry's nephews and nieces rushed to join the war effort. Julius Goldman's brilliant daughters, Agnes and Hetty, joined the Red Cross. Paul Sachs, who was deemed too short for military service, deployed to France as a medic. Walter Sachs, Henry's favorite nephew, applied for and was rejected from officer candidate school. Both of Henry's sons, Robert and Henry Jr., known as Junie, enlisted as naval officers.

Yet even as Goldmans and Sachses joined the rest of the country in mobilizing for war, Henry's pro-German "tirades continued," Walter Sachs remembered. He persisted even as he alienated those closest to him, including his old friend Philip Lehman. Animosity built within the firm through the summer and fall of 1917. Finally, rather than renounce his views, Goldman resigned from Goldman Sachs, withdrawing his substantial capital contribution from the partnership. He would be the last Goldman to work for the firm that his father had started nearly a half century earlier.

His exit caused a bitter rift between members of the Goldman and Sachs clans. "He and Samuel Sachs never spoke again," Henry's granddaughter, June Breton Fisher, wrote in her biography of her grandfather. "Neither did Henry and his sister Louisa, Sachs's wife." Worsening the feud, according to Fisher, Louisa and her sisters-in-law broadcast gossip of a supposed affair between Henry's wife, Babette, and Sam's younger brother Barney, a Mount Sinai neurologist. "Until ten or twenty years ago," recalled Henry Goldman's grandson, Henry Goldman III, "there was never a picture of Henry Goldman at the Goldman Sachs headquarters."[35]

The estrangement became multigenerational, though not all the Goldmans and Sachses fell out of touch. In the 1880s, Julius Goldman and Julius Sachs both built homes in Keene Valley, located in the High Peaks region of the Adirondacks. Goldman's Felsenhöh ("high on the rocks") and Sachs's Waldfried ("peace of the woods") have been passed down through the generations and remain treasured retreats where Goldman and Sachs descendants continue to vacation and to bond over their shared heritage.[36] "There is still quite a lot of connection between various elements of the Goldman-Sachs family," said Marcus Moench, grandson of Agnes Goldman Sanborn (daughter of Julius Goldman). "You know, it's long after any of us have had any connection with the firm. But there's still a lot of connections, a lot of that coming through Keene Valley, but not only through Keene Valley."[37]

In late October 1917, after deciding to sever himself from the partnership at the end of the year, Goldman informed Kleinwort Sons of his forthcoming departure, attempting to spin the news in the most positive light. "Since many months I have been revolving in my mind to withdraw from active business life," he wrote. "I am not in sympathy with many trends which are now stirring the world and which are now shaping public opinion. Moreover, the world's war has deeply affected my view-point of life. . . . It goes without saying that I retire with the best of feeling towards the firm (and all of its members) with which I have been associated for thirty-five years and to which I have given all there is in me."

Reflecting the times with which Goldman now felt so out of step, he announced his resignation on company stationery that, in embossed red lettering, prominently displayed an exhortation to aid the war effort: "SAVE AND SERVE—BUY LIBERTY BONDS!"[38]

24

HERO LAND

To Herbert Lehman, America's entry into World War I came nearly two years too late. Like many others of his generation, he considered the sinking of the *Lusitania* an act of war and believed the Wilson administration should have responded accordingly. Wilson's ambivalence troubled him, but as a loyal Democrat, he nevertheless backed Wilson's 1916 candidacy. On election night he and his brother Irving watched the nail-biting returns trickle in until four a.m. at the Democratic Party's national headquarters in New York.

Unlike some of his peers, Herbert held not even a passing attachment for Germany. If anything, Mayer Lehman had instilled in his children an enduring distrust of his native country and its ruling class, born of the traumatic formative experiences that drove him from Bavaria to the American South. "He hated Germany," Herbert remembered.[1]

Itching to see combat and swept up in the "preparedness" fervor that overtook the nation in the months before the United States joined the Allies, Herbert tramped afternoon after afternoon to Governors Island, where he and other aspiring soldiers drilled with broomsticks in place of rifles, storming wooden boxes that represented enemy machine-gun positions.[2] He channeled much of his remaining free time into Jewish relief work. One of the youngest officers of the Joint Distribution Committee, he served as the organization's treasurer and wrangled the bickering Jewish factions alongside

Felix Warburg, whom Herbert recalled as an "unusually fine man" and "one of the most loved men I've ever known."[3]

When the Wilson administration declared war on Germany, Herbert, then thirty-nine, hurriedly applied for admission to the army's officer training camp in Plattsburgh, New York. He was accepted but, because of his age, never called. Impatient to serve and worried the war might end before he got the opportunity, he handed off his Joint responsibilities to his brother, Arthur, and relocated to Washington, where he secured a civilian navy post overseeing the procurement of textiles for uniforms, blankets, and other military uses. In this position, he served under Franklin Delano Roosevelt, then assistant secretary of the navy, whose penchant for taking bold action—"he had no hesitation at all about getting things done even if it meant cutting corners"—Herbert admired.

Lehman finally received an army commission as a captain in August 1917. He was handed another contracting assignment, though he continued to press for overseas orders. When an opportunity came up for him to deploy to France as head of the army's chemical warfare division, he thought he had found his ticket to the war zone. "I was as well qualified to become a chemical warfare officer as I was to develop a sputnik!" he later recalled. "I knew absolutely nothing at all about it. But I welcomed the call." His commanding officer, General George Goethals, the army's quartermaster, quashed the appointment, claiming that Lehman was indispensable to his operation. Herbert remained in Washington for the duration of the war, rising quickly through the ranks to become a lieutenant colonel.

If his D.C. assignment kept him out of the military theater, it brought him closer to the political action. And after returning to New York, he grew active in Democratic Party politics. During his first bid for office, in 1928, he ran for New York's lieutenant governorship on the same ticket as the red-tape-slashing navy official he'd gotten to know in Washington, FDR.

James Warburg, Paul's son, also spent the war unhappily confined to Washington. He too would later work in politics, also alongside FDR, whom he advised on economic policy during the first year of Roosevelt's presidential administration.[4]

Whip-smart, handsome, and smooth, with a surfeit of youthful confidence and a bohemian streak, Jimmy dabbled in poetry and had scholarly aspirations inspired by his uncle and namesake,

James Loeb, with whom he sometimes corresponded in Latin.[5] He also exuded an air of self-importance and possessed a "Warburgian arrogance . . . a particular type of arrogance," said his granddaughter, the novelist Katharine Weber. "He knew better than anybody about everything."[6] It was this cocksure quality that led to his split with FDR, whose New Deal policies he pilloried in a rapid-fire succession of four books.

In what had become a family tradition, Jimmy attended Harvard, a member of the class of 1917. He would later recall the university's "very definite social anti-Semitism," but he nevertheless thrived there. "Several clubs invited me to join although they had never taken in any Jews," he remembered. "I took the same position in each case, which was, 'If you're giving up your prejudice, okay. But if you're making an exception then no, I'm not going to be anybody's pet Jew.'"[7] Even so, his connection to Judaism remained tenuous, and like other Jewish banking scions, he strove for acceptance in the gentile world. "He had this sort of WASP anxiety," said Weber. "He loved Protestant enclaves where no Jews were allowed except for him, because he was almost not a Jew."

Elected by his peers an editor of the university's prestigious newspaper, the *Crimson*, he spearheaded an editorial campaign in favor of establishing a military training regiment at Harvard. Hundreds of students, including Jimmy, signed up, and the regiment was later folded into the army's new Reserve Officers' Training Corps program.[8]

Jimmy had initially supported Germany. But at Harvard the atmosphere was decidedly pro-Allies, and his perspective had started to change. He recalled the moment that "crystallized my interventionist, pro-Ally sentiment." One day Archie Roosevelt, Jimmy's Harvard classmate, invited him to breakfast with his father. Though Paul Warburg "loathed" Teddy Roosevelt, Jimmy considered him a hero, and he was swayed by the former president's forceful denunciation of the "evil" Kaiser and equally powerful sermonizing on the "righteousness" of the Allied cause.[9]

Jimmy's newfound enthusiasm for preparedness—a first step toward waging war with Germany—placed him at odds with his father who, because of his German sympathies, emphatically favored neutrality. "That was the first and only serious split which I ever had with my father and it worried me a good deal," Jimmy later said.[10]

Jimmy cruised through Harvard in three years, then spent the next six months working for one of Kuhn Loeb's railroad clients in preparation for a career in finance. He planned to officially graduate with his Harvard class in the spring of 1917, but he never got the opportunity. By then, America was at war.

Bent on joining the navy's embryonic aviation division, he and a group of Harvard pals obtained their pilots' licenses at a flight school in Newport News, Virginia. Prior to enlisting, he visited his parents in Washington to inform them of his decision. They recoiled at the news, and Jimmy recalled that a "long and painful" discussion followed. "My father drew a sharp distinction," he would later write, "between doing one's duty if called up for military service and needlessly volunteering for what he called 'the horrible business of killing people.'" Paul also objected to his son's choice of what was perhaps the most hazardous military profession—even the training, in those early days of aviation, could be deadly.[11]

Nina eventually persuaded her husband to come around, and not yet twenty-one, Jimmy headed off to the air station at Hampton Roads, where he trained to become a fighter pilot and, after his first near crash, hired a prostitute to ensure he would not die a virgin.[12]

Jimmy's cousin, Frederick, two years behind him at Harvard, was also eager to join the fight. He "has gone through a number of training camps and has received in Harvard extraordinarily good marks in military tactics," Felix bragged to a relative.[13]

Eager to display his own patriotism after the United States joined the war, Felix formulated a plan to boost navy recruitment, which he presented to navy secretary Josephus Daniels.[14] And he donated his motorboat to the navy's "mosquito fleet," a collection of civilian vessels mobilized to patrol the coastline for German submarines. "You might call her the 'War Bug,'" he joked to the navy representative who visited to thank him for his contribution to the war effort.[15] Felix—like his brother Paul—was far less enthusiastic to contribute his eldest son to military service, though he resigned himself to its inevitability. However, he warned Freddy, "I am determined that until you are twenty-one you will not join the aggressive forces."[16] By the time Freddy came of age, to Felix and Frieda's relief, the bloodshed had ended.

Jimmy Warburg also never saw combat. While many of his fellow fliers headed to Europe—a number of friends never returned—he got stuck training new cadets and was later detailed to the navy's navigational instruments department in Washington, ostensibly to perfect and patent a new type of flight compass he had devised in flight school. Why was Jimmy grounded when his compatriots went off to war? One reason may have been a vision defect that he had tried to conceal from the navy, but Jimmy also learned that his father had played a role in his Washington purgatory.[17] Paul, it turned out, had made a private request to Secretary Daniels that his son not be sent overseas where, after all, Jimmy might be called upon to bomb his German relatives. "This infuriated me and would long remain the one thing for which I could never quite forgive my father," Jimmy said.[18]

Deeply stung by his father's intervention, he responded, the day after discovering it, with an impulsive act of rebellion, proposing to Katharine "Kay" Swift, a young and peppy brunette he had met in the summer of 1917, when she performed with her classical music trio at Fontenay, his parents' Westchester retreat, located on the grounds of Felix and Frieda's sprawling estate.[19] Paul and Nina liked Kay—a beautiful and talented pianist and composer, whose late father was a well-known New York music critic—but they had warned their son he was too young to commit to her. Paul and Nina ultimately gave their blessing to the marriage, and if they had misgivings that Swift was not Jewish, they did not bring them up. But Jimmy's uncle, Jacob Schiff, could not refrain from commenting on her background. He responded to news of their engagement with a haughty telegram wishing his nephew "joy," while simultaneously professing himself "deeply disturbed by your action in marrying out of the faith in view of its probable effect upon my own progeny."[20]

Under Kay's influence, Jimmy indulged his artistic side. After the war, he fulfilled family expectations by embarking on a banking career. But he also published poetry under the nom de plume Paul James, and he penned the lyrics to some of Kay's most popular songs. Together the couple wrote the score to the hit musical *Fine and Dandy*. During the 1920s, their brownstone on East 70th Street was often the site of boozy soirées attended by artists, musicians, and café society types. Jimmy frequently returned home from the buttoned-down world of Wall Street to play bartender at impromptu gatherings featuring a revolving crew of young talent, including the composer George Gershwin, who was a constant presence.

Ultimately, the marriage did not last. Due in part to infidelities on both sides, including Swift's long-term affair with Gershwin, the couple divorced in Reno in 1934. Kay's dalliance with Gershwin humiliated Jimmy, who long remained embittered by their split. "He was vicious about her privately," according to Weber. He married twice more, fathering the youngest of his seven children in 1959, at the age of sixty-three.

Paul Warburg found wartime Washington stifling, but for different reasons than his son. A private man, Paul felt uncomfortable in the fishbowl of public life. He and Nina partook grudgingly of the capital's social rituals—the formal entertaining and calling-card visits—while forging close ties with only a few couples, among them FDR and his wife Eleanor. "He's really a beautiful looking man, but he's so dumb," Nina remarked of the future president.[21]

D.C. life disagreed with him, but Paul loved the work, throwing himself wholeheartedly into the task of building and improving the institution he had helped to push into existence.

The Federal Reserve jolted to life at a fortuitous moment, stepping into the breach (with still-limited powers) to steady the war-roiled financial system and, once the United States entered the conflict, stimulating the sale of war bonds by providing low-interest loans to member banks. But the war that forged the Federal Reserve into a mighty financial player delivered a traumatic blow to its most tireless advocate.

Because of Paul's personal (German, Jew) and professional (Wall Street) pedigree, a shadow hung over him from the start. A House Democrat from Texas, Joe Eagle, summed up the whispers echoing around Washington when, during one 1916 meeting, he lobbied Treasury secretary William McAdoo against Warburg's elevation to the chairmanship of the Federal Reserve Board: "Tell the president for God's sake not to designate Warburg. He is a Jew, German, banker, and an alien."[22] Ultimately, Wilson named him the Fed's vice-governor, a decision that rankled Warburg, who believed he deserved the top spot.

British and French officials viewed Warburg with suspicion—and he did himself no favors by openly consorting with Count Bernstorff, the German ambassador. When in late 1916 the Federal Reserve issued its circular cautioning banks against investing in foreign treasuries, the astounded British ambassador rushed over to meet with the board's chairman, Charles Hamlin. Cecil Spring Rice (like the partners of J.P. Morgan & Co.) faulted Warburg for the decision. He accused Warburg and Kuhn Loeb of helping to perpetrate a German scheme to starve the Allies of war funding and thereby pressure them toward peace negotiations brokered by Wilson. According to Hamlin, Spring Rice claimed his government had intercepted letters showing that "Warburg and Kuhn, Loeb & Co. were plotting" along these lines.[23]

Around this time, Hamlin complained in his diary about Warburg, with whom he often clashed. "While he talks fairly I cannot but feel he is so prejudiced against the Allies that he will go to almost any extreme to injure them," he wrote. In a separate entry, Hamlin also questioned whether Warburg had even voted for Wilson's reelection. "Warburg showed no pleasure at the result of the election—has never said how he voted. Secretary McAdoo told me he was satisfied that Warburg voted for [Charles Evans] Hughes, no matter what he might say."[24]

Warburg's role in shaping American financial policy led to some awkward moments when British and French financial emissaries visited Washington for talks with the Wilson administration in late April 1917, weeks after the United States officially joined the Allies. When McAdoo hosted the head of the Bank of England, he deliberately did not invite Warburg, so as not to upset his British guests. During a luncheon held by the Federal Reserve, French officials were so wary of disclosing confidential information in Warburg's presence that they conspicuously steered clear of the subject they had been invited to discuss—financing the war.[25]

The following spring, his four-year term nearing an end, Warburg foresaw a looming clash over his reappointment led by congressional Federal Reserve opponents and others who intended to use his nationality as a political bludgeon.

The war had unleashed a cresting wave of nativism. And in the hothouse climate of the conflict, immigration restrictionists gained new ground, attracted new allies, and mounted another attempt to impose a literacy test. The measure, also adding new categories of undesirables barred from the country, passed Congress in early 1915. Wilson struck it down. A version passed again the following year. Again, Wilson unsheathed his veto pen. This time Congress surmounted his opposition, and the anti-immigration law took effect in February 1917, two months before America's entrance into the world war.

But as xenophobia disguised itself as patriotism, the backlash extended beyond those whom politicians wanted to keep out to immigrants already living in the United States. It also took aim at the notion that a U.S. citizen, a true American, could embody more than one nationality. Theodore Roosevelt, a prominent opponent of what he called "hyphenated Americanism," summed up this sentiment in a 1915 speech: "There is no such thing as a hyphenated American who is a good American. The only man who is a good American is the man who is an American and nothing else."[26] Even Wilson adopted this position, declaring that "any man who carries a hyphen about with him carries a dagger that he is ready to plunge into the vitals of this Republic whenever he gets ready." In its way, this rhetoric mirrored the dual-loyalties trope brandished against Jews for centuries, used by successive empires and nation-states to disenfranchise them of human and civil rights because, as Jews, they supposedly held competing allegiances that prevented them from serving as faithful subjects or citizens.

Such was the atmosphere when, in late May, Warburg wrote Wilson a face-saving letter giving the president an out if he chose not to renominate him.

> Certain persons have started an agitation to the effect that a naturalized citizen of German birth, having near relatives prominent in German public life, should not be permitted to hold a position of great trust in the service of the United States. (I have two brothers in Germany who are bankers. They naturally now serve their country to the utmost of their ability, as I serve mine.) . . .
>
> These are sad times. For all of us they bring sad duties, doubly hard indeed for men of my extraction. But, though, as in the Civil War, brother must fight brother, each must follow the straight path of duty, and in this spirit I have endeavored to serve during the four years that it has been my privilege to be a member of the Federal Reserve Board. . . .
>
> Much to my regret, Mr. President, it has become increasingly evident that should you choose to renominate me this might precipitate a harmful fight which, in the interest of the country, I wish to do anything in my power to avoid and which, even though resulting in my confirmation, would be likely to leave an element of irritation in the minds of many whose anxieties and sufferings may justify their intense feelings. On the other hand, if for reasons of your own, you should decide not to renominate me it is likely to be construed by many as an acceptance by you of a point of view which I am certain you would not wish to sanction. In these

circumstances, I deem it my duty to state to you myself that it is my firm belief that the interests of the country will best be served if my name be not considered by you in this connection.[27]

While offering to sacrifice himself for the good of the country, Warburg craved Wilson's reassurance that his ongoing presence on the Federal Reserve Board was vital. Jacob Schiff had advised him not to send the letter at all, arguing this would leave Paul "in a more desirable position."[28] But Warburg, anxious over the approaching expiration of his term, couldn't help himself.

A month passed, then another, his letter unanswered, his dread building. Wilson eventually replied on August 9—the day Warburg's term expired. It also happened to be the day before Warburg's fiftieth birthday. "Your retirement from the Board is a serious loss to the public service," Wilson wrote. "I consent to it only because I read between the lines of your generous letter that you will yourself feel more at ease if you are left free to serve in other ways."[29]

Publicly, Warburg accepted his fate graciously, while internally bitterness consumed him. Immediately after Wilson's decision, Warburg took refuge at Fontenay, far from the expressions of sympathy he could not bear to hear. "My real regret is not for myself, it is for our work," he confided to his friend Benjamin Strong, head of the Federal Reserve Bank of New York. "I need not tell you what I think about that. It is a crime to disorganize that at a time like this. I cannot bear the thought that this work, which has been a part of my life, is to be a thing apart from me in the future. . . . It is too bad for the country that good works should be interfered with in this high handed manner. That I could have been confirmed easily I have no doubt."[30]

Warburg would later write that "it was not—as is generally assumed—my German birth" that brought his Federal Reserve career to an end. Rather, he believed, it was political enemies—including Senator Robert Owen, the Oklahoma Democrat who drafted the Senate version of the Federal Reserve Act—who planned to seize on his nationality as a cover to drive him from office.[31] Indeed, his replacement, Albert Strauss, matched his background in many ways. Though born in New York City, Strauss was of German-Jewish extraction and had also been a partner in a top Wall Street firm, J. & W. Seligman & Co.

His tenure abruptly halted, Warburg pondered his next move, traveling with Nina to Lake Tahoe, by way of the Canadian Rockies, to clear his mind. "As to going back to 'money grabbing,' quite between you and me and the angels, it does not appeal to me at all," he told Strong of his future plans.[32] He resolved to write a history of U.S. banking reform—what would eventually become his two-volume treatise on the origins of the Federal Reserve. Still, he lamented to Colonel House, "It is a pity to write history at this time, when it is so much more satisfactory to do one's share in making it."[33]

Yet he did feel compelled to set forth his place in historic events, especially as others, including Carter Glass, who would succeed McAdoo as Treasury secretary, stepped forward as the true progenitors of the Federal Reserve system. "My father was a very quiet man, and people who didn't know him well said he was an extremely modest man, which wasn't strictly true," Jimmy Warburg recalled. "He was a very diffident and sensitive man—not immodest in the sense that he was vain, but he definitely wanted recognition for what he did, and rarely got his due because he was so diffident." The thought that not only was he robbed of carrying out his life's work, but that lesser contributors to the cause of financial reform were wrapping themselves in his achievements, tormented him. "Another man might either have asserted himself or let it go," Jimmy said. "He couldn't quite do either."[34]

Felix and Kuhn Loeb's other partners hoped to lure Paul back to the firm. "I do say with all sincerity and earnestness that anything it may be in my power to do to make 52 William Street attractive and sympathetic and the fellow sitting at the westerly window soothing and palatable to you, I shall do most gladly and wholeheartedly," Otto Kahn wrote, addressing his letter to "Paulus."[35] But Paul declined the offer to return. "During the eleven years of his partnership in Kuhn, Loeb & Co. I believe he had more worry than satisfaction," Jimmy would later write.[36] Anyway, the war had mostly brought business at his old firm to a standstill.[37] "Business there is none, except financing of the Government's loans, which from time to time gives us something to do," Schiff told his friend, the London banker Max Bonn.[38]

No doubt sensitive to charges that Wall Street was seeking to profit from the conflict, Schiff declared in one speech that "no man should seek to increase his personal fortune for the period of the war. The duty of every American at this time is to devote his whole thought and effort to the needs of the Government and to the needs of those who have been made to suffer through the war."[39] Otto Kahn, meanwhile, announced that he would donate his annual income, after living expenses and taxes, to "charity and war purposes" for the conflict's duration.[40] (Left unmentioned was the grandiose scale on which Kahn and his family lived and that he was then in the process of constructing a hundred-thousand-square-foot estate, Oheka Castle, on Long Island's North Shore.)

When new financing opportunities did arise, Kuhn Loeb's senior partner typically turned them down unless the business served some broader patriotic purpose.[41] Along with Jack Morgan, First National Bank's George Baker, and other Wall Street eminences, Schiff served on a Liberty Loan committee responsible for marketing government securities in New York. He marched in parades and gave frequent speeches exhorting the public to purchase war bonds. His position on the war, by now, had undergone a thorough reversal. Publicly and privately, he opined that the Allies must not only win the war but demolish Germany's military establishment.

Addressing one Liberty Loan rally from the steps of the New York Sub Treasury, an imposing Greek revival edifice situated across the street from the offices of J.P. Morgan & Co., Schiff called for the "utter destruction of Prussian military power, which forms a constant threat to the freedom and peace of the nations of the world." He linked the Great War to the bygone battles that had forged America's unique identity: "We are fighting for the same cause our ancestors battled for at Lexington in 1776, our fathers at Bull Run, and Gettysburg and throughout the Civil War." And he said no price, in blood or treasure, was too hefty to spend to uphold the nation's founding principles: "It may be that this war will last so long that we shall become impoverished, both in material resources and, in what would be worse, our young manhood. But, be it so if it must: it will be better if we give up everything to succeed."[42]

He flung himself into patriotic work with the vigor of a man who had seen his own loyalties questioned, despite his fifty years of U.S. citizenship. Because of his German-Jewish background, he strove that much harder to embody the model of an ideal citizen, placing his American identity above all else. And he grew ever more vocal in his Americanism, even joining Roosevelt and Wilson in their crusade against the dreaded hyphen. "God forbid that we permit a hyphen to be placed between Jew and American," he said.[43]

The war continued to feed nativism—and its accompanying

strains of antisemitism. Schiff could see its ugly specter all around
him. One day a telegram, signed by a Massachusetts banker named
C. W. Taintor, arrived at Kuhn Loeb's offices. It was addressed to:

> Jacob Schiff, Esq.,
> Head of Kuhn, Loeb & Co.,
> Money Changers,
> Shylock,
> Polonius,
> German Agent,
> Head of Camarilla of Vice now holding
> sordid Americans in Bondage[44]

Most worrying to Schiff and his allies were signs of official discrimination. By State Department decree, the Red Cross—to which
Schiff had long been a benefactor and which he had once served as
treasurer of its New York chapter—barred naturalized U.S. citizens
from Germany and Austria from working in its European hospitals.
Following protests by Schiff (who wrote directly to the secretary of
state) and others, the order was eventually rescinded.[45] The American Jewish Committee and other Jewish groups likewise vigorously
objected when they learned that an army manual for use by the medical advisory boards reviewing draftees contained this inflammatory
passage: "The foreign born, especially Jews, are more apt to malinger
than the native born."[46]

Only could Jews defeat antisemitic stereotypes, Schiff believed,
by becoming exemplars of American patriotism and loyalty. Addressing a crowd of thousands at a 1917 rally held by the Jewish League of
American Patriots, an organization formed by lawyer Samuel Untermyer, Schiff called on young men of his faith not just to volunteer for
military service but to seek battlefield postings at the front.[47] At the
same time, he opposed the league's plan to recruit one or more all-
Jewish military regiments on the grounds that it fostered perceptions
of Jewish separatism.[48]

Because of his stature and connections, Schiff frequently received
requests—and he often obliged them—to send recommendation letters on behalf of young men seeking military postings. Philip Lehman
sought Schiff's assistance in getting his son Bobbie, a junior officer in
the army reserves, transferred to active duty.[49] (Bobbie, who would
succeed his father as head of Lehman Brothers, deployed to France
as a captain in a field artillery unit.) Julius Goldman asked Schiff to

recommend his nephew, Henry Jr., for the Aviation Corps. (Tellingly, this request did not come from Henry Sr.; the younger Goldman would serve as a navy lieutenant.)[50]

Schiff's own son sought a military appointment with increasing desperation, as he watched friends and colleagues head off to Washington or deploy to the war zone. His lack of success baffled and embarrassed both father and son, especially since they had canvassed high-level business and political contacts seeking a military role for Morti. They had even reached out to two of Wilson's closest advisers—Colonel House and Secretary McAdoo, the president's son-in-law. "I am sure you fully understand my own anxiety that my son's earnest wish to make himself in any possible way useful to the country be taken advantage of by the Administration," the elder Schiff wrote McAdoo. "Indeed, the fact that, for some reason unfathomable both to him and to me, this has not been done, notwithstanding all the efforts to that end my son has made these many months, is a source of great discouragement to him and mortification to both of us."[51]

"I shall be very happy to help him in every way I can," McAdoo assured Schiff, but a position, military or civilian, never materialized.[52] (Morti would have to wait more than a decade for the military commission he coveted. In 1929, President Herbert Hoover appointed him a major in the military intelligence division of the army reserves.)[53]

Shut out of a military post, Morti busied himself with volunteer work. He served as an alternate on the Liberty Loan Committee, assisted the Treasury Department's war savings stamp drive, and succeeded his father as a member of the Federal Milk Commission, organized to control the pricing of dairy products. A vice-president of the recently established Boy Scouts of America—both he and his son John would later serve as presidents of the organization—he helped to mobilize its nearly four hundred thousand members behind the war effort. Scouts sold hundreds of millions of dollars' worth of war bonds and savings stamps, planted "war" gardens to feed the troops, and volunteered as air-raid spotters. Part of the goal of this effort was to prepare boys on the cusp of manhood to trade one uniform for another when they came of age.

One of the main thrusts of Morti's charitable service was the Jewish Welfare Board, an organization formed in 1917 to provide religious, social, and recreational respite to the nation's sailors and soldiers. Founded with the help of a $1 million fundraising campaign led by Morti's father, the organization, serving American military personnel of all faiths, established a presence on hundreds of military outposts throughout the country and, eventually, in Europe. It undertook a wide range of initiatives, from recruiting and vetting Jewish chaplains for the army and organizing religious services, to teaching English classes to immigrant soldiers and sponsoring shows and movie nights. The organization distributed 6.4 million sheets of writing paper, 370,000 packs of cigarettes, 155,000 magazines, and 100,000 books. During Passover, it shipped 300,000 pounds of matzo to Europe.[54]

Morti, working alongside Walter Sachs and Irving Lehman on the welfare board's executive committee, coordinated its efforts with those of other organizations providing similar services in military camps, including the YMCA, the Salvation Army, and the Knights of Columbus—a task no less maddening than synchronizing the at-odds contingents within the Joint Distribution Committee. Nevertheless, as vice-chairman of the United War Work Campaign, Morti led a joint effort by the Jewish Welfare Board and six other charitable groups that raised some $200 million for America's troops.

So much of his time was consumed by fundraising and speech-giving, he told a Philadelphia YMHA chapter, that he no longer had time to prepare remarks for his speaking appearances. "I am engaged in so many welfare enterprises," he joked, "and incidentally I pretend to be a businessman."[55]

In the fall of 1917, the Schiff family suffered its first war casualty when one of Morti's British cousins, the only son of Jacob's late brother Hermann, was reported missing in action during combat in France. The British infantryman, also named Mortimer, was last seen during a raid on German trenches. He had recently written to Jacob announcing his promotion to captain and giving some flavor of his time at the front: "No one who has not been there can have the slightest idea of the fearful and wanton destruction of the French countryside."[56] Captain Schiff was later declared dead.

A few days after Schiff's nephew disappeared in no-man's-land came another family tragedy. Out for his customary early morning ride at his country home in Irvington, Ike Seligman toppled from his horse, fracturing his skull. Passersby discovered him unconscious, and he was rushed to Mount Sinai Hospital. Barney Sachs, Sam's neurologist brother, stood by in the operating room while a colleague performed emergency surgery. But Seligman never regained consciousness.[57]

Jacob Schiff was close with his brother-in-law. Just weeks earlier they had been tramping together through the woods of Mount Desert Island.[58] Now he was looking upon Ike's funeral bier, alongside Paul and Nina Warburg and other close family members, while the Ethical Culture Society's Felix Adler eulogized Seligman for his "equanimity" and "love of human beings."[59]

"We all were warmly attached to this splendid man," Schiff lamented, following the service, "who knew naught but love and service to others, and who left none but friends behind him."[60]

Seligman also left behind substantial debts and departed owing $600,000 to his wife's brother, James Loeb.[61] This reflected what had been an open secret among friends and family: J. & W. Seligman & Co. was in precarious financial shape. The previous year, when Ike's firm had led a syndicate that underwrote shares in the Cuba Cane Sugar Corporation, Felix Warburg wrote to Loeb, pointing out that "for the first time, after quite a long interval," the Seligmans "have made a good deal of money." He added, "I leave it to you, on the strength of this, to throw a hint about re-paying some loans."[62] But at the time of Ike's death, few of these debts had been paid back.

J. & W. Seligman & Co.'s fortunes had steadily faded since the 1907 panic. With the firm already in weakened form, World War I presented a new and alarming threat.[63] Seligman & Stettheimer, the Seligman brothers' Frankfurt branch, had closed in 1900 when Henry Seligman retired to pursue charitable work, but members of the family continued to operate the London and Paris partnerships. William Seligman's death in 1910, at the age of eighty-eight, left Seligman Frères & Cie under the leadership of his son David W. The Paris partnership did a heavy lending business with Berlin, Petrograd, and Vienna, placing it in immediate financial peril when the war started and it was unable to collect outstanding debts. Ike was a partner in the French business and spent "fearful days" in Paris after Germany's declaration of war trying to save the house from collapse—a debacle that could in turn drag down the credit of the New York and London firms because of his association with them.[64]

Ike needed out of the Paris partnership—quickly. In the fall of 1914, he struck a deal with David W., who had come to New York seeking a bailout, which would allow Ike to extricate himself from the firm in exchange for advancing Seligman Frères millions of francs to see it through the crisis. In order not to spook the Paris firm's clients,

Ike told his cousin Charles, a partner in the London operation, "We will state that the reason of my retirement from S. F. & Co. is due to the fact that we are a neutral firm, and desire not to be involved in any eventualities, etc."[65]

But Ike traded one problem for another. Propping up the Paris firm drained J. & W. Seligman's resources and forced it to forgo other business opportunities. His frustration spiraled into rage when he learned David W. made risky investments with funds J. W. Seligman & Co. had loaned the Paris house. At one point, he threatened to turn his back on Seligman Frères altogether and leave it to its fate.[66] Such were the worries weighing on Ike when he plunged from his horse.

The floundering Paris partnership outlived Ike Seligman, though only by a few years. By 1921, the firm had dissolved, a drawn-out process complicated by the U.S. government's Office of the Alien Property Custodian, which during the war confiscated the assets of individuals and entities deemed U.S. enemies, including those of some of Seligman Frères's debtors. The same office, run initially by A. Mitchell Palmer (who would become U.S. attorney general in 1919), also snarled Seligman's debts to James Loeb in years of red tape. Though Loeb was an American citizen, he was residing in Germany (and experiencing another protracted nervous breakdown, exacerbated by the war). Palmer, "after investigation," labeled Loeb an enemy. His office seized Loeb's American holdings, including the late Ike Seligman's promissory notes.[67]

Though Seligman didn't share Schiff's rigid religious convictions, he and his brother-in-law were kindred spirits in philanthropy and frequent collaborators in seeking to uplift the Jewish people, particularly those living within Russia. He sat by Schiff's side in Portsmouth, where they had pressed Sergei Witte over the regime's treatment of their brethren. And like Schiff, Seligman was a longtime member of the Friends of Russian Freedom, which sought the ouster of the czar. Together, they had celebrated the downfall of the Romanov empire.

But in the final months of Seligman's life, it became clear that Russia's struggles were far from over, as Vladimir Lenin's Bolshevik Party gained traction. Ike's death came on the cusp of a moment of seismic upheaval, and a period of great hope and extraordinary peril for the Jews. Nineteen-seventeen itself was an epoch-shaping year—America's entrance into the war marked a turning point in the nearly three-year-old conflict, the women's suffrage movement verged on victory, and the nation's immigration policy veered sharply toward exclusion—and it was bookended by events that dramatically inflected modern Jewish history. Early that year the Russian Revolution freed what was at the time the world's largest Jewish population from an oppressive and autocratic regime. And another monumental development came as 1917 drew to a close, when the British government, in a sixty-seven-word statement, suddenly made feasible the wild-eyed Zionist dream of a Jewish homeland in Palestine. The message was contained in a brief November 2 letter from Foreign Secretary Arthur Balfour to Baron Walter Lionel Rothschild, a prominent leader of British Jewry. It read:

> His Majesty's government view with favour the establishment in Palestine of a national home for the Jewish people, and will use their best endeavours to facilitate the achievement of this object, it being clearly understood that nothing shall be done which may prejudice the civil and religious rights of existing non-Jewish communities in Palestine, or the rights and political status enjoyed by Jews in any other country.

The Balfour Declaration was the product of months of talks between Zionist leaders and British officials. It was negotiated at a time when revolution had thrown Russia's future in the world war into question (Lenin's Bolsheviks were agitating for an immediate withdrawal) and when, after formally entering the conflict, the depth of the Wilson administration's commitment remained unclear. (The American Expeditionary Forces did not fight at the front until October 1917; it wasn't until November 3, incidentally the day after Balfour wrote Rothschild, that America sustained some of its first combat casualties.) Given these worrying circumstances, the British hoped to strengthen the resolve of the Russian and U.S. governments by leveraging the support of the Jewish populations of both countries.

No sooner was the Balfour Declaration made public than the Russian Revolution entered a disconcerting new phase. On November 7, 1917, the Bolsheviks seized power from the provisional government in a coup. Lenin hastened to pull Russia out of the war, as he had promised, and Leon Trotsky, appointed the Bolshevik regime's first commissar of foreign affairs, took charge of the peace talks with the Central Powers. Russia eventually exited the conflict, as a blood-drenched civil war consumed the country, leading to the rise of the

Soviet Union and the establishment of a collection of sovereign states in territory that had previously fallen under the czar's dominion.

The Balfour Declaration came as the British-led Egyptian Expeditionary Forces, under the command of General Edmund Allenby, battled Ottoman troops for control of southern Palestine, where both sides had previously fought to a stalemate. Known as "the Bull" because of his temper and powerful frame, Allenby had commanded a cavalry division in France before his reassignment to the Middle East theater. He had recently lost his only son to combat on the Western Front, and he channeled his grief into a relentless drive toward Jerusalem. By late November, Allenby's troops had pursued retreating Ottoman forces into the Judean hills outside the city and were steadily advancing.

Jerusalem on the brink of British control, St. Petersburg in political turmoil—such was the disorienting state of world affairs on November 28, when Jewish Relief Day kicked off at Hero Land, a two-week patriotic bazaar and pageant at the Grand Central Palace, a sprawling exhibition hall in midtown Manhattan. Hero Land—in which dozens of war relief groups participated—featured an array of elaborate tableaus: the streets of Baghdad, a Versailles ballroom, a segment of the Hindenburg trench system. The attractions also included a captured German submarine—rechristened *U-Buy-a-Bond* by the Liberty Loan Committee.[68]

The Joint Distribution Committee adopted a colonial motif, dubbing its exhibit "Old Bowling Green." Therese Schiff headed the Joint's Hero Land entertainment committee, and on Jewish Relief Day she organized an extravaganza that included matinee performances by Harry Houdini and Irving Berlin and an evening pageant, dubbed *On the Road to Victory*, featuring more than three hundred performers.[69]

The British government dispatched a general to speak to the Hero Land throng. He read a congratulatory message from Lord Reading ("himself a Jew"), then declared, "The Jewish race have found in Britain a country where they have been able to enjoy the privileges of citizenship and liberty for which the allied nations are now fighting. The Jews have proved themselves worthy of that liberty. . . . The world knows that America is repaid by the same spirit of loyalty, devotion, and patriotism which Britain has received from the Jewish race."[70]

On December 11, the day before Hero Land closed its run, General Allenby dismounted his horse outside Jerusalem's Jaffa Gate and entered on foot, a gesture of respect toward the people of the holy city and the beginning of a new and turbulent chapter for the Jews.

Not long after Jerusalem came under British control, Julius Goldman's youngest daughter, Agnes, a thirty-one-year-old bacteriologist, deployed there with the Red Cross. On a compound of old buildings with vaulted ceilings and endless corridors, she helped to establish a lab and medical clinic to treat refugees and the Red Cross's own malaria-stricken employees. Like many in her wealthy German-Jewish social circle, she opposed Zionism. But after touring Jewish settlements in Palestine, she confided in one letter to her father, "I would be sacrificing candor for the sake of appearing consistent, if I proclaimed myself totally unaffected by what I have seen. . . . It is after all impossible to deny the evidence of one's eyes, and when one sees the stubborn soil bearing fruit in response to the efforts of a band of enthusiasts, one can not have the courage to deny the impulse that brought them here."[71]

British support for a Jewish homeland, coupled with developments in Russia over the previous year, caused many Jews to reappraise Zionism. Somewhat surprisingly, given the bitter battles he had waged with his Zionist critics, this included Jacob Schiff.

Schiff's evolving position became evident in April 1917. Heartened by events in Russia but worried about the erosion of Jewish traditions and teachings there and elsewhere in the world, he announced in a speech that he had concluded that "the Jewish people should at last have a home land of their own." Zionists pounced on his statement to trumpet his conversion to their cause, but they sidestepped an important caveat that came in the next line of his remarks: "I do not mean by that that there should be a Jewish nation."[72] Schiff remained firmly opposed to political Zionism and the creation of a Jewish state, which embodied the very type of nationalism he found so dangerous. He supported establishing a Jewish cultural and religious center in Palestine, with the territory itself governed as the protectorate of another nation, perhaps Great Britain.

Throughout much of 1917, Schiff entered a delicate dance with Zionist officials and intermediaries. The Zionists hoped to land the support of the man universally considered the nation's foremost Jewish leader. Schiff sought a path toward Jewish unity.

Schiff's talks with Zionist leaders, including Louis Brandeis, intensified in the fall of 1917, to the point where Schiff prepared a letter, intended for release by the Zionist Organization of America, which "need form part and parcel of my 'conversion.'" Schiff's December 3 letter—drafts of which passed between him and Julian Mack, a federal judge and the incoming president of the Zionist Organization— explained that his "quarrel has never been with Zionism itself but, as I have pointed out, with so-called Jewish Nationalism, the endeavor to reestablish in Palestine an independent Jewish Nation, not for the purpose of a perpetuation of the Jewish people as the bearers of their religion but prompted primarily by political motives and aspirations." He also stated he could "not view with enthusiasm a Jewish resettlement of Palestine, if in this endeavor the religious motive be relegated to the background."[73]

When seven weeks passed and the Zionists had not publicized his missive, the offended banker rescinded his offer to join the movement. "I shall have to continue to remain on the threshold," Schiff wrote Mack, who contended that their talks had been "unofficial."[74] Despite ongoing efforts to persuade Schiff to "pay the shekel"— the nominal fee that would formalize his Zionist membership—the banker remained on the outskirts of the movement.

In the spring of 1918, while Julian Mack continued his efforts to court Schiff, Louis Brandeis contacted Otto Kahn after reading *Right Above Race*, a collection of essays the banker had recently published. In the preface, Teddy Roosevelt called the book, adapted from Kahn's speeches, "an admirable plea for Americanism."

"Possibly you may be interested in the enclosed address on 'Americanization,' in which I attempted to develop the thought of 'Right Above Race'—the thought which led me and I hope may some day lead you—to Zionism," the Supreme Court justice wrote.[75]

Brandeis was an unlikely Jewish leader. A secular Jew and prominent social reformer, he was raised without formal religious training and embraced Zionism late in life. He was almost fifty-eight when, in August 1914, he accepted the chairmanship of the Provisional Executive Committee for General Zionist Affairs. "I am very ignorant of things Jewish," he admitted at the time, explaining that his rationale for accepting the role was his realization that Jewish ideals were the same as those "which we of the twentieth century seek to develop in our struggle for justice and democracy." As the war wrought chaos on the cradle of international Jewry, he believed it was imperative to preserve the Jewish people and that "it is our duty to pursue that method of saving which most promises success." Where critics of Zionism (including Schiff) contended that its nationalist aims were inconsistent with Americanism, Brandeis argued that the "Jewish spirit" was "essentially American" and that seeking to strengthen these values was the ultimate expression of patriotism.[76]

Kahn remained unpersuaded, replying to Brandeis, "I fear I must confess that I have not yet found the way to Zionism; perhaps, to be frank, because I have heretofore made no earnest effort to discover it." Nor would he.[77]

Kahn, like Brandeis, had an irreligious upbringing. His Jewishness was so tenuous that some contemporaries joked he was the "flyleaf between the old and new testaments." He was not ashamed of being Jewish, but he did feel confined by it. He and his wife Addie often avoided the German-Jewish circles that families such as the Schiffs moved in, lest they be ghettoized there and (further) alienated from New York's beau monde. The Kahns baptized their four children in the Episcopal Church to save them from social ostracism. Rumors persisted for years that Otto himself had converted. He never did—and always corrected that misperception when asked about it—though, throughout his life, he considered the possibility.[78] Ultimately, he was no more able to formally accept Christianity than Schiff was to officially adopt Zionism.

Kahn had developed a reputation as a generous philanthropist, and while he contributed to Jewish (as well as Christian) causes, his primary passion was the arts, in particular the Metropolitan Opera. In 1903, Jacob Schiff had declined an offer to join the Metropolitan's board, recommending Kahn in his place. Kahn quickly ascended to the chairmanship, helping to modernize the opera company and cementing its place as an iconic New York institution.

The war brought new challenges to his role at the Metropolitan. In 1914 he booked the renowned Russian Ballet, which arrived in New York early the following year minus its star dancer, Vaslav Nijinsky, who was under house arrest in Budapest as an enemy alien. To save the show, Kahn canvassed his diplomatic contacts, including the secretary of state, seeking the dancer's release. When the dancer was finally freed, Kahn navigated a comical series of obstacles (which included paying off Nijinky's debts) to finally get him to the Metropolitan stage.[79]

After the United States joined the conflict, Kahn and his board faced the question of whether the Metropolitan should continue to perform German operas, including those already scheduled for the fall season. The matter became so internally divisive that Kahn sought the guidance of the highest authority in the land—President Wilson himself.[80] Some board members, he told Wilson, felt performances by German artists might "affront . . . the patriotism of Americans," while others contended that "the flag of art should be neutral." Ultimately, Kahn's Metropolitan compromised by performing German works in translation, including Wagner's *Parsifal*. A purist, Kahn overcame this offense to his artistic sensibilities in the name of American patriotism.[81]

After waffling for years, Kahn became a U.S. citizen in February 1917, two months before the Wilson administration declared war. From the start of the conflict, Kahn had never wavered in his support for the Allies. But as a newly minted American and with internal disagreements over the war no longer paralyzing Kuhn Loeb, Kahn finally felt liberated to be more vocal. "I have been eager for a long time to speak out publicly my hatred and loathing of Prussianism and my wholehearted allegiance to the Allied cause, but as long as I was not an American, I naturally had to hold my peace as far at least as public utterance was concerned," Kahn told his friend Lord Beaverbrook, the British newspaper mogul.[82]

Kahn did more than merely speak out. Assuming the role of unofficial patriotic spokesman, his pen and voice became omnipresent, as he traveled the country assailing what he called the "sinister transmutation" of Prussianism and denouncing Germany's "ruling caste" for instilling "into the nation the demoniacal obsession of power-worship and world-dominion."[83] Meanwhile, he issued a stream of articles and pamphlets, which bore titles such as "The Poison Growth of Prussianism." He often addressed his remarks directly to German Americans, exhorting them to join him in condemning Prussianism's "malignant growth."[84] Because of Kahn's stature, his anti-German diatribes were a powerful propaganda tool. A group calling itself the Friends of German Democracy, created with assistance of the U.S. government's newly formed propaganda agency, the Committee on Public Information, churned out thousands of copies of Kahn's articles and speeches (along with some of Schiff's) which the French government airdropped over the German front lines.[85]

Some found Kahn's—and Schiff's—patriotic zeal hard to swallow. "Does it ever occur to you the Germans are putting things over on us right under our noses?" a broker with the Wall Street firm of Chandler & Co. wrote in a 1918 letter included in a file maintained by the Bureau of Investigation, which secretly probed Kahn for German financial ties and leanings.

> Do you suppose Kahn attempted to break into the British Parliament for his health? There is a lot of talk over here about these things. People don't understand why Kahn and Schiff should be telling them how to be Americans. People are wondering how it comes about that Kahn, Schiff, and [Paul] Warburg should be trusted with everything in this country. Schiff is down here on the steps of the sub-Treasury last Saturday making a speech, two years and six months ago he was buying bonds issued by Germany.[86]

Kahn, of course, was no German agent. He was, however, a British intelligence asset. He was in close contact with Sir William Wiseman and his deputy, Norman Thwaites, the brash young operatives who were overseeing Britain's U.S. spy operation during the war from their outpost in New York.

A Cambridge-educated baronet, Wiseman had worked as a reporter for the London *Daily Express* and dabbled in banking in Canada and Mexico. He joined the British Army at the start of the war and, in July 1915, while serving with a light infantry unit at Ypres, was gassed and briefly blinded. He returned to England to convalesce, where a fortuitous meeting with the chief of the British secret service—a navy buddy of his father's—led to his New York assignment: he and Thwaites led a secret war against German saboteurs and spies while trying to guide the Wilson administration into the Allied camp. In one operation, they succeeded in shutting down a bomb factory established by Franz von Rintelen during his brief but eventful mission in America. In another memorable intelligence coup, Wiseman and Thwaites managed to obtain a compromising picture of Ambassador Bernstorff. The photo, taken in the Adirondacks, featured the German plenipotentiary wearing a swimsuit with his arms around the waists of two women, neither of them his wife. Distributed to the press, the photo deeply embarrassed the German diplomat, making him appear unserious and suggesting he had time for sunbathing and frivolity during wartime. "As a piece of anti-enemy propaganda, I have no hesitation in saying that this incident was more effective than pages of editorial matter which the British were alleged to inspire in the Press of the United States," Thwaites recalled.[87] Wiseman's son

John, the youngest of his five children, recalled hearing little of his father's clandestine exploits during the war. But a relative did once divulge a tale of Wiseman fatally shooting an enemy agent during a standoff at an ammo dump on Long Island.[88]

With youthful round features and a trim mustache, Wiseman was a dapper gentleman-spy with a chummy knack for cultivating useful friends. This included Woodrow Wilson's confidant and adviser Colonel House, with whom Wiseman developed such an extraordinary rapport—even renting an apartment in the same building—that, at just thirty-two, he came to serve as a surrogate ambassador and liaison between the U.S. and British governments. "The thing that I am most proud of in my life is that President Wilson was a close friend," Wiseman would later say. "He admitted me when not even ambassadors could get in."[89]

Wiseman also grew friendly with some of the partners of Kuhn Loeb, including Otto Kahn and Morti Schiff—so friendly, in fact, that shortly after the war, he joined the firm, eventually becoming its first non-Jewish partner. (No doubt hiring a prominent British official helped Kuhn Loeb smooth over ruffled feathers in Great Britain after the war.) Wiseman's personal papers include a memorandum that lists intelligence sources utilized by Thwaites. "Otto Kahn of Kuhn Loeb & Company, William Street, is useful for financial information," the document notes.[90] In his memoir *Velvet and Vinegar*, Thwaites described a close relationship with the banker. "Often, during the years 1917 to 1920, when delicate decisions had to be made, I consulted Mr. Kahn, whose calm judgement and almost uncanny foresight as to political and economic tendencies proved very helpful," he wrote.[91]

Kahn found U.S. officials less receptive to his sage counsel. The secretary of war named Kahn to a military entertainment advisory council that organized performances for the troops, but Kahn aspired to a more consequential assignment, perhaps an "official or semi-official mission" on behalf of the Wilson administration.[92] Sensing little interest for his services, he finally traveled to Europe in 1918 on his own accord to survey the war zone and size up the prospects for peace.

Kahn stopped first in London, where he met with Prime Minister David Lloyd George and where Lord Beaverbrook, who had recently been appointed minister of information, sought the banker's advice on "propaganda matters."[93] Kahn traveled on to France in late May, where he toured American military bases, inspected supply lines, and lunched with General John Pershing, commander of the American Expeditionary Forces.[94]

Earlier that spring, the Germans had signed a peace treaty with Russia's new Bolshevik government; with its troops on the Eastern Front now freed up, the Reich deployed manpower into a renewed assault on France. The German Army had advanced within some fifty miles of Paris, close enough to bombard the city with long-range artillery. But in the weeks after Kahn's visit, Pershing's troops helped to repel the German offensive in the battles of Château-Thierry and Belleau Wood. Kahn would write a pamphlet titled *When the Tide Turned*, arguing that these decisive engagements set the stage for Germany's eventual defeat that fall.

Kahn's fact-finding mission also took him to Spain, where he was received by King Alfonso XIII. Though Spain remained neutral, Kahn found it a hotbed of "German intrigue, unscrupulous plotting and propaganda," and during his visit he managed to pick up a piece of valuable intelligence. He learned the Spartacus League, a movement of German revolutionaries that would later become the Communist Party of Germany, was plotting an imminent uprising. Kahn quickly passed this tip along to the British and U.S. governments. "He did us a great service by reporting on this affair," a British cabinet minister said later.[95]

Wilson had not formally sanctioned the banker's trip, but when Kahn returned, the president requested a debrief; Kahn happily complied. The press widely covered his European adventure and his thoughts on conditions there after arriving home. In August, capping his well-publicized mission, the French government bestowed on Kahn the rare distinction of decorating him as a Chevalier of the Legion of Honor. Similar awards in Italy and Belgium followed.

As the war ended, the world-renowned financier and arts patron added a coveted new title to his résumé: statesman.

Several months after Kahn returned from Europe, Morti Schiff embarked on his own mission to the war zone as a member of the Committee of Eleven, a panel established by the War Department to oversee the expenditure of relief funds raised during the United War Work Campaign. By now, the conflict was over. A sustained Allied counteroffensive steadily pushed the depleted German forces back, and as the reality of Germany's imminent defeat set in, a revolution led by Spartacists and other socialist revolutionaries erupted, forcing Kaiser Wilhelm II to abdicate the throne and flee the country. On November 11, 1918, German and Allied military commanders finalized the terms of an armistice.

Morti reached London a month later and soon hitched a ride to France aboard a U.S. Navy destroyer. "Paris is chuck full of American men and it gets me perfectly disgusted that I was not able to get over here in uniform, while the war was on," he wrote home to his wife.[96]

On New Year's Eve, he drove out to the now-quiet battlefields east of the city, traveling over the Voie Sacrée, or Sacred Road, a pivotal supply route that had conveyed fresh troops and armaments to the front during the Battle of Verdun. In Verdun, he climbed to the top of a hill and looked out over the deserted city. No building was unscathed. Roofs and walls were punched with holes. Not a windowpane appeared intact. For miles around, he saw a sea of mud and barbed wire, etched with trenches pooled with standing water. Here and there dead horses decomposed, and graves dotted the landscape.

His party traveled as far as U.S.-occupied Koblenz. Food was in short supply, and the shops were largely bare of merchandise, with most of their stock displayed in their front windows. Morti bought a pack of cigarettes and after lighting one realized it didn't contain tobacco.[97] "Did I tell you that the entire time I was 'chez le Boche,' I did not see a single dog?" he wrote Adele (using a derogatory term for German). "I wonder if they ate them. God, how I hate the Boches, they are too dreadful."[98]

Morti spent the remainder of his trip in Paris. During working hours, he attempted to sort out the organizational morass created by competing relief groups sharing the same pot of money. ("The Yids are pestering me a lot," he complained, referring derisively to members of the Jewish Welfare Board.) He tried to line up deals for Kuhn Loeb and took meetings with business and military leaders, including General Pershing. At night, he kept up an active social calendar, mingling with French aristocrats, such as Édouard and Maurice de Rothschild. "I am . . . devoting myself more particularly to 'schmoozing' with the more or less important people, as that is really more worth while," he told Adele. "In other words, I am acting à la Kahn, which you always recommend."[99]

Paris and its environs, the site of international peace talks that formally kicked off at the Quai d'Orsay in mid-January 1919, was brimming with VIPs and familiar faces. "It is like Washington, only more so," Morti marveled in a letter to Felix.[100] Woodrow Wilson, with Colonel House by his side, had arrived in December to negotiate on behalf of the United States and to press his plan to create a League of Nations to avert future conflicts. Because of his close rapport with Wilson and House, spy-cum-diplomat William Wiseman accompanied the British delegation to Paris. Max Warburg, in part due to his American banking connections, joined Germany's contingent to the peace conference as a financial expert.

The Armistice brought great relief but also new anxieties to the Warburgs of Hamburg and New York. Germany was in the grip of revolutionary turmoil, and M.M. Warburg, its interests so closely intertwined with those of the government, was on the precipice of a dark period, one that would compel Felix and Paul to dig deeply into their own fortunes to rescue the family firm from extinction.

"After not communicating with you for nearly two years, it is not without emotion that I dictate these lines, which naturally bring to you, to Mother and the whole family the fondest love," Felix wrote days after the Armistice in his first postwar letter to Max. Mail between the United States and Germany remained embargoed, but Felix handed off his missive to Lewis Strauss, then a twenty-two-year-old assistant to Herbert Hoover, head of the U.S. Food Administration. Strauss—whom Felix soon recruited to work for Kuhn Loeb—was headed to Europe with his boss to oversee relief efforts, and Felix offered up his brother as an authority on humanitarian conditions. "I cannot let this opportunity pass without telling you how happy we are that this horrible nightmare is over," Felix wrote, "and by the time this reaches you, I hope that conditions surrounding you have quieted down."[101]

But reports that trickled back from Germany about food shortages and Spartacist violence made Felix increasingly fearful for his family. In March 1919, as Max prepared to head to France, Paul and Nina threw a birthday dinner for Frieda at their Upper East Side home. The guests included Lloyd Thomas, an American war correspondent who had recently returned from Germany, where he had visited Max in Hamburg and witnessed Spartacists rallying in the streets. "He gave a most appalling description of living conditions—if one may call them that—in Germany," Felix recounted to his son Gerald. "The depression which prevailed, he says, in the minds of the people of some education and the hopelessness that drives the masses to follow any orator or agitator while dressed in paper, imitation suits and eating all kinds of worthless substitutes, is beyond description."

Felix was conflicted about Max's role in the peace talks. Given Max's past ties to the government of Kaiser Wilhelm II, his selection by the leaders of the new Weimar Republic represented "a great vote of confidence in his impartiality and wisdom." Yet Felix also wondered how his brother would cope with the "interesting but painful task" of negotiating on behalf of his defeated and demoralized nation. "Paris to him and Alice has always meant the most cheerful life and most successful business transactions and the warmest reception by friends all around," he told Gerald. "For him to go to Versailles, where he has had so many jolly dinner parties, as a supplicant for his country is a changed role indeed."

Moreover, Felix believed Max and his colleagues were marching into a no-win situation they would later be vilified for, no matter the outcome. "It can make very little difference what their opinions and their desires are—they will have to sign what is placed before them, perhaps under protest, if they are permitted to voice it. Whatever they sign, they will be blamed for afterwards."[102]

His prediction turned out to be tragically prophetic.

25

THE FIRST PART OF A TRAGEDY

In the summer of 1919, Jacob Schiff received a flood of old correspondence from Germany, some dating back to late 1915. The confiscated letters, finally relinquished by government censors, carried now-antiquated family news and salutations for occasions long-since passed. One old missive from Max congratulated Schiff on his granddaughter Carola's engagement. She was now the mother of a toddler.

On both sides of the ocean, on opposing ends of the conflict, their friendship existed in a kind of stasis while their countries were at war. Between these old friends there was much to say—and much that needed to remain unsaid. "I know you have done much high-minded and patriotic work for your own country," Schiff wrote Max once mail service was restored between the United States and Germany. "Our feelings and opinions no doubt and very naturally, greatly differ as to the events of the past few years and I am sure you will agree with me that it will be better if we do not enter upon any discussions of these events." What mattered now was the present and the future, the task of rebuilding from the physical and political wreckage of Europe. "And now we face a different world, in which we all, but you more so, will have to face our way anew," Schiff wrote.[1]

Max had been slow to reckon with the new realities of the postwar era and Germany's place in it. Initially, he still "believed in the full restoration of prewar Germany," according to a nephew.[2] The peace conference would erase these delusions.

Asked to attend the Paris talks as a representative of the German Treasury, Max had first demurred. He foresaw, as Felix did, the potential for blowback and worried "anti-Semitic attacks" would be the inevitable result. He also questioned the wisdom of sending bankers to the conference instead of Finance Ministry bureaucrats.[3] When the government pressed, Max finally agreed to attend as a member of the finance delegation, offering up his M.M. Warburg deputy, Carl Melchior, to chair this group and to serve in the higher-profile role of representing Germany at the bargaining table.

The spirit of retribution that infused the peace conference announced itself shortly after the 180-person German delegation crossed into France. Their train slowed to a crawl when it reached the war-devastated countryside, forcing the Germans to take in the full scale of the destruction. It was an obvious psychological tactic, though no less effective for its lack of subtlety.[4]

Installed first at Château de Villette, an estate completed by the same architect who built Versailles, Max and his colleagues lived as virtual prisoners. Under the watch of two hundred soldiers, ostensibly to ensure their safety, they were forbidden from communicating with outsiders or leaving the grounds. Meanwhile they were under constant surveillance by listening devices concealed throughout the property and by servants who spied on their conversations.

Max anticipated "damned hard" peace terms, but the Allies' demands for reparations and territorial concessions were even more punitive than he imagined. On April 16, 1919, following a negotiating session at Château de Villette, Max pulled aside Thomas Lamont, a well-connected J.P. Morgan partner attending the peace conference as a representative of the U.S. Treasury Department.

"Germany's only hope of a just peace is in America," Max implored the banker, emphasizing the precarious state of his country, where Bolshevik agitators were gaining ground and hundreds of men, women, and children perished daily from starvation due to the yet-to-be-lifted blockade. His countrymen were frightened and angry.

Max handed Lamont an eleven-page memo expressing his views on the peace process and describing the alarming conditions in Germany. The document, strident and at times tone deaf, likened the "sufferings of the totality of the German people" with those of the French and Belgians. Max condemned the ongoing blockade against his country as "a crime" responsible for the deaths of more than one hundred thousand German citizens. And he warned that, as a result of the ongoing privation, his country might soon be "driven into the arms of Bolshevism."

It was hard to tell whether Max's memo was intended to persuade or to provoke. Lamont marveled at his brazenness. "The nerve that these boches have is something terrible," he remarked, as he circulated Max's jeremiad to financier Bernard Baruch, who was advising Wilson in Paris.[5]

That Max focused on swaying the Americans was natural. Of the Big Four, the quartet of American, British, French, and Italian leaders guiding the peace talks, Woodrow Wilson stood alone as a voice of restraint. In his "Fourteen Points" address to Congress in January 1918, he declared his desire for a "just and stable peace" with Germany, stating, "We do not wish to injure her or to block in any way her legitimate influence or power." During negotiating sessions, Wilson opposed the most severe terms and at times sparred heatedly with his counterparts, particularly French prime minister Georges Clemenceau. On one occasion, after Wilson opposed the French demand for control of the coal-rich Saar Basin in southwestern Germany, an enraged Clemenceau called him "pro-German" and stormed out of a meeting. Things grew so tense that more than once Wilson threatened to leave the peace conference altogether.

Then in early April 1919, Wilson suddenly fell ill with a severe case of the flu, part of the same pandemic that had rampaged across the globe over the previous year, eventually killing some 50 million people, including nearly seven hundred thousand Americans. Bedridden for several days, Wilson recovered, but to his aides he seemed like a different man. Along with a general weariness, the virus seemed to cause lingering neurological effects. Wilson grew absentminded—he kept leaving behind his briefcase, containing sensitive documents—and seemed to have difficulty grasping information he previously had no trouble processing. Herbert Hoover, who was then spearheading U.S. relief efforts in Europe, later commented on Wilson's "unwilling mind."

Wilson became paranoid and fixated on strange matters, such as the arrangement of the furniture in his Paris quarters. Odder still, he suddenly caved on many of the issues he had recently fought against so ardently, including imposing staggering reparations and a treaty clause, pushed by Clemenceau, that forced Germany to formally accept the blame for starting the war.[6]

The proposed peace terms, presented to the German delegation in early May, stunned Max and his colleagues. He wrote to his wife, Alice, in despair and disbelief: "To announce a new era to the world, to speak of love and justice, and then to perpetrate pillage on a global scale, to sow the seeds of future conflicts and kill all hope of better times, is to commit the greatest sin in the world."

Max helped craft the German delegation's counterproposal, which in a cover letter expressed shock at the terms and stated that "the demands in the Treaty go beyond the strength of the German people." He remained convinced, however, that the Allies would not bargain. Days after submitting the German response, he poured out his frustrations in satirical verse, titling his tragicomic work after the luxurious prison where the fatal peace terms had been foisted on the Germans: *Die Villettiade (Der Tragödie erster Teil)*—"The Villettiade (The First Part of a Tragedy)."[7]

"June 28, 1919 will be a great day in Jewish history," Louis Marshall wrote Jacob Schiff from Paris. Two days earlier, on what was the fifth anniversary of Archduke Franz Ferdinand's assassination, U.S. and European statesmen gathered around a horseshoe-shaped table in the Hall of Mirrors at Versailles to sign the peace treaty formally ending World War I. Marshall was referring not to the main agreement signed by German diplomats but to a related treaty that was initialed moments later by the leaders of the recently established Republic of Poland, which had reclaimed territory partitioned more than a century earlier by Austria-Hungary, Germany, and Russia.

The splintering of those empires had led to the establishment of a collection of independent nations in Eastern Europe and the Baltic region, their boundaries drawn at the Paris bargaining table. And Marshall had spent the last three months working to ensure protections for Jews living in Europe's newly constituted republics. Poland, whose territory included a large swath of the Pale of Settlement, was now home to Europe's largest Jewish population and was thus a focus of Marshall's advocacy.

Officially representing the American Jewish Congress, Marshall had arrived in Paris on March 27, accompanied by Cyrus Adler, who was deployed on behalf of the American Jewish Committee. Marshall and Adler spent arduous weeks pinballing between meetings with diplomats and world leaders, eventually including President Wilson himself, to press their case that minority protections for the Jews should be formally spelled out through the peace process.

On reaching France, Marshall was also thrust into a parallel set of peace talks, mediating between rival Jewish factions with competing agendas at the Paris conference. The Zionists hoped to strengthen their claim to Palestine in the wake of the Balfour Declaration. Emissaries representing the Eastern European masses—suddenly subsumed into the new cartography of Europe—pushed for expansive national rights, including Jewish representation at the League of Nations. Wary of Jewish nationalism, delegates representing the more established and assimilationist Jewish communities of Britain and France sought more general protections for all minority groups living in the new nations seeking formal recognition through the Paris talks.

"The work has been nerve-racking and has demanded infinite patience and self-control of which I never suspected myself," Marshall complained to Schiff, to whom he and Adler wrote frequently of their progress and setbacks.[8] In mid-May they reported "hopeful" developments, cabling to New York a proposed clause in the German peace treaty stating that "such special provision where as are necessary to protect racial linguistic or religious minorities shall be laid down in" a supplemental treaty with Poland that would form the model for accords with other Eastern European nations, including Romania and the newly established Czechoslovakia.[9]

Recent outbreaks of anti-Jewish violence in territory contested by Polish and Ukrainian nationalists, as well as the Russian Red Army, added a sense of urgency to the case for Jewish safeguards. Polish forces and civilians had killed dozens of Jews in late November 1918 after gaining control of the city of Lemberg (now Lviv, Ukraine), which had been claimed as the capital of the newly declared West Ukrainian People's Republic. Shortly after Adler and Marshall's arrival in Paris came news of another massacre, this one in Pinsk, where Polish soldiers executed thirty-five Jews suspected of Bolshevik ties.

The episode at first received little publicity, but by May it had ignited international outrage. In New York, Jewish leaders mobilized a large antipogrom campaign, and on May 21, the Lower East Side exploded in protest. Men and women walked off the job at factories to join demonstrators parading through the streets; schoolchildren left their classrooms. The protesters doffed black armbands in commemoration of their brethren murdered in Poland. When the supply of armbands ran out, people tore the fabric from umbrellas and tied on the frayed pieces. By one estimate, the crowd topped 150,000.

The protest preceded a mass meeting convened by Jewish leaders that evening at Madison Square Garden, where the speakers included Charles Evans Hughes and Jacob Schiff, who declared that Poland should not be admitted to the League of Nations unless it could protect its Jewish citizens and grant them equal rights. Though Schiff and the other speakers addressed a crowd of thousands, the rally's intended audience was far smaller: it was the Big Four, which in addition to Wilson and Clemenceau included Britain's David Lloyd George and Italy's Vittorio Orlando.[10] The following week, when Marshall sat down with Wilson ("he sees practically nobody, because of the intensity of his labors," the lawyer boasted of his ability to wrangle a meeting), he carried with him a nearly two-thousand-word cable from Schiff describing the massive New York demonstration, which Marshall summarized as he pressed the president to support strong protections for the Jews. "He said he would give the subject and others the most careful consideration," Marshall recounted in a letter to Schiff, in which he also noted the delicate status of his diplomacy: "A breath can upset all that we have wrought so faithfully during all of these anxious weeks."[11]

Though not present in Paris, Schiff was nevertheless pulled into its intrigues. In early June 1919, weeks before the treaty's signing, the Senate Foreign Relations Committee subpoenaed Schiff, Paul Warburg, and four other financiers as it probed allegations that confidential drafts of the peace terms had circulated among "special interests"—namely, New York bankers with an intense interest in the financial particulars. Also called to testify were J.P. Morgan partners Jack Morgan, Henry Davison, and Thomas Lamont (who was en route home from advising the Wilson administration in Paris) and the National City Bank's retiring president Frank Vanderlip.[12] Driving the "leak" controversy were two fierce critics of Wilson's League of Nations, Republican senators Henry Cabot Lodge, the Foreign Relations Committee's chairman, and William Borah; later that year the two lawmakers would lead the Republican opposition to the Versailles Treaty, eventually thwarting its ratification in the Senate and, in a major blow to Wilson, preventing the United States from joining the League of Nations.

Citing poor health, for which he said he was "constantly under medical treatment," and his doctor's admonition against "overexertion," Schiff asked to be excused from making the trip to Washington. He said he had never seen a copy of the treaty and had no knowledge of illicit copies in circulation. Warburg similarly denied possessing any inside information.[13]

Their testimony, it turned out, was unnecessary. Davison admitted receiving a copy of the treaty from his partner, Lamont, in Davison's role as a top Red Cross official. Wilson, in a letter to Lamont, formally exonerated him of any wrongdoing in disclosing the document.[14]

Still, Borah seemed reluctant to let Schiff off the hook. Before releasing the banker from testifying, he quizzed Schiff in writing about the "extent" to which Kuhn Loeb had sold European securities over the previous five years. He also asked about Schiff's contributions to an organization called the League to Enforce Peace, which had heavily promoted the League of Nations in the United States. Borah was convinced that "international bankers" lurked behind the effort. Schiff complied by sending the information Borah requested, and he noted that while he remained Kuhn Loeb's senior partner, he was "no longer very active in the management of the firm, other than in an advisory capacity."[15]

In Jewish life, too, Schiff had begun to take a step back, playing a supporting role while Adler and Marshall were at the center of the action in Paris (where Schiff might have been had he been younger and healthier). In a letter to the British author and Zionist Israel Zangwill, Schiff praised both men for "their valuable work in Paris" and noted that "Louis Marshall has become a big force in Jewry."[16]

A hero's welcome awaited Marshall when he returned to New York the month after the signing of the Versailles Treaty and its Polish companion, sometimes known as "Little Versailles." A group of admirers calling themselves the Louis Marshall Reception Committee met his steamer at the docks with a boat chartered for the occasion, and the following week, with Schiff serving as toastmaster, they fêted Marshall at a thousand-person banquet at the Waldorf Astoria.[17]

Marshall and Schiff triumphed in the consecration of the Polish treaty, but it was not the monumental victory for Jewish rights that it at first seemed. The minority protections it enshrined were far less expansive than the "Jewish bill of rights" Marshall had set out to advance in Paris. "Not only were the citizenship and religious protection clauses extremely vague and weak, but every shred of a Jewish *national* identity had been omitted from the final text," the Ohio State University historian Carole Fink pointed out in her study of

Marshall's diplomacy in Paris. Also left out: language protecting the rights of Jews to conduct trade on Sundays, an important proviso for Jewish shopkeepers and merchants who kept the Sabbath and closed their businesses on Saturdays while those of their Christian counterparts remained open.[18]

These hard-fought if tepid protections had unintended and self-defeating consequences, breeding resentment among Poles—angered by the intrusion into the new nation's sovereignty—and contributing to the surge of antisemitism that blighted postwar Europe in the years to follow. Polish leaders bitterly pointed out the hypocrisy of being forced to adopt minority protections by the United States, a country with an appalling record of state-sanctioned racism against Blacks and Asian immigrants. Indeed, not long after inking a nonaggression pact with Adolf Hitler's Germany in 1934, Poland renounced Little Versailles. Its foreign minister contended before the League of Nations that Poland would abide by the treaty only if other member nations submitted themselves to the same scrutiny.

Meanwhile, as Felix and Max had feared, the German peace treaty fueled antisemitism among a humiliated, fearful, and war-weary populace. And Max, despite his effort to take a lower-profile role within the peace delegation, became a convenient scapegoat. The anti-Jewish reverberations were felt even before German foreign minister Hermann Müller signed the accord, when news circulated of the proposed reparations the German delegation had offered: 100 billion marks. "Ultra-Conservative circles took advantage of the fact that such Jewish bankers as Melchior, Warburg, and [Max von] Wasserman were included among the delegation experts, to start an anti-Semitic agitation," wrote Victor Schiff (no relation to Jacob), a journalist who accompanied the German delegation to Paris, in his account of the peace conference. "Even on the Hamburg bourse, where Melchior and Warburg are a power, there were anti-Semitic demonstrations. It naturally made no difference to such circles that purely 'Aryan' and even Conservative financiers . . . had helped to draft our replies. These Versailles weeks saw the earliest symptoms of the recrudescence of anti-Semitism all over Germany."[19]

A pamphlet distributed at the Hamburg bourse linked Max to the reparations offer and decried the "Warburg Jewish Peace."[20] It mattered little that Warburg, Melchior, and the rest of the German financial delegation resigned in disgust on June 18, 1919—ten days before the treaty was signed—convinced that its terms were so impossibly onerous that acceding to them could only lead to their country's economic collapse.[21]

In the late summer of 1919, Felix and Paul separately returned to Europe and to their shell-shocked homeland, reuniting with family for the first time since the war had started.[22] Felix's trip wasn't purely personal. He was on a Joint Distribution Committee–sponsored fact-finding expedition to gather information about relief and reconstruction efforts. Visiting Great Britain, France, Germany, and the Netherlands, Felix met with various Jewish leaders and gathered field reports on conditions within Jewish enclaves throughout Eastern Europe. Representatives of Europe's struggling Jewish communities were urging a summit to compare notes on their unique and collective plights. Felix sensed a danger in this. "At a time when international Jewry is accused of all kinds of impossible, underhand actions, the calling of a conference representing so many nations might furnish fuel for the idiotic claims and do harm," he mused.

The Joint had so far pumped some $30 million into aid work, and Felix reported to his colleagues in New York that their efforts had "saved hundreds of thousands of lives, not vaguely speaking, but as an actual fact." Yet the need remained staggering. "We have by no means reached the period where relief can be dispensed with. The cries of old Russia can be heard and the children of Poland and many other countries are utterly destitute."[23]

The Joint had largely worked through local aid organizations, but by early 1920 it began dispatching its own relief workers to Europe, with the first unit deploying to Poland attired in modified army uniforms. To oversee its expanding aid work, Felix's close friend and fellow JDC official Julius Goldman placed his legal practice on hold and took up a post in Paris as the organization's first director general for Europe, a grueling job requiring equal measures of diplomatic finesse and logistical wizardry.

While Felix surveyed the humanitarian scene, Paul studied the financial picture. The war had upended what Paul referred to as "the world's balance sheet," creating a tangle of debts that were potentially ruinous not just to the vanquished Central Powers but to the European continent as a whole. France had borrowed heavily from the United States and Britain to finance the war effort. Repaying these debts would require crippling reparations, one reason why

Georges Clemenceau had pushed for the steepest possible recompense. Neutral nations that had extended credit to Germany during the hostilities, meanwhile, also jockeyed for repayment. With European nations focused on self-preservation, they risked a chain reaction of default that could tank the European economy.

"The finance problem of the world, placed before us by the war, is so enormous that it is beyond human power to solve it as a whole," Paul concluded. He believed the only place to begin was by straightening out the German financial situation so that "we may safely treat his indebtedness as a sound asset in the balance-sheet of his creditors." Placing Germany on solid economic footing, subject to reparations it could realistically pay, would "create a healing centre, from which healing will spread over other countries, in the same manner as the conflagration spread from one country to another after the outbreak of the war."[24] There was still time to avert a financial calamity. The treaty compelled Germany to make an initial reparation payment of 20 billion marks, but it had not spelled out exactly how much the country owed, leaving that job in the hands of a newly established reparations commission.

Before departing for Europe that summer, Paul received an invitation from his friend Dr. Gerard Vissering, president of the Dutch central bank, to attend a small conference on the financial perils ushered in by the Versailles Treaty. Paul eagerly accepted, and on the morning of October 13, 1919, he showed up at Vissering's grand home in Amsterdam overlooking the Keizersgracht (or Emperor's Canal). Along with several of Vissering's colleagues, also in attendance was the Parisian banker Raphaël-Georges Lévy, who the following year would be elected to the upper chamber of the French parliament; Fred Kent, a Federal Reserve official and expert on foreign exchange who had been appointed to the reparations commission; and John Maynard Keynes, the British economist known for his towering stature (he stood nearly six foot seven) and intellect.

Then thirty-six, Keynes had worked throughout the war for the British treasury, and he had attended the Paris talks as one of his government's chief financial representatives. In order to pave the way for Europe's economic recovery, Keynes had pushed a plan to cancel war debts, which he called "a menace to financial stability everywhere." Woodrow Wilson and his administration strongly opposed the proposal.[25] The United States, unlike its allies, emerged from the war stronger than it had gone in—it was now a bona-fide global superpower. A creditor nation for the first time in its history, it held some $10 billion in Allied debt. Nor did Wilson take kindly to the idea that America should make further sacrifices, after coming to the rescue of its European allies to begin with.

In late May 1919, exhausted and depressed by the course of the Paris negotiations, Keynes resigned in disgust. "The Peace is outrageous and impossible and can bring nothing but misfortune behind it," he vented at the time. "Certainly if I was in the Germans' place I'd rather die than sign such a Peace." He returned to England—"I am slipping away from this scene of nightmare," he informed British prime minister David Lloyd George before departing—and began work on *The Economic Consequences of the Peace*, the treatise that launched him to international renown.[26] The book's bland title belied an impassioned polemic that denounced the Big Four for ignoring the "economic problems of a Europe starving and disintegrating before their eyes," and it warned of the consequences of their shortsightedness. "If we aim deliberately at the impoverishment of Central Europe, vengeance, I dare predict, will not limp," he wrote. "Nothing can then delay for very long that final civil war between the forces of Reaction and the despairing convulsions of Revolution, before which the horrors of the late German war will fade into nothing, and which will destroy, whoever is victor, the civilization and progress of our generation."[27]

The book was still two months from publication at the time of the Amsterdam conference, but Keynes brought with him a draft of the third chapter, which contained a ruthless portrayal of Wilson as a "blind and deaf Don Quixote" who in Paris had been woefully outplayed by his more sophisticated counterparts.[28] One afternoon in his hotel room, Keynes read aloud from the chapter to Paul Warburg and Carl Melchior, whom Keynes had invited to Amsterdam. Paul, now as contemptuous of Wilson as Keynes was, chuckled at the economist's filleting of the president. Melchior, on the other hand, appeared on the verge of tears.[29]

Gerard Vissering, host of the Amsterdam confab, had once served as president of the Bank of Java, and his study was decorated with curios from his travels in Asia.[30] His guests assembled around a table across from a small fireplace. Coal was in short supply throughout Europe, and the fire smoldered so weakly that its warmth barely reached

Warburg, seated on the table's far side. With servants popping in occasionally to offer cocoa, coffee, or tea to dull the chill, the men bantered for hours about Europe's financial predicament.

"The bankers of Europe ought to come together and judge the present situation like doctors over a case," Warburg said, after the meeting had gone on for some time. "The Commission des Réparations holds in its hands the future of Europe."

Keynes continued to press his debt forgiveness agenda, calling for a "general outwiping" of Allied liabilities. "Germany is the key to the whole solution," he stressed at one point.

"If people in Germany could only get a germ of hope that their situation is seriously considered by the other countries, it would do it a lot of good," Warburg replied. He proposed one way to ignite that hope: an appeal, signed by prominent men throughout Europe and America, that expressed the dire reality of Europe's financial situation and called for an international conference of financiers and statesmen to forge a realistic path forward. Warming to the idea, Warburg's colleagues nominated him to draft the proclamation. He at first begged off, noting his involvement would ensure that the initiative was branded pro-German. Instead, he recommended Keynes, who also demurred, citing his forthcoming broadside, which would surely make him unpopular in many quarters. So Warburg suggested a collaboration, joking that if Keynes supplied the whiskey and he the water, together they were "likely to propose a pretty acceptable drink."[31]

By the next day they had pulled together a draft. It warned that penalizing Germany into bankruptcy would have grave consequences and that runaway inflation threatened to spread "anarchy" throughout Europe. "Is it not necessary to free the world's balance sheet from some of the fictitious debts which now inflate it and lead to fear or despair on the part of some, and to recklessness on the part of others?" the appeal asked. "Would not a deflation of the world's balance sheet be the first step towards a cure?" And it concluded, "No time must be lost if catastrophes are to be averted."[32]

After returning to New York the following month—this time accompanied by Felix, who met him in Holland—Paul immediately began lining up signatories.[33] His initiative garnered widespread support. Politicians including Elihu Root, the former New York senator and secretary of state, Herbert Hoover, and William Taft signed on. Jack Morgan, Andrew Mellon, and Jacob Schiff lent their names to the effort. But the appeal hit a snag when Warburg shared the document with the Treasury Department, now run by his onetime nemesis Carter Glass. Alarmed by the language about purging "the world's balance sheet"—a reference to the debt forgiveness the Wilson administration so vehemently opposed—assistant Treasury secretary Norman Davis, Wilson's top financial adviser in Paris, protested. The paragraph was ultimately stricken from the U.S. version.

The original proclamation was also addressed to the League of Nations and called on the newly formed body to convene the international conference the letter prescribed, but the Wilson administration balked at this as well. At the time, Senate Republicans, with William Borah and Henry Cabot Lodge at their vanguard, were waging political battle over the ratification of the peace treaty. And as Paul recalled, "the Administration was scared beyond words of anything that might pour oil on the flames. Anything that would show that we were about to be entangled with the League of Nations before we had entered it, was, therefore, to be avoided like the plague."[34] So instead of the League of Nations, the final appeal was addressed to the reparations commission.

With tepid support from the White House, the International Financial Conference, as it was called, convened in Brussels in the fall of 1920. Yet little came of the effort, spearheaded by Keynes and Warburg, to head off an economic catastrophe. The following year the reparations commission set the compensation owed by Germany at 132 billion gold marks (about $33 billion), plus a 26 percent tax on German exports. The value of the mark collapsed, and the country entered a two-year period of hyperinflation during which its currency became all but worthless.

Returning from a visit to Germany in August 1922, Henry Goldman told reporters the country was on the brink of collapse. "It is obvious that the architects of the Treaty of Versailles built a treaty which is falling down over their own heads. It foreshadows some great catastrophe, the nature of which no man can define. It is like Götterdämmerung"—the twilight of the gods—"for them."[35]

In the fall of 1922, for the first time since the war started, Max and his wife, Alice, sailed to the United States, where Max hoped to advocate for lesser reparations. There was also another reason for his visit. Earlier that summer members of an ultra-nationalist paramilitary group had gunned down Max's friend Walther Rathenau, a Jewish politician then serving as Germany's foreign minister, as he drove through Berlin in his chauffeured NAG convertible. And, Max learned, his name also featured on a list of high-profile Jews targeted by these terrorists.

In Washington, Paul organized meetings for Max with top officials in the fledgling Harding administration, including Secretary of State Charles Evans Hughes. The brothers hoped to win support for a plan to deploy a group of independent experts to Germany to study the economic situation and make recommendations on reparations. Paul still hoped the United States would step up and play "umpire" among the European powers. Instead, he found "Washington did not dare or care to play the part."[36]

In the following months, he and Max watched helplessly as Germany convulsed with economic and political unrest. By late 1922, as Max returned to Hamburg despite the exhortations of his brothers to remain longer in America, Germany had begun defaulting on reparations payments. Early the next year, in a bid to force repayment of its debts, French and Belgian troops streamed into the Ruhr Valley, occupying Germany's industrial heartland and touching off a new international crisis. "As it was, appeals to reason did not prevail," Paul later lamented. "Insanity had to run its course until finally, after the Occupation of the Ruhr, the German finances had been thrown into complete chaos."[37] At the peak of the financial bedlam in late 1923, one U.S. dollar equaled 4.2 trillion German Reichsmarks.

Über-nationalism and far-right zealotry flourished in the fearful and downtrodden atmosphere of the Weimar Republic. And a young and charismatic firebrand, the leader of the fledgling National Socialist German Workers Party, proved especially adept at exploiting the anxious and uncertain climate. A master of propaganda, Adolf Hitler began making a name for himself with speeches that denounced the Versailles Treaty, for emasculating Germany and squelching its "resurrection," and Jews, for supposedly exploiting the German people, economically and otherwise, and polluting the "old Nordic racial spirit." He often linked these issues—one of his early speeches was titled "Political Phenomenon, Jews and the Treaty of Versailles."

Hitler's improbable ascent had begun directly in the wake of the peace treaty's signing. He joined what would become the Nazi Party in September 1919, and in a letter penned that month, he offered a chilling preview of the virulent antisemitism that defined his murderous reign as Germany's Führer more than a decade later. In this missive, he described Jews as a "racial tuberculosis of the nations" who lusted for "gold and domination," and he raised the prospect of legislation whose "ultimate objective" would be "the irrevocable removal of the Jews in general."

Hitler's rise and the resurgence of antisemitism in postwar Germany—a prejudice of a familiar, medieval vintage—paralleled a troubling swell of American antisemitism, this a modern strain of an ancient poison built upon the themes of *The Protocols of the Elders of Zion*, which by the 1920s had entered widespread circulation throughout the United States and Europe. It placed Jews at the center of an international financial conspiracy, and at the nucleus of that supposed plot, it identified firms such as Kuhn Loeb, M.M. Warburg, J. & W. Seligman & Co., and Goldman Sachs. In this fever dream, the Jews controlled governments, dominated the press, and manipulated world events like wily chess masters. They sparked wars, including the most recent one, to add to their ill-gotten fortunes, this deranged worldview contended. Jewish bankers had likewise authored the Paris peace terms, managing, once more, to turn the world's misery to profit.

Amplifying these conspiracy theories—so loudly, so relentlessly that they continue to sound, a century on, undiminished—was a somewhat unlikely figure. A renowned, if quirky industrialist, he was an icon whose name would become a byword for American enterprise and innovation. His technique for mass-producing cars transformed the nation's transportation system. But his complicated legacy also included a darker aspect: his pivotal role in ushering in a new era of antisemitic hate.

26

HENRY FORD

In late 1922, *The New York Times* reported the "rumor," passing through German political circles, that Henry Ford was bankrolling Adolf Hitler and his curiously well-funded political movement, which now operated from a spacious and "splendidly decorated" Munich headquarters, dispensed large salaries to its officials, and possessed a thousand-man paramilitary wing outfitted in new uniforms and armed with gleaming revolvers and blackjacks.[1]

The *Times* story did include some circumstantial evidence, reporting that the wall of Hitler's office featured a large picture of the American mogul. German translations of a book that bore Ford's byline littered a table in the office's anteroom. Titled *The International Jew: The World's Foremost Problem*, the volume featured a compendium of articles published by Ford's *Dearborn Independent* newspaper, which two years earlier had launched an unrelenting crusade to expose Jews for their supposed "financial and commercial control, usurpation of political power, monopoly of necessities, and autocratic direction of the very news that the American people read." Couched as a dispassionate investigation of the "Jewish question"—"we give the facts as we find them"—the *Dearborn Independent*'s series, heavily influenced by the *Protocols* and spanning some ninety-two issues, concluded blithely that the "International Jew and his satellites," these "world controllers," were "the conscious enemies of all that Anglo-Saxons mean by civilization" and lurked behind virtually all the world's ills: labor unrest, the rise of Bolshevism, financial panics, and wars.[2] The conspirators at the heart of these concentric plots, according to the *Independent*, were Jewish financiers. Jacob Schiff, Otto Kahn, and the Warburgs in particular were irresistible targets for the paper's jeremiads. Their legacies still carry the taint of Ford's spurious attacks. His malign impact on the Jewish people was incalculably profound, feeding a dynamo of hatred that only gained in intensity.

Hitler denied receiving financial backing from the U.S. industrialist but made clear he considered Ford an inspiration. "We look on Heinrich Ford as the leader of the growing *Fascisti* movement in America," Hitler said. "We admire particularly his anti-Jewish policy which is the Bavarian *Fascisti* platform. We have just had his anti-Jewish articles translated and published. The book is being circulated to millions throughout Germany." Indeed, copies of *Der internationale Jude* were ubiquitous in German bookshops.[3] In his 1925 manifesto, *Mein Kampf*, Hitler cited Ford's paper and praised him for his stand against American Jews.

How did America's most celebrated automaker become its leading purveyor of antisemitic conspiracies and influence the rise of Nazism? Ford's biographers have wrestled with that question, trying to trace the origins of his antisemitism to its insidious wellspring. Some have pointed to the atmospheric prejudice of his midwestern upbringing, including the occasionally antisemitic passages interwoven into the McGuffey Readers textbooks that formed a staple of Ford's educational diet.[4] Others have noted the profound influence of Ford's personal secretary, Ernest Liebold, who held viciously antisemitic views and who was investigated as a suspected German spy during World War I.[5]

Ford himself suggested that the clarifying moment occurred in late 1915, when he was steaming to Norway on a quixotic mission to broker an end to the Great War. The conflict had turned him into an outspoken peace activist who declared to *The New York Times* earlier that year, "I am opposed to war in every sense of the word." In the same interview, he stated that "two classes benefit by war— militarists and money lenders," and claimed "Wall Street bankers" were behind the "preparedness" movement that aimed to ready the United States for war.[6] Ford subsequently announced that he would channel $1 million of his fortune into a peace campaign. This had led to a meeting between Ford and a Hungarian feminist and pacifist named Rosika Schwimmer, with whom Ford hatched the ill-fated freelance diplomacy effort. Ford chartered the ocean liner *Oscar II*, invited the nation's best-known pacifists to join him, and set off from Hoboken on December 15. Newspapers derided the idealistic undertaking, calling it "Ford's Folly" and the "Ship of Fools."[7] Ford fell ill with the flu during the trip and spent much of the voyage in his cabin. Shortly after arriving in Europe, he abruptly and mysteriously abandoned his compatriots and returned home to Michigan, dooming the effort.[8]

Schwimmer, the originator of the initiative, was Jewish, as were other members of the peace delegation. Six years after this embarrassing episode, Ford claimed that it was his Jewish traveling companions who had opened his eyes to the supposedly pervasive power of the Jews. "On the Peace Ship were two very prominent Jews," Ford explained. "We had not been at sea 200 miles before they began telling me of the power of the Jewish race, of how they controlled the world through their control of gold, and that the Jew and no one but the Jew could end the war. . . . They said, and they believed, that the Jews started the war, that they would continue it as long as they wished. . . . I was so disgusted I would have liked to turn the ship back."[9]

Ford's explanation for his antisemitic awakening, however, does not square with Schwimmer's account. She recalled that during her first meeting with Ford, a month before they sailed for Europe, he not once but twice declared unprompted, "I know who caused the war—German-Jewish bankers! I have the evidence here. Facts! The German-Jewish bankers caused the war."[10]

There was another major influence on Ford's anti-Jewish crusade and on modern antisemitism itself: a Russian expatriate named Boris Brasol. Described as "a small, pallid, nervous, effeminate man, with a slanting forehead, prominent nose, and dark, brooding eyes," Brasol was a literary critic and lawyer who had worked for the Russian Ministry of Justice.[11] He was a member of the Black Hundreds, the ultranationalist organization of Romanov loyalists whose followers were frequently at the center of Russia's anti-Jewish pogroms. At the outset of World War I, he served as a lieutenant in the Russian Imperial Guard. He later received a diplomatic post in the United States, which he resigned in the aftermath of the Russian Revolution. His country in turmoil—and his life possibly in jeopardy if he returned—he remained in the United States, becoming a leader among White Russian émigrés and forming the Union of Czarist

Army and Navy Officers, a counterrevolutionary outfit composed of fellow Black Hundreds members and supporters of the Russian monarchy.[12]

Refined and aristocratic, Brasol became a prominent anti-Bolshevik speaker and polemicist, his writings oozing antisemitic venom. To Brasol, Judaism was synonymous with Bolshevism: he wrote of "the struggle against Bolshevism; that is to say, against Judaism," and promoted the myth of "Jewish Bolshevism."[13]

Brasol's conspiratorial ravings would have amounted to little had they not found an audience with Ford and at senior levels within U.S. military intelligence. Following the Russian Revolution, Brasol volunteered his services to the War Trade Board's intelligence bureau, where he was appointed a special investigator. By 1919, Brasol had become an adviser to Brigadier General Marlborough Churchill, chief of the War Department's Military Intelligence Division.[14]

The Russian Revolution touched off a wave of anti-Communist hysteria in the United States, and the MID led a national effort to root out subversives and radicals of all stripes, particularly the agitators and foreign anarchists believed to be the source of the nation's worsening labor and racial strife. The first "Red Scare" escalated following a series of bombings, carried out by followers of an Italian anarchist named Luigi Galleani, who targeted prominent businessmen, including Jack Morgan, and government officials. In June 1919 a Galleanist bombed the home of Attorney General A. Mitchell Palmer. Palmer subsequently launched a series of raids that targeted thousands of leftists, many of them immigrants.

That was the national atmosphere as Brasol supplied his intelligence community overlords with a steady flow of startling information on the group he considered the most subversive element of all: the Jews. Brasol fixated on Jacob Schiff, Otto Kahn, and the Warburgs, alleging that they were helping to orchestrate an effort to manufacture worldwide chaos in preparation for a global takeover. He was almost certainly the intelligence officer known as "B-1"—identified only as a Russian working for the War Trade Board—whose prodigious reports wove elaborate conspiracy theories, including some accusing the Joint Distribution Committee and the American Jewish Committee of serving as conduits for illicit financial transactions. One of B-1's unsupported allegations was that Schiff, the Warburgs, and others had covertly financed Leon Trotsky with the aim of orchestrating a "social revolution" and that they were the hidden hand behind the rise of Bolshevism.[15]

Brasol was also responsible for the widespread dissemination of the touchstone of modern antisemitism: *The Protocols of the Elders of Zion*. The fabricated document claimed to be the product of secret conclaves convened by Jewish leaders in the late nineteenth century as they devised a plan to destroy Christian civilization and gain global control.

The *Protocols* were first published in serialized form in 1903 in *Znamya*, a St. Petersburg newspaper founded by Pavel Krushevan, the fervently antisemitic journalist and Black Hundreds member who helped to incite the Kishinev pogrom. The authorship of the forged document, which contained passages lifted from several sources, has long remained murky. It has been attributed to the Paris-based chief of the Okhrana, the Russian secret service, but newer research, including by Stanford University professor Steven Zipperstein, points to Krushevan as the author or co-author of the *Protocols*.[16]

The text remained obscure and did not circulate widely until after the Russian Revolution, when Brasol and other czarists promoted the document in a bid to prove that the uprising—and Bolshevism itself—was but one prong of a broader Jewish scheme. In 1918, Brasol provided a copy of the *Protocols* to Harris Houghton, a military intelligence officer "obsessed by the Jewish threat to America's war effort," according to Judaica scholar Robert Singerman, who penned an authoritative study on the American origins of the document.[17] In addition to Brasol's antipathy for Jews, Houghton shared the Russian's obsession with Schiff. At one point, he dispatched an investigator to find a link between the financier and America's unsuccessful and scandal-plagued effort to mass-produce military aircraft during the war; Houghton also probed Schiff's partners Otto Kahn and Felix Warburg for alleged subversive activities.[18]

By late 1918, the translated *Protocols* were circulating widely within the Wilson administration, thanks to the efforts of both Houghton and Brasol. In addition to supplying the document to high-ranking intelligence officials, Houghton furnished it to several members of Wilson's cabinet. Wilson himself was informed of the *Protocols* during the Paris Peace Conference.[19] Around this time, Wilson was alerted to another trove of startling documents, also originating in Russia, that purported to show that Trotsky, Vladimir Lenin, and other leading Bolsheviks were German agents deployed to orchestrate the Russian Revolution and engineer Russia's withdrawal from the war. Consisting of sixty-eight circulars and letters professing to be from German banks, government officials, and others, this collection of documents was purchased in St. Petersburg by Edgar Sisson, a journalist and onetime editor of *Cosmopolitan* who was posted in the Russian city as a representative of the Committee on Public Information, the U.S. government agency created to oversee wartime propaganda.[20]

Some of the records contained references to Max Warburg, suggesting that he and his bank had served as a financial link to the Bolsheviks. One letter, supposedly from a leader of the German Spartacists to a Bolshevik revolutionary, stated that "the banking house M. Warburg has opened . . . an account for the undertaking of Comrade Trotsky." On its face, this missive appeared to be proof of both German (Max was all but working for the government during the war) and Jewish involvement in the Bolshevik revolution, and it seemed to confirm some of the "intelligence" Boris Brasol had fed to the MID. In fact, the files were an apparent disinformation operation mounted by Bolshevik opponents.

In 1956 the diplomat and historian George Frost Kennan—a relative of the journalist George Kennan, with whom Schiff was friendly—published a definitive debunking of the Sisson documents, exposing them as an elaborate fraud. But there were doubts about their authenticity from the start. In 1918 the British government examined the same material and determined it was largely fake, with some documents from supposedly different sources produced using the same typewriter.[21] Yet the Wilson administration came to a different conclusion—with Wilson even green-lighting the publication of the documents in a Committee on Public Information pamphlet titled "The German-Bolshevik Conspiracy," placing the U.S. government's stamp of legitimacy on the phony papers.

Once again Brasol had played a behind-the-scenes part in making sure a set of fraudulent documents was given credence. In their 1946 book *The Great Conspiracy: The Secret War Against Soviet Russia*, Michael Sayers and Albert Kahn note that Brasol and his White Russian allies were "in close touch with the State Department and supplied it with much of the spurious data and misinformation on which the State Department based its opinion of the authenticity of the fraudulent 'Sisson Documents.' "[22]

By 1919, when, despite his best efforts, his allegations of a worldwide Jewish conspiracy had failed to gain sufficient traction within the Wilson administration, Brasol began scouring for a U.S. publisher for the *Protocols*. After repeated rejections, a small Boston publishing house agreed to issue the English translation. Titled *The Protocols and*

World Revolution and published in July 1920, the 149-page volume was augmented with anonymous commentary penned by Brasol. The translated *Protocols* comprise less than half the tome. In the remaining chapters, the unnamed author—that is, Brasol—marshaled the "evidence" that the *Protocols* were genuine, and that Bolshevism was a Jewish contrivance. Among the incriminating information cited were the Sisson documents, "published by the United States Government." The Warburg-Trotsky letter was reprinted in full as proof that "certain powerful Jewish bankers were instrumental and active in spreading Bolshevism." It was a nesting doll of fraudulence—forged document reinforcing forged document. Nevertheless, the myth of a worldwide Jewish plot soon went global, as versions of the *Protocols* were published from Denmark to Japan.[23] Hitler invoked the *Protocols* in *Mein Kampf*, and its message and themes would become a staple of Nazi propaganda.

In 1921, having published *The Protocols and World Revolution* and another Jew-baiting tract, Brasol bragged: "Within the last year I have written three books, two of which have done the Jews more injury than would have been done to them by ten pogroms."[24] If anything, he underestimated his malevolent impact.

In May 1920, several months before the publication of Brasol's edition of the *Protocols*, Henry Ford's *Dearborn Independent* published the first installment of its "International Jew" series, signaling the start of a seven-year antisemitic campaign inspired deeply by the Russian propagandist.

Though it's not certain how their paths first intersected, Brasol had found a fellow traveler in Ford's top lieutenant, Ernest Liebold. Edwin Pipp, the *Independent*'s onetime editor, recalled that Liebold took an unusually keen "interest" in Brasol's "writings and affairs" and recommended that Pipp get in touch with the Russian. This resulted in an article by Brasol, titled "The Bolshevik Menace to Russia," which appeared in the pages of the *Independent* a year before the paper launched its anti-Jewish fusillade. And Pipp recalled that Brasol visited on several occasions with Liebold and Ford.[25] With Brasol's help, Liebold shaped the *Independent*'s editorial mission into one that was almost single-mindedly focused on unraveling the Jewish conspiracy.[26]

"There is no question as to the connection between [Ford's] secretary and Boris Brasol and other Jew-baiters," Pipp recounted.

"They helped fan the flame of prejudice against the Jews in Ford's mind."[27] The timing of the "International Jew" series itself suggested a connection to Brasol, for around the same time the Russian's version of the *Protocols* was published, the *Independent* wrote extensively about the text, including in an article titled "An Introduction to the 'Jewish Protocols.'"

Liebold had purchased the *Independent*, a financially strapped weekly in Ford's hometown, in late 1918 on Ford's behalf. At the time, Ford had just narrowly lost a Senate bid in a contest in which his opponent had muddied him with attacks focused on his pacifism and the draft exemption obtained by his son, Edsel. Convinced that victory had been underhandedly stolen from him and embittered by his treatment by the press, which had ridiculed his antiwar posture, Ford sought a platform for his populist message, unfiltered by media skeptics and naysayers. The paper's tagline captured its Ford-inspired ethos: "Chronicler of the Neglected Truth." Only it would become the nation's leading tribune of antisemitic lies.

Masquerading as sober-minded analysis and dot-connecting, the *Independent*, week after week, explored such loaded topics as "Does a Definite Jewish World Program Exist?," "Did the Jew Foresee the World War?," and "Does Jewish Power Control the World Press?" (Yes, yes, and also yes, according to Ford's paper.) And it scrutinized Jewish organizations such as the American Jewish Committee and the New York Kehillah, writing that both outfits were "notable for their concealment as for their power" and composed a "complete instance of a government within a government in the midst of America's largest city."[28]

Jewish bankers were frequently the objects of *Independent* coverage. Goldman Sachs and J. & W. Seligman & Co. were mentioned in passing, but perhaps reflecting Brasol's preoccupations, Schiff and his partners featured regularly in the *Independent*, their activities—philanthropic, financial, political—refracted through a sinister lens and depicted as wily machinations in service of some Jewish master plan. An article on "How Jewish International Finance Functions"—unbylined like the rest of its scurrilous companions in the "International Jew" series—mused ominously about the "far-sighted manner in which the house of Kuhn, Loeb & Company disposes itself over world affairs" and suggested that the differing sympathies of its partners during the war were in fact a clever ploy to consolidate the firm's influence. "It is a great international orchestra, this Jewish financial firm; it can play The Star Spangled Banner, Die Wacht am Rhein,

the Marseillaise, and God Save the King in one harmonious rendering, paying obsequious attention to the prejudices of each."[29]

The article cast the globetrotting Otto Kahn as the very archetype of the "International Jew," a financier-statesman who at various
points held American, British, and German citizenship. "Of just how
many countries Mr. Kahn has been a citizen is a question not easy to
determine," the paper sniped, stating that his "allotted portion of the
world seems to be Great Britain and France."[30]

The binational Warburg clan came under particular suspicion.
In the *Independent*'s telling, Paul's efforts to modernize the American
financial system had nothing to do with economic stability but was
rather an underhanded initiative intended to foster economic subser-
vience. In an article on the "Jewish idea" behind the Federal Reserve
system, the paper highlighted passages from the *Protocols* that, it contended, laid bare Warburg's true aims:

> In the Twentieth Protocol, wherein the great financial plan
> of world subversion and control is disclosed, there is another
> mention of the rulers' ignorance of financial problems. It is a
> coincidence that, while he does not use the term "ignorance,"
> Mr. Warburg is quite outspoken concerning the benighted
> state in which he found this country. . . . He admitted that
> it was his ambition from the moment he came here an alien
> Jewish-German banker, to change our financial affairs more
> to his liking. More than that, he has succeeded.[31]

Not only did Paul co-opt the American financial system, according to Ford's paper, he and brother Max had all but brokered the
Versailles Treaty. "The brother from America and the brother from
Germany both met at Paris as government representatives in deter-
mining the peace. There were so many Jews in the German delegation that it was known by the term 'kosher,' also as 'the Warburg
delegation,' and there were so many Jews in the American delegation that the delegates from the minor countries of Europe looked
upon the United States as a Jewish country."[32] (Of course, the assertion that the Warburgs had conspired to shape the peace talks, presumably on behalf of international Jewry, was outlandishly false. For
one thing, Paul did not attend the Paris conference, and both he
and Max despaired at the outcome and tried fruitlessly to blunt the
impact of the treaty's most punitive financial measures.)

The Warburg conspiracy unspooled by the *Independent* went

deeper still. "Max Warburg was a factor" in the "establishment of Bolshevism in Russia," the paper reported, citing the phony Sisson document that identified M.M. Warburg "as being one whence funds were forwarded to Trotzky for use in destroying Russia. Always against Russia, not for German reasons, but for Jewish reasons, which in this particular instance coincided. Warburg and Trotzky—against Russia!"[33]

In the plot to bring down the Russian Empire, the *Independent* identified Schiff as the kingpin, liberally mingling fact, fiction, and conjecture to paint an ominous picture of the financier's activism and advocacy. Schiff had supposedly wielded his mighty influence to force Congress to sever America's treaty with Russia—and thus "compel all business between the United States and Russia to pass through German-Jewish hands." He had bankrolled Japan's war against the czar and seeded Russian POWs with the "basic notions of what is now known as Bolshevism." Schiff's "apostles of destruction" eventually succeeded in carrying out his plan to "undermine the Russian Empire," savagely murdering Czar Nicholas and his family in the process.

"It was a family enterprise, this international campaign," the *Independent* contended. "Jacob Schiff swore to destroy Russia. Paul M. Warburg was his brother-in-law; Felix Warburg was his son-in-law. Max Warburg, of Hamburg, banker to the Bolsheviks, was thus brother-in-law to Jacob Schiff's wife and daughter." Case closed![34]

The *Independent*'s barrage of libels reached an increasingly wide audience. With Ford's substantial backing, its initial circulation of seventy thousand rose to a peak of nine hundred thousand, making it one of the largest papers in the country. The *Independent* was ubiquitous in Ford dealerships, which were pressured to hawk the publication alongside the latest Model Ts. And that was just the start: Ford's paper anthologized the "International Jew" series in four volumes, printing millions of copies and distributing them throughout the world.

Ford's onslaught plunged American Jewry into immediate crisis. Jewish leaders were predictably outraged, but they were also somewhat befuddled. Had Ford himself approved publication of these slanderous articles? In early June 1920, after two inflammatory issues of the *Independent* had appeared, Louis Marshall, now head of the American Jewish Committee, wrote to Ford directly, wondering "whether these offensive articles have your sanction" and calling on the industrialist to disavow them. "They constitute a libel upon an entire people who had hoped that at least in America they might be spared the insult, the humiliation, and the obloquy which these articles are scattering throughout the land and which are echoes from the dark Middle Ages," Marshall wrote.

A bellicose reply came promptly, signed in the name of the Dearborn Publishing Company: "Your rhetoric is that of a Bolshevik orator. . . . These articles shall continue."[35] And continue they did.

On June 23 the American Jewish Committee convened an emergency session of its executive committee to determine how to respond to Ford's attacks, which Marshall had called "the most serious episode in the history of American Jewry."[36] Schiff did not attend, but his friend Cyrus Adler read a letter from the financier (who had not yet personally become a target of the Ford paper's screeds).[37] Two years earlier Schiff had declared it "better all around to take preventative measures than to have, later on, when the threatened mischief has been done, to endeavor to take curative action." And throughout his life Schiff had been known for his hot-tempered eruptions in defense of his people. But now, faced with Ford's outrageous provocations, he recommended an uncharacteristically meek approach.

"If we get into a controversy we shall light a fire, which no one can foretell how it will become extinguished, and I would strongly advise therefore that no notice be taken of these articles and the attack will soon be forgotten," he counseled.[38] The AJC largely followed the course Schiff prescribed, hoping to starve the controversy with silence. But Schiff—and others on the AJC executive committee who wanted to avoid a direct clash with Ford—had badly misread the situation. The fire was already lit—and it has never ceased blazing.

Google "Schiff," and it will become evident what Ford—and Boris Barsol, whose intelligence memo linking Schiff to the Bolshevik revolution leaked to the press in 1925 and whose relentless promotion of the *Protocols* stoked antisemitism the world over—helped to unleash. Schiff, along with his Warburg in-laws, would feature in pernicious conspiracy theories concerning their role in the Russian Revolution (and other nefarious acts) that have grown more grandiose with the passage of time. These meritless claims hold that Schiff almost singlehandedly masterminded the revolution with help from the Warburgs (who were clandestinely working on behalf of the Rothschild family); that Trotsky was Schiff's "loyal agent," and that Schiff and Max Warburg had facilitated the passage of Trotsky and Vladimir Lenin to

Russia to carry out the Bolshevik revolution; and most absurdly, that the Russian czar and his family were executed on direct orders from Schiff, an "illuminati Jewish banker."

Dan Kramarsky, a grandson of Dolly Schiff, recalled being confronted with wild allegations concerning his great-great-grandfather when searching online for information about the Order of the Rising Sun medal Jacob received from the Japanese government: "When you start going into that corner of the web, you see the conspiracy theorists, they're out in force there."[39] A Warburg descendant described the family's ongoing discomfort with the conspiracy theories about the clan that populate online forums and Wiki entries. "Our family feels very sensitized to anything about the family," she said, describing the troubling "spillover" from the early twentieth century that continues to plague the Warburgs.[40]

"It's a wonder they haven't come to my house and firebombed it, given the kind of hatred that is said specifically about Paul Warburg," said his great-granddaughter Katharine Weber. Her grandfather, Jimmy, would end up linked to outlandish plots, ranging from the Lindbergh kidnapping to the establishment of the CIA's MK-Ultra program, the agency's mind control experiments utilizing LSD.[41]

After the Schiff-Warburg conspiracy theories first appeared in the pages of *The Dearborn Independent*, demagogues continually revived the allegations in the ensuing decades. Most notably, in 1938 right-wing "radio priest" Father Charles Coughlin, who contended that American-Jewish bankers were responsible for the ascendance of Russian Communism, made Schiff and his Kuhn Loeb partners a focus of his antisemitic broadcasts. The Michigan-based broadcaster told his listeners Schiff had "fomented" the Russian Revolution and that he had financed Trotsky "to bring about the social revolution."[42] Coughlin claimed to be in possession of a Secret Service document supporting these charges, though it turned out he was parroting his claims almost verbatim from a Nazi propaganda bulletin.[43] Trotsky himself responded to Coughlin's claims, denying that Schiff had funded him. "The name Jacob Schiff means nothing to me," he said. "I, personally, never received money from Jacob Schiff."[44]

The Trotsky connection made little sense. Schiff, of course, was jubilant at the overthrow of the Romanov regime and had made no secret of his opposition to the czar. In the aftermath of the revolution, Schiff supported the provisional government led by Alexander Kerensky, a moderate who hoped to establish a constitutional democracy. Over the course of 1917, Schiff's attitude toward events in Russia shifted from exultant to trepidatious to despondent as the Bolsheviks seized power. In an August 1917 letter to Louis Marshall, he was dismissive of Trotsky and lamented that Jews were associated with the Bolshevik movement, accurately predicting an antisemitic backlash.

> We all know that a good many Jews, in name at least, with Trotsky at their head, have been in the Bolshevik Movement and while these no doubt have only been a small minority in this insidious agitation . . . it is unfortunately very likely that the not very highly intelligent Russian peasantry will of their own accord or in consequence of the agitation of others, make the Jews in general, responsible for the misfortune which has been brought upon them. Because of this, dark days may indeed be in store for our coreligionists in Russia. But what is even worse, the danger exists even in our own country, that this tale of the Jews being back of the Bolshevik movement . . . may find considerable credence, which if we can, we should prevent.[45]

Why would Schiff have penned such a letter if he had been aiding Trotsky and the Bolsheviks? Kenneth Ackerman, who authored a book on the ten-week period Trotsky spent in New York between January and March 1917—the supposed time period in which Schiff met and financed the exiled revolutionary—wrote that "even a cursory look at the facts" upends the Schiff-Trotsky tale. "When Lenin and Trotsky seized power for themselves in November 1917," he pointed out, "Schiff immediately rejected them, cut off further loans, started funding anti-Bolshevist groups, and even demanded that the Bolsheviks pay back some of the money he'd loaned Kerensky."[46]

Yet this bunk story endured, with the amount Schiff supposedly advanced to Trotsky and his Bolshevik allies increasing with each new telling—from $10,000 to $12 million to $20 million. The first reference to the latter figure appeared in 1949 in the *New York Journal-American*'s pseudonymous Cholly Knickerbocker gossip column, then authored by journalist Igor Cassini, whose aristocratic family had fled Russia in the wake of the revolution when he was a toddler. "Who do you think financed Lenin, Stalin & Co. in Russia?" Cassini's squib read. "Old man Jacob Schiff, then New York banker, boasted that his money had been one of the causes of the first Russian Revolution of 1905. Today it is estimated even by Jacob's grandson,

John Schiff, a prominent member of New York Society, that the old man sank about $20,000,000 for the final triumph of Bolshevism in Russia."[47]

In the 1950s, as other publications began citing the Knickerbocker item, John Schiff finally issued a statement disputing the remarks attributed to him: "I never said it. I couldn't have, because why would I say something that was completely untrue."[48] This did little to slow down the claim, printed repeatedly over the years, including in Pat Robertson's conspiracy-riddled 1991 book, *The New World Order*, in which the televangelist added a new twist on the fable: Schiff "personally transport[ed]" $20 million in gold to the Bolsheviks.[49]

Ford's paper disfigured Schiff's legacy so thoroughly that when Cyrus Adler was posthumously assembling the banker's biography, he and Morti debated whether it was wise to delve into the *real* role Schiff had played in taking on the czar. "I do not know whether you keep up with Mr. Ford, but you are the only favorite in the family upon whom the vials of his wrath do not descend," Adler wrote. "That your father aided the revolutionary cause in Russia is in my mind certain. He was apparently closely associated with the Friends of Russian Freedom and supplied them with funds, and part of these funds were used in propaganda among the Russian prisoners in Japan. It was part of his settled purpose to liberalize the Czaristic government." Adler concluded that omitting these facts about Schiff's life—he personally considered any role Schiff had played in toppling the czar a "glory"—risked inviting "much more severe" antisemitic attacks. "I do not feel that we have to alter our lives or our writings simply because these mad beasts are about. Let us rather go ahead unafraid and take our chances."[50]

Eventually, the "mad beasts" of the *Independent* were brought to heel by legal action.

In 1923 the journalist Herman Bernstein filed a libel suit against Ford, who had remarked in an interview that it was Bernstein who had told him aboard the "peace ship" that Jewish financiers were at the root of the war. "He told me most of the things that I have printed," Ford had claimed.[51] In early 1925 another subject of the *Independent*'s defamatory broadsides sued Ford and his paper. The plaintiff was a charismatic California lawyer and activist, Aaron Sapiro, a pioneer in organizing farming cooperatives. In an article on "Jewish Exploitation of Farmers' Organizations," the *Independent* had cast Sapiro as the chief villain. Kuhn Loeb's Otto Kahn also made a cameo in this conspiracy, as a member of the Jewish banking cartel facilitating Sapiro's plot.

A few years earlier, as the *Independent* became increasingly fixated on Kuhn Loeb, the firm had contemplated filing its own case against Ford. Julius Goldman produced a thirty-six-page memo weighing the merits of a civil suit. "The plain accusation emerges that your firm here and abroad, in peace and in war, has been part of a Jewish conspiracy for world war, world revolution and world domination," Goldman wrote, calling the charges "as serious as any that I have ever seen in print." The case would be time-consuming and enormously expensive, the lawyer determined, but Kuhn Loeb would probably prevail. Yet "the great publicity the suit might involve might well have unpleasant features," he warned, potentially forcing the partners to divulge "private matters of business which all men conducting such great and important affairs as you desire to keep private."[52] Ultimately, Kuhn Loeb did not move forward with litigation, though in Germany, Max Warburg successfully sued Theodor Fritsch, publisher of German translations of *The International Jew* and the *Protocols*, for libel.

Ford dodged service in the Bernstein case, drawing the matter out, but the Sapiro case went to trial in March 1927. Shortly before Ford was expected to take the stand, he had a mysterious accident, in which his car was forced off the road and sent careering down an embankment, leaving him unable to testify. Sapiro contended Ford "faked" his accident and claimed the mogul had "lost his nerve . . . at the collapse of his case."[53] The proceedings ended in a mistrial, but Sapiro pressed forward with his case. Ford, however, was done fighting. In addition to enmeshing him in pricey litigation, the *Independent*'s anti-Jewish attacks were costing Ford in other ways, fueling negative publicity and sparking boycotts against his businesses.

That summer, shortly before the judge scheduled the Sapiro case for a new trial, Ford representatives enlisted Louis Marshall to help bring the "International Jew" chapter to a close. Marshall drafted, and Ford signed, a statement apologizing for his paper's antisemitic campaign. It read in part: "I am deeply mortified that this journal, which is intended to be constructive and not destructive, has been made the medium for resurrecting exploded fictions, for giving currency to the so-called *Protocols of the Wise Men of Zion* . . . and for contending that the Jews have been engaged in a conspiracy to control the capital and the industries of the world."[54] Ford settled separately with Sapiro and Bernstein, retracting the statements he and his paper had made about them. And he shuttered the *Independent*, which published its final issue in December 1927.[55]

If Ford's statement suggested contrition, his future actions indicated that his views remained largely unaltered. In the last decades of his life, he kept company with Nazi sympathizers including the aviator Charles Lindbergh and Gerald L. K. Smith, founder of the America First Party. And he lunched regularly with Father Coughlin.[56] Hitlerites also populated the ranks of the Ford Motor Company, among them Heinz Spanknöbel, who fronted the American branch of the Nazi Party, and Fritz Kuhn, leader of the German American Bund.[57] On Ford's seventy-fifth birthday in 1938, Hitler's government awarded the automaker—who had established a German subsidiary, with Heinrich Albert, onetime paymaster of the Reich's American spy network, as chairman of the board—the Grand Service Cross of the Supreme Order of the German Eagle, the highest honor awarded to foreign citizens.

As World War II loomed, Ford continued to decry "international financiers" for causing labor unrest and fueling "war scares" for profit. He was typically careful to omit the word *Jewish* from his fulminations against the "Wall Street crowd." But in June 1940, the year before the United States entered World War II, the mask slipped during a conversation with an Associated Press reporter, and Ford remarked: "I still think this is a phony war made by the international Jewish bankers."[58]

Ford did eventually reckon with the lethal hatred he had helped to whip up, according to Josephine Gomon, who oversaw female personnel at a Ford plant. She was among a group of executives who joined Ford in May 1946 for a screening of *Death Stations*, a government-produced film documenting the liberation of Hitler's concentration camps. For an hour, horrifying images flashed across the screen—a crematorium at Poland's Majdanek, torture chambers, a warehouse filled with the confiscated belongings of murdered Jews. When the film ended and the lights rose, Ford's colleagues found him clinging to consciousness. He had suffered a major stroke. Ford died the following year at the age of eighty-three.

It is impossible to know what thoughts flickered through his mind in the moments before he was afflicted, but Gomon believed he was deeply disturbed by the footage. Finally, Ford "saw the ravages of a plague he had helped to spread," she wrote in her unpublished memoir. "The virus had come full circle."[59]

27

THE WORLD TO COME

From the first moments of 1920, an aura of angst and upheaval suffused American life.

The day after the New Year, federal agents in thirty-five cities stormed homes, meeting halls, social clubs, cafés, and other venues, rounding up thousands of suspected Communists and left-wing radicals, most of them immigrants, in a second round of raids authorized by A. Mitchell Palmer and overseen by a young J. Edgar Hoover. Prohibition took effect a couple of weeks later, the result of a national panic over the country's fraying moral fabric.

In March the Senate rejected, for the second and final time, the Versailles Treaty, dooming Wilson's League of Nations and badly tarnishing his political legacy. In May, Massachusetts police arrested Nicola Sacco and Bartolomeo Vanzetti, Italian immigrant anarchists and suspected followers of Luigi Galleani, and later charged them with first-degree murder, sparking one of the most controversial prosecutions in the nation's history. Later that month striking coal miners in West Virginia skirmished with private detectives hired to evict them from their company homes, leading to the deaths of ten people in what would be known as the Battle of Matewan. That June a southern publicist named Edward Young Clarke began overseeing the revival of the Ku Klux Klan, which had been all but squelched during Reconstruction, attracting millions of new members in the coming years. And that summer, of course, the *Dearborn Independent* ramped up its anti-Jewish attacks, and the first version of the *Protocols* was published in the United States.

Hate and prejudice—directed at Blacks, at Jews, at immigrants— was on the rise. The palpable tension almost seemed to be building toward something. Finally, during the lunch hour on Thursday, September 16, the citadel of American capitalism exploded.

The blast, originating from a horse-drawn cart parked across the street from the headquarters of J.P. Morgan & Co., packed with one hundred pounds of dynamite and five hundred pounds of cast-iron sash weights (to ensure maximum human carnage), loosed a curtain of flame down Wall Street. Traders, bank tellers, and runners were lifted off their feet and sent flying through the air. Shattered glass blanketed the ground like fresh snow. The concussion broke windows a half mile away.

Thirty-eight people died in the attack, including J.P. Morgan's twenty-four-year-old chief clerk, William Joyce. Junius Morgan, Jack's eldest son, was among the three hundred wounded. A century later the shrapnel lacerations remain visible on the Corner's marble exterior. The Wall Street bombing, which remains unsolved but was thought to be the work of Galleanists, was the nation's deadliest act of domestic terrorism until the Oklahoma City bombing in 1995. The human toll and physical wreckage were enormous; the psychic wound the attack inflicted upon the nation was equally profound. Coming in the wake of a string of anarchist bombing attempts targeting prominent politicians and businessmen, it confirmed the worst fears of Americans who believed the country was on the verge of a Bolshevik-style takeover.

The bombing added fuel to the atmosphere of intolerance that had been building rapidly across the country, and it helped inspire new and severe immigration restrictions, including a 1924 law that imposed a "national origins" quota system. As a result, Jewish immigration slowed to a trickle. As Europe's Jews fled Hitler's genocide, the nation would remain largely closed to them when they most needed sanctuary.

Meanwhile, quota systems appeared elsewhere too, most notably at Ivy League colleges, such as Harvard, whose president, A. Lawrence Lowell, spun his proposal to cap Jewish attendance at 15 percent of the student body as an effort to reduce growing antisemitism. "The antisemitic feeling among the students is increasing, and it grows in proportion to the increase in the number of Jews," he sanctimoniously declared. "If their number should become 40 percent of the student body, the race feeling would become intense."[1]

Jacob Schiff—who had gifted to Harvard a museum of Semitic studies—did not survive to witness this insult against his people, the final triumph of the restrictionists he had spent most of his life battling, or Hitler's horrifying ascent. But in his final days, the state of the world was grim. The accumulation of crises, and the strain of the war and its aftermath, seemed to weigh physically on the financier. "Personally, I am deeply affected by conditions not only in Russia but throughout the world and, at times, my nerves are very considerably upset by it," he confided in early 1920 to A. J. Sack, head of the anti-Bolshevik Russian Information Bureau, to which Schiff contributed and served as an "honorary adviser."[2]

Over the past few years, Schiff's health had steadily declined. He was now largely deaf, suffering from heart disease and crippling bouts of insomnia. His breathing was becoming labored, and he found sitting upright more comfortable than reclining. Late at night, his chauffeur took him on long drives. Sometimes, lulled by the fresh air and the hypnotic rhythms of the vehicle, Schiff dozed off.[3]

Outside Schiff's family, few knew he was ailing. In public, he put on a good show of vigor, and there were fleeting periods when he did regain his strength. During the summer of 1919, Jacob and Therese made their annual visit to Bar Harbor, where Schiff disregarded his doctor's advice against strenuous activity and spent hours trekking through the woods with his grandchildren and other hiking companions. (Had Senator Borah witnessed Schiff in action, he might have found reason to question Schiff's excuse for avoiding traveling to Washington to testify in the treaty "leak" hearing that June.)[4]

He decided against returning to Maine the following August, blaming the last summer's exertions for aggravating his heart condition and saying he could not "withstand the temptation of going up at least some of the superb hills there."[5] Schiff thought his health might benefit from a "somewhat higher altitude," so he and Therese instead spent the month of August in New Hampshire's White Mountains, before returning in September to their summer home in Sea Bright. Once again Schiff's health seemed to improve slightly, and he briefly began venturing back to his office at Kuhn Loeb.[6] But when Louis Marshall visited Schiff in mid-September 1920 on the day before Rosh Hashanah, the Jewish New Year, he knew something was wrong. Schiff fretted that he might not be able to attend synagogue during the upcoming High Holidays. He had been forbidden from walking and considered it sacrilegious to be driven.[7]

The following week Schiff fasted as usual on Yom Kippur. The next day he was afflicted by severe heart pain and that evening slipped into a state of partial consciousness. He remained in that condition for the next two days, until finally succumbing at six-thirty p.m. on Saturday, September 25, as the last rays of the Sabbath sun disappeared over Fifth Avenue.[8]

"It is with the greatest of grief that we inform you of the death of our beloved senior," Kuhn Loeb cabled its clients and contacts around the world. Benjamin Buttenwieser, then a young Kuhn Loeb staffer, remembered, "It did not even give the name because that would have seemed denigrating even to imply the recipients didn't know who Kuhn Loeb's Senior Partner was."[9]

The fortune Schiff left behind was initially estimated to be as high as $150 million. In fact, it was less than a quarter of that—about $35 million (not including a $6 million trust fund he had established for his wife). Of Schiff's varied assets, the largest chunk, about $6.4 million, was held in U.S. victory notes that supported the war effort. "The fact that Mr. Schiff left only about $10 million more than Andrew Carnegie, who devoted the later years of his life in an effort to die poor, and less than a third of the fortune amassed by J. Pierpont Morgan, whose contemporary he was . . . will occasion general surprise," *The New York Times* commented, after a full accounting of his assets, down to the sixty-nine dollars he had in his pocket at the time of his death, was submitted to New York tax authorities. "The estate is less than half that of Henry Clay Frick and Anthony N. Brady, whose activities in large financial operations did not approach those of Mr. Schiff, but Mr. Schiff, like Mr. Carnegie, was a constant benefactor of religious and charitable organizations and individuals during his lifetime."[10]

Schiff's posthumous charitable gifts, totaling $1.35 million, spanned four pages in his will. The nineteen recipients of his largesse reflected the wide spectrum of his philanthropic interests, ranging from the Jewish Theological Seminary and the Montefiore Home to New York University, Harvard, the Metropolitan Museum of Art, and Booker T. Washington's Tuskegee Institute. Even in death, Schiff exerted rigid control over his philanthropic gifts. Rather than make these bequests outright, he directed in his will that they be treated as endowments, with only the income available to the organizations to spend. In the case of the largest recipient of his charity,

the Federation for the Support of Jewish Philanthropies, founded
and led by Schiff's son-in-law Felix Warburg, accepting the banker's
$500,000 bequest required changing its bylaws, which expressly pro-
hibited legacies. Schiff stated in his will that he was "convinced that
it will be in the interest of the Federation to repeal this provision."
He added, in classic Schiff fashion, that he had "no desire to exercise
any pressure" on the group while doing exactly that. Schiff's request
was the subject of intense debate within the federation, but its bylaws
were ultimately amended.[11]

A fastidious man who saw to every detail, Schiff also left behind
a letter to his survivors "to be opened promptly after my death" that
detailed his burial wishes and how he hoped to be mourned by his
loved ones. It read:

> To my beloved Wife, children, & survivors,
>
> Knowing, that at some time, I shall have to leave you to
> enter into eternal life, I express the following wishes, which
> I ask you to have carried out upon my passing away: Have
> every precaution taken that life is extinct, either by opening
> the veins, embalming or other method. The casket in which
> I am buried should be <u>most simple</u>; a lavish display of flowers
> should be avoided. The ceremonies may take place in a
> temple or other place of worship, but should be confined to
> the reading of the burial service and to music.
>
> The "Tefilin" . . . which I have been using upon the
> anniversary of the death of my parents, I wish to have laid
> into the coffin in which I am buried.
>
> I hope, that my children will say "Kaddish" during the
> first eleven months after my death on Saturdays, whenever
> they can <u>conveniently</u> do this, but they must not feel, that if
> for any reason, they are prevented from doing so, they have
> not carried out my wishes. If they can honor my memory, by
> likewise publicly saying "Kaddish" annually on the Saturday
> preceding the anniversary of my death I think it will give
> them satisfaction.
>
> In life and in death
>
> your loving
>
> Jacob H. Schiff

. . .

A new age dawned for Kuhn Loeb and for the nation, which entered a period of unprecedented prosperity as spectacular as the 1929 economic collapse that marked its conclusion.

The stewardship of Kuhn Loeb passed to the third generation. Though Schiff at times questioned his son's judgment—and had a habit of treating him harshly—he had always hoped Morti would inherit his throne. But the internationally famous, headline-dominating Otto Kahn, bolder in business and in most other respects than his partner, would not happily play a subordinate role. "Since the death of Jacob H. Schiff, nobody was considered a senior member of the firm and each partner's position and influence depended upon what he himself made of it," Morti later acknowledged.[12] For all practical purposes, he and Kahn took joint command of the firm, which then included only two other partners: Jerome Hanauer and Felix, who by that time was involved only nominally in Kuhn Loeb's affairs.

During the 1920s, the firm largely stuck to the path established by Jacob Schiff, overseeing $3 billion of industrial and sovereign bond issues, though Otto Kahn, following his bohemian interests, also steered the partnership into financing the burgeoning film industry.[13] At a time when many Wall Street firms were wary of bankrolling movie studios, Kahn spearheaded a deal for Kuhn Loeb to underwrite a $10 million stock issue for the Famous Players–Lasky Corporation, later known as Paramount.

Entering the postwar era with its prestige diminished, Kuhn Loeb clung to its place in the investment banking world's upper ranks, even as it faced competition from unlikely quarters.

Shortly before Jacob Schiff's death, Paul Warburg had approached him about funding a new venture he was forming called the International Acceptance Bank, which Paul viewed as a vehicle to finance German reconstruction and to get back into business with his brother Max. The firm would specialize in acceptances—a type of short-term exchange bill guaranteed (or "accepted") by a bank and that could be bought and sold on the secondary market. These credit instruments, seen as less risky than other types of exchange bills because a bank (not an individual or business) was liable for payment, had long financed international trade in Europe, but a market was just forming in the United States thanks to the creation of the Federal Reserve, which was newly empowered to purchase acceptances from member banks.

Kuhn Loeb's partners were leery of Warburg's proposal, foresee-
ing possible conflicts with their own business. Still Schiff, for largely
sentimental reasons, agreed to Paul's offer of a 10 percent stake in the
business. The IAB began operating in 1921, with Paul serving as its
chairman and his son Jimmy as the company's vice-president.

The problems began almost immediately, as Paul's new firm
strayed from its commercial banking mandate into terrain occupied
(and zealously guarded) by Kuhn Loeb, including the issue and place-
ment of foreign securities. Soon the IAB was directly approaching
Kuhn Loeb's clients and connections. "For instance," Morti wrote
in a fourteen-page memo documenting the dyspeptic relationship,
"James Warburg urged N.M. Rothschild & Sons, London, not to
ship gold exclusively to Kuhn, Loeb & Co., but to send some of
it to the International Acceptance Bank. He also stated to various
European connections . . . that the relations between Kuhn, Loeb &
Co. and the International Acceptance Bank were so close, that it did
not matter to which of the two proposals were addressed and thus
attempted to strengthen the position of the International Acceptance
Bank."

Alarmingly, Paul's bank seemed to be trying to assert itself as
M.M. Warburg's primary American contact, a role Kuhn Loeb had
played for decades. "Gradually friction arose," Morti explained diplomatically. The partnership limped on uneasily until 1927, when the
Warburgs finally informed Morti that the IAB "must have full freedom of action to do any and all kind of business in any manner it saw
fit." As a result, Morti recalled, Max, "because of family reasons,"
felt "compelled to choose the International Acceptance Bank as their
intimate New York connection."

This dispute placed Felix in an awkward spot. He had never been
very active in Kuhn Loeb's business dealings—Morti remembered
him handling mostly menial jobs "such as supervision and care of
securities" and "signing of mail"—but, as a partner, he nevertheless
shared in its substantial profits. He was also a board member and
shareholder of his brother's bank. These roles were now clashing. In
one case, Felix had transferred $1 million to the IAB without con-
sulting his Kuhn Loeb partners; Morti strongly suspected that these
funds had helped bankroll the IAB's merger with the Bank of Manhattan. (Later, after another merger, the combined entity was known
as Chase Manhattan.) At this point, Felix's partners viewed any deal
that strengthened Paul's bank as a threat. According to Morti, Felix
was unapologetic about his support for his brother's firm, telling his

partners "he reserved to himself the right to support the interests of the International Acceptance Bank . . . even though this should be detrimental to the interests of Kuhn, Loeb & Co."

The business rivalry between Kuhn Loeb and the IAB tested the family relationship in other ways. Frederick Warburg, Felix and Frieda's eldest son, had gone to work for Kuhn Loeb in 1922, fresh from an M.M. Warburg apprenticeship and a stint inspecting the Joint Distribution Committee's Eastern European relief efforts. The job, like Felix's, was largely a sinecure, since Frederick lacked "business sense" and initiative, according to Morti (his uncle). As business disagreements multiplied with the IAB, Morti told Felix, perhaps too bluntly, that Frederick was "unfitted" for banking and keeping him on was doing everyone a disservice. Wounded, as any father would be, Felix pulled Frederick from the partnership and placed him at Lehman Brothers (which maintained a close relationship with Kuhn Loeb and its partners). Felix considered resigning himself, broaching the subject with his brother Max and later with Morti. Schiff's partners had been quietly petitioning him to encourage Felix to retire. But fearing a widening rift with the Warburgs, Morti navigated Felix toward a deal in which he could remain a member of Kuhn Loeb, with no real business responsibilities and with the ability to come and go as he pleased, in exchange for a reduced share of the partnership's profits.

If Paul impinged on Kuhn Loeb's business, he also helped the firm avert catastrophe in the 1929 crash. Long before the inevitable reckoning, he had seen it coming, watching the market inflate with growing unease. During the boom years of the 1920s, the soaring stock market attracted an influx of new investors, many of them purchasing shares on margin to maximize their profits. The prevailing attitude among the financial world's leading minds seemed to be that what went up did not have to come down. Meanwhile investment banks had hatched a risky new vehicle to cater to the nation's growing appetite for playing the market. A more freewheeling version of today's mutual funds, investment trusts were corporations that sold shares to the public and used the proceeds for stock market speculation. In the years leading up to the Great Depression, hundreds of investment trusts were formed and marketed to investors.

Paul was horrified both by the speculative frenzy and by the lack of action by the Federal Reserve, which possessed the power to cool off the overheated market but was instead standing by idly while the U.S. economy headed toward a meltdown. He convinced Morti to cash out some of his personal holdings. And based on Paul's advice, Kuhn Loeb reduced its call loans—so named because bankers could call back these debts at any time—to brokers, and it exchanged some of its riskier assets for more stable municipal bonds.[14]

Kuhn Loeb also abstained from the investment trust craze, unlike many of its peers. "We did not join in the general scramble to create affiliates and to create securities corporations," Otto Kahn would later tell the Senate Banking and Currency Committee, which in 1932 launched a probe into the causes of the stock market crash. "Not one of them bears our trade mark. Not one of them was set up by us."[15]

Tired of waiting for the Federal Reserve to get off the sidelines, Paul issued a public warning. In a statement printed in papers across the country, the banker excoriated the Fed for allowing speculators to consume the nation's credit supply and for turning over the "rudder" of the nation's credit system to "Stock Exchange operators." The central bank had the authority to slow the flood of borrowed money entering the stock market by raising interest rates and "must exercise its influence quickly and forcefully," Warburg said. The outcome would be dire if it failed to do so: "If orgies of unrestrained speculation are permitted to spread too far, however, the ultimate collapse is certain not only to affect the speculators themselves, but also to bring about a general depression involving the entire country."[16]

On September 3, 1929, the Dow Jones Industrial Average reached a record-breaking 381—a high it would not see again for another twenty-five years.

The crash did not come all at once but in a series of convulsive trading sessions late that October. On the morning of October 24 ("Black Thursday"), the market plunged by 11 percent. Suddenly, the irrational exuberance that had sent Wall Street to new heights was replaced by gnawing desperation, and the floor of the New York Stock Exchange became a gladiator pit of fear and frenzy. The pace of the massive sell-off overwhelmed the ticker tape, which was spitting out quotes that lagged more than an hour behind. Wild (and false) rumors spread through the exchange and beyond—one claimed that speculators were committing suicide in droves. When a man was spotted on top of a nearby building, a crowd gathered on Broad Street assuming he planned to leap. He turned out to be a repairman.[17] The market recovered that afternoon, but the panic intensified the following week. On October 28 (Black Monday), the market fell by almost 13 percent. The following day (Black Tuesday), it dropped by another 12. This time it did not bounce back, beginning a slow and painful slide that would take the Dow to a low of 41 in July 1932.

One day in the midst of the panic, Jeff Seligman appeared on the floor of the exchange. Crisply dressed in striped pants and a frock coat, a freshly cut flower in the lapel, the eccentric Seligman scion looked every inch the banking eminence, even though by then, and for many years prior, his role at J. & W. Seligman & Co. had mostly consisted of collecting checks and amusing junior colleagues with his quirky habits. Recently, his name had been plastered all over the papers due to an embarrassing scandal. A showgirl named "Kittens," whom the elderly banker had started courting when she was sixteen, was suing Seligman for $100,000 for reneging on his promise of marriage.[18]

Jeff had come downtown to witness the pandemonium, like some disaster tourist. But the presence of the prominent banker, who was spotted taking in the spectacle with serene detachment, temporarily seemed to calm the market, one paper noted at the time.[19]

Earlier that year J. & W. Seligman & Co. had established two investment trusts. And in the wake of the crash the company saw hefty declines that forced it to embark on a round of cost-cutting and layoffs. It nevertheless fared better than many competitors since it had not borrowed money to fuel speculative buying.[20]

Far harder hit were Lehman Brothers and Goldman Sachs, which had both ridden the stock market boom of the 1920s to new heights, only to be laid low by the collapse. Following Henry Goldman's departure, Goldman Sachs's underwriting partnership with the Lehmans gradually unraveled. In 1926 the firms formally brokered a divorce, divvying up their list of underwriting clients, which now numbered sixty, with the majority remaining with Goldman Sachs.

Both firms were now dominated by new personalities. Though Philip Lehman remained the titular head of Lehman Brothers into the 1930s, he increasingly handed the reins over to his Yale-educated son Robert. Bobbie had joined Lehman Brothers in 1919, following his military service in France with the American Expeditionary Forces. An art connoisseur, he had helped to curate and expand his father's collection of masterpieces. "In the same way Bobbie collected people," remembered Lehman partner Herman Kahn, who joined the firm in 1928 as an office boy. "When one caught his fancy, he would buy him and bring him into the firm." Kahn noted that Bobbie was "obviously more interested in art than banking" and his "genius was to assemble able people who understood the intelligent use of money." And he added: "Bobbie wasn't a technician. He couldn't set up a financing. But he opened every door."[21]

Bobbie's stormy personal life included three marriages, and to his partners, he seemed particularly keen on ingratiating himself into Christian society. "Bobbie wanted to be Episcopalian," one partner said. "He was a Jewish antisemite."[22] Another recalled: "Bobbie was very keen on social distinction and on moving across Jew-Gentile lines. It was a big day for him when I became a director of SOCAL [Standard Oil Company of California]. Not because it meant much money. . . . But because the Lehmans, a Jewish firm, had caught one of the big oil companies which were known to deal only with gentiles."[23]

At Goldman, the Sachses had recruited Waddill Catchings, a Harvard friend and classmate of Arthur Sachs, to fill the void left by Henry Goldman's departure. A Tennessee-born lawyer, Catchings was slender, handsome, and charming. He could also be ruthless and imperious. Awed by his brilliance, Walter Sachs took a deferential posture toward Catchings, who led Goldman Sachs into risky ventures that would have made the partnership's cautious founder, Marcus Goldman, quake.[24] One of them was the creation, in December 1928, of the Goldman Sachs Trading Corporation, which, under Catchings's leadership, sired another investment trust, the Shenandoah Corporation, that in turn established a third trust, the Blue Ridge Company. The Goldman Sachs Trading Corporation initially issued $100 million worth of stock (1 million shares, each with a face value of $100). The shares hit the market at $104 and quickly rose, more than doubling by February 1929.

In his book on the 1929 crash, the economist John Kenneth Galbraith points out that the ballooning share price "was not the undiluted result of public enthusiasm for the financial genius of Goldman, Sachs." Rather, the Trading Corporation was artificially inflating its own share price by "buying heavily of its own securities." Effectively, the daisy chain of trusts fueled one another.[25]

Lehman Brothers, meanwhile, created the Lehman Corporation, debuting the new investment trust the month before the market plunged. By 1930, shares in the Lehman Corporation had shed half their value and the partnership had lost an estimated $13 million in the debacle.[26] But the losses sustained by the Goldman Sachs Trading Corporation were stratospheric: $121.4 million. It accounted for a

staggering 70 percent of the bloodletting by the fourteen top investment trusts.[27] The Sachses finally pushed Catchings out of the firm,
and Walter Sachs, alongside Sidney Weinberg, the onetime office
boy groomed by Paul Sachs, began the arduous task of unwinding the
Trading Corporation. Walter rose at four a.m. and worked until ten
p.m., repeating the exhausting ritual day after day. "As the markets
were improving, we began to sell, sell, and sell."[28]

Goldman Sachs, its reputation shattered, faced a cascade of investor lawsuits. Retired from the business, Sam Sachs remained largely
oblivious to the ruinous damage done to the firm. "His mind began
to fail with age," Walter remembered. "He thought he knew what
was going on, but he always said to me, 'So long as the name isn't
hurt.' But poor man, he didn't know—thank fortune, he didn't realize . . . the name had been hurt." When the elder Sachs died in 1935,
at eighty-three, the firm was still years away from reclaiming its good
name.[29]

Decades after the crash, Walter reflected on what had caused his
firm to act so recklessly in the late 1920s. "To conquer the world!
Not only greed for money, but power sparked it, and that was the
great mistake because I confess to the fact that we were all influenced
by greed."[30]

Any schadenfreude Henry Goldman may have experienced from
seeing the Sachses writhe was tempered by his horror at witnessing the firm that bore his family name become a national punch line
and a mascot of unscrupulous finance. Even before the crash, Henry
had an inkling that Catching was leading the firm in a bad direction.
"I know you do not like flattery," art dealer Joseph Duveen wrote
to him in 1928, "but I am constantly hearing from prominent men
downtown that Goldman Sachs is not at all top drawer today. People
say their way of business is not entirely on the up-and-up."

"I am, of course, egotistical enough to be glad if it is true that I
am missed," Henry replied, "but I am equally sorry that a great old
name, which I did so much to build up, is on the toboggan."[31]

According to Henry's granddaughter, June Breton Fisher, he
weathered the crash largely unscathed: "Henry's personal resources
remained untouched by the debacle. He had steered clear of any participation in the trusts, considering them too risky."[32] After retiring
from Goldman Sachs, Henry had joined the firm Arthur Lipper &
Co., which was seeking to build up its underwriting business, though
he increasingly devoted his time to his own artistic and philanthropic
pursuits.[33] He and his wife Babette took an interest in the career of

Yehudi Menuhin, after watching him perform with the New York Philharmonic, presenting the twelve-year-old violin prodigy with a $60,000 Stradivarius. And with Elena Gerhardt, the German mezzo-soprano and queen of *Lieder*, as their near-constant traveling companion, the Goldmans crisscrossed Europe scouring art dealers and auction houses for antiquities and masterworks to add to their collection.

Germany's plight never strayed far from Henry's mind. As its economy faltered, he stepped in to personally fund the work of some of the country's leading physicists, including Max Born, who later won a Nobel Prize for his pioneering quantum mechanics research. Albert Einstein became a good friend. To mark the mathematician's fiftieth birthday, Goldman and two other wealthy admirers gifted Einstein a twenty-three-foot sailboat dubbed the *Tümmler*. (The Gestapo later seized the boat, along with the rest of Einstein's property, after he renounced his German citizenship in 1933.)

"He thought that the Americans and French and English were quite wrong to give all the guilt for the First World War to the Germans," Born remembered. "He didn't believe that it was quite equally distributed, and he wanted to help the Germans." In addition to scientific funding, Henry sent over dozens of boxes containing clothing and shoes, which Born's wife distributed to the poor.[34]

Henry vocally denounced the Versailles Treaty—an increasingly uncontroversial position among bankers—and during his extended European sojourns, he often consulted with cabinet officials, business leaders, and central bankers as he sought a path toward financial stability for Germany and the rest of the continent. For his considerable efforts on the Fatherland's behalf, the German government awarded him honorary citizenship in 1922.

The more he studied the European financial situation, the more pessimistic he became. "All Europe is ablaze," he said in Berlin the following year, after spending the previous five weeks examining European economic conditions. "Unless some unexpected curb can be found for the causes, there will be such uprisings and blood-letting as will astound the world and set it back many decades."[35]

By the early 1920s, Henry's already poor eyesight had deteriorated. He experienced the world largely in shadow, yet still took immense pleasure in the pictures and sculptures that crowded his Fifth Avenue apartment. Max Born recalled visiting the Goldmans at their home when some Harvard scholars dropped by to view their collection. Henry gave them a tour, describing each piece in encyclopedic detail. Afterward, as he was showing them out, he walked straight into a partially closed door.

The academics were perplexed. "What is wrong with Mr. Goldman," they asked Born. "Doesn't he see well?"

"He sees nothing," the physicist replied, explaining that Goldman loved his collection so much that he knew every piece from memory.[36]

The Goldmans engaged Glenway Wescott, a young writer who would later win acclaim for his novels and essays, as Henry's companion and factotum. He accompanied the Goldmans on their travels, including that 1923 trip to Europe, spending hours a day reading to Henry (often in German) and, in the evenings, when Henry liked to gamble, leading him home from the baccarat table. Wescott peppered his florid correspondence to his longtime companion Monroe Wheeler with references to life with the Goldman family, with whom he had a love-hate relationship. "He has gigantic excellences of character," he wrote of Henry. "I am sometimes amazed with my affection and respect, fantastic as he almost always seems." Though, on other occasions, he found Henry "pitiable & unendurable at once," complained of his "moralizing & bullying & indelicate habits," and commented, "It's a wonder I don't kill him."[37]

Henry loved to debate—that is, to argue, sometimes bitterly—about politics, art, and philosophy. This tendency toward rhetorical blood sport, one can imagine, was a factor in his acrimonious exit from Goldman Sachs and his estrangement from part of his family. Because they spent so much time together, Wescott became Henry's captive sparring partner. "I am slaughtered," he wrote Wheeler. "Whole night arguing about modern art with H.G. Ravenous preposterous talk which is his pleasure." After another round of verbal combat, he vented: "H.G. is one of those men who asserts every opinion, argues imperturbably but arrogantly every shade of difference, till one is hysterical with the constant shock & impact."[38]

Of Babette, he wrote that "a fitful dark aura of displeasure" surrounded her, and he suggested she displayed a certain coolness toward Henry, once remarking of the financier's "powerless adoration of Mrs. Goldman, whose bedroom is always locked against him."[39]

Wescott's 1942 short story "Mr. Auerbach in Paris" is a loosely fictionalized account of his travels with Henry. The title character, like Goldman, is a nearly blind, retired financier of German-Jewish extraction, who occupies himself with art collecting and has a chip on his shoulder about Germany's defeat in the Great War. The narrator, based on Wescott, is Auerbach's "seeing eye and strong young right arm." In the story, Auerbach shocks his young companion by remarking, "I tell you, my boy, Paris is the most beautiful city in the world. And I tell you it would be the greatest city in the world too if the Germans had it. What a pity they lost the war!"[40]

"It was a history lesson for me," the narrator relates. "The point of it was the extraordinary lack of foresight of so many well-meaning Germans and German-Jews, caring for nothing in the world so much as the recovery of that injured, invalid Reich which was to grow too strong for them, so soon."[41]

Goldman, like Wescott's Auerbach, had a blind spot when it came to the sinister developments unfolding in Germany. In April 1932, Henry had a forty-five-minute private audience with President Paul von Hindenburg, gushing afterward that "his mind is as alert as that of a man of 25 years younger" and saying their meeting "was one of the most remarkable experiences I ever had."[42] Even after Hindenburg appointed Hitler as Germany's chancellor, in January 1933, Goldman failed to grasp the lethal transformation underway. The following month James G. McDonald, who that year would be named chair of the League of Nations' High Commission for Refugees (Jewish and Others) Coming from Germany, met with Goldman in New York. "He is fairly optimistic about German conditions," McDonald wrote in his diary afterward. "Thinks that anti-Semitism there is merely a different manifestation of a nearly universal feeling of anti-Semitism. He does not think it is worse than here, though different in its form."[43]

The terrifying reality of Hitler's Germany confronted Henry in April 1933 when he visited Berlin, where swastika-wearing brown-shirts patrolled the streets, old associates shunned him, and he was roughly jostled by passersby.[44] He wrote to his brother Julius of what he was witnessing:

> If I were to attempt to give you a picture of only a small part of what I am seeing, studying, and learning here I would be compelled to write you a volume instead of a letter and for obvious reasons if this is to reach you I cannot say all I would like to tell you. While the American press informs you quite accurately it nevertheless does not bring you anything like the real story so far as the Jews here are concerned. The foreign correspondents are naturally, if they desire to continue to function, considerably handicapped. The press here

is completely and hermetically muzzled and the government now in power controls every avenue of publicity to the effect that a system of intimidation and terror obtain. In the main I know you quite sense this, but to be here and to witness it all is to me a very trying ordeal. Nevertheless I am seeing it through from a sense of duty because I am probably one of a very few Hebrews now here who may be able to give the information that will be necessary in the relief action which Americans, Jews and Gentiles, may wish and feel called upon to undertake. Thousands of intellectuals, teachers, professors, jurists, medical men, are being ruthlessly thrown out and being made breadless, and tens of thousands of men of business are in the most macchiavellian [*sic*] way rendered unable to carry on. To give you just one example of how they go to work here—all drugstores received instructions not to sell medicines produced by a Jewish factory, to the effect that such concerns are practically put out of business over night. All Jewish physicians are barred from the system of *krankenkassen* [public health funds], which constitutes 60 to 80% of their practice. All teachers of Jewish origin unto the third generation are barred from activities and put into the street overnight without pensions. A refined system of cruelty has been meted out to the jurists to the effect that the old will be partially permitted to carry on until by natural processes they die out, but so that no aftergrowth will be possible, to the effect that after a comparatively short time there will be none. I could go on indefinitely if space permitted.

Still, despite everything he experienced, Henry's mind could not conjure the horrifying terminus to which this was all building.

This is the present status, and yet I feel convinced that it cannot last very long. I am of the same opinion which I held when I last spoke to you that the real trend here is far to the right and that the present is a bridge to the reestablishment of monarchy, and I am inclined to think that that is what they probably need here. I encounter many people who are from conviction democrats, but who now sigh for such a change.[45]

Nine months later, in January 1934, Goldman held an hourlong meeting with James McDonald, who was then overseeing efforts to rescue Jews from Germany and relocate refugees. "He is opposed to attempting to bring the children or younger people out of Germany," McDonald scrawled in his diary. "He thinks that they must bear their cross."[46]

Goldman died three years later, at seventy-nine. An intensely private man, he decreed that his personal papers be incinerated.[47] Spared the ultimate horror that would befall the Jewish people, Goldman was nevertheless spiritually shattered by what had become of Germany. "He was completely broken down, for he had such a faith in the Germans, and now there was an anti-Semitic movement and he couldn't understand it at all," Max Born recalled. "He died . . . as a broken man."[48]

On Wednesday, June 3, 1931, Morti Schiff seemed in especially good spirits. In two days, it would be his fifty-fourth birthday. In addition to his renown as a banker, Morti served as president of the Boy Scouts of America and a few years earlier had graced the cover of *Time* magazine. He left his office that afternoon for Northwood, his C.P.H. Gilbert–designed estate that spanned hundreds of acres in Long Island's Oyster Bay. He played a round of golf with his daughter Dolly at the nearby Piping Rock Club, and when he was called down for dinner that evening, he took the stairs two at a time.[49]

He and Dolly retired to the smoking room after dinner. He lit a cigar and sipped kümmel; she had a brandy. Adele was in Paris. Dolly's brother John, who was also staying at Northwood, was out that evening. Other than the help, they had the house to themselves. As they chatted, Morti opened up to his daughter in a way he hadn't before. He told her of the British noblewoman he had bedded during his banking apprenticeship in London—and his shock at later receiving bills from her Parisian dressmakers. He turned melancholy as he reflected on his legacy, confessing that he considered himself a failure—at least in his father's eyes. Under his stewardship, Kuhn Loeb wasn't exactly gaining in prestige. And he confided that the '29 crash had wiped out nearly half his fortune. He gave generously to Jewish causes because that was what was expected of him, but he was not the revered figure that Jacob had been.[50]

They spoke for hours before finally turning in. At seven the next morning, Dolly could hear the butler, William, knocking insistently on Morti's door. Finally William called for Dolly. "I don't seem to be able to rouse your father," he said. Morti, wearing a silk dressing gown, was seated in an armchair with a woolen lap blanket draped over his legs and his hands on his knees. He had died of a heart attack. He left behind a $30 million fortune.[51]

Five months earlier John Schiff had become a Kuhn Loeb partner, along with Gilbert Kahn, Otto's son, and Frederick Warburg, who had returned to the firm from Lehman Brothers with a bit more banking experience under his belt. The third generation took their places at the firm none too soon: a few years after Morti's untimely exit, in March 1934, Otto Kahn would fall dead of a heart attack himself while eating lunch with his partners in Kuhn Loeb's dining room.[52] This left Felix the firm's seniormost partner, a position that bemused him. "I was never born to be a banker," he said after Kahn's death. "I buried nine partners, and now end up as the sole survivor of this big firm, with nothing but young people about me."[53] But Kuhn Loeb soon interred a tenth partner: in October 1937, Felix was also felled by a heart attack (his second in four years). Even in her fog of grief, Frieda thought of others who had loved her husband. Though she had ignored her husband's philandering, now she enlisted her son Edward to deliver the sad news to his retinue of mistresses.[54] Felix's *New York Times* obituary, crammed with his many philanthropic good deeds, consumed the better part of a page in the newspaper.[55]

Paul was gone, too. He had died in January 1932, vindicated in his warnings about the Wall Street debauch but laid low through his exertions in the wake of the crisis. He had suffered a stroke that December, but it was a bout of pneumonia that took him.[56] The New York Warburgs pinned some of the blame for the untimely deaths of Paul and Felix on Max, on whom they had expended large reserves of energy and cash as they sought to save M.M. Warburg.

The U.S. financial crisis had quickly spread to Central Europe, and soon Max's bank was clinging to life. Felix and Paul urged their brother to consider a merger with another bank, but Max refused. In 1931 they deployed Jimmy Warburg to Germany to examine M.M. Warburg's financial condition. He reported back to his father that the firm was a lost cause and that sinking any money into it would be akin to lighting it on fire. Still, Paul could not desert the older brother whom he idolized. Together, he and Felix pumped nearly $9 million into their family firm. The rescue operation burned through more than half of Paul's holdings. The strain of trying to save M.M. Warburg was compounded by their anger when Max continued to spend lavishly, despite his firm's predicament.[57] "M.M. Warburg was eventually rescued from its difficulties, but at the cost of my father's health," Jimmy remembered.[58] Paul's daughter Bettina "felt that he died of a broken heart, pained by everything Max had put them through and the greediness," said Katharine Weber, Jimmy's grand-daughter. "He hardly said thank you."[59]

Soon saving the bank seemed a secondary concern.

Max had been slow to recognize the threat Adolf Hitler posed, and slower still to realize his family, whose roots in Germany stretched back to the sixteenth century, would no longer have a place in their homeland. In 1929, after hearing Hitler address a rapt crowd during a visit to Germany, Jimmy picked up a copy of *Mein Kampf* and read it with growing alarm, warning his uncles that the demagogue they wrote off as an "idiot" was a real danger. But Max and Fritz shrugged off Jimmy's entreaties to read Hitler's book and see for themselves.[60]

Yet there was no ignoring the Nazi Party's electoral gains the following year. In 1930 it won ninety-five seats in the Reichstag, boosting its numbers to 107. Two years later, after winning 123 more seats, the Nazis displaced the Social Democrats as Germany's largest political party, leading to Hitler's elevation as chancellor and his purge of his political rivals. Felix and other family members pleaded with Max to liquidate M.M. Warburg and leave Germany, but he stubbornly refused. "I was determined to defend my firm like a fortress," Max recalled in his memoir.[61] The firm's headquarters at Ferdinandstrasse 75 would come to feel like a bunker, as M.M. Warburg was slowly stripped of its defenses.

Starting in 1933, Max and his partners were systematically removed from the numerous corporate and cultural boards on which they served. Max was bounced from the Reichsbank's advisory council and ousted from the boards of the Hamburg-America line and the German-Atlantic Telegraph Company. He was no longer welcomed by the Hamburg Chamber of Commerce, the Philharmonic Society, or the Board of Higher Education.[62] Similar indignities befell his partners.

Even as Max relocated his late brother Aby's vast library to London, lest its precious volumes become tinder for a Nazi bonfire, he refused to abandon his firm or his coreligionists. (Aby had died in 1929.) Rather, Max and his son Eric poured their energy into efforts to help German Jews flee the country. Early in Hitler's reign, one of the biggest impediments to Jewish emigration was the extortionary flight tax levied on capital leaving the country. In late 1933, Zionist leaders, who hoped to attract immigration to Palestine, and Nazi officials, who wanted to rid Germany of as many Jews as possible, forged a pact that served both of their interests. Under the Haavara (Transfer) Agreement, German Jews could deposit their assets in Reichsmarks in restricted accounts that could be used only to purchase products from German exporters; once these goods were resold in Palestine, the emigrants could reclaim their assets in the local currency. In Germany, M.M. Warburg served as the main financial intermediary for this convoluted and controversial plan, which allowed tens of thousands of Jews to escape while also financially aiding Nazi Germany.

Eric also managed to persuade the American consulate general to move its offices, located down the street, to Ferdinandstrasse 75, which "was very beneficial for his efforts to obtain immigration visas for Jews," his daughter Marie Warburg recalled. "All in all," she noted, "my grandfather, great uncle [Felix] and my father managed to get 40,000 Jews out of Germany into the United States and other countries—as you can imagine—against enormous odds."[63] For all his efforts to aid emigration from Germany, Max privately argued that Jews should remain in their homeland, holding fast to the misbegotten belief that German Jewry would outlast the Nazi takeover.[64]

In 1936, amid his ongoing pressure campaign to get Max to leave Germany, Felix scored a slight victory when his brother accepted an invitation from Takahashi Korekiyo, Japan's long-serving finance minister, to visit the Far East. Max and Takahashi had struck up a friendship decades earlier during the Russo-Japanese war financing, which M.M. Warburg had joined in conjunction with Kuhn Loeb, together helping to underwrite a significant portion of Japan's expenditures in the conflict. But then as the trip neared, Max received word that two members of Japan's Imperial Guard had murdered Takahashi in his bed during an attempted coup, one pumping him full of bullets, the other hacking him with a sword.[65] No corner of the world, it seemed, was safe from violent upheaval.

Increasingly, Max and his firm featured prominently in Nazi propaganda. *Der Stürmer*, the Nazi-aligned tabloid, revived the bogus accusations that Max had schemed with his American brother to sell out Germany at Versailles.[66] And in an issue rehashing the *Protocols*, Max was pictured next to a photograph of Karl Marx.[67] More ominously still, a caricature of the Hamburg banker, alongside those of other Jewish "betrayers of Germany," was painted on the whitewashed wall of the cafeteria at Dachau, the concentration camp first built to confine political prisoners.[68]

In 1937, the Nazi regime ramped up its "Aryanization" campaign to purge Jews from German economic life, in hopes of forcing them from the country itself. The government promulgated so many anti-Jewish laws and regulations that M.M. Warburg's eight-person legal staff could barely keep up with the latest restrictions. The firm's offices were eerily quiet; there was no new business to attend to or to discuss. On his way to work, people whom Max had typically greeted with a doff of the hat averted their eyes. Finally, he was forced to relinquish control of the bank. Like a parent giving up custody of a child, he managed to place the firm in the care of the best possible custodians: Dr. Rudolf Brinckmann, an M.M. Warburg office manager who had power of attorney, and Hamburg merchant Paul Wirtz. To erase its remaining traces of Jewishness, the firm, by Nazi decree, subsequently changed its name to Brinckmann, Wirtz & Co.[69]

"According to the law, the firm is the name under which the merchant carries on his business and issues his signature," Max declared in an emotional farewell speech to his partners and employees in late May 1938. "But it can be more, it should be more, and for us it was much more." The firm was a living entity, he mused, of which they were just its "temporary representatives," charged with ensuring its long-term survival. "There were two paths between which we had to choose," he said, "either we had to give up the business, go into liquidation and transfer the clientele to another banking firm; or place the structure itself above persons and maintain the firm, departing ourselves and transferring the management to our successors. We chose the second path, because we did not wish this firm, which has been our life's work up till today, to be destroyed."[70]

In August 1938, Max and his wife, Alice, departed for New York, fully expecting to return to Hamburg sometime that fall. Then in November came *Kristallnacht*. In the sitting room of Frieda's Fifth Avenue mansion, Max digested the news of the explosion of anti-Jewish violence throughout Germany—dozens killed, hundreds of synagogues burned to the ground, thousands of stores and businesses ransacked, tens of thousands of Jewish men rounded up. He turned to his son Eric. "Now it is finished," he said ruefully.

During the 1920s, Eric had lived for three years in the United States learning the banking business, and in the process he earned resident status, which he had wisely maintained with frequent trips back to New York. That allowed him to apply for citizenship in 1938. As the parents of an American citizen, Max and Alice were granted preference under the strict quota system established by the Immigration Act of 1924. They too were eventually able to naturalize, sparing them the tragic destiny that belonged to the thousands of Jewish refugees to whom the nation remained obstinately closed.

Eric, fresh from high school, had served briefly in the German Army at the end of World War I. As a newly minted American, he didn't wait for the United States to enter the Second World War before joining the U.S. Air Force as an intelligence officer. Due to his language skills and background, he became a valuable military interrogator, questioning various high-ranking Nazi captives, including the powerful Luftwaffe commander and Reichstag president Hermann Göring.

While Eric was deployed throughout the military theaters of Europe and North Africa, Max spent his last years writing and rewriting his memoirs, as if trying to make sense of the unexpected path his life had taken. He lived to see the downfall of Hitler and Nazism, though he never returned to Germany. He died in late 1946, two months after the conclusion of the Nuremberg trials. He was buried at Sleepy Hollow Cemetery in Westchester, next to his brother Paul.

The Warburg bank miraculously survived Hitler's regime: in the late 1940s, Eric reclaimed his family's place at the firm, and its name was eventually restored. Eric's son, Max, named for his grandfather, later assumed his place in the family business, marking the sixth generation of family stewardship. More than two centuries after its founding, M.M. Warburg continues to operate out of its long-standing headquarters on Ferdinandstrasse, a quiet side street a block from the Inner Alster Lake.

Improbably, M.M. Warburg outlasted Kuhn Loeb, which fell victim to the same industry vicissitudes that extinguished the names of many vaunted financial houses. The tipping point came in 1969, when a plucky, decade-old investment banking partnership named Donaldson, Lufkin & Jenrette filed for an IPO, challenging an old New York Stock Exchange rule barring member firms from going public.[71] The rollback of that prohibition and other financial reforms imposed in the wake of the Great Depression spurred an orgy of mergers and stock flotations, upending the partnership model that had bound firms and families for more than a century and radically changing the incentives and risk tolerance of Wall Street's biggest players. These new firms now answered to shareholders, no longer guided by partners zealously guarding the firms that bore their family names. "The old days of investment banking no longer exist today," mused David Schiff, Jacob's great-grandson and a former Kuhn Loeb partner. "Certainly, your handshake was your word. That was true of most of the firms, of the older firms anyway. But that's certainly not true today. I think it went away when Donaldson Lufkin became public."[72]

In late 1977, Kuhn Loeb, still highly regarded but faltering as it struggled for business against bigger competitors, sought refuge in a merger with Lehman Brothers. It was an unhappy pairing marked by clashing outsize personalities and competing visions. In the early 1980s, the merged company, known as Lehman Brothers Kuhn Loeb, merged again, selling itself for $360 million to Shearson, the brokerage arm of American Express. The new company was dubbed Shearson Lehman—the Kuhn Loeb name, for more than a century a Wall Street fixture, was all but erased. A few years later a former Lehman partner named William C. Morris spearheaded the takeover of J. & W. Seligman & Co., buying out the shares of the firm's forty-three partners. (The company was later purchased by Ameriprise Financial.)

Lehman Brothers reemerged in the early 1990s, spun off as a public company. By now, it was just a brand name and bore no resemblance to the partnership forged by Emanuel and Mayer Lehman. Their descendants were horrified by the investment bank's ignominious collapse in 2008, linking the Lehman name with reckless financial practices that helped to ignite a financial meltdown. Of the mighty German-Jewish financial houses that had defined an epoch of American finance, only Goldman Sachs, which waited until 1999 to go public, survived the consolidation frenzy intact, rising to become the world's preeminent investment bank.

Well before Kuhn Loeb's name disappeared from Wall Street, the memory of Jacob Schiff had begun to fade. For a man with a healthy ego—and at times, an air of self-importance—he seemed to care little about his name living on. After his death, *The New York Times* tried and failed to assemble a portrait of Schiff's major philanthropic gifts "because of their number . . . and because so many were anonymous."[73] Nor did Schiff attempt to attach his name to the investment bank he led to international renown.

But whether they knew it or not, the moguls who dominated Wall Street in the years after Schiff's death walked in his shadow.

Bridging the old world and the new, he defined a period of finance and philanthropy from which the modern world, as we know it, germinated. Few could lay claim to a legacy half as profound.

"No man can take his place," the rabbi and Zionist leader Stephen Wise, who had once decried Schiff's stranglehold over Jewish philanthropy, sermonized days after his death. "No man ought to dream of filling his place—that place which Schiff sought not, that place of power that was forced upon him. . . . Schiff is gone, and with him passes the Schiff era."[74]

During Schiff's lifetime, "52 William Street had become a euphemism like the White House and 10 Downing Street and the Quai d'Orsay," recalled Morris Waldman, whose involvement with the Galveston Movement and other Jewish philanthropic projects brought him in close contact with Schiff. And he noted, "there cannot be anything like the Schiff Era today. . . . It was the philanthropic era of Jewish life."[75]

Yet Schiff's singular place in Jewish life was not attributable either to his phenomenal wealth or to his philanthropic giving alone. "Philanthropy is nothing more than a returned penny for a stolen dollar," the *Forward*, the avowedly socialist Yiddish-language daily, declared in its tribute to Schiff.

We have always revered Schiff not because he was a financial giant; not because he was a power in the capitalist class which we are seeking to abolish from this earth; not because he gave vast sums to Jewish charitable institutions because there are other Jewish millionaires who gave as much if not more than he did, and whose charities have found no responsive echo in our hearts. What affected us in his death, what inspired reverence and love was the character, the personality of the man. We were not impressed with his great contributions to charity but by the personal interest which actuated him in this work. If other millionaires had no millions there would be no philanthropies—there would be no wish to give. Schiff would have won respect and reverence if he had been a cloakmaker or peddler.[76]

Resonating far beyond Jewish circles, Schiff's death was an occasion of national mourning, met with an almost royal ceremoniousness. Newspapers across the country celebrated his life on their front pages. Tributes and messages of condolence poured in from around the world. Woodrow Wilson lamented the loss of one of the nation's "most useful citizens." Wilson's predecessor, William Howard Taft, praised Schiff's "never-ending" generosity. Japan's foreign minister Viscount Uchida cabled his government's "deep and sincere regrets" at the loss of "one our country's best friends." In a letter to Therese Schiff, the journalist Oswald Villard said that in his twenty-five-year career, he had never seen a similar "outpouring of regret and sorrow."[77]

On the Monday after Schiff's death, ten thousand people showed up at 52 William Street seeking one of two thousand admission cards to Schiff's funeral services, to be held the following day at Temple Emanu-El.

Witnessing the pomp, Edward Warburg, twelve years old at the time, understood for the first time his grandfather's towering status. Along with his siblings and cousins, he was led to the doorway of Schiff's bedroom for a final glimpse of the great man lying in state, his body framed by rows of purple asters.

"My Mother and the other ladies of the family were in full black," Edward remembered. "When going to and coming from the house, they draped themselves in heavy crepe veils, making them unrecognizable and indistinguishable, one from the other. All the men wore black arm bands and black neckties."[78]

On Tuesday, September 28, the day of Schiff's funeral, thousands of spectators thronged the streets around Temple Emanu-El. More than 350 police officers were on hand to manage the swelling crowd, and several blocks surrounding the synagogue were closed to traffic.

Within Emanu-El, not a pew was unoccupied. Prominent bankers, trust company presidents, and industrialists sat shoulder to shoulder with communal workers, rabbis, and Jewish immigrants. "In front of me was a banker from Wall Street, on my right were two of our old people from the Lower East Side, poor people with their black skull caps," one attendee remembered.[79] Among the crowd were New York governor Alfred E. Smith, who traveled down from Albany, and New York City mayor John Hylan. Japan dispatched its U.S. consul to attend. John D. Rockefeller, Jr., paid his respects. So did Western Union head Newcomb Carlton. Delegations arrived from the vast spectrum of organizations Schiff had supported during his lifetime: the Baron de Hirsch Fund, the Hebrew Orphan Asylum, the Henry Street Settlement, the Montefiore Home, Mount Sinai Hospital, the Red Cross, and others.[80]

At ten a.m. an organ swelled, and the mournful notes of Kol

Nidre filled the sanctuary, as the Metropolitan Opera baritone Robert Leonhardt sang the verses of the Jewish declaration of absolution (typically performed only at the start of Yom Kippur). Schiff's casket, nearly invisible under a mountain of white roses, asters, and lilies of the valley, was carried down the long center aisle toward the altar. (The floral display draping Schiff's coffin was perhaps a technical violation of the banker's last wishes, though the remainder of the temple was mostly unadorned.)

The burial rites, at Schiff's request, were simple, no different from those held for any other Jewish citizen. No words were uttered of his business career, of his role in reorganizing the railroads, capitalizing American industry, and elevating the United States from a developing country into a first-tier financial power. He was lauded neither for his philanthropy, the millions he had poured into Jewish and secular causes, nor for the smaller acts of generosity he had offered to individuals. There was no mention of his feats as a Jewish or civic leader. There were no eulogies at all. Was there really any need to attest to his greatness?

When the service concluded, thousands of mourners accompanied Schiff's casket up Park Avenue, as the funeral procession wound its way solemnly to Salem Fields. Temple Emanu-El's laboriously landscaped "city of the dead" had been carefully etched with neat roads and winding pathways populated by ornate mausoleums whose size and grandeur reflected the earthly status of their inhabitants. One of the grandest monuments, not just here but in all the nation, belonged to Jacob Schiff. Resembling a pantheon, it stood alone high on a hill, flanked on either side by colonnades. From the portico, you could see clear to Long Island's Jamaica Bay. Constructed in the 1890s, it was considered "perhaps the largest and most imposing mausoleum in this country," according to one newspaper account at the time, which pegged its cost at $130,000 and reported that its "walls are absolutely proof against body snatchers, for it would take them several days . . . to chisel through the granite blocks."[81]

"On the mountaintop, all paths unite," Schiff had been fond of saying. Rich or poor, life's journey led everyone to the same destination, though few reposed in such kingly surroundings. At Salem Fields, Schiff took his place among Solomon Loeb, Marcus Goldman, Joseph and Jesse Seligman, and the brothers Lehman, architects, each in his own way, of what America was and what it would become.

Salem Fields Revisited

On a clear, mild January morning nearly a century after Schiff's death, I accompanied David Schiff and his sons, Drew and Scott, to Salem Fields. The eldest son of John Schiff, grandson of Morti, and great-grandson of Jacob, David, then eighty-two, was slim and patrician, with a sometimes-mischievous sense of humor. He wore a tan overcoat over a navy suit and a gold pinky ring on his left hand. David had last visited the cemetery some thirty years earlier, when his aunt Dolly's ashes were interred in the family mausoleum. Drew and Scott were making their first pilgrimage to their great-great-grandfather's grave site.

The present-day Schiffs are descended from not one but two great banking dynasties—David's mother, Edith, was a Baker, granddaughter of First National Bank chairman George Baker, a pivotal figure in American finance during the Gilded Age who was worth some $75 million at the time of his death in 1931.[1] "There's an irony for me that Jacob Schiff's grandson married George Baker's granddaughter, because they weren't on the same side of the fence back then," said Scott, whose middle name is Baker.[2] Not only was George Baker a close ally of Schiff's sometime rival J. P. Morgan, he was also a WASP. The intermarriage, uniting separate social and business spheres, would have been almost unthinkable decades earlier. And it's probable that Jacob, had he been living, would have fiercely opposed the union, fearing, as did many observant Jews, it would dilute his family's Jewish faith. Such concerns would not have been meritless: today the Schiff family, while appreciating their Jewish roots, are Episcopalians.

Because of his Schiff-Baker pedigree, David's career in investment banking was all but preordained. Shortly after graduating from Yale in 1958 with a degree in mechanical engineering, he joined Kuhn Loeb and was made partner in 1966. He remained with the firm through its turbulent 1977 merger with Lehman Brothers, finally exiting the partnership in the early 1980s, shortly before Lehman Brothers Kuhn Loeb sold itself to Shearson. Not only did the Kuhn Loeb name vanish in the deal, but also gone was much of the firm's historical record: to the horror of Kuhn Loeb's librarian, Lehman Brothers purged old ledgers and correspondence dating back to the days of Kuhn Loeb's founding.[3] To ensure the Schiff family retained something of the company their forebears had built, Harvey Krueger, a top Lehman executive who had been president and CEO of Kuhn Loeb before the mergers, later arranged to return the rights to the Kuhn Loeb name to David.[4] "Harvey tried to get as much as he could, and he gave a lot of stuff to me that he was able to rescue from Lehman," David said.[5]

The legacy of the firm—and of Jacob Schiff—remains deeply imprinted on the family. Emails from David sometimes come from a kuhnloebco.com address. One of Scott's most treasured possessions is a box of matchbooks from Kuhn Loeb's boardroom, and the foyer of his Upper East Side apartment is a shrine to his paternal ancestors. On one wall hangs a portrait of Jacob Schiff, purchased at auction, that had originally been presented to the New York Chamber of Commerce, by stipulation of Schiff's will, after the banker's death. He also displays a 1918 fundraising appeal signed by Schiff ("In this blackest tragedy of our race, I ask your aid") and a photograph of Jacob, Morti, and John, alongside a picture of the next three generations: his father, himself, and his son.

Along with their historic connection to high finance, the Schiffs have maintained ties to some of the charitable organizations Jacob nurtured during his lifetime. For more than a decade, David chaired the board of the Wildlife Conservation Society, which oversees New York City's four zoos and one aquarium and pursues conservation projects around the world. Jacob was a founding member of the organization, originally known as the New York Zoological Society; Morti and later John served as trustees. Scott, the cofounder of private wealth management firm BCS, has carried the family's association with the Wildlife Conservation Society into the fifth generation, joining its board in 2014.

Drew, the eldest of the brothers, has meanwhile kept up the family's relationship with the organizations founded by Lillian Wald that Jacob helped get off the ground: the Henry Street Settlement, where Drew is an emeritus board member, and the Visiting Nurse Service of New York, where he serves as chairman.

Driving through the majestic stone archway that marks the entrance to Salem Fields, row upon row of grand mausoleums stretched out before us. Guggenheim and Lewisohn, Bloomingdale and Straus, Shubert and Tishman—here the history of New York, of the United States, was chiseled into marble and granite, inscribed on kaleidoscopic panes of Tiffany glass. "This is more impressive than Sleepy Hollow," David commented, referring to the historic Westchester County cemetery where Max and Paul Warburg are buried, "or where the Bakers are" in Valhalla, New York.

We wound up a steep, narrow drive. Near the top of the hill, the Schiff-Loeb family mausoleum came into view, standing out, amid a sea of impressive monuments, for its size and elaborate Doric architecture. The edifice, rising more than thirty feet and stretching back some forty, would not look out of place on Mount Olympus.

We stepped inside the tomb, through a pair of ornamental brass doors, oxidized with age. Each side of the mausoleum holds sixteen crypts. Loeb family members, including Solomon and Betty, are interred on the right. Schiffs and Warburgs occupy the left, with Jacob side by side with Therese, and a row up, Felix beside Frieda.

Inscribed on the far wall in raised letters was the final line of "Auferstehung" (Resurrection), by the nineteenth-century German poet Emanuel Geibel:

WAS DU EWIG LIEBST
IST EWIG DEIN

"What you love forever, is yours forever." Gazing at the inscription, Drew thought back to the German phrase he had heard often growing up and which had been the family's unofficial credo for generations: *Pflicht und Arbeit* (Duty and Work).

Nearby, David's eyes flickered over the marble tablets etched with the names of his ancestors, lingering on the plaque of his father's cousin, Paul Felix Warburg, who everyone called Piggy. "Piggy was very funny," he mused, explaining that his father was particularly close to him because they were born within months of each other. "It is almost horrifying how many of these people I knew," he added. The mausoleum was also notable for who was not there: David's grandfather, Morti. In what was perhaps a final act of rebellion, Morti was buried on the grounds of his Oyster Bay estate.

Standing a few feet from Jacob's crypt, Scott felt the weight of his family's heritage—a mixture of gratitude and pride, but also the ever-present pressure of living up to the standard set by a paterfamilias who helped to define the twentieth century. "To say that Jacob Schiff still plays a role in our family would be an understatement," he told me later. "We are all clearly quite fortunate, and grateful, to have been born into privilege made possible by Jacob, but more importantly, and I think this is rather significant, we are aware that this is a privilege and not a right. Our family has always been instilled with a feeling of respect, gratitude, duty, and tradition. The shadow of Jacob's philanthropy and philosophy has lasted five generations and does not seem to be waning."[6]

Later, I strolled the grounds with Drew, who wore a Patagonia parka over his gray suit. Unassuming and affable, he is a Cornell-trained doctor who practiced internal medicine for six years before taking his medical background to the finance world. He is a managing partner of Aisling Capital, a venture firm focused on pharmaceuticals and biotech. In 1997, when he was in his thirties, Drew married into one of the country's most prominent political dynasties, wedding Karenna Gore, the eldest daughter of then vice president Al Gore. Aretha Franklin serenaded the couple at the banquet, held on the grounds of the U.S. Naval Observatory, where the vice-presidential residence is located. The couple, who have three children together, later divorced. Drew had recently remarried; any day he was expecting the birth of his first child, a son, with new wife Alexandra Wolfe, a journalist who is the daughter of the late literary icon Tom Wolfe.

Down the hill from the Schiff-Loeb mausoleum, we peered into the hulking Seligman tomb, a hexagonal, domed structure that houses forty crypts. Visible through the gates was the vibrant stained-glass window on the far wall depicting an angel breaking free of the mortal world. Beneath was the inscription: AND I WILL MAKE THE VALLEY OF TRIBULATION FOR A GATE OF HOPE. Farther on, we passed the far-smaller Sachs family sepulchre, located a short distance from the Goldman mausoleum. "Amazing, right?" Drew said. "It's interesting to see history all condensed in one spot. All these names that you've heard of—to see them lined up. It gives you a sense of how close they all were."[7]

We rejoined David and Scott, piled back into the car, and drove out of the gray, granite stillness of Salem Fields and onto the busy thoroughfare of Jamaica Avenue. History yielded to modernity, the past to the present, and we headed back to Manhattan, to a world etched so deeply by the legacy of Jacob Schiff and the money kings.

ACKNOWLEDGMENTS

When I began this book, my eldest son, Wes, was an infant, and I can still vividly recall cradling him with one arm and with the other thumbing through Cyrus Adler's two-volume biography of Jacob Schiff. Wes—who has since been joined by a brother, Reid—will be entering third grade by the time *The Money Kings* is published. Which is to say, this has been a long road, and I am deeply indebted to the many people who helped me along the way.

My fascination with Schiff was the somewhat circuitous result of my curiosity about my father's life. How had a poor immigrant family established itself so quickly in America? How had a kid from a McKibbin Street tenement house wound up practicing law on Fifth Avenue? Exploring these questions eventually led me to the overlapping worlds of the German-Jewish elite and of the refugees of Russian and Eastern European persecution. My dad, who died last fall, did not get to see the final product of my research, but in many ways this book is a tribute to him. Thank you, Dad, for starting me on this journey, and for so much more.

Howard Yoon, my longtime agent and friend, championed this project from the outset. He understood what I was trying to accomplish with a clarity that even I did not possess in the beginning, helping to nurture the seed of an idea into a fully formed narrative. He is one of the most levelheaded and generous people I know, and I consider myself lucky to have him in my corner as an advocate and a collaborator. His colleagues at the Ross Yoon Agency (now part of WME) are equally extraordinary. Gail Ross, Dara Kaye, Jennifer Manguera, and Elizabeth DeNoma have my deep gratitude.

It's fitting (and quite humbling) that this book found a home at Knopf, whose founder was the son of Jewish immigrants from Eastern Europe and who overcame antisemitism to play a pathbreaking role in publishing. My superb editors Andrew Miller and Todd Portnowitz made the manuscript immeasurably better with their sharp line edits, big-picture guidance, and historical insights. I hope they are as proud of *The Money Kings* as I am. I'm extremely grateful to publisher Reagan Arthur, and her predecessor, the late Sonny Mehta, for seeing the promise of this project and for placing their confidence in me. Production editor Nicole Pedersen, text designer Soonyoung Kwon, jacket designer Jenny Carrow, publicists Jessica Purcell and Elka Roderick, marketer Ellen Whitaker, and copyeditor Janet Biehl also have my heartfelt appreciation.

In my experience writing about influential dynasties, I have found some families apprehensive about what historical digging might reveal. This was not the case at all for the Schiff family. From the start, David, Drew, and Scott Schiff were as intrigued by Jacob Schiff as I was. They wholeheartedly supported this project and provided me with unrestricted access to invaluable documents, including Jacob Schiff's private papers. I hope this book contributes meaningfully to their understanding of the legacy of Jacob Schiff and of the extraordinary clan they are descended from. I'm equally indebted to other "money kings" family members who generously provided me with letters, photographs, films, unpublished memoirs, and other records, including: Ann Sachs and Samuel Sachs Morgan; Rusty Sachs; John Loeb, Jr.; Henry Goldman III; Peter Goldman; Tracy Breton; Katharine Weber; Marcus Moench; Ted Lehmann; Stephen Barrett; Wendy Gray; and Dan Kramarsky.

This book benefited greatly from my conversations with an assortment of scholars, historians, and fellow authors, including Jehanne Wake (author of an indispensable history of the British investment bank Kleinwort Benson), Peter Der Manuelian (Harvard), Adam Gower (author of *Jacob Schiff and the Art of Risk*), Rebecca Kobrin (Columbia), the late Mary Ann Neeley (author of various books on the history of Montgomery, Alabama), Susie Pak (of St. John's University and author of the wonderful *Gentlemen Bankers*), Jonathan Sarna (Brandeis), and Steven Weisman (author of *The Chosen Wars:*

How Judaism Became an American Religion). My thanks as well to the late Harvey Krueger and to Yves-Andre Istel for their recollections of their years at Kuhn Loeb. And to John Wiseman for sharing with me the papers of his late father, William Wiseman.

My research took me from Berlin and London to Norman, Oklahoma (where the papers of J. & W. Seligman & Co. improbably ended up), in pursuit of archival records, unpublished manuscripts, and long out-of-print tomes. Dozens of archivists and librarians helped me along the way, pointing me toward vital documents, recommending new sources of information, and otherwise assisting my historical detective work. I'm particularly grateful to the American Jewish Archives (especially Gary Zola, Dana Herman, and Joe Weber) for awarding me a research fellowship. I'd also like to acknowledge the phenomenal staffs of the Alabama Department of Archives and History; the American Jewish Historical Society; the British Library; the British National Archives; Boston University's Howard Gotlieb Archival Research Center; Columbia University's Rare Book and Manuscript Library; the German Foreign Office Political Archive; the Schlesinger Library at Harvard's Radcliffe Institute; Harvard Business School's Baker Library (Melissa Murphy); the Leo Baeck Institute; the Library of Congress; the London Metropolitan Archives; the New York Public Library (special thanks to Andrea Felder, Lyudmila Sholokhova, and Amanda Seigel for unearthing a lost picture of the Schiff and Loeb families); Princeton University's Rare Books and Manuscripts Library; the Rothschild Archive (Justin Cavernelis-Frost); the Yale University Library and Beinecke Rare Book and Manuscript Library; and the Warburg Institute Archive (Claudia Wedepohl).

In Germany, journalist Almut Schoenfeld assisted me with research, combing various archives and turning up incredible material, including on German intelligence operations targeting German-Jewish financiers during World War I. She and her family also showed me incredible hospitality during my visit to Berlin. This book was improved greatly by her contributions. Some of the correspondence I obtained was written in *Kurrentschrift*, an archaic form of German cursive that is indecipherable to most modern-day German speakers. Leo Baeck Institute archivist Dianne Ritchey, an expert on old German scripts, translated these letters. Jörg and Martina Peters, my wonderful German relatives (and authors themselves), also assisted with translation. So did my friend and former colleague Aaron Wiener. Hannah and Luba Levintova lent their Russian-language chops to the effort. Daniel Park, at the time a student at Auburn University, gave me a hand with research in Montgomery, Alabama.

My pals (and fellow authors) Bruce Falconer and Andy Kroll provided insightful feedback on the manuscript. And my old friend Matt Mahoney, who fact-checked the book, spared me from embarrassing errors. Daniel King, who possesses unrivaled copyediting skills, proofed the manuscript and likewise saved me from mistakes that might have otherwise slipped through.

I'm thankful to my wonderful friends and colleagues at *Mother Jones* for making it so damn fun and fruitful to go to work every day. The whole organization has my gratitude, but I would especially like to acknowledge David Corn (who introduced me to my agent years ago and provided helpful comments on a draft of the manuscript), Monika Bauerlein, Clara Jeffery, and Marianne Szegedy-Maszak.

I was at work on this book for so long that surely my friends and family grew tired of hearing about it. Some may have begun to wonder whether I would complete it at all. Their love, support, and encouragement no doubt helped push me across the finish line. Thank you to my mother, Linda Schulman; to the Cooke, Silverman, and Schulman families; to the Colburn, Pieczarka (yes, Ray, the book is done), and Skouteris families; and to Andy Arch, Brett Warwick, Clayton Hainsworth, and the Connelly, Goncalves, Jaeger, Kass, Maguire, Reed, Ross, and Toubman clans.

Being married to an author, it turns out, isn't especially glamorous. For this project, I was away frequently on research trips, sometimes for weeks at a time. During those absences, my incredible wife, Stacey—organized and capable in ways I could never hope to be—cared for our two young boys and kept our household running seamlessly, all while managing a demanding job, a doctoral program, and a mountain of other responsibilities. And it's not just the travel. A book, however large or small, consumes a lot of emotional and intellectual space. You live with it, which means your loved ones must live with it as well. To them, I imagine it begins to feel like a visiting relative who was entertaining at first but who has long since overstayed their welcome—in this case, for eight years! To Stacey, Wesley, and Reid, I thank you for your love, your laughter, and your patience. You are my heart, my lodestar, and I could not have done this without you.

NOTES

ARCHIVAL SOURCES AND RECORDS COLLECTIONS

Aby Warburg Papers, Warburg Institute Archive (London, U.K.)
Adolph Ochs Papers, New York Public Library (New York, N.Y.)
Agnes Goldman Sanborn Papers, Schlesinger Library, Radcliffe Institute, Harvard
    University (Boston, Mass.)
American Jewish Committee Oral History Collection, New York Public Library
    (New York, N.Y.)
Auswärtiges Amt, Federal Foreign Office Political Archive (Berlin, Germany)
Averell Harriman Papers, Library of Congress (Washington, D.C.)
Benjamin Strong, Jr., Papers, Federal Reserve Bank of New York (New York, N.Y.)
Boris Brasol Papers, Library of Congress (Washington, D.C.)
Charles Hamlin Papers, Library of Congress (Washington, D.C.)
David T. Schiff Papers (private collection)
Dorothy Schiff Papers, Archives and Manuscript Collection, New York Public
    Library (New York, N.Y.)
Edwin Robert Anderson Seligman Papers, Columbia University Rare Book and
    Manuscript Library (New York, N.Y.)
Felix and Frieda Warburg Family Collection, American Jewish Archives (Cincinnati,
    Ohio)
Felix M. Warburg Papers, American Jewish Archives (Cincinnati, Ohio)
George S. Hellman Papers, Archives and Manuscript Collection, New York Public
    Library (New York, N.Y.)
Glenway Wescott Papers, Beinecke Rare Book and Manuscript Library, Yale
    University (New Haven, Conn.)
Herbert H. Lehman Papers, Columbia University Rare Book and Manuscript
    Library (New York, N.Y.)
Jacob H. Schiff Papers, American Jewish Archives (Cincinnati, Ohio)
James J. Hill Papers, Minnesota Historical Society (St. Paul, Minn.)
John Wiseman Papers (private collection)
Joint Distribution Committee Archives (New York, N.Y.)
Joseph Kraft Papers, Columbia University, Rare Book and Manuscript Library (New
    York, N.Y.)
Judah Magnes Papers, American Jewish Archives (Cincinnati, Ohio)

Kleinwort Benson Papers, London Metropolitan Archives (London, U.K.)
Knute Nelson Papers, Minnesota Historical Society (St. Paul, Minn.)
Lehman Brothers Collection, Baker Library, Harvard Business School (Boston, Mass.)
Lewis L. Strauss Papers, American Jewish Historical Society (New York, N.Y.)
Lord Beaverbrook Papers, U.K. Parliamentary Archives (London, U.K.)
Lord Reading Papers, British Library (London, U.K.)
Nelson W. Aldrich Papers, Library of Congress (Washington, D.C.)
Oral History Collection, Niels Bohr Library & Archives, American Institute of Physics (College Park, Md.)
Oscar Straus Papers, Library of Congress (Washington, D.C.)
Otto H. Kahn Papers, Princeton University Rare Books and Manuscripts Library (Princeton, N.J.)
Paul M. Warburg Papers, Manuscripts and Archives, Yale University Library (New Haven, Conn.)
Philip Cowen Papers, American Jewish Historical Society (New York, N.Y.)
Seligman Collection, University of Oklahoma (Norman, Okla.)
Seligman Family Correspondence, American Jewish Archives (Cincinnati, Ohio)
Seligman Family Papers, New-York Historical Society (New York, N.Y.)
Stephen Birmingham Papers, Howard Gotlieb Archival Research Center, Boston University (Boston, Mass.)
Theodore Roosevelt Papers, Library of Congress (Washington, D.C.)

LIST OF ABBREVIATIONS: ARCHIVES

AA	Auswärtiges Amt (German Foreign Office)
AIP	American Institute of Physics
AJA	American Jewish Archives
AJCOHC	American Jewish Committee Oral History Collection
AJHS	American Jewish Historical Society
BL-HBS	Baker Library at Harvard Business School
BU	Boston University
CURBML	Columbia University Rare Book and Manuscript Library
FRBNY	Federal Reserve Bank of New York
HU	Harvard University
IFS	Institut für Stadtgeschichte Frankfurt
JDC	Joint Distribution Committee Archives
LBI	Leo Baeck Institute
LMA	London Metropolitan Archives
LOC	Library of Congress
MHS	Minnesota Historical Society
NA	National Archives
NYHS	New-York Historical Society
NYPL	New York Public Library
PA	Parliamentary Archives
PU	Princeton University
UO	University of Oklahoma
WIA	Warburg Institute Archive
YU	Yale University

LIST OF ABBREVIATIONS: PEOPLE AND FIRMS

AGS   Agnes Goldman Sanborn; also Agnes Goldman Sanborn Papers
AH   Averell Harriman; also Averell Harriman Papers
AO   Adolph Ochs; also Adolph Ochs Papers
AW   Aby Warburg; also Aby Warburg Papers
BB   Boris Brasol; also Boris Brasol Papers
CH   Charles Hamlin; also Charles Hamlin Papers
DS   Dorothy Schiff; also Dorothy Schiff Papers
DTS   David T. Schiff; also David T. Schiff Papers
ERAS Edwin R. A. Seligman; also Edwin R. A. Seligman Papers
FMW   Felix M. Warburg; also Felix M. Warburg Papers
GH   George Hellman; also George Hellman Papers
GW   Glenway Wescott; also Glenway Wescott Papers
HL   Herbert Lehman; also Herbert Lehman Papers
INS   Isaac Newton Seligman
JHS   Jacob Henry Schiff; also Jacob Henry Schiff Papers
JJH   James J. Hill; also James J. Hill Papers
JK   Joseph Kraft; also Joseph Kraft Papers
JM   Judah Magnes; also Judah Magnes Papers
JW   John Wiseman; also John Wiseman Papers
KB   Kleinwort Benson; also Kleinwort Benson Papers
KN   Knute Nelson; also Knute Nelson Papers
LB   Lehman Brothers; also Lehman Brothers Collection
LR   Lord Reading; also Lord Reading Papers
LS   Lewis L. Strauss; also Lewis L. Strauss Papers
MLS   Mortimer Leo Schiff; also Mortimer Leo Schiff Papers
MMW   Max Moritz Warburg
NWA   Nelson W. Aldrich; also Nelson W. Aldrich Papers
OHK   Otto H. Kahn; also Otto H. Kahn Papers
OS   Oscar Straus; also Oscar Straus Papers
PC   Philip Cowen; also Philip Cowen Papers
PMW   Paul M. Warburg; also Paul M. Warburg Papers
SB   Stephen Birmingham; also Stephen Birmingham Papers
TR   Theodore Roosevelt; also Theodore Roosevelt Papers
WW   Woodrow Wilson; also Woodrow Wilson Papers

INTRODUCTION SALEM FIELDS

1. "Jacob Schiff Is Buried," Associated Press, September 28, 1920; "Schiff's Death Brings Gloom to East Side," *New-York Tribune*, September 27, 1920.
2. "Jacob H. Schiff, a 'World-Representative of His Race,'" *Literary Digest*, October 16, 1920.
3. "Thousands Gather at Schiff Funeral," *New York Times*, September 29, 1920.
4. Birmingham, *Our Crowd*, 8.
5. Geoffrey T. Hellman to Cass Canfield, May 26, 1967, Box 226, DS-NYPL.
6. Weiner, *What Goes Up*, 39.
7. SB to Geoffrey T. Hellman, February 6, 1967, Box 33, SB-BU.

1 & BROS.

1. Hellman, "Story of Seligmans," 182; Hellman, "Joseph Seligman, American Jew," 28.
2. Wells, "House of Seligman," 6. Wells, a print and radio journalist, worked briefly for J. & W. Seligman & Co., where in 1931 he prepared a 713-page confidential history of the firm for the partners.
3. Wells, "House of Seligman," 8.
4. Muir and White, *Over the Long Term*, 32.
5. Wells, "House of Seligman," 12.
6. "Marine List," *Evening Post* (N.Y.), September 25, 1837.
7. Editorial, *Evening Post* (N.Y.), September 25, 1837.
8. Wells, "House of Seligman," 16.
9. Diner, *Roads Taken*, 128, 136.
10. Muir and White, *Over the Long Term*, 33.
11. "James Seligman, Aged Banker, Dies," *New York Times*, August 21, 1916; James Seligman, "Reminiscences on the Occasion of His 86th Birthday," April 14, 1910, AJA.
12. "James Seligman, Aged Banker, Dies," *New York Times*, August 21, 1916; Muir and White, *Over the Long Term*, 35.
13. Seligman, *In Memoriam: Jesse Seligman*, 124.
14. Muir and White, *Over the Long Term*, 35.
15. Seligman, *In Memoriam: Jesse Seligman*, 9.
16. Ibid.
17. Wells, "House of Seligman," 22–24.
18. "New Goods," *Alabama Beacon*, June 7, 1845.
19. "New Fall Goods," *Alabama Beacon*, October 25, 1845.
20. Muir and White, *Over the Long Term*, 36.
21. Hellman, "Story of Seligmans," 35.
22. Muir and White, *Over the Long Term*, 36.
23. "Last Call," *Alabama Beacon*, May 6, 1848.

2 THE PEDDLERS' PROGRESS

1. *Alabama*, 20:28, R.G. Dun & Co. credit report volumes, BL-HBS.
2. HL to Edgar B. Stern, February 2, 1948, Box 162, HL-CURBML.
3. Flade, *Lehmans*, 44.
4. Edgar B. Stern to Frank Manheim, January 23, 1948, Box 162, HL-CURBML.
5. John Langeloth Loeb, Jr., interview by the author.
6. Campbell, *Southern Business Directory*, 8.
7. Manheim, "Seed and Tree," 38.
8. Birmingham, *Our Crowd*, 54.
9. Young, "Sketch of the First Jewish Settlers of Montgomery," 1.
10. Olitzky and Raphael, *American Synagogue*, 33.
11. Moses, "The History of the Jews of Montgomery," 85; Young, "Sketch of the First Jewish Settlers of Montgomery," 3.
12. Manheim, "Seed and Tree," 23.
13. Ibid.
14. Landman, *Universal Jewish Encyclopedia*, 596.
15. Flade, *Lehmans*, 51.
16. Register of vessels arriving at the port of New York from foreign ports, 1789–1919, NA.

17. "The Storm," *Brooklyn Daily Eagle*, July 19, 1850.
18. Campbell, *Southern Business Directory*, 10.
19. HL, "Reminiscences of Herbert Lehman," Part 1, 4:2.
20. Bill of sale, March 16, 1854, Box 14, JK-CURBML.
21. Manheim, "Seed and Tree," 38.
22. Evans, *Judah P. Benjamin*, 97.
23. *Alabama*, 20:28, R.G. Dun & Co. credit report volumes, BL-HBS.
24. Moore, *Emergence of the Cotton Kingdom*, 233.
25. "Yellow Fever in Montgomery," *Tuskegee Republican*, September 27, 1855.
26. Manheim, "Seed and Tree," 28.
27. HL, "Reminiscences of Herbert Lehman," Part 1, 4:3.
28. "In Memoriam: Mayer Lehman," 14.
29. "In Memoriam: Emanuel Lehman," 32.
30. HL, "Reminiscences of Herbert Lehman," Part 1, 4:73.
31. Ibid.
32. Seligman, "Reminiscences of Isaac Seligman," 13.

3   MANIFEST DESTINY

1. Grant, *Personal Memoirs*, 37.
2. Seligman, *Jesse Seligman: In Memoriam*, 10.
3. "The Watertown Fire," *Watertown Journal Extra*, May 13, 1849.
4. Seligman, *Jesse Seligman: In Memoriam*, 11.
5. Ibid., 12.
6. Wells, "House of Seligman," 34.
7. Seligman, *Jesse Seligman: In Memoriam*, 12.
8. Muir and White, *Over the Long Term*, 41.
9. Wells, "House of Seligman," 35.
10. Voorsanger, *Chronicles of Emanu-El*, 36.
11. "Abraham Seligman Dead," *Daily Alta*, January 22, 1885.
12. Muir and White, *Over the Long Term*, 42.
13. Bancroft, *Popular Tribunals*, 211.
14. "The Vigilance Suit in San Francisco," *Sacramento Daily Union*, July 20, 1860.
15. Williams, *History of the Committee of Vigilance*, 210.
16. Wells, "House of Seligman," 38.
17. Muir and White, *Over the Long Term*, 42.
18. Ibid.; Seligman, *Jesse Seligman: In Memoriam*, 12.
19. Ethington, *Public City*, 161–63.
20. Hellman, "Story of Seligmans," 51.
21. *New York*, 319:500A, R.G. Dun & Co. credit report volumes, BL-HBS.
22. HL to Irwin J. Miller, December 30, 1953, Box 162, HL-CURBML.
23. HL, "Reminiscences of Herbert Lehman," Part 1, 4:17–18.
24. Herbert Lehman to James L. Loeb, April 15, 1947, Box 162, HL-CURBML.
25. HL, "Reminiscences of Herbert Lehman," Part 1, 4:4.
26. *New York*, 319:500A, R.G. Dun & Co. credit report volumes, BL-HBS.
27. Douglas B. Ball to JK, September 22, 1984, Box 13, JK-CURBML.
28. *Alabama*, 20:28, R.G. Dun & Co. credit report volumes, BL-HBS.
29. Ibid.

1. Libo, *Lots of Lehmans*, 8.
2. *New York*, 319:500A, R.G. Dun & Co. credit report volumes, BL-HBS.
3. Manheim, "Seed and Tree," 30.
4. *New York*, 319:500A, R.G. Dun & Co. credit report volumes, BL-HBS.
5. "Important from Montgomery; Speech of Hon. Jefferson Davis," *New York Times*, February 18, 1861.
6. Manheim, "Seed and Tree," 39.
7. Grant, *Papers of Grant*, 7:56–57.
8. Sarna, *When Grant Expelled Jews*, 32.
9. Ibid., 30.
10. Douglas B. Ball to JK, September 22, 1984, Box 13, JK-CURBML.
11. *New York*, 319:500A, R.G. Dun & Co. credit report volumes, BL-HBS.
12. "The Union Forever: Immense Demonstration in This City," *New York Times*, April 21, 1861.
13. Wells, "House of Seligman," 72.
14. Seligman, "Reminiscences of Isaac Seligman," 13
15. Wells, "House of Seligman," 55.
16. Seligman, "Reminiscences of Isaac Seligman," 11.
17. Wells, "House of Seligman," 56.
18. Muir and White, *Over the Long Term*, 26–27.
19. Ibid., 27–28.
20. Ibid., 29.
21. Ibid., 39; Markens, *Abraham Lincoln and Jews*, 31.
22. Hellman, "Joseph Seligman, American Jew," 35.
23. Joseph Seligman to brothers, February 2, 1863, Seligman Family Papers-NYHS.
24. Joseph Seligman to brothers, February 20, 1863, and Joseph to Isaac Seligman, April 29, 1863, Seligman Family Papers-NYHS.
25. "The Draft," *New York Times*, September 4, 1864.
26. "A Letter from One of the Rioters," *New York Times*, July 15, 1863.
27. Hellman, "Story of Seligmans," 80–81.
28. Ibid., 71.
29. Joseph Seligman to brothers, February 20, 1864, Seligman Family Papers-NYHS.
30. Hellman, "Story of Seligmans," 87.
31. Ibid., 53.
32. Joseph Seligman to brothers, February 5, 1863, Seligman Family Papers-NYHS.
33. Joseph Seligman to brothers, January 29, 1863, Seligman Family Papers-NYHS.
34. Ibid.
35. Joseph Seligman to brothers, February 18 and 20, 1864, Seligman Family Papers-NYHS.
36. Ibid.
37. Joseph Seligman to brothers, April 30, 1863, Seligman Family Papers-NYHS.
38. Joseph Seligman to brothers, April 6, 1863, Seligman Family Papers-NYHS.
39. Hellman, "House of Seligman," 72.
40. Seligman, "Reminiscences of Isaac Seligman," 14.
41. U.S. War Department, *War of the Rebellion*, 1223.
42. Flynt, *Alabama Baptists*, 116.
43. "Fresh in the River," *Richmond Dispatch*, January 11, 1865.
44. Krick, *Civil War Weather in Virginia*, 147–49.
45. U.S. War Department, *War of the Rebellion*, 1223–24.
46. Jones, *Rebel War Clerk's Diary*, 2:382.

47. U.S. War Department, *War of the Rebellion*, 365.
48. Ibid., 69–70.
49. Ibid., 166.
50. "Rev. Mr. Tichenor's Address," *Montgomery Advertiser*, March 5, 1865.
51. Douglas B. Ball to JK, September 22, 1984, Box 13, JK-CURBML.
52. Thian, *Correspondence of Treasury Department*, 823.
53. "Evacuation of Montgomery," *Montgomery Daily Mail*, April 17, 1865.
54. Rogers, *Confederate Home Front*, 144.
55. "Evacuation of Montgomery," *Montgomery Daily Mail*, April 17, 1865.
56. *Louisiana*, 12:180, R.G. Dun & Co. credit report volumes, BL-HBS.
57. Manheim, "Seed and Tree," 43.
58. Libo, *Lots of Lehmans*, 12.
59. "Evacuation of Montgomery," *Montgomery Daily Mail*, April 17, 1865.
60. "Application of Mayer Lehman for Amnesty & Pardon," August 4, 1865, and "Application of Emanuel Lehman for Amnesty & Pardon," February 20, 1866, Amnesty Papers, NA.
61. Edgar B. Stern to Frank Manheim, January 23, 1948, Box 162, HL-CURBML.
62. *Louisiana*, 12:180, R.G. Dun & Co. credit report volumes, BL-HBS.
63. *Louisiana*, 20:28, R.G. Dun & Co. credit report volumes, BL-HBS.
64. Muir and White, *Over the Long Term*, 51.
65. *New York*, 417:148, R.G. Dun & Co. credit report volumes, BL-HBS.

5 CITY OF EMPIRES

1. Dietz, *Stammbuch der Frankfurter Juden*, 257.
2. Freimann and Kracauer, *Frankfort*, 237–44; Adler, *Schiff: His Life and Letters*, 1:2.
3. Adler, *Schiff: His Life and Letters*, 1:3.
4. IFS; Dietz, *Stammbuch der Frankfurter Juden*, 205.
5. Adler and Singer, *Jewish Encyclopedia*, 96.
6. Deutsch, *Scrolls*, 2:253.
7. Adler, *Schiff: His Life and Letters*, 1:1.
8. Dr. Otto Driesen, headmaster of the Frankfurt Philanthropin, speech, April 1, 1925.
9. Cohen, *Schiff: Study in Leadership*, 2.
10. Ibid., 1.
11. Warburg, *Reminiscences of Long Life*, 8.
12. Ibid., 4.
13. JHS passport, March 3, 1965, IFS.
14. Adler, *Schiff: His Life and Letters*, 1:5.
15. Cohen, *Schiff: Study in Leadership*, 3.
16. Adler, *Schiff: Biographical Sketch*, 23.
17. Adler, *Schiff: His Life and Letters*, 1:6.
18. Louis Marshall, address to Temple Emanu-El congregation, December 19, 1920, Box 244, DS-NYPL.
19. Max J. Bonn, memo, June 29, 1926, Reel 684, JHS-AJA.
20. Adler, *Schiff: His Life and Letters*, 1:7; Cohen, *Schiff: Study in Leadership*, 4.
21. "Review of the Month," *Commercial and Financial Chronicle*, January 4, 1868; Sobel, *Big Board*, 71, 78, 82.
22. Wells, "House of Seligman," 99–100; Gurock, *Central European Jews in America*, 139.
23. Hickling, *Men and Idioms of Wall Street*, 5.
24. Warburg, "Book for Jimmy, Jennifer," 49.

25. Warburg, *Reminiscences of Long Life*, 12.

26. Ibid., 14–15.

27. *Ohio*, 78:262, R.G. Dun & Co. credit report volumes, BL-HBS.

28. Loeb, *Our Father*, 10.

29. Ibid., 7.

30. Ibid., 9–10.

31. Wells, "House of Seligman," 102.

32. Warburg, "Book for Jimmy, Jennifer," 44; Loeb, *Our Father*, 11.

33. Sachs, *One Hundred Years at Rushing Brook*, 6.

34. Sachs, "Autobiography," 2–3.

35. Ibid., 4.

36. Ibid.; Sachs, "Reminiscences of Walter Sachs," Part 2, 53.

37. *New York*, 417:200VV, R.G. Dun & Co. credit report volumes, BL-HBS.

38. Sachs, "Autobiography," 4.

39. *New York*, 417:200RR, R.G. Dun & Co. credit report volumes, BL-HBS.

40. Manheim, "Seed and Tree," 47; *New York*, 19:500G, R.G. Dun & Co. credit report volumes, BL-HBS.

41. HL, "Reminiscences of Herbert Lehman," Part 1, 4:4.

42. HL to Irwin J. Miller, December 30, 1953, Box 162, HL-CURBML.

43. "Description of House—5 East 62nd Street," Box 163, HL-CURBML.

44. Manheim, "Seed and Tree," 50.

45. Ibid., 51.

46. U.S. House, *Reports of Committees for the Second Session of the Forty-third Congress, 1874–75*, 271.

47. "Commercial Report," *New York Herald*, November 18, 1888.

48. "In Memoriam: Mayer Lehman," 15.

49. "In Memoriam: Emanuel Lehman," 29.

50. Ibid., 7.

51. *New York*, 319:500 A/13 and 500U, R.G. Dun & Co. credit report volumes, BL-HBS.

52. *New York*, 418:235, R.G. Dun & Co. credit report volumes, BL-HBS.

53. Henry Budge, memo, October 10, 1925, Reel 684, JHS-AJA.

6 PANIC!

1. "Securing 'Financial Opinions,'" *Road*, July 1, 1875.

2. "A Western Jim Fisk," *New York Times*, December 8, 1872; "The Rockford Road," *Chicago Tribune*, June 19, 1875.

3. *New York*, 418:235, R.G. Dun & Co. credit report volumes, BL-HBS.

4. Arnsberg, *Henry Budge*, 19–20.

5. *New York*, 420:477, R.G. Dun & Co. credit report volumes, BL-HBS.

6. Office of the mayor, memo to the Frankfurt Senate, December 22, 1866, IFS.

7. Wells, "House of Seligman," 102, 121.

8. White, *Money and Banking*, 176.

9. Geisst, *Wheels of Fortune*, 15.

10. Wells, "House of Seligman," 122.

11. U.S. House, *Reports of Committees for the Second Session, 1869–70*, No. 31, 235.

12. Muir and White, *Over the Long Term*, 57.

13. Ackerman, *Gold Ring*, 88.

14. Wells, "House of Seligman," 123, 134.

15. Ibid., 123.

16. "The Gold Excitement," *New York Times*, September 25, 1869.

17. Ibid.
18. U.S. House, *Reports of Committees for the Second Session of the Forty-first Congress*, No. 31, 240.
19. Ibid., 238.
20. Ibid., 239–40.
21. Ibid., 241.
22. "Failure of Jay Cooke & Co.," *New-York Tribune*, September 19, 1873; "The Panic," *New York Times*, September 19, 1873.
23. *History of the Terrible Financial Panic of 1873*, 8.
24. Oberholtzer, *Jay Cooke*, 2:308.
25. Ibid., 2:196, 215.
26. Ibid., 2:424.
27. Ibid., 2:428.
28. "The Germans," *New York Times*, October 19, 1872.
29. Wells, "House of Seligman," 591.
30. Muir and White, *Over the Long Term*, 68.
31. Wells, "House of Seligman," 225.
32. Ibid., 218.
33. Ibid., 219.
34. Perkins, "Eye of the Storm," 1135.
35. Wells, "House of Seligman," 222.
36. Ibid., 213.
37. Ibid., 224–25.
38. Ibid., 237.
39. Ibid., 239.
40. Muir and White, *Over the Long Term*, 75.
41. Seligman, "Reminiscences of Isaac Seligman," 7.
42. Seligman, "Some Recollections of Sir Charles Seligman," 2.
43. *New York*, 319:500 A/13, R.G. Dun & Co. credit report volumes, BL-HBS.
44. *New York*, 420:418, R.G. Dun & Co. credit report volumes, BL-HBS.

7   THE LITTLE GIANT

1. Henry Budge, memo, October 10, 1925, Reel 684, JHS-AJA.
2. Adler, *Schiff: His Life and Letters*, 1:9.
3. Warburg, *Reminiscences of Long Life*, 9.
4. Articles of Co-partnership, November 29, 1874, Folder 3, Box 517, LB-BL-HBS.
5. Loeb, *Our Father*, 14–15.
6. Warburg, *Reminiscences of Long Life*, 14, 16.
7. Ibid., 9.
8. Ibid.
9. Sachs, "Reminiscences of Walter Sachs," Part 2, 53.
10. Wedding menu and congratulatory telegrams, Felix and Frieda Warburg Family Collection-AJA.
11. Warburg, *Reminiscences of Long Life*, 44.
12. Ibid., 10.
13. David Schiff, interview by the author.
14. Potter, *Men, Money and Magic*, 19.
15. Warburg, *Long Road Home*, 19.
16. Warburg, *Reminiscences of Long Life*, 52.
17. Louis Marshall, address, December 20, 1920, Box 244, DS-NYPL.

18. Warburg, "Reminiscences of Schiff."
19. Warburg, *Reminiscences of Long Life*, 43.
20. Warburg, "Reminiscences of Schiff."
21. Loeb, *Our Father*, 12.
22. "Biographical data about the Kuhns and Loebs by James K. Senior, a grandson of Samuel Kuhn," Box 243, DS-NYPL.
23. Manuscript draft of Adler, *Schiff: His Life and Letters*, 935, Box 1861, JHS-AJA.
24. Ibid., 927–28.
25. "Secretary Sherman's Visit," *New York Times*, April 10, 1878.
26. "The Great Syndicate Bid," *New York Times*, April 19, 1879.
27. "P.R.R. Files Tell of Banking Shift," *New York Times*, December 23, 1937.
28. Henry Tatnall to MLS, November 14, 1925, Reel 684, JHS-AJA.
29. "Jacob H. Schiff," Box 244, DS-NYPL.
30. Warburg, *Reminiscences of Long Life*, 45.
31. Ibid., 74.
32. Ibid., 52.
33. Ibid., 57.
34. Warburg, *Reminiscences of Long Life*, 57; Loeb, *Our Father*, 12–13.
35. Loeb, *Our Father*, 19.
36. Warburg, *Reminiscences of Long Life*, 19; Loeb, *Our Father*, 20.
37. Ibid., 13.
38. Ibid., 17.
39. Ibid., 21–22.
40. Warburg, "Book for Jimmy, Jennifer," 46.

8 THE GILDED GHETTO

1. Muir and White, *Over the Long Term*, 66.
2. Wells, "House of Seligman," 358.
3. Hellman, "Joseph Seligman, American Jew," 33.
4. Wells, "House of Seligman," 308.
5. Hellman, "Story of Seligmans," 253.
6. Wells, "House of Seligman," 306.
7. Rock and Moore, *Haven of Liberty*, 164.
8. Dinnerstein, *Anti-Semitism in America*, 26.
9. Bogen, *Luckiest Orphans*, 6.
10. Ibid., 17.
11. Ibid., 14–15.
12. Ibid., 12.
13. Seligman, *In Memoriam: Jesse Seligman*, 93.
14. Bogen, *Luckiest Orphans*, 49–50.
15. "Report of the Committee: Instructed with the Investigation of the Charges Proffered Against the Management of the Hebrew Orphan Asylum of the City of New York," *American Israelite*, January 15, 1875.
16. "Persecution of the Roumania Jews," *New York Herald*, July 2, 1870.
17. "Persecutions of the Israelites in the Danubian Principalities," *Daily Phoenix* (Columbia, S.C.), February 22, 1870.
18. Sarna, *When Grant Expelled Jews*, 110.
19. Ibid., 115–16.
20. "Historical Sketches of the Jewish Congregations of the United States," *New Era*, March 1874.
21. "Sunday Services for Hebrews," *New York Times*, May 19, 1879.

22. Cowen, *Memories of American Jew*, 94.
23. Kittelstrom, *Religion of Democracy*, 270.
24. Wells, "House of Seligman," 309.
25. Denby, *Grand Hotels*, 42.
26. Wells, "House of Seligman," 309.
27. "A Sensation at Saratoga," *New York Times*, June 19, 1877.
28. "A Reply to Judge Hilton," *New York Times*, June 20, 1877.
29. Manheim, "Seed and Tree," 93.
30. "A Sensation at Saratoga," *New York Times*, June 19, 1877.
31. "Judge Hilton's Position," *New York Times*, June 20, 1877.
32. "Mr. Seligman's Friends," *New York Times*, June 21, 1877.
33. "Mr. Jesse Seligman's Opinion," *New York Times*, June 20, 1877.
34. "Among the Proscribed," *New York Times*, June 20, 1877.
35. "Judge Hilton's Position," *New York Times*, June 20, 1877.
36. "A Cry from Newport," *New York Times*, June 20, 1877.
37. "The Position of New-York Hotels," *New York Times*, June 20, 1877.
38. "The Long Branch Hotel Keepers," *New York Times*, June 20, 1877.
39. Eaton, *Hour with American Hebrew*, 53, 66, 69.
40. Lynch, *"Boss" Tweed*, 407.
41. "A Sensation at Saratoga," *New York Times*, June 19, 1877.
42. Dinnerstein, *Anti-Semitism in America*, 5.
43. Ibid., 15.
44. Dobkowski, *Tarnished Dream*, 82.
45. *Alabama*, 20:28, R.G. Dun & Co. credit report volumes, BL-HBS.
46. Dinnerstein, *Anti-Semitism in America*, 36.
47. Diner, *Jews of the United States*, 170.
48. Klein, *Life and Legend of Gould*, 11.
49. "The Jewish Question," *New York Times*, June 23, 1877.
50. Muir and White, *Over the Long Term*, 76; Seligman, "Some Recollections of Sir Charles Seligman," 1.
51. Wells, "House of Seligman," 316.
52. Hellman, "Story of Seligmans," 165H.
53. "War on the Jews," *Times* (Philadelphia), July 23, 1879.
54. "Mr. Corbin and the Hebrews," *Baltimore Sun*, July 24, 1879.
55. Wells, "House of Seligman," 323.
56. Ibid., 303.
57. David Seligman to ERAS, January 27, 1880, Seligman Family Correspondence-AJA.
58. Hellman, "Story of Seligmans," 195.
59. Wells, "House of Seligman," 324.
60. Letter to ERAS, April 30, 1880, Seligman Family Correspondence-AJA; Muir and White, *Over the Long Term*, 78; INS to ERAS, April 29, 1880, Box 62, ERAS-CURBML.
61. "Obituary: Joseph Seligman," *New York Times*, April 27, 1880.
62. ERAS, Biographical memo, 1928, Box 40, GH-NYPL.
63. Alfred Seligman to ERAS, April 28, 1880, Box 62, ERAS-CURBML.
64. INS to ERAS, April 29, 1880, Box 62, ERAS-CURBML.
65. Ibid.
66. "Funeral Service of Mr. Seligman," *New York Times*, May 3, 1880.
67. Felix Adler, "Memorial Words, Spoken over the Remains of Joseph Seligman," May 3, 1880, NYHS.
68. Stern, *Rise and Progress of Reform Judaism*, 202.
69. "Obituary: Joseph Seligman," *New-York Tribune*, April 27, 1880.

9 AMERICAN MONTEFIORE

1. Friedman, *What Went Wrong?*, 42.
2. "The Committee of Fifty," *New York Times*, December 6, 1882; "Determined for Reform," *New York Times*, October 23, 1882.
3. Adler, *Schiff: His Life and Letters*, 1:345.
4. Ibid., 1:350.
5. Mount Sinai Hospital, annual report, 1921.
6. Sankovitch, *Signed, Sealed, Delivered*, 9.
7. HL, "Reminiscences of Herbert Lehman," Part 1, 4:20.
8. Irving Lehman to MLS, November 25, 1925, Reel 684, JHS-AJA.
9. "Mount Sinai Hospital," *American Hebrew*, December 23, 1881.
10. "Suicide of Moses G. Hanauer," *New York Times*, January 8, 1883.
11. "Jacob Schiff and Mount Sinai Hospital," May 15, 1984, Box 244, DS-NYPL.
12. Levenson, *Montefiore*, 15.
13. Ibid.
14. Manheim, "Seed and Tree," 80.
15. Ibid.
16. Adler, *Schiff: His Life and Letters*, 1:370.
17. Cohen, *Schiff: Study in Leadership*, 68.
18. Ibid., 64.
19. JHS to Henry Solomon, "Memoranda in regard to Jacob H. Schiff from Montefiore Hospital Directors," January 22, 1899, Reel 684, JHS-AJA.
20. S. G. Rosenbaum, "Memoranda in regard to Jacob H. Schiff from Montefiore Hospital Directors," October 29, 1925, Reel 684, JHS-AJA.
21. M. D. Goodman, "Memoranda in regard to Jacob H. Schiff from Montefiore Hospital Directors," October 13, 1925, Reel 684, JHS-AJA.
22. "Diamonds and Vulgarity," *New York Times*, July 31, 1887.
23. Warburg, *Reminiscences of Long Life*, 57.
24. Ibid., 55.
25. Samuel Sachs to Cyrus Adler, August 31, 1925, Reel 684, JHS-AJA.
26. Sachs, "Reminiscences of Walter Sachs," Part 1, 1.
27. Fisher, *When Money Was in Fashion*, 12.
28. Sachs, *One Hundred Years at Rushing Brook*, 7.
29. "English, Hebrew, German and Mathematical Institute," *Baltimore Sun*, August 26, 1856.
30. Sachs, *One Hundred Years at Rushing Brook*, 12.
31. Ibid., 16.
32. Josef Kleinhenz, "Herr Sachs aus Rödelmaier," *Jüdische Allgemeine*, February 19, 2009.
33. Sachs, *One Hundred Years at Rushing Brook*, 16.
34. Warburg, *Reminiscences of Long Life*, 86.
35. HL, "Reminiscences of Herbert Lehman," Part 1, 4:26.
36. Sachs, *One Hundred Years at Rushing Brook*, 8.
37. Samuel Sachs to Cyrus Adler, August 31, 1925, Reel 684, JHS-AJA.
38. S. G. Rosenbaum, "Memoranda in regard to Jacob H. Schiff from Montefiore Hospital Directors," October 29, 1925, Reel 684, JHS-AJA.
39. "Stewardship During One's Lifetime," *Jewish Messenger*, September 29, 1893.
40. Waldman, *Nor by Power*, 328.
41. Warburg, *Reminiscences of Long Life*, 52.
42. "Memoranda in regard to Jacob H. Schiff from Montefiore Hospital Directors," Leopold Stern, August 10, 1925, Reel 684, JHS-AJA.

43. JHS to Ernest Cassel, March 6, 1888, Reel 676, JHS-AJA; Marcus, *United States Jewry*, 477.
44. "American Notes," *Jewish World*, November 18, 1898.
45. Joseph Buttenwieser to MLS, August 1, 1925, Reel 684, JHS-AJA.
46. Waldman, *Nor by Power*, 323.
47. Ibid., 328.
48. Warburg, "Book for Jimmy, Jennifer," 49–50.
49. Feld, *Lillian Wald*, 32–33.
50. Wald, *House on Henry Street*, 4–8.
51. Daniels, *Always a Sister*, 35.
52. "Jacob H. Schiff," *Survey*, October 2, 1920.
53. Ibid.; Adler, *Schiff: His Life and Letters*, 1:292.
54. Adler, *Schiff: His Life and Letters*, 1:317–18.
55. "Jacob H. Schiff," *Survey*, October 2, 1920.
56. Cohen, *Schiff: Study in Leadership*, 72, 74; Weschler, *Qualified Student*, 131.
57. McClellan, *Gentleman and Tiger*, 276–77.
58. Meyer, *Barnard Beginnings*, 102–3.
59. Annie Nathan Meyer, memo, May 1, 1926, Reel 684, JHS-AJA.

10 EXODUS

1. "The Exiles from Russia," *Jewish Messenger*, August 19, 1881.
2. "Hebrew Emigrant Aid Society of the U.S.," *American Hebrew*, December 2, 1881.
3. "Aid for Hebrew Immigrants," *New York Times*, November 28, 1881.
4. Osofsky, "Hebrew Emigrant Aid Society," 176.
5. Pomper, *Lenin's Brother*, 124.
6. Radzinsky, *Alexander II*, 413–16.
7. Klier, *Pogroms*, 39–40.
8. Dubnow, *History of Jews in Russia and Poland*, 18.
9. Montefiore, *Romanovs*, 463.
10. Reinharz and Mendes-Flohr, *Jew in Modern World*, 380.
11. Howe, *World of Our Fathers*, 24.
12. "Aid Needed for Hebrew Refugees," *New York Times*, June 24, 1882.
13. "Too Many Immigrants," *Chicago Tribune*, June 26, 1882.
14. Manners, *Poor Cousins*, 86.
15. "A Riot Among the Russian Jews," *New York Times*, October 15, 1882.
16. Manners, *Poor Cousins*, 85.
17. Osofsky, "Hebrew Emigrant Aid Society," 183.
18. Ibid., 177.
19. Ibid., 181; Wischnitzer, *Visas to Freedom*, 31.
20. Eisenberg, *Jewish Agricultural Colonies*, 75.
21. Osofsky, "Hebrew Emigrant Aid Society," 179.
22. Sachar, *History of Jews in America*, 135.
23. Frankel, "Jewish Charities," 50.
24. Wischnitzer, *Visas to Freedom*, 32.
25. Ibid.
26. Joseph, *History of Baron de Hirsch Fund*, 25.
27. "Montefiore Home for Chronic Invalids," *American Hebrew*, April 6, 1888.
28. "For Work Among Hebrews," *New York Times*, November 9, 1891.
29. Cowen, *Memories of American Jew*, 92.

30. "Opening of the Harvard Semitic Museum," *American Hebrew*, February 12, 1892.

31. Marcus, *United States Jewry*, 55.

32. Joseph, *History of Baron de Hirsch Fund*, 11.

33. Adler, *Schiff: His Life and Letters*, 2:83.

34. Ibid., 2:85, 87.

35. Joseph, *History of Baron de Hirsch Fund*, 35.

36. Ibid., 28.

37. Adler, *Schiff: His Life and Letters*, 2:83.

38. Julius Goldman to MLS, October 29, 1925, Reel 684, JHS-AJA.

39. "To Restrict Immigration," *New York Times*, February 27, 1892.

40. Cohen, *Schiff: Study in Leadership*, 154.

41. "The Russian Jew Problem," *New York Times*, August 2, 1891.

42. Max Kohler to MLS, October 14, 1925, Reel 684, JHS-AJA.

43. "Mr. Nettleton Retires," *New York Times*, April 8, 1892.

44. Markel, *Quarantine!*, 23; Schulteis, *Report on European Immigration*, 12.

45. Best, *To Free a People*, 24–25.

46. Ibid., 34; Travis, *Kennan and American-Russian Relationship*, 212.

47. Best, *To Free a People*, 24.

48. Straus, *Under Four Administrations*, 106–7.

49. Best, *To Free a People*, 31.

50. U.S. Immigration Commission, *Report of the Commissioners of Immigration*, 52, 80, 91, 100–101.

51. Best, *To Free a People*, 34.

52. Ibid., 32.

53. Benjamin Harrison, State of the Union address, 1891.

54. Markel, *Quarantine!*, 27.

55. "Disease Was Her Cargo," *Middletown Times-Press* (N.Y.), February 16, 1892.

56. Markel, *Quarantine!*, 76–77.

57. Ibid., 79.

58. Adler, *Schiff: His Life and Letters*, 2:76–78.

59. American Public Health Association, *Public Health Papers and Reports*, vol. 18, *Presented at the Twentieth Annual Meeting of the American Public Health Association, Mexico, Mex., Nov. 29, 30, Dec. 1, 2, 1892* (reprint: FB&C, 2017), 343.

60. Waldman, *Nor by Power*, 323.

11 END OF AN ERA

1. "Jesse Seligman Honored," *New York Times*, October 2, 1891; "The Seligman Banquet," *Jewish Messenger*, October 9, 1891.

2. "Jesse Seligman's Mission," *New York Times*, October 31, 1891; "Mr. Seligman's Mission," *New York Times*, November 24, 1891.

3. "The Silver Question Again," *North American Review*, January 1891.

4. "The Seligman Banquet," *Jewish Messenger*, October 9, 1891; "Jesse Seligman Honored," *New York Times*, October 2, 1891.

5. Hellman, "Story of Seligmans," 291.

6. Seligman, *In Memoriam: Jesse Seligman*, 40–41.

7. Walker, *Preliminary Report of the Isthmian Canal Commission*, 16.

8. McCullough, *Path Between Seas*, 127.

9. "The Panama Canal," *People's Press* (Winston-Salem, N.C.), October 28, 1880.

10. "Big Pay from De Lesseps," *New York Times*, February 16, 1893.

11. McKinlay, *Panama Canal*, 123.

12. Parker, *Panama Fever,* 162.
13. Ibid., 155; Loizillon, *Bunau-Varilla Brothers and Panama Canal,* 119.
14. Brustein, *Roots of Hate,* 193.
15. Renehan, *Dark Genius of Wall Street,* 249.
16. Wells, "House of Seligman," 621.
17. Renehan, *Dark Genius of Wall Street,* x, 4.
18. "Were Congressmen Bribed?" *Indianapolis Journal,* December 30, 1892.
19. "Big Pay from De Lesseps," *New York Times,* February 16, 1893; "Panama Investigation," *Times-Picayune* (New Orleans), February 16, 1893.
20. "Panama Investigation," *Times-Picayune* (New Orleans), February 16, 1893.
21. Wells, "House of Seligman," 352.
22. "Our New York Letter," *Albany Democrat* (Albany, Ore.), May 5, 1893.
23. "Mr. Seligman Blackballed," *New York Times,* April 15, 1893.
24. "Because He Is a Hebrew," *Indianapolis Journal,* April 16, 1893.
25. "Censure for Union League," *New York Times,* April 21, 1893.
26. Seligman, *In Memoriam: Jesse Seligman,* 22–23.
27. "Death of Jesse Seligman," *New York Times,* April 24, 1893.
28. Seligman, *In Memoriam: Jesse Seligman,* 227.
29. Ibid.
30. Hellman, "Story of Seligmans," 262.
31. "Alfred L. Seligman Dead in Auto Crash," *New York Times,* June 25, 1912.
32. Hellman, "Story of Seligmans," 269–70.
33. "Sorting Out the Seligmans," *New Yorker,* October 30, 1954.
34. Guggenheim, *Out of This Century,* 3.
35. "The Cat Out of the Bag," *Lincoln Evening Call* (Neb.), March 28, 1887 ; "Young Seligman's Deed," *Chicago Tribune,* March 21, 1887.
36. "Charged with Attempting Suicide," *Altoona Tribune* (Penn.), May 21, 1903.
37. "Washington Seligman Suicide in a Hotel," *Brooklyn Daily Eagle,* February 12, 1912.
38. "Seligman Kills Wife and Himself," *New York Times,* December 17, 1915.
39. "Lt. Comdr. Seligman Ends Life in Florida," *New York Times,* April 8, 1944.
40. Wells, "House of Seligman," 390.
41. Ibid., 395, 404, 416.
42. "In Memoriam: Mayer Lehman," 9; "Mayer Lehman Buried," *New York Times,* June 25, 1897.
43. Manheim, "Seed and Tree," 77.
44. Ibid., 103.
45. Ibid., 85–88.
46. Ibid., 102–3.
47. Ibid., 103.
48. HL, "Reminiscences of Herbert Lehman," Part 1, 4:13–14; Leopold Strauss to Emile Semple, August 18, 1932, Box 164, HL-CURBML.
49. Bryan, *Speeches of Bryan,* 248–49; Bensel, *Passion and Preferences,* 233.
50. Manheim, "Seed and Tree," 72.
51. Nevins, *Lehman and His Era,* 17.
52. HL, "Reminiscences of Herbert Lehman," Part 1, 4:35.
53. Paul Sachs to Allan Nevins, February 25, 1960, Box 163, HL-CURBML.
54. Herbert Lehman to Clifford W. Hall, August 7, 1847, Box 162, HL-CURBML.
55. Nevins, *Lehman and His Era,* 36.
56. Mayer Lehman to HL, September 27, 1895, Box 163, HL-CURBML.
57. Nevins, *Lehman and His Era,* 39.
58. Emanuel Lehman to executors, February 3, 1898, Box 591, LB-BL-HBS.
59. Manheim, "Seed and Tree," 108.

60. Herman Kahn interview notes, February 15, 1984, Box 15, JK-CURBML.
61. Manheim, "Seed and Tree," 117.
62. "Automobile Cabs Barred," *New York Times*, December 16, 1899; "Hurrying Bankers Stopped," *New York Times*, April 28, 1902.
63. "Auto Accident Stirs Crowd," *New York Sun*, January 2, 1906; "Orlando H. Peck Dead," *New York Sun*, January 9, 1906; "News Jottings," *Times Union* (Brooklyn, N.Y.), February 6, 1906.

12 MERGERS AND ACQUISITIONS

1. Adler, *Schiff: His Life and Letters*, 1:30; Rosenbaum and Sherman, *Warburg & Co.*, 36.
2. Warburg, "Book for Jimmy, Jennifer," 27, 31.
3. Chernow, *Warburgs*, 10.
4. Farrer, *Warburgs*, 19, 22.
5. Warburg, "Book for Jimmy, Jennifer," 23, 25; Chernow, *Warburgs*, 7.
6. Chernow, *Warburgs*, 13.
7. Warburg, "Under Seven Stars," 1.
8. Farrer, *Warburgs*, 35.
9. Paul Warburg calling card, 1892, AW-WIA.
10. Rosenbaum and Sherman, *Warburg & Co.*, 93.
11. Chernow, *Warburgs*, 38.
12. Warburg, *Reminiscences of Long Life*, 29.
13. PMW to AW, June 14, 1891, AW-WIA.
14. Warburg, "Book for Jimmy, Jennifer," 40.
15. Ibid., 66.
16. Edward M. M. Warburg oral history, October 1989, 1, AJCOHC-NYPL.
17. MLS, memorandum, December 1, 1928, DTS.
18. Warburg, "Under Seven Stars," 10.
19. Edward M. M. Warburg oral history, October 1989, 1, AJCOHC-NYPL.
20. Warburg, *Reminiscences of Long Life*, 82, 87, 90.
21. Ibid., 87–88.
22. FMW to AW, July 22, 1894; FMW to Charlotte and Moritz Warburg, July 30, 1894; AW to Charlotte and Moritz Warburg, August 1, 1894, AW-WIA.
23. Warburg, *Reminiscences of Long Life*, 89.
24. Potter, *Men, Money, and Magic*, 20.
25. Warburg, *Reminiscences of Long Life*, 61–62.
26. Ibid., 90.
27. Charlotte Warburg to AW and siblings, September 2, 1894, AW-WIA.
28. Warburg, *Reminiscences of Long Life*, 90.
29. Charlotte Warburg to AW and siblings, September 17, 1894; AW to Charlotte and Moritz Warburg, August 1, 1894, AW-WIA.
30. Charlotte Warburg to AW and siblings, September 17, 1894, AW-WIA; Warburg, *Reminiscences of Long Life*, 90.
31. Warburg, *Reminiscences of Long Life*, 91.
32. "For a Consumptives' Home," *Evening World* (N.Y.), February 25, 1895.
33. Warburg, *Reminiscences of Long Life*, 92, 97.
34. Ibid., 93.
35. Ibid., 24.
36. Seating chart, FMW Miscellaneous File, AJA.
37. Warburg, *Reminiscences of Long Life*, 94.
38. Ibid., 94–95.

39. Ibid.
40. Chernow, *Warburgs*, 53.
41. Warburg, "Book for Jimmy, Jennifer," 47.
42. Warburg, *Reminiscences of Long Life*, 95.
43. Ibid., 19.
44. Chernow, *Warburgs*, 79.
45. Ibid., 63.
46. Ibid., 65.
47. INS to AW, March 16, 1896, AW-WIA.
48. "Weddings Past and to Come," *New-York Tribune*, October 2, 1892.
49. Warburg, "Under Seven Stars," 5.
50. Warburg, "Reminiscences of James Paul Warburg," 15–16.
51. MLS to JHS and Therese Schiff, October 25, 1896, DTS.
52. Warburg, *Reminiscences of Long Life*, 74.
53. Ibid., 75.
54. Cohen, *Schiff: Study in Leadership*, 4.
55. Warburg, *Reminiscences of Long Life*, 82.
56. MLS to JHS and Therese Schiff, March 5, 1893, DTS.
57. MLS to JHS and Therese Schiff, March 5, 1893, and April 16, 1893, DTS.
58. Nicolson, *Dwight Morrow*, 28.
59. "Plea for the Immigrant," n.d., DTS.
60. Stearns, *Amherst Boyhood*, 123–24.
61. Warburg, *Reminiscences of Long Life*, 83.
62. MLS to JHS, November 14, 1895, DTS.
63. MLS to JHS, December 1, 1895, DTS.
64. MLS to JHS and Therese Schiff, November 10 and 11, and December 1, 1895, DTS; Potter, *Men, Money, and Magic*, 23.
65. J. J. Hill to JHS, May 21, 1896, DTS.
66. MLS to JHS and Therese Schiff, October 29, 1896, DTS.
67. MLS to JHS, November 16, 1896, DTS.
68. Chernow, *Warburgs*, 67.
69. MLS to JHS and Therese Schiff, July 4, 1897, DTS.
70. MLS to JHS and Therese Schiff, July 8, 1897, DTS; Chernow, *Warburgs*, 68.
71. MLS to JHS and Therese Schiff, May 24, 1897, DTS.
72. MLS to JHS and Therese Schiff, October 25, 1896, DTS.
73. MLS to JHS and Therese Schiff, May 24, 1897, DTS.
74. MLS to JHS and Therese Schiff, July 4, 1897, DTS.
75. MLS to JHS and Therese Schiff, July 26, 1897, DTS.
76. MLS to Therese Schiff, October 1, 1897, DTS.
77. MLS to JHS and Therese Schiff, August 31, 1897; MLS to JHS, September 9, 1897, DTS.
78. Warburg, *Reminiscences of Long Life*, 84.
79. MLS to JHS and Therese Schiff, January 21, 1898, DTS.
80. MLS to JHS, February 15, 1898, DTS.
81. MLS to JHS, May 24, 1898, DTS.

13 PARTNERS AND RIVALS

1. Fisher, *When Money Was in Fashion*, 33.
2. Sachs, "Autobiography," 43.
3. Ibid., 29.
4. Ibid., 33.

5. Ibid., 40.
6. Ibid., 34.
7. Fisher, *When Money Was in Fashion*, 52.
8. Wells, "House of Seligman," 82.
9. "Checks for Wedding Presents," *New York Times*, January 4, 1884.
10. Dinkelspiel, *Towers of Gold*, 57.
11. Ibid., 152–53.
12. Sachs, "Reminiscences of Walter Sachs," Part 1, 41.
13. Fisher, *When Money Was in Fashion*, 53.
14. Sachs, "Autobiography," 45.
15. Ibid., 47.
16. Alef, *Henry Goldman*, 19.
17. Sachs, "Autobiography," 49.
18. Ibid., 51.
19. Kobler, *Otto the Magnificent*, 9.
20. Forbes, *Men Who Are Making America*, 216; Kobler, *Otto the Magnificent*, 12.
21. Collins, *Otto Kahn*, 37.
22. Phillips-Matz, *Many Lives of Kahn*, 12.
23. Liebmann, *Fall of House of Speyer*, 8.
24. Kobler, *Otto the Magnificent*, 21.
25. Adler, *Schiff: His Life and Letters*, 1:17.
26. Buttenwieser, "Reminiscences of Benjamin Buttenwieser," 284.
27. Ibid., 306–7.
28. Adler, *Schiff: His Life and Letters*, 1:17.
29. Manuscript draft of Adler, *Schiff: His Life and Letters*, 1056, Box 1861, JHS-AJA.
30. "A Silent Wall Street Man," *Star Tribune* (Minneapolis), November 30, 1900.

14 JUPITER'S SHADOW

1. Klein, *Union Pacific*, 27.
2. Kennan, *E. H. Harriman*, 1:119.
3. Haeg, *Harriman vs. Hill*, 47.
4. "Stories of the Late James J. Hill," *Michigan Manufacturer and Financial Record*, June 24, 1916.
5. Kennan, *E. H. Harriman*, 1:119.
6. Chernow, *House of Morgan*, 104.
7. U.S. Industrial Commission on Transportation, *Report*, 9:770.
8. Cohen, *Schiff: Study in Leadership*, 9.
9. Kobler, *Otto the Magnificent*, 23.
10. Adler, *Schiff: His Life and Letters*, 1:92.
11. Kennan, *E. H. Harriman*, 1:121.
12. Klein, *Union Pacific*, 22–23.
13. "Pacific Railroads Funding Bill," *Los Angeles Herald*, April 30, 1896.
14. Kennan, *E. H. Harriman*, 1:123.
15. Klein, *Life and Legend of Harriman*, 110.
16. Kennan, *E. H. Harriman*, 1:90.
17. Casson, *History of Telephone*, 205.
18. Kennan, *E. H. Harriman*, 1:124–25.
19. "Proceedings of Congress," *New York Times*, December 23, 1896; "Morgan's New Bill," *Salt Lake Tribune*, January 8, 1897.
20. "Defeat for the Lobby," *Chicago Tribune*, January 12, 1897.
21. Adler, *Schiff: His Life and Letters*, 1:94.

22. JHS to Robert Fleming, April 29, 1897, Folder 15, Box 437, JHS-AJA.
23. Klein, *Life and Legend of Harriman*, 113; "Has a Ten Million Interest," *Argus-Leader* (Sioux Falls, S.D.), May 20, 1897.
24. "Morgan Makes an All Day Speech on Union Pacific Affairs," *Courier-Journal* (Louisville, Ky.), July 13, 1897.
25. JHS to Robert Fleming, July 14, 1897, Folder 15, Box 437, JHS-AJA.
26. Kennan, *E. H. Harriman*, 124–25.
27. Kahn, *Our Economic and Other Problems*, 19–21.
28. "Sale of Union Pacific," *New York Times*, September 2, 1897.
29. JHS to MLS, September 23, 1897, DTS.
30. "Confirming the Steal," *World* (N.Y.), October 19, 1897.
31. Klein, *Life and Legend of Harriman*, 114.
32. "World's Biggest Auction," *Nebraska State Journal*, November 2, 1897.
33. Kennan, *E. H. Harriman*, 1:138.
34. Klein, *Union Pacific*, 65.
35. Ibid., 51.
36. Kahn, *Our Economic and Other Problems*, 25.
37. OHK to Horace Burt, February 18, 1898, Folder 5, Box 8, AH-LOC.
38. JHS to Horace Burt, February 23, 1898, Folder 5, Box 8, AH-LOC.
39. JHS to Horace Burt, March 30, 1898, Folder 5, Box 8, AH-LOC.
40. JHS to Robert Fleming, May 2, 1898, Folder 6, Box 437, JHS-AJA.
41. "Astor Battery Enroute," *Wichita Daily Eagle*, June 16, 1898.
42. OHK to Horace Burt, June 17, 1898, Folder 5, Box 8, AH-LOC.
43. Horace Burt to OHK, June 23, 1898, Folder 5, Box 8, AH-LOC.
44. Klein, *Union Pacific*, 67–68.
45. Kennan, *E. H. Harriman*, 1:134.
46. "Owners of America," *Cosmopolitan*, June–November 1909.
47. Klein, *Union Pacific*, 23.

15 A PERFECT PEACE

1. JHS to Horace Burt, February 7, 1898, Folder 5, Box 8, AH-LOC.
2. Pyle, *Life of James Hill*, 45.
3. Klein, *Union Pacific*, 100.
4. MLS to JHS, November 3, 1895, DTS.
5. Pyle, *Life of James Hill*, 10.
6. James J. Hill to JHS, October 11, 1895, JJH-MHS.
7. Haeg, *Harriman v. Hill*, 38.
8. Adler, *Schiff: His Life and Letters*, 1:102.
9. "Proposed Extension of the C., B. & Q.," *Indianapolis Journal*, November 20, 1899.
10. "The Burlington Heading for the Coast," *Anaconda Standard* (Mont.), April 17, 1900.
11. Haeg, *Harriman vs. Hill*, 72.
12. Klein, *Life and Legend of Harriman*, 216.
13. Haeg, *Harriman vs. Hill*, 73.
14. Adler, *Schiff: His Life and Letters*, 1:102–3.
15. Ibid., 1:91; Haeg, *Harriman vs. Hill*, 89.
16. Klein, *Life and Legend of Harriman*, 219.
17. Pyle, *Life of James Hill*, 104.
18. "Harriman Syndicate Gets Southern Pacific," *New York Times*, February 1, 1901.
19. "Leased to Great Northern," *New York Times*, March 13, 1901.

20. Haeg, *Harriman vs. Hill*, 94.
21. Adler, *Schiff: His Life and Letters*, 1:103.
22. "That Rumored C. B. & Q.," *Des Moines Register*, March 30, 1901.
23. Adler, *Schiff: His Life and Letters*, 1:105.
24. Ibid., 1:104.
25. Kennan, *Harriman*, 1:296–97.
26. Paine, *George Fisher Baker*, 202.
27. Kennan, *Harriman*, 1:296.
28. OHK, memorandum, November 24, 1925, Reel 684, JHS-AJA.
29. Ibid.
30. Schiff remained on the Great Northern's board until December 1901. "American and Canadian," *Herapath's Railway Journal*, December 6, 1901.
31. Haeg, *Harriman vs. Hill*, 108–9.
32. "Another Exciting Day on the Stock Exchange," *New York Times*, April 30, 1901.
33. Haeg, *Harriman vs. Hill*, 134.
34. Warburg, *Reminiscences of Long Life*, 75.
35. Otto Kahn, in a memo written more than twenty years later, pegged the date of this meeting as May 2. In a letter to J. P. Morgan written two weeks after the fact, Schiff said the meeting occurred on May 3.
36. Haeg, *Harriman vs. Hill*, 135.
37. Ibid., 156; Klein, *Life and Legend of Harriman*, 239.
38. Adler, *Schiff: His Life and Letters*, 1:106.
39. Kennan, *Harriman*, 1:303.
40. Klein, *Life and Legend of Harriman*, 231.
41. Kennan, *Harriman*, 1:305.
42. OHK, memorandum, November 24, 1925, Reel 684, JHS-AJA.
43. *Brooklyn Daily Eagle*, May 7, 1901.
44. Haeg, *Harriman vs. Hill*, 180.
45. Julius Goldman, memorandum, October 29, 1925, Reel 684, JHS-AJA.
46. Baruch, *Baruch: My Story*, 2:144.
47. "Scenes of Disorder in Stock Exchange," *New York Times*, May 10, 1901.
48. OHK, memorandum, November 24, 1925, Reel 684, JHS-AJA.
49. "Northern Pacific Corner Exposed," *New York Times*, May 10, 1910.
50. Allen, *Lords of Creation*, 89.
51. "The Northern Pacific Settlements Effected," *New York Times*, May 11, 1901.
52. "Dies in Vat of Hot Beer," *New York Times*, May 10, 1901.
53. "The Struggle for Control," *New York Times*, May 10, 1901.
54. "Morgan Will Hurry to New York," *St. Louis Post-Dispatch*, May 12, 1901.
55. "A Game of Wreckers Says James J. Hill," *St. Louis Post-Dispatch*, May 12, 1901.
56. "Quick Recovery Follows Panic," *Chicago Tribune*, May 11, 1901.
57. OHK, memorandum, November 24, 1925, Reel 684, JHS-AJA.
58. Adler, *Schiff: His Life and Letters*, 1:107.
59. Ibid.
60. William Ripley to George Kennan, March 19, 1916, Folder 3, Box 140, OHK-PU.
61. U.S. Industrial Commission on Transportation, *Report*, 9:769.
62. Ibid., 9:770.
63. Ibid., 9:772.
64. Haeg, *Harriman vs. Hill*, 166–67.
65. U.S. Industrial Commission on Transportation, *Report*, 9:772.
66. Klein, *Union Pacific*, 107.
67. Josephson, *Robber Barons*, 443.
68. Strouse, *Morgan*, 431.

69. Adler, *Schiff: His Life and Letters,* 1:110.
70. JHS to TR, telegram, September 10, 1901, TR-LOC.
71. TR, *Addresses and Messages of Roosevelt,* 290, 296.
72. Goodwin, *Bully Pulpit,* 299.
73. JHS to Lucius Littauer, March 24, 1902, TR-LOC.
74. TR to JHS, March 27, 1902, TR-LOC.
75. Adler, *Schiff: His Life and Letters,* 1:47.
76. Best, *To Free a People,* 44–46.
77. "Mr. Schiff's Views," *Wall Street Journal,* December 15, 1904.
78. "Small Talk of the Week," *Sketch,* December 19, 1906.
79. "The New Money King," *Philadelphia Press,* August 22, 1903.
80. Cohen, *Schiff: Study in Leadership,* 11.
81. "'On Pleasure Bent Are We,'" *Los Angeles Times,* November 30, 1904.
82. Nicholas Murray Butler to TR, December 23, 1903, TR-LOC.
83. JHS to TR, January 31, 1904, TR-LOC.
84. Morris, *Theodore Rex,* 309.
85. JHS to Louis Lipsky, October 5, 1904, Folder 29, Box 1, PC-AJHS.
86. "Safe and Sane," *Wall Street Journal,* June 25, 1904.
87. Zipperstein, *Pogrom,* 98.
88. Best, *To Free a People,* 82.
89. Muraoka, "Jews and Russo-Japanese War," 11.
90. Best, *To Free a People,* 74–75.
91. TR to Oscar Straus, July 19, 1904, TR-LOC.
92. TR to Cornelius Bliss, July 14, 1904, TR-LOC.
93. Sachar, *History of Jews in America,* 226.

16 THE SINEWS OF WAR

1. Adler, *Schiff: Biographical Sketch,* 46.
2. Adler, *Selected Letters,* 2:38.
3. "Jacob Schiff Talks," *Los Angeles Times,* April 14, 1904.
4. "An American 'Slave' Becomes Japan's Premier," *Literary Digest,* February 18, 1922.
5. Takahashi Korekiyo to MLS, July 24, 1925, Reel 684, JHS-AJA.
6. Smethurst, *Foot Soldier to Finance Minister,* 20.
7. Takahashi Korekiyo to MLS, July 24, 1925, Reel 684, JHS-AJA.
8. Best, "Schiff's Early Interest in Japan."
9. Smethurst, *Foot Soldier to Finance Minister,* 151.
10. Ibid., 155.
11. Ibid., 150.
12. Ibid., 151.
13. "Japanese War Loan," *Lewiston Evening Teller* (Idaho), May 10, 1904.
14. Best, "Financing a Foreign War," 315.
15. PMW, memorandum, November 19, 1925, Reel 684, JHS-AJA.
16. MLS to JHS, May 27, 1901, DTS.
17. PMW to AW, July 16, 1901; PMW to AW, December 15, 1901, AW-WIA.
18. Katharine Weber, interview by the author; Weber, *Memory of All That,* 163.
19. MMW to AW, March 16, 1901, AW-WIA.
20. MLS, memorandum, December 1, 1928, DTS.
21. Warburg, *Reminiscences of Long Life,* 15.
22. Chernow, *Warburgs,* 88.
23. PMW, memorandum, November 20, 1925, Reel 684, JHS-AJA.

24. Therese Schiff to MLS, December 4, 1895, DTS.
25. PMW, memorandum, November 19, 1925, Reel 684, JHS-AJA; Warburg, *Long Road Home*, 18.
26. Muraoka, "Jews and Russo-Japanese War," 106.
27. Takahashi Korekiyo to MLS, July 24, 1925, Reel 684, JHS-AJA.
28. Sherman, "German-Jewish Bankers in World Politics," 73.
29. Adler, *Schiff: His Life and Letters*, 2:121.
30. "Reminiscences from an Old Friend," *American Hebrew*, October 8, 1920.
31. PC, *Memories of American Jew*, 285.
32. Adler, *Schiff: His Life and Letters*, 2:121–22.
33. PC, *Memories of American Jew*, 286.
34. "Finance," *Forum*, July 1904–June 1905.
35. Adler, *Schiff: His Life and Letters*, 2:125–26.
36. Best, *To Free a People*, 100.
37. Albert Strauss to Gregory Wilenkin, March 20, 1905, Albert Strauss letter book 2, SC-UO.
38. J. & W. Seligman & Co. to Gregory Wilenkin and Baron Wrangel, December 13, 1904, Albert Strauss letter book 2, SC-UO.
39. Albert Strauss to Henry Grove, December 10, 1904, Albert Strauss letter book 2, SC-UO.
40. Albert Strauss to Henry Grove, March 8, 1905, Albert Strauss letter book 2, SC-UO.
41. "Kuhn Loeb & Co.'s New Quarters," *New York Times*, May 12, 1903.
42. "New Japanese Loan Several Times Taken," *New York Times*, March 30, 1905.
43. Muraoka, "Jews and Russo-Japanese War," 107.
44. Takahashi Korekiyo to MLS, July 24, 1925, Reel 684, JHS-AJA.
45. Best, "Financing Foreign War," 313.
46. Herman Bernstein, "Personal Memories of Mr. Schiff," *American Hebrew*, October 8, 1920.
47. Keene, *Emperor of Japan*, 612.
48. Matsumura, *Baron Kaneko and Russo-Japanese War*, 342.
49. Witte, *Memoirs of Count Witte*, 135.
50. Morris, *Theodore Rex*, 391.
51. INS to Seligman Frères et Cie, July 19, 1905, SC-UO.
52. Muraoka, "Jews and Russo-Japanese War," 5, 17.
53. INS to Seligman Brothers, August 8, 1905, SC-UO.
54. Warburg, *As I Recall*, 21.
55. JHS to PC, August 7, 1905, Folder 29, Box 1, PC-AJHS.
56. Witte, *Memoirs of Count Witte*, 163–64.
57. Kraus, *Reminiscences and Comments*, 156–57; "Witte Receives Jews in Appeal for Race," *New York Times*, August 15, 1905.
58. "Jewish Representatives and M. De Witte," *Menorah*, January–July 1905.
59. JHS to PC, August 16, 1905, Folder 29, Box 1, PC-AJHS.
60. INS to TR, August 17, 1905, INS letter book, SC-UO.
61. Herman Bernstein, "Personal Memories of Mr. Schiff," *American Hebrew*, October 8, 1920.
62. "To Blow Up Schiff," *Scranton Republican* (Penn.), August 19, 1905.
63. "Not Disturbed," *Boston Globe*, August 19, 1905; "Guarding Schiff's House," *New York Times*, August 19, 1905.
64. "Infernal Machine Incidents in New York," *American Israelite*, August 24, 1905; "An Infernal Machine for Jacob H. Schiff," *New York Times*, September 25, 1906.
65. "How the World Learned the News," *Index*, September 2, 1905.
66. Adler, *Schiff: His Life and Letters*, 1:231–32.

67. Ibid., 1:227.
68. Best, *To Free a People*, 111.
69. Adler, *Schiff: His Life and Letters*, 2:133.
70. "How Russian Soldiers Were Enlightened in Japan," *Outlook*, March 17, 1915.
71. Ibid.
72. "Russian Prisoners Cheer Revolution," *New York Times*, November 12, 1905.
73. George Kennan to JHS, April 11, 1917, Folder 5, Box 2541, JHS-AJA.
74. "Russia Free! Russia Aflame! Woe to the Jew!" *Menorah*, November 1905.
75. "American Jews to Aid Sufferers in Russia," *New York Times*, November 8, 1905.
76. Schachner, *Price of Liberty*, 8.
77. Adler, *Schiff: His Life and Letters*, 2:137–38.
78. Best, *To Free a People*, 120; TR, *Letters of Theodore Roosevelt*, 112.
79. Schachner, *Price of Liberty*, 9.

17 THE HARRIMAN EXTERMINATION LEAGUE

1. "Talks with Big Ones," *Los Angeles Times*, January 13, 1907.
2. "Kuhn, Loeb & Co. Leave All Railroad Boards," *New York Times*, February 27, 1906.
3. Schiff, *Our Journey to Japan*, 1, 8.
4. Klein, *Life and Legend of Harriman*, 330.
5. Ibid., 330.
6. Ibid., 329.
7. "Ryan Now Tells of Harriman Talk," *New York Times*, December 13, 1905.
8. "Equitable Hearing Waits on Mediation," *New York Times*, March 29, 1905.
9. JHS to TR, July 26, 1905, TR-LOC.
10. JHS to Charles R. Flint, April 6, 1896, Box 36, AO-NYPL.
11. JHS to AO, January 5, 1898, Box 36, AO-NYPL.
12. JHS to AO, October 30, 1904; AO to JHS, October 30, 1904, Box 36, AO-NYPL.
13. JHS to AO, February 26, 1905, Box 36, AO-NYPL.
14. JHS to AO, March 31, 1905, Box 36, AO-NYPL.
15. "Too Fast and Too Far," *New York Times*, April 1, 1905.
16. New York State, *Testimony: Business and Affairs of Life Insurance Companies*, 1050.
17. Schiff, *Our Journey to Japan*, 1.
18. Smethurst, "Korekiyo, Rothschilds and War," 6.
19. Griscom, *Diplomatically Speaking*, 263.
20. Muraoka, "Jews and Russo-Japanese War," 110.
21. Schiff, *Our Journey to Japan*, 168.
22. Ibid., 49, 167.
23. Harvey Krueger, interview by the author.
24. Victor Solomon to DS, June 7, 1972, Box 244, DS-NYPL.
25. Yashuda Kawamura to DTS, February 28, 2012, DTS.
26. "How Japan Saved Jews from Hitler," *Washington Post*, November 14, 1982.
27. Warburg, *Reminiscences of Long Life*, 49–51.
28. "Editorial," *American Federationist*, August 1906.
29. Kahn, *Our Economic and Other Problems*, 39–40.
30. Kennan, *Harriman*, 2:182.
31. Ibid., 2:201; Bishop, *Theodore Roosevelt and His Time*, 2:42, 61.
32. Klein, *Life and Legend of Harriman*, 401.
33. "Harriman Facing Federal Inquiry," *Chicago Tribune*, November 9, 1906.
34. Kennan, *Harriman*, 2:174–75.

35. "The Harriman Investigation," *Railroad Gazette*, May 17, 1907.
36. "E. H. Harriman Stands by His Guns in Chicago & Alton," *Wall Street Journal*, March 25, 1907.
37. "Schiff Predicts Panic Unless Money Is Freed," *New York Times*, January 4, 1906.
38. Adler, *Schiff: His Life and Letters*, 1:36.
39. Cohen, *Schiff: Study in Leadership*, 22.
40. Adler, *Schiff: His Life and Letters*, 1:44–45.
41. Ibid.
42. "Mellen Gloats over Harriman," *Eugene Guard* (Ore.), July 16, 1907.
43. U.S. Interstate Commerce Commission, *Reports*, 301.
44. Kennan, *Chicago & Alton Case*, 13, 25.
45. TR, *Address on Laying the Corner Stone of Pilgrim Monument*.
46. Kahn, *Our Economic and Other Problems*, 55–56.
47. Chernow, *House of Morgan*, 122–23, 126–27.
48. "Schiff Declares Trouble Over," *Washington Evening Star*, October 24, 1907.
49. "Jacob Schiff Sounds Warning," *American Israelite*, November 7, 1907.
50. "Zionism's Hope Here, Says Jacob H. Schiff," *New York Times*, July 29, 1907.
51. "Zionism and Patriotism," *Houston Press*, September 22, 1907.
52. "Calls Schiff Traitor," *Washington Post*, September 15, 1907; "Zionists Stirred by Schiff's Trip," *Morning News* (Wilmington, Del.), March 25, 1908.
53. Kennan, *Harriman*, 2:327.
54. Klein, *Life and Legend of Harriman*, 437.
55. OHK to E. H. Harriman, May 23, 1908, Folder 3, Box 8, AH-LOC.
56. "An American in Asia," *Asia*, February 1921.
57. Adler, *Schiff: His Life and Letters*, 2:253.
58. Klein, *Life and Legend of Harriman*, 439.
59. Ibid., 64.

18 "THE GOLD IN GOLDMAN SACHS"

1. Sachs, "Autobiography," 25.
2. Sachs, "Reminiscences of Walter Sachs," Part 1, 11.
3. Ibid., 16.
4. Sachs, "Autobiography," 97.
5. Carr and Bruner, *Panic of 1907*, 30.
6. Sachs, "Autobiography," 96–99.
7. Fisher, *When Money Was in Fashion*, 53.
8. Sachs, "Reminiscences of Walter Sachs," Part 1, 24.
9. Sachs, "Autobiography," 59, 64, 65.
10. Manheim, "Seed and Tree," 133.
11. Endlich, *Culture of Success*, 38.
12. Supple, "Business Elite," 173–74; Manheim, "Seed and Tree," 142; Sachs, "Autobiography," 132–33.
13. Ellis, *Partnership*, 12.
14. Ascoli, *Julius Rosenwald*, 24.
15. Manheim, "Seed and Tree," 153.
16. "Farmers Betrayed to Wall Street," *Hanover Democrat and Enterprise* (Kan.), June 29, 1906.
17. Manheim, "Seed and Tree," 153.
18. Wake, *Kleinwort Benson*, 128.
19. Herman Andreae to Paul Sachs, July 11, 1912, KB-LMA.
20. Goldman Sachs to Kleinwort Sons, December 6, 1910, KB-LMA.

21. Goldman Sachs to Herman Andreae, April 24, 1912, KB-LMA.
22. Paul Sachs to Herman Andreae, June 28, 1912, KB-LMA.
23. Alexander, *Museum in America*, 208.
24. "Portrait of the Artist as a Director," *Harvard Magazine*, September–October 2002.
25. Ibid.
26. Duncan and McClellan, *Art of Curating*, 16.
27. "Portrait of the Artist as a Director," *Harvard Magazine*, September–October 2002.
28. Fisher, *When Money Was in Fashion*, 53.
29. Rusty Sachs, interview by the author.
30. Weber, *Patron Saints*, 26–27.
31. "Mentor for American Museum Men," *New York Times*, November 28, 1948; Kantor, *Barr and Museum of Modern Art*, 73.
32. Valentiner, *Henry Goldman Collection*, 8.
33. "Mr. F. W. Woolworth's Story," *World's Work*, November 1912–April 1913.
34. Manheim, "Seed and Tree," 155.
35. Winkler, *Five and Ten*, 173, 182.
36. "55-Story Building Opens on a Flash," *New York Times*, April 25, 1913; "Wilson Lights Up Woolworth Tower," *Brooklyn Daily Eagle*, April 25, 1913; "Architect Given Signal Courtesy," *Marion Star* (Ohio), April 25, 1913.
37. Sachs, "Reminiscences of Walter Sachs," Part 2, 97.
38. Sachs, "Autobiography," 110.
39. Levy, *Yesterdays*, 246.

19 AND STILL THEY COME

1. Riis, *How the Other Half Lives*, 105, 108.
2. "Bill Is Un-American," *South Bend Tribune*, June 12, 1906; "The Dillingham Immigration Bill," *Burlington Free Press*, April 11, 1906.
3. "Pass Immigration Bill, Cut by Cannon's Order," *New York Times*, June 26, 1906.
4. "Jacob H. Schiff's Chautauqua Address," *American Hebrew and Jewish Messenger*, July 23, 1909.
5. Adler, *Schiff: His Life and Letters*, 2:97; Best, "Schiff's Galveston Movement," 45.
6. "Interview with Mr. Jacob Schiff," *American Hebrew and Jewish Messenger*, June 25, 1909.
7. Adler, *Schiff: His Life and Letters*, 2:87–88; Berman and Schloff, *Jews in Minnesota*, 25.
8. Richardson, *Compilation of Messages and Papers of Presidents*, 1131.
9. Cohen, *Schiff: Study in Leadership*, 160.
10. JHS to Solomon Schechter, September 22, 1907, Box 7, OS-LOC.
11. JHS to OS, October 4, 1907, Box 7, OS-LOC.
12. Adler, *Schiff: His Life and Letters*, 2:97.
13. Marinbach, *Galveston*, 11, 179.
14. Dr. Bernhard Kahn, tribute to Max M. Warburg (1947), LBI.
15. Marinbach, *Galveston*, 14.
16. Best, "Schiff's Galveston Movement," 52.
17. Marinbach, *Galveston*, 23, 24, 42.
18. "Foreign Criminals in New York," *North American Review*, September 1908.
19. Silver, *Marshall and Jewish Ethnicity*, 146; Feldstein, *Land I Show You*, 215.
20. Goren, *New York Jews and Quest*, 28, 30, 34; "Bingham Is Criticized," *Detroit Free Press*, September 10, 1908.

21. "Wrong About Jews Bingham Admits," *New York Times*, September 17, 1908.
22. Goren, *New York Jews and Quest*, 38.
23. Ibid., 49, 51, 54.
24. Ibid., 68.
25. "Memorandum Containing Recollections of Felix Warburg by One of His Children," April 12, 1939, Felix and Frieda Warburg Family Collection-AJA.
26. Warburg, *As I Recall*, 20.
27. Gerald Warburg, "Life with Fizzie," n.d., Felix and Frieda Warburg Family Collection-AJA.
28. Ibid.
29. Chernow, *Warburgs*, 243.
30. "First Draft of Interview with Mr. Sol Stroock in Question of Materials for Biography," December 12, 1940, Felix and Frieda Warburg Family Collection-AJA.
31. Warburg, *As I Recall*, 20.
32. "Memorandum Containing Recollections of Felix Warburg by One of His Children," April 12, 1939, Felix and Frieda Warburg Family Collection-AJA.
33. "First Draft of Transcript of Interview with Mr. Newcomb Carlton in Quest of Materials for Biography of Felix M. Warburg," December 19, 1940, Felix and Frieda Warburg Family Collection-AJA.
34. Buttenwieser, "Reminiscences of Benjamin Buttenwieser," 285.
35. Warburg, *As I Recall*, 19.
36. Memorandum, c. 1917, Reel 2434, JM-AJA.
37. Goren, *New York Jews and Quest*, 164.
38. Robert Adamson to MLS, November 20, 1925, Reel 684, JHS-AJA.
39. Best, *To Free a People*, 171.
40. Ibid., 175.
41. Marinbach, *Galveston*, 59.
42. Max Kohler to MLS, January 6, 1925, Reel 684, JHS-AJA.
43. "Puts Up Bars at Galveston," *Baltimore Sun*, August 21, 1910.
44. Adler, *Schiff: His Life and Letters*, 2:107–8.
45. Best, "Schiff's Galveston Movement," 64.
46. Marinbach, *Galveston*, 107–8.
47. Best, "Schiff's Galveston Movement," 66.
48. JHS to FMW, November 4, 1914, Folder 16, Box 166, FMW-AJA.

20   THE PASSPORT QUESTION

1. Adler, *Schiff: His Life and Letters*, 2:151–52; JHS to AO, April 28, 1911, Box 35, AO-NYPL.
2. Cohen, *Schiff: Study in Leadership*, 147.
3. "The Passport Question," *American Jewish Year Book*, September 23, 1911; Best, *To Free a People*, 183.
4. JHS to Simon Wolf, May 24, 1918, Folder 20, Box 457, JHS-AJA.
5. Wolf, *Presidents I Have Known*, 294–310.
6. William H. Taft to Otto Bannard, June 17, 1911, Reel 684, JHS-AJA.
7. Cohen, *Encounter with Emancipation*, 238.
8. McAdoo, *Crowded Years*, 122.
9. Ibid.; "Break with Russia Demands Public Opinion," *American Israelite*, December 14, 1911.
10. McAdoo, *Crowded Years*, 122.
11. Cohen, *Not Free to Desist*, 79.
12. Best, *To Free a People*, 196–97.

13. Cohen, *Encounter with Emancipation*, 98.
14. "Report of American Jewish Committee," *American Jewish Year Book*, September 21, 1914–September 8, 1915.
15. "Schiff Bares Brandt Plot," *New York Times*, February 27, 1912.
16. "Evidence Which Indicted Brandt," *New York Times*, February 15, 1912.
17. "Thirty Years for Valet," *New-York Tribune*, April 5, 1907.
18. Folke Brandt to KN, March 1, 1909, Box 76, KN-MHS.
19. "The Strange Case of Mr. Schiff's Valet," *St. Louis Post-Dispatch*, January 26, 1912.
20. MLS to KN, July 1, 1909, Box 76, KN-MHS.
21. Howard Gans to MLS, December 13, 1911, Box 220, DS-NYPL.
22. "Gerard Will See Dix About Brandt Tonight," *Brooklyn Daily Eagle*, February 15, 1912.
23. "Jacob Schiff Sails; Silent on the Brandt Case," *Philadelphia Inquirer*, February 22, 1912.
24. L. E. Miller to MLS, October 19, 1922, Box 220, DS-NYPL.
25. Booker T. Washington to MLS, February 19, 1912, Box 220, DS-NYPL.
26. "Schiff Bares Brandt Plot," *New York Times*, February 27, 1912.
27. "Mrs. Schiff Before Grand Jury to Tell Her Story of Brandt," *Evening World* (N.Y.), March 26, 1912.
28. "No Indictment in Brandt Case," *Boston Globe*, March 29, 1912.
29. "Thousands Mourn at Straus Memorial," *New York Times*, May 13, 1912.
30. "Slur Against Woman Is Reason Dix Refuses Pardon," *Star-Gazette* (Elmira, N.Y.), March 1, 1912.
31. Cohen, *Schiff: Study in Leadership*, 152.
32. "Press Assailed by Schiff," *Daily Herald* (Arlington Heights, Ill.), March 22, 1912.
33. "Brandt Retracts; Is Free; Justice, Not Mercy, Rules," *New-York Tribune*, January 18, 1913.
34. Samuel Diehl to MLS, June 16 and October 10, 1913, Box 220, DS-NYPL.
35. William Sulzer to MLS, March 12, 1913, Box 220, DS-NYPL.
36. "Folke Brandt Reported Killed in the War," *Watertown Daily Times* (N.Y.), February 10, 1917.
37. Folke Brandt to MLS and Adele Schiff, August 8, 1927, Box 220, DS-NYPL.
38. M. M. Murphy to Folke Brandt, November 7, 1927, Box 220, DS-NYPL.
39. Ernst Schiff to MLS, March 1928, Box 220, DS-NYPL.
40. Potter, *Men, Money, and Magic*, 39.
41. Warburg, *Reminiscences of Long Life*, 85.
42. Wendy Gray, interview by the author.
43. Potter, *Men, Money, and Magic*, 110.
44. Ibid., 43.
45. "Heavy Gambling on the Deutschland," *New York Times*, August 30, 1901.
46. MLS to JHS and Therese Schiff, September 24, 1901, DTS.
47. Potter, *Men, Money, and Magic*, 74.
48. LS, "Reminiscences of Lewis L. Strauss," 74–75.
49. "To Accuse Gov. Sulzer," *Buffalo Morning Express*, August 1, 1913.

21 THE HUNTING PARTY

1. "To Investigate 'Money Trust,'" *Courier-Journal* (Louisville, Ky.), July 30, 1911.
2. HL, "Reminiscences of Herbert Lehman," Part 1, 4:70, 82.
3. "Morgan Testifies at Pujo Probe; He Denies There Is a Money Trust," *Times Union* (Brooklyn, N.Y.), December 19, 1912.

4. U.S. House of Representatives, *Money Trust Investigation*, 1:1:1052.
5. "Morgan Reveals Business of Firm," *New York Times*, December 19, 1912.
6. U.S. House of Representatives, *Money Trust Investigation*, 3:23:1663, 1691–92.
7. U.S. House of Representatives, *Report of the Committee to Investigate the Concentration of Money*, 56, 129, 131.
8. "Tributes to Morgan," *Buffalo Morning Express* (N.Y.), April 1, 1913.
9. "Schiff's Tribute to Morgan," *New York Times*, April 4, 1913.
10. "Who Will Wear Morgan's Mantle," *Allentown Democrat* (Penn.), April 4, 1913.
11. "The Income Tax Amendment," *Political Science Quarterly*, June 1910.
12. Mehrotra, "Envisioning the Fiscal State," 1860.
13. "To Become British Because of Tax," *New York Times*, March 7, 1914; "British Citizenship Is Easy to Obtain," *New York Times*, March 8, 1914.
14. "Applauds the President," *Pittsburgh Press*, May 6, 1906.
15. "A Tax on Business Incomes," *New York Times*, February 19, 1909.
16. Warburg, *Federal Reserve System*, 1:19.
17. Ibid., 1:12.
18. Ibid., 1:14.
19. Ibid., 1:18–19.
20. Warburg, "Reminiscences of James Paul Warburg," 17.
21. "Warburg, the Revolutionist," *Century Magazine*, May–October 1915; "Attitude of the Public and of the Bankers Toward Monetary Reform Prior to the Panic of 1907," Reel 61, NWA-LOC.
22. "Defects and Needs of Our Banking System," *New York Times*, January 6, 1907.
23. AO to JHS, January 10, 1907, and JHS to AO, January 14, 1907, AO-NYPL.
24. "Aldrich Becomes Converted to Idea of a Central Bank, May–October 1908," Reel 61, NWA-LOC.
25. "Philadelphia Meeting," *New-York Tribune*, December 3, 1907.
26. Seligman, *Currency Problem and Present Financial Situation*, 149.
27. "Aldrich Becomes Converted to Idea of a Central Bank, May–October 1908," Reel 61, NWA-LOC.
28. PMW to NWA, December 31, 1907, Reel 61, NWA-LOC.
29. Lowenstein, *America's Bank*, 76.
30. Adler, *Schiff: His Life and Letters*, 1:286; Lowenstein, *America's Bank*, 82.
31. Warburg, *Federal Reserve System*, 1:56–57.
32. Vanderlip, *Farm Boy to Financier*, 213.
33. Paul Warburg, narrative of the Jekyll Island conference, Reel 61, NWA-LOC.
34. Lowenstein, *America's Bank*, 110.
35. Vanderlip, *Farm Boy to Financier*, 216.
36. Ibid.
37. PMW to Samuel Sachs, January 11, 1911, Folder 1, Box 1, PMW-YU.
38. PMW statement, January 17, 1911, Folder 1, Box 1, PMW-YU.
39. "Wants a Bank Inquiry," *New York Times*, July 9, 1911.
40. "Thin Ice," *New York Times*, June 16, 1911.
41. Lowenstein, *America's Bank*, 148–49, 157.
42. Phillips-Matz, *Many Lives of Kahn*, 147–48.
43. Link, *Wilson*, 1:485.
44. Adler, *Schiff: His Life and Letters*, 1:312.
45. "12,000 Give to Campaign," *Sioux City Journal*, September 9, 1912.
46. U.S. House, *Hearings on Banking and Currency Reform*, 73.
47. Lowenstein, *America's Bank*, 182–83; Link, *Wilson*, 2:202, 204.
48. PMW to E. M. House, April 22, 1913, Folder 4, Box 1, PMW-YU.
49. Lowenstein, *America's Bank*, 202; Warburg, *Federal Reserve System*, 1:92.
50. PMW to E. M. House, July 13, 1913, Folder 5, Box 1, PMW-YU.

51. PMW to E. M. House, July 30, 1913, Folder 5, Box 1, PMW-YU.
52. Link, *Wilson*, 2:239.
53. PMW to Gerard Vissering, December 29, 1913, Folder 12, Box 1, PMW-YU.
54. Lowenstein, *America's Bank*, 268.
55. Warburg, *Long Road Home*, 29.
56. PMW to WW, May 1, 1914, Folder 14, Box 1, PMW-YU.
57. "Schiff to Head the Reserve Board," *Courier-Post* (Camden, N.J.), March 30, 1914; Adler, *Schiff: His Life and Letters*, 1:287.
58. William McAdoo, "Memorandum Concerning the Late Jacob H. Schiff," Reel 684, JHS-AJA.
59. ERAS to WW, March 10, 1914, Folder 19, Box 2, PMW-YU.
60. E. M. House to WW, May 1, 1914, in WW, *Papers of Wilson Digital Edition*.
61. JHS to Ernest Cassel, May 14, 1914, Box 1861, JHS-AJA.
62. William McAdoo to PMW, June 17, 1914, Folder 20, Box 2, PMW-YU.
63. PMW to William McAdoo, June 17, 1914, Folder 20, Box 2, PMW-YU.
64. Atlee Pomerene to PMW, June 24, 1914, Folder 20, Box 2, PMW-YU.
65. PMW to Atlee Pomerene, June 26, 1914, Folder 20, Box 2, PMW-YU; memos, n.d., Folder 21, Box 2, PMW-YU.
66. PMW to WW, July 3, 1914, Folder 21, Box 2, PMW-YU.
67. Carter Glass to PMW, July 8, 1914, Folder 21, Box 2, PMW-YU.

22 RAMPARTS BETWEEN US

1. Sachs, "Reminiscences of Walter Sachs," Part 1, 35–38; Sachs, "Autobiography," 123–25.
2. "Refugees in Boston," *Boston Globe*, August 8, 1914.
3. "Foreign Exchange," *Wall Street Journal*, August 3, 1914.
4. Sachs, "Autobiography," 128.
5. FMW to MMW, January 29, 1915, Folder 3, Box 165, FMW-AJA.
6. FMW to John Henry Hammond, January 21, 1918; Hammond to FMW, January 25, 1918, Folder 29, Box 179, FMW-AJA.
7. Chernow, *Warburgs*, 161.
8. Warburg, "Reminiscences of James Paul Warburg," 8.
9. JHS to James Wilson, October 24, 1914, Folder 7, Box 438, JHS-AJA.
10. "Mr. Schiff's Triple Patriotism," *Maccabean*, February 1913.
11. Weizmann, *Trial and Error*, 184.
12. Adler, *Schiff: His Life and Letters*, 2:182.
13. MLS to JHS and Therese Schiff, August 16, 1914, DTS.
14. MLS to JHS and Therese Schiff, August 6, 1914, DTS.
15. MLS to JHS and Therese Schiff, August 16, 1914, DTS.
16. Roberts, "Conflict of Loyalties," 10.
17. Max Kohler to MLS, October 14, 1925, Reel 684, JHS-AJA.
18. JHS to Takahashi Korekiyo, August 23, 1914, Folder 6, Box 438, JHS-AJA.
19. "Jacob H. Schiff Has Quit Japan Society," *New York Times*, December 2, 1914.
20. "Jacob H. Schiff Points a Way to European Peace," *New York Times*, November 22, 1914.
21. "An Insidious Suggestion," *London Globe*, November 23, 1914; "German Press Campaign," *Times* (London), November 23, 1914.
22. "German Press and Peace," *Scotsman*, November 28, 1914.
23. JHS to MMW, January 28, 1915, Folder 16, Box 444, JHS-AJA; Adler, *Schiff: His Life and Letters*, 2:187–88.
24. Rosenbaum and Sherman, *Warburg & Co.*, 115, 117.

25. Ibid., 113.
26. Weizmann, *Trial and Error*, 184.
27. Rosenbaum and Sherman, *Warburg & Co.*, 114–16.
28. Chernow, *Warburgs*, 156.
29. U.S. Senate, *Brewing and Liquor Interests and German Propaganda*, 1994.
30. Szajkowski, *Jews, Wars, and Communism*, 38.
31. "Bernhard Dernburg: The German Whose Presence Here Has Aroused British Apprehensions," *Current Opinion*, January–June 1915.
32. Feilitzsch, *Secret War on United States*, 125.
33. JHS to MMW, January 28, 1915, Folder 16, Box 444, JHS-AJA.
34. FMW to MMW, January 29, 1915, Folder 3, Box 165, FMW-AJA.
35. FMW to MMW, December 24, 1914, Folder 3, Box 165, FMW-AJA.
36. U.S. Senate, *Brewing and Liquor Interests and German Propaganda*, 2006–7.
37. Memo, August 15, 1914, Reel 20925, AA.
38. FMW to MMW, February 17, 1915, Folder 3, Box 165, FMW-AJA.
39. David de Sola Pool to FMW, December 30, 1914, Folder 15, Box 166, FMW-AJA.
40. Louis Marshall to JHS, December 30, 1914, Folder 1, Box 439, JHS-AJA.
41. FMW to Bernhard Dernburg, December 30, 1914, Folder 3, Box 165, FMW-AJA.
42. Gwynn, *Letters and Friendships of Spring Rice*, 2:242–43.
43. Max Bodenheimer to Carl Diego Ludwig von Bergen, September 16, 1914, AA.
44. Szajkowski, *Jews, Wars, and Communism*, 38.
45. U.S. Senate, *Brewing and Liquor Interests and German Propaganda*, 1448.
46. Feilitzsch, *Secret War on United States*, 137.
47. Isaac Strauss, memo, April 26, 1915, Reel 20945, AA.
48. Doerries, *Imperial Challenge*, 64–66.
49. Ibid.
50. Isaac Strauss, memo, April 26, 1915, Reel 20945, AA.
51. JHS to WW, November 19, 1914, in WW, *Papers of Wilson Digital Edition*.
52. WW to JHS, December 8, 1914, AJA.
53. Henry Morgenthau to JHS, August 31, 1914, JDC.
54. "Jewish War Relief Work," *American Jewish Year Book*, September 17, 1917–September 6, 1918.
55. "Palestine and the War: Impressions on a Relief Trip to the Holy Land," *Survey*, January 2, 1915.
56. "Jewish War Relief Work," *American Jewish Year Book*, September 17, 1917–September 6, 1918.
57. JHS to Louis Brandeis, February 29, 1916, Folder 8, Box 446, JHS-AJA.
58. Cohen, *Not Free to Desist*, 93.
59. Ibid., 90.
60. "Schiff Urges Jews to Be Americans," *New York Times*, May 22, 1916.
61. "Jacob Schiff Quits Jewish Movements," *New York Times*, June 5, 1916.
62. Editorial, *American Jewish Chronicle*, May 19, 1916.
63. Szajkowski, *Jews, Wars, and Communism*, 40.
64. FMW to MMW, June 19, 1916, Reel 20947, AA.
65. MMW to Arthur Zimmermann, July 19, 1916, Reel 20947, AA.
66. "Toluol Leads Him to Ellis Island," *New York Herald*, February 16, 1918; "Berlin Agent Sought Secret of Gas Masks," *New-York Tribune*, April 5, 1918; "Straus Interned," *American Israelite*, April 11, 1918.
67. "To Intern Seven Germans," *Baltimore Sun*, March 14, 1919.
68. Bernstorff, *My Three Years in America*, 139–41.

69. Chernow, *House of Morgan*, 165.
70. Ibid., 196.
71. Nicolson, *Dwight Morrow*, 188–89.
72. Warburg, *Reminiscences of Long Life*, 76.
73. "Cornell Will Drop the Study of 'Kultur,'" *New York Times*, June 25, 1918.
74. M. J. Stroock to MLS, October 3, 1925, Reel 684, JHS-AJA.
75. Adler, *Schiff: His Life and Letters*, 2:190.
76. L. M. Cangrell, report, July 20, 1915, Investigative Reports of the Bureau of Investigation 1908–1922, NA.
77. "Dernburg Off; Pleased with Work," *Central New Jersey Home News*, June 12, 1915.
78. Feilitzsch, *Secret War Council*, xxi–xxii.
79. Von Rintelen, *Dark Invader*, xxxiii; Sachs, "Reminiscences of Walter Sachs," Part 1, 19.
80. Von Rintelen, *Dark Invader*, 66, 74.
81. Sachs, "Reminiscences of Walter Sachs," Part 1, 19–20.

23 ALLIES

1. "To Raise Loan of $500,000," *Boston Globe*, September 10, 1915.
2. Reading, *Rufus Isaacs*, 51.
3. JHS to LR, September 12, 1915, LR-BL.
4. "German-American Banks to Be Asked to Loan to Allies," *Philadelphia Inquirer*, September 15, 1915.
5. OHK memo, n.d., Reel 684, JHS-AJA.
6. Ibid.
7. Adler, *Schiff: His Life and Letters*, 2:252.
8. "Kuhn Loeb & Co., Pro-German Bankers, May Not Aid in Loan," *Evening Public Ledger* (Philadelphia), September 21, 1915.
9. Erich Hossenfelder to Theobald von Bethmann-Hollweg, October 12, 1915, Reel 17358, AA.
10. Johann Heinrich von Bernstorff to Theobald von Bethmann-Hollweg, November 17, 1915, Reel 17359, AA; U.S. Senate, *Brewing and Liquor Interests and German Propaganda*, 2001.
11. Bernstorff to Bethmann-Hollweg, November 17, 1915.
12. Heinrich Albert, Memo on the Prospects of a German Loan in the United States, November 8, 1915, Reel 3101/672, AA.
13. OHK to Lord Beaverbrook, June 26, 1916, C/187A, Beaverbrook Papers-PA.
14. OHK to JHS, September 21, 1916, Folder 4b, Box 449, JHS-AJA.
15. JHS to OHK, September 27, 1916, Folder 4b, Box 449, JHS-AJA.
16. Link, *Wilson*, 5:196.
17. Collins, *Otto Kahn*, 116.
18. JHS to Israel Zangwill, March 15, 1917, Reel 684, JHS-AJA.
19. "Jacob H. Schiff Rejoices," *New York Times*, March 17, 1917.
20. JHS to Pavel Milyukov, March 19, 1917, Folder 22, Box 455, JHS-AJA.
21. JHS to Philipp Schiff, April 6, 1917, Folder 4, Box 450, JHS-AJA.
22. "Pacifists Pester Till Mayor Calls Them Traitors," *New York Times*, March 24, 1917.
23. JHS to MLS, March 20, 1917, DTS.
24. Adler, *Schiff: His Life and Letters*, 2:254.
25. JHS to MLS, March 24, 1917, DTS.

26. Sachs, "Reminiscences of Walter Sachs," Part 1, 39.
27. Herman Andreae to Arthur Sachs, November 25, 1915, CLC/B/140//KS04/02/08/018, KB-LMA.
28. Kleinwort Sons to Goldman Sachs, October 18, 1915, CLC/B/140//KS04/02/08/021, KB-LMA; Wake, *Kleinwort Benson*, 142.
29. Kleinwort Sons to Goldman Sachs, July 12, 1916, CLC/B/140//KS04/02/08/021, KB-LMA.
30. Richard Timmerscheidt to Chief Cabinet, January 27, 1917, M1085, Investigative Reports of the Bureau of Investigation 1908–1922, NA.
31. "German Ends Life After Questioning by U.S. Agents," *New York Tribune*, July 6, 1917.
32. "In re: Henry Goldman Sr.," March 15, 1918, M1085, Investigative Reports of the Bureau of Investigation 1908–1922, NA.
33. Gerhardt, *Recital*, 79.
34. Stephen Barrett to author, January 17, 2019.
35. Henry Goldman III, interview by the author.
36. Fisher, *When Money Was in Fashion*, 112–13.
37. Marcus Moench, interview by the author.
38. Henry Goldman to Kleinwort Sons, October 29, 1917, CLC/B/140//KS04/02/08/005, KB-LMA.

24 HERO LAND

1. HL, "Reminiscences of Herbert Lehman," Part 2, 4:2:606.
2. Ibid., Part 2, 4:2:243.
3. HL, "Reminiscences of Herbert Lehman," Part 1, 4:151.
4. Warburg, "Reminiscences of James Paul Warburg," 44.
5. Ibid., 16.
6. Katharine Weber, interview by the author.
7. Warburg, "Reminiscences of James Paul Warburg," 14.
8. Ibid., 10.
9. Warburg, *Long Road Home*, 31.
10. Warburg, "Reminiscences of James Paul Warburg," 7.
11. Warburg, *Long Road Home*, 37–38.
12. Ibid., 47–48.
13. FMW to John Warburg, March 27, 1918, Folder 33, Box 179, FMW-AJA.
14. FMW to Josephus Daniels, September 19, 1917, Folder 31, Box 175, FMW-AJA.
15. Alice R. Emanuel, memo, September 1963, Felix and Frieda Warburg Family Collection-AJA.
16. Chernow, *Warburgs*, 186.
17. Weber, *Memory of All That*, 142.
18. Warburg, *Long Road Home*, 49.
19. Weber, *Memory of All That*, 138–39.
20. Warburg, *Long Road Home*, 49.
21. Warburg, "Reminiscences of James Paul Warburg," 44.
22. CH diary, entry for August 9, 1916, vol. 3, CH-LOC.
23. CH diary, entry for November 29, 1916, vol. 4, CH-LOC.
24. CH diary, entries for November 25 and August 9, 1916, vol. 4, CH-LOC.
25. CH diary, entries for April 22 and 30, 1917, vol. 3, CH-LOC.
26. TR, *Works of Theodore Roosevelt*, 457.
27. PMW to WW, May 27, 1918, in WW, *Papers of Wilson Digital Edition*.

28. JHS to PMW, May 9, 1918, Folder 1, Box 456, JHS-AJA.
29. WW to PMW, August 9, 1918, Folder 56, Box 4, PMW-YU.
30. PMW to Benjamin Strong, August 13, 1918, Benjamin Strong Papers-FRBNY.
31. Chernow, *Warburgs*, 186.
32. PMW to Benjamin Strong, August 14, 1918, Benjamin Strong Papers-FRBNY.
33. PMW to E. M. House, October 10, 1918, Folder 57, Box 4, PMW-YU.
34. Warburg, "Reminiscences of James Paul Warburg," 16–17.
35. OHK to PMW, August 12, 1918, Folder 8, Box 276, OHK-PU.
36. Warburg, "Book for Jimmy, Jennifer," 52.
37. JHS to Takahashi Korekiyo, July 15, 1918, Folder 14, Box 460, JHS-AJA.
38. JHS to Max Bonn, January 22, 1918, Folder 3, Box 450, JHS-AJA.
39. "Against War Time Wealth," *American Israelite*, November 29, 1917.
40. Kobler, *Otto the Magnificent*, 104.
41. JHS to K. J. Imanishi, October 26, 1917, Folder 2, Box 451, JHS-AJA.
42. "Destroy Prussianism, Jacob Schiff Urges," *New York Times*, April 12, 1918.
43. Cohen, *Schiff: Study in Leadership*, 199.
44. C. W. Taintor to JHS, June 10, 1918, Folder 1, Box 456, JHS-AJA.
45. Cohen, *Schiff: Study in Leadership*, 204–5.
46. "Report of American Jewish Committee," *American Jewish Year Book*, September 25, 1919–September 12, 1920.
47. "Untermyer Joins Protest on Root," *New York Times*, May 4, 1917.
48. "New York Letter," *Reform Advocate*, April 14, 1917.
49. Philip Lehman to JHS, July 13, 1917, Folder 3, Box 451, JHS-AJA.
50. Julius Goldman to JHS, April 6, 1917, Folder 18, Box 452, JHS-AJA.
51. JHS to William McAdoo, May 14, 1918, Folder 5, Box 459, JHS-AJA.
52. William McAdoo to JHS, May 11, 1918, Folder 5, Box 459, JHS-AJA.
53. Certificate of commission, April 11, 1929, DTS.
54. MLS, "The Jewish Welfare Board," speech, May 29, 1919, DTS.
55. MLS, speech to the YMHA of Philadelphia, April 27, 1919, DTS.
56. MLS to JHS, June 6, 1917, Folder 4, Box 450, JHS-AJA.
57. "Fall from Horse Kills I. N. Seligman," *New York Times*, October 1, 1917.
58. JHS to MLS, August 1917, Folder 4, Box 450, JHS-AJA.
59. "Eulogies of Life of I. N. Seligman," *New York Times*, October 3, 1917.
60. JHS to Philipp Schiff, October 3, 1917, Folder 4, Box 450, JHS-AJA.
61. "Presents Seligman Notes," *New York Times*, March 5, 1920.
62. FMW to James Loeb, February 15, 1916, Folder 31, Box 170, FMW-AJA.
63. Wells, "House of Seligman," 503.
64. INS to Mr. Wyler, July 31, 1915, Box 3, SC-UO.
65. Wells, "House of Seligman," 514.
66. Ibid., 516.
67. Central Union Trust Co. to Office of the Alien Property Custodian, September 7, 1918, Box 6, Records of the Office of Alien Property, NA.
68. "U-Boat Street Parade," *New York Times*, October 20, 1917.
69. Hero Land advertisement, *New-York Tribune*, November 28, 1917.
70. "Jewish Relief Day Crowds Hero Land," *New York Times*, November 29, 1917.
71. AGS to Julius Goldman, October 3, 1918, Folder 53, Box 1, AGS-HU.
72. "Schiff Favors Home for Jewish Culture," *New York Times*, April 23, 1917; JHS to David Philipson, May 11, 1917, Box 453, JHS-AJA.
73. JHS to Julian Mack, December 3, 1917, Folder 22, Box 460, JHS-AJA.
74. JHS to Julian Mack, January 29, 1918, and Julian Mack to JHS, January 30, 1918, Folder 22, Box 460, JHS-AJA.
75. Kobler, *Otto the Magnificent*, 91.
76. Schmidt, "Zionist Conversion of Brandeis," 21, 30.

77. Kobler, *Otto the Magnificent*, 91.
78. Ibid., 78, 123; Collins, *Otto Kahn*, 85.
79. Phillips-Matz, *Many Lives of Kahn*, 107–8.
80. OHK to WW, April 6, 1917, Folder 11, Box 284, OHK-PU.
81. Collins, *Otto Kahn*, 123.
82. OHK to Lord Beaverbrook, July 2, 1917, C/187A, Lord Beaverbrook Papers-PA.
83. "Otto Kahn Flays Prussianism," *Brooklyn Daily Eagle*, September 26, 1917.
84. "Otto H. Kahn Says Pan-German Plots Threatened Safety of United States," *Brooklyn Daily Eagle*, October 6, 1918.
85. Kobler, *Otto the Magnificent*, 100.
86. "In Re: Otto H. Kahn (German Activities)," July 28, 1918, M1085, Investigative Reports of the Bureau of Investigation 1908–1922, NA.
87. Thwaites, *Velvet and Vinegar*, 154–55.
88. JW, interview by the author.
89. "Sir William Wiseman, Friend of Wilson, Roney Plaza Guest," *Roney Plaza Daily*, March 8, 1936, JW.
90. Memorandum, n.d., JW.
91. Thwaites, *Velvet and Vinegar*, 255.
92. Collins, *Otto Kahn*, 123.
93. Lord Beaverbrook cable to OHK, n.d., C/187A, Beaverbrook Papers-PA.
94. "Otto Kahn on European Conditions," *Argonaut*, August 10, 1918.
95. Phillips-Matz, *Many Lives of Kahn*, 190.
96. MLS to Adele Schiff, December 20, 1918, Folder 17b, Box 460, JHS-AJA.
97. "With the A.E.F.," Address to the Philadelphia YMHA, April 27, 1919, DTS.
98. MLS to Adele Schiff, January 9, 1919, Folder 16b, Box 461, JHS-AJA.
99. Ibid.
100. MLS to FMW, January 19, 1919, Folder 20, Box 183, FMW-AJA.
101. FMW to MMW, November 15, 1918, Folder 27, Box 10, LS-AJHS.
102. FMW to Gerald Warburg, March 17, 1919, Folder 5, Box 184, FMW-AJA.

25 THE FIRST PART OF A TRAGEDY

1. JHS to MMW, August 26, 1919, Folder 16b, Box 461, JHS-AJA.
2. Chernow, *Warburgs*, 212.
3. Ibid., 210.
4. Schiff, *Germans at Versailles 1919*, 48.
5. Chernow, *Warburgs*, 214.
6. Barry, *Great Influenza*, 385.
7. Ferguson, *Paper and Iron*, 222.
8. Louis Marshall to JHS, May 29, 1919, Box 2364, JHS-AJA.
9. Louis Marshall and Cyrus Adler, cable, May 12, 1919, Box 461, JHS-AJA.
10. "Call on Nations to Protect Jews," *New York Times*, May 22, 1919.
11. Louis Marshall to JHS, May 29, 1919, Box 2364, JHS-AJA; Adler, *Schiff: His Life and Letters*, 2:306.
12. "Senators Call Six Financiers," *New York Times*, June 10, 1919.
13. "Willing to Tell What He Knows of Treaty Leak," Associated Press, June 10, 1919.
14. "President Exonerates Lamont in Peace Treaty Leak," *New York Times*, June 17, 1919.
15. William Borah to JHS, June 17, 1919, and JHS to William Borah, June 19, 1919, Folder 10, Box 461, JHS-AJA.

16. JHS to Israel Zangwill, August 14, 1919, Reel 684, JHS-AJA.
17. "To Honor Louis Marshall," *New York Times*, July 22, 1919.
18. Fink, "Louis Marshall: An American Jewish Diplomat," 37.
19. Schiff, *Germans at Versailles 1919*, 109.
20. Chernow, *Warburgs*, 217.
21. Rosenbaum and Sherman, *Warburg & Co.*, 123.
22. "Warburg Studies Relief," *New York Times*, October 18, 1919.
23. FMW, Report to JDC, November 10, 1919, Folder 13, Box 182, FMW-AJA.
24. PMW, memo, December 5, 1919, Folder 91, Box 7, PMW-YU.
25. Carter, *Price of Peace*, 80.
26. Ibid., 86.
27. Keynes, *Economic Consequences of Peace*, 251.
28. Ibid., 38.
29. Keynes, *Two Memoirs*, 71.
30. Ibid.
31. Minutes of the Conference on the Problem of International Credit and Organization, Box 7, Folder 93, PMW-YU; "History of the European Memorandum," Folder 96, Box 8, PMW-YU.
32. Draft appeal, Folder 94, Box 7, PMW-YU.
33. "Warburg Back from Europe," *Baltimore Sun*, November 6, 1919.
34. "History of the European Memorandum," Folder 96, Box 8, PMW-YU.
35. Fisher, *When Money Was in Fashion*, 127; "Banker Sees Germany on the Verge of Collapse," *New York Times*, August 5, 1922.
36. "History of the European Memorandum," Folder 96, Box 8, PMW-YU.
37. Ibid.

26 HENRY FORD

1. "Berlin Hears Ford Is Backing Hitler," *New York Times*, December 20, 1922.
2. Ford, *International Jew: World's Foremost Problem*, 1:5, 6, 46.
3. Wallace, *American Axis*, 46.
4. Baldwin, *Ford and Jews*, 2.
5. Wallace, *American Axis*, 24.
6. "Commercialism Made This War," *New York Times*, April 11, 1915.
7. "Ford, as Oscar II Sailed, Got Blessing from Edison," *Brooklyn Daily Eagle*, December 5, 1915; "Dubbed 'Ship of Fools,'" *New York Times*, December 4, 1915.
8. Watts, *People's Tycoon*, 234.
9. Wallace, *American Axis*, 19.
10. Baldwin, *Ford and Jews*, 59.
11. Kahn and Sayers, *Great Conspiracy*, 49; Singerman, "American Career of 'Protocols of Elders of Zion,'" 55.
12. Szajkowski, *Jews, Wars, and Communism*, 162.
13. BB to Serge Karasseff, July 13, 1920, Box 17, BB-LOC; BB to Mary Gagarine, December 18, 1920, Box 22, BB-LOC.
14. Singerman, "American Career of 'Protocols of Elders of Zion,'" 56.
15. Bendersky, *Jewish Threat*, 55, 57.
16. Zipperstein, *Pogrom*, 170.
17. Singerman, "American Career of 'Protocols of Elders of Zion,'" 49.
18. "The Inside Story of Henry Ford's Jew-Mania," Part 4, *Hearst's International*, September 1922.
19. Singerman, "American Career of 'Protocols of Elders of Zion,'" 70.

20. Fuller, *Foreign Relations of the United States, 1918, Russia*, 1:215.
21. Kennan, *Russia Leaves the War,* 449.
22. Kahn and Sayers, *Great Conspiracy,* 144.
23. Graves, *Truth About "The Protocols."*
24. "The Inside Story of Henry Ford's Jew-Mania," Part 1, *Hearst's International,* June 1922.
25. Singerman, "American Career of 'Protocols of Elders of Zion,'" 72.
26. "An Ally to the Pogrom Makers," *American Hebrew,* April 1, 1921.
27. Pipp, *Real Henry Ford,* 21.
28. Ford, *International Jew: Jewish Activities in United States,* 137–38.
29. *Jewish Influence in Federal Reserve System,* 46.
30. Ibid., 7.
31. Ibid., 42.
32. Ibid., 47.
33. Ibid., 48.
34. Ibid., 43–44.
35. "Report of the American Jewish Committee," *American Jewish Year Book,* October 3, 1921–September 22, 1922.
36. Wallace, *American Axis,* 14.
37. Baldwin, *Ford and Jews,* 139.
38. Cohen, *Not Free to Desist,* 130–31.
39. Dan Kramarsky, interview by the author.
40. Warburg descendant, interview by the author.
41. Katharine Weber, interview by the author.
42. "Coughlin in Error, Kerensky Asserts," *New York Times,* November 29, 1938.
43. "Church Paper Editor Charges Father Coughlin Uses False Statements," *Leader-Telegram* (Eau Claire, Wis.), December 23, 1938.
44. Trotsky, *Writings of Trotsky,* 148.
45. JHS to Louis Marshall, August 19, 1918, Folder 3, Box 459, JHS-AJA.
46. Ackerman, *Trotsky in New York,* 320.
47. "Cholly Knickerbocker," *New York Journal-American,* February 3, 1949.
48. John Schiff statement, Box 215, DS-NYPL.
49. "Calling All Crackpots," *Washington Post,* October 16, 1994.
50. Adler, *Selected Letters,* 2:38–39.
51. "$200,000 Libel Suit Filed Against Ford," *New York Times,* August 19, 1923.
52. "Memorandum Re Anti-Semitic Articles in the 'Dearborn Independent,'" August 29, 1921, Box 32, LS-AJHS.
53. "Sapiro Sees 'Fake' in Suit," *New York Times,* May 28, 1927.
54. "Statement by Henry Ford," American Jewish Committee, 1927.
55. Ribuffo, "Ford and 'International Jew,'" 469.
56. Baldwin, *Ford and Jews,* 297.
57. Wallace, *American Axis,* 133–34.
58. Watts, *People's Tycoon,* 397.
59. Wallace, *American Axis,* 359.

27 THE WORLD TO COME

1. "Lowell Tells Jews Limit at Colleges Might Help Them," *New York Times,* June 22, 1922.
2. JHS to A. J. Sack, February 9, 1920, Folder 7, Box 463, JHS-AJA.
3. Adler, *Schiff: His Life and Letters,* 2:359.
4. Ibid., 2:357–58.

5. Ibid., 2:359.
6. "Jacob Schiff, Dead," *Reform Advocate*, October 2, 1920.
7. Louis Marshall, address, December 19, 1920, Box 244, DS-NYPL.
8. "Weather Report," *New-York Tribune*, September 25, 1930.
9. Buttenwieser, "Reminiscences of Benjamin Buttenwieser," 280–81.
10. "Jacob H. Schiff Left $34,426,282 Subject to New York Taxes," *New York Times*, March 3, 1922.
11. JHS, Last Will and Testament, Box 244, DS-NYPL; Berman, *American Jewish Philanthropic Complex*, 39.
12. MLS, memorandum, December 1, 1928, DTS.
13. Kuhn, Loeb & Co., *Investment Banking Through Four Generations*, 24.
14. Chernow, *Warburgs*, 309; Collins, *Otto Kahn*, 190.
15. U.S. Senate, *Stock Exchange Practices*, 1007.
16. "Warburg Assails Federal Reserve," *New York Times*, March 8, 1929.
17. Galbraith, *Great Crash*, 99.
18. "Banker Seligman Sued for $100,000 Love Balm Claim," *Brooklyn Daily Eagle*, June 3, 1929; Muir and White, *Over the Long Term*, 133.
19. Muir and White, *Over the Long Term*, 137.
20. Ibid., 137–38.
21. Herman Kahn interview notes, Box 15, JK-CURBML.
22. David Sachs interview notes, Box 15, JK-CURBML.
23. George Ball interview notes, Box 15, JK-CURBML.
24. Sachs, "Reminiscences of Walter Sachs," Part 1, 44.
25. Galbraith, *Great Crash*, 62.
26. Sachs, "Reminiscences of Walter Sachs," Part 1, 48.
27. Ellis, *Partnership*, 28.
28. Sachs, "Reminiscences of Walter Sachs," Part 1, 47.
29. Ibid., Part 1, 52.
30. Ibid., 2:22.
31. Fisher, *When Money Was in Fashion*, 194.
32. Ibid., 238.
33. "Goldman Joins Arthur Lipper & Co.," *New York Times*, May 13, 1919.
34. Max Born, interview by Thomas S. Kuhn, October 18, 1962, Niels Bohr Library & Archives, AIP.
35. "Banker Says 'All Europe Is Ablaze,'" *Buffalo Courier*, May 29, 1923.
36. Max Born interview, Oral History Collection, Niels Bohr Library & Archives, AIP.
37. GW to Monroe Wheeler, May 21, June 10, June 15, and July 2, 1923, Box 3, GW-YU.
38. GW to Monroe Wheeler, May 26 and 30, 1923, Box 3, GW-YU.
39. GW to Monroe Wheeler, May 21, 1923, Box 3, GW-YU.
40. "Mr. Auerbach in Paris," *Harper's*, April 1942.
41. Ibid.
42. "American Amazed at Hindenburg's Perception," Associated Press, April 21, 1932.
43. McDonald, *Advocate for Doomed*, 23.
44. Fisher, *When Money Was in Fashion*, 150.
45. Henry Goldman to Julius Goldman, April 13, 1933, Folder 28, Box 1, AGS-HU.
46. McDonald, *Advocate for the Doomed*, 246.
47. Tracy Breton, interview by the author.
48. Max Born interview, Oral History Collection, Niels Bohr Library & Archives, AIP.
49. "Mortimer L. Schiff Dies Unexpectedly," *New York Times*, June 5, 1931.

50. Potter, *Men, Money, and Magic*, 75.
51. "Schiff Estate $28,718,213 Net," *Times Union* (Brooklyn, N.Y.), April 21, 1933.
52. "Otto Kahn, 67, Dies of a Heart Attack in Bank's Offices," *New York Times*, March 30, 1934.
53. Warburg, *Reminiscences of Long Life*, 100.
54. Chernow, *Warburgs*, 455.
55. "F. M. Warburg Dies at 66 in Home Here," *New York Times*, October 21, 1937.
56. "Paul M. Warburg Dies of Pneumonia," *New York Times*, January 25, 1932.
57. Chernow, *Warburgs*, 328.
58. Warburg, "Book for Jimmy, Jennifer," 56.
59. Katharine Weber, interview by the author.
60. Warburg, "Reminiscences of James Paul Warburg," 53–54.
61. Warburg, *Aus meinen Aufzeichnungen*, 140.
62. Rosenbaum and Sherman, *Warburg & Co.*, 160.
63. Marie Warburg, speech at the San Diego conference of the Eric M. Warburg Chapters of the American Council on Germany, January 25, 2014.
64. Chernow, *Warburgs*, 441.
65. Ibid., 442; Smethurst, *Foot Soldier to Finance Minister*, 297.
66. Farrer, *Warburgs*, 115.
67. Chernow, *Warburgs*, 442.
68. McDonald, *Advocate for Doomed*, 98.
69. Rosenbaum and Sherman, *Warburg & Co.*, 167.
70. Ibid., 168.
71. "When Bankers Started Playing with Other People's Money," *Atlantic*, February 28, 2017.
72. DTS, interview by the author.
73. "Schiff Mourned by Hosts He Aided," *New York Times*, September 27, 1920.
74. "Schiff as a Jew Is Praised by Dr. Wise," *New-York Herald*, October 4, 1920.
75. Waldman, *Nor by Power*, 323, 327.
76. *Forward* editorial, translation, Box 35, AO-NYPL.
77. Oscar Garrison Villard to Therese Schiff, September 28, 1920, Felix and Frieda Warburg Family Collection-AJA.
78. Warburg, *As I Recall*, 23.
79. "Memorial for Jacob Schiff," *Yonkers Herald* (N.Y.), October 2, 1920.
80. "Thousands Pay Last Honors to Jacob H. Schiff," *New-York Tribune*, September 29, 1920.
81. "Some Costly Tombs," *Phillipsburg Herald* (Kan.), October 24, 1895.

EPILOGUE SALEM FIELDS REVISITED

1. "Baker Will Divides $75,000,000 Fortune," *New York Times*, May 14, 1931.
2. Scott Schiff, interview by the author.
3. DTS, interview by the author.
4. Harvey Krueger, interview by the author.
5. DTS, interview by the author.
6. Scott Schiff to the author, January 15, 2019.
7. Drew Schiff, interview by the author.

BIBLIOGRAPHY

Ackerman, Kenneth D. *The Gold Ring: Jim Fisk, Jay Gould, and Black Friday, 1869.* New York: Harper Business, 1990.

———. *Trotsky in New York, 1917: A Radical on the Eve of Revolution.* Berkeley: Counterpoint, 2016.

Adler, Cyrus. *Jacob H. Schiff: His Life and Letters.* 2 vols. Garden City, N.Y.: Doubleday, Doran, 1928.

———. *Selected Letters.* Edited by Ira Robinson. 2 vols. Philadelphia: Jewish Publication Society of America, 1985.

Adler, Cyrus, and Isidore Singer. *The Jewish Encyclopedia: A Descriptive Record of the History, Religion, Literature, and Customs of the Jewish People from the Earliest Times to the Present Day.* New York: Funk & Wagnalls, 1905.

Alef, Daniel. *Henry Goldman: Goldman Sachs and the Beginning of Investment Banking.* Santa Barbara, Calif.: Titans of Fortune, 2010.

Alexander, Edward Porter. *The Museum in America: Innovators and Pioneers.* New York: AltaMira Press, 1997.

Allen, Frederick Lewis. *The Lords of Creation.* New York: Harper & Brothers, 1935.

Arnsberg, Paul. *Henry Budge: Der "geliebten Vaterstadt—Segen gestiftet."* Frankfurt: Kramer, 1972.

Ascoli, Peter M. *Julius Rosenwald: The Man Who Built Sears, Roebuck and Advanced the Cause of Black Education in the American South.* Bloomington: Indiana University Press, 2006.

Baldwin, Neil. *Henry Ford and the Jews: The Mass Production of Hate.* New York: Public Affairs, 2003.

Bancroft, Hubert Howe. *The Works of Hubert Howe Bancroft: Popular Tribunals.* San Francisco: History Company, 1887.

Barry, John M. *The Great Influenza: The Story of the Deadliest Pandemic in History.* New York: Penguin Books, 2005.

Baruch, Bernard Mannes. *Baruch: My Own Story.* 2 vols. New York: Holt, Rinehart & Winston, 1957.

Bendersky, Joseph W. *The Jewish Threat: Anti-Semitic Politics of the American Army.* New York: Basic Books, 2000.

Bensel, Richard Franklin. *Passion and Preferences: William Jennings Bryan and the 1896 Democratic Convention.* New York: Cambridge University Press, 2008.

Berman, Hyman, and Linda Mack Schloff. *Jews in Minnesota.* St. Paul: Minnesota Historical Society Press, 2002.

Berman, Lila Corwin. *The American Jewish Philanthropic Complex: The History of a Multibillion-Dollar Institution*. Princeton, N.J.: Princeton University Press, 2020.

Bernstorff, Johann Heinrich. *My Three Years in America*. New York: Charles Scribner's Sons, 1920.

Best, Gary Dean. *To Free a People: American Jewish Leaders and the Jewish Problem in Eastern Europe, 1890–1914*. Westport, Conn.: Greenwood Press, 1982.

Birmingham, Stephen. *Our Crowd: The Great Jewish Families of New York*. New York: Harper & Row, 1977.

Bishop, Joseph Bucklin, ed. *Theodore Roosevelt and His Time Shown in His Own Letters*. 2 vols. New York: Charles Scribner's Sons, 1920.

Bogen, Hyman. *The Luckiest Orphans: A History of the Hebrew Orphan Asylum of New York*. Urbana: University of Illinois Press, 1992.

Brandeis, Louis Dembitz. *Letters of Louis D. Brandeis*. Edited by Melvin I. Urofsky. Albany: State University of New York Press, 1971.

Brustein, William I. *Roots of Hate: Anti-Semitism in Europe Before the Holocaust*. Cambridge: Cambridge University Press, 2003.

Bryan, William Jennings. *Speeches of William Jennings Bryan*. Edited by Mary Baird Bryan. New York: Funk & Wagnalls, 1911.

Campbell, John P. *The Southern Business Directory and General Commercial Advertiser*. Charleston, S.C.: Press of Walker & James, 1854.

Carr, Sean D., and Robert F. Bruner. *The Panic of 1907: Lessons Learned from the Market's Perfect Storm*. Hoboken, N.J.: Wiley, 2007.

Carter, Zachary D. *The Price of Peace: Money, Democracy, and the Life of John Maynard Keynes*. New York: Random House, 2020.

Casson, Herbert Newton. *The History of the Telephone*. Chicago: A. C. McClurg & Co., 1910.

Chernow, Ron. *The House of Morgan: An American Banking Dynasty and the Rise of Modern Finance*. New York: Grove Press, 1990.

———. *The Warburgs: The Twentieth-Century Odyssey of a Remarkable Jewish Family*. New York: Vintage Books, 1994.

Cohen, Naomi W. *Encounter with Emancipation: The German Jews in the United States, 1830–1914*. Philadelphia: Jewish Publication Society of America, 1984.

———. *Jacob H. Schiff: A Study in American Jewish Leadership*. Hanover, N.H.: Brandeis University Press, 1999.

———. *Not Free to Desist: The American Jewish Committee, 1906–1966*. Philadelphia: Jewish Publication Society of America, 1972.

Collins, Theresa M. *Otto Kahn: Art, Money, and Modern Time*. Chapel Hill: University of North Carolina Press, 2014.

Cowen, Philip. *Memories of an American Jew*. New York: Arno Press, 1932.

Daniels, Doris. *Always a Sister: The Feminism of Lillian D. Wald*. New York: Feminist Press at the City University of New York, 1989.

Dearborn, Mary V. *Mistress of Modernism: The Life of Peggy Guggenheim*. Boston: Houghton Mifflin, 2004.

Denby, Elaine. *Grand Hotels: Reality and Illusion*. London: Reaktion Books, 2002.

Deutsch, Gotthard. *Scrolls: Essays on Jewish History and Literature, and Kindred Subjects*. 2 vols. Cincinnati: Ark Publishing Co., 1917.

Dietz, Alexander. *Stammbuch der Frankfurter Juden: Geschichtliche Mitteilungen über die Frankfurter jüdischen Familien von 1349–1849*. Frankfurt: J. St. Goar, 1907.

Diner, Hasia R. *The Jews of the United States, 1654 to 2000*. Berkeley: University of California Press, 2006.

———. *Roads Taken: The Great Jewish Migrations to the New World and the Peddlers Who Forged the Way*. New Haven, Conn.: Yale University Press, 2015.

Dinkelspiel, Frances. *Towers of Gold: How One Jewish Immigrant Named Isaias Hellman Created California*. New York: St. Martin's Press, 2010.

Dinnerstein, Leonard. *Antisemitism in America*. Oxford: Oxford University Press, 1994.

Dobkowski, Michael N. *The Tarnished Dream: The Basis of American Anti-Semitism*. Westport, Conn.: Greenwood Press, 1979.

Doerries, Reinhard R. *Imperial Challenge: Ambassador Count Bernstorff and German-American Relations, 1908–1917*. Chapel Hill: University of North Carolina Press, 1989.

Dubnow, Simon. *History of the Jews in Russia and Poland*. Philadelphia: Jewish Publication Society of America, 1916.

Duncan, Sally Anne, and Andrew McClellan. *The Art of Curating: Paul J. Sachs and the Museum Course at Harvard*. Los Angeles: Getty Research Institute, 2018.

Eaton, Herbert N. *An Hour with the American Hebrew: Including Rev. Henry Ward Beecher's Sermon on "Jew and Gentile."* New York: J. Haney & Co., 1879.

Eisenberg, Ellen. *Jewish Agricultural Colonies in New Jersey, 1882–1920*. Syracuse, N.Y.: Syracuse University Press, 1995.

Ellis, Charles D. *The Partnership: The Making of Goldman Sachs*. New York: Penguin Press, 2008.

Endlich, Lisa. *Goldman Sachs: The Culture of Success*. New York: Knopf Doubleday, 2013.

Ethington, Philip J. *The Public City: The Political Construction of Urban Life in San Francisco, 1850–1900*. Berkeley: University of California Press, 2001.

Evans, Eli N. *Judah P. Benjamin: The Jewish Confederate*. New York: Free Press, 1989.

Farrer, David. *The Warburgs: The Story of a Family*. New York: Stein & Day, 1975.

Feilitzsch, Heribert von. *The Secret War Council: The German Fight Against the Entente in America in 1914*. Amissville, Va.: Henselstone Verlag, 2015.

———. *The Secret War on the United States in 1915: A Tale of Sabotage, Labor Unrest and Border Troubles*. Amissville, Va.: Henselstone Verlag, 2014.

Feld, Marjorie N. *Lillian Wald: A Biography*. Chapel Hill: University of North Carolina Press, 2012.

Feldstein, Stanley. *The Land That I Show You: Three Centuries of Jewish Life in America*. New York: Anchor Press, 1979.

Ferguson, Niall. *Paper and Iron: Hamburg Business and German Politics in the Era of Inflation, 1897–1927*. Cambridge: Cambridge University Press, 2002.

Fisher, June Breton. *When Money Was in Fashion: Henry Goldman, Goldman Sachs, and the Founding of Wall Street*. New York: Palgrave Macmillan, 2010.

Flade, Roland. *The Lehmans: From Rimpar to the New World: A Family History*. Würzburg: Königshausen & Neumann, 1999.

Flynt, Wayne. *Alabama Baptists: Southern Baptists in the Heart of Dixie*. Tuscaloosa: University of Alabama Press, 1998.

Forbes, Bertie Charles. *Men Who Are Making America*. New York: B. C. Forbes, 1921.

Ford, Henry, ed. *The International Jew: Jewish Activities in the United States*. Dearborn, Mich.: Dearborn Publishing Co., 1921.

———. *The International Jew: The World's Foremost Problem, Being a Reprint of a Series of Articles Appearing in The Dearborn Independent*. Dearborn, Mich.: Dearborn Independent, 1920.

Freimann, Aron, and Isidor Kracauer. *Frankfort*. Translated by Bertha Szold Levin. Philadelphia: Jewish Publication Society of America, 1929.

Friedman, Murray. *What Went Wrong? The Creation and Collapse of the Black-Jewish Alliance*. New York: Free Press, 2007.

Galbraith, John Kenneth. *The Great Crash, 1929*. Boston: Houghton Mifflin, 1955.

Gaynor, William Jay. *Some of Mayor Gaynor's Letters and Speeches*. New York: Greaves, 1913.

Geisst, Charles R. *Wheels of Fortune: The History of Speculation from Scandal to Respectability*. Hoboken, N.J.: Wiley, 2003.

Gerhardt, Elena. *Recital*. London: Methuen, 1953.

Goodwin, Doris Kearns. *The Bully Pulpit: Theodore Roosevelt, William Howard Taft, and the Golden Age of Journalism*. New York: Simon & Schuster, 2013.

Goren, Arthur A. *New York Jews and the Quest for Community: The Kehillah Experiment, 1908–1922*. New York: Columbia University Press, 1970.

Grant, Ulysses Simpson. *The Papers of Ulysses S. Grant*, vol. 7, *December 9, 1862 to March 31, 1863*. Edited by John Y. Simon. Carbondale: Southern Illinois University Press, 1979.

———. *The Papers of Ulysses S. Grant*, vol. 24, *1873*. Edited by John Y. Simon. Carbondale: Southern Illinois University Press, 2000.

———. *Personal Memoirs of U. S. Grant*. New York: C. L. Webster, 1894.

Graves, Philip Perceval. *The Truth About "The Protocols": A Literary Forgery*. London: Times Publishing Co., 1921.

Griscom, Lloyd Carpenter. *Diplomatically Speaking*. Boston: Little, Brown, 1940.

Guggenheim, Peggy. *Out of This Century: The Informal Memoirs of Peggy Guggenheim*. New York: Dial Press, 1946.

Gurock, Jeffrey S., ed. *Central European Jews in America, 1840–1880: Migration and Advancement*. New York: Routledge, 1998.

Haeg, Larry. *Harriman vs. Hill: Wall Street's Great Railroad War*. Minneapolis: University of Minnesota Press, 2013.

Hickling, John, & Co. *Men and Idioms of Wall Street: Explaining the Daily Operations in Stocks, Bonds and Gold*. New York: E. H. Jones, 1875.

History of the Terrible Financial Panic of 1873. Chicago: Western News, 1873.

Howe, Irving. *World of Our Fathers*. New York: Simon & Schuster, 1976.

Jewish Influence in the Federal Reserve System: Six Articles Reprinted from the Dearborn Independent. Dearborn, Mich.: Dearborn Publishing Co., 1921.

Jones, John Beauchamp. *A Rebel War Clerk's Diary at the Confederate States Capital*. 2 vols. Philadelphia: J. B. Lippincott, 1866.

Jordan, David Starr. *Unseen Empire: A Study of the Plight of Nations That Do Not Pay Their Debts*. Boston: American Unitarian Association, 1912.

Joseph, Samuel. *History of the Baron de Hirsch Fund: The Americanization of the Jewish Immigrant*. New York: Baron de Hirsch Fund, 1935.

Josephson, Matthew. *The Robber Barons: The Great American Capitalists, 1861–1901*. New York: Harcourt, Brace & World, 1962.

Kahn, Albert E., and Michael Sayers. *The Great Conspiracy: The Secret War Against Soviet Russia*. Boston: Little, Brown, 1916.

Kahn, Otto Hermann. *Our Economic and Other Problems: A Financier's Point of View*. New York: George H. Doran, 1920.

Kantor, Sybil Gordon. *Alfred H. Barr, Jr., and the Intellectual Origins of the Museum of Modern Art*. Cambridge, Mass.: MIT Press, 2002.

Keene, Donald. *Emperor of Japan: Meiji and His World, 1852–1912*. New York: Columbia University Press, 2005.

Kennan, George. *The Chicago & Alton Case: A Misunderstood Transaction*. Garden City, N.Y.: Country Life Press, 1916.

———. *E. H. Harriman: A Biography*. 2 vols. Boston: Houghton Mifflin, 1922.

Kennan, George Frost. *Russia Leaves the War*. Princeton, N.J.: Princeton University Press, 1956.

Keynes, John Maynard. *The Economic Consequences of the Peace*. London: Macmillan, 1919.

———. *Two Memoirs: Dr. Melchior, a Defeated Enemy, and My Early Beliefs*. New York: A. M. Kelley, 1949.

Kittelstrom, Amy. *The Religion of Democracy: Seven Liberals and the American Moral Tradition*. New York: Penguin Press, 2016.

Klein, Maury. *The Life and Legend of E. H. Harriman*. Chapel Hill: University of North Carolina Press, 2000.

———. *The Life and Legend of Jay Gould*. Baltimore: Johns Hopkins University Press, 1997.

———. *Union Pacific: The Rebirth, 1894–1969*. New York: Doubleday, 1987.

Klier, John Doyle. *Pogroms: Anti-Jewish Violence in Modern Russian History*. Cambridge: Cambridge University Press, 1992.

Kobler, John. *Otto the Magnificent: The Life of Otto Kahn*. New York: Scribner, 1988.

Kraus, Adolf. *Reminiscences and Comments: The Immigrant, the Citizen, a Public Office, the Jew*. Chicago: Toby Rubovits, 1925.

Krick, Robert K. *Civil War Weather in Virginia*. Tuscaloosa: University of Alabama Press, 2007.

Kuhn, Loeb & Co. *Investment Banking Through Four Generations*. New York: Kuhn, Loeb & Co., 1955.

Landman, Isaac. *The Universal Jewish Encyclopedia: An Authoritative and Popular Presentation of Jews and Judaism Since the Earliest Times*. New York: Universal Jewish Encyclopedia, 1939.

Levenson, Dorothy. *Montefiore: The Hospital as Social Instrument, 1884–1984*. New York: Farrar, Straus & Giroux, 1984.

Levy, Louis S. *Yesterdays*. New York: Library Publishers, 1954.

Libo, Kenneth, ed. *Lots of Lehmans: The Family of Mayer Lehman of Lehman Brothers: Remembered by His Descendants*. New York: Center for Jewish History, 2007.

Liebmann, George W. *The Fall of the House of Speyer: The Story of a Banking Dynasty*. New York: Bloomsbury, 2015.

Link, Arthur S. *Wilson*. 5 vols. Princeton, N.J.: Princeton University Press, 1947–65.

Loizillon, Gabriel J. *The Bunau-Varilla Brothers and the Panama Canal*. Morrisville, N.C.: Lulu.com, 2012.

Lowenstein, Roger. *America's Bank: The Epic Struggle to Create the Federal Reserve*. New York: Penguin Press, 2015.

Lynch, Dennis Tilden. *"Boss" Tweed: The Story of a Grim Generation*. New York: Boni & Liveright, 1927.

Manners, Ande. *Poor Cousins*. New York: Coward, McCann & Geoghegan, 1972.

Marcus, Jacob Rader. *United States Jewry, 1776–1985*. Detroit: Wayne State University Press, 1989.

Marinbach, Bernard. *Galveston: Ellis Island of the West*. Albany: State University of New York Press, 2012.

Markel, Howard. *Quarantine! East European Jewish Immigrants and the New York City Epidemics of 1892*. Baltimore: Johns Hopkins University Press, 1999.

Markens, Isaac. *Abraham Lincoln and the Jews*. New York: Self-published, 1909.

Matsumura, Masayoshi. *Baron Kaneko and the Russo-Japanese War (1904–05): A Study in the Public Diplomacy of Japan*. Translated by Ian Ruxton. Morrisville, N.C.: Lulu .com, 2009.

McAdoo, William Gibbs. *Crowded Years: The Reminiscences of William G. McAdoo*. Boston: Houghton Mifflin, 1931.

McCabe, James D. *Lights and Shadows of New York Life: Or, The Sights and Sensations of the Great City*. Philadelphia: National Publishing Co., 1872.

McClellan, George Brinton. *The Gentleman and the Tiger: The Autobiography of George B. McClellan, Jr.* Philadelphia: J. B. Lippincott, 1956.

McCullough, David. *The Path Between the Seas: The Creation of the Panama Canal, 1870–1914*. New York: Simon & Schuster, 2001.

McDonald, James G. *Advocate for the Doomed: The Diaries and Papers of James G. McDonald, 1932–1935*. Edited by Richard Breitman, Barbara McDonald Stewart, and Severin Hochberg. Bloomington: Indiana University Press, 2007.

McKinlay, Duncan E. *The Panama Canal*. San Francisco: Whitaker & Ray-Wiggin Co., 1912.

Meyer, Annie Nathan. *Beginnings of Barnard College*. Boston: Houghton Mifflin, 1935.

Montefiore, Simon Sebag. *The Romanovs: 1613–1918*. New York: Knopf, 2017.

Moore, John Hebron. *The Emergence of the Cotton Kingdom in the Old Southwest: Mississippi, 1770–1860*. Baton Rouge: Louisiana State University Press, 1988.

Morris, Edmund. *Theodore Rex*. New York: Random House, 2001.

Muir, Ross L., and Carl J. White. *Over the Long Term: The Story of J. & W. Seligman & Co.* New York: J. & W. Seligman, 1964.

Nevins, Allan. *Herbert H. Lehman and His Era*. New York: Charles Scribner's Sons, 1963.

Nicolson, Harold. *Dwight Morrow*. New York: Harcourt, Brace, 1935.

Oberholtzer, Ellis Paxson. *Jay Cooke: Financier of the Civil War*. 2 vols. Philadelphia: G. W. Jacobs & Co., 1907.

Olitzky, Kerry M., and Marc Lee Raphael. *The American Synagogue: A Historical Dictionary and Sourcebook*. Westport, Conn.: Greenwood Press, 1996.

Paine, Albert Bigelow. *George Fisher Baker: A Biography*. New York: Knickerbocker Press, 1938.

Pak, Susie J. *Gentlemen Bankers: The World of J. P. Morgan*. Cambridge, Mass.: Harvard University Press, 2013.

Parker, Matthew. *Panama Fever: The Battle to Build the Canal*. London: Hutchinson, 2007.

Phillips-Matz, Mary Jane. *The Many Lives of Otto Kahn*. New York: Pendragon Press, 1984.

Pipp, Edwin Gustav. *The Real Henry Ford*. Detroit: Pipp's Weekly, 1922.

Pomper, Philip. *Lenin's Brother: The Origins of the October Revolution*. New York: W. W. Norton, 2010.

Potter, Jeffrey. *Men, Money, and Magic: The Story of Dorothy Schiff*. New York: Coward, McCann & Geoghegan, 1976.

Pyle, Joseph Gilpin. *The Life of James J. Hill*. New York: Doubleday, Page & Co., 1917.

Quinn, Tom. *Mrs. Keppel: Mistress to the King*. London: Biteback, 2016.

Radzinsky, Edvard. *Alexander II: The Last Great Tsar*. New York: Free Press, 2005.

Reading, Gerald. *Rufus Isaacs: First Marquess of Reading, by His Son the Marquess of Reading*. London: Hutchinson, 1939.

Reinharz, Jehuda, and Paul R. Mendes-Flohr, eds. *The Jew in the Modern World: A Documentary History*. Oxford: Oxford University Press, 2011.

Renehan, Edward J., Jr. *Dark Genius of Wall Street: The Misunderstood Life of Jay Gould, King of the Robber Barons*. New York: Basic Books, 2006.

Richardson, James Daniel, ed. *A Compilation of the Messages and Papers of the Presidents, 1789–1907*. Washington, D.C.: Bureau of National Literature and Art, 1908.

Riis, Jacob August. *How the Other Half Lives: Studies Among the Tenements of New York*. New York: Charles Scribner's Sons, 1890.

Rintelen, Franz von. *The Dark Invader: Wartime Reminiscences of a German Naval Intelligence Officer.* New York: Macmillan, 1933.

Rock, Howard B., and Deborah Dash Moore. *Haven of Liberty: New York Jews in the New World, 1654–1865.* New York: New York University Press, 2012.

Rogers, William Warren, Jr. *Confederate Home Front: Montgomery During the Civil War.* Tuscaloosa: University of Alabama Press, 2001.

Roosevelt, Theodore. *Address of President Roosevelt on the Occasion of the Laying of the Corner Stone of the Pilgrim Memorial Monument.* Washington, D.C.: Government Printing Office, 1907.

———. *Addresses and Presidential Messages of Theodore Roosevelt, 1902–1904.* New York: G. P. Putman's Sons, 1904.

———. *The Letters of Theodore Roosevelt,* vol. 5, *The Big Stick, 1905–1907.* Edited by Elting E. Morison. Cambridge, Mass.: Harvard University Press, 1951.

———. *The Works of Theodore Roosevelt.* Edited by Hermann Hagedorn. New York: Charles Scribner's Sons, 1923.

Rosenbaum, Eduard, and Ari Joshua Sherman. *M. M. Warburg & Co., 1798–1938, Merchant Bankers of Hamburg.* New York: Holmes & Meier, 1979.

Sachar, Howard Morley. *A History of the Jews in America.* New York: Knopf, 1998.

Sachs, Ann. *One Hundred Years at Rushing Brook: Seven Generations in Keene Valley: A Family Story.* New York: Privately printed, 2015.

Samuels, Ernest. *Bernard Berenson: The Making of a Legend.* Cambridge, Mass.: Belknap Press, 1987.

Sankovitch, Nina. *Signed, Sealed, Delivered: Celebrating the Joys of Letter Writing.* New York: Simon & Schuster, 2015.

Sarna, Jonathan D. *When General Grant Expelled the Jews.* New York: Schocken, 2012.

Schachner, Nathan. *The Price of Liberty: A History of the American Jewish Committee.* New York: American Jewish Committee, 1948.

Scharnhorst, Gary, and Jack Bales. *The Lost Life of Horatio Alger, Jr.* Bloomington: Indiana University Press, 1985.

Schiff, Jacob Henry. *Our Journey to Japan.* New York: New York Co-operative Society, 1907.

Schiff, Victor. *The Germans at Versailles, 1919.* London: Williams & Norgate, 1930.

Seligman, Edwin R. A., ed. *The Currency Problem and the Present Financial Situation: A Series of Addresses Delivered at Columbia University, 1907–1908.* New York: Columbia University Press, 1908.

Silver, Matthew. *Louis Marshall and the Rise of Jewish Ethnicity in America: A Biography.* Syracuse, N.Y.: Syracuse University Press, 2013.

Smethurst, Richard J. *From Foot Soldier to Finance Minister: Takahashi Korekiyo, Japan's Keynes.* Cambridge, Mass.: Harvard University Asia Center, 2007.

Sobel, Robert. *The Big Board: A History of the New York Stock Market.* New York: Free Press, 1965.

Spring Rice, Cecil. *The Letters and Friendships of Sir Cecil Spring Rice.* Edited by Stephen Gwynn. 2 vols. London: Constable, 1929.

Stearns, Alfred Ernest. *An Amherst Boyhood.* Amherst, Mass.: Amherst College Press, 1946.

Stern, Myer. *The Rise and Progress of Reform Judaism: Embracing a History Made from the Official Records of Temple Emanu-El of New York.* New York: M. Stern, 1895.

Straus, Oscar Solomon. *Under Four Administrations, from Cleveland to Taft: Recollections of Oscar S. Straus.* Boston: Houghton Mifflin, 1922.

Strouse, Jean. *Morgan: American Financier.* New York: Random House, 2014.

Szajkowski, Zosa. *Jews, Wars, and Communism: The Attitude of American Jews to World War I, the Russian Revolutions of 1917, and Communism (1914–1945)*. Brooklyn, N.Y.: KTAV, 1972.

Thwaites, Norman Graham. *Velvet and Vinegar*. London: Grayson & Grayson, 1932.

Travis, Frederick F. *George Kennan and the American-Russian Relationship, 1865–1924*. Athens: Ohio University Press, 1990.

Trotsky, Leon. *Writings of Leon Trotsky: 1938–1939*. New York: Pathfinder Press, 1969.

Valentiner, Wilhelm Reinhold. *The Henry Goldman Collection*. New York: Privately printed, 1922.

Vanderlip, Frank Arthur, and Boyden Sparkes. *From Farm Boy to Financier*. New York: D. Appleton-Century, 1935.

Voorsanger, Jacob. *The Chronicles of Emanu-El: Being an Account of the Rise and Progress of the Congregation Emanu-El, Which Was Founded in July 1850*. San Francisco: Geo. Spaulding & Co., 1900.

Wake, Jehanne. *Kleinwort Benson: The History of Two Families in Banking*. Oxford: Oxford University Press, 1997.

Wald, Lillian D. *The House on Henry Street*. New York: Henry Holt, 1915.

Waldman, Morris David. *Nor by Power*. New York: International Universities Press, 1953.

Wallace, Max. *The American Axis: Henry Ford, Charles Lindbergh, and the Rise of the Third Reich*. New York: St. Martin's Press, 2004.

Warburg, Edward M. *As I Recall: Some Memoirs*. Clifton, N.J.: Privately printed, 1978.

Warburg, Frieda Schiff. *Reminiscences of a Long Life*. New York: Privately printed, 1956.

Warburg, James P. *The Long Road Home: The Autobiography of a Maverick*. New York: Doubleday, 1964.

Warburg, Max M. *Aus meinen Aufzeichnungen*. Hamburg: E. M. Warburg, 1952.

Warburg, Paul Moritz. *The Federal Reserve System, Its Origin and Growth: Reflections and Recollections*. 2 vols. Boston: Macmillan, 1930.

Watts, Steven. *The People's Tycoon: Henry Ford and the American Century*. New York: Vintage Books, 2006.

Weber, Katharine. *The Memory of All That: George Gershwin, Kay Swift, and My Family's Legacy of Infidelities*. New York: Crown, 2011.

Weber, Nicholas Fox. *Patron Saints: Five Rebels Who Opened America to a New Art, 1928–1943*. New York: Knopf, 2014.

Weiner, Eric J. *What Goes Up: The Uncensored History of Modern Wall Street as Told by the Bankers, Brokers, CEOs, and Scoundrels Who Made It Happen*. Boston: Little, Brown, 2007.

Weintraub, Stanley. *Young Mr. Roosevelt: FDR's Introduction to War, Politics, and Life*. New York: Da Capo, 2013.

Weizmann, Chaim. *Trial and Error: The Autobiography of Chaim Weizmann*. London: H. Hamilton, 1949.

Weschler, Harold S. *The Qualified Student: A History of Selective College Admission in America, 1870–1970*. New York: John Wiley, 1977.

White, Horace. *Money and Banking: Illustrated by American History*. Boston: Ginn & Co., 1895.

Williams, Mary Floyd. *History of the San Francisco Committee of Vigilance of 1851: A Study of Social Control on the California Frontier in the Days of the Gold Rush*. Berkeley: University of California Press, 1921.

Willoughby, Lynn. *Fair to Middlin': The Antebellum Cotton Trade of the Apalachicola/Chattahoochee River Valley*. Tuscaloosa: University of Alabama Press, 2009.

Wilson, Woodrow. *Papers of Woodrow Wilson Digital Edition*. Charlottesville: University of Virginia Press, 2017.

Winkler, John Kennedy. *Five and Ten: The Fabulous Life of F. W. Woolworth*. New York: R. M. McBride, 1940.

Wischnitzer, Mark. *Visas to Freedom: The History of HIAS*. Cleveland: World, 1956.

Witte, Sergei. *The Memoirs of Count Witte*. Garden City, N.Y.: Doubleday Page, 1921.

Wolf, Simon. *The Presidents I Have Known from 1860-1918*. Washington, D.C.: B. S. Adams, 1918.

Zipperstein, Steven J. *Pogrom: Kishinev and the Tilt of History*. New York: Liveright, 2018.

ORAL HISTORIES

Born, Max S. "Interview of Max Born by Thomas S. Kuhn." 1962. Niels Bohr Library & Archives, American Institute of Physics.

Buttenwieser, Benjamin J. "Reminiscences of Benjamin J. Buttenwieser." 1981. Oral History Archives, Columbia University Rare Book and Manuscript Library.

Lehman, Herbert. "Reminiscences of Herbert Henry Lehman." 1961. Box 1308, Herbert Lehman Papers, Columbia University Rare Book and Manuscript Library.

Sachs, Walter E. "Reminiscences of Walter Sachs." Part 1, 1956. Oral History Collection, Columbia University Rare Book and Manuscript Library.

———. "Reminiscences of Walter Sachs." Part 2, 1964. Oral History Collection, Columbia University Rare Book and Manuscript Library.

Strauss, Lewis L. "Reminiscences of Lewis L. Strauss." 1963. Oral History Collection, Columbia University Rare Book and Manuscript Library.

Warburg, James P. "Reminiscences of James Paul Warburg." 1951 and 1952. Oral History Collection, Columbia University Rare Book and Manuscript Library.

UNPUBLISHED MANUSCRIPTS AND TYPESCRIPTS

Hellman, George S. "The Story of the Seligmans." 1945. MS-475, Seligman Family Collection, American Jewish Archives.

Manheim, Frank. "The Seed and the Tree: 100 Years of Lehman Brothers." Box 13, Joseph Kraft Papers, Columbia University Rare Book and Manuscript Library.

Sachs, Walter E. "Autobiography." Box 35, Stephen Birmingham Papers, Howard Gotlieb Archival Research Center, Boston University.

Seligman, Charles. "Some Recollections of Sir Charles Seligman." 1951. Box 40, George Hellman Papers, New York Public Library.

Warburg, Edward. "Reminiscences of Jacob H. Schiff." 1977. SC-10961, American Jewish Archives.

Warburg, Felix M. "Under the Seven Stars." 1926. SC-12702, American Jewish Archives.

Warburg, James P. "A Book for Jimmy, Jennifer and Philip." 1955. Folder 128, Box 10, Paul M. Warburg Papers, Sterling Library, Yale University.

Wells, Linton. "The House of Seligman." 1931. Seligman Family Papers, New York Historical Society.

Young, Leopold. "A Sketch of the First Jewish Settlers of Montgomery." 1901. Courtesy of Temple Beth Or.

SELECTED ARTICLES, PAMPHLETS, AND REPORTS

Adler, Cyrus. *Jacob Henry Schiff: A Biographical Sketch*. American Jewish Committee, 1921.

Best, Gary Dean. "Financing a Foreign War: Jacob H. Schiff and Japan, 1904–05." *American Jewish Historical Quarterly* 61, no. 4 (1972): 313–24.

———. "Ideas Without Capital: James H. Wilson and East Asia, 1885–1910." *Pacific Historical Review* 49, no. 3 (August 1980): 453–70.

———. "Jacob Schiff's Early Interest in Japan." *American Jewish History* 69, no. 3 (1980): 355–59.

———. "Jacob H. Schiff's Galveston Movement: An Experiment in Immigrant Deflection, 1907–1914." April 1978. American Jewish Archives.

Fink, Carole. "Louis Marshall: An American Jewish Diplomat in Paris, 1919." *American Jewish History* 94, no. 1–2 (2008): 21–40.

Frankel, Lee K. "Jewish Charities." *Annals of the American Academy of Political and Social Science* 21 (May 1903): 47–64.

Fuller, Joseph V., ed. *Papers Relating to the Foreign Relations of the United States, 1918, Russia*. Washington, D.C.: Government Printing Office, 1931.

Hellman, George S. "Joseph Seligman, American Jew." *Publications of the American Jewish Historical Society* 41, no. 1 (1951): 27–40.

"In Memoriam: Emanuel Lehman." Privately printed, 1907. Box 163, Herbert Lehman Papers, Columbia University Rare Book and Manuscript Library.

"In Memoriam: Mayer Lehman." Privately printed, 1897. Box 163, Herbert Lehman Papers, Columbia University Rare Book and Manuscript Library.

In Memoriam: Jesse Seligman. New York: Press of P. Cowen, 1894.

Loeb, James. *Our Father: A Memorial*. Privately printed, 1929. Courtesy of David T. Schiff and family.

Mehrotra, Ajay. "Envisioning the Modern American Fiscal State: Progressive-Era Economists and the Intellectual Foundations of the U.S. Income Tax." *UCLA Law Review* (2005): 1793.

Moses, Rabbi Alfred G. "The History of the Jews of Montgomery." *Publications of the American Jewish Historical Society* 13 (1905): 83–88.

Muraoka, Mina. "Jews and the Russo-Japanese War: The Triangular Relationship Between Jewish POWs, Japan, and Jacob H. Schiff." Ph.D. diss., Brandeis University, 2014.

New York State. *Testimony: Taken Before the Joint Committee Senate and Assembly . . . to Investigate and Examine into the Business and Affairs of Life Insurance Companies Doing Business in the State of New York*. New York: J. B. Lyon Co., 1906.

Osofsky, Gilbert. "The Hebrew Emigrant Aid Society of the United States (1881–1883)." *American Jewish Historical Society* 49, no. 3 (March 1960): 173–87.

Perkins, Edwin J. "In the Eye of the Storm: Isaac Seligman and the Panic of 1873." *Business History* 56, no. 7 (2014): 1129–42.

Ribuffo, Leo P. "Henry Ford and 'The International Jew.'" *American Jewish History* 69, no. 4 (1980): 437–77.

Roberts, Priscilla. "A Conflict of Loyalties: Kuhn, Loeb & Company and the First World War, 1914–1917." In *Studies in the American Jewish Experience II: Contributions from the Fellowship Programs of the American Jewish Archives*, ed. Abraham J. Peck and Jacob Rader Marcus. London: Rowman & Littlefield, 1984.

Schmidt, Sarah. "The Zionist Conversion of Louis D. Brandeis." *Jewish Social Studies* 37, no. 1 (1975): 18–34.

Schulteis, Herman J. *Report on European Immigration to the United States of America*. Washington, D.C.: Government Printing Office, 1893.

Seligman, Isaac. "Reminiscences of Isaac Seligman." Privately Printed, 1926. Box 40, George Hellman Papers, New York Public Library.

Sherman, A. J. "German-Jewish Bankers in World Politics: The Financing of the Russo-Japanese War." *Leo Baeck Institute Year Book* 28, no. 1 (January 1983): 59–73.

Singerman, Robert. "The American Career of the 'Protocols of the Elders of Zion.'" *American Jewish History* 71, no. 1 (1981): 48–78.

Sisson, Edgar Grant. *The German-Bolshevik Conspiracy*. Washington, D.C.: Committee on Public Information, 1918.

Smethurst, Richard J. "Takahashi Korekiyo, the Rothschilds and the Russo-Japanese War, 1904–1907." *Rothschild Archive Annual Review*, 2005–2006.

Supple, Barry E. "A Business Elite: German-Jewish Financiers in Nineteenth-Century New York." *Business History Review* 31, no. 2 (1957): 143–78.

Thian, Raphael P., comp. *Correspondence of the Treasury Department of Confederate States of America 1861–1865*. Washington, D.C.: Government Printing Office, 1879.

U.S. House of Representatives. *Hearings Before the Subcommittee of the Committee on Banking and Currency, Charged with Investigating Plans of Banking and Currency Reform and Reporting Constructive Legislation Thereon*. Washington, D.C.: Government Printing Office, 1913.

———. *Money Trust Investigation: Investigation of Financial and Monetary Conditions in the United States Under House Resolutions Nos. 429 and 504, Before a Subcommittee of the Committee on Banking and Currency*. 3 vols. Washington, D.C.: Government Printing Office, 1912.

——— *Report of the Committee Appointed Pursuant to House Resolutions 429 and 504 to Investigate the Concentration of Control of Money and Credit*. Washington, D.C.: Government Printing Office, 1913.

———. *Reports of Committees of the House of Representatives for the Second Session of the Forty-first Congress, 1869–70*. Washington, D.C.: Government Printing Office, 1870.

———. *Reports of Committees of the House of Representatives for the Second Session of the Forty-third Congress*. Washington, D.C.: Government Printing Office, 1875.

U.S. Immigration Commission. *Report of the Commissioners of Immigration Upon the Causes Which Incite Immigration to the United States*. Washington, D.C.: Government Printing Office, 1892.

U.S. Industrial Commission on Transportation. *Report of the Industrial Commission on Transportation*. Washington, D.C.: Government Printing Office, 1901.

U.S. Interstate Commerce Commission. *Reports and Decisions of the Interstate Commerce Commission of the United States*. New York: L. K. Strouse, 1906.

U.S. Senate. *Brewing and Liquor Interests and German Propaganda: Hearings Before a Subcommittee of the Committee on the Judiciary . . . Relating to Charges Made Against the United States Brewers' Association and Allied Interests*. Washington, D.C.: Government Printing Office, 1919.

———. *Stock Exchange Practices: Hearings Before the Committee on Banking and Currency . . . on S. Res. 84*. Washington, D.C.: Government Printing Office, 1932.

U.S. War Department. *The War of the Rebellion: A Compilation of the Official Records of the Union and Confederate Armies*. Washington, D.C.: Government Printing Office, 1880.

Walker, John Grimes. *A Preliminary Report of the Isthmian Canal Commission*. Washington, D.C.: Government Printing Office, 1900.

INDEX

ILLUSTRATION CREDITS

INSERT 1

1 Joseph Seligman: Atlantic Publishing and Engraving Company of New York
1 Jesse Seligman: *Harper's Weekly* (1894)
1 Peddlers: C. G. Bush, Library of Congress
2 Mayer Lehman: Herbert Lehman Collection, Columbia University Rare Book and Manuscript Library
2 Lehman home: Herbert Lehman Collection, Columbia University Rare Book and Manuscript Library
2 Court Square: Alabama Department of Archives and History
3 Mayer Lehman and family: Herbert Lehman Collection, Columbia University Rare Book and Manuscript Library
3 Emanuel Lehman: Herbert Lehman Collection, Columbia University Rare Book and Manuscript Library
3 Herbert Lehman: Herbert Lehman Collection, Columbia University Rare Book and Manuscript Library
4 Jacob Schiff: American Jewish Archives
4 Therese Schiff: American Jewish Archives
4 Schiff/Rothschild home: Universitätsbibliothek Frankfurt am Main
5 Solomon Loeb: American Jewish Archives
5 Abraham Kuhn: American Jewish Archives
5 Betty Loeb: American Jewish Archives
5 Schiff-Loeb Family: The Dorot Jewish Division, The New York Public Library
6 Henry Street Settlement: Jacob Riis/Library of Congress
6 Lillian Wald: Library of Congress
6 Temple Emanu-El: *Harper's Weekly*
7 Walter Sachs: Courtesy of the Sachs Family
7 Marcus Goldman: Wikimedia Commons
7 Goldman-Sachs Family: Courtesy of the Sachs Family
8 Grand Union caricature: Puck/Library of Congress
8 Grand Union Hotel: Library of Congress
8 Grand Union headline: *The New York Times*

INSERT 2

1 Jacob and Therese Schiff: Bain News Service/Library of Congress
1 The Schiff home at 965 Fifth Avenue: *The Architectural Record*
1 Drawing Room of 965 Fifth Avenue: *The Architectural Record*
1 The Sachs' New Jersey shore home, Ellencourt: *Architecture*
1 Morti and Adele Schiff: Bain News Service/Library of Congress
2 Max Warburg and Carl Melchior: National Archives
2 Warburg Brothers: Warburg Institute Archive

2 Representatives of the Joint Distribution Committee and the American Jewish Relief Committee: Joint Distribution Committee Archives

3 Felix and Frieda Warburg's C.P.H. Gilbert–designed mansion: William Roege

3 Felix, Frieda, and Edward Warburg: Bain News Service/Library of Congress

3 Felix Warburg dancing: Joint Distribution Committee Archives

4 John Pierpont Morgan: Library of Congress

4 James J. Hill: Harris & Ewing/Library of Congress

4 Edward H. Harriman: Bain News Service/Library of Congress

5 Otto Kahn in Palm Beach: Lehman Collection, Baker Library, Harvard Business School

5 Otto Kahn with showgirls: Arnold Genthe/Library of Congress

5 Kuhn Loeb boardroom: Anja Elisabeth Witte/Berlinische Galerie

6 Robert Lehman: Lehman Collection, Baker Library, Harvard Business School

6 Jefferson Seligman: Bain News Service/Library of Congress

6 Mortimer Schiff: Harris & Ewing/Library of Congress

6 Philip Lehman: Lehman Collection, Baker Library, Harvard Business School

6 Samuel Sachs: Courtesy of the Sachs family

7 *Dearborn Independent:* Wikimedia Commons

7 *Der Internationale Jude:* Wikimedia Commons

7 *The Protocols of the Elders of Zion:* Wikimedia Commons

7 Propaganda slide 1 (men seated on the podium): United States Holocaust Memorial Museum

7 Propaganda slide 2 (Schiff and Warburg): United States Holocaust Memorial Museum

8 Inaugural board of the Federal Reserve: Bain News Service/Library of Congress

8 Jewish immigrants in Galveston: University of Texas at San Antonio Special Collections

8 Jacob Schiff and Mayor William Gaynor: Bain News Service/Library of Congress

8 The author's grandmother: Schulman family

A NOTE ON THE TYPE

This book was set in Janson, a typeface long thought to have been made by the Dutchman Anton Janson, who was a practicing typefounder in Leipzig during the years 1668–1687. However, it has been conclusively demonstrated that these types are actually the work of Nicholas Kis (1650–1702), a Hungarian, who most probably learned his trade from the master Dutch typefounder Dirk Voskens. The type is an excellent example of the influential and sturdy Dutch types that prevailed in England up to the time William Caslon (1692–1766) developed his own incomparable designs from them.

Composed by North Market Street Graphics,
Lancaster, Pennsylvania

Printed by Berryville Graphics,
Berryville, Virginia

Designed by Soonyoung Kwon